ENVIRONMENT ACT 2021

The Environment Act 2021 is the most wide-reaching and significant new environmental Statute for many years. In this book, the full text of the Act is reproduced, accompanied by commentary and a section-by-section analysis written by 2 of the UK's leading experts in environmental law.

The book comments on and analyses the main provisions of the Act, including:

- A requirement on government to establish long-term environmental targets and environmental improvement plans;
- Legal recognition for the first time in national law of a number of core environmental principles, including the precautionary principle and the polluter pays principle;
- The establishment of a new independent statutory body, the Office for Environmental Protection;
- Substantial provisions on waste including producer responsibility and resource efficiency;
- Provisions on water resource management, water abstraction and drainage and sewerage;
- Strengthening of controls on air quality; and
- New provisions concerning the protection of nature and biodiversity, including the creation of conservation covenants.

This comprehensive and practical guide to the new legislation will be of significant value to anyone involved in environmental law in both the private and public sector, in particular practitioners and those advising on the impact and ambit of environmental law.

Environment Act 2021

Text, Guide and Analysis

Christopher Badger, Barrister
and
Richard Macrory, Hon QC
Emeritus Professor of Environmental Law
University College London

•HART•
OXFORD • LONDON • NEW YORK • NEW DELHI • SYDNEY

HART PUBLISHING

Bloomsbury Publishing Plc

Kemp House, Chawley Park, Cumnor Hill, Oxford, OX2 9PH, UK

1385 Broadway, New York, NY 10018, USA

29 Earlsfort Terrace, Dublin 2, Ireland

First published in Great Britain 2022

A catalogue record for this book is available from the British Library.

Library of Congress Cataloging-in-Publication data

Names: Badger, Christopher, author. | Macrory, Richard, author.

Title: Environment Act 2021 : text, guide and analysis / Christopher Badger, Barrister and Richard Macrory, Hon QC, Emeritus Professor of Environmental Law University College London.

Description: Oxford ; New York : Hart, 2022. | Includes bibliographical references and index.

Identifiers: LCCN 2022010746 (print) | LCCN 2022010747 (ebook) | ISBN 9781509951024 (hardback) | ISBN 9781509951048 (pdf) | ISBN 9781509951031 (Epub)

Subjects: LCSH: Great Britain. Environment Act 2021. | Environmental law–Great Britain. | LCGFT: Law commentaries.

Classification: LCC KD3372.A3282021 B33 2022 (print) | LCC KD3372.A3282021 (ebook) | DDC 344.41/046—dc23/eng/20220430

LC record available at https://lccn.loc.gov/2022010746

LC ebook record available at https://lccn.loc.gov/2022010747

ISBN: HB: 978-1-50995-102-4
ePDF: 978-1-50995-104-8
ePub: 978-1-50995-103-1

Typeset by Compuscript Ltd, Shannon
Printed and bound in Great Britain by CPI Group (UK) Ltd, Croydon CR0 4YY

FSC www.fsc.org MIX Paper from responsible sources FSC® C013604

CONTENTS

TABLE OF CASES

TABLE OF STATUTES

UNITED STATES OF AMERICA

TABLE OF STATUTORY INSTRUMENTS

Introduction

Background and Main Aims

Aside from the Climate Change Act 2008, the Environment Act 2021 is the most significant environmental law for a generation in terms of both scope and substance. It is, importantly, the first major Act concerning the environment passed since the UK left the European Union on 31 January 2020. The Act needs to be seen in that context, and against the background of the Government's broader environmental ambitions set out in its long-term plan for the environment published in January 2018, *A Green Future: Our 25-year Plan to Improve the Environment*. According to the Government's Policy Statement that accompanied the Bill when presented to Parliament, the Act is '*part of the wider government response to the clear and scientific case, and growing public demand, for a step-change in environmental protection and recovery*'.

The Act is divided into eight parts, with 21 schedules.

Part 1: Environmental Governance in England

Part 1 provides for the making of legally binding long-term environmental targets by the Government covering at a minimum air quality, water, biodiversity, and resource efficiency and waste reduction. Targets for $PM_{2.5}$ particulate matter in the air must be set. In addition, a species abundance target must be set, to be reached by 2030.

Long-term environmental plans are to be established with the 25-year plan, *A Green Future*, designated the first such plan. The Government is obliged to publish annual reports on progress in achieving the plan.

The Government must publish a policy statement concerning environment principles. The principles are derived from those contained in The Treaty on the Functioning of the European Union, and while post-Brexit they no longer have the equivalent legal force to the Treaty principles, the Act provides that Ministers must have due regard to the statement when making policy.

Part 1 also establishes a new public body, the Office for Environmental Protection (OEP), with jurisdiction mainly in England and Northern Ireland. The OEP will provide an annual assessment of the Government's progress with its long-term environmental plan, has duties to monitor the implementation of environmental law, and to provide advice on changes to environmental law. In addition, the OEP has enforcement powers against both central and local government, and other public bodies in respect of breaches of environmental law as defined in the Act.

Part 2: Environmental Government in Northern Ireland

Part 2 adapts the provisions concerning environmental improvement plans and environmental principles to apply in Northern Ireland. It also provides for the OEP to have jurisdiction in Northern Ireland.

Part 3: Waste and Resource Efficiency

Part 3 lacks overall coherence, but largely brings together a number of disparate reforms designed to improve and extend existing legislation with the aim of reducing waste and improving resource efficiency.

The existing law on producer responsibility is strengthened and aims to impose on producers the full costs of dealing with products at the end of their life. The Government is given power to regulate for ecodesign and to require producers and manufacturers to provide information about the resource efficiency of their products.

Provision is made for introducing a deposit return scheme for single-use containers and charges for single-use plastic items. Waste collection services by local authorities are to be standardised to improve recycling rates.

Various amendments to existing waste legislation are introduced to provide more effective measures against waste crime, including the introduction of electronic waste tracking, extended powers to regulate the import and export of wastes post-Brexit, and improved enforcement powers concerning waste offences and littering.

Part 4: Air Quality

Part 1 of the Act provides for the making of air quality statutory targets. Part 4 includes provisions to strengthen the provisions of air quality in the Environment Act 1995. The National Air Quality Strategy must now be reviewed at least every five years, and an annual report made by the Secretary of State on progress in meeting air quality standards and objectives. The provisions in the 1995 Act on local air quality management are strengthened, requiring greater cooperation from other public bodies responsible for regulating sources of air pollution and more detail to be contained in local authority action plans.

The provisions on smoke control areas under the Clean Air Act 1993 are strengthened, including the introduction of civil penalties for certain offences.

In the light of the emissions cheating scandal by vehicle manufacturers, new powers are given to the Secretary of State to require the recall of motor vehicles that do not meet prescribed environmental standards.

Part 5: Water

Various amendments are introduced to improve and update existing water legislation. They include provision for greater joint planning by water undertakers and new requirements on sewerage undertakers to develop long-term management plans for sewerage, equivalent to those currently existing for the supply of water. New provisions are introduced into the Water Industry Act concerning discharges from storm overflows, including a duty on the Secretary of State to produce and report on a storm overflow reduction plan and requirements on undertakers to provide more information on discharges from their overflows. A duty is imposed on undertakers to secure a progressive reduction of the adverse environmental and public health impacts caused by overflow discharges.

Amendments are made to the Water Industry Act 1991 giving Ofwat greater power to require information from undertakers and to modify licence conditions without the agreement of undertakers.

New powers are given to the Secretary of State to amend or modify various regulations, largely derived from EU law, concerning water quality.

Amendments are made to the Water Resources Act 1991 giving greater powers to vary or revoke water abstract licences for environmental reasons without the need to pay compensation.

Amendments are made to the Land Drainage Act 1991 allowing regulations to be made to modernise the system of valuation and funding of Internal Drainage Boards.

Part 6: Biodiversity

Growing concern about the decline of biodiversity in the UK has led to a significant range of new provisions. In addition to the duty of the Secretary of State under Part 1 of the Act to produce a long-term species abundance target and for biodiversity to be one of the priority areas for long-term targets, new provisions are introduced into the Town and Country Planning Act requiring developers to provide a biodiversity gain plan to be approved by planning authorities before granting planning permission. The aim of the plan is to secure at least a 10 per cent increase in the habitat value, either through on-site gains, off-site gains or the purchase of biodiversity credits from the Government. Similar requirements will apply to national infrastructure projects.

The general duty under s 40 of the Natural Environment and Rural Communities Act 2006 for public authorities to have due regard to conserving biodiversity is strengthened, including a requirement on local authorities and other designated bodies to produce regular reports on actions taken in respect of biodiversity duties.

New provisions are made for the production of local nature recovery strategies by local authorities to cover the whole of England, and for Species Conservation Strategies to be produced by Natural England. Power is given to the Secretary of State to amend the Habitats Regulations, provided any changes do not reduce the level of environmental protection provided by the Regulations.

Provision is made for new controls over the imports of products from agricultural land converted from forests. They largely stem from concern over the extent of global deforestation, much of it caused by illegal conversion to agricultural use and its impact on climate change. Regulations will define businesses and importers who will be obliged to establish due diligence systems to ensure that relevant local legislation concerned the land in question has been complied with.

Part 7: Conservation Covenants

A new form of land agreement, based on recommendations of the Law Commission, is introduced. Conservation Covenants allow landowners and lessees of more than seven years to make agreements with public bodies and designated environmental organisations to manage the land for conservation purposes, and such agreements can bind successors in title.

Part 8: Amendments of REACH Legislation and Consequential Amendments

Power is given to the Secretary of State to amend the EU Regulation of chemicals as transposed after Brexit provided they are consistent with the overall goal of the Registration, Evaluation, Authorisation and Restriction of Chemicals (REACH) regulation to ensure a high level of human health and environmental protection.

Legislative History

In December 2018 the Government published a draft Environment Principles and Governance Bill. The provisions in the Bill were focused on the policy statement of environmental principles, environmental improvement plans and the proposed Office for Environmental Protection, which now appear in Part 1 of the Act. The Bill was subject to pre-legislative scrutiny in Parliament and two House of Commons Select Committees produced reports following the scrutiny: the Environment Audit Committee (Eighteenth Report Session 2017–19, HC 1951) and Environment Food and Rural Affairs Committee (Fourteenth Report Session 2017–19, HC 1893). Government responses to the Committee's reports were made in October 2019.

The Environment Bill 2019 was published in October 2019, passed second reading on 28 October 2019 but fell at the dissolution of Parliament at the 2019 General Election. The Bill was reintroduced with a number of changes on 30 January 2020 and received its second reading in the House of Commons on 26 February 2020, entering committee stage on 10 March 2020. There were then lengthy delays due to coronavirus, and it received its third reading on 26 May 2021. It had its second reading in the House of Lords on 7 June 2021 and third reading on 13 October 2021. Following various amendments passed by the House of Lords, with the Government proposing amendments in response, the Bill ping-ponged between the Commons and Lords during October and November before receiving Royal Assent on 9 November 2021. The Department of the Environment, Food and Rural Affairs published a 49-page Impact Assessment with 270 pages of Annexes on 3 December 2019 (RPC-DEFRA-4439(1)), which provides a detailed analysis of the rationale for the provisions in the Bill and the costs and benefits of the policy options considered.

Legislative Features

The Act is a mixture of wholly new provisions and complex amendments to existing legislation. A number of common features in the legislative structure are striking:

- The provisions in Part 1, including the setting of long-term statutory environmental targets, the statutory policy statement on environmental principles and the creation of the new Office for Environmental Protection, have been largely designed to fill the perceived gaps in environmental governance arrangements following Brexit. In addition, the Act includes a range of new powers enabling government to amend various existing environmental regulations derived from EU legislation and made under the European Communities Act 1972. Although these have been 'rolled over' under the European Union (Withdrawal) Act 2018, the new powers enable more substantive revision than permitted under the constraints of the 2018 Act, which essentially only permitted amendments that would allow the regulations to operate in a national context.

- Many provisions are designed to reinforce the political accountability of Government to Parliament, with requirements to lay before Parliament various proposals and other matters, and produce regular reports on various aspects of the Act. The aim in many of the provisions to secure longer-term environmental improvements makes the obligation in the Act under s 9 to produce annual progress reports on the environmental improvement plan especially important.
- In common with much of modern legislation, a number of the core provisions in the Act only provide a very broad framework, leaving the substantial detail to be found in subsequent regulations to be made by the Government. Examples include producer responsibility obligations (s 50), electronic waste tracking (s 58), hazardous waste (s 60), environmental recall of vehicles (s 74), amendment of water quality regulations (s 89) and amendment of Habitats Regulations (s 112).
- Civil penalties are introduced as an alternative enforcement tool to criminal prosecution in many areas. Some are based on those contained in the Regulatory Enforcement and Sanctions Act 2008, others are bespoke, but the use of civil sanctions for enforcement is now clearly embedded in domestic environmental law. Examples in the Act include single bottle deposit schemes, electronic tracking of waste, hazardous waste, resource efficiency requirements, producer responsibility obligations, forest risk commodities and emissions in smoke control areas.

Devolution and Application of the Act

The environment is now largely a devolved matter and many of the provisions in the Act extend to England only. But the position is complex and there are examples of provisions in the Act extending throughout the UK, such as those on producer responsibility and the recall of motor vehicles, some applying only to England and Wales, such as hazardous waste and litter enforcement, some only to Northern Ireland, and various other combinations. There are also a growing number of instances where power is exercised by UK Ministers with the consent of the devolved governments. Examples in this Act include producer responsibility (ss 50 and 51), resource efficiency (ss 52 and 53), water quality (ss 89 and 90), consequential provisions (s 142), and REACH (chemicals) (Sch 21).

The devolution settlements allow for 'reserved matters' to remain within the jurisdiction of the UK Parliament and Government, but their extent varies in Scotland, Wales and Northern Ireland. Some of the reserved matters are relevant to environmental protection, but the boundaries can be complex. For example, in relation to Scotland, the licensing of nuclear powers stations is a reserved matter, while any necessary planning permission for a power station and the controls over the disposal of radioactive waste are devolved. Identifying what are and are not reserved matters will be especially important for the respective jurisdictions of the Office for Environmental Protection and Environmental Standards Scotland, and any equivalent body to be established in Wales. In relation to reserved matters, Lord Hope noted in *Imperial Tobacco Ltd v The Lord Advocate* [2012] UKSC 61: '*There is no common characteristic, but there is a common theme. It is that matters in which the United Kingdom as a whole has an interest should continue to be the responsibility of the United Kingdom Parliament at Westminster. They include matters which are affected by its treaty obligations and matters that are designed to ensure that there is a single market within the United Kingdom for the free movement of goods and services*' (para 29).

The United Kingdom Internal Market Act 2020, containing principles for the mutual recognition and non-discrimination of goods, could well lead to political and legal tensions where devolved governments wish to promote different environmental and public health standards.

For a useful analysis, see the House of Commons Library Briefing Paper, *Reserved Matters in the United Kingdom* (CBP 8544, 5 April 2019), which includes a valuable though not exhaustive current list of reserved matters.

S 146 of the Act sets out the territorial extent of the provisions in the Act, but this does not necessarily mean the provisions will actually apply in those jurisdictions. As the Office of Parliamentary Counsel has noted, '*"Extent" should be distinguished from "application", which concerns the persons and matters to which the provision relates. For example, a legal proposition may "extend" to England and Wales – that is, form part of the law of England and Wales – even though it only applies to persons in England*' (Office of the Parliamentary Counsel, *Drafting Guidance*, June 2020, para 10.4.3).

Application of these provisions has to be largely determined from their language and context. Annex A of the Explanatory Notes to the Environment Bill contains a valuable table setting both the extent and application of each section of the Bill as introduced in the House of Commons in January 2020. In the annotations to the Act, the territorial application rather than the extent of the provisions is noted for each section.

'Have Regard To'

General Note

The phrase '*have regard to*' is familiar in British legislation and appears over 30 times in the Environment Act. In seven cases it refers to guidance issued by the Secretary of State (the OEP enforcement policy; collection of waste; litter enforcement; local nature recovery strategies; felling of trees in highways; enforcement of forest risk commodities controls; and enforcement in smoke control areas). Guidance in this context is used where the Government wishes to influence but not dictate decision-making, and can be considered a form of 'soft' law in that it has legal status but is not binding as such. In other cases the '*have regard to*' formula is used to ensure that certain factors or interests are taken into account in decision making.

The phrase has been considered by the courts where it appears in other statutory provisions, and while the case law provides useful guidance on its meaning, courts frequently emphasise that one must consider the statutory context in which it is being used.

In *Howell v SSHCL* [2014] EWHC 3627 (concerning s 17A Norfolk and Suffolk Broads Act 1988 – duty of authority exercising functions to have regard to purposes of conserving and enhancing the natural beauty of the Broads), Cranston J noted: '*To have regard to a matter means simply that that matter must be specifically considered, not that it must be given greater weight than other matters, certainly not that it is some sort of trump card. It does not impose a presumption in favour of particular result or a duty to achieve that result. In the circumstances of the case other matters may outweigh it in the balance of decision-making. On careful consideration the matter may be given little, if any, weight.*'

For an extensive review of the case law, see the decision of Cobb J in *R on the application of the Governing Body of the London Oratory School v Schools Adjudicator* [2015] EWHC 1012, paras 49–61, again emphasising the need to look at the statutory context and background. Lord Justice Laws in *London Borough of Newham* 2004 EWCA Civ 55 noted in relation to a guidance issued by the Secretary of State to which authorities must have regard that authorities '*(a) must take it into account and (b) if they decide to depart from it, give clear reasons for doing so*'.

In the Environment Act 2021 there are examples of a requirement to lay such guidance before Parliament: enforcement guidance to the OEP (both draft and final) waste collection (final), litter enforcement (final) and local nature recovery strategies (final). In *R v Ashworth Hospital Authority* [2005] UKHL (code of practice issued by Secretary of State under s 118 Mental Health Act 1983), the House of Lords gave greater status to a statutory code where the legislation required prior consultation and the code to be laid before Parliament. As Lord Hope noted (paras 68 and 69), '*What does "guidance" mean in this context? There is no statutory obligation to comply with it. But it cannot be divorced from its statutory background, from the process of consultation and from the Parliamentary procedure that must be gone through before it is published under section 118(6) as "the code as for the time being in force". Statutory guidance of this kind is less than a direction. But it is more than something to which those to whom it is addressed must "have regard to" … Parliament by enacting section 118(1) has made it clear that it expects that the persons to whom the Code is addressed will follow it, unless they can demonstrate that they have a cogent reason for not doing so.*'

In one instance, the effect of the statement on environmental principle (s 19), the phrase used is '*have due regard*', which implies a greater legal significance. See the annotations to s 19.

Instances Where 'Have Regard To' Appears in the Act

Office for Environmental Protection (OEP)

In the exercise of its functions, the OEP must '*have regard to the need to act proportionately and transparently*' (s 23(2)(b)), and its statutory strategy must set out how the OEP '*will have regard to the need to act proportionately and transparently*' (s 23(4)(c)).

In considering its enforcement policy, the OEP must '*have regard to the particular importance of prioritising cases that it considers have or may have national implications*' and the importance of prioritising cases relating to other matters specified (s 23(7)).

In preparing its enforcement policy and exercising its enforcement policy, the OEP '*must have regard to the guidance*' issued by the Secretary of State (s 25(2)). There is an equivalent provision in relation to guidance issued by the NI Department of Agriculture, Environment and Rural Affairs (DAERA) in respect of the OEP's enforcement policy as it relates to Northern Ireland.

Where a Minister of the Crown requests that the OEP links information and decision notices, the OEP '*must have regard to that request*' (s 37(2)). Sch 3 para 11(2) contains an equivalent duty where a Northern Ireland Department has requested for linked notices.

In appointing non-executive members of the OEP, the Secretary of State '*must have regard to the desirability of the members*' having experience in certain areas specified (Sch 1 para 2(3)).

In determining the length of a non-executive member's term, the Secretary of State must '*have regard to the desirability of securing that the appointments of non-executive members expire at different times*' (Sch 1 para 2(4)). There is an equivalent duty on the Northern Ireland Department of Environment, Agriculture and Rural Affairs in respect of a Northern Ireland member's term of office.

In exercising functions in relation to the OEP, the Secretary of State '*must have regard to the need to protect its independence*' (Sch 1 para 17). An equivalent duty is placed on DAERA in respect of the OEP's functions in Northern Ireland.

Collection of Waste and Litter Enforcement

Waste collection authorities and other parties arranged to collect waste '*must have regard to the guidance*' issued by the Secretary of State concerning collection arrangements (s 57(4), introducing new s 45AZE Environment Protection Act 1990).

Where the Secretary of State or Welsh Ministers have issued guidance, litter authorities '*must have regard to that guidance when exercising any of its littering enforcement functions*' (s 68, introducing new s 88B Environmental Protection Act 1990).

Resource Efficiency Information

Where the relevant authority makes regulations concerning information requirements on products, the authority must '*have regard to the matters in sub-paragraph (2)*' (Sch 6 para 5(1)(b)). The matters referred to in sub-para (2) encompass the extent to which information is likely to reduce the product's impact on the environment, environmental, social economic and other costs of compliance, and whether exemptions should be given to small businesses.

Appeals Concerning Modification of Appointment Conditions of Water and Sewerage Undertakers

On an appeal to the Competition and Marketing Authority (CMA) concerning the modification of conditions of appointments of water and sewerage undertakers by Ofwat, there are four specified matters to which the CMA must, must not or may have regard to. One of the grounds on which an appeal may be allowed is that Ofwat '*failed properly to have regard to*' its statutory duties and strategic priorities under ss 2 and 2A Water Industry Act 1991 (s 86, introducing new s 12F Water Industry Act 1991).

Biodiversity and Nature Conservation

In determining the amounts payable for biodiversity credits, the Secretary of State '*must have regard to the need to determine an amount which does not discourage the registration of land in the biodiversity gain sites register*' (s 101(4)).

In complying with their general biodiversity duty under s 40(1) and (1A) Natural Environment and Rural Communities Act 2006, authorities '*must in particular have regard to (a) any relevant local nature recovery strategy and (b) any relevant species conservation strategy or protected site strategy prepared by Natural England*' (s 102, introducing new sub-s 2A to s 40 of the 2006 Act).

Where the Secretary of State has issued guidance concerning information and any other matters to be included in a local nature recovery strategy, a responsible authority '*must have regard to the guidance when preparing a local nature recovery strategy*' (s 106).

Where Natural England has prepared a species conservation strategy, local planning authorities and any prescribed authority must in the exercise of their functions '*have regard to a species conservation strategy so far as is relevant to its functions*' (s 109(9)).

Where Natural England has prepared a protected site strategy, '*a person must have regard to a protected site strategy*' so far as relevant to duties under Conservation of Habitats and Species Regulations, and specified duties under the Wildlife and Countryside Act 1981 and the Marine and Coastal Access Act (s 110(9)).

In making regulations to amend the Habitats Regulations, the Secretary of State '*must have regard to the particular importance of furthering the conservation and enhancement of biodiversity*' (ss 112(6) and 113(2)).

Felling of Trees in Highways

Local highway authorities '*must have regard to any guidance given by the Secretary of State to local highway authorities*' about how to discharge its duty to consult the public before felling trees in urban roads. (s 115, introducing s 96A Highways Act 1980).

In deciding whether to make a restocking order following a conviction for illegal felling, '*the court must have regard to (a) the interests of good forestry and agriculture and of the amenities of the district to which the restocking order would relate, and (b) the desirability of promoting the establishment and maintenance of adequate reserves of growing trees in England*' (Sch 16 para 6, introducing new s 24B Forestry Act 1967).

Forest Risk Commodities

In relation to enforcement functions concerning obligations concerning forest risk commodities, an enforcement authority '*must have regard to guidance*' issued by the Secretary of State (Sch 17 para 6(2)).

Air Quality

Designated public authorities, local authorities and county councils '*must have regard to the [national air quality] strategy when exercising any function of a public nature that could affect the quality of air*' (Sch 11 para 4, introducing new s 81A Environment Act 1995).

A local authority '*must have regard to any guidance published by the Secretary of State about the exercise of the authority's functions under this Part*' (Sch 12 para 6, introducing new s 28A Clean Air Act 1993 in Part III of the Act (smoke control areas)).

Annotations

Although this is a work of joint authorship, Christopher Badger took the lead on the annotations of Part 1 Chapter 1 and Part 3. Richard Macrory took the lead on Part 1 Chapter 2 and Parts 4–8. After work had started on the book, Richard Macrory was appointed a non-executive Director of the Office for Environmental Protection. Any views or legal interpretations in the annotations are personal to him, and do not necessarily represent the views of the OEP or any other body.

As far as possible, the annotations are intended to reflect the law as of 9 May 2022.

Commencement Orders

As of 1 April 2022, the following Commencement Orders have been made:

The Environment Act 2021 (Commencement No 1) Regulations 2021. SI 2021/1274.
The Environment Act 2021 (Commencement No 2 and Saving Provision) Regulations 2022. SI 2022/48.
The Environment (2021 Act) (Commencement and Saving Provision) Order (Northern Ireland) 2022 SRNI 2022/54.
The Environment Act 2021 (Commencement No 3) Regulations. SI 2022/518.
The Environment Act 2021 (Commencement No 1 and Saving Provision) (Wales) Regulations 2022/223.

Arrangement of Sections and Schedules

CHAPTER 30

CONTENTS

PART 1

ENVIRONMENTAL GOVERNANCE

CHAPTER 1

IMPROVING THE NATURAL ENVIRONMENT

Environmental targets

Environmental improvement plans

Environmental monitoring

Policy statement on environmental principles

Environmental protection: statements and reports

Chapter 2

The Office for Environmental Protection

The Office for Environmental Protection

The OEP's scrutiny and advice functions

The OEP's enforcement functions

Information

Chapter 3

Interpretation of Part 1

Part 2

Environmental governance: Northern Ireland

Part 3

Waste and resource efficiency

Producer responsibility

Resource efficiency

Managing waste

Local nature recovery strategies

Conservation

Habitats Regulations

Tree felling and planting

Use of forest risk commodities in commercial activity

PART 7

CONSERVATION COVENANTS

Creation of conservation covenant

Effect of conservation covenant

Breach and enforcement

Discharge and modification

Replacement etc of responsible body

Miscellaneous

Supplementary

PART 8

MISCELLANEOUS AND GENERAL PROVISIONS

Regulation of chemicals

Concurrent functions in Wales

General provisions

Text of Act and Commentary

2021 CHAPTER 30

An Act to make provision about targets, plans and policies for improving the natural environment; for statements and reports about environmental protection; for the Office for Environmental Protection; about waste and resource efficiency; about air quality; for the recall of products that fail to meet environmental standards; about water; about nature and biodiversity; for conservation covenants; about the regulation of chemicals; and for connected purposes. [9th November 2021]

BE IT ENACTED by the Queen's most Excellent Majesty, by and with the advice and consent of the Lords Spiritual and Temporal, and Commons, in this present Parliament assembled, and by the authority of the same, as follows:—

Part 1

Environmental governance

Chapter 1

Improving the natural environment

Environmental targets

1 Environmental targets

(1) The Secretary of State may by regulations set long-term targets in respect of any matter which relates to—

(a) the natural environment, or

(b) people's enjoyment of the natural environment.

(2) The Secretary of State must exercise the power in subsection (1) so as to set a long-term target in respect of at least one matter within each priority area.

(3) The priority areas are—

(a) air quality;

(b) water;

(c) biodiversity;

(d) resource efficiency and waste reduction.

(4) A target set under this section must specify—

(a) a standard to be achieved, which must be capable of being objectively measured, and

(b) a date by which it is to be achieved.

(5) Regulations under this section may make provision about how the matter in respect of which a target is set is to be measured.

(6) A target is a "long-term" target if the specified date is no less than 15 years after the date on which the target is initially set.

(7) A target under this section is initially set when the regulations setting it come into force.

(8) In this Part the "specified standard" and "specified date", in relation to a target under this section, mean the standard and date (respectively) specified under subsection (4).

(9) The Secretary of State may not by regulations under this section make any provision which, if contained in an Act of Senedd Cymru, would be within the legislative competence of the Senedd.

Definitions

'natural environment'	s 44
'long-term target'	s 1(6)
'priority areas'	s 1(3)
'specified standard'	s 1(4)(a)
'specified date'	s 1(4)(b)

In force 24 January 2022 Commencement Order No 2

Application E

Background

Part 1 of the Act is intended to provide measures to ensure that there is no environmental governance gap in the UK following the end of the implementation period under the Withdrawal Agreement (see the commentary in the House of Commons Library analysis of the Environment Bill 2019–20, CBP 8824, 18 February 2020). Existing environmental targets have been largely derived from EU law and are retained in domestic legislation in accordance with the EU (Withdrawal) Act 2018 (as amended). In the Memorandum from the Department for the Environment, Food and Rural Affairs (DEFRA) to the Delegated Powers and Regulatory Reform Committee, dated 27 May 2021, DEFRA identified that now that the UK has left the EU, *'it may wish to set its own targets that differ and go beyond those of the EU'*.

When the draft Environment (Governance and Principles) Bill was first introduced in 2018, there was no provision for targets. Instead, the policy paper accompanying the Bill stated:

> *'Overall, the new statutory cycle of environmental planning, monitoring and reporting will incentivise sustained improvement in our natural world and ensure that we deliver our commitments, now and in the future.*
>
> *In addition, we will explore options for including additional cross-cutting targets for environmental improvement as part of this framework. Well-designed targets could offer greater certainty on the strength of the government's ambition and drive action by businesses and wider society.'*

In its report on the draft Environment (Governance and Principles) Bill at that time, the Environmental Audit Committee made the recommendation for a framework of targets and interim milestones: '*We recommend that in addition to the objective of a high level of protection being included on the face of the Bill, the Bill should also include a framework for targets and interim milestones to be achieved by Government Departments. These should be set following stakeholder consultation and parliamentary scrutiny. Once these targets have been established, the Cabinet Office must issue guidance directing Departments to explain how their work programmes will achieve the delivery of these targets in their Single Departmental Plans. This will then assist the Office for Environmental Protection in holding Government Departments to account*' (House of Commons Environment Audit Committee, *Scrutiny of the Draft Environment (Principles and Governance) Bill*, Eighteenth Report of Session 2017–19, HC 1951, 25 April 2019, para 53).

The need for targets was also referred to by the European Commission in its recommendation for a Council Decision authorising the opening of negotiations for a new partnership with the United Kingdom of Great Britain and Northern Ireland (see paras 98–99 of the Annex), itself a broader assessment of what would be required to ensure a common level of environmental protection:

> *'The envisaged partnership should ensure that the common level of environmental protection provided by laws, regulations and practices is not reduced below the level provided by the common standards applicable within the Union and the United Kingdom at the end of the transition period in relation to at least the following areas: access to environmental information; public participation and access to justice in environmental matters; environmental impact assessment and strategic environmental assessment; industrial emissions; air emissions and air quality targets and ceilings; nature and biodiversity conservation; waste management; the protection and preservation of the aquatic environment; the protection and preservation of the marine environment; the prevention, reduction and elimination of risks to human health or the environment arising from the production, use, release and disposal of chemical substances; and climate change. This should take into account the fact that the Union and the United Kingdom share a common biosphere in respect of cross-border pollution. The envisaged partnership should lay down minimum commitments reflecting standards, including targets, in place at the end of the transition period in those areas, where relevant. The envisaged partnership should ensure the Parties respect the precautionary principle and the principles that preventive action should be taken, that environmental damage should as a priority be rectified at source and that the polluter should pay.*
>
> *The envisaged partnership should ensure that the United Kingdom implements a transparent system for the effective domestic monitoring, reporting, oversight and enforcement of its obligations by an independent and adequately resourced body or bodies'* ('Annex to the Recommendation for a Council Decision authorising the opening for a new partnership with the United Kingdom of Great Britain and Northern Ireland', COM(2020) 35 final, Brussels, 3 February 2020).

The Government's response to the recommendation of the Environmental Audit Committee, dated 15 October 2019, agreed with the introduction of a framework for legally binding targets:

> *'We agree with the Committee's recommendation to supplement the statutory cycle of monitoring, planning and reporting with a framework for legally-binding targets. This is in line with our*

commitment laid out in the policy paper that accompanied the publication of the draft Environment Bill in December 2018.

The Environment Bill introduces a comprehensive new environmental governance framework for England. This incorporates a duty on government to set and achieve a suite of far-reaching, long-term targets across priority areas for environmental improvement, in particular air quality, water, biodiversity, and resource efficiency and waste reduction, and to set out measures to achieve those targets in EIPs. The targets will be set following public and stakeholder consultations, and subject to parliamentary scrutiny through the affirmative procedure.

These targets will complement action being taken to implement the government's statutory EIP and provide a long-term trajectory for helping to deliver the EIP's goals. The long-term targets will be accompanied by 5-yearly interim milestones, allowing for monitoring of progress. The progress towards these targets and milestones will be subject to scrutiny by the OEP.

To ensure a comprehensive suite of targets, with sufficient coverage and ambition, is in place and that the government's EIP is able to deliver these, we have included an objective in the clauses that ensures that meeting the targets, set under this and other legislation, and the measures laid out in the EIP will deliver a significant improvement in the natural environment. This provides a clear frame of reference for the duties and powers in this framework as well as providing long-term certainty to businesses and society.

We note the Committee's recommendation that the Cabinet Office should issue guidance directing government departments to explain how their work programmes will achieve the delivery of these targets. We are committed to cross-departmental action in the delivery of any targets and long-term environmental improvement. The Cabinet Office routinely issues guidance to departments on the production of the Single Departmental Plans, which is the core of the Government's planning and performance framework. Departments set out how they will deliver public commitments, such as to the natural environment, in their plans' (House of Commons Environmental Audit Committee Scrutiny of the Draft Environment (Principles and Governance) Bill: Government Response to the Committee's Eighteenth Report of Session 2017–19, First Special Report of Session 2019, HC 238, 23 October 2019, p 6).

Environmental Targets: s 1

This section establishes the power of the Secretary of State to set long-term targets in respect of any matter that relates to the natural environment or people's enjoyment of the natural environment. It requires the Secretary of State to set at least one such target in four priority areas: air quality; biodiversity; water and resource efficiency; and waste reduction. A long-term target must have a minimum duration of 15 years.

Targets must specify a standard to be achieved, which must be capable of being objectively measured, together with a date by which that target is to be achieved. The purpose of this approach is to base targets on environmental outcomes, essentially the intended final results or benefits to the environment. The Government has stated in its policy paper on environmental targets, updated on 6 September 2021, that it recognised that this may not always be possible, and in cases, where an environmental outcome cannot easily be measured, an action-based target may be more appropriate. However, in light of sub-s (4), the statutory basis for this proposition is not entirely clear.

DEFRA has stated as follows (Memorandum from the Department for the Environment, Food and Rural Affairs to the Delegated Powers and Regulatory Reform Committee, 27 May 2021): *'The Department's view is that the amount of technical detail on targets, the standard to be achieved, and the deadline for achievement will be such that it is appropriate for it to be set out in secondary, not primary legislation. The target-setting cycle is intended to be an iterative and ongoing process, for which these measures set a framework. As such, it is envisaged that targets may be, and may need to be, amended over time in order to reflect changes in scientific knowledge and evidence. Also, targets may need to be set in new areas. It would be unduly onerous for primary legislation to be introduced every time a target needed to be amended, even slightly, or created. A Bill with appropriate scope would need to be found each time.'*

S 1(2) does not specify when the duty must be exercised. But in response to a proposed amendment at committee stage, Rebecca Pow, Parliamentary Under Secretary of State at the Department for Environment, Food and Rural Affairs, stated that a target would be set in each priority area by 31 October 2022 following a process of *'robust evidence-gathering, consultation and engagement with experts, advisers and the public'* (Environment Bill Deb 17 March 2020, col 171). Sub-s (5) identifies that Regulations *'may'* make provisions about *'how the matter in respect of which a target is set is to be measured'*. The use of the word 'may' indicates a degree of flexibility.

The meaning of natural environment is set out at s 44 and includes plants, wild animals and other living organisms, their habitats, land (except buildings or other structures), air and water, and the natural systems, cycles and processes through which they interact. The restriction of the ambit of the 'natural environment' is very specific. For example, it is likely to exclude interference with a person's enjoyment of the natural environment through noise nuisance. Such an interference would fall under the statutory nuisance regime, currently found in the Environmental Protection Act 1990. The effect is to align the targets set by the Environment Bill to the principal objective of the OEP. In effect, the two run in tandem. Widening the definition of 'natural environment' would have the effect of widening the remit of the OEP. The examples given in s 44 should be regarded as an exhaustive list. In light of the wording of s 44, it is unlikely that Courts will accede to arguments seeking to introduce environmental protections to areas that do not clearly involve the natural environment as defined.

Buildings and other structures are excluded from the definition of 'natural environment'. The provisions are not intended to be used to protect historical or cultural assets of man-made structures.

See further the annotations to ss 44–46.

The policy paper that accompanied the Bill identified that the setting of legally binding targets would provide a strong mechanism for delivering long-term environmental outcomes. The targets bind current and future governments. The wording of the legislation does not preclude more than one target being set in each priority area. The purpose of the long-term targets is also stated to be to support wider environmental aims, such as reaching the net zero climate target by 2050. The OEP will be able to recommend additional targets in its annual report.

The means by which to achieve an individual target will result in policy initiatives that inevitably require 'taxation, spending or the allocation of resources within government', notably an area excluded from the definition of environmental law found in s 46 of the Act. Although the setting of a target is not directly concerned with the allocation of resources, it can be said to be indirectly concerned. There could therefore be a tension in the legislation between allocating the resources necessary for the achievement of any particular target and the overarching intention to improve the environment through the attainment of environmental outcomes. However, it is likely that the possibility of tension is overstated. In the opinion of the authors, it would be highly unlikely in a judicial review or an environmental review concerning a failure to reach a target that the Government could claim a lack of resources, or that resource issues were totally excluded from consideration because of the definition and exclusions in s 46. These are absolute duties, imposed on the Government, whereby the breach of environmental law would be the failure to meet the target.

See s 5 below as to the legal effect of the targets.

2 Environmental targets: particulate matter

(1) The Secretary of State must by regulations set a target ("the $PM_{2.5}$ air quality target") in respect of the annual mean level of $PM_{2.5}$ in ambient air.

(2) The $PM_{2.5}$ air quality target may, but need not, be a long-term target.

(3) In this section "$PM_{2.5}$" means particulate matter with an aerodynamic diameter not exceeding 2.5 micrometres.

(4) Regulations setting the $PM_{2.5}$ air quality target may make provision defining "ambient air".

(5) The duty in subsection (1) is in addition to (and does not discharge) the duty in section 1(2) to set a long-term target in relation to air quality.

(6) Section 1(4) to (9) applies to the $PM_{2.5}$ air quality target and to regulations under this section as it applies to targets set under section 1 and to regulations under that section.

(7) In this Part "the $PM_{2.5}$ air quality target" means the target set under subsection (1).

Definitions

'$PM_{2.5}$ air quality target'	s 2(1)
'$PM_{2.5}$'	s 2(3)

In force	24 January 2022 Commencement Order No 2
Application	E

Background

This section requires a target to be set for $PM_{2.5}$. Fine particulate matter is recorded in the Environment Bill's policy statement as having the most significant impact on human health. It is formed of tiny particles that can get into lungs and blood that can be transported around the body, lodging in the heart, brain and other organs, classified according to size. It is not a single compound, but is made up of a mixture of solid and liquid particles or organic and inorganic chemicals (World Health Organisation Fact Sheet, *Ambient (Outdoor) Air Quality and Health*, September 2016). The smaller the particle, the further it can penetrate into the lungs through inhalation ('Air Pollution in the UK, 2016', published September 2017).

The UK has already adopted legally binding targets to reduce overall national emissions for five air pollutants by 2020 and 2030, found in the National Emission Ceilings Regulations 2018, including $PM_{2.5}$. In January 2019 the UK published its Clean Air Strategy, which stated that air pollution was the top environmental risk to human health in the UK and the fourth greatest risk to public health after cancer, heart disease and obesity. As of 9 December 2020, the UK had committed to a 46 per cent reduction in $PM_{2.5}$ in 2030 and in each subsequent year, recorded in Sch 3 of the National Emission Ceilings Regulations 2018.

However, the World Health Organization's *Air Quality Guidelines* recommend a considerably lower level for annual mean $PM_{2.5}$ than the legal limit in the UK and across Europe.

At the time of writing, following an update in 2021, the WHO states that annual average concentrations of $PM_{2.5}$ should not exceed 5 μg/m^3, while the 24-hour mean average exposure should not exceed 15 μg/m^3 more than 3–4 days per year. In the UK, the Air Quality Standards Regulations 2010, as amended by the Environment (Miscellaneous Amendments) (EU Exit) Regulations 2020, require that the concentrations of $PM_{2.5}$ must not exceed an annual average of 20 μg/m^3. The gross disparity between national limits and WHO guidelines was referenced in the 'Prevention of Future Deaths' report published by the Coroner of Southwark following the 2021 inquest touching on the death of Ella Adoo Kissi Debra. The evidence at the inquest was that there was no safe level for particulate matter and that the WHO guidelines should be seen as the minimum requirements. Central Government Departments, including DEFRA, were required to report on this concern by 17 June 2021.

In its response, published on 17 June 2021, the Government committed to a public consultation on new legal targets for $PM_{2.5}$ and other pollutants in early 2022, with the aim of setting new targets in legislation by October 2022. In addition to a simple concentration target on $PM_{2.5}$, the Government also stated that it is developing a more sophisticated population exposure reduction target, aiming to drive reductions not just in pollution hotspots, but in all areas.

At the time that the Environment Bill was introduced, the WHO annual mean guideline limit was 10 μg/m^3, but, as noted above, this limit was revised in September 2021. Previous government research, notably *Air Quality: Assessing Progress Towards WHO Guideline Levels of $PM_{2.5}$ in the UK* (Department of Environment, Food and Rural Affairs, 23 July 2019), concluded that *'it would be technically feasible to meet the WHO guideline level for $PM_{2.5}$ across the UK in the future'*, although challenging. In response to the revised WHO limit the Government stated that it will set ambitious targets on air quality through the Environment Act, but it has not yet committed to the revised WHO limit.

Previously, the Clean Air Strategy set out the Government's ambition as follows: *'[The Government] will progressively cut public exposure to particulate matter pollution as suggested by the World Health Organization. We will set a new, ambitious, long-term target to reduce people's exposure to $PM_{2.5}$ and will publish evidence early in 2019 to examine what action would be needed to meet the WHO annual mean guideline limit of 10 μg/m^3. By implementing the policies in this Strategy, we will reduce $PM_{2.5}$ concentrations across the UK, so that the number of people living in locations above the WHO guideline level of 10 μg/m^3 is reduced by 50% by 2025'* (Department of Environment, Food and Rural Affairs, *Clean Air Strategy 2019*, p 7). It can be anticipated that the landscape has changed considerably since that was published.

The target for $PM_{2.5}$ is not a long-term target as under s 1. Although there is no explicit rationale for the target for $PM_{2.5}$ not needing to be a long-term target, it may be that, given the urgency of the problem, tackling $PM_{2.5}$ cannot afford the minimum period of 15 years associated with a long-term target. In addition, it is likely that the inclusion of $PM_{2.5}$ here as a specific priority reflects the importance attributed to the problem.

Other, potentially long-term, targets for air quality can be set as a result of this legislation, irrespective of the fact that other specific targets are not directly referred to in the legislation. By way of example of the areas that could be considered, the National Emission Ceilings Regulations 2018 also set binding targets for SO_2, NO_x, non-methane volatile organic compounds and NH_3.

The term 'ambient air' is to be defined in regulations (s 2(4)). The US Environmental Protection Agency (EPA) defined 'ambient air' in the Clean Air Act, 42 USC § 7401 et seq (1970), as *'that portion of the atmosphere, external to buildings, to which the general public has access'* (Title 40, Code of Federal Regulations, § 50.1(e)). In applying that definition, the EPA has followed a policy that allows excluding certain areas of a source's property, located outside of a building, from ambient air. As a result, atmosphere over land owned or controlled by the stationary source may be excluded from the definition of ambient air where measures are employed to preclude access to the land by the general public. This has proved controversial, as it is considered that the policy approach of the EPA allows industry to emit pollution into the outdoors as long as the pollution technically goes into the air at the site that it owns and some measures, for example warning signs, have been taken to prevent general public access. Given that the definition of 'natural environment' in s 44 does not include buildings or other structures (and potentially their curtilage), it is likely that the same issues could arise in the UK, perhaps even to a greater extent.

See s 5 below as to the legal effect of the targets.

3 Environmental targets: species abundance

(1) The Secretary of State must by regulations set a target (the "species abundance target") in respect of a matter relating to the abundance of species.

(2) The specified date for the species abundance target must be 31 December 2030.

(3) Accordingly, the species abundance target is not a long-term target and the duty in subsection (1) is in addition to (and does not discharge) the duty in section 1(2) to set a long-term target in relation to biodiversity.

(4) Before making regulations under subsection (1) which set or amend a target the Secretary of State must be satisfied that meeting the target, or the amended target, would halt a decline in the abundance of species.

(5) Section 1(4) to (9) applies to the species abundance target and to regulations under this section as it applies to targets set under section 1 and to regulations under that section.

(6) In this Part "the species abundance target" means the target set under subsection (1).

Definitions

'species abundance target'	s 3(1)
'long-term target'	s 1(6)
'specified date'	s (1)(4)(a)

In force	24 January 2022 Commencement Order No 2
Application	E

Background

The Act establishes long-term environmental targets in four priority areas, including biodiversity. It does not state what these targets must be, but that they must be laid before Parliament in draft statutory instruments before 31 October 2022 (see s 4(9)).

When the Act was originally laid before Parliament, there was no reference to a 'species abundance target'. In contrast, the 25 Year Environment Plan makes 75 references to the word 'species' and commits, at p 26, to '*take action to recover threatened, iconic or economically important species of animals, plants and fungi, and where possible to prevent human-induced extinction or loss of known threatened species in England and the Overseas Territories'*. The amendment to the Bill, as it then was, was introduced on 23 June 2021. The House of Commons Library notes that the amendment sets a short-term species abundance target for 31 December 2030 and applies to species across the country and not just protected sites. (*Environment Bill 2021–22: Lords Amendments and "Ping Pong" Stages*, No 09345, 15 November 2021).

During the parliamentary debates on the Bill in the House of Lords, Lord Goldsmith, House of Lords Environment Minister, stated: *'The 2030 species target will be subject to the same requirements as the long-term legally binding targets set under the Bill. Our focus now must be on the detailed work to develop a fully evidenced target. I met stakeholders on this issue just last week. We are developing the scientific and economic evidence to underpin this target, and will consult on all our proposed targets early next year'* (HL Deb 23 June 2021, vol 813, col 313).

Species Abundance Target: s 3

This section requires a target to be set for species abundance. In accordance with s 4(9), a draft of the statutory instrument setting out the target must be laid before Parliament on or before 31 October 2022.

The wording 'in respect of a matter relating to the abundance of species' found in s 3(1) is vague. When the amendment was moved in the House of Lords on 23 June 2021, Lord Goldsmith stated: *'We hope that this measure will be the net zero equivalent for nature, spurring action of the scale required to address the biodiversity crisis. As noble Lords know, nature has been in decline for decades, and tackling that long-term decline will be challenging. But through this new target we are committing ourselves to that objective. A domestic 2030 species target will not only benefit species; the actions necessary to achieve it will also help drive wider environmental improvements – for example, to the habitats in which they live, and on which they depend'* (HL Deb 23 June 2021, vol 813, col 313).

In light of concerns that the wording was not specific enough, the wording of sub-s (4) was subsequently amended from *'the Secretary of State must be satisfied that meeting the target, or the amended target, would further the objective of halting a decline in the abundance of species'* to the more specific wording now found in the Act that the *'Secretary of State must be satisfied that meeting the target, or the amended target, would halt a decline in the abundance of species'*.

See s 5 below as to the legal effect of the species abundance target.

4 Environmental targets: process

(1) Before making regulations under sections 1 to 3 the Secretary of State must seek advice from persons the Secretary of State considers to be independent and to have relevant expertise.

(2) Before making regulations under sections 1 to 3 which set or amend a target the Secretary of State must be satisfied that the target, or amended target, can be met.

(3) The Secretary of State may make regulations under sections 1 to 3 which revoke or lower a target (the "existing target") only if satisfied that—

(a) meeting the existing target would have no significant benefit compared with not meeting it or with meeting a lower target, or

(b) because of changes in circumstances since the existing target was set or last amended the environmental, social, economic or other costs of meeting it would be disproportionate to the benefits.

(4) Before making regulations under sections 1 to 3 which revoke or lower a target the Secretary of State must lay before Parliament, and publish, a statement explaining why the Secretary of State is satisfied as mentioned in subsection (3).

(5) Regulations lower a target if, to any extent, they—

(a) replace the specified standard with a lower standard, or

(b) replace the specified date with a later date.

(6) Regulations under section 2 may not revoke the $PM_{2.5}$ air quality target (but may amend it in accordance with this section).

(7) For the purposes of this Part a target is met if the specified standard is achieved by the specified date.

(8) Regulations under sections 1 to 3 are subject to the affirmative procedure.

(9) A draft of a statutory instrument (or drafts of statutory instruments) containing regulations setting—

(a) each of the targets required by section 1(2),

(b) the $PM_{2.5}$ air quality target, and

(c) the species abundance target,

must be laid before Parliament on or before 31 October 2022.

Definitions

'the $PM_{2.5}$ air quality target'	s 2(1)
'the species abundance target'	s 3(1)

In force	24 January 2022 Commencement Order No 2
Application	E

S 4(3) permits the Secretary of State to make regulations that revoke or lower a target only if satisfied that (a) meeting that target would have no significant benefit with not meeting it or with meeting a lower target or (b) where, because of a change in circumstances, the environmental, social, economic or other costs of meeting it would be disproportionate to the benefits.

It may be of note that the 'or' between (a) and (b) is disjunctive, as it provides the Secretary of State with two routes by which to revoke or lower an existing target. As to the first, since the word 'significant' is not defined, it is not clear how the term will be assessed, and the section leaves open what kind of 'benefit' is intended to be encompassed. On one view it would make some sense to the provision to confine 'benefit' in sub-s 3(a) to mean health benefits, leaving wider economic and other considerations to the second limb, but there is no guarantee that a court would interpret the provision in this way and, importantly, such a restriction may simply be too narrow an interpretation. As to the second limb, the existence of a further 'or other costs' would appear to allow for significant latitude in the assessment of relevant 'costs' in the calculation of proportionality, or at the very least allow for a multitude of factors to be considered by the Secretary of State as part of the assessment of proportionality.

There is the potential for further latitude as in many cases the 'benefits' are, at present, unknown or speculative. In principle, the application of the precautionary principle referred to in s 17 should, if the Government statement on principles is consistent with previous interpretation at EU level, require that these benefits should be treated as being concrete (even where there is some uncertainty) and that any target should aim to achieve the best possible case scenario in respect of these benefits (see the approach taken by the Court of First Instance towards the applicability of the precautionary principle as a general principle informing the interpretation of EU law in *Artegodan GmbH and Others v Commission of the European Communities* [2002] ECR II-04945, paras 181–86). That in itself creates the possibility of an inherent tension between the application of the precautionary principle and the requirement on the Secretary of State to have an eye on proportionality. There is a risk that the fact that the 'benefits' may be difficult to quantify will make any substantive legal challenge difficult in the event that the Secretary of State attempts to lower or revoke an existing target.

Proportionality as a ground for judicial review has been discussed extensively by the courts, mainly in the context of EU law and the European Convention on Human Rights, and any case law has been considered in that light. In the context of human rights, Lord Sumption in *Bank Mellat v Her Majesty's Treasury (No 2)* [2013] UKSC 39 summarised the principle as meaning in relation to any particular measure: '*(i) whether its objective is sufficiently important to justify the limitation of a fundamental right; (ii) whether it is rationally connected to the objective; (iii) whether a less intrusive measure could have been used; and (iv) whether, having regard to these matters and to the severity of the consequences, a fair balance has been struck between the rights of the individual and the interests of the community*' (para 20).

The benchmark for the assessment of proportionality is also not defined, subject to the direct connection to 'the benefits'. In light of the stated policy of using environmental outcomes as the primary means of setting targets, it may be envisaged that the outcome itself and the reasoning behind the selection of that environmental outcome are likely to be directly relevant to any assessment of proportionality.

Regulations made under sub-ss (1)–(3) are subject to the affirmative procedure. The result is that statutory instruments laid under the affirmative procedure must be actively approved by both Houses of Parliament. This should ensure greater scrutiny of environmental targets and issues surrounding benefit and proportionality.

5 Environmental targets: effect

It is the duty of the Secretary of State to ensure that—

(a) targets set under section 1 are met,

(b) the $PM_{2.5}$ air quality target set under section 2 is met, and

(c) the species abundance target set under section 3 is met.

In force 24 January 2022 Commencement Order No 2

Application E

This section places a positive duty on the Secretary of State to ensure that targets set under s 1 are met and that the $PM_{2.5}$ air quality target and the species abundance target set under ss 2 and 3 are also met. S 5 contains no qualifications or weaker forms of obligation, nor does it restrict the Secretary of State to what is reasonable or practicable, or cross-refer to other functions.

The wording largely mirrors s 1 of the Climate Change Act 2008 in the setting of a mandatory target. Outcome duties are absolute obligations to ensure that a certain outcome is achieved, requiring an aggregation of legal, financial, policy and practical measures taken by the Secretary of State over a prolonged period. There is domestic precedent for outcome duties to be taken at face value. *R (Client Earth) v Secretary of State for the Environment, Food and Rural Affairs* [2015] PTSR 909 concerned Art 13(1) of Directive 2008/50, whereby, in the absence of a derogation, it was an automatic consequence of non-compliance that the relevant authority should establish a plan as required by the Directive. Even arguments for the impossibility of compliance were 'unfounded', and it was held by Lord Carnwath at para 19 of the judgment that it was the duty of national courts to require the relevant authority to deal with the problems as swiftly as possible.

On the outcome duty in the Climate Change Act 2008, *De Smith's Judicial Review* notes: *'Had Parliament wanted to create a duty to take reasonable steps, it could have done so expressly. Had Parliament wanted to exclude or reduce the scope for judicial review challenge, it could have done so expressly. The better view is that a court called upon to review whether a hard-edged strategic outcome duty has been fulfilled should do so on the basis of evidence; the answer is either yes or no'* (para 5-082, 8th edn, 2018).

There is a constitutional argument that long-term targets are inherently undemocratic because they extend significantly beyond the life of Parliament and hence bind the hands of future governments to ensure compliance. This recent style of legislation was addressed in *R (Friends of the Earth) v Secretary of State for Business, Enterprise and Regulatory Reform* [2010] Env LR 11 when the court considered the cost of eradicating fuel poverty and noted that '*This style of legislation is of recent origin. Historically, central Government has announced and developed its policies primarily through political rather than statutory or legal channels and the consequences of failure have been political rather than justiciable*' (para 2). However, the real challenge in that case was not the style of the legislation but the fact that the duty to achieve the relevant target was qualified by the phrase 'as far as reasonably practicable'. No such qualification exists in s 5.

Ensuring that the duty is met will inevitably be dependent on factors that may be beyond the control of the Secretary of State. The creation of multiple absolute targets can lead to conflicts in the allocation of resources. In addition, it is not inconceivable that the achievement of one target may impact on the Government's ability to achieve a different target, but there is no scope within s 5 for a hierarchy of targets. Absolute targets remain absolute.

The date by when the target is met is the end date, to be specified in accordance with s 1(4)(b) of the Act. However, the duty needs also to be read in the context of the s 6 reporting duties to Parliament, and these provisions, which envisage the possibility of failure, may inhibit a court from granting more prescriptive remedies beyond a declaration (see annotations to s 6).

The environmental improvement plan (EIP) provisions under ss 9, 12 and 15 set requirements for consideration of the progress made towards meeting targets, and for consideration of the need to introduce new measures to meet targets, when reviewing and renewing EIPs. There is no explicit sanction in s 5 on the Secretary of State in the event that a target is not on course to be met, though failure to reach the target would be subject to judicial review or to enforcement action by the Office for Environmental Protection (see below).

6 Environmental targets: reporting duties

(1) Regulations under section 1, 2 or 3 must specify a reporting date for any target set under that section.

(2) On or before the reporting date the Secretary of State must lay before Parliament, and publish, a statement containing the required information about the target.

(3) The required information about a target is (as appropriate)—

(a) that the target has been met,

(b) that the target has not been met, or

(c) that the Secretary of State is not yet able to determine whether the target has been met, the reasons for that and the steps the Secretary of State intends to take in order to determine whether the target has been met.

(4) Where the Secretary of State makes a statement that the target has not been met the Secretary of State must, before the end of the 12 month period beginning with the date on which the statement is laid, lay before Parliament, and publish, a report.

(5) The report must—

(a) explain why the target has not been met, and

(b) set out the steps the Secretary of State has taken, or intends to take, to ensure the specified standard is achieved as soon as reasonably practicable.

(6) Where the Secretary of State makes a statement that the Secretary of State is not yet able to determine whether the target has been met the Secretary of State must, before the end of the 6 month period beginning with the date on which the statement is laid, lay before Parliament, and publish, a further statement containing the required information.

(7) Subsections (3) to (6) apply to further statements under subsection (6) as they apply to a statement under subsection (2).

Definitions

'required information'	s 6(3)

In force	24 January 2022 Commencement Order No 2
Application	E

S 6 provides for the reporting duties of the Secretary of State to Parliament when a long-term target is set under s 1 for the $PM_{2.5}$ air quality target or a species abundance target is set pursuant to ss 2 and 3. The regulations specifying the targets must provide for a reporting date (sub-s (1)). However, there is nothing within the section prohibiting the Secretary of State from reporting before the reporting date and, were it thought appropriate, regulations could set multiple reporting dates in respect of the individual targets.

Where a target has not been met, this section allows for parliamentary scrutiny of that failure.

Sub-s 4 allows for the Secretary of State to take 12 months before publishing a report that sets out why a particular target has not been met and the steps that are to be taken to ensure that the target is met as soon as reasonably practicable. This is consistent with the environmental outcomes approach adopted by the legislation. Nonetheless, it is not made clear why a period of 12 months has been allowed, nor how 12 months is consistent with ensuring targets are met as soon as reasonably practicable.

Other than parliamentary scrutiny and the need to identify steps towards achieving the target as soon as reasonably practicable, there is no explicit sanction for a failure to meet a target, other than an action for judicial review or enforcement action by the Office for Environmental Protection. Such an action would be likely to focus on whether or not an adequate plan was in place to meet the target in question.

The Act leaves open the question of the effect of an explicit provision contemplating a failure to meet a particular target and it is unclear precisely what will be the effect if the Secretary of State fails in their duty to ensure that a target is met. It may be argued that, given the fact that the failure to meet the target results in a report to that effect to Parliament, the only sanction available for a failure to meet a target is a political one. In such circumstances, a court might go so far as to make a declaration that the target had been met, with the consequent breach of duty on the part of the Secretary of State, but decline to make a remedial order, choosing to leave the issue of remedy to Parliament to determine what action to take in light of the report. In other words, the ability of the court to require that the Secretary of State determine an immediate plan to address the deficiencies in meeting the target would be inhibited by the existence of parliamentary scrutiny. However, such an interpretation ignores the duties on national courts to ensure that those who are directly or indirectly affected by a breach of legal duty are able to obtain a legal remedy through the court process. It may be that the better interpretation would be that the existence of these provisions enables a court to require that an immediate plan to achieve compliance is formulated by the Secretary of State, leaving Parliament to debate and influence the details of the steps to be taken to ensure compliance. This latter interpretation would be commensurate with the significance to which the need to meet environmental targets is attributed.

Under the Climate Change Act 2008 there is a similar potential tension between absolute legal duties to achieve greenhouse gas reduction targets and a duty on government to report to Parliament on failure to meet the target and the steps to be taken to secure the reductions.

The reporting duty is part of the Government's 'triple lock system'. Rebecca Pow, Parliamentary Under Secretary of State at the Department for Environment, Food and Rural Affairs, stated during the parliamentary debates on the Bill: '*To be clear, we have a little mechanism called the triple lock, which is the key to driving short-term progress. The Government must have an environmental improvement plan, which sets out the steps they intend to take to improve the environment, and review it at least every five years. In step 2, the Government must report on progress towards achieving the targets every year. In step 3, the OEP [Office for Environmental Protection] will hold us to account on progress towards achieving the targets, and every year it can recommend how we could make better progress, if it thinks better progress needs to be made. The Government then have to respond. If progress seems too slow, or is deemed to be too slow, the Government may need to develop new policies to make up for that when reviewing their EIPs. They will not wait until 2037 to do that; these things can be done as a continuous process, and that is important*' (Environment Bill Deb 17 March 2020, col 211).

This statement ignores the potential for judicial pressure resulting from a successful judicial review or environmental review challenge.

7 Environmental targets: review

(1) The Secretary of State must review targets set under sections 1 to 3 in accordance with this section.

(2) The purpose of the review is to consider whether the significant improvement test is met.

(3) The significant improvement test is met if meeting—

(a) the targets set under sections 1 to 3, and

(b) any other environmental targets which meet the conditions in subsection (8) and which the Secretary of State considers it appropriate to take into account,

would significantly improve the natural environment in England.

(4) Having carried out the review the Secretary of State must lay before Parliament, and publish, a report stating—

(a) whether the Secretary of State considers that the significant improvement test is met, and

(b) if the Secretary of State considers that the test is not met, the steps the Secretary of State intends to take in relation to the powers in sections 1 to 3 to ensure that it is met.

(5) The first review must be completed by 31 January 2023.

(6) Subsequent reviews must be completed before the end of the 5 year period beginning with the day on which the previous review was completed.

(7) A review is completed when the Secretary of State has laid and published the report.

(8) The conditions mentioned in subsection (3)(b) are that—

(a) the target relates to an aspect of the natural environment in England or an area which includes England,

(b) it specifies a standard to be achieved which is capable of being objectively measured,

(c) it specifies a date by which the standard is to be achieved, and

(d) it is contained in legislation which forms part of the law of England and Wales.

(9) In this section "England" includes—

(a) the English inshore region, and

(b) the English offshore region,

within the meaning of the Marine and Coastal Access Act 2009 (see section 322 of that Act).

Definitions

'significant improvement test'	s 7(3)
'natural environment'	s 44
'England'	s 7(9)

In force	24 January 2022 Commencement Order No 2
Application	E

This section requires the Secretary of State to conduct periodic reviews to consider whether the significant improvement test, defined in sub-s (3), is met. The first review must be completed by 31 January 2023, the initial targets having to be set by October 2022. Subsequent reviews will then take place every five years.

It is to be assumed that the purpose of the review is to ensure that the targets that have been set are sufficiently stringent to ensure that they serve a significant benefit to the natural environment. As with s 4, the word 'significant' is undefined.

The requirement for significant improvement with respect of the targets set under ss 1 and 2 is not explicitly referred to in either of those two earlier sections. On the face of it, this omission in the drafting gives rise to two potential interpretations. On the one hand, the process of selecting a target set under ss 1–3 must satisfy some as yet undefined concept of significant improvement, otherwise, at any first review, the targets would fall foul of the significant improvement test and could be revoked by the Secretary of State under s 4. On the other hand, any target set under ss 1–3 can be said to define the environmental outcome, resulting in a significant environmental improvement. Adopting this latter interpretation, ss 4 and 6 are mechanisms to be used to ensure that targets are properly met rather than a gateway for the Secretary of State to reduce or remove environmental obligations.

The section does not explicitly state that any revision cannot allow for any reduction in existing targets, but this is a likely interpretation of the provisions. S 7(2) and (3) provides that the purpose of the review is to consider whether the existing targets set would *'significantly improve the natural environment in England'*. After carrying out the review, the Secretary of State must publish and lay a report before Parliament, stating whether the Secretary of State considers the targets do significantly improve the environment, and if the Secretary of State considers they do not, what steps will be taken to make new regulations on targets under ss 1–3. It would be a perverse reading of the powers that would allow the Secretary of State to consider that an existing target does not significantly improve the natural environment but that a revised lower target does do so.

During the parliamentary debates on the Bill, Rebecca Pow, Parliamentary Under Secretary of State at the Department for Environment, Food and Rural Affairs, stated that *'I want to offer reassurance that the target-setting process is an ongoing process. It is not a one-off thing, where we set one target and that is the end of that. That is why we will also need to consider what other targets might be needed to ensure that we can significantly improve the natural environment in England'* (Environment Bill Deb 17 March 2020, col 172). She confirmed that when the first statutory Environment Improvement Plan review takes place, the Government would review whether any other targets that had not been set to date might be required, with an outcome reported by 31 January 2023. She also stated that the Office for Environmental Protection would be able to recommend additional targets in its annual report (ibid col 202).

Environmental improvement plans

8 Environmental improvement plans

(1) The Secretary of State must prepare an environmental improvement plan.

(2) An "environmental improvement plan" is a plan for significantly improving the natural environment in the period to which the plan relates.

(3) That period must not be shorter than 15 years.

(4) An environmental improvement plan must set out the steps Her Majesty's Government intends to take to improve the natural environment in the period to which the plan relates.

(5) It may also set out steps Her Majesty's Government intends to take to improve people's enjoyment of the natural environment in that period (and if it does so references in this Part to improving the natural environment, in relation to that plan, include improving people's enjoyment of it).

(6) The Secretary of State's functions in relation to environmental improvement plans are not exercisable in relation to the natural environment in Wales.

(7) The document entitled "A green future: our 25 year plan to improve the environment" published by Her Majesty's Government on 11 January 2018 is to be treated as an environmental improvement plan prepared by the Secretary of State under this section.

(8) References in this Part—

(a) to the first environmental improvement plan, are to that document;

(b) to the current environmental improvement plan, are to the environmental improvement plan for the time being in effect.

Definitions

'environmental improvement plan'	s 8(2)
'natural environment'	s 44
'first environmental improvement plan'	s 8(8)
'current environmental improvement plan'	s 8(8)

In force	24 January 2022 Commencement Order No 2
Application	E

The Secretary of State must set an environmental improvement plan (EIP), which must set out the steps that are intended to be taken by the Government to improve the natural environment in the period to which the plan relates (which must be at least 15 years). In this way, the Act places the 25 Year Environment Plan, first published on 11 January 2018, on a legislative footing as the first EIP. There is no limit to the number of EIPs that can be made under this section save that, per sub-s (8), only one EIP can be 'in effect' at any one time. Steps for the review, amendment or revocation of EIPs are set out in the following sections.

There is no indication in the section of the level of detail required in an EIP. Sub-s (4) identifies that steps to improve the natural environment within an EIP are mandatory. Conversely, steps to improve people's enjoyment of the natural environment within an EIP are only discretionary, as identified in sub-s (5).

There is no specific link between the environmental improvement plan and the target-setting powers provided for in the Act. It was commented at committee stage that to link the EIP to the specified targets would single out aspects of the environment ahead of others. It was thought that the EIP would allow the Government to take a more holistic approach to the environment.

It must therefore follow that it is expected that the EIP will go beyond the simple targets set out in the Act. This supports the idea that the targets are for priority areas but that they are not the only focus for environmental improvement.

A further difference can be drawn from the fact that targets must be objectively measurable whereas there is no such requirement for this to be the case for EIPs. EIPs prima facie mark a shift away from established legal frameworks and effectively reflect government strategy. If it is accepted that the definition of significant environmental improvement is defined by reference to environmental outcomes achieved through the setting of specific targets, then the apparent difference between EIPs and targets takes a different hue. EIPs, as plans for significantly improving the natural environment in the period to which they apply, can be seen as the complementary side of targets and should document (in more detail than the targets) the policy and steps that will be taken in the lifespan of the EIP.

9 Annual reports on environmental improvement plans

(1) The Secretary of State must prepare annual reports on the implementation of the current environmental improvement plan.

(2) An annual report must—

(a) describe what has been done, in the period to which the report relates, to implement the environmental improvement plan, and

(b) consider, having regard to any data obtained under section 16, whether the natural environment has, or particular aspects of it have, improved during that period.

(3) In considering the matters in subsection (2)(b) an annual report must consider the progress that has been made towards achieving—

(a) any targets, or any relevant targets, set under sections 1 to 3, and

(b) any interim targets, or any relevant interim targets, set under sections 11 and 14.

(4) The first annual report on the first environmental improvement plan may relate to any 12 month period that includes the day on which this section comes into force.

(5) The first annual report on a subsequent environmental improvement plan must relate to the first 12 months of the period to which the plan relates.

(6) Subsequent annual reports on an environmental improvement plan must relate to the 12 month period immediately following the 12 month period to which the previous annual report relates.

(7) An annual report must be laid before Parliament before the end of the 4 month period beginning immediately after the last day of the period to which the report relates.

(8) The Secretary of State must publish annual reports laid before Parliament under this section.

Definitions

'first environmental improvement plan'	s 8(8)
'current environmental improvement plan'	s 8(8)
'natural environment'	s 44

In force	24 January 2022 Commencement Order No 2
Application	E

This section requires the Secretary of State to prepare annual reports on the implementation of the current EIP and progress towards targets.

An annual report must both describe what has been done to implement the EIP and consider, having regard to any data obtained under s 16, whether the natural environment has improved. The section does not identify the benchmarks against which improvement should be objectively measured, save for reference to the specific targets, albeit these are unlikely to reflect or require an environmental outcome in all areas of the natural environment.

The Natural Capital Committee was an independent advisory committee which ran from 2012 to December 2020. The key focus during its final term was on advising the Government on the implementation of the 25 Year Environment Plan. The final response of the Natural Capital Committee to the second 25 Year Environment Plan Progress Report was highly critical of the Government's assessment of progress, highlighting that it was crucial to use the right framework and metrics or risk multiple policy failures, including the success of the 25 Year Environment Plan and future EIPs (Natural Capital Committee, *Final Response to the 25 Year Environment Plan Progress Report*, October 2020).

It therefore may be of note that the requirement on the Secretary of State to produce an annual report does not specify any criteria on how to measure improvement, save for by reference to the progress towards the specific targets set under ss 1–3 or interim targets set under ss 11 and 14. However, this section should be read closely together with s 16, which requires the Secretary of State to make arrangements for the obtaining of data for the purposes of monitoring whether the natural environment is improving and whether progress is being made towards meeting targets under ss 1–3 or interim targets under ss 11 and 14.

Under s 28 below, the Office of Environmental Protection must also monitor progress with the environmental improvement plan and publish and lay before Parliament annual reports (see annotations to s 28).

10 Reviewing and revising environmental improvement plans

(1) The Secretary of State must—

(a) review the current environmental improvement plan in accordance with this section, section 11 and section 12, and

(b) if the Secretary of State of State is required to revise the plan under section 11, or considers it appropriate to revise the plan as a result of the review, revise the plan.

(2) The period to which a revised plan relates must end at the same time as the period to which the current plan relates.

(3) The first review of the first environmental improvement plan must be completed by 31 January 2023.

(4) The first review of a subsequent environmental improvement plan must be completed before the end of the 5 year period beginning with the day on which it replaces the previous plan (see section 13(4)).

(5) Subsequent reviews of an environmental improvement plan must be completed before the end of the 5 year period beginning with the day on which the previous review was completed.

(6) If as a result of a review the Secretary of State revises the environmental improvement plan, the Secretary of State must lay before Parliament—

(a) the revised environmental improvement plan, and

(b) a statement explaining the revisions and the reasons for them.

(7) If as a result of a review the Secretary of State does not revise the environmental improvement plan, the Secretary of State must lay before Parliament a statement explaining that and the reasons for it.

(8) The Secretary of State must publish the documents laid under subsection (6) or (7).

(9) A review is completed when the Secretary of State has laid and published the documents mentioned in subsection (6) or (7).

(10) References in this Act to an environmental improvement plan include a revised environmental improvement plan.

Definitions

'current environmental improvement plan'	s 8(8)
'first environmental improvement plan'	s 8(8)
'natural environment'	s 44

In force	24 January 2022 Commencement Order No 2
Application	E

Ss 10–12 set out the process by which the Secretary of State is to undertake reviews and revisions of EIPs. S 10 considers reviews of EIPs, with supplemental requirements provided by s 12. Following review, the Secretary of State must follow the steps in s 11 to revise any interim targets.

As a minimum, reviews are mandatory and are triggered simply by the passage of time, but there is no limitation on the number of reviews that the Secretary of State may undertake provided that they adhere to the correct procedural steps.

11 Reviewing and revising plans: interim targets

(1) On the first review of the first environmental improvement plan, the Secretary of State must revise the plan so as to—

(a) set at least one interim target in respect of each relevant matter, and

(b) secure that there is at all times, until the end of the 5 year period beginning with the relevant date, an interim target set by the plan in respect of each relevant matter.

(2) On any other review of an environmental improvement plan, the Secretary of State must make any revisions to the plan which are necessary in order to—

(a) set at least one interim target in respect of any matter that has become a relevant matter since the previous review, and

(b) secure that there is at all times, until the end of the 5 year period beginning with the relevant date, an interim target set by the plan in respect of each relevant matter.

(3) A "relevant matter" means any matter in respect of which there is a target under sections 1 to 3.

(4) Subsection (2)(b) does not apply in respect of a matter if the specified date for the target under sections 1 to 3 in respect of that matter is before the end of the 5 year period beginning with the relevant date.

(5) On a review of an environmental improvement plan, the Secretary of State may revise or replace any interim targets set by the plan in respect of a relevant matter (subject to subsection (2)(b), where it applies in respect of the matter).

(6) An interim target in respect of a matter must specify—

(a) a standard to be achieved, which must be capable of being objectively measured, and

(b) a date by which it is to be achieved.

(7) The date must be no later than the end of the 5 year period beginning with—

(a) for the first interim target in respect of a matter, the relevant date;

(b) for subsequent interim targets in respect of a matter, the later of the relevant date and the date specified for the previous interim target.

(8) Before setting or revising an interim target in respect of a matter the Secretary of State must be satisfied that meeting the target, or the revised target, would make an appropriate contribution towards meeting the target under sections 1 to 3 in respect of that matter.

(9) The "relevant date" is the date on which the review is completed.

Definitions

'first environmental improvement plan'	s 8(8)
'environmental improvement plan'	s 8(8)
'relevant matter'	s 11(3)
'relevant date'	s 11(9)

In force	24 January 2022 Commencement Order No 2
Application	E

The Secretary of State is required to revise the existing EIP in different ways depending on whether he is reviewing the first EIP or any subsequent EIP. With respect to the first EIP, the Secretary of State is required to set an interim target for each matter in respect of which there is a pre-existing long-term target concerning priority areas (s 1), the target for particulate matter (s 2) and the species abundance target (s 3). If any of these interim targets are achieved having been the only target concerning a given relevant matter, they must be replaced with a new interim target. When reviewing subsequent EIPs, the Secretary of State is afforded the flexibility to make new interim targets with respect to new relevant matters that have gained significance in the intervening period. Any interim target set by the Secretary of State must set out a standard to be achieved and be capable of objective measurement.

S 11(8) requires that, before setting or revising an interim target, the Secretary of State is satisfied that meeting that interim target would make an 'appropriate contribution' towards meeting the related long-term target under ss 1–3. The Act is silent on what constitutes an 'appropriate contribution' for these purposes. It is consistent with the outcome approach of the Act that the 'appropriate contribution' must support a direction of travel that will meet the target's dates. It is arguable that it would not be appropriate (and potentially legally challengeable) to set an interim target that would result in a path that unreasonably risked, by reference to the scientific knowledge and understanding at the relevant time, meeting the eventual environmental outcome, particularly if that eventual outcome was defined in the legislation as a priority target.

In contrast to the long-term targets pursuant to s 1, there is no legal duty on the Secretary of State to meet interim targets. Interim targets may therefore be considered a method of measuring progress towards the achievement of long-term targets, rather than legally enforceable outcomes in their own right. Nonetheless, it may well become palpably clear through the assessment of interim targets whether the Government is on track to meet the binding requirements of the Environment Act. In this way, interim targets may provide the backbone of any challenge to the Government for lack of progress.

It is consequently unlikely that there can be any form of environmental review for failing to meet an interim target if there is no duty on the Secretary of State to meet that interim target. Nonetheless, the Office for Environmental Protection must report annually on progress towards achieving targets (in accordance with s 28), and the Secretary of State is required to respond to those reports and lay that response before Parliament. See further the annotations to s 28.

12 Reviewing and revising plans: other requirements

(1) In reviewing an environmental improvement plan under section 10, the Secretary of State must consider—

(a) what has been done to implement the plan in the period since it was published or (if it has been reviewed before) last reviewed,

(b) whether, having regard to data obtained under section 16 and reports made by the OEP under section 28, the natural environment has, or particular aspects of it have, improved during that period, and

(c) whether Her Majesty's Government should take further or different steps to improve the natural environment (compared to those set out in the plan) in the remainder of the period to which the plan relates.

(2) In considering the matters in subsection (1)(b) the Secretary of State must consider the progress that has been made towards meeting—

(a) any targets, or any relevant targets, set under sections 1 to 3, and

(b) any interim targets, or any relevant interim targets, set under sections 11 and 14.

(3) In considering the matters in subsection (1)(c) the Secretary of State must consider whether Her Majesty's Government should take further or different steps towards meeting those targets (compared to those set out in the plan).

Definitions

'environmental improvement plan'	s 8(8)
'natural environment'	s 44

In force	24 January 2022 Commencement Order No 2
Application	E

The further obligations in s 12 are non-specific in terms of what they require of the Secretary of State. The Secretary of State need only consider, rather than act upon, the implementation steps, resultant data and steps open to the Government. It appears, by means of sub-ss (1)(c) and (3) of s 12, that there is scope for wholesale change in the way that the Government responds to issues for the remaining duration of the term of the plan. The way in which these changes can be actioned is not made clear.

Sub-s (2) risks binding the improvement of the natural environment to the priority areas. This is an unnecessarily restrictive interpretation. The Government has stressed that a holistic approach to environmental improvement is to be facilitated by the Environment Act. The fact that targets must be considered as part of the assessment of the natural environment does not limit the concept of improvement to those specific targets.

S 12 underlines the importance of the reports under ss 16 and 28. At the same time, it should be noted that a report on improvement does not necessarily translate into a report on what further steps should be taken.

S 28 gives the OEP important responsibilities to provide regular independent assessments of the Government's progress in meeting the statutory environmental improvement plans and might be considered similar to the role of the Climate Change Committee in relation to climate change targets and interim budgets. Reports by the OEP are likely to include commentary on the adequacy of available data and specifically 'how' progress might be improved. The quality of those reports, their independence and expertise will therefore have an important role to play in ensuring political and public accountability of the Government. See further the annotations to s 28.

13 Renewing environmental improvement plans

(1) Before the end of the period to which an environmental improvement plan (the "old plan") relates, the Secretary of State must prepare a new environmental improvement plan (the "new plan") for a new period in accordance with this section, section 14 and section 15.

(2) The new period must begin no later than immediately after the end of the period to which the old plan relates.

(3) At or before the end of the period to which the old plan relates the Secretary of State must lay before Parliament, and publish, the new plan.

(4) The new plan replaces the old plan when—

(a) it has been laid and published, and

(b) the period to which it relates has begun.

Definitions

'environmental improvement plan'	s 8(8)
'new plan'	s 13(1)

In force	24 January 2022 Commencement Order No 2
Application	E

This section requires that a new EIP be prepared before the end of the period to which the old EIP relates and that the new plan begin no later than immediately after the period to which the old plan relates. It is axiomatic that the preparatory steps that need to be taken in order to prepare a new EIP should begin sometime before the old EIP is due to end.

As with the first EIP, any new plan does not require parliamentary approval. At first glance, this may appear peculiar. However, an EIP is essentially a government policy document, and whilst the Act gives an EIP a foundation in legislation, it does not require cross-party support.

14 Renewing plans: interim targets

(1) A new plan prepared by the Secretary of State under section 13 must—

(a) set at least one interim target in respect of each relevant matter, and

(b) secure that there is at all times, until the end of the 5 year period beginning with the relevant date, an interim target set by the plan in respect of each relevant matter.

(2) A "relevant matter" means any matter in respect of which there is a target under sections 1 to 3.

(3) Subsection (1) does not apply in respect of a matter if the specified date for the target under sections 1 to 3 in respect of that matter is before the end of the 5 year period beginning with the relevant date.

(4) An interim target in respect of a matter must specify—

(a) a standard to be achieved, which must be capable of being objectively measured, and

(b) a date by which it is to be achieved.

(5) The date must be no later than the end of the 5 year period beginning with—

(a) for the first interim target set by the new plan in respect of a matter, the relevant date;

(b) for subsequent interim targets set by the new plan in respect of a matter, the date specified for the previous interim target.

(6) Before setting an interim target in respect of a matter, the Secretary of State must be satisfied that meeting it would make an appropriate contribution towards meeting the target under sections 1 to 3 in respect of that matter.

(7) The "relevant date" is the first day of the period to which the new plan relates.

(8) In this section references to the "new plan" are to be read in accordance with section 13.

Definitions

'new plan'	s 13(1)
'relevant matter'	s 14(2)

Application	E W
In force	24 January 2022 Commencement Order No 2

This section considerably overlaps with s 11, save that it applies to new plans.

15 Renewing plans: other requirements

(1) In preparing a new plan under section 13 the Secretary of State must consider—

(a) what has been done to implement the old plan,

(b) whether, having regard to data obtained under section 16 and reports made by the OEP under section 28, the natural environment has improved since the beginning of the period to which the old plan relates, and

(c) whether Her Majesty's Government should take further or different steps (compared to those set out in the old plan) to improve the natural environment in the period to which the new environmental improvement plan relates.

(2) In considering the matters in subsection (1)(b) the Secretary of State must consider the progress that has been made towards meeting—

(a) any targets set under sections 1 to 3, and

(b) any interim targets set under sections 11 and 14.

(3) In considering the matters in subsection (1)(c) the Secretary of State must consider whether Her Majesty's Government should take further or different steps (compared to those set out in the old plan) towards meeting any targets set under sections 1 to 3.

(4) In this section references to the "new plan" and the "old plan" are to be read in accordance with section 13.

Definitions

'new plan'	s 13(1)
'old plan'	s 13(1)

In force	24 January 2022 Commencement Order No 2
Application	E

This section considerably overlaps with s 12, save that it applies to new plans.

Environmental monitoring

16 Environmental monitoring

(1) The Secretary of State must make arrangements for obtaining such data about the natural environment as the Secretary of State considers appropriate for the purpose of monitoring—

(a) whether the natural environment is, or particular aspects of it are, improving in accordance with the current environmental improvement plan,

(b) the progress being made towards meeting any targets set under sections 1 to 3, and

(c) the progress being made towards meeting any interim targets set under sections 11 and 14.

(2) The Secretary of State must lay before Parliament, and publish, a statement setting out the kinds of data to be obtained under subsection (1).

(3) The first statement must be laid before the end of the 4 month period beginning with the day on which this section comes into force.

(4) The Secretary of State may revise the statement at any time (and subsection (2) applies to any revised statement).

(5) The Secretary of State must publish any data obtained under subsection (1).

Definitions

'natural environment'	s 44

In force	24 January 2022 Commencement Order No 2
Application	E

This section is intended to identify that the responsibility for obtaining data necessary for the purposes of monitoring falls on the Secretary of State.

Under most EU Environmental Directives and regulations, the UK and Member States were required to provide regular reports on implementation based on questionnaires provided by the Commission – for example, how many facilities were regulated, the situation and progress in attaining the objectives and targets defined by legislation, the profile and intensity of environmental pressures and the effectiveness of responses to environmental pressures. Obligations varied by topic and legislation. At EU level, monitoring fulfilled numerous purposes. In addition to compliance and effective implementation, monitoring also assisted with evaluating the level playing field of the internal market and best practice and improving decision making, for example through policy evaluations or impact assessments.

The European Commission's *Better Regulation Guidelines* defined monitoring as the process that generates evidence of an intervention's activities and impacts over time in a continuous and systematic way. Such (regulatory) monitoring allowed the European Commission to review the Member States' efforts when implementing EU law. The act of monitoring assisted with identifying whether a policy was being applied on the ground as expected, addressing any implementation problems and identifying what further actions were required in order to ensure that the respective policy could reach its intended objectives (European Commission, *Better Regulation Guidelines*, Commission Staff Working Document SWD (2017) 350).

The Guidelines stipulate that a fit-for-purpose environmental monitoring and reporting system should follow five 'governing principles'. It should be comprehensive, proportionate, timely, minimise overlap and provide accessibility.

S 16 now places much of the legal responsibility for environmental monitoring on the Secretary of State, while the OEP has a general duty to review the implementation of environmental law (see s 29 below). S 16, though, is notable by its lack of reference to the wider uses to which monitoring can be put. In this section, monitoring is for the purpose of identifying whether the natural environment is improving in accordance with the EIP and whether progress is being made towards meeting targets or interim targets. That rather narrow focus is not ameliorated by the discretion set out in sub-s (2) afforded to the Secretary of State in determining the kinds of data to be obtained. In this way, the mandatory obligation on the Secretary of State to make arrangements for the obtaining of data is tempered by the purposes for which that data is to be obtained. The wording of this section does not lend itself to an argument that the Secretary of State has breached his duty if he does not have regard to the potential wider purposes for which such data can be put, nor if the Secretary of State does not put in place arrangements for obtaining data that mirror the types of arrangements that the European Commission has in place or replicates the aims or intentions of the European Commission in monitoring as outlined above.

S 16 does not limit in any way the use that can be made of the data that is to be obtained, and, for example, the Office for Environmental Protection could make use of the material in carrying out its functions.

Policy statement on environmental principles

17 Policy statement on environmental principles

(1) The Secretary of State must prepare a policy statement on environmental principles in accordance with this section and section 18.

(2) A "policy statement on environmental principles" is a statement explaining how the environmental principles should be interpreted and proportionately applied by Ministers of the Crown when making policy.

(3) It may also explain how Ministers of the Crown, when interpreting and applying the environmental principles, should take into account other considerations relevant to their policy.

(4) The Secretary of State must be satisfied that the statement will, when it comes into effect, contribute to—

(a) the improvement of environmental protection, and

(b) sustainable development.

(5) In this Part "environmental principles" means the following principles—

(a) the principle that environmental protection should be integrated into the making of policies,

(b) the principle of preventative action to avert environmental damage,

(c) the precautionary principle, so far as relating to the environment,

(d) the principle that environmental damage should as a priority be rectified at source, and

(e) the polluter pays principle.

Definitions

'environmental principles'	s 20(e)

In force	10 May 2022 Commencement Order No 3
Application	E

Background

Given that so much domestic environmental legislation has derived from EU law, there was concern raised that the UK's departure from the EU could result in a weakening of environmental standards. On Brexit, the Government's initial focus was concerned with the rollover of existing EU legislation in the interests of ensuring a period of regulatory certainty, but this process was concerned with the black letter of the law and, in the environmental context, ignored the potential policy and legal significance of the core environmental principles that appeared in the Treaty on the Functioning of the European Union.

In May 2018 the Government published a consultation entitled *Consultation on Environmental Principles and Accountability for the Environment.* Paras 4 and 5 read:

> *'We believe it will be beneficial to underpin environmental regulation and policymaking with a clear set of principles. Environmental principles are a specific set of principles which have been used to guide and shape modern environmental law. They are reflected in international instruments such as Agenda 21, a non-binding action plan of the United Nations with regard to sustainable development, and the Convention on Biological Diversity. Environmental principles are also set out in the EU Treaties as the basis for EU environmental law.*
>
> *Whilst these principles are central to government policy, at a national level we do not currently set them down in one place, or define their role in policy-making or delivery. So, as we leave the EU, we will create a new statutory statement of the environmental principles which will guide us, drawing on the current international and EU environmental principles. It will remain government's responsibility to set policy within the framework of these principles.'*

Subsequently, s 16 of the European Union (Withdrawal) Act 2018, as introduced, required the Secretary of State to publish a draft Bill by 26 December 2018 consisting of a set of environmental principles, a duty to publish a policy statement in relation to their application and interpretation, a duty to ensure Ministers of the Crown must have regard to the policy statement and provisions for the establishment of what would subsequently become the Office for Environmental Protection.

The draft Environment (Principles and Governance) Bill was subsequently published on 19 December 2018, and was subject to pre-legislative scrutiny. In its report following the pre-legislative scrutiny, the House of Commons Environment, Food and Rural Affairs (EFRA) Committee noted that

> *'It is essential that environmental principles continue to guide environmental policy making and legislation after the UK's departure from the European Union. We therefore support the list of principles included in Clause 2 of the draft Bill. However, the Government has not included within the list of principles a clear overarching objective for the UK's future environmental governance. Notably, the Government has not carried across the objective of "a high level of protection for the environment" as currently stated in Art 191(2) of the Treaty on the Functioning of the European Union. This is a surprising omission given the Secretary of State's clear commitment to improving the state of the environment.*
>
> *We are also concerned that the Bill turns what are currently legal provisions for environmental principles into a policy statement which will be much weaker and easier to revise. In reducing the legal status of the principles, the draft Bill therefore marks a significant regression on the current levels of protection guaranteed under the European Union treaties.*
>
> *We recommend that Clauses 1–4 of the draft Bill are redrafted to provide a stronger legal commitment to the protection of the environment. An overarching objective to ensure a "high level of protection for the environment", as is currently outlined in the Treaty on the Functioning of the European Union, should be inserted into the draft Bill to underpin the other environmental principles. The interpretation and application of the environmental principles in Clause 2 should not be left to just a policy statement but should be further outlined on the face of the Bill. Given the importance it has placed on the policy statement, the Government should also clarify and reinforce in the draft Bill the timescales and process for drafting, consulting on, publishing and reviewing the statement. This is essential for effective public and parliamentary scrutiny'* (*Pre-legislative Scrutiny of the Draft Environment (Principles and Governance) Bill*, House of Commons Environment Audit Committee, Fourteenth Report of Session 2017–19, HC 1893, paras 24–26).

The Environment Act contains several significant changes from the draft Environment (Principles and Governance) Bill. In particular, the Act requires that the Secretary of State must be satisfied that the policy statement on environmental principles will, when it comes into effect, contribute to the improvement of environmental protection and sustainable development (s 17(4)) and that a Minister of the Crown must have 'due regard' to the policy statement on environmental principles when making policy (s 19(1)).

In a letter to the chair of the House of Commons EFRA Committee, date 15 October 2019, Theresa Villiers, then Secretary of State for the Environment, Food and Rural Affairs, commented on the Government's approach to the environmental principles by stating: '*We are committed to ensuring that the principles are placed on a clear legal footing which is why the list of principles is included on the face of the Bill. We have strengthened the current duty in the Bill from "have regard" to "have due regard" with the aim of ensuring that the policy statement is used effectively across departments. Strengthening the duty in this way means that Ministers of the Crown will be required to give fuller consideration to the principles as the policy statement will be given greater weight. This change strengthens the duty in line with the Public Sector Equality Duty in the Equality Act 2010. We have added a requirement that the Secretary of State must be satisfied that the statement will contribute to the improvement of environmental protection and sustainable development.*'

Policy Statement on Environmental Principles: s 17

This section gives some legal effect for the first time in domestic legislation to a number of general environmental principles. The principles listed in s 17(5) have been derived from EU law. The integration principle, reflected in s 17(5)(a), is contained in Art 11 of the Treaty on the Functioning of the European Union (TFEU), which states: '*Environmental protection requirements must be integrated into the definition and implementation of the Union's policies and activities, in particular with a view to promoting sustainable development.*' The other principles, contained in s 17(5)(b)–(e) are derived from Art 191(2) TFEU: '*Union policy on the environment shall aim at a high level of protection taking into account the diversity of situations in the various regions of the Union. It shall be based on the precautionary principle and on the principles that preventive action should be taken, that environmental damage should as a priority be rectified at source and that the polluter should pay.*'

The principles stated in s 17(5) do not have direct legal effect in domestic law, but must be reflected in the statement issued by the Secretary of State. It is the statement which has some legal effect as defined in s 18 below. Although the Secretary of State has considerable discretion in the drafting of the statement, he must be satisfied under sub-s (4) that the statement will contribute to the improvement of environmental protection and sustainable development (a term not defined in the Act).

S 17(2) provides that the statement must explain how the principles are to be interpreted and applied proportionately. This gives considerable discretion, and clearly does not require the Secretary of State to blindly follow, say, specific rulings of the European Court of Justice on their meaning. It does, however, raise the question of how far the Secretary of State could depart from existing interpretation of the principles in both EU and international law, even though there has not always been consistency in their meaning or implications. The principles are stated in s 17(5) as principles in their own right. A statement that, say, wholly reinterprets the accepted understanding of a principle could be subject to challenge in the courts on the grounds of *Wednesbury* unreasonableness. Against this context it is worth considering how environmental principles have been treated in EU law.

EU Environmental Principles

In EU law environmental principles are binding, their mandatory nature reflected in the use of the words 'must' and 'shall'. According to Professor Nicholas de Sadeleer, '*EU measures not complying with these principles are likely to be subject to judicial review*' (Pro Natura, *The Polluter-Pays Principle in EU Law – Bold Case Law and Poor Harmonisation*, Festskrift til H-C Bugge, Oslo, Universitetsforlaget, 2012, p 407). Member States are obliged to apply these principles when carrying out action in the environment field that has been harmonised by secondary EU law (Case C-127/02 *Waddenzee* [2005] ECR I-6515, para 44).

The Integration Principle

The integration principle stands out as a clear reminder to policymakers of the need to properly take into account environmental considerations. Environmental protection is an objective of universal application across all potential policy areas. Under the Act, its interpretation and proportionate application by Ministers of the Crown will be influenced by the forthcoming policy statement on environmental principles. The principle does not mandate that environmental requirements must trump all other considerations.

The differences between the phrase 'environmental protection requirements' found in Art 11 and the phrase 'environmental protection' found in s 17(5)(a) do not immediately suggest any form of substantive divergence in meaning and effect – both phrases are extremely wide and would include environmental policy objectives in addition to the policies themselves. Nonetheless, it may be considered that Art 11 goes a little further than sub-s (5)(a), in that Art 11 applies to both the activities of the EU and its policies, rather than just its policies, as well as, in particular, having a view to promoting sustainable development. This latter consideration is reflected in sub-s (4), which requires the policy statement on environmental principles to contribute to sustainable development, rather than mandating that individual Government policies are required to positively contribute to sustainable development.

Preventative Action

Both the principle of preventative action and the polluter pays principle were considered in the Opinion of Advocate General Kokott in *Fipa Group and others* (Case C-534/13), in which he stated, in the context of considering who should pay for remedying pollution caused by third parties:

> *'If polluters know that they are liable in full for damage, they will take the necessary preventative measures so that damage does not occur in the first place. In general, the polluters are the parties who are able to take the most effective measures.*
>
> *In addition, the principle of preventative action, just like the principle that environmental damage should be rectified at source as a matter of priority, nevertheless requires that, irrespective of any contributions by the owners to the causes, measures can be taken on polluted sites to prevent further spread of the damage. In certain circumstances, it may also be necessary for the owner to support these measures using his better knowledge of the site. Otherwise it would clearly be more difficult, if not impossible, to prevent such spread. On the other hand, in general neither of these principles requires that these owners should themselves be called on to carry out the remedial work.*
>
> *Moreover, the principle of preventative action suggests that owners of sites should be required, in certain cases, to take preventative measures against risks for which third parties are essentially responsible. It would be conceivable, for example, to require the owner of a site subject to repeated dumping of illegal waste to fence in that site in order to prevent further offences.'*

The principle of preventative action was considered further in *Criminal proceedings against Paolo Lirussi* (Case C-175/98) and *Francesca Bizzaro* (Case C-177/98). At para 51 of the judgment, the Court held that the principle required *'the Community and the Member States to prevent, reduce and, in so far as is possible, eliminate from the outset, the sources of pollution or nuisance by adopting measures of a nature such as to eliminate recognised risks'*.

The Precautionary Principle

The essence of the precautionary principle is that it may be legitimate to take action to prevent environmental harm even where no direct link in causation has been demonstrated between the activity in question and the harm.

The precautionary principle has been considered in a number of cases at the European level. In *Artegodan GmbH and Others v Commission of the European Communities* (European

Court Reports, 2002, II-04945), most relevantly at paras 181–86, it was held to be a '*general principle of Community law requiring the competent authorities to take appropriate measures to prevent specific potential risks to public health, safety and the environment, by giving precedence to the requirements related to the protection of those interests over economic interests*'. The precautionary principle implies that '*where there is uncertainty as to the existence or extent of risks to human health, the institutions may take precautionary measures without having to wait until the reality and seriousness of those risks become fully apparent*'. For institutions, we should now read Ministers of the Crown.

The precautionary principle was also considered in the context of the Habitats Directive in *Landelijke Vereniging tot Behoud van de Waddenzee and Nederlandse Vereniging tot Bescherming van Vogels v Staatssecretaris van Landbouw, Natuurbeheer en Visserij* (Case C-127/02, para 44): '*In the light, in particular, of the precautionary principle, which is one of the foundations of the high level of protection pursued by Community policy on the environment, in accordance with the first subparagraph of Article 174(2) EC, and by reference to which the Habitats Directive must be interpreted, such a risk exists if it cannot be excluded on the basis of objective information that the plan or project will have significant effects on the site concerned (see, by analogy, inter alia Case C-180/96 United Kingdom v Commission [1998] ECR I-2265, paragraphs 50,105 and 107). Such an interpretation of the condition to which the assessment of the implications of a plan or project for a specific site is subject, which implies that in case of doubt as to the absence of significant effects such an assessment must be carried out, makes it possible to ensure effectively that plans or projects which adversely affect the integrity of the site concerned are not authorised, and thereby contributes to achieving, in accordance with the third recital in the preamble to the Habitats Directive and Article 2(1) thereof, its main aim, namely, ensuring biodiversity through the conservation of natural habitats and of wild fauna and flora.*'

The precautionary principle is not without its detractors. The UK Innovation Strategy, for example, states: '*When applied disproportionately the precautionary principle can err too much on the side of caution, reversing the burden of proof and placing it on the Innovator to demonstrate no possible harm from an innovation … The precautionary principle can be interpreted in ways that can produce more harm than good. In some cases, the precautionary principle has become a policy of blocking all potential harms, even a possibility of harm, without a balanced analysis of likely benefits*' (Department for Business, Energy and Industrial Strategy, *UK Innovation Strategy: Leading the Future by Creating It*, July 2021, p 34).

In the Divisional Court, when rejecting the contention that the precautionary principle imposed obligations on Member States to act in a particular way, Smith LJ stated in *R v Secretary of State for Trade and Industry, ex p Duddridge* [1995] Env LR 151 at p 167: '*[The obligation to apply the precautionary principle] would entail the need to conduct cost–benefit analyses in respect of every known risk of damage to the environment and every known risk to human health from the environment. They would then be obliged to legislate in every case in which the cost–benefit analysis showed that action would be reasonable. All of this would be obligatory as a matter of national initiative, in the absence of any definition of the precautionary principle and before any formulation of a coherent policy on the environment. I find quite remarkable the proposition that each state should be obliged to act alone on the basis of so general a statement of objectives and considerations.*'

The Court of Appeal upheld the ruling that the precautionary principle did not place any obligation on the national government. That position has now changed, by virtue of the principle being placed on the statute book in s 17(5)(c). The extent of the need to conduct extensive cost–benefit analyses will presumably be a factor addressed in the forthcoming policy statement.

Rectification at Source

There is no known authority, either domestically or at the European level, defining in any detail the 'rectification at source' principle, despite its existence in Art 191(2). The 'Information Paper on the Policy Statement on Environmental Principles' published in December 2018 reads: *'The rectification at source principle means that environmental damage should, as a priority, be addressed by targeting its original cause and taking preventative action at the origin of the problem. This principle places the responsibility for managing environmental damage on the polluter or the source of environmental harm. It reinforces the responsibility for managing environmental damage at the source of that damage – therefore linking it to the polluter. The principle also encourages processes that are inherently clean rather than approaches which treat the problem as or after it occurs'* (Department of Environment, Food and Rural Affairs, December 2018, p 12).

In *Re Imports of Waste: EC Commission v Belgium* (Case C-2/90), the rectification at source principle was used to uphold a ban on the import of waste where the influx of waste caused a threat to the environment in view of the limited capacity, locally, for dealing with that waste. Rectification at source required Member States to take appropriate measures to collect, treat and dispose of its own waste.

The Polluter Pays Principle

The 'polluter pays' principle is already established with respect to environmental liabilities within the insolvency régime in Scotland following *Re Doonin Plant Hire Ltd (in liquidation)* [2018] CSOH 89. In that case, the *pari passu* principle that the property of insolvents should be divided equally amongst their unsecured creditors was regarded as much 'attenuated' and in effect trumped by the principles of environmental protection to be gleaned from Scottish regulations and the Water Framework Directive that they implemented. Lord Doherty considered the continuing liability of the company in liquidation to be mandated by the 'polluter pays' principle. This judgment clearly predates the Act, but is indicative of the scope of applicability of the principles.

Relevance of EU Case Law on Principles Post-Brexit

Under s 6(2) of the EU (Withdrawal) Act 2018, UK Courts and tribunals are not bound by any principles laid down by, or any decisions of, the European Court of Justice (CJEU) after 31 December 2020, but they may have regard to anything done by the CJEU, another EU entity or the EU itself so far as is relevant to any matter before the court or tribunal.

As a consequence, whilst the policy statement should set out how the principles are to be interpreted and proportionately applied, it would appear to be unlikely that sub-s (2) can completely exclude the application of EU law and precedent concerning the principles to the issue of interpretation in relation to EU retained law. As a result, whilst it may be the aim of the UK as part of this legislation to 'anglicise' the environmental principles, it will still be possible to derive support for their meaning from European case law and precedent.

Retained EU case law is limited to any principles laid down by, and any decisions of, the CJEU as they have effect in EU law immediately before 31 December 2020. The Supreme Court can depart from retained EU case law in circumstances where any appellate court considers that it is right to do so, the same test as applied for when the Supreme Court can depart from one of its own decisions (see s 6 of the European Union (Withdrawal Act) 2018). However, the principles do not form part of any UK statute or statutory instrument designed to implement EU law when it was binding in the UK. Nor do these principles form part of EU Regulations with direct effect in the UK. As a result, it cannot be said that the principles themselves form part of retained EU law.

The Trade and Cooperation Agreement

Under the EU–UK Trade and Cooperation Agreement (TCA), each party has the right to set its policies and priorities, to determine the environmental levels of protection and climate level of protection it deems appropriate and to adopt or modify its law and policies in a manner consistent with that party's international commitments. Nonetheless, there are a number of articles within the TCA that are directly relevant to the interpretation of the environmental principles.

Art 391(2) prohibits the UK from weakening or reducing, in a manner affecting trade or investment between the parties, its environmental levels of protection or its climate level of protection below the levels that are in place at the end of the transition period, including by failing to effectively enforce its environmental law or climate level of protection.

This article explicitly links environmental protection to 'trade or investment between the Parties'. Insofar as, for example, divergence in the application of the precautionary principle affects trade and investment between the parties, it is not open to the UK to weaken its environmental levels of protection. The contrast with the Innovation Strategy here is stark. The TCA is silent on the whether the phrase 'in a manner affecting trade or investment between the Parties' extends to indirect effects caused by trade agreements not involving the EU. For rather more clearly worded provisions concerning investment and environmental non-regression, see Art 24.5 of the 2016 Comprehensive Economic and Trade Agreement (CETA) between Canada and the European Union. For consideration of the meaning of the phrase 'in a manner affecting trade or investment between the Parties', see pages 50–66 of the final arbitral decision in *United States v Guatamala*, dated 14 June 2017.

The environmental principles set out in s 17 are expressly identified in Art 393 of the TCA. The UK has committed to respecting these principles, the extent of which can be expected to be addressed in the forthcoming policy statement.

The issue to be determined is whether the commitments made by the UK in the TCA, in particular on non-regression, as well as the UK's adoption of essentially European environmental principles, combine to require the UK to maintain at least 'equivalence' with the EU on environmental protection, in circumstances where the UK has already been directly critical of EU environmental policy hampering innovation and progress.

The 2021 Draft Policy Statement

On 10 March 2021 the Department for Environment, Food and Rural Affairs published a draft environmental principles policy statement for consultation. The consultation closed on 2 June 2021 and, at the time of writing, the Government was still analysing the feedback.

The draft policy statement was explicit that it did not seek to dictate a set formula for how environmental principles should be applied to policymaking. Instead, it aimed to empower Ministers and those working on their behalf to think creatively and use environmental principles *'as an innovative and forward-thinking way to protect and enhance the environment whilst supporting innovation and economic growth'*.

In a somewhat circular fashion, the draft statement identified that it will contribute to the improvement of environmental protection *'by setting out how the principles should be interpreted and proportionately applied by Ministers so that they are used effectively and embedded in policy to protect the environment'*.

The draft policy statement went on to identify how to assess whether a particular policy would have an environmental impact, noting that it is not expected that policymakers carry out a 'deep-dive' assessment into all environmental impacts as these may not be known. 'Proportionate' allows for policymakers to apply the policy statement in a 'lighter-touch way', and a 'holistic, common sense approach' should be adopted.

Notably, the draft policy statement did not consider any case law or precedent on the interpretation of the principles, but defined them as follows:

- The *integration principle* is the principle that policymakers should look for opportunities to embed environmental protection in other fields of policy that have impacts on the environment. It is an overarching objective which is relevant in all circumstances where the legal duty to have due regard to the policy statement applies.
- The *prevention principle* means that government policy should aim to prevent, reduce or mitigate environmental harm.
- The *rectification at source principle* means that if damage to the environment cannot be prevented it should be tackled at its origin.
- The *polluter pays principle* is the principle that those who cause pollution or damage to the environment should be responsible for mitigation or compensation.
- The *precautionary principle* states that where there are threats of serious or irreversible environmental damage, a lack of full scientific certainty shall not be used as a reason for postponing cost-effective measures to prevent environmental degradation.

Any initial reaction will focus on the phrase 'overarching objective' in reference to the integration principle, potentially according it greater applicability than the other principles, as well as the phrase 'cost-effective measures' in reference to the precautionary principle, whereas 'appropriate measures' might have been considered more consistent with a European approach.

The draft policy statement then goes on to describe the application of each principle in turn by reference to proportionality and the above holistic approach but without any significant detail on the contribution expected to environmental protection from the application of each principle. Possible actions following consideration of the principles, where action is considered necessary, included:

- Amending the policy options, reflecting consideration of the environmental principles;
- Reframing the policy to accommodate the environmental principles,
- Embedding a principle in law or guidance;
- Postponing a policy until further evidence is gained.

Numerous responses to the consultation were received. In particular, the interim Office for Environmental Protection has recommended that the draft policy statement is strengthened in a number of areas and requested that greater guidance be given on linking the policy statement with the Government's environmental goals, such as those in the 25 Year Environment Plan and the natural capital guidance set out in the Green Book (www.theoep.org.uk/reports-publications, accessed 12 December 2021).

18 Policy statement on environmental principles: process

(1) The Secretary of State must prepare a draft of the policy statement on environmental principles.

(2) The Secretary of State must consult such persons as the Secretary of State considers appropriate in relation to the draft statement.

(3) The Secretary of State must lay the draft statement before Parliament.

(4) If before the end of the 21 day period—

(a) either House of Parliament passes a resolution in respect of the draft statement, or

(b) a committee of either House of Parliament, or a joint committee of both Houses, makes recommendations in respect of the draft statement,

the Secretary of State must produce a response and lay it before Parliament.

(5) The Secretary of State must prepare and lay before Parliament the final statement, but not before—

(a) if subsection (4) applies, the day on which the Secretary of State lays the response required by that subsection, or

(b) otherwise, the end of the 21 day period.

(6) The final statement has effect when it is laid before Parliament.

(7) The Secretary of State must publish the statement when it comes into effect.

(8) The "21 day period" is the period of 21 sitting days beginning with the first sitting day after the day on which the draft statement is laid under subsection (3).

(9) "Sitting day" means a day on which both Houses of Parliament sit.

(10) The requirements in subsections (1) and (2) may be met by the preparation of a draft statement, and consultation, before this section comes into force.

(11) The Secretary of State may prepare a revised policy statement on environmental principles at any time (and subsections (1) to (9) apply in relation to any revised statement).

Definitions

'environmental principles'	s 17(5)

In force	10 May 2022 Commencement Order No 3
Application	E

Any policy statement must be made pursuant to a specific process. The Secretary of State must prepare a draft after any consultation that the Secretary of Statement considers to be appropriate and lay this before Parliament, which can comment upon it, prompting a response by the Secretary of State.

19 Policy statement on environmental principles: effect

(1) A Minister of the Crown must, when making policy, have due regard to the policy statement on environmental principles currently in effect.

(2) Nothing in subsection (1) requires a Minister to do anything (or refrain from doing anything) if doing it (or refraining from doing it)—

(a) would have no significant environmental benefit, or

(b) would be in any other way disproportionate to the environmental benefit.

(3) Subsection (1) does not apply to policy so far as relating to—

(a) the armed forces, defence or national security,

(b) taxation, spending or the allocation of resources within government, or

(c) Wales.

(4) Subsection (1) applies to policy relating to Scotland only so far as relating to reserved matters.

(5) Section 14(2) of the UK Withdrawal from the European Union (Continuity) (Scotland) Act 2021 (asp 4) (UK Ministers must have regard to guiding principles on the environment in making policies extending to Scotland) does not apply to policies so far as relating to reserved matters.

(6) In this section "reserved matters" has the same meaning as in the Scotland Act 1998.

Definitions

'policy statement on environmental principles'	s 17(2)
'environmental principles'	s 17(5)

In force	S19(5) and (6): 10 May 2022 Commencement Order No 3
Application	E

This section defines the legal effect of the statement of environmental principles and how it applies to any Minister making policy. There are extensive references in the Act to duties to *'have regard to'* (see Introduction), but this is the only section in the Act imposing a duty to *'have due regard to'*. It was the result of a conscious Government amendment made before the draft Environment Bill was put before the Commons where the earlier provision was simply 'have regard to'. Given this background, a court would feel entitled to consider that it was intended to impose a stronger test.

Have Due Regard To

There is no definition in the legislation of the phrase *'have due regard'*. But given the similarities between environmental law and aspects of human rights law, involving as they do fundamental and procedural rights and including the importance of proportionality as a means of review, as well the explicit reference by the then Secretary of State for the Environment, Food and Rural Affairs to the Equality Act 2010 in the 2019 letter to the Chair of the House of Commons EFRA Committee (see annotation to s 17), it is reasonable to try to interpret the phrase '*have due regard to*' in light of the case law arising from the duty in s 149 of the Equality Act 2010. Four relevant principles arise from *R (Brown) v Secretary of State for Work and Pensions* [2008] EWHC 3158 (Admin). First, those making the relevant decisions must be made aware of their duty to have 'due regard' to an identified goal. An incomplete or erroneous appreciation of the duty will mean that 'due regard' has not been given to it. Second, the duty to have due regard means that the duty must be considered both before and at the time when a particular policy is being determined. Attempts to justify a decision as being consistent with the exercise of the duty when the duty was not, in fact, considered before the decision are not enough to discharge the duty. Third, the duty must be 'exercised in substance, with rigour, and with an open mind' rather than simply being a question of 'ticking boxes'. Finally, it is good practice for the decision maker to explain what steps were taken to demonstrate compliance with the duty.

The principles from case law were helpfully summarised by McCombe LJ in *R (on the application of Bracking) v Secretary of State for Work and Pensions* [2013] EWCA 1345 at para 26:

'(1) As stated by Arden LJ in R (Elias) v Secretary of State for Defence [2006] 1 WLR 3213; [2006] EWCA Civ 1293 at [274], equality duties are an integral and important part of the mechanisms for ensuring the fulfilment of the aims of anti-discrimination legislation.

(2) An important evidential element in the demonstration of the discharge of the duty is the recording of the steps taken by the decision maker in seeking to meet the statutory requirements: R (BAPIO Action Ltd) v Secretary of State for the Home Department [2007] EWHC 199 (QB) (Stanley Burnton J (as he then was)).

(3) The relevant duty is upon the Minister or other decision maker personally. What matters is what he or she took into account and what he or she knew. Thus, the Minister or decision maker cannot be taken to know what his or her officials know or what may have been in the minds of officials in proffering their advice: R (National Association of Health Stores) v Department of Health [2005] EWCA Civ 154 at [26–27] per Sedley LJ.

(4) A Minister must assess the risk and extent of any adverse impact and the ways in which such risk may be eliminated before the adoption of a proposed policy and not merely as a "rearguard action", following a concluded decision: per Moses LJ, sitting as a Judge of the Administrative Court, in Kaur & Shah v LB Ealing [2008] EWHC 2062 (Admin) at [23–24].

(5) These and other points were reviewed by Aikens LJ, giving the judgment of the Divisional Court, in R (Brown) v Secretary of State for Work and Pensions [2008] EWHC 3158 (Admin), as follows:

- *i) The public authority decision maker must be aware of the duty to have "due regard" to the relevant matters;*
- *ii) The duty must be fulfilled before and at the time when a particular policy is being considered;*
- *iii) The duty must be "exercised in substance, with rigour, and with an open mind". It is not a question of "ticking boxes"; while there is no duty to make express reference to the regard paid to the relevant duty, reference to it and to the relevant criteria reduces the scope for argument;*
- *iv) The duty is non-delegable; and*
- *v) Is a continuing one.*
- *vi) It is good practice for a decision maker to keep records demonstrating consideration of the duty.*

(6) "[G]eneral regard to issues of equality is not the same as having specific regard, by way of conscious approach to the statutory criteria." (per Davis J (as he then was) in R (Meany) v Harlow DC [2009]

EWHC 559 (Admin) at [84], approved in this court in R (Bailey) v Brent LBC [2011] EWCA Civ 1586 at [74–75].)

(7) Officials reporting to or advising Ministers/other public authority decision makers, on matters material to the discharge of the duty, must not merely tell the Minister/decision maker what he/she wants to hear but they have to be "rigorous in both enquiring and reporting to them": R (Domb) v Hammersmith & Fulham LBC [2009] EWCA Civ 941 at [79] per Sedley LJ.

(8) Finally, and with respect, it is I think, helpful to recall passages from the judgment of my Lord, Elias LJ, in R (Hurley & Moore) v Secretary of State for Business, Innovation and Skills [2012] EWHC 201 (Admin) (Divisional Court) as follows:

(i) At paragraphs [77–78]

"[77] Contrary to a submission advanced by Ms Mountfield, I do not accept that this means that it is for the court to determine whether appropriate weight has been given to the duty. Provided the court is satisfied that there has been a rigorous consideration of the duty, so that there is a proper appreciation of the potential impact of the decision on equality objectives and the desirability of promoting them, then as Dyson LJ in Baker (para [34]) made clear, it is for the decision maker to decide how much weight should be given to the various factors informing the decision.

[78] The concept of 'due regard' requires the court to ensure that there has been a proper and conscientious focus on the statutory criteria, but if that is done, the court cannot interfere with the decision simply because it would have given greater weight to the equality implications of the decision than did the decision maker. In short, the decision maker must be clear precisely what the equality implications are when he puts them in the balance, and he must recognise the desirability of achieving them, but ultimately it is for him to decide what weight they should be given in the light of all relevant factors. If Ms Mountfield's submissions on this point were correct, it would allow unelected judges to review on substantive merits grounds almost all aspects of public decision making."

(ii) At paragraphs [89–90]

"[89] It is also alleged that the PSED in this case involves a duty of inquiry. The submission is that the combination of the principles in Secretary of State for Education and Science v Tameside Metropolitan Borough Council [1977] AC 1014 and the duty of due regard under the statute requires public authorities to be properly informed before taking a decision. If the relevant material is not available, there will be a duty to acquire it and this will frequently mean than some further consultation with appropriate groups is required. Ms Mountfield referred to the following passage from the judgment of Aikens LJ in Brown (para [85]):

'… the public authority concerned will, in our view, have to have due regard to the need to take steps to gather relevant information in order that it can properly take steps to take into account disabled persons' disabilities in the context of the particular function under consideration.'"

Although the 'due regard' duty means that the environmental principles cannot be lightly ignored when making policy, they do not in themselves determine the final content of the policy. Sub-s (2) reinforces this approach by providing that the duty does not require a Minister to do anything or refrain from doing anything if doing it or refraining from doing it would have no significant environmental benefit, or would be in any other way disproportionate to the environmental benefit.

Exemptions

The exemptions mirror the definition given of environmental law in s 46.

The exemption in sub-s (3)(a) for the armed forces, defence or national security is intended to reflect that these are highly sensitive matters that are vital for the UK's protection.

On first reading, the exemption in s 19(3)(b) relating to taxation, spending or the allocation of spending within government could be interpreted very broadly. Nevertheless, the carve-out may not be as dramatic as it might appear. Funding allocations should follow from the making of policies rather than the other way round, and the statement of principles clearly applies to policy determination. Rebecca Pow, Parliamentary Under Secretary of State at the Department for Environment, Food and Rural Affairs, clarified at Environment Bill Deb 3 November 2020 that the exemption for taxation, spending or the allocation of resources within government is intended to apply only to central spending decisions, such as budget allocations, while individual policy decisions would need to consider the statement:

> *'It is important to be clear that this exemption only refers to central spending decisions, because at fiscal events and spending reviews such decisions must be taken with consideration to a wide range of public priorities. These include public spending on individual areas such as health, defence, education and the environment, as well as sustainable economic growth and development, financial stability and sustainable levels of debt.*
>
> *There is no exemption for individual policy interventions simply because they require spending. Ministers should still have due regard to the policy statement when developing and implementing all policies to which the statement is applicable. This means that while the policy statement will not need to be used when the Treasury is allocating budgets to Departments, it will be used when Departments develop policies that draw upon that budget. This is the best place for the use of the policy statement to effectively deliver environmental protection'* (Environment Bill Deb 3 November 2020, col 272).

Environmental protection: statements and reports

20 Statements about Bills containing new environmental law

(1) This section applies where a Minister of the Crown in charge of a Bill in either House of Parliament is of the view that the Bill as introduced into that House contains provision which, if enacted, would be environmental law.

(2) The Minister must, before Second Reading of the Bill in the House in question, make—

- (a) a statement to the effect that in the Minister's view the Bill contains provision which, if enacted, would be environmental law, and
- (b) a statement under subsection (3) or (4).

(3) A statement under this subsection is a statement to the effect that in the Minister's view the Bill will not have the effect of reducing the level of environmental protection provided for by any existing environmental law.

(4) A statement under this subsection is a statement to the effect that—

- (a) the Minister is unable to make a statement under subsection (3), but
- (b) Her Majesty's Government nevertheless wishes the House to proceed with the Bill.

(5) In making a statement under this section the Minister may in particular take into account the possibility that a Bill, by making provision that is different from existing environmental law, might provide for the same or a greater level of environmental protection.

(6) For the purposes of this section—

(a) references to environmental protection provided for by any existing environmental law includes any protection which could be provided for under powers conferred by the existing environmental law, and

(b) in considering the effect of a Bill, any powers conferred by the Bill to provide for any environmental protection may be taken into account.

(7) A statement under this section must be in writing and be published in such manner as the Minister considers appropriate.

(8) "Existing environmental law", in relation to a statement under this section, means environmental law existing at the time that the Bill to which the statement relates is introduced into the House in question, whether or not the environmental law is in force.

Definitions

'environmental law'	s 46
'existing environmental law'	s 20(8)

In force	10 May 2022 Commencement Order No 3
Application	E W S NI

This section concerns laws that are mainly to do with environmental protection, with the exception of the excluded matters set out in s 46(2).

The Government resisted proposals during the passage of the Bill that there should be a general non-regression provision, especially from existing EU environmental legislation. The section, however, at least alerts Parliament where proposed environmental legislation will reduce levels of environmental protection provided by existing environmental law (whether domestic or EU derived). The Minister must make a statement either that the proposed new environmental legislation does not reduce existing environmental protection or, where that is not the case, that the Government still wants Parliament to approve the new law. The obligation applies only to environmental law provisions appearing in a Bill. There are many examples in the Environment Act giving very broad power to make regulations, and new regulations would not be covered by this duty.

In contrast to other sections of the Act that require consultation between the Secretary of State and other expert bodies, sub-s (3) merely requires the individual Minister to form a 'view' as to the prospective effect of the proposed legislation. Even then, sub-s (4) would appear to be able to circumvent this requirement. It is to be implied that such a 'view' is a rational one.

This section is consistent with one of the key themes pervading the Environment Act. A critical element of the Environment Act is the level of political accountability that is to be read into the various sections. It is apparent, for example, in both targets and interim targets; in environmental improvement plans; and in both the OEP's functions and the Secretary of State's requirement to respond in relation to reports on progress reporting and monitoring of environmental law. That accountability, taken together with the obligation to integrate environmental protection into the making of policies (a principle of universal application across Government), might be considered to be part of the Act's key strengths.

Non-regression and the Trade and Cooperation Agreement with the EU

It is worthwhile cross-referring to Art 391 TCA, which states: *'A Party shall not weaken or reduce, in a manner affecting trade or investment between the Parties, its environmental levels of protection or its climate level of protection below the levels that are in place at the end of the transition period, including by failing to effectively enforce its environmental law or climate level of protection.'*

The TCA expressly recognises that the parties may have their own environmental priorities and are entitled to make bona fide decisions on the allocation of environmental enforcement resources. Art 391 is entitled 'Non-regression from levels of protection', but is notable for the following:

i) Environmental protection is explicitly linked in the TCA to trade and investment 'between the Parties'. No explanation is provided as to whether this is limited to trade conducted directly between the parties or whether the phrase is intended to extend to indirect impacts from trade agreements with other countries. For clearer provisions concerning investment and environmental non-regression, see Art 24.5 CETA. For consideration of the meaning of the phrase 'in a manner affecting trade or investment between the Parties', see pages 50–66 of the final arbitral decision in *United States v Guatamala*, dated 14 June 2017.
ii) The Article would appear to permit a weakening of environmental protection where such action does not affect trade and investment between the parties.
iii) The transition period ended on 31 December 2020, whereas the Environment Bill was introduced to the House of Commons on 20 January 2020.

21 Reports on international environmental protection legislation

(1) The Secretary of State must report on developments in international environmental protection legislation which appear to the Secretary of State to be significant.

(2) "International environmental protection legislation" means legislation of countries and territories outside the United Kingdom, and international organisations, that is mainly concerned with environmental protection.

(3) The Secretary of State must report under this section in relation to each reporting period.

(4) The reporting periods are—

(a) the 2 year period beginning with the day on which this section comes into force, and

(b) each subsequent 2 year period.

(5) A report under this section may consider—

(a) particular countries, territories or international organisations, or

(b) particular aspects of environmental protection, as the Secretary of State considers appropriate.

(6) A report under this section must be laid before Parliament, and published, as soon as reasonably practicable after the end of the reporting period to which it relates.

In force 1 April 2022 Commencement Order No 2

Application E W S NI

This section requires the Secretary of State to publish and lay before Parliament reports on developments in international environmental protection. There is a wide ambit afforded to the Secretary of State, who must determine which developments in international environmental protection legislation are 'significant' (s 21(1)). The Secretary of State must also determine which geographic areas or international organisations and which aspects of environmental protection are considered appropriate to be included in the report. There is further uncertainty arising from the need for international environmental protection legislation to be 'mainly concerned' with environmental protection, although this mirrors the definition of environmental law given in s 46.

Bearing this in mind, it is reasonable to infer that the starting point for the Secretary of State would be to report on international developments that overlap directly with the targets set under ss 1–3. Conceivably, this could be in the imposition of more stringent targets in other countries (which could precipitate an amendment of domestic targets), or of scientific development in measurement techniques or similar.

However, the legislation does not limit the Secretary of State to consideration of priority targets, but leaves open the possibility of other environmental outcomes playing their part in the determination of what is 'significant'.

CHAPTER 2

THE OFFICE FOR ENVIRONMENTAL PROTECTION

The Office for Environmental Protection

22 The Office for Environmental Protection

(1) A body corporate called the Office for Environmental Protection is established.

(2) In this Act that body is referred to as "the OEP".

(3) Schedule 1 makes further provision about the OEP.

In force 17 November 2021. Commencement Order No 1

Application UK (reserved matters) E NI (but see s 49 in relation to NI)

This section establishes a new non-departmental public body, the Office for Environmental Protection. It is not to be regarded as a servant or agent of the Crown, and its members and employees are not civil servants of the state (Sch 1, para 16). Dame Glenys Stacey, formerly Chief Regulator at Ofqual and Her Majesty's Chief Inspector of Probation, was appointed first chairman by the Secretary of State for Environment, Food and Rural Affairs, following pre-scrutiny appointment hearings by the House of Commons EFRA and Environment Audit Committees. Unlike bodies such as the Environment Agency and Natural England, the Secretary of State has no power to issues directions, either general or specific, to the OEP, but has the power to issue guidance on its enforcement strategy (see s 25). Para 17 of Sch 1 provides that in exercising any functions relating to the OEP, the Secretary of State must have regard to the need to protect its independence.

Administrative Structure

Sch 1 deals with the OEP's administrative structure and financial arrangements. It provides that the OEP shall consist of the Chair, two to five non-executive members, the chief executive and at least one (up to a maximum of three) other executive members. The Chair and non-executive members are appointed by the Secretary of State, while the first chief executive is appointed by the Chair, and other members by the OEP. Subsequent chief executives are appointed by the non-executive members. If the OEP has jurisdiction in Northern Ireland (see 'Jurisdiction of the OEP' below), the provisions are amended to provide for one Northern Ireland non-executive member appointed by the NI Department of Agriculture, Environment and Rural Affairs, following consultation with the Secretary of State and the Chair of the OEP (Sch 3, para 29(3)).

In practice, many of the OEP's functions will be carried out by its staff under delegated arrangements, but unusually para 10(4) of Sch 1 provides that certain key functions may not be delegated and will therefore have to be taken by the board. These are more extensive than equivalent provisions found for most non-departmental public bodies, and include: approving the s 23 strategy and enforcement policy, s 28 annual reports on government progress in meeting its Environment Improvement Plan and environmental targets, s 29 reports on the implementation of environmental law and s 30 advice to Ministers; and making key decisions in its enforcement functions – issuing of a s 35 Information Notice and s 36 Decision Notices, applying to the courts for a s 38 environmental review, applying for a judicial or statutory review in urgent cases or intervening in a judicial review taken by another party (s 39).

Para 8 gives a general power to the OEP to do anything it thinks appropriate for the purposes of or in connection with its functions, other than accepting gifts of money, land or other property, or forming or participating in companies, joint ventures or similar arrangements. See, for example, *Attorney General v Lower Hutt City* [1964] NZLR 438 at 461: *'In deciding what can fairly be regarded as incidental to express powers, the courts do not think narrowly. They bear in mind the public nature of the obligations of a local body and the requirements of its community, and they take a liberal view of the power under consideration.'* But for a rather less generous interpretation, see *Crédit Suisse v Allerdale Borough Council* [1997] QB 306 at 359D–360F: *'The authorities … establish the general proposition that when a power is claimed to be incidental, the provisions of the statute which confer and limit functions must be considered and construed. The authorities also show that a power is not incidental merely because it is convenient or desirable or profitable.'*

Para 22 provides that the OEP will be subject to the jurisdiction of the Parliamentary Ombudsman under the Parliamentary Commissioner Act 1967.

Funding

Para 12 deals with funding arrangements. The Secretary of State must pay grant-in-aid to the OEP that is reasonably sufficient to carry out its functions, and provide any further financial assistance by way of grants, loans, guarantees or indemnities subject to conditions. These powers could be used to fund specific activities or projects required by the Secretary of State. During the development of the Bill and its pre-legislative scrutiny, there were considerable concerns as to whether reliance on the standard departmental grant-in-aid model would be sufficient to guarantee the OEP's independence and protection against departmental budgetary cuts. During the parliamentary progress of the Bill, Lord Goldsmith, House of Lords Environment Minister, noted that, *'The Government have committed to a ring-fenced multiannual funding envelope within the remits of the spending review, which will be regularly reviewed. For added transparency and to enable further parliamentary scrutiny, the OEP's budget will be set out as a separate line in Defra's supply estimate*' (HL Deb 28 June 2021, vol 813, col 613). Apart from Lord Goldsmith's statement, many commitments were made by the Government to Parliament concerning the OEPs funding, including: Government response to the Environment Audit Committee's 18th Report of Session 2017–19 (15 October 2019); Government response to the EFRA Committee's 14th Report of Session 2017–19 (15 October 2019); Minister Pow in Environment Bill (2017–2019 session) second reading debate (HC Deb 28 October 2019, vol 667, col 129); Minister Pow in Environment Bill second reading Debate (HC Deb 26 February 2020, vol 672, col 426); Speech of Chief Whip Docherty in Environment Bill Committee (HC Deb 3 November 2020, vol 683, col 308); Letter from Lord Goldsmith to Peers (10 June 2021); Response of Minister Pow to a written question submitted by Caroline Lucas MP (16 July 2021); Ministerial Statement to the House of Commons by Minister Pow (7 September 2021); Ministerial Statement to the House of Lords by Lord Goldsmith (7 September 2021); Speech by Lord Goldsmith in Environment Bill Report (HL Deb 8 September 2021, vol 814, col 889).

The provisions relating to the OEP's annual accounts in para 14 provide that the OEP must include an assessment by the OEP as to whether the Secretary of State and the Northern Ireland Department of Agriculture, Environment and Rural Affairs (see further annotations to s 49 on the OEP and Northern Ireland) have provided sufficient funding during any financial year to carry out its functions. Annual accounts are laid before Parliament, and this provision, which is not replicated in provisions about annual accounts for bodies such as the Environment Agency, will allow the OEP to highlight to Parliament where it considers funding insufficient, although there is no obligation on Parliament or the Government to act on the OEP's assessment.

Jurisdiction of the OEP

The OEP's jurisdiction formally covers the whole of the UK, but in practice the majority of its operations will relate to England and Northern Ireland (where it has been given jurisdiction, under s 49 of the Act). Most environmental matters are devolved, and under s 46 the definition of environmental law does not include a devolved legislative provision, other than for the purposes of s 20 (ministerial statements about Bills containing new environmental laws). The OEP's jurisdiction in Scotland and Wales is therefore confined to reserved matters. A House of Commons Library Briefing Paper (CBP 8544, April 2019) provides a useful review of the issue, including case law of the Supreme Court on the subject together with a table of reserved powers, though this is not intended to be exhaustive. To take one example, the licensing of nuclear power installations would be a reserved matter and to the extent that any licensing provisions are mainly concerned with environmental protection would fall within the jurisdiction of the OEP throughout the UK. Planning permissions required for such installations would be devolved, as would the regulation of any disposal of radioactive waste. The OEP will also have jurisdiction in marine waters beyond the territorial jurisdictions of the devolved administrations. The position is made more complex by the increasing use of executive devolution powers, whereby UK Ministers may exercise powers in devolved areas with the consent of the devolved government – see, for example, the provisions in this Act on producer responsibility (s 50) and water quality regulations (s 85(4) and (5)). The OEP would not have jurisdiction in such areas.

In relation to Northern Ireland, Sch 3 provides specific provisions applying the OEP's functions and powers in Northern Ireland, but also amends a number of the main provisions in the Act to include appropriate reference to Northern Ireland.

In Scotland, Environmental Standards Scotland has been established under Chapter 2 of the UK Withdrawal from the European Union (Continuity) (Scotland) Act 2021. Environment Standards Scotland will perform a similar function of independent scrutiny as does the OEP, but there are some significant differences in some of the provisions, such as the enforcement procedures and the definition of failing to comply with environmental law.

In Wales, an independent Environmental Protection Assessor was appointed on 1 March 2021 as an interim measure while the Welsh Government considers whether to develop a more permanent oversight body.

23 Principal objective of the OEP and exercise of its functions

(1) The principal objective of the OEP in exercising its functions is to contribute to—

(a) environmental protection, and

(b) the improvement of the natural environment.

(2) The OEP must—

(a) act objectively and impartially, and

(b) have regard to the need to act proportionately and transparently.

(3) The OEP must prepare a strategy that sets out how it intends to exercise its functions.

(4) In particular, the strategy must set out—

(a) how the OEP will further its principal objective,

(b) how the OEP will act objectively and impartially, and

(c) how the OEP will have regard to the need to act proportionately and transparently.

(5) The strategy must also set out—

(a) how the OEP intends to avoid any overlap between the exercise of its functions and the exercise by the Committee on Climate Change of that committee's functions, and

(b) how the OEP intends to co-operate with devolved environmental governance bodies.

(6) The strategy must contain an enforcement policy that sets out—

(a) how the OEP intends to determine whether failures to comply with environmental law are serious for the purposes of sections 33(1)(b) and (2)(b), 35(1)(b), 36(1)(b), 38(1)(b) and 39(1)(a) and (7),

(b) how the OEP intends to determine whether damage to the natural environment or to human health is serious for the purposes of section 39(2),

(c) how the OEP intends to exercise its enforcement functions in a way that respects the integrity of other statutory regimes (including statutory provision for appeals),

(d) how the OEP intends to avoid any overlap between the exercise of its functions under sections 32 to 34 (complaints) and the exercise by each relevant ombudsman of their functions, and

(e) how the OEP intends to prioritise cases.

(7) In considering its enforcement policy the OEP must have regard to the particular importance of prioritising cases that it considers have or may have national implications, and the importance of prioritising cases—

(a) that relate to ongoing or recurrent conduct,

(b) that relate to conduct that the OEP considers may cause (or has caused) serious damage to the natural environment or to human health, or

(c) that the OEP considers may raise a point of environmental law of general public importance.

(8) The OEP's "enforcement functions" are its functions under sections 32 to 41.

(9) For the purposes of this Part, each of the following is a "relevant ombudsman"—

(a) the Commission for Local Administration in England;

(b) the Parliamentary Commissioner for Administration.

In force	17 November 2021. Commencement Order No 1
Application	UK (reserved matters) E NI (but see s 49 in relation to NI)

S 23(1) provides that the principal objective of the OEP is the exercise of functions that contribute towards environmental protection and the improvement of the natural environment. The terms 'environmental protection' and 'natural environment' must be read in the light of the definitions of these terms in ss 44 and 45, respectively. Coupled with the definition of environment law in s 46, it is clear that many of the OEP's functions, including its enforcement powers, are not intended to deal with all aspects of environmental protection, or policies and decisions which may have environmental implications but do not involve environmental law as defined. The protection of human health is not explicitly mentioned within the OEP's principal objective, though it is clear that public health considerations fall within its jurisdictional scope. The definition of the environmental protection in s 45 includes 'the protection of people from the effects of human activity on the environment'. The provision on prioritisation in s 24(7) includes reference to conduct that may cause serious damage to human health, and the provision in s 39 (urgent judicial reviews applications by the OEP) also makes reference to serious damage to public health as well as the environment.

S 23(2) imposes a general duty on the OEP to act objectively and impartially, and to have regard to the need to act proportionately and transparently. Proportionality as a concept has appeared in other domestic legislation. See, for example, ss 21–24 Legislative and Regulatory Reform Act 2006 and the Regulators Code, which says: '*Regulators should avoid imposing unnecessary regulatory burdens through their regulatory activities and should assess whether similar social, environmental and economic outcomes could be achieved by less burdensome means. Regulators should choose proportionate approaches to those they regulate, based on relevant factors including, for example, business size and capacity.*' In the domestic courts it only appears to have been discussed in detail to date in the context of EU law and the European Convention on Human Rights, and any case law has been considered in that light. In the context of human rights, Lord Sumption in *Bank Mellat v Her Majesty's Treasury (No 2)* [2013] UKSC 39 summarised the principle as meaning in relation to any particular measure: '*(i) whether its objective is sufficiently important to justify the limitation of a fundamental right; (ii) whether it is rationally connected to the objective; (iii) whether a less intrusive measure could have been used; and (iv) whether, having regard to these matters and to the severity of the consequences, a fair balance has been struck between the rights of the individual and the interests of the community*' (para 20). The OEP's principal objective is to contribute to environmental protection and improve the natural environment, as defined in the legislation. The proportionality duty applies to all the actions of the OEP, whether or not human rights are engaged, and essentially implies the need to have regard to other interests that may be affected by its actions, and that less intrusive measures could not be taken to achieve the objective concerned.

The OEP Strategy

The Strategy that the OEP is obliged to produce under s 23(3) will be a key policy document of the organisation, and will contain an enforcement policy relating to the OEP's formal enforcement powers under ss 31–41 below.

Overlap and Coordination with Other Public Bodies, Including the Climate Change Committee

One of the functions of the Strategy is to provide a statement of how the OEP will avoid unnecessary overlap with the Climate Change Committee and the Ombudsmen. The Committee on Climate Change established under the Climate Change Act 2008 has powerful advisory and reporting functions, but no enforcement powers as such. In addition to the need for the strategy to state how the OEP will avoid overlap with the Climate Change Committee's functions (sub-s 5(a)), the OEP and the Committee must prepare a memorandum of understanding on how they will cooperate and avoid overlap (s 26). In evidence on the pre-legislative scrutiny of the Environment Bill, the chief executive of the Climate Change Committee noted in particular the potential issues of overlap in respect of climate change adaptation (House of Commons EFRA Committee, Pre-legislative Scrutiny of the Draft Environment Bill, Evidence Session, 6 March 2019). These provisions concerning overlap include the enforcement functions of the OEP but go wider, and in particular will include the OEP's duty to monitor progress on environmental improvement plans and targets under s 28, where there could well overlap with the Committee's reporting function. In relation to enforcement, climate change law is included within the OEP's jurisdiction, but the OEP must inform the Committee where it commences potential enforcement action with the issue of an Information Notice in relation to environmental law relating to emissions of greenhouse gases (s 35(7)). Further overlap is prevented by prohibiting the OEP from reporting on the implementation of environmental law in relation to matters within the remit of the Climate Change Committee (s 29(3) and (4)).

The Local Government and Parliamentary Ombudsmen frequently deal with complaints about public authorities and environmental law, and the enforcement policy must state how the OEP will avoid overlap with their functions in the handling of public complaints (s 23(6)). A memorandum of understanding with the Ombudsmen is not a legal requirement, but may prove advisable.

The Strategy must also set out how the OEP intends to cooperate with devolved environmental governance bodies (s 23(5)(b)). In accordance with the definition in s 47, this means devolved bodies with functions similar to those of the OEP. At present, such bodies would include Environment Standards Scotland and the Welsh Protection Assessor. Cooperation is likely to prove especially important where there are cross-border environmental enforcement issues raised, or where the OEP wishes to act because it is dealing with reserved matters.

Respecting Integrity of Other Statutory Regimes

The enforcement policy must state how the OEP will respect the integrity of other statutory regimes, including appeals (s 23(6)(c)). According to the Explanatory Notes to the Bill, this implies that *'In normal circumstances it is expected that the OEP would allow the usual regulatory processes to take their course, where they could affect a matter concerning a possible failure to comply with environmental law, before taking enforcement action'* (para 221). This would apply, for example, where an appeal had been made to the Secretary of State concerning a decision of a planning authority or the Environment Agency. The principle would also appear to apply where, say, a judicial review or statutory review has been taken by another party concerning a failure of environmental law, and the OEP would probably refrain from taking enforcement action in relation to the same matter until proceedings are completed, or might decide to intervene in the case under its powers in s 39(7) if it considers the failure to be serious.

Enforcement Priorities and Government Guidance

It is clear that the OEP will not be able to investigate or take enforcement action against every alleged breach of environmental law by public bodies. The enforcement provisions repeatedly refer to the need for the breach to be 'serious', a term not defined in the Act. The OEP is required in its enforcement policy to provide criteria on how it will determine what breaches are considered 'serious', and it is given considerable leeway is so doing. But s 25 below gives power to the Government to issue guidance on the OEP's enforcement policy that is not legally binding but to which the OEP must have regard. The Government rejected a recommendation from the House of Commons EFRA Select Committee to provide a statutory definition of 'serious', arguing that *'it is impracticable to establish such a definition that could reasonably cover all areas of environmental law and contexts in which OEP will need to judge seriousness'* (House of Commons EFRA Committee Pre-legislative Scrutiny of the Draft Environment Bill: Government Response to the Committee's Fourteenth Report of Session 2017–19, p 11, HC 95, 17 October 2019). 'Serious' in this context does not necessarily mean only breaches of law with serious impacts on the natural environment. The OEP could, for example, judge that a blatant breach of environmental law duties by an authority or repeated breaches by an authority were 'serious' even if they did not have significant impacts on the environment. Similarly, the Government has a duty under s 9 to make an annual progress report on the Environment Improvement Plan. Failure to produce such a report could be considered serious, even if the failure could not be said to cause environmental damage. Similarly, the OEP could consider that where a significant legal provision of importance requires testing, this could be included within the seriousness criteria. In contrast, the power of the OEP to take judicial review actions in urgent cases under s 39 requires that such action is required to prevent or mitigate 'serious damage to the natural environment or human health'. The enforcement policy must also define how the OEP will determine this requirement (s 23(6)(b)).

S 23(7) provides a number of criteria concerning the prioritising of cases for enforcement action by the OEP. It includes reference to cases relating to ongoing or recurrent conduct, and those raising points of environmental law of general public importance. They are not exclusive nor legally binding, but the OEP must have regard to them when drawing up its enforcement policy, and the provisions reinforce the broad interpretation that can legitimately be given to the concept of a serious failure. See the Introduction for further consideration on 'have regard to'.

24 The OEP's strategy: process

(1) The OEP must—

(a) arrange for the strategy prepared under section 23 to be laid before Parliament, and

(b) publish it.

(2) The OEP may revise the strategy at any time (and subsection (1) applies to any revised strategy).

(3) The OEP must review the strategy at least once in every review period.

(4) "Review period" means—

(a) in relation to the first review, the period of 3 years beginning with the day on which the strategy was first published, and

(b) in relation to subsequent reviews, the period of 3 years beginning with the day on which the previous review was completed.

(5) Before preparing, revising or reviewing the strategy, the OEP must consult such persons as it considers appropriate.

Definitions

'review period'	s 23(4)

In force	17 November 2021. Commencement Order No 1
Application	UK (reserved matters) E NI (but see s 49 in relation to NI)

This section provides further requirements concerning the OEP Strategy. In drawing up the Strategy, the OEP must consult such persons it considers appropriate, and it must be laid before Parliament and published. It may be revised at any time, and must be reviewed (but not necessarily revised) at least every three years. On 25 January 2022 OEP published for consultation a draft Strategy including an Enforcement Policy.

25 Guidance on the OEP's enforcement policy and functions

(1) The Secretary of State may issue guidance to the OEP on the matters listed in section 23(6) (OEP's enforcement policy).

(2) The OEP must have regard to the guidance in—

(a) preparing its enforcement policy, and

(b) exercising its enforcement functions.

(3) The OEP's "enforcement functions" are its functions under sections 32 to 41.

(4) Before issuing the guidance, the Secretary of State must—

(a) prepare a draft, and

(b) lay the draft before Parliament.

(5) If before the end of the 21 day period—

(a) either House of Parliament passes a resolution in respect of the draft guidance, or

(b) a committee of either House of Parliament, or a joint committee of both Houses, makes recommendations in respect of the draft guidance,

the Secretary of State must produce a response and lay it before Parliament.

(6) The Secretary of State may prepare and lay before Parliament the final guidance, but not before—

(a) if subsection (5) applies, the day on which the Secretary of State lays the response required by that subsection, or

(b) otherwise, the end of the 21 day period.

(7) The final guidance has effect when it is laid before Parliament.

(8) The Secretary of State must publish the guidance when it comes into effect.

(9) The "21 day period" is the period of 21 sitting days beginning with the first sitting day after the day on which the draft guidance is laid under subsection (4).

(10) "Sitting day" means a day on which both Houses of Parliament sit.

(11) The Secretary of State may revise the guidance at any time (and subsections (4) to (10) apply in relation to any revised guidance).

In force	24 January 2022. Commencement Order No 2
Application	UK (reserved matters) E

This was a politically controversial clause introduced by the Government during the committee stage of the Bill because it was seen as impinging on the independence of the OEP. It gives power to the Secretary of State to issue and revise guidance to the OEP concerning its enforcement policy and exercise of enforcement functions. In exercising any functions relating to the OEP, the Secretary of State is also under a duty under para 17 of Sch 1 'to have regard to the need to protect its independence'.

The OEP 'must have regard to the guidance', implying that the Guidance has legal significance but is not legally binding. 'Must have regard' is a familiar phrase in statutory provisions, though case law must be read with care as much depends on the particular context in which the provision appears. See further on 'have regard to' in the Introduction.

As part of the response to parliamentary concerns, Government at a late stage introduced sub-ss (4)–(6), which require the draft of any guidance to be laid before Parliament, allowing time for a resolution of either House of Parliament, or for a committee or joint committee to make recommendations. The Secretary of State must produce a response to the resolution or recommendations to be laid before Parliament.

The final guidance must be published and laid before Parliament. The case law on 'have regard to' indicates that the fact it has been laid before Parliament gives the Guidance more weight – see the Introduction.

The Guidance may only relate to the matters listed in s 23(6) (how the OEP will determine seriousness, how the OEP will determine serious damage to the environment or human health, how it will respect the integrity of other statutory regimes, how it will avoid overlap with the relevant Ombudsmen in handling complaints and how it intends to prioritise cases).

During the parliamentary debates, the Government confirmed that the Guidance could not be used to preclude the OEP from investigating a broad category of cases or particular subject areas: '*This is not a power that could be used simply to divert the OEP away from investigating issues that could be in some way inconvenient to the Government. The provision for guidance on how the OEP intends to exercise its functions means that the guidance will, by its nature, be on the OEP's approach to those issues, rather than defining specific areas to prioritise or deprioritise*' (Rebecca Power, Parliamentary Under Secretary of State, HC Deb 8 November 2021, vol 703, col 84). The Government went on to confirm that it would not issue any Guidance before the OEP had had the chance to develop its first enforcement policy (ibid, col 85).

26 Memorandum of understanding

(1) The OEP and the Committee on Climate Change must prepare a memorandum of understanding.

(2) The memorandum must set out how the OEP and the Committee intend to co-operate with one another and avoid overlap between the exercise by the OEP of its functions and the exercise by the Committee of its functions.

In force	17 November 2021. Commencement Order No 1
Application	UK (reserved matters) E, NI

This provision reinforces the need for the OEP and the Committee for Climate Change to cooperate with each other and avoid undue overlap of functions by requiring them to prepare a memorandum of understanding. This will cover not just the enforcement functions of the OEP, but perhaps more importantly its duty to report on environmental improvement plans and targets under s 28. There is no specific requirement in this legislation to publish the memorandum, though, given its general duty to have regard to the need to act transparently under s 23(1)(b), the OEP may decide to do so. See further the annotations to s 23 above on the relationship between the OEP and the Climate Change Committee.

27 Co-operation duties of public authorities and the OEP

(1) A person whose functions include functions of a public nature must co-operate with the OEP, and give it such reasonable assistance as it requests (including the provision of information), in connection with the exercise of its functions under this Act.

(2) Subsection (1) does not apply to—

- (a) a court or tribunal,
- (b) either House of Parliament,
- (c) a devolved legislature,
- (d) the Scottish Ministers, the Welsh Ministers, a Northern Ireland department or a Minister within the meaning of the Northern Ireland Act 1998,
- (e) a person exercising a parliamentary function, or
- (f) a person whose only public functions are devolved functions.

(3) A person whose public functions include devolved functions is only required to co-operate with the OEP by virtue of subsection (1) to the extent that co-operation is in relation to functions that are not devolved functions.

(4) If the OEP considers that a particular exercise of its functions may be relevant to the exercise of a devolved environmental governance function by a devolved environmental governance body, the OEP must consult that body.

Definitions

'public authority'	s 31(3)
'devolved environmental governance body'	s 47
'devolved function'	s 47
'devolved environmental governance function'	s 47
'devolved legislature'	s 47

In force	24 January 2022. Commencement Order No 2
Application	UK (reserved matters) E NI

This provision provides a general duty of cooperation of public bodies with the OEP, although it is qualified by the ambiguous phrase 'such reasonable assistance' – what appears reasonable to the OEP may not appear so to the authority concerned, though, especially where a failure of legal duties is suspected, the level of cooperation required by this duty would probably be fairly substantial. It applies not only to the OEP's enforcement functions, but also to its other functions, including reviewing progress reports on environmental improvement plans and the implementation of environmental law where information from public authorities may be extremely valuable to the OEP in carrying out an implementation review. According to the Explanatory Notes, '*The intention of the duty to cooperate is to help the OEP and public authorities resolve issues constructively, and to share relevant information*' (para 233). Certain bodies are excluded, and the duty does not apply to bodies carrying out devolved functions, subject to sub-s (3), where cooperation is needed in relation to non-devolved functions (reserved matters). There may be circumstances where the OEP considers a body carrying out devolved environmental functions, such as the Scottish Environmental Protection Agency, has relevance – for example, where it is investigating a breach of duties in England with transboundary environmental impacts. Here the OEP must consult the body concerned, though there is no formal duty for that body to cooperate. Although defined as a legal duty, there is no specific provision on its enforcement should an authority be unwilling to cooperate. But the duty is in connection with the OEP's functions and should therefore fall within the definition of environmental law, and could be subject to the enforcement procedures of the OEP.

The definition of a public authority in s 31(3) encompasses bodies 'carrying out any function of a public nature that is not a devolved function'. Statutory bodies such as water utilities and other utilities would be included in respect of their public functions – see *Fish Legal v Information Commissioner* [2015] UKUT 0052 AAC, where the Upper Tribunal held that water companies were public authorities within the meaning of the Environment Information Regulations 2004 because of their special powers, and *Marcic v Thames Water Authority* [2003] UKHL 66, where a statutory sewerage undertaker was treated as a public authority for the purposes of the Human Rights Act. Contrast *Cameron v Network Rail Infrastructure Ltd* [2006] EWHC 1133, where the defendant was held not be a public authority under the Human Rights Act. See also Lord Nichols in *Aston Cantlow with Billesley PCC v Wallbank and anor* [2004] I AC 546: '*Factors to be taken into account include the extent to which in carrying out the relevant function the body is publicly funded, or is exercising statutory powers, or is taking place of central government or local authorities or is providing a public service.'* See also *The A-G for the Prince of Wales v the Information Commissioner and Burton* [2016] UKUT 0154 (AAC), where the Upper Tribunal held that the Duchy of Cornwall was not a public authority for the purposes of the Environmental Information Regulations except to the extent (as was conceded by the Attorney-General) that the Duke of Cornwall acted as the harbour and lighthouse authority at St Mary's on the Isles of Scilly.

The OEP's scrutiny and advice functions

28 Monitoring and reporting on environmental improvement plans and targets

(1) The OEP must monitor progress—

(a) in improving the natural environment in accordance with the current environmental improvement plan,

(b) towards meeting any targets set under sections 1 to 3, and

(c) towards meeting any interim targets set under sections 11 and 14.

(2) The OEP must prepare a progress report for each annual reporting period.

(3) A progress report for an annual reporting period is a report on progress made in that period in or towards the matters listed in subsection (1).

(4) An annual reporting period is a period for which the Secretary of State must prepare a report under section 9 (a "section 9 report").

(5) In reporting on progress made in an annual reporting period, the OEP must consider—

(a) the section 9 report for that period,

(b) the data published by the Secretary of State under section 16 that relates to that period, and

(c) any other reports, documents or information it considers appropriate.

(6) A progress report for an annual reporting period may include—

(a) consideration of how progress could be improved, and

(b) consideration of the adequacy of the data published by the Secretary of State under section 16.

(7) The OEP must—

(a) arrange for its reports under this section to be laid before Parliament, and

(b) publish them.

(8) A progress report for an annual reporting period must be laid no later than 6 months after the section 9 report for that period is laid before Parliament.

(9) The Secretary of State must—

(a) respond to a report under this section, and

(b) lay before Parliament, and publish, a copy of the response.

(10) Where a report under this section contains a recommendation for how progress could be improved, the response must address that recommendation.

(11) The response—

(a) must be laid no later than 12 months after the report is laid, and

(b) may be included in a section 9 report.

Definitions

'current environment improvement plan'	s 8(8)
'environment improvement plan'	ss 8 and 10(10)

In force	24 January 2022. Commencement Order No 2
Application	UK (reserved matters) E

S 28 gives the OEP important responsibilities to provide regular independent assessments of the Government's progress in meeting its statutory environmental improvement plans and longer-term and interim environmental targets under Chapter 1. The functions extend considerably beyond the implementation and enforcement of environmental law, and in many ways will perform a similar role to that of the Climate Change Committee in relation to climate change targets and interim budgets. The main difference is that under the Climate Change Act 2008 it is the prime responsibility of the Climate Change Committee to produce annual progress reports. In contrast, under s 9 of the Environment Act, the Secretary of State has a duty to produce annual progress reports; in that context, the OEP's assessments under s 28 are likely to provide an independent critique of the Government's own assessments.

According to the Explanatory Notes, '*This monitoring and reporting function will hold the government to account on its environment improvement commitments*' (para 239). In 2020 the National Audit Office published a report on how the Government had set itself up to deliver its long-term environmental goals as set out in the 25 Year Environment Plan, published in 2018 (National Audit Office, *Achieving Government's Long-Term Environmental Goals*, HC 958, 11 November 2020). Although only the Climate Change Committee and the Ombudsmen are expressly mentioned, the requirements to avoid overlap are contained in the OEP Strategy (see ss 22((5) and 22(6)(b) above), but in practice there is likely to be a need in future to avoid duplication of auditing functions of the National Audit Office and the OEP under this section.

As part of its reports, the OEP must consider and report the Government's progress on the environmental improvement plan. In doing so, it must consider the Government's own annual progress report on the environmental improvement plan, data used and published by the Secretary of State under s 16 to assess progress, and any other relevant reports and information.

The OEP progress review must also consider progress in meeting the statutory targets established under ss 1–3, and while there is a duty on the Government to set a final duty to report on whether or not it has achieved the targets, there is no explicit duty equivalent to that on environmental improvement plans for the Government to provide annual progress reports. The longer-term targets could be included in the environmental improvement plan, though there is no obligation to do so. On the first review and revision of the environmental improvement plan, however, the Government must include an interim target for each of the matters for which a target has been set under ss 1–3 (see s 11). Once included in the plan, the interim targets will be included as matters to be considered as part of the Government's annual progress report. In turn, the OEP must, as part of its review on the progress of the plan, consider progress in meeting the interim targets (sub-s (1)(c)) as well as the longer-term targets, whether or not they are included in the plan.

The OEP reports may – though they are not obliged to – include both consideration of the adequacy of the data and how progress could be improved. The extent to which the OEP engages in detailed critical review of the effectiveness of government policy in meeting its goals and targets will therefore very much depend on the discretion and judgement of the OEP.

The OEP report must be laid before Parliament within six months of the Government's own annual progress report being laid before Parliament. The Government is not obliged to comply with any recommendations in the OEP's reports, but the Secretary of State is obliged to respond to the reports within 12 months, and must address any recommendations made by the OEP for improving progress. Essentially, the process is designed to reinforce the political and public accountability of the Government by providing a regular and independent assessment of the Government's progress.

29 Monitoring and reporting on environmental law

(1) The OEP must monitor the implementation of environmental law.

(2) The OEP may report on any matter concerned with the implementation of environmental law.

(3) But the OEP must not monitor the implementation of, or report on, a matter within the remit of the Committee on Climate Change.

(4) A matter is within the remit of the Committee on Climate Change if it is a matter on which the Committee is, or may be, required to advise or report under Part 1, sections 34 to 36, or section 48 of the Climate Change Act 2008.

(5) The OEP must—

(a) arrange for its reports under this section to be laid before Parliament, and

(b) publish them.

(6) The Secretary of State must—

(a) respond to a report under this section, and

(b) lay before Parliament, and publish, a copy of the response.

(7) The response to a report under this section must be laid no later than 3 months after the report is laid.

Definitions

'environmental law'	s 45

In force	24 January 2022. Commencement Order No 2
Application	UK (reserved matters) E

This section gives an important role for the OEP to monitor and report on the implementation of environmental law. Systematic monitoring of implementation has rarely been a feature of UK environmental law, and there are few instances of legal provisions in national environmental legislation that require regular reporting on implementation (though for an unusual example, see para 17 of Sch 17 in this Act relating to forest risk commodities). In contrast, most EU Environmental Directives have required the European Commission to produce regular reports on their implementation within Member States – see Directive 91/692 standardising and rationalising reports on the implementation of certain Directives relating to the environment.

The term 'implementation' is not defined, and while it would include the enforcement of environmental law (ensuring that the law is complied with), it is often considered to go much wider and could include, inter alia, the design of the legislation in question, training, staffing levels and funding. At an international level, implementation has been described as encompassing '*the enactment of executive regulations and guidelines; establishing institutions, designating their responsibilities and coordinating their activities with remits to oversee implementation. To enable effective implementation, the laws and regulations need to be clearly stated (ie capable of being identified and evaluated as having been implemented, or not); feasible technically, economically and socially (ie fit-for-purpose at the level they are required to be implemented); and provide for appropriate sanctions in case of violations. In order to sustain itself, effective implementation requires training and capacity building as much as awareness raising and education*' (Global Water Partnership, Implementation and Enforcement (A2.02) www.gwp.org/en/learn/iwrm-toolbox/The-Enabling-Environment/Legal-Framework/Implementation-and-Enforcement/).

S 29(1) is expressed as a duty on the OEP, but clearly gives the OEP considerable discretion in choosing which areas of environmental law to investigate and how it should go about the task. In carrying out a review, the OEP may need to obtain information from local authorities and other public bodies, and the general duty of cooperation under s 27 would apply. Information from complaints under s 32 below where no enforcement action is pursued might also suggest areas where an investigation under this section is required. The OEP reports on implementation must be published and laid before Parliament, and although its conclusions and recommendations will not be binding, the Secretary of State is obliged to respond, and publish and lay the response before Parliament.

Concerns about possible overlap with the functions of the Climate Change Committee are reinforced in s 29(3) and (4), which prohibit the OEP from reporting on those matters under the Climate Change Act 2008 on which the Climate Change Committee advises or reports – including advice in connection with carbon budgets, advice on emissions from international aviation, reports on progress in meeting carbon budgets and advice on regulations concerning emissions trading. See further the commentary on s 23 above.

30 Advising on changes to environmental law etc

(1) The OEP must give advice to a Minister of the Crown about—

(a) any proposed change to environmental law, or

(b) any other matter relating to the natural environment, on which the Minister requires it to give advice.

(2) The Minister may specify matters which the OEP is to take into account in giving the required advice.

(3) The OEP may give advice to a Minister of the Crown about any changes to environmental law proposed by a Minister of the Crown.

(4) Advice under this section is to be given in writing to the Minister concerned.

(5) The OEP must publish—

(a) its advice, and

(b) if the advice is given under subsection (1), a statement of the matter on which it was required to give advice and any matters specified under subsection (2).

(6) The Minister concerned may, if the Minister thinks fit, lay before Parliament—

(a) the advice, and

(b) any response the Minister may make to the advice.

Definitions

'environmental law'	s 46
'Minister of the Crown'	s 47
'natural environment'	s 44

In force	24 January 2022. Commencement Order No 2
Application	UK (reserved matters) E

Sub-s (1) and (2) give the OEP an obligation to give advice to any Minister on proposed changes in environmental law as defined in s 46, or on other matters relating to the natural environment in response to a requirement from the Minister to provide such advice. Sub-s (3) allows the OEP to give advice on proposed changes in environmental law by any Minister. Even where no specific advice has been sought, the OEP reports on the implementation of environmental law under s 29 could legitimately include recommendations to change existing environmental law if considered relevant to more effective implementation.

The advice must be published by the OEP (together with a summary of the Minister's request for advice if applicable), but, in contrast to the OEP reports on implementation, there is no obligation on the relevant Minister to respond or lay a response before Parliament; rather, it is at the Minister's discretion. There is a requirement for Ministers introducing a Bill containing environmental law provisions to make a statement under s 20 as to whether or not the Bill would reduce the level of environmental protection provided by existing environmental law, but this duty is confined to Bills, and would not include, as here, regulations – the definition of environmental law in s 46 includes 'any legislative provision'.

The OEP's enforcement functions

31 Failure of public authorities to comply with environmental law

(1) Sections 32 to 41 make provision about functions of the OEP in relation to failures by public authorities to comply with environmental law.

(2) For the purposes of those sections, a reference to a public authority failing to comply with environmental law means the following conduct by that authority—

(a) unlawfully failing to take proper account of environmental law when exercising its functions;

(b) unlawfully exercising, or failing to exercise, any function it has under environmental law.

(3) In this Part "public authority" means a person carrying out any function of a public nature that is not a devolved function, a parliamentary function or a function of any of the following persons—

(a) the OEP;

(b) a court or tribunal;

(c) either House of Parliament;

(d) a devolved legislature;

(e) the Scottish Ministers, the Welsh Ministers, a Northern Ireland department or a Minister within the meaning of the Northern Ireland Act 1998.

Definitions

'devolved function'	s 47
'devolved legislature'	s 47
'environmental law'	s 46
'parliamentary function'	s 47
'public authority'	s 31(3)

In force	24 January 2022. Commencement Order No 2
Application	UK (reserved matters) E

The following sections (ss 31–41) give the OEP specific enforcement powers against public authorities for failures to comply with environmental law. In many ways, the core procedures are designed to replicate and replace the processes used by the European Commission to ensure the implementation of EU environmental law by Member States. Similar to the Commission procedures under Arts 258 and 259 Treaty on the Functioning of the European Union, which involve a three-stage process (infringement letter, Reasoned Opinion and referral to the European Court of Justice), the provisions here introduce a stepped process (service of Information Notice, service of Decision Notice and referral to court by way of environmental review) designed to encourage resolution before court action. As with Commission infringement letters and Reasoned Opinions, the Information and Decision Notices are not legally binding in the sense that failure to comply gives rise to sanctions, but there are statutory duties to cooperate and respond, and the knowledge that this is essentially a one-way ratchet that could lead to court action means that authorities would be ill-advised not to treat such Notices with seriousness. The position can be contrasted to that in Scotland, where a compliance notice issued by Environmental Standards Scotland (ESS) is binding unless appealed against. Where there is a failure without reasonable excuse to comply with the notice, ESS can report the matter to the Court of Session, which may make an appropriate order and/or treat the failure as contempt of court (ss 36 and 37 UK Withdrawal from the European Union (Continuity) (Scotland) Act 2021).

A failure to comply with environmental law is defined in s 31(2) as unlawfully failing to take proper account of environmental law when exercising functions, or unlawfully exercising or failing to exercise any function under environmental law. S 38(5) provides that where enforcement action by the OEP comes before a court by way of environmental review, the court must apply the principles of judicial review in determining whether an authority has failed to comply with environmental law. The use of the term 'unlawfully' in the definition would therefore appear to imply no more than that the failure is contrary to judicial review principles. In *Council of Civil Service Unions v Minister for the Civil Service* [1985] AC 374 Lord Diplock made a well-known division of three broad grounds of judicial review: 'illegality' (failure to apply the law correctly), 'procedural irregularity' and 'irrationality' (*Wednesbury* unreasonableness). If 'illegality' were equated with 'unlawfulness', this might suggest the enforcement powers of the OEP were confined to the first category only, but this seems an unnecessarily strained reading, and in any event subsequent case law has held that Lord Diplock's categorisation is neither exhaustive nor mutually exclusive.

The first half of the definition would apply where authorities are under a legal duty to take into account matters falling within the definition of environmental law – for example, in this Act the duty of Ministers to have due regard to the statutory statement on environmental principles (s 19), or the duty to have regard to a relevant protected site strategy (s 102(5)). See further commentary on 'have regard to' in the Introduction.

Certain bodies are excluded from the remit of the OEP, including bodies carrying out devolved functions. Public authorities are given a broad definition in s 31(3), and would therefore appear to apply to statutory undertakers where they are carrying out public functions – see annotations to s 27 above.

32 Complaints

(1) A person may make a complaint to the OEP under this section if the person believes that a public authority has failed to comply with environmental law.

(2) The OEP must prepare and publish a document which sets out the procedure by which complaints can be made.

(3) A complaint under this section must be made in accordance with that procedure (as most recently published).

(4) A complaint under this section may not be made by any person whose functions include functions of a public nature.

(5) A complaint about a public authority may not be made under this section if—

(a) the authority operates a procedure for considering complaints ("an internal complaints procedure") under which the complaint could be considered, and

(b) that procedure has not been exhausted.

(6) A complaint under this section may not be made after the later of—

(a) the end of the 1 year period beginning with the day on which the alleged failure that is the subject of the complaint last occurred, and

(b) if the substance of the complaint was subject to an internal complaints procedure, the end of the 3 month period beginning with the day on which that procedure was exhausted.

(7) The OEP may waive the time limit in subsection (6) if it considers that there are exceptional reasons for doing so.

Definitions

'environmental law'	s 46
'failed to comply with environmental law'	s 31(2)
'public authority'	s 31(3)

In force	24 January 2022. Commencement Order No 2
Application	UK (reserved matters) E

S 32 requires the OEP to establish a complaints procedure allowing members of the public, environmental organisations, industries and any other person to complain to the OEP that a public authority has failed to comply with environmental law. The OEP is not obliged to investigate every complaint sent to it (see s 33) and its enforcement policy will provide an indication of the types of cases it is likely to examine further. Complaints are likely to be an important source of information for the OEP about alleged breaches of environmental law, and even if they do not lead to formal investigations and enforcement may indicate areas of environmental law where a report on implementation under s 29 would be desirable.

There are certain restrictions on the complaint procedure. Authorities carrying out public functions, including bodies such parish councils, may not make complaints (sub-s (4)). The restriction (applicable to 'persons') would encompass individuals carrying out such functions, and therefore could be interpreted to preclude 'whistleblowers' employed by public bodies from formally making a complaint. S 43B of the Employment Rights Act 1996 permits disclosure of information by workers to prescribed bodies if they have a reasonable belief that, amongst other matters listed, the employer is failing to comply with a legal obligation. At present, the OEP is not listed within the bodies prescribed under s 43F of the same Act, though it might be in the future (see Public Interest Disclosure (Prescribed Persons) Order 2014). The provisions in s 32(4) may not be as restrictive as they first appear, since the OEP may initiate investigations under s 33 on the basis of complaints or 'other information' it possesses (s 33(3)). Even if material provided by an employee of a public authority could not be accepted as a formal complaint, it could be treated as 'other information'.

If the authority against which a complaint has been made operates an internal complaints procedure covering the issue in question, the complainant must first exhaust that procedure (sub-s (5)). Authorities are not obliged to establish internal complaints procedures, but if they have, complainants must use these first. The rationale is that this may resolve the issue being complained about without the need to go further. The requirement to exhaust the internal complaints procedure could lead to problems where that procedure has no specific time limits for resolution, especially as, unlike the provisions concerning the time limits for making complaints to the OEP in sub-s (7) below, the OEP has no power to override these provisions in special circumstances. For example, the internal complaints procedure and Customer Service Commitment of the Environment Agency provides that it will 'aim to respond' to complaints within 10 working days but that sometimes it may need longer to respond. If the complainant is not satisfied with the response, the Agency will escalate it to a manager, who will 'review your complaint and write to you again'. Where, in effect, the complainant appears to be caught up in a lengthy internal complaints procedure, it appears that the OEP, after being alerted to the issue, could still use its powers under s 33(2) below to launch an investigation even though the complaint has not been formally accepted because of the condition about exhausting an internal complaints procedure in sub-s (5).

The complaint must concern a failure of environmental law as defined in s 46, and relate to a public authority as defined in s 31(3). Generally, the complaint must be made within 12 months of the alleged failure and three months from the exhaustion of any internal complaints procedure. The OEP has the discretion to override these time limits where it considers there are 'exceptional' reasons. This might apply, for example, where the environmental effects of an alleged breach do not become apparent until after the time limit has elapsed. There is no provision for the OEP to charge complainants for using the complaint procedure.

33 Investigations

(1) The OEP may carry out an investigation under this section if it receives a complaint made under section 32 that, in its view, indicates that—

(a) a public authority may have failed to comply with environmental law, and

(b) if it has, the failure would be a serious failure.

(2) The OEP may carry out an investigation under this section without having received such a complaint if it has information that, in its view, indicates that—

(a) a public authority may have failed to comply with environmental law, and

(b) if it has, the failure would be a serious failure.

(3) An investigation under this section is an investigation into whether the public authority has failed to comply with environmental law.

(4) The OEP must notify the public authority of the commencement of the investigation.

(5) The OEP must prepare a report on the investigation and provide it to the public authority.

(6) The OEP is not required to prepare a report until it has concluded that it intends to take no further steps under this Chapter in relation to the alleged failure to comply with environmental law that is the subject of the investigation.

(7) The OEP is not required to prepare a report if it has applied for an environmental review, judicial review or statutory review (see sections 38 and 39) in relation to the alleged failure.

(8) The report must set out—

(a) whether the OEP considers that the public authority has failed to comply with environmental law,

(b) the reasons the OEP came to that conclusion, and

(c) any recommendations the OEP may have (whether generally or for the public authority) in light of those conclusions.

(9) The OEP may publish the report or parts of it.

(10) If the public authority is not a Minister of the Crown, the OEP must also—

(a) notify the relevant Minister of the commencement of the investigation, and

(b) provide the relevant Minister with the report prepared under subsection (5).

(11) In this Part "the relevant Minister", in relation to a failure (or alleged failure) of a public authority to comply with environmental law, means the Minister of the Crown that the OEP considers appropriate having regard to the nature of the public authority and the nature of the failure.

Definitions

'environmental law'	s 46
'failure to comply with environmental law'	s 31(2)
'Minister of the Crown'	s 47
'public authority'	s 31(3)
'relevant Minister'	s 33(11)

In force	24 January 2022. Commencement Order No 2
Application	UK (reserved matters) E

S 33 gives the power to carry out investigations into potential failures of environmental law by public authorities, whether as a result of information from a public complainant or from its own sources of information. The failure must, in the OEP's view, be 'serious', and the enforcement policy of the OEP must include consideration of how the OEP will determine whether a failure is serious or not (s 23(6)(a) above). The OEP does not need to carry out a s 33 investigation as a condition of starting formal enforcement procedures under s 35 with an Information Notice, but the procedure is designed to assist the OEP in establishing whether or not there has been a serious breach, and potentially to resolve the situation without initiating formal enforcement action.

The OEP must notify the relevant public authority that it has commenced the investigation, as well as the relevant Minister where the body concerned is not part of central government, and authorities will be under the general duty of cooperation with the OEP under s 27 above. See also s 42 below, which contains provisions about disclosure of information by public authorities and provides, subject to some exceptions, that any obligation of secrecy imposed by statute or otherwise shall not prevent the disclosure of information to the OEP in connection with s 33 investigation, a s 35 Information Notice or a s 36 Decision Notice.

The report on the investigation must be provided to the authority concerned and must state whether the OEP considers that there has been a failure of environmental law, its reasons for so doing and any recommendations the OEP has in the light of these conclusions. Recommendations are not legally binding on authorities, but may assist in resolution of an issue without the need to take the matter further. Recipient authorities will need to give serious weight to the reports, and would probably need rational reasons for rejecting them. See *R (Bradley) v Secretary of State for Works and Pensions* [2008] EWCA Civ 36, where Sir John Chadwick held that, in relation to a report by the Ombudsman under the Parliamentary Commissioner Act 1967, *'I am not persuaded that the Secretary of State was entitled to reject the Ombudsman's finding merely because he preferred another view which could not be characterised as irrational. As I have said, earlier in this judgment, it is not enough that the Secretary of State has reached his own view on rational grounds: it is necessary that his decision to reject the Ombudsman's findings in favour of his own view is, itself, not irrational having regard to the legislative intention which underlies 1967 Act: he must have a reason (other than simply a preference for his own view) for rejecting a finding which the Ombudsman has made after an investigation under the powers conferred by the Act'* (para 91).

Reports are not required if the OEP concludes that it intends to take no further enforcement action or where it has commenced formal enforcement before the courts (application for an environmental review under s 38 or application for judicial or statutory review in urgent cases under s 39). Under this section, the OEP has the discretion whether to publish the whole or part of a report, though it will still be subject to requirements under the Freedom of Information Act 2000 and the Environmental Information Regulations 2004, and has a general duty to act transparently under s 23(2)(b) above. Where it has published a report, it must provide the complainant with a copy if the investigation has resulted from a public complaint (s 34(2)(e) below).

34 Duty to keep complainants informed

(1) Where a person makes a complaint to the OEP alleging that a public authority has failed to comply with environmental law, the OEP must keep the complainant informed about its handling of the complaint.

(2) In particular, the OEP must—

(a) notify the complainant if it does not intend to consider the complaint because the complaint was not made in accordance with section 32;

(b) notify the complainant if it has concluded that it will not be commencing an investigation under section 33 in relation to the complaint;

(c) notify the complainant if it commences an investigation under section 33 in relation to the complaint;

(d) if such an investigation is commenced, notify the complainant—

(i) where it provides a report under section 33(5) to the public authority that is the subject of the investigation, that it has provided it;

(ii) where it applies for an environmental review (see section 38), for permission to apply for judicial review or for statutory review (see section 39), in relation to the alleged failure to comply with environmental law that is the subject of the investigation, that it has made such an application;

(e) provide the complainant with a copy of any document published under section 33(9) in relation to any investigation in relation to the complaint.

Definitions

'environmental law'	s 46
'environmental review'	s 38
'failure to comply with environmental law'	s 31(2)
'public authority'	s 31(3)

In force	24 January 2022. Commencement Order No 2
Application	UK (reserved matters) E

This section imposes duties on the OEP to inform a complainant of how it has handled a complaint, including a decision to reject the complaint on grounds, for example, that the complaint does not raise issues of environmental law, or that any internal complaints procedure of the authority concerned have not first been exhausted. No statutory time limits are provided for making notifications to the complainant under this section, though the OEP may well develop a customer services policy that addresses this issue.

35 Information notices

(1) The OEP may give an information notice to a public authority if—

(a) the OEP has reasonable grounds for suspecting that the authority has failed to comply with environmental law, and

(b) it considers that the failure, if it occurred, would be serious.

(2) An information notice is a notice which—

(a) describes an alleged failure of a public authority to comply with environmental law,

(b) explains why the OEP considers that the alleged failure, if it occurred, would be serious, and

(c) requests that the authority provide such information relating to the allegation as may be specified in the notice.

(3) The recipient of an information notice must—

(a) respond in writing to the notice, and

(b) so far as is reasonably practicable, provide the OEP with the information requested in the notice.

(4) The recipient of an information notice must comply with subsection (3) by—

(a) the end of the 2 month period beginning with the day on which the notice was given, or

(b) such later date as may be specified in the notice.

(5) The written response to an information notice must set out—

(a) the recipient's response to the allegation described in the notice, and

(b) what steps (if any) the recipient intends to take in relation to the allegation.

(6) The OEP may—

(a) withdraw an information notice;

(b) give more than one information notice in respect of the same alleged failure of a public authority to comply with environmental law.

(7) Where the OEP intends to give an information notice to a public authority in respect of an alleged failure to comply with environmental law which relates to emissions of greenhouse gases (within the meaning of the Climate Change Act 2008), the OEP—

(a) must notify the Committee on Climate Change of its intention before it gives the notice to the authority, and

(b) must provide that Committee with such information relating to the alleged failure as the OEP considers appropriate.

Definitions

'environmental law'	s 46
'failure to comply with environmental law'	s 31(2)
'public authority'	s 31(3)

In force	Day to be appointed by Secretary of State
Application	UK (reserved matters) E

The service of an Information Notice is the first formal step in the OEP's bespoke enforcement powers against public authorities, and must be issued before the OEP moves on to the second stage, the service of a Decision Notice under s 36 (see s 36(5)). It is not necessary for the OEP to carry out a s 33 investigation before serving an Information Notice, though in practice it may often do so, and Information Notices do not have to be issued only in response to a public complaint if the OEP has other sources of information giving it reasonable grounds for suspecting a failure to comply with environmental law. The failure must be considered 'serious' by the OEP before service of an Information Notice, a term that will be elaborated in the OEP's Enforcement Policy.

The Information Notice will describe the alleged failure and why it is considered serious, and request any further information that the OEP requires. Authorities must respond to the Notice within two months or any later period specified in the Notice, and provide any information requested in the Notice as far as reasonably practicable. Authorities will also be under the general duty of cooperation under s 27, and see also s 42 below about disclosure of information. There is no particular mechanism for enforcing the duty to respond, but once the time limits have passed, the OEP could move to the next stage of enforcement, the service of a Decision Notice. Alternatively, since this section should be considered to fall within the definition of environmental law under s 46 below, the OEP could use the enforcement mechanisms here to enforce the duty to respond.

The use of an Information Notice reflects the general policy underlying enforcement by the OEP, which is designed to encourage resolution of issues without the need for court proceedings. In its response to an Information Notice, an authority must set out any steps (if any) it intends to take in respect of the alleged failure. If it accepts there has been a failure that is serious and takes appropriate steps, this may be sufficient to warrant no further enforcement action. But any steps that an authority may be able to take in relation to the breach will depend on the nature and circumstances of the breach in question. If, for example, the breach relates to a specific decision of the authority, the authority may be *functus officio* and unable to revisit that decision without an order quashing the decision from a court. See, for example, *Flaxby Park Ltd v Harrogate Borough Council* [2020] EWHC 3204 (a local authority cannot review its decision to adopt a local plan under the Planning and Compulsory Purchase Act 2004). In *R (Sambotin) v London Borough of Brent* [2018] EWCA Civ 1826, Jackson LJ noted that, '*Once a public authority exercising a statutory power has decided how the power is to be exercised, it will lack further authority and be functus officio. Any later attempt will be outside the authority's powers (ultra vires). Aside from these limits on powers, there is a strong and obvious policy interest in finality, which allows individuals to rely upon statutory decisions without having to worry that they may later be changed.*' But the court noted that, in the interests of justice and of good administration, there were limited exceptions allowing reconsideration, notably where there had been fraud or a fundamental mistake of fact. Furthermore, for the principle to apply, the decision in question must be final, a question that depends on the statutory scheme in question. Should the authority be *functus officio* in relation to the issue, then presumably the OEP would need to move on to an application to the court for an environmental review having first served a Decision Notice, or consider an application for a judicial review under 39 below where the application is necessary to prevent serious damage to the environment or public health.

Climate change law falls within the definition of environmental law, but the OEP must inform the Climate Change Committee of its intention to issue an Information Notice with respect to the emissions of greenhouse gases. The provisions do not require the OEP to take into account any representations by the Climate Change Committee, though the procedure may be elaborated upon in the memorandum of understanding between the OEP and the Climate Change Committee required under s 26.

36 Decision notices

(1) The OEP may give a decision notice to a public authority if—

(a) the OEP is satisfied, on the balance of probabilities, that the authority has failed to comply with environmental law, and

(b) it considers that the failure is serious.

(2) A decision notice is a notice that—

(a) describes a failure of a public authority to comply with environmental law,

(b) explains why the OEP considers that the failure is serious, and

(c) sets out the steps the OEP considers the authority should take in relation to the failure (which may include steps designed to remedy, mitigate or prevent reoccurrence of the failure).

(3) The recipient of a decision notice must respond in writing to that notice by—

(a) the end of the 2 month period beginning with the day on which the notice was given, or

(b) such later date as may be specified in the notice.

(4) The written response to a decision notice must set out—

(a) whether the recipient agrees that the failure described in the notice occurred,

(b) whether the recipient intends to take the steps set out in the notice, and

(c) what other steps (if any) the recipient intends to take in relation to the failure described in the notice.

(5) The OEP—

(a) may not give a decision notice to a public authority unless it has first given at least one information notice relating to the failure of the authority to comply with environmental law that is described in the decision notice;

(b) may withdraw a decision notice.

Definitions

'environmental law'	s 46
'failure to comply with environmental law'	s 31(2)
'public authority'	s 31(3)

In force	24 January 2022. Commencement Order No 2
Application	UK (reserved matters) E

If matters have not been resolved following the service of an Information Notice, the OEP is entitled to move to the second and more serious stage of the enforcement process, the service of a Decision Notice. Service of an Information Notice under s 35 requires the OEP to have 'reasonable grounds for suspecting that the authority has failed to comply with environmental law'. For Decision Notices under this section the evidential test is rather higher, in that the OEP must be satisfied on the balance of probabilities that the failure has occurred (sub-s 1(a)). This reflects the seriousness of this step in the enforcement process.

As with the Information Notice, the Decision Notice will describe the failure to comply with environmental law and explain why it is considered serious. But unlike the Information Notice, the Decision Notice must also set out the steps that the OEP considers should be taken in relation to the failure. This is in contrast with the position of statutory nuisance abatement notices under s 80 Environmental Protection Act 1980, where local authorities may, but are not obliged to, specify the steps needed to abate the nuisance: *R v Falmouth & Truro ex parte South West Water* [2001] QB 445. However, under Reg 37(4) Environmental Permitting (England and Wales) Regulations 2010 (now the 2016 regulations) a suspension notice issued by the Environment Agency must specify the steps that must be taken to remove the risk: *R (European Metal Recycling Ltd) v EA* [2013] Env LR 14. Again, s 36(2)(c) is consistent with the aim of an enforcement process that seeks a resolution without the issue having to go to court.

The OEP is given wide discretion in determining the steps it considers appropriate in the light of the particular breach. The Explanatory Notes give a number of examples, including cancelling or amending a particular decision, preparing a new strategy and undertaking remedial action. In determining steps, the OEP would have regard to its principal objective – to contribute to environmental protection and the improvement of the natural environment (s 23(1)) – but also its duty to act proportionately under s 23(2). For example, specifying that the authority should quash the granting of a planning decision before development is complete under s 97 Town and Country Planning Act 1971 (or a discontinuance order under s 102 of the Act where development is completed), which would oblige the authority to pay a large amount of compensation, might, depending on the circumstances, be considered disproportionate compared to, say, taking steps to ensure that the failure does not reoccur. See also *Health and Safety Executive v Wolverhampton City Council* [2012] UKSC 34, where Lord Hope noted that in deciding whether or not to exercise powers to revoke under s 47 Town and Country Planning Act, an authority was entitled to take into consideration the costs involved: '*As custodian of public funds, the authority not only may, but generally must, have regard to the cost on the public of its actions, at least to the extent of considering in any case whether the cost is proportionate to the aim to be achieved*' (para 25). See also *Revocation of Planning Permission*, Briefing Paper 00905 (House of Commons Library, 2016). In setting out steps, the OEP must also ensure that the steps proposed can legitimately be taken by the authority. Depending on the nature of the breach, it may be unable to revisit a decision taken under statutory powers as being *functus officio* – see annotations to s 35 above. In such a case, the OEP might focus on steps to ensure that no repetition takes place.

Authorities are not legally bound to comply with the steps specified by the OEP, and may, if they accept that a failure has occurred, describe alternative steps they intend to take. The legislation is not entirely clear about what happens when the authority admits the breach but there is disagreement as to the appropriate steps to be taken to remedy the situation. There are no appeal provisions for the authority to challenge the Decision Notice other than by way of ordinary judicial review. Presumably, in those circumstances, the OEP, if it felt the response by the authority was not satisfactory, could still bring an environmental review before the courts under s 38 with a focus on securing appropriate judicial remedies, provided it considered that, despite the remedial steps offered, the failure was still serious enough to meet the threshold test of s 38. See further commentary on s 38 below.

The authority must respond to a Decision Notice within two months, or any later date specified in the Notice (sub-s (3)). See also s 42 below on disclosures of information. If it fails to respond, the OEP is entitled to commence legal proceedings by way of an environmental review under s 38 below. S 36 should be considered to fall within the definition of environmental law under s 46, and if the OEP considered that information from the authority was essential before taking further action, it could initiate enforcement proceedings under these provisions in respect of that failure to respond.

37 Linked notices

(1) If the OEP gives an information notice or a decision notice to more than one public authority in respect of the same or similar conduct, it may determine that those notices are linked.

(2) A Minister of the Crown may request that the OEP determine that information notices or decision notices are linked and the OEP must have regard to that request.

(3) The OEP must provide the recipient of an information notice or a decision notice (a "principal notice") with a copy of every information notice or decision notice which is linked to it (and such a notice is referred to in this section as a "linked notice").

(4) The OEP must provide the recipient of a principal notice with a copy of any relevant correspondence, relating to a linked notice, between the OEP and the recipient of that linked notice.

(5) The OEP must provide the recipient of a principal notice with a copy of any relevant correspondence between the OEP and the relevant Minister that relates to a linked notice.

(6) Subsection (5) does not apply where either the recipient of the principal notice or the linked notice is a Minister of the Crown.

(7) The obligation to provide a copy of any notice or correspondence under this section does not apply where the OEP considers that in the circumstances it would not be in the public interest to do so.

(8) For the purposes of this section, correspondence is relevant if—

(a) it is not correspondence in connection with an environmental review or any other legal proceedings (such as judicial review), and

(b) it is not correspondence sent by virtue of section 40(1)(a) or (b).

Definitions

'public authority'	s 31(3)
'Minister of the Crown'	s 47
'relevant Minister'	s 33

In force	24 January 2022. Commencement Order No 2
Application	UK (reserved matters) E

This section allows the OEP to decide that where Information Notices or Decision Notices are sent to more than one authority and are in respect of the 'same or similar conduct' they should be linked. It might apply, for example, where more than one authority in involved in a particular breach. In its Enforcement Policy, the OEP may decide that it would act where there appear to be systematic failings in an area of environmental law by a number of different authorities ('similar failings') and that it is appropriate in such circumstances to have notices linked. Essentially, once notices are linked, the OEP must provide copies of the linked notices to all the authorities concerned, together with copies of correspondence between the OEP and the parties concerned, unless it considers it would not be in the public interest to do so. The example given in the Explanatory Notes is where an Information or Decision Notice relates to matters of national security and it would not be in the public interest to share this with other parties.

38 Environmental review

(1) Where the OEP has given a decision notice to a public authority it may apply to the court for an environmental review, but only if—

(a) it is satisfied, on the balance of probabilities, that the authority has failed to comply with environmental law, and

(b) it considers that the failure is serious.

(2) An environmental review is a review of alleged conduct of the authority that is described in the decision notice as constituting a failure to comply with environmental law.

(3) An application for an environmental review may not be made—

(a) before the earlier of—

(i) the end of the period within which the authority must respond to the decision notice in accordance with section 36(3), and

(ii) the date on which the OEP receives the authority's response to that notice, or

(b) before the expiry of any time limit which applies to the commencement of judicial review or other similar legal proceedings for questioning the alleged conduct.

(4) Any restriction imposed by or under any other enactment on questioning the conduct of a public authority in legal proceedings does not apply to an environmental review.

(5) On an environmental review the court must determine whether the authority has failed to comply with environmental law, applying the principles applicable on an application for judicial review.

(6) If the court finds that the authority has failed to comply with environmental law, it must make a statement to that effect (a "statement of non-compliance").

(7) A statement of non-compliance does not affect the validity of the conduct in respect of which it is given.

(8) Where the court makes a statement of non-compliance it may grant any remedy that could be granted by it on a judicial review other than damages, but only if Condition A or Condition B is met.

(9) Condition A is that the court is satisfied that granting the remedy would not—

(a) be likely to cause substantial hardship to, or substantially prejudice the rights of, any person other than the authority, or

(b) be detrimental to good administration.

(10) Condition B is that Condition A is not met but the court is satisfied that—

(a) granting the remedy is necessary in order to prevent or mitigate serious damage to the natural environment or to human health, and

(b) there is an exceptional public interest reason to grant it.

(11) In deciding whether to grant a remedy the court must (subject to subsection (8)) apply the principles applicable on an application for judicial review; but this does not require the court to apply section 31(2A) of the Senior Courts Act 1981 (High Court to refuse to grant relief where the outcome for the applicant not substantially different) on an environmental review in England and Wales.

(12) If, on an environmental review, the court has made a statement of non-compliance in respect of a public authority, and the statement has not been overturned on appeal, the authority must publish a statement that sets out the steps it intends to take in light of the review.

(13) A statement under subsection (12) must be published before the end of the 2 month period beginning with the day the review (including any appeal) concludes.

(14) In this section—

"the court" means—

(a) in relation to an environmental review arising under the law of England and Wales or Northern Ireland, the High Court, or

(b) in relation to an environmental review arising under the law of Scotland, the Court of Session;

"enactment" has the same meaning as in the European Union (Withdrawal) Act 2018;

"the principles applicable on an application for judicial review" means, in relation to an environmental review, the principles that would apply on an application for judicial review in the jurisdiction under which the environmental review arises;

"remedy" includes any relief or order.

Definitions

'enactment'	s 38(12)
'environmental law'	s 46
'failure to comply with environmental law'	s 31(2)
'principles application on an application for judicial review'	s 38(12)
'public authority'	s 31(3)
'remedy'	s 38(12)
'the court'	s 38(12)

In force	24 January 2022. Commencement Order No 2
Application	UK (reserved matters) E

Where matters have not been resolved at the earlier stages of the enforcement process, the OEP may take the matter to court, the final stage in the procedure. The OEP must be satisfied on the balance of probabilities that there has been a failure to comply with environmental law, and that the failure to comply is serious. The criteria for seriousness will be contained in the OEP's Enforcement Policy under s 23(6) above. Although it is termed an environmental review, this is essentially a form of judicial review before the High Court (and for reserved matters where the breach has taken place in Scotland, the Court of Session), and the court is required to apply normal principles of judicial review (sub-s (9)). The term 'environmental review' is used because some of the conditions applicable to ordinary judicial review (such as requirement of leave and time limits) do not apply. The Civil Procedure Rules will be amended to reflect the distinctive nature of Environmental Reviews – see *Amending the Civil Procedure Rules to establish environmental review: Consultation Outcome. Summary of Responses and Government Response*, March 2022.

Time for Making Application

Under sub-s (3)(b), the OEP may not make an application before the expiry of the time limit that would be applicable to a judicial review or similar action in relation to the conduct (generally 'promptly', or within six weeks for a planning decision or three months for other decisions, unless the court considers there are exceptional circumstances). This is intended to ensure that an environmental review does not pre-empt other proceedings. If, say, judicial review proceedings have been commenced by a third party, the OEP has the power to intervene in such proceedings where it considers the alleged failure to be serious (s 38(6) and (7)). Alternatively, the OEP might persuade a party that has commenced proceedings to abandon them to allow the OEP to take over the case by way of an environmental review. This could be attractive to third parties in terms of reducing exposure to costs, but the OEP would still have to go through the Information and Decision Notice stages before making an application for an environmental review, and the delays involved (a minimum of four months before an application could be made) might discourage a third party from abandoning their own proceedings. Alternatively, if the condition for urgent cases were met (see s 39 below), it could make an application direct for judicial review.

The OEP may not commence an environmental review before the date required for a response to a Decision Notice (normally two months unless the OEP specifies otherwise) or when the authority makes a response (which might be within the time limits specified).

Restrictions in other legislation that may require, for example, that legal challenges may only be made by judicial review do not apply. The provisions do not require a prior leave stage of the court, nor does the OEP have to show sufficient standing in the matter.

Involvement of Ministers in Environmental Reviews

When the OEP makes an application for an environmental review against authorities other than central government, it must inform the Minister under s 40(3) that the OEP considers it appropriate, having regard to the particular authority concerned and the nature of the failure (the 'relevant Minister' as defined in s 33(11)). In doing so, it may state that it considers that the Minister should participate in the environmental review. This might apply, for example, where the OEP considers it would be helpful for the court to understand the level of government funding provided to the authority concerned. There is no obligation on the Minister to comply with such a request.

Mandatory Declaration by Court

In dealing with an environmental review, the court must apply ordinary principles of judicial review, and if it finds there has been a failure to comply with environmental law, it must make a declaration to this effect. There is considerable case law on the use and purpose of declarations in judicial review – see, for example, *R v Ministry of Agriculture Fisheries and Food, ex p dairy Trade Federation Ltd* [1998] EuLR 253: *'Declarations are a useful discretionary remedy, and the courts are increasingly adopting a flexible and pragmatic approach to their use'* (Dyson J). But most of the case law concerns their use as a discretionary remedy, and here there is an obligation to make a declaration if the court finds there has been a failure. S 38(7) provides that the declaration itself does not affect the legal validity of the authority's conduct, and this reflects the fact that the OEP may commence enforcement proceedings in respect of conduct by an authority that had taken place a long time before. Complaints by the public to the OEP must be made within one year of the alleged conduct (or three months from the exhaustion of any internal complaints procedure), but where the OEP commences enforcement proceedings by way of an Information Notice and this is followed by a Decision Notice, there are no time limits as to the date of alleged failure. The authority is obliged to publish a statement within two months on the steps it will take in response to the declaration (s 38(10) and (11)), another provision designed to ensure that enforcement by the OEP will lead to practical results. There is no particular provision to enforce the duty to make a statement, but since it would fall within the definition of environmental law under s 46 the OEP could initiate enforcement proceedings in relation to the breach of the duty.

Other Remedies

In making a declaration of non-compliance, the court may grant any remedy that could be granted on judicial review with the exclusion of damages, ie a mandatory, prohibiting or quashing order or an injunction (sub-s (8)). Damages may be awarded in ordinary judicial reviews but only to the applicant, and here it is considered that the OEP itself will have suffered no damage, and the remedy is therefore inappropriate. In its Decision Notice, the OEP must specify steps that it considers the authority should take in response to the breach, including steps designed to remedy, mitigate or prevent reoccurrence of the failure (see s 36(2)(c) above). Whether the courts will be more prepared to grant mandatory orders (described by Lord Scarman *in R v Inland Revenue Commissioners ex p National Federation of Self-Employed and Small Businesses Ltd* [1982] AC 617 as *'the most elusive of the prerogative writs and orders'*) reflecting those sorts of steps remains to be seen. But see *R (Client Earth v Secretary of State for the Environment, Food and Rural Affairs* [2015] UKSC 28, where the Supreme Court made a mandatory order requiring the production of revised air quality plans with a timetable specified in the order.

Restrictions of Granting of Remedy

Other than the requirement to make a declaration of non-compliance, the court has discretion as to the appropriate remedy to choose, but subject to the statutory restrictions contained in sub-ss (8)–(10). As originally drafted, the provision was that a court can only grant a remedy where satisfied it would not be likely to cause substantial hardship or prejudice to a third party (such as someone in receipt of planning permission) or be detrimental to good administration. The language (substantial hardship or prejudice, or detrimental to good administration) is the same as in s 31(6) Senior Courts Act 1981 relating to applications for judicial review and for substantial relief, but there it is limited to where the court considers there has been undue delay in making the application, and the court still retains the discretion as to whether to grant a remedy. Here, in contrast, once the court is satisfied about the conditions, it cannot grant a remedy other than a declaration. Further, although the provisions partly reflect the fact that the OEP's enforcement action can be taken in respect of failures that have taken place a considerable time before matters reach the court, questions of substantial hardship or prejudicial or good administration are not triggered solely when there has been delay. But also note *R v Secretary of State for Health ex p Furneaux* [1994] 2 All ER 652, where the Court of Appeal held that there was no requirement in s 31(6) Senior Courts Act 1981 for a causal connection between the substantial prejudice and the delay, but there did need to be a connection between the prejudice and the relief being sought.

During the parliamentary passage of the Bill, there was considerable concern that this provision unduly interfered with judicial discretion, and that since third party interests might often be involved or affected in the sort of cases the OEP might bring, this could have a chilling effect of the effectiveness of the environmental review procedure. As a result, during the late stages of the Bill, the Government introduced amendments in sub-ss (9) and (10). Condition A in sub-s (9) preserves the original restrictions on granting a remedy. But Condition B in sub-s (10) in effect provides that the court may ignore the restrictions if it is satisfied that granting the remedy is necessary to prevent or mitigate serious environmental or human health damage and there is exceptional public interest in so doing. In introducing the amendment, the Government noted that *'The amendment will ensure that a high bar is still set for the granting of remedies where third parties may be affected. This is set out in condition A of our amendment. But, critically, it will also provide that, even where condition A is not met, if the court is satisfied that it is necessary in order to prevent or mitigate serious damage to the natural environment or human health, and there is an exceptional public interest reason to do so, the court will be able to grant a remedy. This is set out in condition B. It gives the court discretion to undertake a real and meaningful, albeit weighted, balancing exercise. It means that there would no longer be a blanket prohibition on the granting of remedies where third parties are likely to suffer substantial hardship or prejudice'* (Rebecca Pow, Parliamentary Under Secretary of State, HC Deb 8 November 2021, vol 903, col 86).

Detrimental to Good Administration

The meaning of 'detrimental to good administration' has been considered by the courts in the context of s 31(6) Senior Courts Act. See, for example, *R (Thornton Hall Hotel Ltd v Wirral Metropolitan Borough Council* [2019] EWCA Civ 737: *'The concept of detriment to good administration is not tightly defined, but will generally embrace the length of delay in bringing the challenge, the effect of the impugned decision before the claim was issued, and the likely consequences of it being reopened'* (Sir Terence Etherton MR), and Lord Goff in *R v Dairy Produce Quota Tribunal for England and Wales ex parte Caswell and another* [1990] 2 AC 738: *'I do not consider that it would be wise to attempt to formulate any precise definition or description of what constitutes detriment to good administration. This is because applications for judicial review may occur in many different situations, and the need for finality may be greater in one context than in another. But it is of importance to observe that section 31(6) recognises that there is an interest in good administration independently of hardship, or prejudice to the rights of third parties, and that the harm suffered by the applicant by reason of the decision which has been impugned is a matter which can be taken into account by the court when deciding whether or not to exercise its discretion under section 31(6) to refuse the relief sought by the applicant. In asking the question whether the grant of such relief would be detrimental to good administration, the court is at that stage looking at the interest in good administration independently of matters such as these. In the present context, that interest lies essentially in a regular flow of consistent decisions, made and published with reasonable dispatch; in citizens knowing where they stand, and how they can order their affairs in the light of the relevant decision.'* S 31(2A)–(2B) Senior Courts Act 1981 (in the absence of exceptional public interest, the court must refuse relief in a judicial review if it considers that outcome for the applicant would not have been substantially different if the breach had not occurred) does not apply to an environmental review (and is also disapplied where the OEP applies for judicial review in urgent cases under s 39).

Disagreement about Remedial Steps

An authority may accept that it is in breach but disagree with the remedial steps specified by the OEP in its Decision Notice. The original version of the Bill provided that the OEP could bring an environmental review in respect of further conduct by the public authority that had taken place after the Decision Notice and was similar to the conduct specified in the Notice. The Explanatory Notes state that this was intended to deal with the situation where the authority accepted the failure, had committed to remedial steps but had failed to take the steps needed to address the failure, and relieved the OEP from recommencing fresh enforcement proceedings with a new Decision Notice. However, this provision was removed by a government amendment to the Bill (there was no explanation or debate in the Public Bill Committee on this amendment). Although the point may have been tested in law, it would seem that the OEP should be able to continue its original environmental review provided it was satisfied that the remedial steps proposed or carried out by the authority did not properly address the failure, which remained serious. The focus of the court proceedings would then be on an appropriate remedy to address the breach.

Failure to Comply with a Court Order

Failure to comply with a court order would be punishable as contempt of court, and according to *De Smith's Judicial Review*, '*In theory all the normal sanctions are at the disposal of the court – imprisonment, sequestration, fine*' (para 18.045, 8th edn, London, Sweet & Maxwell, 2018). In practice, a court may feel that a finding of contempt without further penalty is sufficient to mark the gravity of the situation – see *M v Home Office* [1994] I AC 377, where Lord Woolf noted: '*Although it is to be expected that it will be rare indeed that the circumstances will exist in which such a finding would be justified, I do not believe there is any impediment to a court making such a finding, when it is appropriate to do so, not against the Crown directly, but against a government department or a Minister of the Crown in his official capacity*' (p 34).

In the case of government departments, it would normally be the Minister rather than civil servants who could be liable in contempt, but in *Beggs v Scottish Ministers* [2007] UKHL 3, Lord Hope noted that civil servants who wilfully act or failed to act in breach of a court order against a Minister '*exposes them to the risk of being held in contempt*' (para 11). Under Rule 70.2A of the Civil Procedure Rules, where a court order has not been complied with, the court may direct that the act specified in the order be done by another person, with the costs of so doing charged to the person failing to comply with the order.

Statement by Authority Following Finding of Non-compliance

Where an authority has been held by the court to be in breach of environmental law following an application under this section, the authority must publish a statement within two months of the steps it intends to take in the light of the decision. If the finding is upheld on appeal, the period starts from the conclusion of the appeal. This is not a statutory requirement under ordinary judicial review proceedings, and is consistent with the general policy underlying the provisions in this Part that enforcement, including court proceedings, should lead to effective outcomes in practice. The fact that the authority is obliged to publish a statement of the steps it will take in response to a finding of breach could influence the court's approach to the granting of remedies and their terms. A court might be tempted to withhold any remedy because of the statutory requirement of the authority to respond. Equally, they might be tempted to grant a remedy but suspend its operation until the authority had made a satisfactory response of the steps it will take. Victorian courts, for example, often make use of suspensory injunctions in nuisance cases, thereby giving an opportunity for public authorities to develop the most appropriate response – see B Pontin, *Nuisance Law and Environmental Protection* (Witney, Lawtext Publishing, 2013).

39 Judicial review: powers to apply in urgent cases and to intervene

(1) The OEP may apply for judicial review, or a statutory review, in relation to conduct of a public authority (whether or not it has given an information notice or a decision notice to the authority in respect of that conduct) if—

(a) the OEP considers that the conduct constitutes a serious failure to comply with environmental law, and

(b) the urgency condition is met.

(2) The urgency condition is that making an application under subsection (1) (rather than proceeding under sections 35 to 38) is necessary to prevent, or mitigate, serious damage to the natural environment or to human health.

(3) Section 31(2A), (3C) and (3D) of the Senior Courts Act 1981 (High Court to refuse to grant leave or relief where the outcome for the applicant not substantially different) does not apply to an application for judicial review made under subsection (1) in England and Wales.

(4) If, on an application for judicial review or a statutory review made by virtue of subsection (1), there is a finding that a public authority has failed to comply with environmental law, and the finding has not been overturned on appeal, the authority must publish a statement that sets out the steps it intends to take in light of the finding.

(5) A statement under subsection (4) must be published before the end of the 2 month period beginning with the day the proceedings relating to the application for judicial review or the statutory review (including any appeal) conclude.

(6) Subsection (7) applies to proceedings (including any appeal) that—

(a) are in respect of an application for judicial review or a statutory review, and

(b) relate to an alleged failure by a public authority to comply with environmental law (however the allegation is framed in those proceedings).

(7) If the OEP considers that the alleged failure, if it occurred, would be serious, it may apply to intervene in the proceedings (whether it considers that the public authority has, or has not, failed to comply with environmental law).

(8) In this Part—

(a) except in section 38, reference to an application for judicial review includes an application for the permission of the High Court or, as the case may be, the Court of Session to apply for judicial review;

(b) "statutory review" means a claim for statutory review under—

(i) section 287 or 288 of the Town and Country Planning Act 1990,

(ii) section 63 of the Planning (Listed Buildings and Conservation Areas) Act 1990,

(iii) section 22 of the Planning (Hazardous Substances) Act 1990, or

(iv) section 113 of the Planning and Compulsory Purchase Act 2004.

Definitions

'environmental law'	s 46
'failure to comply with environmental law'	s 31(2)
'judicial review'	s 47
'natural environment'	s 44

'public authority'	s 31(3)
'statutory review'	s 39(8)(b)

In force	24 January 2022. Commencement Order No 2
Application	UK (reserved matters) E

S 39 allows the OEP to apply for judicial review or statutory review without first having to go through the steps of serving an Information Notice and Decision Notice. To do so, the OEP must consider that the failure to comply with environmental law is serious (in accordance with criteria in its enforcement policy), but also the application must be urgent as defined in sub-s (2) – ie the application is necessary to prevent or mitigate serious damage to the environment or human health. The bespoke enforcement process leading to a possible environmental review is fairly lengthy – at least four months – to allow an authority to respond to the Information Notice and Decision Notice, and this provision allows the OEP to bring court proceedings where delay would lead to serious environmental consequences. Unlike an environmental review, leave must be obtained from the court to bring the application. However, the requirement in s 31(2)(A)–(C) Senior Courts Act 1981 in ordinary judicial review proceedings that the court must, in the absence of exceptional public interest, refuse relief (and refuse leave) if it appears that the outcome of the case would not have been substantially different if the breach had not occurred does not apply.

As with an environmental review, where the OEP makes an application under this section against an authority other than central government, s 40 requires it to inform the Minister that the OEP considers it appropriate in the light of authority concerned and the nature of the breach (the 'relevant Minister').

The OEP may invite the Minister to be a party to the proceedings.

As with Environmental Reviews, the authority must publish a statement of what steps it will take in the light of a finding of non-compliance by the court (s 39(4) and (5). See annotations to s 38.

Application by the OEP to Intervene

Sub-ss (6) and (7) allow the OEP to apply to intervene in any judicial or statutory review relating to an alleged failure of environmental law considered by the OEP to be serious. The requirement for urgency does not apply. Intervention by third parties in judicial review proceedings have become increasingly common in recent years – as noted by Ousely J in *R (Air Transport Association Inc) v Secretary of State for Energy and Climate Change* [2010] EWHC 1554: *'It has been the practice of this court for a number of years, well established and beneficial, to allow interventions by groups or bodies, or individuals who have particular knowledge and expertise in the area, whether in terms of the effect which the action at issue may have upon them and their interests, or by virtue of the work which they carry out or through close study of the law, practice and problems in an area, or because of the campaigning experience and knowledge which their activities have brought'* (para 8). The OEP would not be obliged to support or oppose the case, but could, for example, explain its importance from a broader environmental context, which may be helpful to the court.

40 Duty of the OEP to involve the relevant Minister

(1) Where the recipient of an information notice or a decision notice is not a Minister of the Crown, the OEP must—

(a) provide the relevant Minister with—

(i) a copy of the notice and,

(ii) a copy of any correspondence between the OEP and the recipient of the notice that relates to the notice (apart from correspondence sent by virtue of paragraph (b)), and

(b) provide the recipient of the notice with a copy of any correspondence between the OEP and the relevant Minister that relates to the notice (apart from correspondence sent by virtue of paragraph (a)).

(2) The obligation to provide a copy of any notice or correspondence under subsection (1) does not apply where the OEP considers that in the circumstances it would not be in the public interest to do so.

(3) Where the OEP makes an application for an environmental review, judicial review or statutory review in which the relevant Minister is not a party, it must provide the relevant Minister with—

(a) a copy of the application, and

(b) a statement of whether the OEP considers the relevant Minister should participate in the review (for example, by applying to be a party).

Definitions

'Minister of the Crown'	s 47
'relevant Minister'	s 33

Application	UK (reserved matters) E
In force	24 January 2022 Commencement Order No 1

This section obliges the OEP, where it is taking enforcement action against an authority other than the central government, to keep the relevant Minister informed. The relevant Minister is defined in s 33 as the Minister the OEP considers appropriate in the light of the authority concerned and the nature of the breach. Copies of Information and Decision Notices and related correspondence must be sent to the Minister, as well as any copies of an application for a s 38 environmental review or a s 39 judicial or statutory review, unless the OEP considers it would not be in the public interest to do so (sub-s (2)).

Where the OEP makes a s 38 or s 39 application for review, it must also issue a statement to the Minister as to whether it considers the Minister should participate in the review (sub-s (3)). Although there is no requirement for the Minister to comply with a request to participate, this is potentially a significant provision. It could be used, for example, where the OEP considers that the level of funding provided by central government to an authority is relevant to the breach, and that the court would benefit from the central government appearing in proceedings.

41 Public statements

(1) Where the OEP gives an information notice or a decision notice, applies for an environmental review, judicial review or statutory review or applies to intervene in a judicial review or statutory review, it must publish a statement that—

(a) states that the OEP has taken that step,

(b) describes the failure (or alleged failure) of a public authority to comply with environmental law in relation to which that step was taken, and

(c) sets out such further information as the OEP considers appropriate.

(2) Subsection (1) does not apply if the OEP considers that in the circumstances it would not be in the public interest to publish a statement.

In force	24 January 2022 Commencement Order No 1
Application	UK (reserved matters) E

The OEP has a general duty under s 22(2)(b) to have regard to the need to act transparently. This section reinforces this duty by requiring the OEP to publish statements where it has issued an Information Notice or Decision Notice, or applied for a s 38 environmental review or a s 39 application for judicial or statutory review. S 41 does not provide any time limits for publishing the statements, though the OEP's enforcement policy could contain commitments as to how soon it will issue such statements. Although the requirements are not explicit on the point, it would be desirable for the OEP to issue statements on the outcome of enforcement proceedings, especially if Information Notices and Decision Notices have led to satisfactory solutions without the need for any court action. Sub-s (2) provides the OEP with the discretion not to publish statements where it would not be in the public interest. According to the Explanatory Notes, this might apply where the protection of personal or confidential data would be prejudiced.

Information

42 Disclosures to the OEP

(1) No obligation of secrecy imposed by statute or otherwise prevents a person from—

(a) in accordance with section 27(1), providing the OEP with information in connection with an investigation under section 33, an information notice or a decision notice, or

(b) providing information to the OEP in accordance with section 35(3)(b).

(2) But nothing in this Part—

(a) requires a person to provide the OEP with information that the person would be entitled to refuse to provide in civil proceedings on grounds of legal professional privilege (or, in Scotland, confidentiality of communications), or

(b) requires a person to provide the OEP with information that the person would be entitled, or required by any rule of law, to refuse to provide in civil proceedings on grounds of public interest immunity.

(3) No obligation of secrecy imposed by statute or otherwise prevents a relevant ombudsman from providing information to the OEP—

(a) for purposes connected with the exercise of the OEP's functions under section 33;

(b) for purposes connected with the co-ordination of the OEP's functions that relate to investigations under section 33 and the ombudsman's functions that relate to investigations by the ombudsman.

(4) Nothing in this Part requires or authorises a disclosure of information that would contravene the data protection legislation (but in determining whether a disclosure would do so, take into account the duties imposed and powers conferred by this Part).

(5) In this section "the data protection legislation" has the same meaning as in the Data Protection Act 2018 (see section 3(9) of that Act).

Definitions

'date protection legislation'	s 42(5)
'relevant ombudsmen'	s 47

In force	24 January 2022. Commencement Order No 2
Application	UK (reserved matters) E

This section is intended to assist the OEP in obtaining information in connection with s 33 investigations, or s 35 Information Notices and s 36 Decision Notices. It provides that, with the exception of contraventions of data protection legislation, those responding are not inhibited from doing so by any obligation of secrecy imposed by legislation or otherwise. Exceptions are provided in sub-s (2) for legal professional privilege and public interest immunity.

43 Confidentiality of proceedings

(1) The OEP must not disclose—

(a) information obtained under section 27(1) or 35(3)(b), or

(b) correspondence between the OEP and a public authority that—

(i) relates to a particular information notice or decision notice, or

(ii) is, or contains, such a notice.

(2) Subsection (1) does not apply to a disclosure—

(a) other than a disclosure of an information notice or a decision notice, made with the consent of the person who provided the information or correspondence;

(b) made for purposes connected with the exercise of the OEP's functions under section 33 (investigations);

(c) made for purposes connected with the co-ordination of the OEP's functions that relate to investigations under section 33 and a relevant ombudsman's functions that relate to investigations by that ombudsman;

(d) made for the purposes of any publication of a report (or part of it) on an investigation under section 33;

(e) made for purposes connected with the exercise of the OEP's functions under sections 35 to 41 (enforcement);

(f) made to a devolved environmental governance body for purposes connected with the exercise of a devolved environmental governance function;

(g) made for purposes connected with the protection of the natural environment in a country or territory outside the United Kingdom, to an authority of that country or territory, or an international organisation, that has functions in connection with the protection of the natural environment in that country or territory;

(h) of information, or correspondence, that relates only to a matter in relation to which the OEP has concluded that it intends to take no further steps under this Chapter.

(3) A public authority must not disclose correspondence between the OEP and that, or any other, public authority that—

(a) relates to a particular information notice or decision notice, or

(b) is, or contains, such a notice.

(4) Subsection (3) does not apply to a disclosure—

(a) made—

(i) in the case of a disclosure of correspondence between another public authority and the OEP other than correspondence that is, or contains, an information notice or a decision notice, with the consent of that authority and the OEP, or

(ii) in any other case, with the specific or general consent of the OEP;

(b) made for purposes connected with co-operating with any investigation under section 33;

(c) made for purposes connected with responding to any information notice or decision notice;

(d) made for purposes connected with any proceedings in relation to an environmental review, judicial review or statutory review.

(5) The OEP may not give a person consent to disclose an information notice or a decision notice unless that notice relates only to a matter in relation to which the OEP has concluded that it intends to take no further steps under this Chapter.

(6) If a public authority requests the consent of the OEP to disclose correspondence that relates only to a matter in relation to which the OEP has concluded that it intends to take no further steps under this Chapter, the OEP may not withhold that consent.

(7) If information referred to in subsection (1) and held by the OEP, or referred to in subsection (3) and held by a public authority, is environmental information for the purposes of the Environmental Information Regulations 2004 (S.I. 2004/3391) or the Environmental Information (Scotland) Regulations 2004 (S.S.I. 2004/520), it is held by that person, for the purposes of the application of those regulations to that information, in connection with confidential proceedings.

Definitions

'devolved environmental governance body'	s 47
'devolved environmental governance function'	s 47
'judicial review'	s 47
'natural environment'	s 44
'public authority'	s 31(3)
'relevant ombudsmen'	s 47
'statutory review'	s 39(8)(b)

In force	24 January 2022 Commencement Order No 1
Application	UK (reserved matters) E

This section imposes various duties of confidentiality on both the OEP and public authorities in their dealings with the OEP. Sub-s (1) imposes confidential duties on the OEP in respect of information obtained under the general duty of cooperation by public authorities (s 27), requested under an Information Notice (s 35(3)), or correspondence in connection with a s 35 Information Notice or a s 36 Decision Notice. But there are a wide number of exceptions contained in sub-s (2), reflecting the overall duty on the OEP to act transparently, and the requirements of public access to information concerning the environment. This information, to the extent it is 'environmental information' under the Environmental Information Regulations 2004, is to be treated as being held in connection with confidential proceedings under those regulations, meaning that the OEP may refuse to disclose to the extent that disclosure would adversely affect the confidentiality of the proceedings, and in all the circumstances where the public interest in maintaining the exception outweighs the public interest in disclosure. This is subject to the general requirement in the regulations that a public authority should apply a presumption in favour of disclosure. See, for example, *DBERR v IC and O'Brian* [2004] EWHC 164, where Wyn Williams J noted, *'although a heavy weight is to be accorded to the exception, it must not be so heavy that it is in effect elevated into an absolute exemption'*.

Sub-s (3) imposes a duty on public authorities not to disclose correspondence with the OEP in connection with its investigatory and enforcement functions other than with the consent of the OEP. With relation to Information and Decisions Notices, consent cannot be given until the OEP has concluded that no further enforcement action will be taken on the matter, and if it has reached such a conclusion consent must be granted (s 43(5) and (6)).

Chapter 3

Interpretation of Part 1

44 Meaning of "natural environment"

In this Part the "natural environment" means—

(a) plants, wild animals and other living organisms,

(b) their habitats,

(c) land (except buildings or other structures), air and water,

and the natural systems, cycles and processes through which they interact.

In force	17 November 2021. Commencement Order No 1
Application	UK (reserved matters) E

See annotations to s 46.

45 Meaning of "environmental protection"

In this Part "environmental protection" means—

(a) protection of the natural environment from the effects of human activity;

(b) protection of people from the effects of human activity on the natural environment;

(c) maintenance, restoration or enhancement of the natural environment;

(d) monitoring, assessing, considering, advising or reporting on anything in paragraphs (a) to (c).

In force	17 November 2021. Commencement Order No 1
Application	UK (reserved matters) E

See annotations to s 46.

46 Meaning of "environmental law"

(1) In this Part "environmental law" means any legislative provision to the extent that it—

(a) is mainly concerned with environmental protection, and

(b) is not concerned with an excluded matter.

(2) Excluded matters are—

(a) disclosure of or access to information;

(b) the armed forces or national security;

(c) taxation, spending or the allocation of resources within government.

(3) The reference in subsection (1) to "legislative provision" does not include devolved legislative provision, except for the purposes of section 20.

(4) "Devolved legislative provision" means—

(a) legislative provision contained in, or in an instrument made under, an Act of the Scottish Parliament, an Act or Measure of Senedd Cymru, or Northern Ireland legislation, and

(b) legislative provision not within paragraph (a) which—

(i) if contained in an Act of the Scottish Parliament, would be within the legislative competence of the Parliament;

(ii) if contained in an Act of Senedd Cymru, would be within the legislative competence of the Senedd, or

(iii) if contained in an Act of the Northern Ireland Assembly, would be within the legislative competence of the Assembly and would not require the Secretary of State's consent.

(5) The Secretary of State may by regulations provide that a legislative provision specified in the regulations is, or is not, within the definition of "environmental law" in subsection (1) (and this Part applies accordingly).

(6) Before making regulations under subsection (5) the Secretary of State must consult—

(a) the OEP, and

(b) any other persons the Secretary of State considers appropriate.

(7) Regulations under subsection (5) are subject to the affirmative procedure.

Definitions

'devolved legislative provision'	s 45(4)

In force	17 November 2021. Commencement Order No 1
Application	UK (reserved matters) E

The interpretation section on the meanings of 'natural environment', 'environmental protection' and 'environmental law' are interconnected, and highly important in determining the boundaries of the OEP's responsibilities, as to both its general objectives under s 23 and its particular functions, notably its duty to monitor and investigate the implementation of environmental law and its enforcement powers concerning the failure of public authorities to comply with environmental law.

The definitions of natural environment and environmental protection taken together are broad, but certain areas are clearly excluded, though there are bound to be some ambiguities in practice. The protection of agricultural livestock and domestic animals would fall outside the definitions, while noise or other human activity affecting wild animals would be included. It is, though, questionable whether noise or smell nuisances affecting humans are included. It could be argued that noise to the extent that it takes the form of vibration in the air is an 'effect', albeit harmless, on the natural environment under s 44(b), but this seems to be straining the language of the legislation. The conservation and protection of historic and other buildings falls outside the definition. 'Land' includes land covered by water (Interpretation Act 1978) and therefore should encompass the seabed. 'Water', perhaps surprisingly, is not defined, but the Explanatory Notes state that this will include the marine environment.

The definition of 'environmental law' is rather open-ended in that it is defined to mean any legislative provision to the extent that it is 'mainly' concerned with environmental protection, and is subject to a number of specific exceptions in sub-ss (2) and (3). 'Mainly' will be a matter of judgement initially for the OEP, and ultimately the courts, though under sub-s (5) the Secretary of State is given power to define in regulations whether any particular legislative provision falls within or without the definition. To take some examples from recent legislation, the power of the Secretary of State to give financial assistance under s 1 Agricultural Act 2020 is confined to 10 specified purposes, six of which could be said to fall with the definition of environmental protection. Similarly, six of the eight 'Fisheries Objectives' under s 1 Fisheries Act 2020 would fall with the definition of environmental protection.

Many actions and decisions of public authorities (such as a decision to grant planning permission, or to promote infrastructure) may have significant and potentially harmful environment effects. But in themselves such decisions would fall outside the ambit of the OEP jurisdiction even if illegality is alleged, unless this involved specific legislative provisions mainly concerned with environmental protection. This could apply to regulations operating within the ambit of the legislation concerned, such as environmental assessment requirements, or could encompass a particular legislative provision within the legislation concerned (such as a specific duty to have regard to biodiversity). According to the Explanatory Notes, a legislative provision refers to UK legislation whether an Act of Parliament, regulations or other subordinate legislation, but does not include international law unless the national legislation is implementing international law. In carrying out a review of the implementation of environmental law under s 28, it seems unlikely the definition would preclude the OEP from considering policy and guidance documents directly connected with the implementation of the law in question.

The reference to a legislative provision implies that requirements of the common law relating to the environment, such as common law nuisance, are excluded from the OEP's jurisdiction. The OEP could be faced with a situation where a planning authority, say, grants planning permission for a development that is likely at some point in the future to lead to a breach of air quality standards. Depending on the details of the legislative requirements, the OEP might argue the authority granting permission was in breach because it unlawfully failed to take proper account of environmental law (s31(2)(a)). Aside from this, it could not bring enforcement action in respect of the prospective breach of air pollution standards because this had not yet occurred, though presumably the OEP could still warn the authority that it might well do so in the future if the authority went ahead with its decision.

A number of specific exceptions are provided in s 45(2) ('excluded matters'). Access to environmental information is excluded to prevent overlap of jurisdiction with the Information Commissioner. Taxation, spending or allocation of resources within the Government are excluded. According to the Explanatory Notes, this should be read in a general sense, meaning that specific fees and charges imposed under environmental regulatory schemes are not excluded. It is less clear whether legislation concerning a specific environmental tax such as the Landfill Tax is completely excluded. A better reading might that the rates of tax imposed by the Treasury and how they are used is excluded, but that the detailed operation of the taxation regime that is concerned with environmental protection would be included. The definition refers to the allocation of resources within the Government rather than by the Government. According to Minister Pow in the Public Bill Committee, '*If a public authority were to argue that it did not have adequate resources to implement an environmental law, that would not stop the legislative provisions in question being environmental law, although the authority's comments on its resources could, of course, be considered during the OEP's investigation'* (Public Bill Committee 10 November 2020, col 385).

47 Interpretation of Part 1: general

In this Part—

"application for judicial review" is to be read in accordance with section 39(8);

"current environmental improvement plan" has the meaning given by section 8(8);

"decision notice" means a notice given under section 36;

"devolved environmental governance body" means a person on whom a devolved environmental governance function has been conferred;

"devolved environmental governance function" means a devolved function that is similar to a function conferred on the OEP under this Part;

"devolved function" means—

(a) a function exercisable in or as regards Wales that could be conferred by provision falling within the legislative competence of Senedd Cymru (see section 108A of the Government of Wales Act 2006);

(b) a function exercisable in or as regards Scotland, the exercise of which would be within devolved competence (within the meaning of section 54 of the Scotland Act 1998);

(c) a function exercisable in or as regards Northern Ireland that could be conferred by provision included in an Act of the Northern Ireland Assembly made without the consent of the Secretary of State (see sections 6 to 8 of the Northern Ireland Act 1998);

"devolved legislature" means the Scottish Parliament, Senedd Cymru or the Northern Ireland Assembly;

"environmental improvement plan" has the meaning given by section 8 (and see also section 10(10));

"environmental principles" has the meaning given by section 17; "environmental review" has the meaning given by section 38;

"first environmental improvement plan" has the meaning given by section 8(8);

"improving the natural environment", in relation to an environmental improvement plan, is to be read in accordance with section 8(5);

"information notice" means a notice given under section 35; "judicial review" means—

(a) in England and Wales or Northern Ireland, an application to the High Court for judicial review, or

(b) in Scotland, an application to the supervisory jurisdiction of the Court of Session;

"making" policy includes developing, adopting or revising policy; "met", in relation to a target set under sections 1 to 3, has the meaning given by section 4(7);

"Minister of the Crown" has the same meaning as in the Ministers of the Crown Act 1975;

"OEP" has the meaning given by section 22;

"parliamentary function" means a function in connection with proceedings in Parliament or a devolved legislature;

"policy" includes proposals for legislation, but does not include an administrative decision taken in relation to a particular person or case (for example, a decision on an application for planning permission, funding or a licence, or a decision about regulatory enforcement);

"policy statement on environmental principles" has the meaning given by section 17;

"public authority" has the meaning given by section 31(3); "relevant Minister" has the meaning given by section 33; "relevant ombudsman" has the meaning given by section 23;

"specified date" and "specified standard", in relation to a target set under sections 1 to 3, have the meaning given by section 1(8);

"statutory review" has the meaning given by section 39(8).

In force 17 November 2021. Commencement Order No 1

Application UK (reserved matters) E

PART 2

ENVIRONMENTAL GOVERNANCE: NORTHERN IRELAND

48 Improving the natural environment: Northern Ireland

Schedule 2 makes provision about—

(a) environmental improvement plans, and

(b) policy statements on environmental principles, in Northern Ireland.

In force 25 July 2022. Northern Ireland Commencement Order 2022. Sch 2 para 8 (Departmental duty to have due regard to policy statement on environmental principles) in force 6 months after final statement laid before Assembly

Application NI

Background

In 2018, during the period when the Northern Irish Assembly had been suspended between January 2017 and January 2020, the Permanent Secretary for the NI Department of Agriculture, Environment and Rural Affairs (DAERA) requested the UK Government to consult on extending some aspects of the Bill to Northern Ireland to address gaps in environmental governance in NI that would occur following Brexit – notably the role of environmental principles and the extension of the jurisdiction of the Office of Environmental Protection to replicate the role of the European Commission in the enforcement of environmental law. The appropriateness of an environmental improvement plan for Northern Ireland should also be considered. See the letter of the Permanent Secretary dated 27 February 2019 to the Chair of the House of Commons Environment Audit Committee and referenced in *Analysis of the Environment Bill 2019–2020* (House of Commons Library Briefing Paper CBP 8824, February 2020, pp 19–20). S 48 introduces Sch 2, which makes provisions for environmental improvement plans and policy statements on environmental principles in Northern Ireland, while s 49 makes provisions for extending the OEP's remit to Northern Ireland.

Environment Improvement Plan (Sch 2, Part 1)

The provisions largely replicate the provisions concerning environmental improvement plans for England in Part 1 of the Act (ss 8–16), with appropriate adjustments for the application to Northern Ireland.

Preparation

DAERA must prepare an environmental improvement plan, defined as a plan for 'significantly improving the natural environment' and covering the period specified in the plan, or indeed no specified period (Sch 2 para 1(3)). The discretion as to the period to be covered contrasts with the position in England, where the environmental improvement plan is intended to be a long-term plan, covering a period no shorter than 15 years (s 18(3)). The plan must set out the steps that DAERA and any other Department intends to take to improve the natural environment and may also include steps that any Department intends to take to improve people's enjoyment of the natural environment.

The first plan must be laid before the Northern Ireland Assembly within 12 months of this provision coming into force. On 11 November 2021 DAERA published for consultation the draft *Environment Strategy for Northern Ireland*, which is intended to be the first environmental improvement plan under these provisions. The draft includes Strategic Environmental Outcomes covering six broad areas – air, water, land and neighbourhood quality; healthy and accessible environment and landscapes; nature and wildlife; sustainable production and consumption; zero waste and a circular economy; and a fair contribution to the UK's net zero greenhouse gas emissions target and improved climate resilience and adaptability.

Annual Reports

DAERA must prepare annual reports describing what has been done to implement the plan, and the extent to which the natural environment has improved during the period of review. Reports are to be laid before the NI Assembly (Sch 2 para 2).

Reviews

Within five years of the publication of the first plan or any subsequent revisions, DAERA must review the plan and revise it if considered appropriate. In carrying out the review, DAERA must consider what has been done to implement the plan and the extent to which the natural environment has improved, and consider whether any NI Department should take further or different steps to improve the natural environment. Any revised plan must be laid before the NI Assembly with a statement explaining the rationale for the revisions (Sch 2 para 3). The first revision of the English environmental improvement plan must include various interim targets relating to those established under ss 1–3 of the Act (s 11). Since there are no equivalent provisions for statutory environmental targets in Northern Ireland, there is no duty to make reference to targets on the NI environmental improvement plan.

New Plans

Where an environment improvement plan specifies a period to which it relates, DAERA must prepare a new, replacement plan before the end of that period. Similar to the provisions on revising a plan, in doing so DEARA must consider what was done to implement the existing plan, the extent to which the natural environment has improved during the period of the existing plan and whether any Northern Ireland Department should take further or different steps than those in the existing plan to improve the natural environment. Other Departments must be consulted, and the replacement plan laid before the NI Assembly (Sch 2 para 4).

Environmental Data and Monitoring

DAERA must make arrangements for obtaining data about the natural environment that it considers appropriate for assessing whether the natural environment has improved in accordance with the environmental improvement plan in accordance with the requirements concerning annual reports, reviews and new plans above. A statement setting out the kinds of data being obtained must be laid before the NI Assembly within four months of this provision coming into force (Sch 2 para 5).

Environmental Principles (Sch 2 Part 2)

Part 2 of Sch 2 contains provisions concerning environmental principles which replicate almost word for word the provisions in ss 17–19 but with appropriate reference for the Northern Ireland context. The annotations on ss 17–19 will be relevant. Following the approach taken in England, the principles, though derived from the EU Treaty on the Functioning of the European Union, no longer have any independent legal effect but will be reflected in the Policy Statement. But in relation to those parts of European Union law still applicable to Northern Ireland under the 2020 Protocol on Ireland/Northern Ireland, the EU principles and how they have been interpreted by the Court of Justice of the European Union will still be relevant to the applicable EU legislation (see especially Art 12 of the Protocol, and Annex 2 for a list of EU legislation, including environmental legislation, that is applicable).

Policy Statement on Environmental Principles

DAERA must prepare a policy statement on environmental principles (Sch 2 para 6). The five principles as defined in para 6(5) are the same as those relating to the English statement: environmental protection should be integrated in the making of policies; preventative action to avert environmental damage; the precautionary principle as it relates to the environment; environmental damage should be rectified at source; and the polluter pays principle. The statement must explain how the principles are to be interpreted and proportionately applied by Northern Ireland Departments and Departments and Ministers of the Crown when making policy relating to Northern Ireland. The statement must also explain how Departments and Ministers of the Crown should take into account other considerations when interpreting and applying the principles. There is a duty for DAERA to be satisfied that the statement will contribute to the improvement of environmental protection and sustainable development.

Process of Making the Policy Statement

DAERA must consult other NI Departments, the Secretary of State and anyone else considered appropriate on the drafting of the statement and lay the draft before the NI Assembly, giving it the opportunity to pass a resolution within three weeks. The resolution is not binding, but DAERA must publish a response if one is passed. DAERA must publish and lay before the Assembly the final statement, but not before it has made a response to a resolution, or after the end of the three-week period if no resolution is made.

Effect of the Policy Statement

Sch 2 para 8 describes the effect of the statement in identical words to s 19 of the Act relating to the statement by the Secretary of State. It provides that when making policy, a Northern Ireland Department must have due regard to the policy statement on environmental principles. See the Introduction concerning the legal meaning of 'have regard to'. But the duty does not require a Department or Crown Minister to do anything or refrain from doing anything that would have no environmental benefit, or would in any other way be disproportionate to the environmental benefit. The obligations concerning the effects of the statement do not apply to policies relating to taxation, spending, the allocation of resources within government, the armed forces, defence or national security. These are identical to the exclusions in s 19 of the Act.

Interpretation

Paras 9 and 10 contain interpretations of the meaning of 'natural environment' and 'environmental protection' for the purposes of this Schedule, and are in the same terms as the definitions in ss 44 and 45 of the Act. Para 11 contains a more general list of interpretations relevant to the Schedule.

49 The Office for Environmental Protection: Northern Ireland

Schedule 3—

(a) makes provision about the functions of the OEP in, or as regards, Northern Ireland, and

(b) amends this Act to reflect those functions.

In force	Day to be determined by order by Department of Agriculture, Environment and Rural Affairs, Northern Ireland, but draft order must be approved by resolution of Northern Ireland Assembly
Application	NI

S 49 introduces Sch 3, which relates to the OEP's functions in Northern Ireland. Most of the provisions are worded almost identically to those in Chapter 2 of this Act concerning the OEP with adjustments for the Northern Ireland context. The annotations to that chapter will provide a useful cross-reference.

Monitoring and Reporting on Northern Ireland's Environmental Improvement Plan

Para 1 of Sch 3 relates to the duties of the OEP concerning Northern Ireland's environmental improvement plan (and any revisions or renewals) produced by the NI Department of Agriculture, Environment and Rural Affairs (DAERA). The OEP must prepare an annual progress report on the Plan within six months of DAERA producing its own annual progress report.

The OEP progress report is defined in para 1(3) as a report on the progress made during the annual reporting plan in improving the natural environment in accordance with the current improvement plan. The provisions concerning the OEP's monitoring and annual reports in England must include considering progress on meeting interim and long-term statutory environmental targets established under ss 1–7 of the Act. There are no equivalent provisions in Northern Ireland, so the annual report will be confined to the NI environmental improvement plan.

The OEP progress report may include consideration of how progress could be improved and the adequacy of environmental data published by DAERA under Sch 2(5). The reports must be published and laid before the Northern Ireland Assembly, and a response made by DAERA within 12 months. Where the OEP has made recommendations for improvement progress, the response must address these.

Monitoring and Reporting on Environmental Law

Para 2 of Sch 3 imposes a duty on the OEP to monitor the implementation of environmental law in Northern Ireland. The core provisions are in identical terms to the OEP's monitoring functions under s 29 of the Act, and the annotations to that section are therefore relevant. The OEP has discretion about how to go about the task and the subject areas to choose, though they must fall within the definition of Northern Ireland environmental law as provided in para 18 of the Schedule. This refers to any Northern Ireland legislation provision 'mainly concerned with environmental protection', with 'environmental protection' defined in para 2 of Sch 2 (see above). Access to information and taxation, spending or the allocation of resources within government are excluded from the definition (para 18(3)), which also follow the definition's provisions in s 46 of the Act. As with s 29, the OEP may not monitor or report on matters falling within the remit of the Climate Change Committee.

The reports must be published and laid before the Northern Ireland Assembly and a response made by DAERA within three months.

Advising on Changes to Northern Ireland Environment Law etc

Para 3 of Sch 3 concerns advice by the OEP to Northern Ireland Departments and is equivalent to the advice functions in s 30 of the Act. If requested, the OEP must give advice to any Northern Ireland Department about proposed changes to Northern Ireland environmental law as defined in para 18, or on any matter relating to the natural environment, defined in Sch 2 para 2. The OEP also has the discretion, even if not requested, to advise any Department on proposed changes to Northern Ireland law.

The advice must be published by the OEP. The advice is not binding and, as with s 30 advice, there is no obligation to respond. Departments have the discretion to lay before the Northern Ireland Assembly the advice and any response made to it (para 3(5) and (6)).

Enforcement of Breaches of Environmental Law

Paras 4–17 contain provisions concerning the OEP's enforcement functions in Northern Ireland and again largely replicate the provisions in ss 31–43 of the Act, but with appropriate adjustments for Northern Ireland. Reference can be made to the annotations of these sections.

Scope of Enforcement Provisions

The provisions apply to Northern Ireland Departments, persons carrying out Northern Ireland's devolved functions and any other person carrying out any function of a public nature in or as regards Northern Ireland ('relevant public authority'). Courts, tribunals and the NI Assembly are excluded. See definitions of 'relevant Northern Ireland public authority' and 'relevant public authority' in para 5(3) and (4). They relate to 'failures' of environmental law, with failure defined in the same terms as s 31(2) of this Act – see annotations to s 31.

For Northern Ireland Departments and persons carrying out devolved functions, the failure may be in respect of UK or Northern Ireland environmental law (see para 18for definitions). For other persons carrying out functions in or as regards Northern Ireland, the failure must relate only to Northern Ireland environmental law.

Public Complaints (para 6)

The OEP must establish a public complaint procedure allowing any person to make a complaint if they believe a relevant public authority has failed to comply with environmental law. The same time limits and the need to first go through an internal complaints procedure if established by the authority as those contained in s 32 apply. Again, as with s 32, a complaint may not be made by any person carrying out functions of a public nature. See the annotations to s 32 as to whether this would encompass individual whistleblowers. Under para 8 complainants must be kept informed of progress with their complaint, and in particular whether or not the OEP has decided to initiate an investigation under para 7.

Investigations (para 7)

The OEP may carry out an investigation if it considers that a complaint or any other information it possesses indicates that there has been a 'serious' failure of environmental law by the authority concerned. The criteria for determining whether a failure is serious or not is to be determined in accordance with the OEP enforcement policy, and is not necessarily confined to cases where there is potential serious damage to the environment or public health.

The OEP is not obliged to carry out an investigation before commencing enforcement proceedings under the following provisions. The procedure is most likely to be used to help establish the facts of a case, but, depending on the circumstances, it is possible that resolution could be achieved at this stage without the need for more formal enforcement proceedings. The report on the investigation must be provided to the authority concerned, setting out whether and why the OEP considers there has been a failure to comply with environmental law, and any recommendations it may have. The OEP has the discretion as to whether to publish the report.

The s 27 duty of cooperation with the OEP will apply by amendments introduced under para 27, and will include Northern Ireland Departments and implementation bodies within the meaning of the Northern Ireland Act 1998 in relation to functions exercisable in or relating to Northern Ireland.

Information Notice (para 9)

An information notice is the first formal stage of the OEP's enforcement process, and may be given to the relevant public authority where it has 'reasonable grounds for suspecting' there has been a serious failure of an environmental law duty. The provisions in para 9, including time limits for responses (generally two months unless otherwise specified in the notice), mirror those concerning information notices in s 35 of the Act. Again, the procedure is clearly intended to encourage a resolution of the issue if possible without the need for further proceedings.

Decision Notice (para 10)

If matters have not been resolved following the service and response to an Information Notice, the OEP may proceed to the next enforcement stage, the service of a Decision Notice, where it is satisfied on the balance of probabilities that there has been a serious failure to comply with relevant environmental law. Again, the provisions mirror those in s 36 of the Act. The evidential burden on the OEP – satisfaction on the balance of probabilities rather than reasonable grounds for suspecting – is rather higher than that for an Information Notice, reflecting the seriousness of this step.

Recipients of a Decision Notice must respond within two months (or later if specified in the notice), setting out whether they agree that the failure has occurred, whether they intend to take any of the steps specified in the notice by the OEP in relation to the failure (which can include steps to remedy, mitigate or prevent reoccurrence) and any other steps they intend to take. Depending on the nature of the failure, the authority may not be empowered to revisit a particular decision under attack because of the doctrine of *functus officio* (see annotations to s 35 above), though this would not prevent the authority from specifing steps to prevent a similar reoccurrence in the future.

Linked Notices (para 11)

Linked Information or Decision Notices may be sent to more than one authority in respect of the same or similar conduct, and para 11 mirrors the provisions in s 37 on linked notices. Essentially, once notices are linked, the OEP must provide copies of the linked notices to all the authorities concerned, together with copies of correspondence between the OEP and the parties concerned, unless it considers it would not be in the public interest to do so.

Review Application (para 12)

If the issue has not been resolved at the Information or Decision Notice stage, the OEP may proceed to an application for a review before the High Court. Again, the provisions are very similar to those in s 38, though there the terminology is an environmental review rather than a Review Application as here. The OEP may not commence an application before either the date on which the OEP receives a response to the Decision Notice, or the period specified in the Notice for response, whichever is the earlier.

The Review Application is defined as an application for judicial review (under s 38 for an environmental review the court must apply the principles of ordinary judicial review). As with s 38, the time limits for commencing a judicial review do not apply (para 12(4)), but leave for application must first be sought from the court (para 12(10)), contrasting the position for s 38 environmental reviews, where no leave to apply is required.

The provisions in s 38 requiring a court to make a statement of non-compliance if it finds that there has been a failure of environmental law do not apply here. The court may grant any remedy available in judicial review – see ss 18–20 Judicature (Northern Ireland Act) 1978 – but subject to the restrictions in para 12(19) and (20). Originally these provisions, which now mirror those in s 38(9) and (10) on environmental reviews, would have restricted the grant of the remedy where it was likely to cause substantial hardship or prejudice to the rights of third parties, and although they reflected the concern that there was no time limit for the OEP to bring an application, the provisions were not restricted to where delay was the cause of the prejudice. Following extensive parliamentary debate, and concerns that this was inhibiting judicial discretion, the Government introduced amendments to qualify the restriction (see annotations to s 38), which are reflected here. The restriction on granting a remedy where this would cause substantial hardship or prejudice to a third party or would be detrimental to good administration remain. They can, however, be overridden where the court is satisfied that granting the remedy is necessary to prevent or mitigate serious damage to the environment or human health and there is an exceptional public interest in granting the remedy. If a court feels unable to override the restriction, presumably it might feel able to grant a declaration rather than quashing the decision concerned.

Where the court has found there has been a failure of environmental law, the authority concerned must within two months (or within two months of an unsuccessful appeal) publish a statement of the steps it intends to take in the light of the finding. This provision is not found in ordinary judicial reviews, and again reflects the underlying policy of the enforcement provisions designed to resolving issues at a practical level, and indeed preventing repetition.

Urgent Judicial Review and Interventions (para 13)

The bespoke enforcement provisions take some time before an application to a court can be made – a minimum of four months following the service of an information and decision notice. The OEP is therefore given power to take urgent judicial reviews without the need first to serve an Information and Decision Notice. The conditions for doing so are the same as in s 39. The OEP must consider that there has been a serious failure of environmental law, and that the application, rather than going through the bespoke enforcement process, is necessary to prevent or mitigate serious damage to the environment or human health. If the application is successful, the authority concerned must within two months of the decision (or a decision on appeal) publish a statement of the steps it intends to take in the light of the decision.

The OEP is also given the power to intervene in any judicial review relating to an alleged failure by public authorities to comply with environmental law, provided it considers the failure, if such has occurred, to be serious – the condition that there is the likelihood of serious environmental or human health damage serious is not necessary for an intervention. Intervention by third parties in judicial review proceedings have become increasingly common in recent years, as noted by Ousely J in R *(Air Transport Association Inc) v Secretary of State for Energy and Climate Change* [2010] EWHC 1554: 'It has been the practice of this court for a number of years, well established and beneficial, to allow interventions by groups or bodies, or individuals who have particular knowledge and expertise in the area, whether in terms of the effect which the action at issue may have upon them and their interests, or by virtue of the work which they carry out or through close study of the law, practice and problems in an area, or because of the campaigning experience and knowledge which their activities have brought.' The OEP is not obliged to support or oppose the case, but could, for example, explain its importance from a broader environmental context, which may be helpful to the court.

Duty to Involve Relevant Department (para 14)

Para 14 replicates the duty in s 40, and requires the OEP to keep a relevant Department informed of proceedings it takes against authorities other than a Department. This includes sending copies of any Information or Decision Notice, and copies of any application for a review or for an urgent judicial review.

Where the OEP makes an application for a review or urgent judicial review, it may also make a statement to say that it considers the Department should participate in proceedings (for example, by become a party to proceedings). This might be appropriate where, say, the OEP considers guidance or funding provided by a Department to the authority concerned is relevant, and the court needs to be informed about this. There is no obligation on the Department to agree to such a request.

Public Statements by the OEP on Proceedings (para 15)

Para 15 replicates s 41, and requires the OEP, unless it considers it would not be in the public interest to do so, to publish a statement saying that it has served an Information Notice or Decision Notice, or made an application for a review or urgent judicial review, and describing the alleged failures and any other information it considers appropriate.

Disclosure of Information and Confidentiality of Proceedings (paras 16 and 17)

Paras 16 and 17 replicate ss 42 and 43 of the Act. Para 16 is intended to assist the OEP in obtaining information in connection with investigations, Information Notices and Decision Notices. It provides that, with the exception of contraventions of data protection legislation, those responding are not inhibited from doing so by any obligation of secrecy imposed by legislation or otherwise. Exceptions are provided in sub-s (2) for legal professional privilege and public interest immunity.

Para 17 concerns various duties of confidentiality on both the OEP and public authorities in their dealings with the OEP. Sub-s (1) imposes confidential duties on the OEP in respect of information requested under an Information Notice (para 9(3)(b)) or correspondence in connection with an Information or Decision Notice. But there are a wide number of exceptions contained in sub-s (2), reflecting the overall duty on the OEP to act transparently and the requirements of public access to information concerning the environment. This information, to the extent that it is 'environmental information' under the Environmental Information Regulations 2004, is to be treated as being held in connection with confidential proceedings under those regulations, meaning that the OEP may refuse to disclose to the extent that disclosure would adversely affect the confidentiality of the proceedings, and in all the circumstances where the public interest in maintaining the exception outweighs the public interest in disclosure. This is subject to the general requirement in the regulations that a public authority should apply a presumption in favour of disclosure. See, for example, *DBERR v IC and O'Brian* [2004] EWHC 164, where Wyn Williams J noted that, *'although a heavy weight is to be accorded to the exception, it must not be so heavy that it is in effect elevated into an absolute exemption.'*

Para 17 (3) imposes a duty on public authorities not to disclose correspondence with the OEP in connection with its investigatory and enforcement functions other than with the consent of the OEP. In relation to Information and Decision Notices, consent cannot be given until the OEP has concluded that no further enforcement action will be taken on the matter, and if it has reached such a conclusion consent must be granted.

Definitions (paras 18 and 19)

Para 18 contains definitions of UK and Northern Ireland environmental law applicable to this part of the Schedule. Para 19 defines other terms used in the Schedule.

Office of Environment Protection (paras 20–30)

Paras 20–30 contain a complex set of amendments to the provisions in the Act relating to the Office for Environmental Protection to extend their geographical scope to Northern Ireland should DAERA make an order bringing these provisions into force. The making of such an order requires the consent of the Northern Ireland Assembly (s 147(9)), and the consent of the Secretary of State is also required (s 147(7)).

Key changes include the following:

- The OEP's Strategy, including its enforcement policy, must be laid before the Northern Ireland Assembly as well as Parliament.
- The Enforcement Policy must set out how the OEP intends to determine whether failures are serious for the purposes of the enforcement functions in Northern Ireland, and whether damage to the natural environment or human health is serious enough for urgent judicial reviews under Sch 2 para 13.
- The Strategy must set out how the OEP's public complaints process will avoid overlapping with the functions of the Northern Ireland Public Services Ombudsmen.
- A new s 25A is inserted giving power to DAERA to issue and revise guidance to the OEP concerning its enforcement policy. A draft of the Guidance is to be laid before the NI Assembly, giving it the opportunity to make a resolution which requires a response from DAERA. The OEP must have regard to the guidance. See further the annotations to s 25, and the Introduction for the legal meaning of 'have regard to'. A parliamentary commitment was made by the Government in relation to s 25 that it would not issue any guidance before the OEP had published its first enforcement policy.
- The duty of cooperation of public authorities with the OEP under s 37 will apply to Northern Ireland and include Northern Ireland Departments.
- An additional Northern Ireland non-executive board member of the OEP is to be appointed by DAERA with the consent of the Secretary of State.
- Other than the first chair of the OEP, the chair is to be appointed jointly by the Secretary of State and DAERA.
- DAERA must contribute to the funding of the OEP, as agreed with the Secretary of State.
- The OEP annual reports must be laid before the NI Assembly as well as Parliament, and must include an assessment as to whether the funding by both the Secretary of State and DAERA is sufficient to carry out its functions.
- The duty of the Secretary of State in Sch 1 para 17 to have regard to the need to protect the independence of the OEP extends to DAERA.

PART 3

WASTE AND RESOURCE EFFICIENCY

Producer responsibility

50 Producer responsibility obligations

(1) In Schedule 4—

(a) Part 1 confers power on the relevant national authority to make regulations about producer responsibility obligations;

(b) Part 2 confers power on the relevant national authority to make regulations about the enforcement of regulations made under Part 1.

(2) In this section and that Schedule "relevant national authority" means—

(a) in relation to England, the Secretary of State;

(b) in relation to Wales, the Welsh Ministers or the Secretary of State;

(c) in relation to Scotland, the Scottish Ministers or the Secretary of State;

(d) in relation to Northern Ireland, the Department of Agriculture, Environment and Rural Affairs in Northern Ireland or the Secretary of State.

(3) Regulations under Schedule 4 made by the Secretary of State may not contain provision that could be contained in regulations under that Schedule made by another relevant national authority, unless that authority consents.

(4) Regulations under Schedule 4 that contain only provision for, or in connection with, the variation of targets specified in the regulations are subject to the negative procedure.

(5) Otherwise, regulations under Schedule 4 are subject to the affirmative procedure.

(6) The following are repealed—

(a) in the Environment Act 1995, sections 93 to 95;

(b) the Producer Responsibility Obligations (Northern Ireland) Order 1998 (S.I. 1998/1762 (N.I. 16)).

Definitions

'producer responsibility obligations'	Sch 4 para 1(3)
'relevant national authority'	s 50(2)

In force	E: 24 January 2022; W: 7 March 2022; S: day to be appointed by Secretary of State; NI: 28 February 2022
Application	E W S NI

This section repeals ss 93–95 of the Environment Act 1995 as well as the Producer Responsibility Obligations (Northern Ireland) Order 1998 (SI 1998/1762 (NI 16)).

Background

Ss 93–95 of the Environment Act 1995 provided for regulations to be made, following consultation, imposing 'producer responsibility' obligations on certain classes of person. The relevant legislation started with the Producer Responsibility Obligations (Packaging Waste) Regulations 1997 (SI 1997/648), subsequently replaced by the Producer Responsibility Obligations (Packaging Waste) Regulations 2005 (SI 2005/3468), which was in turn repealed and replaced by the Producer Responsibility Obligations (Packaging Waste) Regulations 2007 (SI 2007/871), as amended. In Northern Ireland, the current Regulations are the Producer Responsibility Obligations (Packaging Waste) Regulations (Northern Ireland) 2007 (SI 2007/198).

The regulations were designed to implement the Packaging and Packaging Waste Directive 94/62/EC, which required Member States to meet a number of specific targets in relation to the recovery and recycling of packaging waste. The 1994 Directive was amended by the Amending Packaging Waste Directive 2018 (2018/852), which increased the recycling target to 70 per cent by weight for packaging waste by 2030, with an interim target of 65 per cent by 2025. It also introduced a new plastic packaging recycling target of 55 per cent to be reached by 2030.

The regulations required producers over a certain size to register with the appropriate national regulator and report on packaging data annually, unless the producer joined a registered exemption scheme. Producers, or the registered scheme, were required to take reasonable steps to achieve specific recycling and recovery targets. The design and manufacturing aspects of packaging are regulated by the Packaging (Essential Requirements) Regulations 2015 (SI 2015/1640), as amended. At the time of writing, the Government had initiated a review of these Regulations and was likely to consult on further amendments.

According to the House of Commons Library Briefing Paper on the Act (*Commons Library Analysis of the Environment Bill 2019–20*, CBP 8824, 18 February 2020), 7002 companies registered as having packaging obligations across the UK. Relevant businesses discharge their responsibilities by collecting evidence of waste packaging recycling and recovery equivalent to the weight of their obligations from accredited reprocessors and exporters. Packaging Recovery Notes (PRNs) or Packaging Export Recovery Notes (PERNs) are issued by accredited businesses and provide the only means of evidence of compliance.

The system has been the subject of abuse. In 2016 an operator was convicted of fraud after Environment Agency officers discovered that falsified paperwork was used to illegitimately claim that TLC Recycling Ltd, a Leeds-based firm, had collected and recycled over 19,500 tonnes of household electrical waste in 2011. In fact, the company had never handled that amount of waste and was not entitled to receive money through the Government-backed Producer Compliance Scheme. Money had been claimed for waste collections from streets and properties that did not exist, and some documents showed vast amounts of waste being collected by vehicles that could not carry such loads: one trip by moped was said to have carried 991 TVs and 413 fridges between businesses. Terence Dugbo was sentenced to 7 years, 6 months and made the subject of a £1.3 million confiscation order. See www.gov.uk/government/news/convicted-waste-fraudster-has-more-than-9-years-added-to-jail-time-for-failing-to-repay-1-3-million-in-ill-gotten-gains.

In 2018 the National Audit Office published its report *The Packaging Recycling Obligations* (Session 2017–19, HC 1386, 23 July 2018), in which it expressed concern that there were no checks to ensure that exported material was actually recycled and that there were risks of fraud and error in the current system. The report stated that the Environment Agency, despite having a range of activities to help prevent or detect companies that break the rules, did not have a good understanding of the extent of fraud and error that remained in the system to determine whether or not its approach was proportionate. The report also stated that the Government had no evidence that the system has actually encouraged companies to minimise packaging or to make it easy to recycle.

The House of Commons Environmental Audit Committee examined the packaging producer responsibility scheme in its report *Plastic Bottles: Turning Back the Plastic Tide* (First Report of Session 2017–19, HC 339, 22 December 2017). The report noted that taxpayers, rather than producers, cover around 90 per cent of the costs of packaging waste disposal, indicating that the scheme was not working as it should. The same report also called for the Environment Agency to be given greater regulatory control and for waste processors to be held accountable to the Environment Agency for how they spend packaging revenue.

In December 2018 the Government published a waste and resources strategy for England, *Our Waste, Our Resources: A Strategy for England*. The Strategy recognised that the current system did not sufficiently incentivise design for greater reuse or recyclability, and noted the fact that less than one-tenth of the costs of managing household packaging waste are covered by producers. It recorded the concerns that the system favoured the export of packaging waste for recycling and concluded that the current system was not comprehensive enough, lacked transparency and fell short of the Government's objectives.

The Government published a consultation entitled *Reforming the Packaging Producer Responsibility System* on 18 February 2019, undertaken jointly by the UK, the Scottish and Welsh Governments and the Department of Agriculture, Environment and Rural Affairs in Northern Ireland. The summary of responses and next steps was published on 23 July 2019, and the Government confirmed that it would introduce an extended producer responsibility system for packaging in 2023 (p 8).

On 24 March 2021 a second consultation, entitled *Extended Producer Responsibility for Packaging*, was published jointly by the Department of Environment, Food and Rural Affairs, the Scottish and Welsh Governments and the Northern Ireland Department of Agriculture, Environment and Rural Affairs. This set out proposals for the introduction of extended producer responsibility for packaging and sought views on the details of implementing the Government's preferred approaches. This second consultation revised both the overarching principles and the governing principles for packaging extended producer responsibility, first set out in the 2019 consultation.

The Government noted that responses to the 2019 consultation showed a strong support for a set of an overarching principles for packaging extended producer responsibility. The overarching principles proposed at para 4.3 of the 2021 Consultation are:

1. Producers are incentivised through the fees they pay or by other complementary measures to reduce unnecessary and difficult-to-recycle packaging, to design and use packaging that is recyclable and to promote reusable or refillable packaging where it is a feasible option.
2. Producers will pay into the system either directly or through the price they are charged by others in the supply chain consistent with the 'polluter pays' principle.
3. Producers will bear the full net cost of managing the packaging they handle or place on the market, including at end-of-life to achieve agreed targets and outcomes.
4. Costs paid by producers will support a cost-effective and efficient system for managing packaging waste, including the collection of a common set of packaging materials for recycling from households and businesses.
5. Actions by producers will enable consumers to play their part and correctly manage packaging waste through access to good services, labelling and other means that tell consumers how to recycle and dispose of packaging, and enhanced communications campaigns.

There was also strong support for principles for the scheme of governance for extended producer responsibility, and these are listed also at para 4.3 of the 2021 Consultation:

1. A UK-wide approach that provides Government-level accountability and supports delivery of the wider policy context in England, Northern Ireland, Scotland and Wales; that provides the flexibility to tailor scheme implementation to different parts of the UK where this is necessary; and which enables broad parity in the distribution of producer funding and treatment of local authorities and businesses across the UK.
2. Clear outcomes and UK-wide targets for packaging extended producer responsibility to be set by Government to encourage long-term investment and innovation across the packaging value chain.
3. Scheme governance arrangements to be approved by Government in accordance with established procedures and procurement processes.
4. Those involved in scheme governance to have a fiduciary duty to obligated producers in line with best business practice.

5. All sectors in the value chain to be clear on their roles and responsibilities in contributing to the delivery of an efficient and effective system.
6. Measures put in place to increase transparency of material and financial flows, encourage effective competition, drive efficiency and improve quality along the value chain. This is so that costs to producers do not exceed those necessary to provide packaging waste services in a cost-efficient way, and that payments to local authorities and other service providers are fair and transparent and they understand any conditions that apply.
7. Measures are put in place to promote compliance and limit opportunities for fraud and waste crime and ensure packaging waste is managed in an environmentally responsible way both in the UK and when exported.

The 2021 Consultation went on to elaborate on outcomes. Packaging extended producer responsibility outcomes are set out in para 4.4 as:

- That unnecessary packaging – packaging that is not required to protect a product or excess packaging – is avoided; this will help reduce packaging and packaging waste
- That opportunities to replace single-use packaging with reusable or refillable packaging increase, particularly for consumer products
- That more packaging is designed to be recyclable, so packaging that cannot be recycled because of the material or the materials it is made from, or due to its format, will cease to be used where it can be avoided
- That packaging waste recycling increases. It is proposed that by 2030, 73% of all packaging placed on the UK market and in scope of packaging extended producer responsibility will be recycled
- That the quality of packaging materials presented for recycling increases across the packaging value chain and more packaging is recycled into higher value and closed loop applications
- That packaging extended producer responsibility and the deposit return scheme contribute to less packaging being littered.

Broader system outcomes are identified in para 4.5 as:

- That there is additional reprocessing capacity available in the UK to handle the increasing quantities of packaging waste that will be available for recycling;
- That the system for managing packaging waste becomes more efficient and effective in delivering the environmental outcomes;
- That people's knowledge of the packaging they can and can't recycle increases and it is easier for them to recycle.

In order to comply with the Protocol on Ireland/Northern Ireland Protocol under the EU Withdrawal Agreement, the UK Government must ensure that Northern Ireland continues to transpose the Packaging and Packaging Waste Directive, as amended. The Directive was most recently amended by the Waste Circular Economy Package, which requires extended producer responsibility for packaging.

Schedule 4

Under Sch 4, relevant national authorities – the Secretary of State in all parts of the UK or, as relevant, the Welsh Ministers, the Scottish Ministers or the Department of Agriculture, Environment and Rural Affairs in Northern Ireland – are empowered to make regulations about producer responsibility obligations (Part 1 regulations) and about the enforcement of such regulations (Part 2 regulations). Where regulations are made by the Secretary of State but could have been made by another relevant national authority, they may not contain a provision in the absence of consent of that other authority.

Generally, regulations made under Sch 4 are subject to the affirmative procedure. However, those that contain only provision for, or in connection with, the variation of targets specified in the regulations are subject to the negative procedure. General provisions regarding the power to make regulations are set out in s 143.

Part 1 Regulations

Purpose and Scope of Regulations

Regulations may be made to apply producer responsibility obligations to specific persons in respect of specified products or materials and specific obligations regarding those products or materials, including a product or material at a time when it becomes, or has become, waste. There is no statutory definition of product or material. The regulations may be made only for the purpose of preventing a product or material becoming waste, reducing the amount of a product or material that becomes waste or sustaining a minimum level of, or promoting or securing an increase in, the reuse, redistribution, recovery or recycling of products or materials.

The provisions for a revised, extended packaging producer responsibility scheme seek to make producers responsible for the full net costs (as opposed to just some of the costs) of managing their products at end of life. The Act provides a framework for powers to design a system using modulated fees that incentivise producers to design their products with reuse and recycling in mind, to prevent materials from becoming waste and to aid the redistribution of surplus products or materials.

Para 2 provides that regulations may make provision for persons to be subject to producer responsibility obligations, the products and materials to be included, the obligations involved, targets to be achieved in relation to the proportion of products or materials to be reused, redistributed, recovered or recycled; and the circumstances in which producer responsibility obligations may be met by financial payment. The wording of the heading 'Examples of provisions that may be made' strongly suggests that para 2 is a non-exhaustive list of areas that might be covered by the regulations, suggesting greater flexibility in the scope of regulations provided that the regulations themselves do not go beyond the boundaries of para 1(2).

The Explanatory Notes explain that waste management is based on the 'waste hierarchy', which sets a priority order when shaping waste policy and managing waste. It gives top priority to preventing waste in the first place. When waste is created, it gives priority to preparing it for reuse, then recycling, then recovery and last of all disposal (for example, landfill). This is reflected in the word order of para 1(2)(b) of Sch 4.

S 93(1) of the Environment Act 1995 did not explicitly identify that the prevention of products and materials from becoming waste was an identifiable purpose behind producer responsibility obligations. Instead, s 93 focused on the promotion of the goals of reuse, recovery and recycling. In contrast, the Environment Act 2021 is explicit in declaring that the prevention of waste creation is a positive reason to make regulations. 'Redistribution' has also been added to the goals of reuse, recovery and recycling. These are very deliberate amendments, made according to the 'Environment Bill, Memorandum from the Department for the Environment, Food and Rural Affairs to the Delegated Powers and Regulatory Reform Committee', dated 27 May 2021, in order to clarify that regulations imposing producer responsibility obligations can be made for the purposes of prevention of products becoming waste or the redistribution of products, in addition to 're-use, recovery or recycling of' products. Although it is not immediately obvious what is added by the term 'redistribution', the Waste and Resources Action Programme (WRAP) has previously published numerous reports identifying that redistributing surplus food is one of the best ways that businesses can help to reduce the amount of food that ends up as waste, and Food Standards Scotland, in conjunction with Zero Waste Scotland, published a 'Surplus Food Redistribution Guide' in July 2020.

Registration and Compliance Schemes

Para 3 of Sch 4 provides that regulations may require persons who are subject to a producer responsibility obligation to be registered.

Paras 4–7 address compliance schemes. Regulations may require persons who are subject to a producer responsibility obligation to become members of a compliance scheme, which may be registered in a manner specified by regulations, or, if not a member of such a scheme, to provide certificates of compliance to an enforcement authority. The Environment Act 2021 is silent on the determination of fees related to compliance schemes and also on guidance relating to appeals against refusal of registration. Operators of compliance schemes may be directed to take or not take (as appropriate) a specific action to ensure compliance with an international agreement to which the UK is a signatory. Any such direction on the application of the relevant national authority is enforceable by injunction or, in Scotland, by interdict or order for specific performance.

The use of compliance schemes is not a new feature for producer responsibility. For example, producers of portable batteries that place those batteries on the UK market for the first time are already required to join a battery compliance scheme by virtue of the Waste Batteries and Accumulators Regulations 2009. Producers are required to join by a specific date, pay various fees, provide information about the batteries placed on the market and receive evidence notes for the collection, treatment and recycling of waste portable batteries. Failure to comply with the relevant regulations governing the scheme and its requirements can result in prosecution and financial penalties.

Consultation before Making Regulations

Paras 8–10 deal with the requirement for the relevant national authorities to undertake consultation prior to making regulations. Persons must appear before the relevant national authority to represent the interests of those likely to be affected and (save for regulations made to implement an international agreement to which the UK is a party) the relevant national authority must be satisfied that making the regulation(s) would be likely to achieve one or more of the purposes in para 1(2) and produce environmental or economic benefits that are significant as against the likely costs. The relevant national authority must be further satisfied that any burdens imposed on businesses are the minimum necessary to secure those benefits. Any burdens are to be imposed on the persons most able to make a contribution to securing those benefits and a producer responsibility obligation may be imposed on any class or description of person to the exclusion of others. The relevant national authority must also make regulations in the way it considers best calculated to avoid the restriction, distortion or prevention of competition, and to the extent that such an effect is unavoidable it must be no greater than is necessary for achieving the above environmental or economic benefits.

Consultation requirements are drafted in slightly broader terms than under s 93(2) Environment Act 1995, which refers to bodies, or their representatives, whose interests are likely to be 'substantially affected'. Here the reference is to representatives of 'interests likely to be affected'.

Amendments to the relevant regulations have tended to be reactionary. Reviews took place following volatility in the glass recycling market in 2012 and in respect of plastic packaging in 2014. There is currently little mandate for the Environment Agency to monitor or regulate the market for evidence notes and, consequently, the mechanism for trading evidence notes and the individual commercial activities of compliance schemes are not, on the face of it, the subject of significant scrutiny by the Environment Agency. The fact that the pricing of evidence notes can prove volatile in any given compliance year has again been demonstrated by huge fluctuations in the price for evidence notes for the recycling of glass throughout 2020, at least partly attributable to the pandemic. Any obvious change in approach does not immediately jump out from the wording of Sch 4, but para 5 includes provision for conditions to be attached to the registration of compliance schemes. This would appear to provide sufficient scope for the Environment Agency to be tasked with a more interventionalist approach, but, as is evident from the above, any such regulatory change would be subject to consultation.

Part 2 Regulations

Enforcement and Sanctions

The relevant national authority may, by Part 2 regulations, make provision for the enforcement of requirements imposed by Part 1 regulations. According to para 20 of Sch 4, before making Part 2 regulations, the relevant national authority must consult any persons it considers appropriate. Part 2 regulations may involve conferring functions on an 'enforcement authority', who may be empowered to exercise discretion and/or further delegate the exercise of functions to persons authorised in accordance with Part 2 regulations. Enforcement authorities may be required to issue guidance about the exercise of its functions.

Para 14 of Sch 4 states that Part 2 regulations may include provision conferring on an enforcement authority the function of monitoring compliance with requirements imposed by Part 1 regulations.

Para 15 of Sch 4 outlines potential provisions concerning the requirement for persons subject to Part 1 regulations to keep records and provide such records (and/or other information) to an enforcement authority, who, in turn, may be required to make reports or provide information to the relevant national authority.

Para 16 of Sch 4 provides that enforcement authorities may be conferred powers of entry, inspection, examination, search and seizure. Part 2 regulations must secure that the authority of a warrant issued by a justice of the peace, sheriff, summary sheriff or lay magistrate is required for enforcement authorities to enter premises by force, enter private dwellings without consent of the occupier, or search and seize material.

Paras 17–18 of Sch 4 set out the civil and criminal sanctions in respect of failure to comply with regulations or the obstruction of or failure to assist an enforcement authority. The sanctions are primarily financial, but civil sanctions also include discretionary requirements, stop notices and enforcement undertakings. Sanctions may be imposed whether or not the relevant conduct constitutes an offence, or whether the enforcement authority is a regulator for the purposes of Part 3 of the Regulatory Enforcement and Sanctions Act 2008.

Prior to the introduction of civil sanctions by virtue of the Regulatory Enforcement and Sanctions Act 2008, the only sanction for a breach of the relevant regulations was a criminal prosecution for what was a strict liability offence – a sanction that may have been considered to be the equivalent of using a sledgehammer to crack a nut but which still caught out a number of corporate organisations, which had in some cases been careless at most. The toolkit available now to regulators for such breaches has been considerably extended. Prosecutions for breaches of producer responsibility regulations are now rare and the more favoured enforcement response is the use of civil sanctions.

The fact that Part 2 regulations may include provision for the imposition of civil sanctions for conduct irrespective of whether the conduct constitutes 'an offence' appears to be a curious attempt at an extension of the civil sanction regime. Civil sanctions under the Regulatory Enforcement and Sanctions Act 2008 are dependent on whether or not the regulator considers that a criminal offence has been committed. Criminal sanctions plainly cannot be imposed unless a criminal offence has been committed. The wording of Sch 4 para 18 envisages civil sanctions being imposed for conduct relating to a failure to comply with Part 1 or Part 2 regulations but which would not amount to a criminal offence.

There is no specific mention of offences committed by a body corporate as provided in s 95(2) Environment Act 1995, but the breadth of the wording in paras 17(2) and 18 should be sufficient to create such offences under the regulations. Equally, regulations could provide that offences committed by an individual as a consequence of the act or default of some other person may lead to proceedings against both persons (as contained in s 95(4) Environment Act 1995).

Para 19 of Sch 4 deals with charges that may be payable to an enforcement authority as a means of recovering costs incurred in performing its function. These charges may be imposed directly by Part 2 regulations or by a court or tribunal under the terms of a Part 2 regulation.

51 Producer responsibility for disposal costs

(1) Schedule 5 confers power on the relevant national authority to make regulations requiring the payment of sums in respect of the costs of disposing of products and materials.

(2) In this section and that Schedule "relevant national authority" means—

(a) in relation to England, the Secretary of State;

(b) in relation to Wales, the Welsh Ministers or the Secretary of State;

(c) in relation to Scotland, the Scottish Ministers or the Secretary of State;

(d) in relation to Northern Ireland, the Department of Agriculture, Environment and Rural Affairs in Northern Ireland or the Secretary of State.

(3) Regulations under Schedule 5 made by the Secretary of State may not contain provision that could be contained in regulations under that Schedule made by another relevant national authority, unless that authority consents.

(4) Regulations under Schedule 5 are subject to the affirmative procedure.

Definitions

'disposal costs'	Sch 5 para 2(1), 2(3), 2(4)
'disposal'	Sch 5 para 2(2)
'relevant national authority'	s 51(2)

In force	E W S: 9 January 2022; NI: 28 February 2022
Application	E W S NI

Schedule 5

Under Sch 5, relevant national authorities are conferred the power to make regulations requiring the payment of sums in respect of the costs of disposing of products and materials. Any such regulations are to be subject to the affirmative procedure. Regulations may be made only for the purpose of securing that those involved in manufacturing, processing, distributing or supplying products or materials meet, or contribute to, the disposal costs of the products or materials.

The Need for Reform

One of the identified problems of the scheme at the time that the Act was introduced was that producers did not pay for full costs of disposal, with local authorities often paying the majority of costs involved. According to the House of Commons Environmental Audit Committee's report *Plastic Bottles: Turning Back the Plastic Tide* (First Report of Session 2017–19, HC 339, 22 December 2017),

> *'Throughout this inquiry we have heard evidence from environmental researchers and local authorities that the UK's compliance fee contributes less than 10% of the cost of collecting, sorting and disposing of packaging waste. The Local Government Association noted:*
>
> *The UK's limited packaging producer compliance scheme generated £111 million of compliance revenue in 2013, only £37 million of which went towards collection. This compares to the £550 million cost to local authorities for collection and sorting of packaging material'* (para 38).

As noted above, the Department for the Environment, Food and Rural Affairs (DEFRA) ran a consultation between March and June 2021 on its plans to introduce an extended producer responsibility scheme for packaging, with the intended result that packaging producers will be required to pay the full cost of managing packaging once it becomes waste. This part of the Environment Act clearly extends further than packaging, applying as it does to the disposal costs of products and materials.

Politically, the use of producer responsibility schemes, building upon a domestic packaging responsibility scheme in existence since 1997, may be considered attractive, as placing the cost of waste disposal onto producers might be seen as financially beneficial for the Treasury whilst achieving a positive environmental outcome at the same time. In addition, the Commons Library Analysis of the Environment Bill 2019–20 (CBP 8824, 18 February 2020) records that the provisions on the extended producer responsibility scheme were largely welcomed by waste professionals and quotes the chief executive of Suez Recycling and Recovery UK, who said: '*Producer responsibility schemes, as envisaged by the Government, are an essential tool to ensure we move, as a nation, from a throwaway society to a reuse and recycle-based economy that gives new lives to products we consume – which must go with efforts to minimise our overall consumption of the planet's finite resources*' (p 79).

Part 1 Regulations

Regulations can specify that payment is made by specific persons, in respect of specified products or materials. A person (or persons) may be appointed to administer provision made by the regulations and this person may be required to register with an enforcement authority. The specific details as regards applications for registrations, the duration of registration, the cancellation of registration, the fees payable to register and the publication of any such registers may be specified by regulations. Before making regulations, the relevant national authority must consult persons appearing to it to represent the interests of those likely to be affected.

Para 2 makes provision for determining what disposal costs are. These costs may include the costs of collecting, transporting, sorting and treating products or materials for disposal. They may also include the costs of providing the public with information about the disposal of products, for example through communication campaigns. Costs in relation to products or materials that have been disposed of unlawfully may also be included (for example, the costs of clearing up products or materials that have been littered or fly-tipped). Sub-para (2) clarifies that 'disposal' includes the reuse, redistribution, recovery and recycling of products or materials. Sub-para (4) allows for disposal costs to be calculated in accordance with provision made in the regulations.

Para 3 allows for the amount to be paid to be calculated in accordance with the regulations and for this amount to vary according to the design or composition of a product or materials, or the methods by which they were made. For example, a producer of easily recycled products might pay less, and producers of unrecyclable products might pay more.

This is an extension to the approach taken to producer responsibility so far, foreshadowed by the DEFRA consultation between March and June 2021. To date, the financial obligations placed on producers have covered the costs of recycling/recovery but not the full costs of managing products at end of life. The intention is to make producers think about the impacts that their products will have once they have been discarded by consumers.

Paras 6–9 outline the scope of regulations with respect to the payment and distribution of sums. Regulations may specify that monies be paid to an administrator, who may then hold them or distribute them among persons who have incurred disposal costs or, in some cases, repay the monies to the persons by whom they were payable. There may also be provision made for the payment of charges to the administrators, which are a means of recovering costs incurred by administrators in performing functions under the regulations.

Part 2 Regulations

The relevant national authority may by Part 2 regulations make provision about the enforcement of requirements imposed by Part 1 regulations. The wording of Sch 5 effectively mirrors that of Sch 4, set out in the previous section, save in respect of criminal offences.

Part 2 includes the provision for creating criminal offences, but it is notable that, in contrast to Sch 4, such criminal offences set out in Part 2 are limited to failing to comply with civil sanctions that have been imposed as a result of a breach or for an offence of obstruction or failing to assist an enforcement authority. The latter offence is one that is likely to be viewed considerably more seriously than, for example, a failure to register with a scheme. However, where the schedules differ is that, under Sch 5, there is no scope for criminal offences to be created to reflect a breach of the relevant regulations.

This difference may reflect the history of prosecutions for breaches of producer responsibility regulations, for example in the field of packaging, and the move from criminal prosecutions to the more prevalent use of civil sanctions.

On a general level, the distinction in possible enforcement response may reflect the fact that these types of regulations are considered to be more technical in nature and designed to achieve an environmental outcome at an economic cost to the producer, and consequently any economic benefit obtained by virtue of a breach can be adequately marked through the use of a civil penalty linked to that financial advantage. However, it is not immediately clear why producer responsibility for disposal costs should fall into a different category than the broader producer responsibility obligations found in Sch 4 or, indeed, the duties imposed by the Producer Responsibility Obligations (Packaging Waste) Regulations 2007.

Resource efficiency

52 Resource efficiency information

(1) In Schedule 6—

(a) Part 1 confers power on the relevant national authority to make regulations about the provision of resource efficiency information;

(b) Part 2 confers power on the relevant national authority to make regulations about the enforcement of regulations made under Part 1.

(2) In this section and that Schedule "relevant national authority" means—

(a) in relation to England, the Secretary of State;

(b) in relation to Wales, the Welsh Ministers or the Secretary of State;

(c) in relation to Scotland, the Scottish Ministers or the Secretary of State;

(d) in relation to Northern Ireland, the Department of Agriculture, Environment and Rural Affairs in Northern Ireland or the Secretary of State.

(3) Regulations under Schedule 6—

(a) made by the Welsh Ministers, may contain only provision which, if contained in an Act of Senedd Cymru, would be within the legislative competence of the Senedd;

(b) made by the Scottish Ministers, may contain only provision which, if contained in an Act of the Scottish Parliament, would be within the legislative competence of the Parliament;

(c) made by the Department of Agriculture, Environment and Rural Affairs in Northern Ireland, may contain only provision which, if contained in an Act of the Northern Ireland Assembly, would be within the legislative competence of the Assembly and would not require the Secretary of State's consent.

(4) Regulations under Schedule 6 made by the Secretary of State may not contain provision that could be contained in regulations under that Schedule made by another relevant national authority, unless that authority consents.

(5) Regulations under Schedule 6 are subject to the affirmative procedure.

Definitions

'resource efficiency information'	Sch 6 para 2(1), 2(2)
'relevant national authority'	s 52(2)

In force	E W S: 9 January 2022; NI: 28 February 2022
Application	E W S NI

Background

The Government's Resource and Waste Strategy published in December 2018 set out a policy aim of setting minimum requirements through ecodesign to encourage resource-efficient product design: '*Ecodesign is a way of designing products which takes a preventative approach to protecting our natural capital by considering whole lifecycle impacts. To date minimum Ecodesign requirements have been used in the EU to transform the design of energy-using products to reduce energy consumption. Recently Member States voted to include eco-design requirements in product regulation for resource efficiency, taking into account the potential to design for disassembly, repair and recyclability. Through similar mechanisms to the EU Ecodesign system we will seek to drive change in product standards by gradually removing from the market the least resource efficient products and demanding a certain level of resource efficiency. We will match or where economically practicable exceed the ambition of the EU's Ecodesign standards which to some extent currently allow for material efficiency standards, by legislating to expand the scope to cover more resource intensive product groups, such as textiles and furniture. We will also explore using this mechanism to mandate that spare parts be made available for repair. We will also look to address the presence of harmful chemicals in products, to ensure they neither end up in secondary products, where they may pose a high risk due to increased exposure, nor prevent recycling altogether owing to their presence in the waste stream*' (p 40).

At the European level, the Ecodesign Directive 2009/125/EC aims to provide consistent EU-wide rules for improving the environmental performance of products, such as household appliances, information and communication technologies and engineering. The Directive sets out minimum mandatory requirements for the energy efficiency of these products. The intention is to help prevent the creation of barriers to trade and improve product quality and environmental protection. The Ecodesign Directive is implemented through product-specific regulations, directly applicable in all EU countries. Ecodesign and energy labelling regulations are complemented by harmonised European standards. These technical specifications indicate that a product complies with the mandatory requirements that enable the manufacturer to affix the CE marking and sell the product in the EU. National market surveillance authorities verify whether products sold in the EU follow the requirements laid out in ecodesign and energy labelling regulations. Consequently, the term 'ecodesign' encompasses both environmental ambition and minimum standards to achieve trade consistency and product quality.

Sch 6 of the Environment Act is principally concerned with resource efficiency information. Sch 7 is concerned with resource efficiency requirements.

Part 1 Regulations

Sch 6 permits the relevant national authority to make regulations to make provision for the purposes of requiring specified persons, in specified circumstances, to provide specified information about the resource efficiency of specified products (subject to specific exceptions set out in para 1(2)).

Para 2 of Sch 6 identifies that information about resource efficiency is information about:

(a) the expected life of the product;
(b) aspects of the products design which affect its expected life;
(c) the availability or cost of component parts, tools, or anything else required to repair or maintain the product;
(d) whether the product can be upgraded, and the availability or cost of upgrades;
(e) any other matter relevant to repairing, maintaining, remanufacturing or otherwise prolonging the expected life of, the product;
(f) the ways in which the product can be disposed of at the end of its life (including whether and to what extent it can be recycled, and whether materials used in it can be extracted and reused or recycled)

or

(a) the materials from which the product is manufactured;
(b) the techniques used in its manufacture;
(c) the resources consumed during its production or use;
(d) the pollutants, including greenhouse gases, released or emitted at any stage of the product's production, use or disposal.

Such information is relevant to the product's impact on the natural environment.

Such regulations may only impose a requirement on a person to provide such information if they are connected with the manufacture, import, distribution, sale or supply of the product (Sch 6 para 3).

Examples are given at para 4. Regulations may include provision:

(a) about how information about a product is to be provided;
(b) conferring on specified persons the function of determining whether specified products or materials have specified properties or characteristics;
(c) specifying a scheme for classifying products;
(d) requiring information provided about a product to be determined according to specified criteria.

Consultation must be with any persons the relevant national authority considers appropriate.

According to the House of Commons Briefing Paper that accompanied the introduction of the Environment Bill (CBP 8824, 18 February 2020), the Government wants to encourage producers to think about resource-efficient product design, so that less material is used, greater circularity is achieved and more efficient business models are adopted. The intention of ecodesign standards are part of the wider producer responsibility reforms.

The Ecodesign for Energy-Related Products and Energy Information (Amendment) (EU Exit) Regulations 2019, in force as of 31 December 2020, amended the Ecodesign for Energy-Related

Products Regulations 2010 to allow for mandatory product standards (which may relate to energy efficiency and resource efficiency) to be set by the government for energy-related products. The Act is intended to complement these provisions by enabling resource efficiency standards to be set for non-energy-related products. The Act also allows for clear labelling to enable consumers to identify products that are more durable, repairable and recyclable. These measures are aimed at reducing the consumption of materials.

Part 2 Regulations

The relevant national authority may by Part 2 regulations make provision about the enforcement of requirements imposed by Part 1 regulations. The wording of Sch 6 effectively mirrors that of Sch 5, set out previously. The same observations on the lack of criminal sanctions apply compared to the broader options permitted by Sch 4.

53 Resource efficiency requirements

(1) In Schedule 7—

(a) Part 1 confers power on the relevant national authority to make regulations about resource efficiency requirements;

(b) Part 2 confers power on the relevant national authority to make regulations about the enforcement of regulations made under Part 1.

(2) In this section and that Schedule "relevant national authority" means—

(a) in relation to England, the Secretary of State;

(b) in relation to Wales, the Welsh Ministers or the Secretary of State;

(c) in relation to Scotland, the Scottish Ministers or the Secretary of State;

(d) in relation to Northern Ireland, the Department of Agriculture, Environment and Rural Affairs in Northern Ireland or the Secretary of State.

(3) Regulations under Schedule 7—

(a) made by the Welsh Ministers, may contain only provision which, if contained in an Act of Senedd Cymru, would be within the legislative competence of the Senedd;

(b) made by the Scottish Ministers, may contain only provision which, if contained in an Act of the Scottish Parliament, would be within the legislative competence of the Parliament;

(c) made by the Department of Agriculture, Environment and Rural Affairs in Northern Ireland, may contain only provision which, if contained in an Act of the Northern Ireland Assembly, would be within the legislative competence of the Assembly and would not require the Secretary of State's consent.

(4) Regulations under Schedule 7 made by the Secretary of State may not contain provision that could be contained in regulations under that Schedule made by another relevant national authority, unless that authority consents.

(5) Regulations under Schedule 7 are subject to the affirmative procedure.

Definitions

'resource efficiency requirements'	Sch 7 para 2
'relevant national authority'	s 53(2)

In force:	E W S: 9 January 2022; NI: 28 February 2022
Application	E W S NI

Ecodesign requirements are part of a bigger producer responsibility agenda, intended to mirror or exceed EU Ecodesign standards. In the provisions here, resource efficiency requirements mirror those concerning resource efficiency information in s 52, save the word 'requirement' is substituted for 'information'. The relevant national authority may, by regulations, make provision for the purposes of requiring specified products, in specified circumstances, to meet specified resource efficiency requirements. Regulations can prohibit products being distributed, sold or supplied if requirements are not met. The schedule contains a consultation requirement and sets conditions on when the regulation can be used. Resource efficiency requirements may only be imposed on a person if that person is connected with the manufacture, import, distribution, sale or supply of the product.

54 Deposit schemes

(1) Schedule 8 confers power on the relevant national authority to make regulations establishing deposit schemes.

(2) In this section and that Schedule "the relevant national authority" means—

(a) in relation to a deposit scheme relating to the purchase of products in England, the Secretary of State;

(b) in relation to a deposit scheme relating to the purchase of products in Wales, the Welsh Ministers or the Secretary of State;

(c) in relation to a deposit scheme relating to the purchase of products in Northern Ireland, the Department of Agriculture, Environment and Rural Affairs in Northern Ireland or the Secretary of State.

(3) Regulations under Schedule 8—

(a) made by the Welsh Ministers, may contain only provision which, if contained in an Act of Senedd Cymru, would be within the legislative competence of the Senedd;

(b) made by the Department of Agriculture, Environment and Rural Affairs in Northern Ireland, may contain only provision which, if contained in an Act of the Northern Ireland Assembly, would be within the legislative competence of the Assembly and would not require the Secretary of State's consent.

(4) Regulations under Schedule 8 made by the Secretary of State may not contain provision that could be contained in regulations under that Schedule made by another relevant national authority, unless that authority consents.

(5) Regulations made by a relevant national authority under Schedule 8 are subject to the affirmative procedure if they—

(a) are the first regulations under paragraph 1, or the first regulations under paragraph 5, made by the authority;

(b) provide for conduct to be a criminal offence which is not a criminal offence under existing regulations made by the authority under that Schedule;

(c) provide for conduct to be subject to a civil sanction (within the meaning given by paragraph 5(3) of that Schedule) which is not subject to a civil sanction under existing regulations made by the authority under that Schedule;

(d) increase the amount or maximum amount of a fine or monetary penalty, or change the basis on which such an amount or maximum is to be determined.

(6) Otherwise, regulations under Schedule 8 are subject to the negative procedure.

(7) In this section "deposit scheme" has the meaning it has in Schedule 8.

Definitions

'deposit schemes'	Sch 8 para 1(2)
'deposit'	Sch 8 para 1(2)(a)
'deposit item'	Sch 8 para 1(3)
'relevant national authority'	s 54(2)

In force	E W: 9 January 2022; NI: 28 February 2022
Application	E W NI

Background

The *Litter Strategy for England* (HM Government, April 2017) laid the groundwork to examine the case for economic incentives to reduce litter. Referencing the success of the 5p carrier bag charge introduced in 2015, the Strategy recorded: '*As well as voluntary models, the working group will consider regulatory options and measures to target particular types of item or product. For its first piece of work, Ministers will ask the group to consider the advantages and disadvantages of different types of deposit and reward and return schemes for drinks containers, and to provide advice by the end of 2017. In taking forward this work, the group will gather evidence from relevant industries and independent experts, and analyse the full costs impacts and benefits of these tools when put together. This should include looking at the administrative costs of such schemes, the effect on consumer prices, and the impact on consumers who responsibly dispose of such products via their council-provided household recycling service*' (para 3.3.2).

In February 2018, the independent Voluntary and Economics Incentives Working Group established by DEFRA published its report *Voluntary and Economic Incentives to Reduce*

Littering of Drinks Containers and Promote Recycling. The key conclusions on deposit return schemes were:

- there was some evidence from other countries that well-designed and well-run deposit return schemes can deliver increased amounts of containers collected for recycling;
- there was little direct evidence on the impacts of a deposit return scheme on litter;
- there was scope for increasing collection of high-quality material from drinks containers consumed outside the home, to complement that currently being collected through kerbside and other bring-back systems; and
- more work was needed on the implications and impacts of a deposit return scheme.

On 28 March 2018, the Government announced plans for a deposit return scheme in England for single-use drinks containers, including plastic, glass and metal, subject to consultation. The announcement referenced similar schemes that operate in countries such as Denmark, Sweden and Germany, which see the consumer pay an up-front deposit when they buy a drink, ranging from 8p in Sweden to 22p in Germany, which is redeemed on return of the empty drink container, often through a network of 'reverse vending machines' – the consumer inserts a bottle and the machine returns the money.

The initial consultation on introducing a deposit return scheme in England, Wales and Northern Ireland opened on the 18 February 2019 and closed on 13 May 2019. This set out the aims of introducing a deposit return scheme, with a view to reducing the amount of littering, boosting recycling levels and offering an enhanced possibility of collecting high-quality materials in greater quantities and promoting recycling through clear labelling and consumer messaging.

The response to this initial consultation was published on 23 July 2019, with high levels of interest in introducing a deposit return scheme for drinks containers. The 2019 Conservative Party Manifesto, published in November of that year, contained an explicit commitment to a deposit return scheme to incentivise people to recycle plastic and glass.

However, as a result of the COVID-19 pandemic, the Government has run a second consultation, which opened in March 2021, in order to assess whether there is a continued appetite for a deposit return scheme in a 'post-COVID' context. It is anticipated that the introduction of such a scheme in England, Wales and Northern Ireland would not take place until late 2024 at the earliest.

- The broad themes of the scheme proposed in the consultation include:
- The scope of the scheme should be determined based on material, not product.
- It is proposed that the scheme should capture PET plastic bottles, glass bottles and steel and aluminium cans.
- There are different views between the Welsh Government and others on whether the scheme should be an all-in scheme (including drinks containers up to 3 litres in size) or should be an on-the-go scheme (including drinks containers under 750ml in size but excluding multipack containers).
- There should be an obligation on the deposit management organisation to be created to achieve a 90 per cent collection rate after three years from the scheme's introduction.
- It is not considered that there should be recycling targets in addition to collection targets, but rather that there is a legal obligation on the deposit management organisation to pass on and evidence collected material to a reprocessor.
- The deposit management scheme will be funded through material revenue, producer registration fees and unredeemed deposits.

- Secondary legislation should be passed to set a minimum and maximum deposit level, leaving it to the deposit management organisation to change the deposit level as a lever for meeting targets.
- All retailers that sell in-scope containers should host a return point.
- Mandatory labelling should be legislated for as part of the deposit return scheme.
- Environmental regulators in England, Wales and Northern Ireland are best placed to be scheme regulators.

Interestingly, the Impact Assessment accompanying the consultation assumed a deposit level of 20p, up from 15p proposed in the 2019 consultation.

Scotland has implemented its own plans for an all-in deposit scheme following its own consultation in June 2018. The Deposit and Return Scheme for Scotland Regulations 2020 are partly in force, with the parts relevant to the scheme itself due to come into force on 1 January 2022. The deposit level will be set at 20p. Consequently, this part of the Environment Act has no part to play in Scotland. Nevertheless, the form of the Scottish deposit return scheme is likely to influence the final form of the scheme in the rest of the UK, particularly as there will inevitably be issues for producers if there is a lack of consistency between schemes that will turn on in which nation a particular container was placed on the market.

Schedule 8

Sch 8 empowers the relevant national authority, through regulations, to establish deposit schemes for sustaining, promoting or securing an increase in the recycling or reuse of materials or for reducing the incidence of littering or fly-tipping.

The essence of a deposit scheme is that a person supplied with a deposit item, for example a plastic bottle, by a scheme supplier pays the supplier an amount known as 'a deposit'. On provision of that deposit item to a scheme collector, that person is then entitled to a refund of the deposit. The value of the deposit may be (a) specified or described in a deposit scheme, (b) determined and published by the relevant national authority or (c) determined by the scheme administrator. The Schedule does not make clear what the material difference is between (a) and (c).

Para 2 allows for the deposit scheme to impose requirements on a scheme supplier, including requirements to take steps to ensure that deposits are paid and markings are made on deposit items so as to identify them as deposit items.

Para 3 allows for a deposit scheme to impose requirements on a scheme collector, including requirements to pay the refund and for deposit schemes to be interchangeable. The latter aspect is likely to be important, as ease of use is likely to be critical to the future success of any such deposit schemes.

Para 4 allows for a person to be appointed as an administrator of a deposit scheme and to confer functions on that person, including the power to charge fees for registration and use such fees to meet the costs of exercising its functions. The paragraph is silent on whether an administrator of a deposit scheme would be entitled to make a commercial profit through the use of such fees, although it may be implied by para 2(c) that this is not permitted.

Para 5 permits the relevant national authority to make regulations about the enforcement of requirements under deposit schemes. These include the potential for the imposition of civil sanctions in respect of failures to comply with relevant requirements and the creation of criminal offences for failures to comply with civil sanctions or in connection with obstruction of those tasked with the role of enforcement. As before, it is interesting that it is clearly anticipated that relevant breaches will be dealt with by way of a civil sanction, rather than the option of a criminal prosecution.

55 Charges for single use items

(1) Schedule 9 confers powers on the relevant national authority to make regulations about charges for single use items.

(2) In this section and that Schedule the "relevant national authority" means—

(a) in relation to England, the Secretary of State;

(b) in relation to Wales, the Welsh Ministers;

(c) in relation to Northern Ireland, the Department of Agriculture, Environment and Rural Affairs in Northern Ireland.

(3) Regulations made by a relevant national authority under Schedule 9 are subject to the affirmative procedure if they—

(a) are the first regulations made by the authority under that Schedule;

(b) contain provision about charging for a new item;

(c) provide for conduct to be subject to a civil sanction (within the meaning of paragraph 9(3) of that Schedule) which is not subject to a civil sanction under existing regulations made by the authority under that Schedule;

(d) increase the amount or maximum amount of a monetary penalty, or change the basis on which such an amount or maximum is to be determined.

(4) Otherwise, regulations under Schedule 9 are subject to the negative procedure.

(5) A "new item" means an item in relation to which there are no existing regulations made by the relevant national authority under Schedule 9.

Definitions

'single use plastic items'	Sch 9 para 1(2)–(5)
'relevant national authority'	s 55(2)
'new item'	s 55(5)

In force	E W: 9 January 2022; NI: 28 February 2022
Application	E W NI

Background

The number of single-use carrier bags has fallen dramatically after a charge was introduced on 5 October 2015. WRAP (the Waste and Resources Action Programme) has published data indicating that carrier bags issued by seven large supermarkets fell from 12.6 billion in 2006 to 8.5 billion in 2014, prior to the introduction of the charge, to 'just' 0.6 billion in 2018/19.

The Government's Waste and Resources Strategy (*Our Waste, Our Resources: A Strategy for England*, December 2018) records that more than 15.6 billion fewer plastic bags have been used since the charge was introduced.

The Strategy goes on to state that, '*In general, we prefer to help people and companies make the right choice, rather than banning items outright. There may, however, be times when a ban is appropriate as part of a wider strategic approach. We have already banned the sale of plastic microbeads, consulted on banning plastic drinking straws, stirrers and cotton buds, and are assessing the impact of banning other single use plastic items. We will continue to review the latest evidence on problematic products and/or materials to take a systematic approach to reducing the use of unnecessary single-use plastic products including problematic packaging materials, in line with our commitment to match and where economically practicable exceed the ambition of the EU in this regard*' (para 2.1.3).

The approach adopted by the Environment Act 2021 is to allow relevant national authorities in England, Wales and Northern Ireland to impose charges on single-use plastic items 'to incentivise consumers to choose more sustainable alternatives' (Environment Bill: Memorandum from the Department for the Environment, Food and Rural Affairs to the Delegated Powers and Regulatory Reform Committee, 30 January 2020). It is intended that these powers, whilst new, will be modelled on existing powers to make regulations about carrier bag charges in s 77 and Sch 6 of the Climate Change Act 2008 (Environment Bill: Memorandum from the Department for the Environment, Food and Rural Affairs to the Delegated Powers and Regulatory Reform Committee, 27 May 2021).

Schedule 9

Single-use plastic items, within the meaning of this part of the Act, are defined as those items made wholly or partly of plastic, supplied in connection with goods or services and likely to be used only once, or used only for a short period of time, before being disposed of.

The phrase 'likely to be' is therefore critical to the definition. The Act does not identify how this is to be assessed (ie subjectively or objectively), and if the issue came before a court, it is to be anticipated that an objective test would be applied. Nonetheless, the definition might be considered problematic. Plastic takeaway boxes, for example, are capable of being washed and used as boxes for storage, but they might be considered an obvious example of single-use plastic.

Recognising the need for careful scrutiny of those items that will become the subject of a charge, the first set of regulations made under the power is subject to the affirmative procedure; in addition, regulations imposing a charge on a new single-use plastic item will also be subject to the affirmative procedure. In justifying the requirement for the affirmative procedure in relation to new single-use plastic items, DEFRA has stated: '*This further safeguard is necessary because single-use plastic items do not need to be made wholly of plastic so there is, potentially, a larger number of single-use items in relation to which regulations could be made. The Department considers that this warrants closer Parliamentary scrutiny and time for debate, and so has proposed that regulations imposing a charge in relation to a new item (a plastic takeaway container as opposed to a disposable cup made of paper but with a plastic lining) should also be subject to the affirmative procedure. This will give Parliament the opportunity to scrutinise how that power is used in relation to different items*' (Environment Bill: Memorandum from the Department for the Environment, Food and Rural Affairs to the Delegated Powers and Regulatory Reform Committee, 27 May 2021).

An item is supplied in connection with goods or services if it is supplied at the place the goods or services are sold or provided, for the purpose of enabling the goods to be taken away, used or consumed, enabling the services to be received or enabling goods to be delivered.

The definition of 'supplied in connection with goods' includes, in particular, a container or other packaging into which goods are placed at the point of sale.

The regulations may make provision requiring sellers of goods or services to charge for items specified in the regulations. In doing so, the cost is passed on to the consumer. The term 'seller' will ultimately have the meaning given by the regulations, but Sch 9 specifically identifies that the definition may be made by reference (in particular) to a person's involvement in selling the goods and services, a person's interest in goods and services or a person's interest in the place at or from which the goods or services are sold or provided, or any combination of these factors.

The regulations may specify the minimum amount that a seller must charge for an item specified in the regulations or provide for that amount to be determined in accordance with the regulations. Sellers may be required to register with an administrator, to whom they would have to pay fees. The administrator may be provided with powers to enforce the regulations and may be able to issue civil sanctions.

At the European level, the Single Use Plastic Directive was required to be transposed into the laws of Member States by 3 July 2021, banning 10 specific single-use plastic products and imposing compulsory marking on certain disposable plastic products placed on the market. This section of the Environment Act does not make any attempt to mirror that Directive, as foreshadowed by the Resources and Waste Strategy, raising interesting issues on the possibility of divergence. A consultation on proposals to ban commonly littered single-use plastic items in England closed on 12 February 2022.

56 Charges for carrier bags

In Schedule 6 to the Climate Change Act 2008 (power to impose carrier bag charge) after paragraph 6 insert—

"Registration

6A (1) This paragraph applies to regulations made by—

(a) the Secretary of State, or

(b) the Department of Agriculture, Environment and Rural Affairs in Northern Ireland.

(2) The regulations may require sellers to register with an administrator.

(3) The regulations may make provision—

(a) about applications for registration,

(b) about the period for which registration has effect,

(c) about the cancellation of registration.

(4) The regulations may require sellers to pay to the administrator, in connection with their registration, fees of an amount determined by, or by the administrator in accordance with, the regulations.

(5) The regulations may provide for the amount of the fees to be such as to recover the costs incurred by the administrator in performing its functions under the regulations."

In force E W: 9 January 2022; NI: 28 February 2022

Application E W NI

S 56 of the Environment Act 2021 allows for regulations to be made to require sellers of single-use carrier bags to register with an administrator. Sch 6 to the Climate Change Act 2008 allows for the appointment of that administrator to administer provision made by regulations in respect of the power to impose a charge for carrier bags and to confer or impose on them powers and duties.

Rationale for a Registration System

According to the Government, '*The purpose of registration is to enable an accurate record to be kept of those who are required to charge for single-use carrier bags. Requiring payment of a registration fee will ensure that the costs of administering (record keeping, the database system and compliance checks) a carrier bag charge are borne by sellers of single-use plastic carrier bags rather than by government. The registration fee may be set at an amount sufficient to cover the costs of the administrator in performing its functions under the regulations, which accords with the polluter pays principle (those who produce pollution should bear the costs of managing it). Some sellers may respond to the new duty to register (and pay a registration fee) by ceasing to provide single-use plastic carrier bags. Such action would be consistent with the reduction in single-use plastic bag use since regulations made under the single-use carrier bag power were introduced and which has seen some supermarket sellers removing single-use plastic bags from their stores. It would also be consistent with government policy set out in its 25 Year Plan to eliminate avoidable plastic waste*' (Environment Bill: Memorandum from the Department for the Environment, Food and Rural Affairs to the Delegated Powers and Regulatory Reform Committee, 30 January 2020, p 31).

Related Consultation in December 2018

In 2018 the Government published a consultation in which it was proposed that the charge for single-use carrier bags would be extended to include all retailers (Department of Environment, Food and Rural Affairs, *Single Use Carrier Bags: Extending and Increasing the Charge*, 27 December 2018). At present, the regulations impose requirements on businesses who sell goods with over 250 employees, and micro-, small and medium enterprises are excluded from the mandatory obligation to charge. Some 82 per cent of members of the public and 81 per cent of organisations supported the proposed extension and, as a result, the Government at the time stated that the proposal would be introduced. This section does *not* enact that consultation proposal, but it is anticipated that the extension might be found in future legislation.

Managing waste

57 Separation of waste

(1) The Environmental Protection Act 1990 is amended as follows.

(2) In section 30 (definitions of authorities), after subsection (4) insert—

"(4A) In this Part—

"English waste collection authority" means a waste collection authority whose area is in England;

"English waste disposal authority" means a waste disposal authority whose area is in England."

(3) In section 33ZA (fixed penalty notices), in subsection (12) omit the definition of "English waste collection authority".

(4) For section 45A substitute—

"45A England: separate collection of household waste

(1) This section applies in relation to arrangements made under section 45(1)(a) for an English waste collection authority to collect household waste, unless they are arrangements in relation to which section 45AZA applies.

(2) The arrangements must meet the conditions in subsections (3) to (8) (subject to any provision in regulations under section 45AZC).

(3) The first condition is that recyclable household waste must be collected separately from other household waste.

(4) The second condition is that recyclable household waste must be collected for recycling or composting.

(5) The third condition is that recyclable household waste in each recyclable waste stream must be collected separately, except so far as provided by subsection (6).

(6) Recyclable household waste in two or more recyclable waste streams may be collected together where—

(a) it is not technically or economically practicable to collect recyclable household waste in those recyclable waste streams separately, or

(b) collecting recyclable household waste in those recyclable waste streams separately has no significant environmental benefit (having regard to the overall environmental impact of collecting it separately and of collecting it together).

(7) But recyclable household waste within subsection (10)(a) to (d) may not be collected together with recyclable household waste within subsection (10)(e) or (f).

(8) The fourth condition is that recyclable household waste which is food waste must be collected at least once a week.

(9) Household waste is "recyclable household waste" if—

(a) it is within any of the recyclable waste streams, and

(b) it is of a description specified in regulations made by the Secretary of State.

(10) For the purposes of this section the recyclable waste streams are—

(a) glass;

(b) metal;

(c) plastic;

(d) paper and card;

(e) food waste;

(f) garden waste.

45AZA England: separate collection of household waste from relevant non-domestic premises

(1) This section applies in relation to arrangements for household waste to be collected from relevant non-domestic premises in England by a person who, in collecting the waste—

(a) is acting in the course of a business (whether or not for profit), or

(b) is exercising a public function (including a function under section 45(1)(a)).

(2) The arrangements must meet the conditions in subsections (3) to (7) (subject to any provision in regulations under section 45AZC).

(3) The first condition is that recyclable household waste must be collected separately from other household waste.

(4) The second condition is that recyclable household waste must be collected for recycling or composting.

(5) The third condition is that recyclable household waste in each recyclable waste stream must be collected separately, except so far as provided by subsection (6).

(6) Recyclable household waste in two or more recyclable waste streams may be collected together where—

(a) it is not technically or economically practicable to collect recyclable household waste in those recyclable waste streams separately, or

(b) collecting recyclable household waste in those recyclable waste streams separately has no significant environmental benefit (having regard to the overall environmental impact of collecting it separately and of collecting it together).

(7) But recyclable household waste within subsection (10)(a) to (d) may not be collected together with recyclable household waste within subsection (10)(e).

(8) The person who presents household waste from the premises for collection under the arrangements must present it separated in accordance with the arrangements.

This subsection does not apply so far as the person is subject to an equivalent duty by virtue of a notice under section 46.

(9) Household waste is "recyclable household waste" if—

(a) it is within any of the recyclable waste streams, and

(b) it is of a description specified in regulations made by the Secretary of State.

(10) For the purposes of this section the "recyclable waste streams" are—

(a) glass;

(b) metal;

(c) plastic;

(d) paper and card;

(e) food waste.

(11) For the purposes of this section "relevant non-domestic premises" means—

(a) a residential home;

(b) premises forming part of a university or school or other educational establishment;

(c) premises forming part of a hospital or nursing home;

(d) premises of a description specified in regulations made by the Secretary of State.

(12) Regulations under subsection (11)(d) may not specify domestic properties (within the meaning of section 75(5)(a)).

45AZB England: separate collection of industrial or commercial waste

(1) This section applies in relation to arrangements for industrial or commercial waste to be collected from premises in England by a person who, in collecting the waste—

(a) is acting in the course of a business (whether or not for profit), or

(b) is exercising a public function (including a function under section 45(1)(b) or (2)).

(2) So far as they relate to waste which is similar in nature and composition to household waste ("relevant waste") the arrangements must meet the conditions in subsections (3) to (7).

This is subject to any provision in regulations under section 45AZC.

(3) The first condition is that recyclable relevant waste must be collected separately from other relevant waste.

(4) The second condition is that recyclable relevant waste must be collected for recycling or composting.

(5) The third condition is that recyclable relevant waste in each recyclable waste stream must be collected separately, except so far as provided by subsection (6).

(6) Recyclable relevant waste in two or more recyclable waste streams may be collected together where—

(a) it is not technically or economically practicable to collect recyclable relevant waste in those recyclable waste streams separately, or

(b) collecting recyclable relevant waste in those recyclable waste streams separately has no significant environmental benefit (having regard to the overall environmental impact of collecting it separately and of collecting it together).

(7) But recyclable relevant waste within subsection (10)(a) to (d) may not be collected together with recyclable relevant waste within subsection (10)(e).

(8) The person who presents relevant waste from the premises for collection under the arrangements must present it separated in accordance with the arrangements.

This subsection does not apply so far as the person is subject to an equivalent duty by virtue of a notice under section 47.

(9) Relevant waste is "recyclable relevant waste" if—

(a) it is within any of the recyclable waste streams, and

(b) it is of a description specified in regulations made by the Secretary of State.

(10) For the purposes of this section the "recyclable waste streams" are—
(a) glass;
(b) metal;
(c) plastic;
(d) paper and card;
(e) food waste.

45AZC Sections 45A to 45AZB: powers to exempt and extend

(1) The Secretary of State may by regulations provide—
(a) for exemptions from the condition in section 45A(5), 45AZA(5) or 45AZB(5);
(b) for exemptions from the application of section 45AZA or 45AZB;
(c) for exemptions from the application of section 45AZA or 45AZB in relation to household waste or relevant waste in recyclable waste streams specified in the regulations.

(2) The Secretary of State may exercise the power in subsection (1)(a) in relation to two or more recyclable waste streams only if satisfied that doing so will not significantly reduce the potential for recyclable household waste or recyclable relevant waste in those waste streams to be recycled or composted.

(3) The Secretary of State may by regulations amend sections 45A to 45AZB so as to—
(a) add further recyclable waste streams, and
(b) make provision about the extent to which recyclable household waste or recyclable relevant waste in any of those waste streams may or may not be collected together with recyclable household waste or recyclable relevant waste in another recyclable waste stream.

(4) The Secretary of State may exercise the power in subsection (3)(a) in relation to a waste stream only if satisfied that—
(a) there is waste in that waste stream which is suitable for recycling or composting, and recycling or composting it will have an environmental benefit,
(b) all English waste collection authorities can make arrangements for collecting waste in that waste stream which comply with the conditions in section 45A, 45AZA or 45AZB (as appropriate), taking account of any amendments to be made under subsection (3)(b), and
(c) there is a market for it after its collection.

(5) Before making regulations under this section the Secretary of State must consult—
(a) the Environment Agency,
(b) English waste collection authorities,
(c) English waste disposal authorities, and
(d) anyone else the Secretary of State considers appropriate.

(6) The requirement in subsection (5) may be met by consultation carried out before this section comes into force.

45AZD Sections 45A to 45AZB: duties of waste collectors

(1) Subsection (2) applies where—

(a) a person collects or proposes to collect waste under arrangements to which section 45A, 45AZA or 45AZB applies, and

(b) the arrangements include arrangements to collect recyclable household waste or recyclable relevant waste in two or more recyclable waste streams together in reliance on section 45A(6), 45AZA(6) or 45AZB(6).

(2) The person must prepare a written assessment of why the person considers that the section relied on applies.

45AZE Sections 45 to 45AZD: guidance

(1) The Secretary of State may issue guidance about the duties imposed by sections 45 to 45AZD.

(2) The guidance may in particular deal with—

(a) the circumstances in which it may not be technically or economically practicable to collect recyclable household waste or recyclable relevant waste in recyclable waste streams separately, or in which separate collection may not have significant environmental benefit;

(b) the frequency with which household waste other than recyclable household waste which is food waste should be collected;

(c) the kinds of waste which are relevant waste for the purposes of section 45AZB;

(d) assessments under section 45AZD.

(3) The guidance may make different provision in relation to sections 45A, 45AZA and 45AZB.

(4) Before issuing guidance under this section the Secretary of State must consult—

(a) the Environment Agency,

(b) English waste collection authorities,

(c) English waste disposal authorities, and

(d) anyone else the Secretary of State considers appropriate.

(5) The requirement in subsection (4) may be met by consultation carried out before this section comes into force.

(6) A waste collection authority, and any party to arrangements to which section 45AZA or 45AZB applies, must have regard to the guidance

(7) The Secretary of State must lay before Parliament, and publish, the guidance.

45AZF Sections 45AZA and 45AZB: compliance notices

(1) This section applies where the Environment Agency considers that a person other than an English waste collection authority—

(a) is a party to arrangements for the collection of household waste which fail to comply with section 45AZA,

(b) is a party to arrangements for the collection of relevant waste which fail to comply with section 45AZB, or

(c) is failing to comply with section 45AZA(8) or 45AZB(8).

(2) It may give that person a notice (a "compliance notice") requiring them to take specified steps within a specified period to secure that the failure does not continue or recur.

(3) A compliance notice must—

(a) specify the failures to comply with section 45AZA or 45AZB,

(b) specify the steps which must be taken for the purpose of preventing the failure continuing or recurring,

(c) specify the period within which those steps must be taken, and

(d) give information as to the rights of appeal (including the period within which an appeal must be brought).

(4) A person who fails to comply with a compliance notice commits an offence.

(5) A person who commits an offence under subsection (4) is liable on summary conviction or conviction on indictment to a fine.

45AZG Sections 45AZA and 45AZB: appeals against compliance notices

(1) A person who is given a compliance notice may appeal to the First-tier Tribunal against—

(a) the notice, or

(b) any requirement in the notice.

(2) The notice or requirement has effect pending the determination of the appeal, unless the tribunal decides otherwise.

(3) The tribunal may—

(a) quash the notice or requirement,

(b) confirm the notice or requirement,

(c) vary the notice or requirement,

(d) take any steps the Environment Agency could take in relation to the failure giving rise to the notice or requirement, or

(e) remit any matter relating to the notice or requirement to the Environment Agency."

(5) In section 46(2) (receptacles for household waste) for the words from "subject to" to the end substitute—

"(a) subject to that, a waste collection authority whose area is in Wales may require separate receptacles or compartments of receptacles to be used for waste which is to be recycled and waste which is not;

(b) an English waste collection authority may require separate receptacles or compartments of receptacles to be used for the purposes of complying with its duties under section 45A or 45AZA."

(6) In section 47(3) (receptacles for commercial or industrial waste) at the end insert ", but an English waste collection authority may require separate receptacles or

compartments of receptacles to be used for the purposes of complying with section 45AZB so far as it applies to waste of the kind in question."

(7) In section 160A(2) (regulations and orders) (as inserted by section 63), in the Table, at the appropriate place insert—

"45AZC (separation of waste) | any regulations under that section."

(8) In section 41(1) of the Environment Act 1995 (powers to make charging schemes) after paragraph (r) (as inserted by section 64) insert—

"(s) as a means of recovering costs which are incurred by it in performing functions relating to sections 45A to 45AZB of the Environmental Protection Act 1990, the Agency may require the payment to it of such charges as may from time to time be prescribed;".

(9) In section 108(15) of the Environment Act 1995 (powers of entry), in the definition of "pollution control functions" in relation to a waste collection authority, in paragraph (a) for ", 45A" substitute "to 45AZD".

Definitions

'Recyclable household waste'	s 45A(9)
'Recyclable waste streams'	s 45A(10)
'Relevant non-domestic premises'	s 45AZA(11)
'Domestic properties'	s 75(5)(a) Environmental Protection Act 1990
'Relevant waste'	s 45AZB(2)

In force	E: on such date appointed by regulations
Application	E

This section amends the duties imposed on English waste collection authorities set out in the Environmental Protection Act 1990.

Background

The Waste Framework Directive (2008/98/EC) required the UK to increase household recycling rates to 50 per cent by 2020. The Resources and Waste Strategy, *Our Waste, Our Resources: A Strategy for England* (HM Government, December 2018), set a target of increasing municipal waste recycling rates to 65 per cent by 2035. But official figures appear to show that, at the time of publication, UK recycling rates have stalled and are hovering around the 45 per cent mark.

Reg 13 of the Waste (England and Wales) Regulations 2011 (SI 2011/988), as amended, requires a waste collection authority which collects waste paper, metal, plastic or glass to collect them separately. This duty, however, only applies where it is both:

- necessary to ensure that waste undergoes recovery operations in accordance with Arts 4 and 13 of the Waste Framework Directive and to facilitate or improve recovery; and
- technically, environmentally and economically practicable.

In practice, this means that many councils offer commingled collections of recycled materials where the cost of separate collections is prohibitively high.

The Resources and Waste Strategy committed the Government to:

- improving recycling rates by ensuring that a consistent set of dry recyclable materials is collected from all households and businesses;
- reducing greenhouse gas emissions from landfill by ensuring that every householder and appropriate business has a weekly separate food waste collection, subject to consultation; and
- improving urban recycling rates, working with business and local authorities.

In February 2019, the Government published its *Consultation on Consistency in Household and Business Recycling Collections in England*. The response to that consultation, published in July 2019, identified that there was overwhelming support for a requirement that all local authorities should collect a core set of dry recyclable materials from houses and flats at the kerbside. The Government stated that it would seek to amend legislation to require all English local authorities to collect at least the following dry materials from 2023:

- glass bottles and containers – including drinks bottles, condiment bottles, jars;
- paper and card – including newspaper, cardboard packaging, writing paper;
- plastic bottles – including clear drinks containers, HDPE (milk containers), detergent, shampoo and cleaning products;
- plastic pots tubs and trays; and
- steel and aluminium tins and cans.

The Consultation also noted that China's ban on the import of post-consumer plastic waste and paper reinforced the need both to improve the quality of what is collected for recycling and to reduce contamination.

The response to the consultation noted that whilst there was strong support from individuals that food and drink cartons, as well as plastic bags and film, should be included in the core set, there was significantly less support for this from local authorities. In total, 80 per cent of individual respondents and 72 per cent of stakeholder responses (including 68 per cent of local authorities who responded) agreed that there should be at least a weekly collection of food waste. As a result, the Government confirmed it would legislate to ensure that every local authority provides householders with a separate food waste collection.

The response identified that it was the Government's preference for a separate weekly collection of food waste and not mixed with garden waste, but it stated that further consideration was needed in respect of local circumstances. Particular considerations include providing a separate food waste collection for properties in densely populated areas, especially flats and properties above commercial premises, as well as very rural areas.

Separate Collection of Household Waste: s 45A

Prior to the amendments introduced by this section, s 45A of the Environmental Protection Act 1990 required English waste collection authorities to make arrangements for the collection of at least two types of recyclable waste together or individually separated from the rest of the household waste, unless the cost of doing so would be unreasonably high or comparable alternative arrangements were available. In practice, this allowed a large degree of variation amongst local authorities in the way they actually carried out their duties.

The duty has now changed to introduce a greater degree of consistency amongst local authorities.

All recyclable household waste, rather than just two types, as under the previous legislation, must now be collected separately from other household waste. Household waste is defined as 'recyclable household waste' if it is within any of the recyclable waste streams, and furthermore is specified in regulations. The six 'recyclable waste streams' listed in the Act are:

- glass
- metal
- plastic
- paper and card
- food waste
- garden waste

Regulations will provide detail about which materials within a recyclable waste stream are suitable for recycling, because *'some materials may on the face of it fall within a subsection (10) waste stream, but will not in fact be suitable for recycling or composting'* (Environment Bill Explanatory Notes, para 412).

It is a condition that recyclable household waste must be collected for recycling or composting. No such condition existed previously.

It is a condition that each recyclable waste stream must be collected separately, save for some exceptions. The exceptions are where it is not technically or economically practicable to collect recyclable household waste in those recyclable waste streams separately or where to do so would have no significant environmental benefit. Food waste must be collected at least once a week.

The section introduces a bar on collecting food waste or garden waste together with other specific waste streams, namely glass, metal, plastic and paper and card.

S 45 of the Environmental Protection Act 1990 continues to apply, which will mean that the requirements of the new s 45A do not apply in case of

- waste which is situated in a place which in the opinion of the authority is so isolated or inaccessible that the cost of collecting it would be unreasonably high; or
- waste for which the authority is satisfied that adequate arrangements for its disposal have been or can reasonably be expected to be made by a person who controls it.

Separate Collection of Recyclable Waste from Certain Non-domestic Premises: s 45AZA

The section applies to those making arrangements for household waste to be collected from certain non-domestic premises in the course of a business or where exercising a public function. Pursuant to s 45AZA(11), relevant non-domestic premises include residential homes, premises forming part of a university, school or other educational establishment and premises forming part of a hospital or nursing home. The Secretary of State may add further categories by regulations (aside from applying the provision to domestic premises).

The conditions mirror the new s 45A, save that there is no explicit reference to garden waste and, under sub-s (8), that they require that the waste be presented for collection already separated.

Separate Collection of Industrial and Commercial Waste Similar to Household Waste: s 45AZB

This section impacts on arrangements for industrial or commercial waste to be collected from premises in England by those acting in the course of a business or exercising a public function, so far as the waste that is collected is similar in nature and composition to household waste. The conditions mirror s 45AZA.

Exemptions and Amendments: s 45AZC

This section provides the Secretary of State power, through regulations, to make exemptions or amendments to ss 45A, 45AZA and 45AZB. This includes an express ability to add further recyclable waste streams and how waste caught by these sections may be collected.

Adding an additional recyclable waste stream requires an identifiable environmental benefit, an assessment that English waste collection authorities can make arrangements that comply with the relevant sections and that there is a market for the waste stream after its collection. No threshold for any of these tests is identified, but before such regulations are made, consultation must take place.

Written Assessment Required by Two or More Waste Streams Collected Together: s 45AZD

This section imposed a requirement on a waste collector subject to s 45A, 45AZA or 45AZB to produce a written assessment of why it is considered that two or more waste streams are to be collected together.

Guidance on Duties: s 45AZE

S 45AZE identifies that the Secretary of State may produce guidance about the duties imposed by ss 45 to 45AZD. There is a requirement to consult before issuing such guidance. Waste collection authorities and any party to arrangements to which s 45AZA or 45AZB applies must have regard to the guidance. For the legal meaning of 'have regard to', see the Introduction.

Compliance Notices: s 45AZF

This section empowers the Environment Agency to issue compliance notices, requiring a person other than an English waste collection authority to take specified steps within a specified period to rectify a failure to comply with s 45AZA(8) or s 45AZB(8) (requirements to present waste separated).

The Environment Agency cannot issue a compliance notice to an English waste collection authority itself. A waste collection authority would fall within the jurisdiction of the OEP and potentially could be subject to enforcement action by the OEP where it has failed in its legal duties.

Appeals against Compliance Notices: s 45AZG

Any appeal against a compliance notice can be made to the First-tier Tribunal. Such an appeal does not suspend the notice. No grounds of appeal are specified, but the tribunal is provided with a wide range of options following determination of the appeal.

Sub-s (5) amends s 46(2) of the Environmental Protection Act 1990, distinguishing between England and Wales, but permitting both English and Welsh waste collection authorities to require the use of separate receptacles. However, it is only the English waste collection authorities that may require separate receptacles to be used for the purpose of complying with s 45A or 45AZA.

Sub-s (6) amends s 47(3) to account for the requirement to comply with s 45AZB.

Sub-s (8) permits the Environment Agency to charge for costs incurred in performing functions pursuant to ss 45A to 45AZB, via an amendment to s 41(1) of the Environment Act 1995.

Sub-s (9) amends s 108(15) of the Environment Act 1995 to ensure that ss 45A to 45AZD are included within the definition of pollution control functions in relation to a waste collection authority.

58 Electronic waste tracking: Great Britain

(1) The Environmental Protection Act 1990 is amended in accordance with subsections (2) and (3).

(2) After section 34C insert—

"Electronic waste tracking

34CA Electronic waste tracking

(1) The relevant national authority may by regulations make provision for the purpose of tracking relevant waste, including provision about the establishment of an electronic system ("the system") for that purpose.

(2) The regulations may impose requirements on relevant waste controllers, or a waste regulation authority, to take specified steps to secure the entry into the system of specified information about, or which is relevant to the tracking or regulation of, specified relevant waste.

(3) The information which may be specified includes information about—

(a) the processing, movement or transfer to another person of relevant waste or waste processing products;

(b) persons to whom relevant waste or waste processing products have been transferred;

(c) the carrying out of any activity by relevant waste controllers in relation to, or in connection with, relevant waste or waste processing products;

(d) relevant waste controllers.

(4) The regulations may impose requirements on relevant waste controllers to take specified steps to enable physical identification of specified relevant waste or waste processing products.

(5) The regulations may allow relevant waste controllers, or a waste regulation authority, to make arrangements for other persons to discharge their obligations under the regulations, and may impose requirements on such persons in connection with such arrangements.

(6) The regulations must provide for an exemption for digitally excluded persons from any requirement that would involve the use of electronic communications or the keeping of electronic records, but may impose alternative requirements on those persons that do not involve either.

(7) The regulations may designate a person to establish, operate or maintain the system and may confer functions on such a person.

(8) The regulations may make provision about how information held on the system is to be used including provision—

(a) about who may access the information;

(b) permitting, or requiring, the disclosure, publication or transfer to another electronic system of such information;

(c) imposing requirements on persons who obtain such information not to further disclose it.

(9) The regulations may impose fees or charges, payable to a person designated by, or in accordance with, the regulations, on persons subject to any requirement imposed by the regulations.

(10) The amount of such fee or charges may reflect the costs of establishing, operating or maintaining the system and any other costs incurred in connection with the tracking of relevant waste by a person designated to establish, operate or maintain the system.

(11) The relevant national authority may provide grants or loans to a person designated to establish, operate or maintain the system.

(12) In this section—

"digitally excluded person" means a person—

(a) who is a practising member of a religious society or order whose beliefs are incompatible with using electronic communications or keeping electronic records, or

(b) for whom it is not reasonably practicable to use electronic communications or to keep electronic records for any reason (including age, disability or location);

"extractive waste"—

(a) in relation to regulations made in relation to England or Wales, has the meaning it has in this Part (as it extends to England and Wales);

(b) in relation to regulations made in relation to Scotland, has the meaning it has in the Management of Extractive Waste (Scotland) Regulations 2010 (S.S.I. 2010/60);

"relevant national authority" means—

(a) in relation to England, the Secretary of State;

(b) in relation to Wales, the Welsh Ministers;

(c) in relation to Scotland, the Scottish Ministers; "relevant waste" means controlled waste or extractive waste;

"relevant waste controller" means any person who—

(a) is subject to the duty in section 34(1) (duty of care as respects controlled waste),

(b) imports, produces, carries, keeps, treats, manages or disposes of extractive waste or, as a dealer or broker, has control of such waste, or

(c) exports relevant waste;

"specified" means specified or described in the regulations;

"waste processing product" means any product of the processing of relevant waste, including material which is not relevant waste or which is not derived from relevant waste.

34CB Further provision about regulations under section 34CA

(1) Regulations under section 34CA(1) may make provision about the enforcement of requirements imposed by or under the regulations.

(2) The regulations may include provision—

(a) creating criminal offences punishable with a fine in respect of failures to comply with the regulations;

(b) about such offences.

(3) The regulations may include provision—

(a) for, about or connected with the imposition of civil sanctions by an enforcement authority;

(b) in the case of a civil sanction that requires the payment of an amount, for that amount—

(i) to be specified in the regulations;

(ii) to be determined by an enforcement authority in accordance with the regulations;

(c) for such a determination to be made by reference to factors specified or described in the regulations which may include, for example, the turnover of a business or the costs of complying with the requirement being enforced (and the regulations may provide that the amount to be paid may exceed the amount of those costs);

(d) about appeals against the imposition of a civil sanction.

(4) In this section "civil sanction" means a sanction of a kind for which provision may be made under Part 3 of the Regulatory Enforcement and Sanctions Act 2008 (fixed monetary penalties, discretionary requirements, stop notices and enforcement undertakings).

(5) The regulations may include provision for the imposition of sanctions of that kind whether or not—

(a) the conduct in respect of which the sanction is imposed constitutes an offence,

(b) the enforcement authority is a regulator for the purposes of Part 3 of the Regulatory Enforcement and Sanctions Act 2008, or

(c) the relevant national authority may make provision for the imposition of sanctions under that Part.

(6) The regulations may make different provision for different purposes.

(7) The regulations may make consequential, supplementary, incidental, transitional or saving provision, including provision amending, repealing or revoking primary legislation or retained direct EU legislation.

(8) In this section—

"enforcement authority" means the Environment Agency, the Natural Resources Body for Wales, a waste collection authority for an area in England or Wales or the Scottish Environment Protection Agency;

"primary legislation" means—

(a) in relation to regulations made by the Secretary of State, an Act of Parliament;

(b) in relation to regulations made by the Welsh Ministers, an Act of Parliament or an Act or Measure of Senedd Cymru;

(c) in relation to regulations made by the Scottish Ministers, an Act of Parliament or an Act of the Scottish Parliament."

(3) In section 160A(2) (regulations and orders) (as inserted by section 63), in the Table, at the appropriate place insert—

"34CA (electronic waste tracking)	regulations that— (a) are the first set of regulations to be made by the relevant national authority (within the meaning given by section 34CA(12)) under section 34CA,

(b) provide for conduct to be a criminal offence which is not a criminal offence under existing regulations made by that authority under that section,

(c) increase the maximum penalty for a criminal offence under existing regulations made by that authority under that section,

(d) provide for conduct to be subject to a civil sanction (within the meaning given by section 34CB(4)) which is not subject to a civil sanction under existing regulations made by that authority under that section, or

(e) amend, repeal or revoke a provision contained in primary legislation (within the meaning given by section 34CB(8)) or retained direct principal EU legislation."

(4) In section 41(1) of the Environment Act 1995 (powers to make charging schemes) after paragraph (d) insert—

"(da) as a means of recovering costs incurred by it in performing functions conferred by regulations made under section 34CA of the Environmental Protection Act 1990 (electronic waste tracking) the Agency, the Natural Resources Body for Wales or SEPA may require the payment to it of such charges as may from time to time be prescribed;".

Definitions

'digitally excluded person'	s 34CA(12)
'extractive waste'	s 34CA(12)
'relevant national authority'	s 34CA(12)
'relevant waste'	s 34CA(12)
'relevant waste controller'	s 34CA(12)
'specified'	s 34CA(12)
'waste processing product'	s 34CA(12)
'civil sanction'	s 34CB(4)
'enforcement authority'	s 34CB(8)
'primary legislation'	s 34CB(8)

In force	9 January 2022
Application	E W S

Background

S 58 amends the Environmental Protection Act to add specific provisions on electronic waste tracking. The amendment forms part of a government commitment to clamp down on illegal movements of waste at home and abroad. A review commissioned by the Home Office (*Independent Review into Serious and Organised Crime in the Waste Sector*, November 2018) found that the lack of digital record-keeping is exploited by organised criminals, who mislabel waste to avoid landfill tax or illegally export it. The review made recommendations that included mandatory electronic tracking of waste and a national database of registered brokers.

The Resources and Waste Strategy published (HM Government, *Our Waste, Our Resources: A Strategy for England*, December 2018) identified at p 92 areas of concern where it was considered that electronic waste tracking could help identify:

- waste that does not reach the next stage, which implies illegal dumping;
- waste descriptions that change, which implies Landfill Tax or regulatory regime avoidance;
- strange patterns of waste transfers, which may indicate fraud.

A waste tracking project was first announced by DEFRA back in February 2019, following funding provided through the GovTech Catalyst fund, a £20 million fund aimed at helping tech firms deliver innovative solutions to public sector challenges.

Rebecca Pow, Parliamentary Under Secretary of State, stated on 20 October 2020, in response to a parliamentary question, that the Budget committed the Government to investing £7.2 million in the development of electronic waste tracking. A Government consultation on the introduction of mandatory digital waste tracking opened on 21 January 2022.

Electronic Waste Tracking: s 34CA

The new s 34CA allows for regulations to be made for the purpose of tracking 'relevant waste', defined as controlled waste or extractive waste. The wording of the section is such that relevant waste controllers or a waste regulation authority will be required to take specified steps to secure the entry into the system of information relevant to the tracking of waste, potentially including, amongst other things, information about the movement or transfer of waste, identifying persons to whom waste has been transferred, waste activities and waste controllers.

The regulations may also require relevant waste controllers to take specified steps to enable the physical identification of specified relevant waste or waste processing products. They may also allow for the possibility of delegating the obligation to comply.

Enforcement: s 34CB

Enforcement is dealt with at new s 34CB and includes the fact that regulations may create criminal offences punishable by a fine for failures to comply. On its face, electronic waste tracking is so intrinsically linked to the duty of care and the auditing of waste transfers that penalties could easily mirror each other. Whilst the wording of the Act limiting any penalty to a financial penalty is understandable and whilst a financial penalty is likely to be unlimited, there is a risk that, in practice, limiting the penalty to a purely financial one may lead to a lack of interest in pursuing criminal offences for failures to comply with waste tracking legislation. Often there is little appetite to pursue criminal offences that fall at the bottom end of the scale, due to the cost in doing so. Given the availability of civil sanctions, set out in s 34CB(3), it must be open to considerable doubt whether the criminal sanction is ever likely to be widely used.

59 Electronic waste tracking: Northern Ireland

(1) The Waste and Contaminated Land (Northern Ireland) Order 1997 (S.I. 1997/2778 (N.I. 19)) is amended as follows.

(2) After Article 5F insert—

"Electronic waste tracking

5G Electronic waste tracking

(1) The Department may by regulations make provision for the purpose of tracking relevant waste, including provision about the establishment of an electronic system ("the system") for that purpose.

(2) The regulations may impose requirements on relevant waste controllers, or the Department, to take specified steps to secure the entry into the system of specified information about, or which is relevant to the tracking or regulation of, specified relevant waste.

(3) The information which may be specified includes information about—

(a) the processing, movement or transfer to another person of relevant waste or waste processing products;

(b) persons to whom relevant waste or waste processing products have been transferred;

(c) the carrying out of any activity by relevant waste controllers in relation to, or in connection with, relevant waste or waste processing products;

(d) relevant waste controllers.

(4) The regulations may impose requirements on relevant waste controllers to take specified steps to enable physical identification of specified relevant waste or waste processing products.

(5) The regulations may allow relevant waste controllers, or the Department, to make arrangements for other persons to discharge their obligations under the regulations, and may impose requirements on such persons in connection with such arrangements.

(6) The regulations must provide for an exemption for digitally excluded persons from any requirement that would involve the use of electronic communications or the keeping of electronic records, but may impose alternative requirements on those persons that do not involve either.

(7) The regulations may designate a person to establish, operate or maintain the system and may confer functions on such a person.

(8) The regulations may make provision about how information held on the system is to be used including provision—

(a) about who may access the information;

(b) permitting, or requiring, the disclosure, publication or transfer to another electronic system of such information;

(c) imposing requirements on persons who obtain such information not to further disclose it.

(9) The regulations may impose fees or charges, payable to a person designated by, or in accordance with, the regulations, on persons subject to any requirement imposed by the regulations.

(10) The amount of such fees or charges may reflect the costs of establishing, operating or maintaining the system and any other costs incurred in connection with the tracking of relevant waste by a person designated to establish, operate or maintain the system.

(11) The Department may provide grants or loans to a person designated to establish, operate or maintain the system.

(12) In this Article—

"digitally excluded person" means a person—

(a) who is a practising member of a religious society or order whose beliefs are incompatible with using electronic communications or keeping electronic records, or

(b) for whom it is not reasonably practicable to use electronic communications or to keep electronic records for any reason (including age, disability or location);

"extractive waste" has the meaning it has in the Planning (Management of Waste from Extractive Industries) Regulations (Northern Ireland) 2015 (S.R. 2015 No. 85);

"relevant waste" means controlled waste or extractive waste; "relevant waste controller" means any person who—

(a) is subject to the duty in Article 5(1) (duty of care as respects controlled waste),

(b) imports, produces, carries, keeps, treats, manages or disposes of extractive waste or, as a dealer or broker, has control of such waste, or

(c) exports relevant waste;

"specified" means specified or described in the regulations; "waste processing product" means any product of the processing of relevant waste, including material which is not relevant waste or which is not derived from relevant waste.

5H Further provision about regulations under Article 5G

(1) Regulations under Article 5G may make provision about the enforcement of requirements imposed by or under the regulations.

(2) The regulations may include provision—

(a) creating criminal offences punishable with a fine in respect of failures to comply with the regulations;

(b) about such offences.

(3) The regulations may include provision—

(a) for, about or connected with the imposition of civil sanctions by the Department;

(b) in the case of a civil sanction that requires the payment of an amount, for that amount—

(i) to be specified in the regulations;

(ii) to be determined by the Department in accordance with the regulations;

(c) for such a determination to be made by reference to factors specified or described in the regulations which may include, for example, the turnover of a business or the costs of complying with the requirement being enforced (and the regulations may provide that the amount to be paid may exceed the amount of those costs);

(d) about appeals against the imposition of a civil sanction.

(4) In this Article "civil sanction" means a sanction of a kind for which provision may be made under Part 3 of the Regulatory Enforcement and Sanctions Act 2008 (fixed monetary penalties, discretionary requirements, stop notices and enforcement undertakings).

(5) The regulations may include provision for the imposition of sanctions of that kind whether or not the conduct in respect of which the sanction is imposed constitutes an offence.

(6) The regulations may make consequential, supplementary, incidental, transitional or saving provision, including provision amending, repealing or revoking any statutory provision."

(3) In Article 82 (regulations etc) after paragraph (1A) insert—

"(1B) Paragraph (1) does not apply to regulations made by the Department under Article 5G that—

(a) are the first set of regulations made under that Article,

(b) provide for conduct to be a criminal offence which is not a criminal offence under existing regulations under that Article,

(c) increase the maximum penalty for a criminal offence under existing regulations under that Article,

(d) provide for conduct to be subject to a civil sanction (within the meaning given by Article 5H(4)) which is not subject to a civil sanction under existing regulations under that Article,

(e) amend or repeal a provision contained in Northern Ireland legislation or an Act of Parliament, or

(f) amend or revoke a provision contained in retained direct principal EU legislation.

(1C) Regulations to which paragraph (1) does not apply by virtue of paragraph (1B) may not be made unless a draft of the regulations has been laid before and approved by a resolution of the Assembly."

Definitions

'digitally excluded person'	Art 5G(12)
'extractive waste'	Art 5G(12)
'relevant national authority'	Art 5G(12)
'relevant waste'	Art 5G(12)
'relevant waste controller'	Art 5G(12)
'specified'	Art 5G(12)
'waste processing product'	Art 5G(12)
'civil sanction'	Art 5H(4)

In force	28 February 2022
Application	NI

S 59 mirrors the previous section, applying as it does to Northern Ireland, amending the Waste and Contaminated Land (Northern Ireland) Order 1997.

60 Hazardous waste: England and Wales

(1) The Environmental Protection Act 1990 is amended in accordance with subsections (2) to (4).

(2) After section 62 insert—

"62ZA Special provision with respect to hazardous waste in England and Wales

(1) The relevant national authority may, by regulations, make provision for, about or connected with the regulation of hazardous waste in England and Wales.

(2) Provision that may be made in the regulations includes provision—

(a) prohibiting or restricting any activity in relation to hazardous waste;

(b) for the giving of directions by waste regulation authorities with respect to matters connected with any activity in relation to hazardous waste;

(c) imposing requirements about how hazardous waste may be kept (including requirements about the quantities of hazardous waste which may be kept at any place);

(d) about hazardous waste that originated outside England or Wales;

(e) about the registration of hazardous waste controllers or places where activities in relation to hazardous waste are carried out;

(f) for the keeping of records by hazardous waste controllers;

(g) for the inspection of those records by waste regulation authorities or specified persons;

(h) for the provision by hazardous waste controllers of copies of, or information derived from, those records to waste regulation authorities or specified persons;

(i) for hazardous waste controllers to inform waste regulation authorities, or specified persons, when carrying out activities in relation to hazardous waste;

(j) about the circumstances in which waste which is not hazardous waste, but which shares characteristics with hazardous waste, is to be treated as hazardous waste;

(k) for, about or connected with criminal offences;

(l) for, about or connected with the imposition of civil sanctions.

(3) The regulations may not provide for an offence to be punishable—

(a) on summary conviction, by imprisonment, or

(b) on conviction on indictment, by a term of imprisonment exceeding two years.

(4) For the purposes of this section "civil sanction" means a sanction of a kind for which provision may be made under Part 3 of the Regulatory Enforcement and Sanctions Act 2008 (fixed monetary penalties, discretionary requirements, stop notices and enforcement undertakings).

(5) The regulations may make provision for, about or connected with the imposition of a sanction of that kind whether or not—

(a) the conduct in respect of which the sanction is imposed constitutes an offence, or

(b) the person imposing it is a regulator for the purposes of Part 3 of the Regulatory Enforcement and Sanctions Act 2008.

(6) The regulations may also include provision—

(a) for the supervision by waste regulation authorities—

(i) of activities in relation to hazardous waste, or

(ii) of hazardous waste controllers;

(b) about the keeping of records (which may include registers of hazardous waste controllers and places where hazardous waste may be kept or processed) by waste regulation authorities;

(c) as to the recovery of expenses or other charges for the treatment, keeping or disposal or the re-delivery of hazardous waste by waste regulation authorities or hazardous waste controllers;

(d) as to appeals to the relevant national authority from decisions of waste regulation authorities.

(7) This section is subject to section 114 of the Environment Act 1995 (delegation or reference of appeals etc).

(8) Regulations under this section may confer functions (including functions involving the exercise of a discretion) on the relevant national authority or a waste regulation authority.

(9) The regulations may—

(a) make different provision for different purposes;

(b) make incidental, supplementary, consequential, transitional or saving provision.

(10) For the purposes of this section "mixing" in relation to hazardous waste means—

(a) diluting it (with any substance);

(b) mixing it with other hazardous waste of a different type, or that has different characteristics;

(c) mixing it with any other substance or material (whether waste or not).

(11) In this section—

"activity", in relation to hazardous waste, includes—

(a) keeping, collecting, receiving, importing, exporting, transporting or producing hazardous waste;

(b) sorting, treating, recovering, mixing or otherwise processing hazardous waste;

(c) disposing of hazardous waste in any manner (including providing hazardous waste to another person for the purposes of that person carrying out an activity in relation to it);

(d) examining, testing or classifying hazardous waste (including doing any of those things to waste in connection with establishing whether it is hazardous);

(e) acting as a broker of, or dealer in, hazardous waste;

(f) directing or supervising another person in relation to an activity in relation to hazardous waste;

"hazardous waste controller" means a person who carries out any activity in relation to hazardous waste;

"relevant national authority" means—

(a) in relation to England, the Secretary of State;

(b) in relation to Wales, the Welsh Ministers; "specified" means specified in the regulations."

(3) In section 75 (meaning of "waste" etc) for subsection (8A) substitute—

"(8A) In the application of this Part to England, "hazardous waste" means—

(a) any waste identified as hazardous waste in—

(i) the waste list as it applies in relation to England, or

(ii) regulations made by the Secretary of State under regulation 3 of the Waste and Environmental Permitting etc. (Legislative Functions and Amendment etc.) (EU Exit) Regulations 2020 (S.I. 2020/1540), and

(b) any other waste that is treated as hazardous waste for the purposes of—

(i) regulations made by the Secretary of State under section 62ZA, or

(ii) the Hazardous Waste (England and Wales) Regulations 2005 (S.I. 2005/894).

(8B) In the application of this Part to Wales, "hazardous waste" means—

(a) any waste identified as hazardous waste in—

(i) the waste list as it applies in relation to Wales, or

(ii) regulations made by the Welsh Ministers under regulation 3 of the Waste and Environmental Permitting etc. (Legislative Functions and Amendment etc.) (EU Exit) Regulations 2020 (S.I. 2020/1540), and

(b) any other waste that is treated as hazardous waste for the purposes of—

(i) regulations made by the Welsh Ministers under section 62ZA, or

(ii) the Hazardous Waste (Wales) Regulations 2005 (S.I. 2005/1806 (W.138)).

(8C) In subsections (8A) and (8B) "the waste list" means the list of waste contained in the Annex to Commission Decision of 3 May 2000 replacing Decision 94/3/EC establishing a list of wastes pursuant to Article 1(a) of Council Directive 75/442/EEC on waste and Council Decision 94/904/EC establishing a list of hazardous waste pursuant to Article 1(4) of Council Directive 91/689/EEC on hazardous waste (2000/532/EC)."

(4) In section 160A(2) (regulations and orders) (as inserted by section 63), in the Table, at the appropriate place insert—

"62ZA (regulation of hazardous waste in England and Wales)	regulations that— (a) provide for conduct to be a criminal offence which is not a criminal offence under existing regulations made by the relevant national authority (within the meaning given by section 62ZA(11)) under section 62ZA, (b) increase the maximum penalty for a criminal offence under existing regulations made by that authority under that section, or (c) provide for conduct to be subject to a civil sanction (within the meaning given by section 62ZA(4)) which is not subject to a civil sanction under existing regulations made by that authority under that section."

(5) In section 41(1) of the Environment Act 1995 (power to make charging schemes), before paragraph (d) insert—

"(cc) as a means of recovering costs incurred by it in performing functions conferred by regulations made under section 62ZA of the Environmental Protection Act 1990 (special provision with respect to hazardous waste), the Agency or the Natural Resources Body for Wales may require the payment to it of such charges as may from time to time be prescribed;".

(6) In section 114 of the Environment Act 1995 (delegation or reference of appeals etc), in subsection (2)(a)(iii) before ", 78L" insert "62ZA(6)(d)".

Definitions

'activity'	s 60(11)
'hazardous waste controller'	s 60(11)
'relevant national authority'	s 60(11)
'specified'	s 60(11)

In force	E: 24 January 2022; W: 7 March 2022
Application	E W

Background

This section amends the Environmental Protection Act 1990 in respect of hazardous waste. Much of the current law on hazardous waste has stemmed from EU law. S 62 of the Environmental Protection Act 1990 had previously given the Government the power to regulate hazardous waste through secondary legislation. However, it was considered that retaining the power in s 62 was unnecessary since it was expected that any future regulation of this area would be achieved via powers in the European Communities Act 1972 to implement EU obligations. Now that the UK has left the EU, separate legislative power is necessary to be able to amend or replace regulations that govern how hazardous waste is managed.

Annex III of the Waste Framework Directive sets out the properties that render waste hazardous, and these are further specified by EU Commission Decision 2000/532/EC (as amended) establishing a 'List of Waste'.

The European List of Waste is the waste classification system in the EU for administration purposes, ie for permitting and supervision in the field of waste generation and management. The List of Waste defines approximately 839 waste types, which are structured into 20 chapters, mainly according to the source of the waste. Each waste type is characterised by a six-digit code. Full and compliant classification enables businesses and competent authorities to identify whether waste is hazardous or not. In this respect, the List of Waste recognises three types of entries:

- 'absolute hazardous entries': wastes which are assigned to absolute hazardous entries cannot be allocated to non-hazardous entries and are hazardous without any further assessment;
- 'absolute non-hazardous entries': wastes which are assigned to absolute non-hazardous entries cannot be allocated to hazardous entries and are non-hazardous without any further assessment; and
- 'mirror entries': where waste from the same source might under the List of Waste be allocated to a hazardous entry or to a non-hazardous entry depending on the specific case and on the composition of the waste.

Hazardous waste is defined in the new s 62ZA to include any waste listed in the List of Waste as hazardous, as well as waste listed in regulations made under s 62A(2) of the Environmental Protection Act 1990 and waste treated as hazardous for the purposes of regulations made under s 62ZA of the Environmental Protection Act 1990, the Hazardous Waste (England and Wales) Regulations 2005 or the Hazardous Waste (Wales) Regulations 2005. This is an expansion of the current definition, which limits hazardous waste to that identified as hazardous in the Hazardous Waste (England and Wales) Regulations 2005 (waste identified as hazardous in the waste list and waste to be treated as hazardous pursuant to Regulation 8 of the Hazardous Waste (England and Wales) Regulations 2005). In practice, this would permit the Secretary of State to require, through regulations, other wastes that would not currently fall within the definition of hazardous waste to be treated as hazardous.

There appears to be a typographical error in sub-s (3) in that it states 'the regulations may *not* provide for the offence to be punishable' (emphasis added). A court is likely to disregard the 'not' as an error. See *Inco Europe Ltd and others v First Choice Distribution (a firm) and others* [2000] 1 WLR 586 (HL), where Lord Nicholls noted: *'It has long been established that the role of the courts in construing legislation is not confined to resolving ambiguities in statutory language. The court must be able to correct obvious drafting errors. In suitable cases, in discharging its interpretative function the court will add words, or omit words or substitute words.'*

The definition of mixing found in sub-s (10) is slightly reformulated from the definition of mixing hazardous waste found in Reg 18 of the Hazardous Waste (England and Wales) Regulations 2005 in that it contains an explicit reference to dilution. The purpose is to ensure that any hazardous waste that is mixed or diluted, potentially to the extent that it would no longer be considered to be hazardous, can still be regulated by virtue of regulations made under this section.

61 Hazardous waste: Northern Ireland

(1) The Waste and Contaminated Land (Northern Ireland) Order 1997 (S.I. 1997/2778 (N.I. 19)) is amended as follows.

(2) In Article 30 (special provision with respect to hazardous waste)—

(a) in paragraph (1), for the words from "regulations" to "disposal" substitute "the Department may, by regulations, make provision for, about or connected with the regulation";

(b) in paragraph (2)—

(i) before sub-paragraph (a) insert—

"(za) prohibiting or restricting the treatment, keeping or disposal of hazardous waste or any other activity in relation to such waste;";

(ii) in sub-paragraph (a), after "hazardous waste" insert "or any other activity in relation to such waste";

(iii) after sub-paragraph (g) insert—

"(h) for, about or connected with the imposition of civil sanctions.";

(c) after that paragraph insert—

"(2A) For the purposes of this Article "civil sanction" means a sanction of a kind for which provision may be made under Part 3 of the

Regulatory Enforcement and Sanctions Act 2008 (fixed monetary penalties, discretionary requirements, stop notices and enforcement undertakings).

(2B) The regulations may include provision for, about or connected with the imposition of a sanction of that kind whether or not—

(a) the conduct in respect of which the sanction is imposed constitutes an offence, or

(b) the person imposing it is a regulator for the purposes of Part 3 of the Regulatory Enforcement and Sanctions Act 2008.";

(d) after paragraph (3) insert—

"(3A) The regulations may make consequential, supplementary, incidental, transitional or saving provision."

(3) In Article 82 (regulations etc) after paragraph (1C) (as inserted by section 59) insert—

"(1D) Paragraph (1) does not apply to regulations made by the Department under Article 30 that provide for conduct to be subject to a civil sanction (within the meaning given by Article 30(2A)) which is not subject to a civil sanction under existing regulations under that Article.

(1E) Regulations to which paragraph (1) does not apply by virtue of paragraph (1D) may not be made unless a draft of the regulations has been laid before and approved by a resolution of the Assembly."

In force 28 February 2022

Application NI

This section amends the Waste and Contaminated Land (Northern Ireland) Order 1997, providing for the making of regulations that make provision for, about or connected with the regulation of hazardous waste, defined as controlled waste that is or may be dangerous or difficult to treat. This is a revised and expanded power on the previous drafting, which was limited to regulations controlling the management of hazardous waste.

The amendments include the prospect of the imposition of civil sanctions.

62 Transfrontier shipments of waste

(1) Section 141 of the Environmental Protection Act 1990 (power to prohibit or restrict the importation or exportation of waste) is amended in accordance with subsections (2) to (8).

(2) In the heading—

(a) for "prohibit or restrict" substitute "regulate";

(b) after "waste" insert "or the transit of waste for export".

(3) For subsection (1) substitute—

"(1) The Secretary of State may, by regulations, make provision for, about or connected with the regulation of the importation or exportation of waste or the transit of waste for export.

(1A) Provision that may be made in regulations under this section includes provision prohibiting or restricting—

(a) the importation of waste;

(b) the landing and unloading of waste in the United Kingdom;

(c) the exportation of waste;

(d) the loading of waste for exportation;

(e) the transit of waste for export.

(1B) The provision that may be made by virtue of subsection (1A) includes provision which relates to—

(a) the intended final destination of waste, or

(b) the countries or territories it is intended to pass through before reaching that destination."

(4) For subsection (3) substitute—

"(3) Regulations under this section may confer functions on the Secretary of State or a waste regulation authority, including functions—

(a) involving the exercise of a discretion;

(b) relating to enforcement."

(5) Omit subsection (4).

(6) In subsection (5)—

(a) omit paragraph (a);

(b) after that paragraph insert—

"(aa) provide for the Secretary of State to issue general directions as to the exercise by waste regulation authorities of their functions in connection with the regulation of the importation or exportation of waste or the transit of waste for export;";

(c) in paragraph (b) omit "prescribed in or under the regulations";

(d) after paragraph (b) insert—

"(ba) provide for the charging by waste regulation authorities of fees or charges payable by persons involved in the importation or exportation of waste or the transit of waste for export;

(bb) provide that such fees or charges may be used by waste regulation authorities to meet costs incurred in exercising their functions in connection with the regulation of those activities;";

(e) in paragraph (d), for the words from "to" to the end substitute ", with or without modifications, to section 108(4) of the Environment Act 1995 (powers of entry and seizure) on persons authorised by the Secretary of State or a waste regulation authority;";

(f) in paragraph (e), for "authorities under the regulations" substitute "waste regulation authorities";

(g) after paragraph (f) insert—

"(fa) make provision authorising the disclosure of information by Officers of Revenue and Customs to waste regulation authorities;

(fb) confer, on persons designated as general customs officials under section 3(1) of the Borders, Citizenship and Immigration Act 2009, functions relating to the seizure and detention of waste that has arrived at, or entered into, the United Kingdom or is to leave the United Kingdom;";

(h) after paragraph (g) insert—

"(h) make provision for, about or connected with the imposition of civil sanctions."

(7) After subsection (5A) insert—

"(5B) For the purposes of this section "civil sanction" means a sanction of a kind for which provision may be made under Part 3 of the Regulatory Enforcement and Sanctions Act 2008 (fixed monetary penalties, discretionary requirements, stop notices and enforcement undertakings).

(5C) The regulations may make provision for, about or connected with the imposition of a sanction of that kind whether or not—

(a) the conduct in respect of which the sanction is imposed constitutes an offence, or

(b) the person imposing it is a regulator for the purposes of Part 3 of the Regulatory Enforcement and Sanctions Act 2008.

(5D) Regulations under this section may make provision in relation to any area of sea or seabed or its subsoil within the seaward limits of—

(a) the area designated by Order in Council under section 1(7) of the Continental Shelf Act 1964 (designation of continental shelf), or

(b) the area designated by Order in Council under section 41(3) of the Marine and Coastal Access Act 2009 (designation of exclusive economic zone).

(5E) Regulations under this section may make consequential, supplementary, incidental, transitional or saving provision, including provision amending, repealing or revoking primary legislation or retained direct EU legislation."

(8) In subsection (6), at the appropriate places insert—

""exportation", in relation to waste, means causing it to leave the United Kingdom;";

""importation", in relation to waste, means causing it to arrive at, or enter into, the United Kingdom;";

""primary legislation" means—

(a) an Act of Parliament,

(b) a Measure or Act of Senedd Cymru,

(c) an Act of the Scottish Parliament, or

(d) Northern Ireland legislation;";

""transit of waste for export" means the transportation or keeping of waste, that has arrived at, or has entered, the United Kingdom, for the purpose of facilitating its leaving the United Kingdom;".

(9) In section 160A(2) of the Environmental Protection Act 1990 (regulations and orders) (as inserted by section 63), in the Table, at the appropriate place insert—

"section 141 (imports, exports and transit of waste)	regulations that— (a) confer powers of entry, seizure or detention in circumstances where there is no such power under existing regulations under section 141, (b) provide for the charging of fees or charges that are not chargeable under existing regulations under that section, (c) provide for conduct to be a criminal offence which is not a criminal offence under existing regulations under that section, (d) increase the maximum penalty for a criminal offence under existing regulations under that section, (e) provide for conduct to be subject to a civil sanction (within the meaning given by section 141(5B)) which is not subject to a civil sanction under existing regulations under that section, or

(f) amend, repeal or revoke a provision contained in primary legislation (within the meaning given by section 141(6)) or retained direct principal EU legislation."

(10) In section 41 of the Environment Act 1995 (power to make schemes imposing charges)—

(a) in subsection (1), for paragraph (d) substitute—

"(d) as a means of recovering costs incurred by it in performing functions in connection with the regulation of the importation or exportation of waste or the transit of waste for export, the Agency, the Natural Resources Body for Wales or SEPA may require the payment to it of such charges as may from time to time be prescribed;";

(b) after subsection (1) insert—

"(1A) In paragraph (d) of subsection (1) "importation", "exportation", "transit of waste for export" and "waste" have the meaning they have in section 141 of the Environmental Protection Act 1990."

(11) In regulation 46 of the Transfrontier Shipment of Waste Regulations 2007 (S.I. 2007/1711), omit paragraph (1).

Definitions

'civil sanction'	s 141(5B) EPA 1990
'importation'	s 141(6) EPA 1990
'exportation'	s 141(6) EPA 1990
'primary legislation'	s 141(6) EPA 1990
'transit of waste for export'	s 141(6) EPA 1990
'waste'	s 141(6) EPA 1990

In force	24 January 2022
Application	E

Background

The 2018 review commissioned by the Home Office (*Independent Review into Serious and Organised Crime in the Waste Sector*, November 2018) recorded that control over our waste exports suffers from the same weakness as the domestic waste management system, with the added complication of international jurisdictions. In particular, the review stated that '*Waste exports provide ample opportunity for organised criminals to operate at scale, with a veil of legitimacy and with limited probability of detection'* (p 11). The review also noted the current inadequacy of data concerning the export of non-hazardous wastes: *'With the exception of hazardous waste exports, which require prior approval from the UK competent authorities, data on the majority of UK waste exports is poor. The EU system requires an exporter to attach an "Annex VII" form to waste exports, similar to a Waste Transfer Note. In contrast to exporters in Scotland and Northern Ireland, exporters in England and Wales are not required to submit Annex VII forms to the Environment Agency. As a result, we do not know how much waste for recycling is leaving the UK, who is exporting it or where it is going. Reliable data is also lacking for all waste exported under Green List controls, because although HMRC estimates the total volume and value from tax receipts, there is no UK-wide obligation for exporters to provide this data to UK regulators'* (p 9).

The 'Green List' refers back to the European Union's Waste Shipment Regulation (1013/2006), which introduced two lists for types of waste shipments: an Amber List and a Green List. The latter concerns the majority of shipments of non-hazardous wastes to EU/OECD countries and some non-OECD countries. These shipments can be imported or exported for recovery without prior written notification or consent from the competent authorities.

Three regimes govern the UK international trade in waste:

- The Basel Convention is concerned with international movements of hazardous waste. The overarching objective of the Basel Convention is to protect human health and the environment against the adverse effects of hazardous wastes. Its scope of application covers a wide range of wastes defined as 'hazardous wastes' based on their origin and/or composition and their characteristics, as well as two types of waste defined as 'other wastes' – household waste and incinerator ash. The provisions of the Basel Convention are focused on or around the following principal aims:
  - the reduction of hazardous waste generation and the promotion of environmentally sound management of hazardous wastes, wherever the place of disposal;
  - the restriction of transboundary movements of hazardous wastes except where it is perceived to be in accordance with the principles of environmentally sound management; and
  - a regulatory system applying to cases where transboundary movements are permissible.
- OECD Decision Rules are concerned with trade in waste which is exported for recovery between OECD countries. Since the creation of the OECD in 1961, around 460 substantive legal instruments have been developed within its framework. The substantive OECD legal instruments can be divided into five categories:
  - Decisions are adopted by the OECD Council and are legally binding on all Members except those who abstain at the time of adoption. The Decisions set out specific rights and obligations, and can contain monitoring mechanisms.
  - Recommendations are adopted by the OECD Council but are not legally binding. They represent a political commitment to the principles they contain and entail an expectation that adherents will do their best to implement them.
  - Substantive Outcome Documents are adopted by individual adherents rather than by an OECD body. They usually set general principles or long-term goals.
  - International Agreements, which are negotiated and concluded within the framework of the Organisation and are legally binding on the parties.
  - Arrangement, Understanding and Others. A catch-all category for other types of substantive legal instruments that have been developed within the OECD framework over time. An example would be the 'International Understanding on Maritime Transport Principles'.

- The EU Waste Shipment Regulations implement the Basel Convention and OECD Decision for EU Member States. These set the procedures and processes that govern the shipment of waste into, within and from the EU.

In the UK, the Transfrontier Shipment of Waste Regulations 2007 were made for the purpose of implementing and enforcing the provision of the Waste Shipment Regulation (1013/2006). The Regulations set out offences and penalties, and designate the competent authorities for enforcing the Waste Shipment Regulation.

In explaining the rationale behind the provisions in s 62, the Government noted the following in relation to s 62: '*Although the government already has a power to prohibit or restrict the import or export of waste under section 141 of the EPA 1990, this power requires amendment so that it can be used to make provision about, or connected with, the regulation of waste imports and exports and the transit of waste for export. This will enable government to amend existing regulations on international waste shipments such as the TSWR 2007. This clause updates the power so that it comprehensively covers issues such as transit of waste for export, civil sanctions and fee charging. In particular, the updated power includes a power for the Secretary of State to make regulations about the transit of waste for export, thus ensuring that the power under section 141 is broad enough to cover the different phases of an international shipment of waste, so that the power can be used effectively. The section 141 power is widened to encompass powers corresponding to provisions already in the TSWR 2007, including powers to create civil sanctions, powers for the Secretary of State to issue general directions as to the exercise by waste regulation authorities of their functions including in connection with the regulation of the transit of waste for export, and powers to provide for the charging by waste regulation authorities of fees or charges payable by persons involved in the importation, exportation or transit of waste for export. The powers further make provision authorising the disclosure of information by Officers of Revenue and Customs to waste regulation authorities, and conferring functions relating to the seizure and detention of waste on customs officials*' (Environment Bill: Memorandum from the Department for the Environment, Food and Rural Affairs to the Delegated Powers and Regulatory Reform Committee, 27 May 2021).

The Transfrontier Shipment of Waste Regulations 2007 were made under s 2(2) of the European Communities Act 1972. In justifying the updated powers, the Government has identified that now that the UK has left the EU, it is appropriate to ensure that there are effective powers to amend or replace those Regulations, to ensure that the manner in which international waste shipments are regulated can '*keep pace with the methods and practices of those engaged in illegal waste shipment activity*' (ibid). The Government cited the fact that the level of Fixed Penalty Notices provided for in the Transfrontier Shipment of Waste Regulations, set at £300, could not be amended without the use of s 2(2) of the European Communities Act 1972, which has now been repealed.

Powers to Regulate the Importation or Exportation of Waste or the Transit of Waste for Export

S 141 of the Environmental Protection Act 1990 contains a power to make regulations to prohibit or restrict waste imports and exports. This section amends s 141 to allow regulations to be made to regulate waste imports or exports or the transit of waste for export.

The key changes are therefore to replace 'prohibit or restrict' with 'regulate' and to expand the scope of the regulations to include transit as defined in sub-s (8). The term 'regulate' includes the possibility of banning or restricting waste imports and exports and making provision on the landing and loading of waste in the UK, loading of waste for export or the transit of waste for export. Functions may be conferred on the Environment Agency, Natural Resources Wales, the Scottish Environment Protection Agency or the Department of Agriculture, Environment and Rural Affairs in Northern Ireland for the enforcement of regulations, including the discretion as to how those functions should be exercised (although these amendments also allow for the possibility of directions being issued on how such functions should be exercised). Fees may be charged in connection with the exercise of those functions.

The latter extension of scope may be considered consistent with the decision of the Court of Appeal in *R v KV* [2011] EWCA Crim 2342, in which it was confirmed that the action of waste leaving the country has both a transactional and a temporal character. The Court held that 'export' is a process commencing once the waste is destined for another country at its point of origin and continuing until the waste reaches its ultimate destination in the foreign country. However, the amendment will also be seen as an expansion on the position at the European level, which excluded the transport of waste through the European Community from the definition of 'export'.

Regulations may be made to allow HMRC to disclose information to the various regulatory bodies and to confer functions on customs officials in relation to seizing or detaining waste that has arrived at or entered into the UK or will leave the UK.

As with many of the regulations permitted under the Environment Act, specific provision for civil sanctions can also be made for conduct relating to the transfrontier shipments of waste.

The section also contains a Henry VIII power to make consequential, supplementary, incidental, transitional or saving provision, including provision amending, repealing or revoking primary legislation or retained direct EU legislation. Any future additional restriction or requirements relating to waste shipments will need to be harmonised with those provisions already contained within the Transfrontier Shipment of Waste Regulations 2007 and any relevant retained direct EU legislation or primary legislation. DEFRA has committed to a review of the regulatory framework covering waste exports and it can be anticipated that this is a key area for future legislation, not least because the introduction of a ban on the export of plastic waste to non-OECD countries was an explicit commitment in the Conservative Party Manifesto for the 2019 General Election.

63 Regulations under the Environmental Protection Act 1990

(1) The Environmental Protection Act 1990 is amended as follows.

(2) After section 160 insert—

"160A Regulations and orders

(1) Regulations and orders under this Act are subject to the negative procedure, other than—

(a) regulations or orders subject to the affirmative procedure by virtue of subsection (2);

(b) regulations made by a Northern Ireland department under section 156 (power to give effect to retained EU obligations and international obligations);

(c) an order under section 164(3) (commencement);

(d) an order under paragraph 4 of Schedule 3 (statutory nuisance).

(2) Regulations or orders made under a section listed in the first column of the following Table that are of the description specified in the second column are subject to the affirmative procedure—

Section	*Description of regulations or orders*
34D (prohibition on disposal of food waste to sewer: Wales)	any regulations under that section.
45AA(10) (separate collection of waste: Wales)	any regulations under that section.
78M(4) (offences of not complying with a remediation notice)	any order under that section.
79(1ZA) (statutory nuisance)	any regulations under that section.
80ZA(11) (fixed penalty notices)	any regulations under that section.
88A (litter from vehicles: England)	regulations that include provision falling within section 88A(3)(a) or (6).

(3) Regulations and orders made under this Act by the Secretary of State or the Welsh Ministers are to be made by statutory instrument, other than an order under paragraph 4 of Schedule 3.

(4) Where regulations or orders under this Act made or to be made by the Secretary of State—

(a) are subject to the negative procedure, the statutory instrument containing them is subject to annulment in pursuance of a resolution of either House of Parliament;

(b) are subject to the affirmative procedure, they may not be made unless a draft of the statutory instrument containing them has been laid before, and approved by a resolution of, each House of Parliament.

(5) Where regulations or orders under this Act made or to be made by the Welsh Ministers—

(a) are subject to the negative procedure, the statutory instrument containing them is subject to annulment in pursuance of a resolution of Senedd Cymru;

(b) are subject to the affirmative procedure, they may not be made unless a draft of the statutory instrument containing them has been laid before, and approved by a resolution of, Senedd Cymru.

(6) See sections 28 and 29 of the Interpretation and Legislative Reform (Scotland) Act 2010 (asp 10) for the meaning of "the negative procedure" and "the affirmative procedure" in relation to regulations or orders under this Act made or to be made by the Scottish Ministers.

(7) Any provision that may be made by regulations or order under this Act subject to the negative procedure may be made subject to the affirmative procedure."

(3) In section 45B omit subsection (3).

(4) In section 78M omit subsection (7).

(5) In section 161 (regulations, orders and directions)—

(a) for the heading substitute "Directions";

(b) omit subsections (1) to (4).

In force 9 November 2021

Application E W S NI

This section inserts a new s 160A into the Environmental Protection Act 1990. Sub-s (1) of the new s 160A sets out the regulations and orders under the Act that are subject to the negative resolution procedure, subject to the exemptions listed in sub-ss (1)(a)–(d). Sub-s (1)(a) sets out that regulations and orders listed in sub-s (2) are subject to the affirmative resolution procedure. Sub-s (1)(b) relates to Northern Ireland. Sub-ss (1)(c) and (d) set out that neither commencement orders nor orders under para 4 of Sch 3 to the Act (statutory nuisance) are subject to the negative resolution procedure. Such orders are not subject to any parliamentary procedure.

The remaining parts of the section provide specific requirements for regulations and orders made under this Act by the Secretary of State or the Welsh Ministers.

Waste enforcement and regulation

64 Powers to make charging schemes

(1) The Environment Act 1995 is amended as follows.

(2) In section 41(1) (powers to make charging schemes) after paragraph (m) insert—

"(n) as a means of recovering costs incurred by it in performing functions conferred by regulations made under Schedule 4 or 5 to the Environment Act 2021, the Agency, the Natural Resources Body for Wales or SEPA may require the payment to it of such charges as may from time to time be prescribed;

(o) as a means of recovering costs incurred by it in performing functions conferred by the End-of-Life Vehicles (Producer Responsibility) Regulations 2005 (S.I. 2005/263), the Agency, the Natural Resources Body for Wales or SEPA may require the payment to it of such charges as may from time to time be prescribed;

(p) as a means of recovering costs incurred by it in performing functions conferred by the Waste Electrical and Electronic Equipment Regulations 2013 (S.I. 2013/3113), the Agency, the Natural Resources Body for Wales or SEPA may require the payment to it of such charges as may from time to time be prescribed;

(q) as a means of recovering costs incurred by it in performing functions relating to section 33(1) of the Environmental Protection Act 1990, the Agency or the Natural Resoucres Body for Wales may require the payment to it of such charges as may from time to time be prescribed;

(r) as a means of recovering costs incurred by it in performing functions relating to regulation 12(1) of the Environmental Permitting (England and Wales) Regulations 2016 (S.I. 2016/1154) in relation to a regulated facility which is a waste operation (within the meaning of those Regulations), the Agency or the Natural Resources Body for Wales may require the payment to it of such charges as may from time to time be prescribed;".

(3) In section 56(1) (interpretation)—

(a) in the definition of "environmental licence", in the application of Part 1 of the Act in relation to an appropriate agency—

(i) in paragraph (j) for the words from "WEEE" to the end substitute "waste operation (within the meaning of those Regulations),";

(ii) omit paragraphs (l) to (o);

(b) in the definition of "environmental licence", in the application of Part 1 of the Act in relation to the Scottish Environment Protection Agency, omit paragraphs (l) to (o).

(4) Until the repeal of section 93 of the Environment Act 1995 ("the 1995 Act") by section 50 of this Act is fully in force, section 41(1)(n) of the 1995 Act has effect as if the reference to Schedule 4 to this Act included a reference to section 93 of the 1995 Act.

In force	E: 24 January 2022; W: 7 March 2022; S: day to be appointed by Scottish Ministers
Application	E W S

Background

Producer responsibility schemes are already in place for four waste streams, namely packaging waste, end-of-life vehicles, batteries and accumulators, and waste electrical and electronic equipment. By the end of 2025 it is intended that DEFRA will have reviewed and consulted on measures for five new waste streams, namely textiles, bulky waste (including furniture and mattresses), construction and demolition materials, vehicle tyres and fishing gear.

Where the Environment Agency or its devolved equivalent is, or is appointed, regulator for a producer responsibility scheme, it will need to charge for the enforcement duties that it undertakes. The Government noted that the *'new powers will allow the Agencies to recover their reasonable costs of appropriate investigation, intervention and enforcement of current producer responsibility systems and, as and when they are established, new, EPR [Extended Producer Responsibility] schemes'* (Environment Bill: Memorandum from the Department for the Environment, Food and Rural Affairs to the Delegated Powers and Regulatory Reform Committee, 27 May 2021).

The Agencies can already charge producers fees for the current schemes that they regulate. However, this happens in different ways and to different extents depending on the scheme. The Commons Library analysis of the Environment Bill 2019–20 (Briefing Paper CBP 8824, 18 February 2020) states that the new charging powers are intended to make charging more consistent across the current producer responsibility schemes, and future new schemes, where one of the Agencies is the regulator (p 100).

In addition to producer responsibility, the 2018 review commissioned by the Home Office (*Independent Review into Serious and Organised Crime in the Waste Sector*, November 2018) identified three priority areas for potential reform in relation to the funding of the Environment Agency. These were:

- Permit fees. It was identified that the charges for permits and licences are set at the level required to secure 'compliance', but that this did not include 'enforcement' activities, such as investigation or prosecution. Enforcement at illegal sites, exempt sites and for illegal waste carriers, brokers and dealers – who do not pay an annual subsistence fee – depends entirely on government funding. It was estimated that if permit revenues were expanded to cover the cost of all waste crime enforcement, permit fees would need to increase by around 50 per cent.
- Tax allocation. This forms the basis of the current business model for the entire waste industry. It was noted that to defend the gains made since the introduction of the Landfill Tax, more rigorous regulation and effective policing of the sector is required.
- Role of industry. It was suggested that industry recognises the value of strengthening defences against illegal activity which undercuts their margins and noted potential support for a voluntary levy.

The report made no reference to the potential for the Environment Agency to recover its costs following a successful prosecution.

In light of these observations, s 64(2)(q) and (r) extends the power of Agencies to make charging schemes for performing functions relating to s 33(1) of the Environmental Protection Act 1990 and reg 12(1) of the Environmental Permitting (England and Wales) Regulations 2016.

Powers to Make Charging Schemes: s 64

Sub-s (2) inserts five new paragraphs into s 41(1) of the Environment Act 1995, which creates powers to make charging schemes. Each of these powers is conferred on some or all of the Agencies.

Para (n) provides a power to make charging schemes to recover costs incurred by the relevant national authority in performing functions conferred by regulations made under Sch 4 relating to producer responsibility obligations.

Paras (o) and (p) provide the same power as (n), but in relation to the End-of-Life Vehicles (Producer Responsibility) Regulations 2005 and the Waste Electrical and Electronic Equipment Regulations 2013.

Paras (q) and (r) provide the power to create charging schemes to recover costs incurred by the Environment Agency and Natural Resources Wales when performing functions in relation to s 33(1) Environmental Protection Act 1990 and Reg 12(1) Environmental Permitting (England and Wales) Regulations 2016. The Explanatory Notes identify that this will allow fees to be charged to site operators for interventions at unpermitted waste sites or those in breach of a permit.

The last two are particularly interesting. By way of example, the Environment Agency already receives fees for applications for environmental permits and subsistence fees, which ought on any view to include a proportion for acting as a regulator (consistent with the observations made by the independent review into serious and organised crime in the waste sector and the recommendation that the Environment Agency and HM Treasury should calculate the cost of ensuring compliance across the sector as a whole, including enforcement action against illegal sites, and consider whether the additional income might be raised in association with the permitting system). Those fees increase for poorly performing sites, justifiable on the grounds that poorly performing sites require additional interventions. However, here scope is being provided to the Environment Agency to charge further fees to site operators, to include situations where there is an identifiable breach of permit or other enforcement issue. Whilst this may be considered similar to the 'Fees for Intervention' scheme operated by the Health and Safety Executive, such an analysis would ignore the existence of the current charging scheme. Care may need to be taken to avoid the risk of double recovery or, alternatively, it may need to be made explicit that certain types of regulatory involvement by the Environment Agency attract multiple fees. It raises the question of how such charges will be determined in the event that the site operator disputes the fact of a permit breach and what will be the interrelationship between any potential charging scheme and the ability to recover costs in criminal courts following a successful prosecution.

Waste sites that are wholly unpermitted are likely to result in further enforcement action, so it will be interesting to consider how any charging scheme will take this into account.

Sub-s (3)(a)(i) extends the interpretation of the definition of 'environmental licence' found in s 56(1)(j) to include any waste operation with a registered exemption, to allow for charges to be prescribed for them under s 41(2) of the Environment Act 1995.

Sub-s (4) ensures that the power to create a charging scheme in the new s 41(1)(n) can apply to functions conferred by regulations made under s 93 of the Environment Act 1995, as well as Sch 4 to this Environment Act, until such time as s 93 is fully repealed.

65 Waste charging: Northern Ireland

(1) In the Waste and Contaminated Land (Northern Ireland) Order 1997 (S.I. 1997/2778 (N.I. 19)), after Article 76 insert—

"Charging schemes

76A Power to make charging schemes

(1) As a means of recovering costs incurred by it in performing any functions mentioned in paragraph (2), the Department may require the payment to it of such charges as may be specified in or determined under a scheme made by the Department under this Article (referred to in this Article as a "charging scheme").

(2) The functions referred to in paragraph (1) are—

(a) functions related to—

(i) Article 4(1); or

(ii) regulation 18(1) of the Waste Management Licensing Regulations (Northern Ireland) 2003;

(b) functions conferred by regulations made under Article 5G;

(c) functions conferred by regulations made under Schedule 4 or 5 to the Environment Act 2021;

(d) functions conferred by the End-of-Life Vehicles Regulations 2003;

(e) functions conferred by the End-of-Life Vehicles (Producer Responsibility) Regulations 2005;

(f) functions conferred by the Waste Batteries and Accumulators Regulations 2009;

(g) functions conferred by the Waste Electrical and Electronic Equipment Regulations 2013;

(h) functions in connection with the regulation of the importation or exportation of waste or the transit of waste for export.

(3) In sub-paragraph (h) of paragraph (2) "importation", "exportation", "transit of waste for export" and "waste" have the meaning they have in section 141 of the Environmental Protection Act 1990.

(4) A charging scheme must specify, in relation to any charge prescribed by the scheme, the description of person who is liable to pay the charge.

(5) A charging scheme may—

(a) make different provision for different cases, including different provision in relation to different persons, circumstances or localities;

(b) provide for the times at which, and the manner in which, charges are to be paid;

(c) revoke or amend any previous charging scheme;

(d) contain supplemental, incidental, consequential or transitional provision for the purposes of the scheme.

(6) Before making a charging scheme the Department must consult such persons as appear to the Department to be appropriate.

(7) The Department must, when it makes or amends a charging scheme—

(a) lay a copy of the scheme or amendments before the Assembly, and

(b) publish the scheme or the amendments."

(2) Until the repeal of Article 3 of the Producer Responsibility Obligations (Northern Ireland) Order 1998 (S.I. 1998/1762 (N.I. 16)) ("the 1998 Order") by section 50 of this Act is fully in force, Article 76A(2)(c) of the Waste and Contaminated Land (Northern Ireland) Order 1997 (S.I. 1997/2778 (N.I. 19)) has effect as if the reference to Schedule 4 to this Act included a reference to Article 3 of the 1998 Order.

(3) The Waste Management Licensing Regulations (Northern Ireland) 2003 (S.R. (N.I.) 2003 No. 493) are amended as follows.

(4) In regulation 17 (exemptions from waste management licensing), in paragraph (4)—

(a) in sub-paragraph (b) for "and the fee (if any) required under regulation 18(12) have" substitute "has";

(b) after sub-paragraph (b) insert "; and

(c) any fee required under regulation 20B has been paid."

(5) In regulation 18 (registration in connection with exempt activities)—

(a) in paragraph (3)(d) for "a payment of any fee in respect of each place where any such exempt activity is being carried on" substitute "payment, in respect of each place where any such exempt activity is being carried on, of any fee that may be required under regulation 20B";

(b) in paragraph (9) for "and 47" substitute ", 47 and 49 to 52";

(c) in paragraph (11)(b) for "specified in accordance with paragraph (12)" substitute "required under regulation 20B";

(d) omit paragraph (12).

(6) After regulation 20A insert—

"20B Fees and charges for registration in connection with exempt activities

(1) There are to be charged by and paid to the Department—

(a) in respect of applications for registration, and

(b) in respect of the subsistence of registrations,

such fees and charges as may be provided for by a scheme under paragraph (2) (but this is subject to regulations 18(4A) and 19(2)).

(2) The Department may make, and from time to time revise, a scheme ("a charging scheme") specifying—

(a) fees in respect of applications for registration, payable to the Department, by the applicant, in respect of each place to which an application relates;

(b) charges in respect of the subsistence of registrations, payable to the Department by persons to whom registrations have been issued.

(3) The Department must, when it makes or amends a charging scheme—

(a) lay a copy of the scheme or amendments before the Assembly, and

(b) publish the scheme or the amendments.

(4) A charging scheme may in particular—

(a) provide for fees or charges payable in respect of applications or the subsistence of registrations to differ according to the activities to which the applications or registrations relate (including by providing for no fee or charge in the case of some activities);

(b) provide for reductions of fees where conditions specified in the scheme are met;

(c) provide for the times at which, and the manner in which, payments of fees or charges are to be made;

(d) make such incidental, supplementary and transitional provision as appears to the Department to be appropriate.

(5) If it appears to the Department that a person to whom a registration has been issued has failed to pay a charge due in respect of the subsistence of the registration, the Department may, by notice in writing served on that person, revoke the registration.

(6) In this regulation—

(a) "registration" means registration under regulation 18;

(b) any reference to an application for registration includes an application for renewal of a registration."

Definitions

'importation'	s 141(6) EPA 1990
'exportation'	s 141(6) EPA 1990
'transit of waste for export'	s 141(6) EPA 1990
'waste'	s 141(6) EPA 1990

In force:	28 February 2022
Application	NI

Background

As set out above, it is intended that regulatory bodies are given the power to create charging schemes to cover existing and new producer responsibility schemes and costs of other functions. The exact basis of the functions for Northern Ireland is slightly different to the functions listed in the previous section as it includes some Northern Ireland-only legislation, but it includes unauthorised disposal and treatment of waste, extended producer responsibility, the registration of exempt waste management activities and the electronic waste tracking system.

Waste Charging: Northern Ireland: s 65

S 65 amends the Waste and Contaminated Land (Northern Ireland) Order 1997 and the Waste Management Licensing Regulations (Northern Ireland) 2003 to supplement existing charging powers available to the Department of Agriculture, Environment and Rural Affairs.

There will be a power to prescribe charges to be paid to the Department in relation to costs incurred by it in performing the functions set out at para (2).

Sub-s (6) creates a new regulation 20B in the Waste Management Licensing Regulations (Northern Ireland) 2003, providing the Department with the power to make a charging scheme in respect of fees and charges for registration in connection with exempt activities. Different fees can be provided for, depending on the nature of the activities, including a reduction in fees where an applicant is applying for multiple exemptions.

66 Enforcement powers

Schedule 10 amends legislation about enforcement powers in relation to waste and other environmental matters.

In force: 9 January 2022

Application E W

Background

The provisions in this section largely derive from recommendation in the 2018 review commissioned by the Home Office (*Independent Review into Serious and Organised Crime in the Waste Sector*, November 2018). The review noted that: '*In England, the [Environment] Agency acts as regulator for the waste sector, and as such, most of its powers relate to ensuring compliance with regulation. Policing criminality in the sector requires a different focus. While the Agency has acquired (and lost) police-type powers during the course of its existence, it relies heavily on police bodies to investigate and prosecute serious criminality. The ability of the Agency to respond to serious and organised waste crime is therefore limited by a lack of powers concerning prevention, investigation and early intervention*' (p 15).

Specific areas of weakness included a lack of surveillance powers, a high burden of evidence prior to the use of stop notices, a requirement for an Agency officer to be present for the police to be able to seize a vehicle involved in waste crime, aged investigatory powers and underused powers of financial investigation.

Directly relevant to this section, the report stated: '*The power for the police to seize vehicles involved in waste crime currently requires an Agency officer to be present, with public funds paying for the recovery of the vehicle. This is in contrast to other types of offence, such as illegal parking, where the offender must cover the costs of storage and recovery of their vehicle*' (p 16).

The review recommended that DEFRA update vehicle seizure provisions to allow police to seize a vehicle involved in waste crime without requiring an Environment Agency or Natural Resources Wales enforcement officer to be present, and to require the offender to cover the costs of storage and recovery of their vehicle.

The review also stated: '*The current powers of entry and inspection require the [Environment] Agency to give seven days' notice to enter residential premises, even with a magistrates' warrant. Officers must also show their authorisation to an occupier before the powers can be exercised. This creates an obvious opportunity to hide, remove or tamper with evidence before inspection can occur, and is a particular issue with remote or unstaffed sites, because the Agency officer must "present the warrant"*' (p 16).

The required notice period raised its head in *R (on the application of Allensway Recycling Ltd) v Environment Agency* [2016] 1 WLR 1903, where the Court of Appeal (Civil Division) held that a warrant obtained under Sch 18 of the Environment Act 1995 did not confer a stand-alone power of entry, free from conditions set down in s 108. Despite the fact that Sch 18(2) allowed a warrant to be issued in circumstances where notice would at best be pointless or undesirable, this did not mean that the interpretation of s 108 could be strained to avoid the clear meaning of the statutory wording. Seven days' notice was still required in the case of residential premises, despite the fact that a warrant had been obtained. The Court commented that, putting the correct construction of s 108 to one side, the fact that the Environment Agency can request the police to apply for a search warrant under the Police and Criminal Evidence Act 1984, authorising entry without notice, was not regarded as a satisfactory alternative to the Environment Agency being able to exercise its own powers under s 108. Nonetheless, that unsatisfactory position did not assist in the correct construction of s 108.

The review recommended that DEFRA should amend s 108 of the Environment Act 1995 to allow the Environment Agency to search premises and seize materials, remove the requirement to give seven days' notice to enter residential properties and remove the requirements for officers to show authorisation at unmanned or remote sites.

The review also recommended a low-level financial penalty, such as a Fixed Penalty Notice, for the clear and deliberate misdescription of waste, and for the Home Office to provide regulations under Part 3 of the Investigatory Powers Act 2016 to allow the Environment Agency to acquire communications data to tackle serious and organised waste crime.

Sch 10 amends existing legislation in relation to enforcement powers.

Seizing Vehicles

Paras 1 and 2 make minor amendments to the practical effects of seizing a vehicle by amending both s 5(6) of the Control of Pollution (Amendment) Act 1989 and s 34B(6) of the Environmental Protection Act 1990, and by not requiring the presence of an authorised officer of an enforcement authority with a police constable at the point of seizure in order to ensure that the vehicle is seized on behalf of that enforcement authority, provided that an authorised officer has requested seizure.

Directions Relating to Waste

Para 3 provides more expansive powers to the Secretary of State or the Welsh Ministers to direct others to require waste to be accepted, treated, disposed of or delivered. Registered waste carriers can be directed to collect waste and deliver it to a specified person on specified terms, and the person keeping such waste on their land or the owner or occupier of the land can be directed to facilitate that collection. The person keeping the waste or the owner or occupier of land can be directed to pay the reasonable costs of the waste carrier and the reasonable costs of the person to whom the waste is delivered.

Entering Premises

The remaining paragraphs of Sch 10 amend s 108 of the Environment Act 1995.

Where an authorised officer has the power to enter premises under s 108(4)(a), namely at any reasonable time (or in an emergency, at any time and, if need be, by force) where he has reason to believe it is necessary for him to enter (and necessity remains a precondition) for the purposes of making such examination and investigation as may in any circumstances be necessary (the second necessity precondition), it is intended that the authorised officer should have the power to search the premises, seize and remove documents or anything else found on the premises, require information stored electronically to be produced in a form in which it can be removed and be able to operate equipment found on the premises for the purposes of producing such information in such a form (for example, a printer).

This clarification is welcome, as it has long been the subject of debate as to the extent of the powers of authorised officers when on premises in circumstances where the authorised officer is not accompanied by the police. The authorised officer does not need a warrant, but must have reasonable grounds for believing that there is evidence of a failure to comply with either pollution control enactments or flood risk activity enactments and that exercising the power is necessary to prevent that evidence from being concealed, lost, altered or destroyed.

This last requirement could be interpreted restrictively. It is possible to foresee that where a person refuses to assist, it can be inferred that there is a risk of losing the information. But what if no one is on the premises? How would the officer come to the conclusion that the information sought would not be provided on request? And what would be the sanction for a breach of this part? In *Walker v Chelmsford City Council* [2020] EWHC 635 (Admin), the High Court held that a power to compel a person to answer questions, found in s 108(4)(j), could not be exercised independently of the power to enter premises and only applied to a face-to-face request for information. This ruling was significant, as para 4 of Sch 18 to the Environment Act 1995 provides that any information obtained in consequence of the exercise of a relevant power under s 108 (subject to s 108(12), privilege against self-incrimination), with or without consent, shall be admissible in evidence against that or any other person. In the context of answers under compulsion, this provides a clear exception to the rules on hearsay in criminal proceedings. The consequence of breach therefore is likely to be an issue on admissibility in legal proceedings. However, even then it is open to a court to rule the material admissible. There is no provision that would render the evidence obtained automatically inadmissible.

A carve-out is provided for 'protected material' – defined as 'privileged material', 'excluded material' within the meaning of s 11 of the Police and Criminal Evidence Act 1984 (which includes personal records which a person has acquired or created in the course of any trade, business, profession or other occupation or for the purposes of any paid or unpaid office and which he holds in confidence) and 'journalistic material' within the meaning of s 13 of the Police and Criminal Evidence Act 1984 that does not fall within the definition of 'excluded material'.

S 11(2) of the Police and Criminal Evidence Act 1984 states that a person holds material other than journalistic material in confidence for the purposes of s 11 if he holds it subject:

(a) to an express or implied undertaking to hold it in confidence; or
(b) to a restriction on disclosure or an obligation of secrecy contained in any enactment, including an enactment contained in an Act passed after the Police and Criminal Evidence Act 1984.

Material that falls within this definition may not be used for the purposes of an examination or investigation under sub-s 108(4)(c) and must be returned to the premises from which it was removed, or to the person who had possession or control of it immediately before it was removed, as soon as reasonably practicable after it is identified as protected material.

A new definition of 'document' that includes anything in which information of any description is recorded (by any means) and any part of such a thing will be added to sub-s (15).

Finally, Sch 18 is amended to permit a warrant to be issued to an English or Welsh authorised person to exercise the powers in s 108(4)(ka) in accordance with that warrant and, if need be, by force, subject to the caveat that there must be reasonable grounds for believing that there is material likely to be of substantial value to an examination or investigation and that either it is impracticable to communicate with a person entitled to grant access or that access is unlikely to be granted unless a warrant is produced.

67 Enforcement powers: Northern Ireland

(1) Article 27 of the Waste and Contaminated Land (Northern Ireland) Order 1997 (S.I. 1997/2778 (N.I. 19)) (power to give directions) is amended as follows.

(2) In paragraph (2) omit the words from "with a view" to the end.

(3) After paragraph (2) insert—

"(2A) The Department may by notice—

(a) direct a registered carrier to collect controlled waste which is being kept in or on specified land and deliver it to a specified person on specified terms;

(b) direct any person who—

(i) is keeping controlled waste in or on any land, or

(ii) owns or occupies land in or on which controlled waste is being kept,

to facilitate collection of the waste by a specified registered carrier to whom a direction in respect of the waste is given under sub-paragraph (a)."

(4) In paragraph (3) for "paragraph (1) or (2)" substitute "this Article".

(5) In paragraph (4), for "of treating or disposing of" substitute "in relation to".

(6) After paragraph (4) insert—

"(4A) A direction under paragraph (2A)(b) may require the person to whom it is given—

(a) to pay to the specified registered carrier the reasonable costs of collecting and delivering the waste;

(b) to pay to the specified person to whom the waste is delivered ("P") the reasonable costs incurred by P in relation to the waste (including any costs P is required by a direction under this Article to pay to another person)."

(7) In paragraph (5) for "paragraph (1) or (2)" substitute "this Article".

(8) In paragraph (6) for "paragraph (1) or (2)" substitute "this Article".

(9) In paragraph (7) for the words from ", where" to the end substitute "pay any costs mentioned in paragraph (4) or (4A)."

(10) For paragraph (8) substitute—

"(8) In this Article—

"specified" means specified in a direction under this Article;

"registered carrier" means a person registered under Article 39 as a carrier of controlled waste."

Definitions

'specified'	s 67(8)
'registered carrier'	s 67(8)

In force:	28 February 2022
Application	NI

Background

Art 27 of the Waste and Contaminated Land (Northern Ireland) Order 1997 provides DAERA with a power to require waste to be accepted, treated, disposed of or delivered in relation to waste management licence holders or in relation to those who keep controlled waste on their land.

The Environment Bill: Memorandum from the Department for the Environment, Food and Rural Affairs to the Delegated Powers and Regulatory Reform Committee, dated 27 May 2021, records that unlike the powers of direction in s 57 of the Environmental Protection Act 1990, Art 27 powers are routinely used by DAERA's Environmental Crime Unit for the remediation of sites, on average four times a month.

However, there is a gap in DAERA's current powers as they are unable to direct a registered waste carrier to collect and transport waste.

Sub-s (2) amends para 2 of Art 27 to account for circumstances in which waste might be taken to an appropriate storage site in the first instance, or otherwise not directly treated or disposed of. The previous wording restricted the direction to circumstances where the receiver of the waste was to treat or dispose of that waste themselves.

Sub-s (3) inserts a new paragraph (2A) into Art 27. This allows the Department to direct a registered carrier of controlled waste to collect specified waste and deliver it to a specified site. Sub-para (b) allows the Department to direct a keeper of controlled waste, or the owner or occupier of the land on which the waste is being kept, to facilitate the collection of the waste by the specified waste carrier.

Sub-s (6) allows for the Department to direct the keeper of the controlled waste or the owner or the occupier of the land on which the waste is being kept to pay the waste carrier's reasonable costs and in (b) the reasonable costs of the person the waste is delivered to.

68 Littering enforcement

(1) Part 4 of the Environmental Protection Act 1990 is amended as follows.

(2) In Section 88 (fixed penalty notices for leaving litter), for subsection (11) substitute—

"(11) The appropriate person may by regulations provide that—

(a) an authorised officer of a litter authority must meet such conditions as may be prescribed in the regulations;

(b) if an authorised officer of a litter authority fails to meet any such condition, the authority must revoke the officer's authorisation.

(12) Regulations under subsection (11) may make different provision for different cases.

(13) Before making regulations under subsection (11), the appropriate person must consult such persons as the appropriate person thinks appropriate."

(3) After section 88A insert—

"88B Guidance on littering enforcement in England and Wales

(1) The appropriate person may issue guidance to litter authorities on the exercise of littering enforcement functions by those authorities and authorised officers of those authorities.

(2) A litter authority must have regard to that guidance when exercising any of its littering enforcement functions.

(3) The appropriate person may revise any guidance issued under this section at any time.

(4) Before issuing guidance, or revised guidance, under this section the appropriate person must consult such persons as the appropriate person thinks appropriate.

(5) The Secretary of State must lay before Parliament and publish guidance, and any revised guidance, issued by the Secretary of State under this section.

(6) The Welsh Ministers must lay before Senedd Cymru and publish guidance, and any revised guidance, issued by the Welsh Ministers under this section.

(7) In this section—

"authorised officer", in relation to a litter authority, means a person who is an authorised officer in relation to that authority for the purposes of—

(a) section 88 (fixed penalty notices for littering, see subsection (10) of that section),

(b) section 88A (fixed penalty notices for littering from vehicles in England, see subsection (4) of that section), or

(c) Schedule 3A (distribution of free printed matter, see paragraph 8 of that Schedule);

"littering enforcement function" means—

(a) any function of a litter authority, or of an authorised officer of that authority, conferred by or under sections 87 to 88A or Schedule 3A, or

(b) any function exercised for purposes connected with any of those sections or that Schedule."

(4) In section 98(1A) (definition of appropriate person), in paragraph (b) for "National Assembly for Wales" substitute "Welsh Ministers".

In force	E: day to be appointed by Secretary of State; W: day to be appointed by Welsh Ministers
Application	E W

Background

The Government's *Litter Strategy for England* (April 2017) identified that there are public misconceptions about enforcement activity against littering. In particular, surveys suggested that many people are unaware that they can be fined for dropping litter. There was a concern that media coverage of enforcement activity focuses on enforcement activity that is perceived as disproportionate and therefore undermines public confidence in its legitimacy.

The Strategy records that, '*Subject to consultation, we also intend to issue stronger guidance to enforcement authorities on the use of these enforcement powers. That guidance will make clear that fixed penalties should only be issued when it is in the public interest to do so, and when it is proportionate to do so. Our policy is clear that under no circumstances should councils view the use of fixed penalties for these offences as a means to generate income*' (para 4.2.1).

Consultation was conducted between April and June 2018. The Government subsequently updated the *Code of Practice on Litter and Refuse* to include an enforcement guidance document.

The Government has identified that the changes introduced by s 68 are to '*ensure that skills, quality and professionalism of authorised officers of litter authorities are maintained*' (Environment Bill: Memorandum from the Department for the Environment, Food and Rural Affairs to the Delegated Powers and Regulatory Reform Committee, 27 May 2021). It is also determined that flexibility is needed to change or update prescribed conditions in future, hence the justification for the use of regulations.

Littering Enforcement: s 68

Sub-s (11) allowed for regulations to prescribe conditions to be satisfied before a parish or community council could authorise an enforcement officer to be able to issue fixed penalty notices for leaving litter.

However, it would appear that it is considered that further steps need to be taken to be able to allow for the possibility of revoking an enforcement officer's authorisation in the event that such conditions are not met. The result is the creation of provisions that are somewhat draconian for an authorised officer of a litter authority – presumably to guard against over-officiousness in the use of fixed penalty notices. However, the conditions on which an authorisation may be revoked are not made clear. One area of contention, in addition to the sense of disproportion identified above, may relate to the fact that income from fixed penalty notices is generally retained by the litter authorities, which may give rise to tension between revenue generation and appropriate enforcement.

The new s 88B raises the prospect of new guidance on the exercise of littering enforcement functions, defined by sub-s (5). It is clear that the scope of the guidance can cover enforcement functions relating to any of the three offences in Part 4 of the Environmental Protection Act 1990, as well as 'any function exercised for purposes connected' with any of those offences. These functions include setting fixed penalty levels, authorising enforcement officers, issuing penalty notices, collecting and processing payments, initiating and pursuing prosecutions, and designating land for the purposes of Sch 3A. It may therefore be expected that the resulting guidance is likely to aim to provide consistency of approach and outcome across the relevant authorities. Litter authorities must have regard to the guidance when exercising any litter enforcement functions (s 88B(2)). For the legal meaning of 'have regard to', see the Introduction.

69 Fixed penalty notices

(1) The Environmental Protection Act 1990 is amended as follows.

(2) In section 33ZA (fixed penalty notices relating to depositing, treatment or disposal of waste: England)—

(a) in subsection (10), for the words from "the period" to the end substitute "a period specified by the authority.";

(b) after that subsection insert—

"(10A) The Secretary of State may by regulations substitute different amounts for the amounts for the time being specified in subsections (9) and (10)."

(3) In section 33ZB (fixed penalty notices relating to depositing, treatment or disposal of waste: Wales)—

(a) in subsection (10), for the words from "the period" to the end substitute "a period specified by the authority.";

(b) after that subsection insert—

"(10A) The Welsh Ministers may by regulations substitute different amounts for the amounts for the time being specified in subsections (9) and (10)."

(4) In section 34ZA (fixed penalty notices relating to transfer of household waste: England)—

(a) in subsection (9), for the words from "within" to the end substitute "before the end of a period specified by the authority.";

(b) after that subsection insert—

"(9A) The Secretary of State may by regulations substitute different amounts for the amounts for the time being specified in subsections (7)(b), (8) and (9)."

(5) In section 34ZB (fixed penalty notices relating to transfer of household waste: Wales)—

(a) in subsection (8), for the words from "the period" to the end substitute "a period specified by the authority.";

(b) after that subsection insert—

"(8A) The Welsh Ministers may by regulations substitute different amounts for the amounts for the time being specified in subsections (7) and (8)."

In force: E: day to be appointed by Secretary of State; W: day to be appointed by Welsh Ministers

Application E W

S 33ZA originally set a time period of 10 days within which a penalty of a lesser amount, not less than £120, could be paid. Sub-s (2)(a) amends this specified time period to provide the Regulator with greater flexibility over the relevant time within which the offender would qualify for the lesser penalty. Sub-s (2)(b) allows for the specified amounts set out in S 33ZA to be amended by regulations.

Sub-s (3) mirrors the changes made above, but in respect of Wales.

Highly similar changes are made to ss 34ZA and 34ZB, referring to fixed penalty notices relating to the transfer of household waste in both England and Wales.

70 Regulation of polluting activities

In Schedule 1 to the Pollution Prevention and Control Act 1999, in paragraph 4 (permits)—

(a) the existing text becomes sub-paragraph (1);

(b) after that sub-paragraph insert—

"(2) In relation to England and Wales, imposing such a prohibition in relation to an activity except where the carrying on of the activity meets conditions determined by the regulators in accordance with the regulations."

In force 9 January 2022

Application E W

Background

Sch 1 of the Pollution Prevention and Control Act 1999 specifies the particular purposes for which regulations may be made by the Secretary of State.

The original purpose set out in para 4 of Sch 1 related to the prohibition of operating an installation or plant of a specified description without a permit – essentially, the ability to make regulations relating to permits and exemptions from permits. This amendment allows the Secretary of State to prohibit an activity unless it meets conditions determined by the Environment Agency and/or Natural Resources Wales in accordance with the regulations. This enables the regulators to set conditions for exempt activities which do not require a permit, but only those activities specified by the Secretary of State and only within the confines of the proposed regulations.

Exemptions have been the subject of concern for some time. They are intended for low-risk activities and, probably as a consequence, exemptions are not necessarily as closely regulated as permits and permit conditions. Concerns do exist that some operators take advantage of exemptions for precisely this reason.

However, exemptions pursuant to the Environmental Permitting (England and Wales) Regulations 2016 have always been subject to conditions, for example relating to how long waste may be stored or the type of waste suitable for use under the exemption. It therefore is not immediately clear what this section adds to current legislation, unless it is a precursor to further, more considerable regulation of exemptions in the future.

71 Waste regulation: amendment of Northern Ireland Order

(1) In Article 2(2) of the Waste and Contaminated Land (Northern Ireland) Order 1997 (S.I. 1997/2778 (N.I. 19)), in the definition of "the Department", for "the Department

of the Environment" substitute "the Department of Agriculture, Environment and Rural Affairs".

(2) To the extent that immediately before the commencement of this section a reference in that Order to "the Department" was to be read as being or including a reference to a department other than the Department of Agriculture, Environment and Rural Affairs (by virtue of Article 9(1) of the Departments (Transfer of Functions) Order (Northern Ireland) 2016 (S.R. (N.I.) 2016 No. 76) or otherwise), it is to continue to be so read.

In force 28 February 2022

Application NI

This section reflects the fact that the Department of the Environment in Northern Ireland has been abolished and replaced by the Department of Agriculture, Environment and Rural Affairs.

PART 4

AIR QUALITY AND ENVIRONMENTAL RECALL

Air quality

72 Local air quality management framework

Schedule 11 contains amendments of Part 4 of the Environment Act 1995 (air quality).

In force Day to be appointed by Secretary of State

Application E

Schedule 11

The amendments made in Sch 11 to the air quality provisions in the Environment Act 1995 are intended to strengthen the overall system of air quality management provided for in the 1995 legislation. The current arrangements place much responsibility on district councils and unitary authorities, but the amendments recognise the role that other public bodies have to play in controlling emissions, and provide for greater coordination and cooperation. The Government's *Clean Air Strategy 2019* (Department of the Environment, Food and Rural Affairs, 2019) provided a background to many of the legal improvements sought.

The key changes introduced by Sch 11 cover the following areas:

National Air Quality Strategy

S 80 Environment Act 1995 introduced a duty on the Secretary of State to produce a National Air Quality Strategy concerning Great Britain, and the current statutory strategy is contained in *The Air Quality Strategy for England, Scotland, Wales, and Northern Ireland* (Department for Environment, Food and Rural Affairs in partnership with the Scottish Executive, Welsh Assembly Government and Department of the Environment Northern Ireland, Cm 7169 NIA 61/-6-07, July

2007). Northern Ireland was included within the Strategy under the cooperation powers within the Environment (Northern Ireland) Order 2002 N0 3153. The National Air Quality Strategy will no longer have to relate to every part of Great Britain. This reflects the fact that air pollution is largely a devolved matter, and that devolved jurisdictions need to produce their own strategies reflecting distinctive challenges and priorities. At the same time, while the UK remains party to a number of international conventions on air pollution, post-Brexit there is no longer the pressure for UK wide approaches under EU air quality legislation. The Scottish Government first published its own strategy in 2015, which was replaced in July 2021 by *Cleaner Air for Scotland 2 (CAFS 2): Towards a Better Place for Everyone*. The Welsh Government published its first strategy in 2020: *The Clean Air Plan for Wales – Healthy Air, Healthy Wales*. In Northern Ireland, a consultation was launched in November 2020 on a *Clean Air Strategy for Northern Ireland*.

S 80 gave the discretion to revise the strategy 'from time to time', but this is now strengthened by requiring the National Air Quality Strategy to be reviewed and, if appropriate, modified by the Secretary of State within 12 months of these amendments coming into force, then at least every five years. A new provision (s 81A) is introduced requiring the Secretary of State to lay an annual statement before Parliament as soon as practicable after every financial year. The statement must contain an assessment of progress on meeting air quality standards and objectives in England, and the steps taken by the Secretary of State to support the meetings of these standards and objectives.

The Environment Act contained provisions for the Environment Agency to have regard to the National Air Quality Strategy when exercising its pollution control functions, but amendments now broaden the scope of this duty to other bodies and wider functions. A new s 81A will require local authorities (unitary authorities, district councils and county councils) and any other public authority designated in regulations made by the Secretary of State to have regard to the Strategy when exercising any public function which could affect air quality. For commentary on the meaning of 'have regard to', see the Introduction.

Local Authority and Air Quality Management

Reviews

S 82 of the 1995 Act requires unitary and district councils to review from time to time the air quality in their area, including an assessment of whether air quality standards and objectives are being or likely to be achieved, and, if not, to identify those parts of their area where there are, or are likely to be, failures. The amendments strengthen the provisions by requiring the review to identify sources of emissions contributing to the failures, identifying other authorities where those sources are within another authority's area and identifying the Environment Agency or other public authorities designated as 'relevant' by the Secretary of State under s 81A where they consider the functions of those bodies to be relevant to the sources of emissions (termed as 'air quality partners').

Air Quality Management Areas

S 83 of the Act requires local authorities to identify areas in which it appears that air quality standards and objectives are not being, or are not likely to be, met, and s 84 requires the authority to prepare action plans in relation to such designated areas to secure the achievement of the objectives and standards. The 1995 Act was not very specific as to the content of action plans, and the provisions are strengthened by a new s 83A, which elaborates the requirements of an action plan in relation to English local authorities. The plan must set out how it will achieve those standards and objectives, and (a new requirement) maintain them after achievement. The action plan must include particular measures the authority will take to secure the standards and objectives, and specify dates for carrying out each measure (the 1995 Act required dates for which the authority 'proposes to implement' measures). The 1995 Act gave the discretion to revise action plans from time to time, but the new 83A obliges authorities to revise the plan where they consider there is a need for further or different measures.

Contribution by Other Public Authorities

S 86 of the 1995 Act provided a role for county councils to use their functions to contribute to reviews and action plans, and these provisions have been strengthened by various amendments to s 86 made in para 9 of the Schedule. The *Clean Air Strategy 2019* identified the need for more coordination amongst local authorities and other public bodies in the development of local air pollution plans (see s 9.2.3 of the Strategy), and during the parliamentary debates on the Bill, Rebecca Pow, Parliamentary Under Secretary of State at the Department for Environment, Food and Rural Affairs, noted that '*local authorities have told us that they need greater-cooperation from a range of bodies in order to deliver meaningful action to bring pollution levels to within statutory limits*' (House of Commons Public Bill Committee, 12 November 2020, para 461). The concept of 'air quality partners' is introduced to help address this challenge. Under a new s 85A, 'air quality partners' (the Environment Agency and other public authorities as designated by the Secretary of State and considered by the district council to be relevant to sources of emissions in their area – see note on s 82 above) have a general duty to assist the local authority in response to reasonable requests. The new s 85B relates to the duties of such partners in relation to an action plan being prepared by a local authority. Partners must provide the authority with proposals for measures they will take to achieve the air quality standards, include dates for measures to be taken, and the plan must include these proposals. Air quality partners are under a duty to carry out their measures 'as far as is reasonably practical' (s 85B(3)). The Secretary of State is given power to give binding directions to partners where the proposals made are considered to be insufficient or inappropriate.

The provisions of the role of the Mayor of London in relation to action plans of London local authorities in s 86A of the 1995 Act have been slightly strengthened by the insertion of a new s 86A. As in the previous provisions, the Mayor must be notified where a London borough is preparing an action plan, and the borough must submit proposals relating to the powers excisable by the Mayor. The proposals must specify a date for carrying out each measure, and there is now a duty to carry them out by the specified dates 'so far as reasonably practicable'.

Following the Local Democracy, Economic Development and Construction Act 2009, local authorities may pool responsibilities by establishing a combined local authority. A new s 86B makes provisions in relation to combined authorities in respect of air quality action plans.

73 Smoke control areas: amendments of the Clean Air Act 1993

Schedule 12 makes provision—

(a) for imposing financial penalties for the emission of smoke in smoke control areas in England,

(b) about offences relating to the sale and acquisition of solid fuel in England,

(c) for applying smoke control orders to vessels in England, and

(d) for authorised fuels and exempted fireplaces to be listed in Wales.

In force	E: 1 May 2022. Commencement Order No 2; W: day to be appointed by Welsh Ministers
Application	E W (in part)

Schedule 12

Sch 12 contains various amendments to the Clean Air Act 1993 designed to strengthen the controls. The main changes apply to England only since the environment is largely a devolved matter in Wales. Under Part 2 of Sch 12 various amendments are made to the Clean Air Act to make specific reference to Welsh Ministers.

Civil Penalties for Emissions in Smoke Control Areas

The emission of smoke from a chimney in a smoke control area designated by a local authority is currently a criminal offence (Level 3 on the standard scale (maximum current fine £1000)) under s 1 Clean Air Act 1993. A new s 19A and Sch 1A are now included, making it easier for local authorities in England to enforce the controls without the need for a criminal prosecution. As the *Clean Air Strategy 2019* noted, *'The current Smoke Control framework is difficult to enforce. We will bring it into the 21st century with more flexible, proportionate enforcement powers'* (p 82). Local authorities are given power to issue civil penalties in respect of such emissions following the procedure prescribed in the Schedule. The minimum penalty is £175 and the maximum £300, though these sums may be amended by regulations made by the Secretary of State (Sch 1A para 3). The authority may issue such penalties where it is satisfied on the balance of probabilities that the emission has occurred (para 2), and appeals are to the First-tier Tribunal. As with the criminal offence, the person liable to such a penalty is the occupier of the building containing the chimney, or, where the chimney serves the furnace of a fixed boiler or industrial plant, the person having possession of the boiler or plant. Domestic householders within a smoke control area are therefore potentially subject to the new civil penalty regime, reflecting growing concern about the domestic contribution to air pollution. According to DEFRA, domestic burning (including wood-burning stoves and coal fires) is now the single largest contributor to the UK's harmful particulate matter emissions, and accounted for 43 per cent of total $PM_{2.5}$ emissions in 2019: https://deframedia.blog.gov.uk/2021/02/17/emissions-from-domestic-burning-in-the-uk. Para 10 of the new Sch 1A gives power to the local authority to delegate 'to a person' exercise of any of its functions under these enforcement provisions. The drafting is very broad, and would appear to allow local authorities to delegate enforcement to private bodies. A new s 28A gives power to the Secretary of State to issue guidance (see below), and guidance may be required regarding the extent to which these powers should be delegated and to whom. Under a new s 19C, the Secretary of State is given power to suspend or relax by order the civil penalty regime in relation to the whole or part of a smoke control area.

Vessels in waters

Various amendments are made concerning vessels in waters. S 44 of the Clean Air Act 1993 applies the prohibition of dark smoke under s 1 of the 1993 Act to vessels on waters within the local authority area (see s 44(3) and (4) for the definition of such waters). In making a smoke control order, a local authority may provide that the provisions concerning the issuing of civil penalties will apply in relation to vessels (new s 44(2) introduced by Sch 12, para 7). Grants for the adaptation in dwellings to ensure compliance within smoke control areas have been available under s 27 of the Act, but a new provision for adaptation grants in respect of vessels is introduced in s 26A. This provides for the local authority to pay 70 per cent of adaptation costs approved by the authority and needed to avoid the imposition of civil penalties. The provisions do not apply to a vessel which has access to mains electricity or gas at its mooring place.

Controlled Solid Fuel

A new s 19B is introduced to strengthen the provisions in s 23 Clean Air Act concerning the acquisition and sale of controlled solid fuel ('controlled solid fuel' is defined as solid fuel which has not been authorised by the Secretary of State: s 19D). S 19B(5) is added, creating the equivalent offence but applicable in England only. Retailers who deliver such fuel are now liable on summary conviction to an unlimited fine (s 19B(7)). These offences relate only to the delivery of fuel by a retailer, but a new offence is created for a retailer who sells controlled fuel to be taken away by the purchaser and who fails to take reasonable steps to notify purchasers that it is an offence to use such fuel in a smoke control area (s 19B(4)). As with selling fuel for delivery, liability on summary conviction is for an unlimited fine, but the provisions concerning civil penalties for the s 1 'dark smoke' offence do not apply here. The Secretary of State is given power to suspend or relax these provisions in relation to the whole or part of a smoke control area (new s 19C).

Secretary of State Guidance

S 19 of the Clean Air Act gives power to the Secretary of State to direct authorities to prepare a smoke control order. A new 28A is introduced which gives broad powers concerning guidance that may be issued by the Secretary of State in England on the exercise of functions under Part III of the 1993 Act (smoke control areas). A local authority is required to have regard to any such guidance about the exercise of the authorities functions under Part III of the Act. See the Introduction for the legal meaning of 'have regard to'.

Statutory Nuisances in Smoke Control Areas

One of the classes of statutory nuisance under s 79 Environmental Protection Act 1990 is smoke emitted from premises so as to be prejudicial to health or a nuisance, but it does not apply to smoke emitted from a private dwelling in a smoke control area. By amendment introduced under Sch 12 para 25, this exemption will no longer apply in England, but in Wales only.

Environmental recall of motor vehicles etc

74 Environmental recall of motor vehicles etc

(1) The Secretary of State may by regulations make provision for, about or connected with the recall of relevant products that do not meet relevant environmental standards.

(2) A "relevant product" is a product specified or described in the regulations.

(3) Only the following types of product may be specified or described in the regulations—

(a) a mechanically propelled vehicle;

(b) a part of a mechanically propelled vehicle;

(c) an engine that is, or forms part of, machinery that is transportable (including by way of self-propulsion);

(d) a part of such an engine, or any other part of such machinery that is connected with the operation of the engine.

(4) A "relevant environmental standard" means a standard that—

(a) by virtue of any enactment, a relevant product must meet,

(b) is relevant to the environmental impact of that product, and

(c) is specified in the regulations,

and the regulations may provide that a reference in the regulations to a standard is to be construed as a reference to that standard as it has effect from time to time.

(5) In subsection (4)(a) "enactment" has the same meaning as in the European Union (Withdrawal) Act 2018.

(6) In subsection (4)(b) "environmental impact", in relation to a relevant product, includes any impact on the environment caused by noise, heat or vibrations or any other kind of release of energy or emissions resulting from the use of the product.

(7) Regulations under subsection (1) are subject to the affirmative procedure.

(8) Sections 75 to 77 make further provision about regulations under subsection (1).

Definitions

'enactment'	s 74(5)
'environmental impact'	s 74(6)
'relevant product'	s 74(2) and (3)
'relevant environmental standard'	s 74(4)

In force	Day to be appointed by Secretary of State
Application	E W S NI

The following ss 74–76 give broad powers to the Secretary of State to make regulations concerning the recall of motor vehicles that fail to meet environmental standards that are specified in the regulations. Manufacturers and distributors may be required to recall vehicles that do not meet certification standards, compensating the consumer where appropriate. The background to the need for new controls was the evidence in 2015 that some car manufacturers had manipulated emission test certification procedures with defeat software systems, with the result that emissions in actual driving conditions could greatly exceed the legal limits. The Road Vehicles (Defeat Devices, Fuel Economy and Type-Approval) (Amendment) Regulations SI 2018/673 were introduced to make it a criminal offence for manufacturers to market motor vehicles fitted with a defeat system, but the potential reach of regulations made under s 73 is much broader. S 73 provides the general scope of regulations which are applicable to 'products' defined in the regulations, encompassing motor vehicles and engines forming part of machinery that is transportable (sub-ss (2) and (3)). The scandals mainly concerned emissions into the air of nitrogen dioxide, but the definition of 'environmental impact' in sub-s (6) is much broader. The regulations relate to standards contained in any 'enactment', defined by reference to its broad interpretation in s 20(1) European Union (Withdrawal) Act 2018, which includes any retained direct EU legislation.

75 Compulsory recall notices

(1) Regulations under section 74(1) may make provision for, about or connected with a power of the Secretary of State to give a compulsory recall notice to a manufacturer or distributor of a relevant product.

(2) A "compulsory recall notice" is a notice that requires the recipient of the notice to organise the return of a relevant product to the recipient, or to any other person specified in the notice, from persons who have been supplied (whether or not directly by the recipient) with the product.

(3) Provision for the Secretary of State to give a compulsory recall notice in relation to a relevant product must not permit the giving of such a notice unless the Secretary of State has reasonable grounds for believing the product does not meet a relevant environmental standard.

(4) The regulations may provide that, where a relevant product forms part of another product, a compulsory recall notice may require its recipient to organise the return of that other product (whether or not it is a relevant product).

(5) The regulations may provide that a compulsory recall notice may impose supplementary requirements on its recipient.

(6) The regulations may confer a power on the Secretary of State to give a recipient of a compulsory recall notice a further notice (a "supplementary notice") that imposes supplementary requirements on its recipient.

(7) The following are examples of supplementary requirements—

(a) to secure that at least a specified proportion of products subject to a compulsory recall notice that are manufactured or distributed by the recipient are returned in accordance with the notice;

(b) to publicise a compulsory recall notice;

(c) to provide information to the Secretary of State;

(d) a prohibition on supplying, or offering or agreeing to supply, a product subject to a compulsory recall notice;

(e) to pay such compensation to a person who returns a product subject to a compulsory recall notice as may be specified;

(f) to make other specified arrangements for the purpose of mitigating the effect of returning a product on the person who returns it;

(g) to destroy, or arrange for the destruction of, a returned product;

(h) to take steps to modify, or arrange for the modification of, a returned product for the purpose of ensuring that the product complies with relevant environmental standards;

(i) to organise the return of a returned product to the person who initially returned it;

(j) to otherwise dispose of the product in such manner as may be specified.

(8) In subsection (7) "specified" means specified, or described, in a compulsory recall notice or a supplementary notice.

(9) The regulations may—

(a) make provision about appeals against a decision to give a compulsory recall notice or a supplementary notice;

(b) make provision about the withdrawal of compulsory recall notices and supplementary notices (including provision about the effect of withdrawal).

Definitions

'compulsory recall notice'	s 75(2)
'distributor' as defined in s 74 regulations	s 77
'manufacturer' as defined in s 74 regulations	s 77
'relevant environmental standard'	s 74(4)
'relevant product'	s 74(2) and (3)
'supplementary notice'	s 75(6)

In force	Day to be appointed by Secretary of State
Application	E W S NI

S 75 provides that s 74 regulations may provide for a new system of compulsory recall notices, and elaborates what may be provided for in the system. Manufacturers and distributors may be required by a compulsory recall notice to recall all or a proportion of vehicles considered by the Secretary of State to fail to meet relevant environmental standards. Regulations may give power to the Secretary of State to provide for supplementary requirements to a compulsory recall notice by means of a supplementary notice. These extra requirements could include, inter alia, payments of compensation to those who return products, rectification of vehicles to meet the required standards or their destruction. The regulations may provide for appeals against notices, and their withdrawal.

76 Further provision about regulations under section 74

(1) Regulations under section 74(1) may impose a duty on a manufacturer or distributor of a relevant product to notify the Secretary of State if the person has reason to consider that the product does not meet a relevant environmental standard.

(2) The regulations may confer a power on the Secretary of State—

(a) to require the provision of information by a manufacturer or distributor of a relevant product for the purpose of enabling the Secretary of State to consider whether, or how, to exercise a power to give a compulsory recall notice or a supplementary notice;

(b) to require the provision of samples of relevant products by such a manufacturer or distributor for that purpose.

(3) The regulations may make provision for, about or connected with the enforcement of requirements imposed by or under the regulations including provision—

(a) for, about or connected with the designation of a person to exercise functions in connection with the enforcement of the requirements ("the enforcement authority");

(b) for the functions of the enforcement authority to be exercised on its behalf by persons authorised in accordance with the regulations;

(c) requiring the provision of information by a manufacturer or distributor of a relevant product for purposes connected with the enforcement of the requirements;

(d) requiring the provision of samples of relevant products by such a manufacturer or distributor for those purposes;

(e) for, about or connected with the imposition of financial penalties by the enforcement authority;

(f) for the amount of financial penalties to be determined by the enforcement authority in accordance with the regulations;

(g) for such a determination to be made by reference to factors specified in the regulations which may include, for example, the turnover of a business or the costs of complying with the requirement being enforced (and the regulations may provide that the amount of a financial penalty may exceed the amount of those costs);

(h) about appeals against the imposition of a financial penalty.

(4) The regulations may confer powers on the enforcement authority—

(a) to enter the premises of a manufacturer or distributor of a relevant product;

(b) to take documents or records from those premises (or make copies of such documents or records);

(c) to take samples of relevant products found on those premises,

where the authority has reasonable grounds for suspecting that the manufacturer or distributor has failed to comply with a requirement imposed by or under the regulations.

(5) The regulations may make provision about warrants in connection with any power conferred by virtue of subsection (4).

Definitions

'distributor' as defined in s 74 regulations	s 77
'enforcement authority' designated in s 74 regulations	s 76(3)(a)
'manufacturer' as defined in s 74 regulations	s 77

'relevant product'	s 74(2) and (3)
'relevant environmental standard'	s 74(4)

In force	Day to be appointed by Secretary of State
Application	E W S NI

S 76 contains further provisions that may be included in s 74 regulations, and in particular their enforcement. A duty is imposed on manufacturers or distributors to notify the Secretary of State if they have reason to believe their product does not meet the relevant environmental standards. Enforcement will be the responsibility of an authority designated in the s 74 regulations, and the regulations may provide for powers of entry and the taking of documents or samples. The authority will be given power to impose financial penalties according to factors specified in the regulations, which may include the turnover of the business concerned.

77 Interpretation of sections 74 to 76

In sections 74 to 76—

"compulsory recall notice" has the meaning given by section 75(2);

"distributor" has the meaning given by regulations under section 74(1), but may only include a person acting in the course of business;

"manufacturer" has the meaning given by regulations under section 74(1) which may define that term by reference (in particular) to—

(a) a person's involvement in the manufacture of a relevant product, or

(b) a person's relationship with a person involved in the manufacture of a relevant product;

"relevant environmental standard" has the meaning given by section 74(4);

"relevant product" has the meaning given by section 74(2);

"supplementary notice" has the meaning given by section 75(6).

In force	Day to be appointed by Secretary of State
Application	E W S NI

Part 5

Water

Background

Following water privatisation in 1989, the core water legislation for England and Wales is currently found in the Water Industry Act 1991, the Water Resources Act 1991 and the Land Drainage Act 1991. In 2011 the Government published a White Paper, *Water for Life* (Cm 8230). While *Water for Life* acknowledged that the environmental quality of many rivers had improved dramatically in recent years, it noted that, due to pollution and over-abstraction of water, only a quarter of rivers and lakes could be described as fully functioning ecosystems. Water supplies were already under stress in some parts of the country, and the combined effects of climate change and a growing population were likely to put increasing pressure on water resources. *Water for Life* identified many issues that would have to be addressed in meeting future challenges, including the need to reform abstraction regulation and the need for longer-term and more coordinated planning by water and sewerage undertakers. The White Paper was followed by the Water Act 2014, which gave effect to some of its proposals, mainly with amendments to the Water Industry Act dealing with the privatised industry. In particular, it introduced into the set of core duties of the Secretary of State and Ofwat under s 2 Water Industry Act 1991 an additional duty to further 'the resilience objective'. The core definition of this objective is *'to secure the long-term resilience of water and sewerage supply systems as regards environmental pressures, population growth and changes in consumer behavior'* (s 2D(A)).

A Green Future, the Government's 25-year plan for the environment published in 2018, identified the need to reform the approach to water abstraction, with indicators suggesting that 20 per cent of surface waters were over-abstracted. Utilities needed to engage in greater longer-term planning for water and personal consumption of water, and the amount of water lost through leakage should be reduced. In March 2020, the Environment Agency published a report, *Meeting our Future Water Needs: A National Framework for Water Resources*, providing a national framework identifying strategic long-term water needs in England. In particular, it called for greater planning at regional level involving extensive cooperation between individual water undertakers and other bodies responsible for water quality and supply. In its 2020 report *Water Supply and Demand Management*, the National Audit Office noted the growing risk of water shortages, and highlighted continuing challenges for government, regulators and the water industry.

In 2019 the Government issued a consultation document containing a range of proposals designed to improve and update existing legislation of water management and regulation, many of which had been identified in *Water for Life* and subsequent reports. The key proposals in *Improving our Management of Water in the Environment – Consultation Proposals* (Department of the Environment, Food and Rural Affairs, January 2019) were:

- Introducing more flexible procedures for the making of water resource management plans by water undertakers under the Water Resources Act 1991.
- Providing for greater joint planning by utilities for water resources.
- A new statutory duty on undertakers to develop longer-term drainage and waste water management plans.
- Improvements to the regulation of water abstraction under the Water Resources Act 1991, giving greater flexibility to change licence conditions or revoke conditions without the need to pay compensation.
- Modernising the system of licensing of water undertakers by Ofwat under the Water Industry Act 1991, giving it more flexibility to vary licences.
- Introducing the new charging methodologies for the calculation of charges by internal drainage boards under the Land Drainage Act 1991, designed to assist internal drainage boards wishing to expand and to encourage the creation of new internal drainage boards.

In July 2019, DEFRA published *Improving Our Management of Water in the Environment – Summary of Responses and Government Response*. The provisions in Part 5 largely give effect to these proposals. There clearly remains no appetite for a complete overhaul of the core 1991 legislation (Water Industry Act, Water Resources Act and Land Drainage Act), and the provisions in the Environment Act are largely by way of introducing amendments to those statutes.

During the passage of the Bill, the issue of storm overflows and the discharge of sewage into rivers became an issue of high political controversy. In response to the amendments proposed in the Lords, which would have imposed express legal duties on sewerage undertakers to deal with the subject, the Government proposed the amendments that are found in s 80 below.

Plans and proposals

78 Water resources management plans, drought plans and joint proposals

(1) Chapter 1 of Part 3 of the Water Industry Act 1991 (general duties of water undertakers) is amended as follows.

(2) In section 37A (water resources management plans)—

(a) in the heading omit ": preparation and review";

(b) in subsection (3)(b) omit from "(also" to the end;

(c) in subsection (4)—

(i) at the beginning insert "Section 39F contains provision about";

(ii) omit "is set out in section 37B below";

(d) in subsection (6) omit the words after paragraph (c);

(e) omit subsection (8);

(f) omit subsection (10).

(3) Omit sections 37B and 37C (water resources management plans: publication and provision of information).

(4) In section 37D (water resources management plans: supplementary)—

(a) in subsection (1), in the words before paragraph (a), for ", 37AA or 37B" substitute "or 37AA";

(b) in subsection (3)—

(i) in paragraph (a) for "to 37C" substitute "and 37AA";

(ii) omit paragraph (b) (and the "and" before it).

(5) In section 39B (drought plans)—

(a) in the heading omit ": preparation and review";

(b) in subsection (4)(b) omit from "(also" to the end;

(c) for subsection (5) substitute—

"(5) Section 39F makes provision about the procedure for preparing and publishing a drought plan (or revised plan).";

(d) in subsection (6)—

(i) in paragraph (c) omit from "in accordance" to the end;

(ii) omit the words after paragraph (c);

(e) omit subsection (7);

(f) in subsection (9), in the words before paragraph (a), omit from "(including" to "above)".

(6) Omit section 39C (drought plans: provision of information).

(7) After section 39D insert—

"39E Joint proposals

(1) The Minister may give a direction to two or more water undertakers to prepare and publish a joint proposal.

(2) A joint proposal is a proposal that identifies measures that may be taken jointly by the undertakers for the purpose of improving the management and development of water resources.

(3) A joint proposal must not contain measures that (if taken) would result in any water undertaker being unable to meet its obligations under this Part.

(4) A direction under this section may, in particular, require that—

(a) a joint proposal takes a specified form;

(b) a joint proposal addresses a specified matter;

(c) a joint proposal be prepared—

(i) in relation to a specified area;

(ii) by reference to specified criteria;

(iii) on the basis of a specified assumption.

(5) Directions under this section are to be given by an instrument in writing.

(6) Each water undertaker to whom a direction applies must comply with the direction.

(7) The duties of a water undertaker under this section are enforceable by the Minister under section 18.

(8) In this section "the Minister" means—

(a) the Secretary of State, in relation to water undertakers whose areas are wholly or mainly in England, and

(b) the Welsh Ministers, in relation to water undertakers whose areas are wholly or mainly in Wales.

(9) In this section "specified" means specified in a direction under this section.

39F Plans and joint proposals: regulations about procedure

(1) The Minister may by regulations make provision about the procedure for preparing and publishing—

(a) a water resources management plan,

(b) a drought plan, and

(c) a joint proposal,

including any revised plans or proposals.

(2) The regulations may provide for the sharing of information and, in particular, may require a water supply licensee to share such information with a water undertaker as may be reasonably requested.

(3) The regulations may make provision about consultation to be carried out by water undertakers, including provision about—

(a) the persons to be consulted,

(b) the frequency and timing of any consultation, and

(c) the publication of statements relating to any consultation.

(4) The regulations may make provision about the preparation and circulation of drafts, including provision for the Minister to require changes to a draft plan or proposal.

(5) The regulations may make provision for the purposes of ensuring that persons likely to be affected by the plan or proposal have a reasonable opportunity to make representations to the Minister.

(6) The regulations may make provision about how representations (and any comments on them by a water undertaker) are to be dealt with, and in respect of a plan mentioned in subsection (1)(a) or (b), the regulations may provide for—

(a) the Minister to cause an inquiry or other hearing to be held in connection with the plan, and

(b) section 250(2) to (5) of the Local Government Act 1972 (local inquiries: evidence and costs) to apply to such an inquiry or hearing (with or without modifications).

(7) The regulations may make provision about commercially confidential information and its publication.

(8) In this section "the Minister" means—

(a) the Secretary of State, in relation to water undertakers whose areas are wholly or mainly in England, and

(b) the Welsh Ministers, in relation to water undertakers whose areas are wholly or mainly in Wales.

39G Regulations under section 39F: directions

(1) Regulations made under section 39F may confer on the Minister power to make provision by directions.

(2) Those directions are to be given by an instrument in writing.

(3) They may be—

(a) general directions applying to all water undertakers, or

(b) directions applying only to one or more water undertakers specified in the directions.

(4) Each water undertaker to whom a direction applies must comply with the direction.

(5) The duties of a water undertaker under this section are enforceable by the Minister under section 18.

(6) In this section "the Minister" has the same meaning as in section 39F.

39H Regulations under section 39F: supplementary

(1) Regulations under section 39F are to be made by statutory instrument.

(2) A statutory instrument containing regulations under section 39F is subject to annulment in pursuance of a resolution of—

(a) either House of Parliament, in the case of regulations made by the Secretary of State;

(b) Senedd Cymru, in the case of regulations made by the Welsh Ministers.

(3) Subsection (4) applies in relation to a statutory instrument containing both—

(a) regulations made by the Secretary of State under section 39F, and

(b) regulations made by the Welsh Ministers under section 39F.

(4) If in accordance with subsection (2)(a) or (b) (negative resolution procedure)—

(a) either House of Parliament resolves that an address be presented to Her Majesty praying that an instrument containing regulations made by the Secretary of State be annulled, or

(b) Senedd Cymru resolves that an instrument containing regulations made by the Welsh Ministers be annulled,

the instrument is to have no further effect and Her Majesty may by Order in Council revoke the instrument.

(5) Section 213(2) to (2B) applies to regulations made by the Welsh Ministers under section 39F as it applies to regulations made by the Secretary of State."

In force — Day to be appointed by Secretary of State so far as relating to undertakers whose areas are wholly or mainly in England; Welsh Ministers so far as relating to undertakers whose areas are wholly or mainly in Wales

Application — E W

Sub-ss (2)–(6) provide various technical amendments to provisions in the Water Industry Act 1991 concerning water management and drought plans to accommodate the more substantial changes introduced in this part of the Act.

Sub-s (7) then introduces new provisions into the Water Industry Act – ss 39E (joint proposals), 39F, 39G and 39H (regulations for procedures).

Joint Proposals by Water Undertakers

The new s 39E gives power to the Minister to issue directions to two or more water undertakers to prepare proposals for joint measures to improve the management and development of resources. Joint proposals do not replace the duty on undertakers to prepare their own water management plans every five years, but are designed to improve cooperation and planning at a wider, regional geographical level. According to the DEFRA Consultation Document, *Improving Our Management of Water in the Environment – Consultation Proposals* (January 2019), water transfers between undertakers remain low, and few strategic water schemes have been developed. In 2018 the National Infrastructure Commission reported that despite established regional coordination groups and some bilateral operations amongst undertakers, the individual water management plans failed to reflect sufficient strategic options: *Preparing for a Drier Future: England's Water Infrastructure Needs*. The Environment Agency's report, *Meeting Our Future Water Needs: A National Framework for Water Resources* (March 2020), further stressed the need for greater regional planning for water resources to meet long-term water needs in the future. The duty to comply with directions is enforceable by enforcement orders made by the Secretary of State or Ofwat under s 18 Water Industry Act. On s 18 enforcement orders, see further the annotations to s 83 below.

Procedures for Making Water Management Plans and Joint Proposals

The Water Industry Act 1991 contained a number of substantive provisions in s 37B and C concerning the procedures for making water management plans, and also provided supplementary powers to the Secretary of State to make regulations on certain aspects of the procedures (see Water Resource Management Plans Regulations 2007, SI 2007/727). These provisions in the Act have now been removed (s 77(3)) and procedures will now be contained in regulations as provided for in new ss 39F, G and H. The overall aim is to provide greater flexibility in the light of changing circumstances and demands (such as the range of statutory consultees). The regulations may also provide for procedures in making joint proposals under s 99E, and making drought plans under s 39B of the Water Industry Act, with amendments made to s 39B to reflect the new powers. Regulations are made in England by the Secretary of State and in Wales by Welsh Ministers (termed 'the Minister' in the provisions).

Under new s 39G, regulations may also provide powers for the Minister to issue directions which can be of general application or issued to specified undertakers. Directions, according to the Explanatory Notes to the Bill, can be of value because some administrative requirements, such as timetables for preparation, revision and publication, are likely to change from planning round to planning round. Undertakers are obliged to comply with directions, a duty enforceable by enforcement orders made by the Secretary of State or Ofwat under s 18 Water Industry Act (s 39G(5)). On s 18 enforcement orders, see further the annotations to s 83 below.

79 Drainage and sewerage management plans

In the Water Industry Act 1991, after section 94 insert—

"94A Drainage and sewerage management plans: preparation and review

(1) Each sewerage undertaker must prepare, publish and maintain a drainage and sewerage management plan.

(2) A drainage and sewerage management plan is a plan for how the sewerage undertaker will manage and develop its drainage system and sewerage system so as to be able, and continue to be able, to meet its obligations under this Part.

(3) A drainage and sewerage management plan must address in particular—

(a) the capacity of the undertaker's drainage system and sewerage system,

(b) an assessment of the current and future demands on the undertaker's drainage system and sewerage system,

(c) the resilience of the undertaker's drainage system and sewerage system,

(d) the measures the undertaker intends to take or continue for the purpose in subsection (2),

(e) the likely sequence and timing for implementing those measures,

(f) relevant environmental risks and how those risks are to be mitigated, and

(g) any other matters specified by the Minister in directions.

(4) Section 94C contains provision about the preparation and publication of a drainage and sewerage management plan (including a revised plan).

(5) Before each anniversary of the date when its plan (or revised plan) was last published, the sewerage undertaker must—

(a) review its plan, and

(b) send a statement of the conclusions of its review to the Minister.

(6) The sewerage undertaker must prepare and publish a revised plan in each of the following cases—

(a) following conclusion of its annual review, if the review indicated a material change of circumstances;

(b) if directed to do so by the Minister;

(c) in any event, not later than the end of the period of 5 years beginning with the date when the plan (or the revised plan) was last published.

(7) The Minister may give directions specifying—

(a) the form which a drainage and sewerage management plan must take;

(b) the planning period to which a drainage and sewerage management plan must relate.

(8) The duties of a sewerage undertaker under this section are enforceable by the Minister under section 18.

(9) In this section references—

(a) to a drainage system of a sewerage undertaker, are to any drainage system (within the meaning of section 114A) maintained or operated by the sewerage undertaker which is not part of its sewerage system;

(b) to the sewerage system of a sewerage undertaker, have the same meaning as in Chapter 1A of Part 2 (see section 17BA(7)).

(10) In this section "the Minister" means—

(a) the Secretary of State, in relation to sewerage undertakers whose areas are wholly or mainly in England, and

(b) the Welsh Ministers, in relation to sewerage undertakers whose areas are wholly or mainly in Wales.

94B Drainage and sewerage management plans: power to amend period

(1) The Minister may by order made by statutory instrument amend the period for the time being specified in section 94A(6)(c).

(2) In subsection (1) "the Minister" means—

(a) the Secretary of State, in relation to sewerage undertakers whose areas are wholly or mainly in England, and

(b) the Welsh Ministers, in relation to sewerage undertakers whose areas are wholly or mainly in Wales.

(3) A statutory instrument containing an order under subsection (1) is subject to annulment in pursuance of a resolution of—

(a) either House of Parliament, in the case of an order made by the Secretary of State;

(b) Senedd Cymru, in the case of an order made by the Welsh Ministers.

(4) Subsection (5) applies in relation to a statutory instrument containing both—

(a) an order made by the Secretary of State under subsection (1), and

(b) an order made by the Welsh Ministers under subsection (1).

(5) If in accordance with subsection (3)(a) or (b) (negative resolution procedure)—

(a) either House of Parliament resolves that an address be presented to Her Majesty praying that an instrument containing regulations made by the Secretary of State be annulled, or

(b) Senedd Cymru resolves that an instrument containing regulations made by the Welsh Ministers be annulled,

the instrument is to have no further effect and Her Majesty may by Order in Council revoke the instrument.

94C Drainage and sewerage management plans: regulations about procedure

(1) The Minister may by regulations make provision about the procedure for preparing and publishing a drainage and sewerage management plan (including a revised plan).

(2) The regulations may provide for the sharing of information and, in particular, may require a sewerage licensee to share such information with a sewerage undertaker as may be reasonably requested.

(3) The regulations may make provision about consultation to be carried out by sewerage undertakers, including provision about—

(a) the persons to be consulted,

(b) the frequency and timing of any consultation, and

(c) the publication of statements relating to any consultation.

(4) The regulations may make provision about the preparation and circulation of draft plans, including provision for the Minister to require changes to a draft plan.

(5) The regulations may make provision for the purposes of ensuring that persons likely to be affected by the plan have a reasonable opportunity to make representations to the Minister.

(6) The regulations may make provision about how representations (and any comments on them by the sewerage undertaker) are to be dealt with, including provision for—

(a) the Minister to cause an inquiry or other hearing to be held in connection with the plan, and

(b) section 250(2) to (5) of the Local Government Act 1972 (local inquiries: evidence and costs) to apply to such an inquiry or hearing (with or without modifications).

(7) The regulations may make provision about commercially confidential information and its publication.

(8) The regulations may confer on the Minister power to make provision by directions.

(9) In this section "the Minister" means—

(a) the Secretary of State, in relation to sewerage undertakers whose areas are wholly or mainly in England, and

(b) the Welsh Ministers, in relation to sewerage undertakers whose areas are wholly or mainly in Wales.

94D Regulations under section 94C: supplementary

(1) Regulations under section 94C are to be made by statutory instrument.

(2) A statutory instrument containing regulations under section 94C is subject to annulment in pursuance of a resolution of—

(a) either House of Parliament, in the case of regulations made by the Secretary of State, and

(b) Senedd Cymru, in the case of regulations made by the Welsh Ministers.

(3) Subsection (4) applies in relation to a statutory instrument containing both—

(a) regulations made by the Secretary of State under section 94C, and

(b) regulations made by the Welsh Ministers under section 94C.

(4) If in accordance with subsection (2)(a) or (b) (negative resolution procedure)—

(a) either House of Parliament resolves that an address be presented to Her Majesty praying that an instrument containing regulations made by the Secretary of State be annulled, or

(b) Senedd Cymru resolves that an instrument containing regulations made by the Welsh Ministers be annulled,

the instrument is to have no further effect and Her Majesty may by Order in Council revoke the instrument.

(5) Section 213(2) to (2B) applies to regulations made by the Welsh Ministers under section 94C as it applies to regulations made by the Secretary of State.

94E Drainage and sewerage management plans: directions

(1) In this section "directions" means directions given under—

(a) section 94A, or

(b) regulations under section 94C.

(2) Directions are to be given by an instrument in writing.

(3) Directions may be—

(a) general directions applying to all sewerage undertakers, or

(b) directions applying only to one or more sewerage undertakers specified in the directions.

(4) Each sewerage undertaker to whom a direction applies must comply with the direction.

(5) The duties of a sewerage undertaker under this section are enforceable under section 18 by—

(a) the Secretary of State, in the case of directions given by the Secretary of State, and

(b) the Welsh Ministers, in the case of directions given by the Welsh Ministers."

In force	Day to be appointed by Secretary of State so far as relating to undertakers whose areas are wholly or mainly in England; Welsh Ministers so far as relating to undertakers whose areas are wholly or mainly in Wales
Application	E W

Drainage and Sewerage Management Plans

S 79 introduces five new sections into the Water Industry Act 1991, ss 94A–E, dealing with drainage and sewerage management plans. Under s 94 of the Water Industry Act, undertakers have a general duty to provide and improve a system of public sewers to ensure their area continues to be effectively drained, and to make provision for effectively dealing with the contents of the sewers. Although there is a supplementary duty to have regard to existing and likely future obligations concerning discharge of trade effluent into sewers, there is no specific statutory obligation to draw up future plans for drainage and sewerage. This contrasts with the position of water undertakers, who must draw up water resource management plans under s 37A Water Industry Act 1991. The 2011 White Paper on water, *Water for Life* (DEFRA, Cm 8230), identified the need for greater long-term planning for sewerage infrastructure, and this was followed by Ofwat and the Environment Agency developing a joint framework for undertakers to use in planning long term strategies (*Drainage Strategy Framework*, May 2013). In September 2018, the industry body, Water UK, in collaboration with government Departments, Ofwat, the Environment Agency and Natural Resources Wales, published *A Framework for the Production of Drainage and Wastewater Plans*. Building upon existing practice within the industry, the framework was designed to assist the production of drainage and sewerage plans on a voluntary basis.

In its *Surface Water Management Action Plan* (DEFRA, July 2018), the Government supported the industry's voluntary development of drainage and waste water management plans, but said it would review progress and consider putting them on a stronger statutory basis if need be. In *Improving Our Management of Water in the Environment – Consultation Proposals* (DEFRA, January 2019), the Government concluded there should be statutory provisions on drainage and sewerage plans. This would help ensure more consistent standards, and avoid the problems of non-statutory plans receiving less attention during the Ofwat price review process and not effectively joining up with statutory plans such as local flood plans.

The new s 94A introduces a duty on every undertaker to prepare, publish and maintain a plan for how it will manage and develop its drainage system and sewerage system to meet its obligations under Part III of the Water Industry Act (see the definition of a plan in s 94A(2)). The issue of storm overflows received much political attention during the passage of the Bill, and specific duties and powers were introduced by late government amendments under s 80 below. Drainage and sewerage management plans are likely to provide an important mechanism for dealing with the issue, and provide evidence that the new duties are being addressed. S 94A(3) specifies matters that must be addressed in the plan, including capacity, future demands, resilience, meeting legal obligations, environmental risks and other matters specified by Ministers in directions. Undertakers must conduct an annual review of the plans, sending conclusions to the Minister, and must revise the plan at least every five years, but earlier if there has been a material change of circumstances or if directed by the Secretary of State in England or Welsh Ministers in Wales (termed 'the Minister'). The minimum five-year period in s 94A(6)(c) may be amended by Ministers by order under s 94B. More flexibility is provided by giving power to the Minister to issue directions as to the form of the plan and the planning period to which the plan must relate (s 94A(7)). Obligations under s 94A are enforceable by enforcement orders made by the Secretary of State or Ofwat under s 18 Water Industry Act.

S 94B gives power to the Minister to amend the provision concerning the five-year minimum period for revisions of plans.

Ss 94C and 94D deal with procedures for the making of plans, and give wide powers to the Ministers to make regulations on the subject, including consultation on draft plans and sharing of information especially between sewerage licensees (granted by Ofwat since 2017 and currently allowing for the provision of sewerage services to non-household premises using the networks operated by sewerage undertakers) and undertakers in the preparation of plans. The Government proposes to align the timing for drainage and sewerage management plans with Ofwat's existing price review mechanisms, with the statutory process starting in December 2022, and to coincide with Ofwat's 2024 price review (*Improving Our Management of Water in the Environment – Consultation Proposals*, p 18).

S 94E gives the power to Ministers to issues directions to undertakers concerning drainage and sewerage management plans, either on a general basis or specifically to one or more undertakers. There is a duty to comply with directions, enforceable by enforcement orders made by the Secretary of State or Ofwat under s 18 Water Industry Act 1991. On s 18 enforcement orders, see further the annotations to s 83 below.

Storm overflows

80 Storm overflows

(1) In Part 4 of the Water Industry Act 1991 (sewerage services), after Chapter 3 insert—

"Chapter 4

Storm overflows

141A Storm overflow discharge reduction plan

(1) The Secretary of State must prepare a plan for the purposes of—

(a) reducing discharges from the storm overflows of sewerage undertakers whose area is wholly or mainly in England, and

(b) reducing the adverse impacts of those discharges.

(2) The reference in subsection (1)(a) to reducing discharges of sewage includes—

(a) reducing the frequency and duration of the discharges, and

(b) reducing the volume of the discharges.

(3) The reference in subsection (1)(b) to reducing adverse impacts includes—

(a) reducing adverse impacts on the environment, and

(b) reducing adverse impacts on public health.

(4) The plan may in particular include proposals for—

(a) reducing the need for anything to be discharged by the storm overflows;

(b) treating sewage that is discharged by the storm overflows;

(c) monitoring the quality of watercourses, bodies of water or water in underground strata into which the storm overflows discharge;

(d) obtaining information about the operation of the storm overflows.

(5) When preparing the plan the Secretary of State must consult—

(a) the Environment Agency,

(b) the Authority,

(c) the Council,

(d) Natural England,

(e) sewerage undertakers whose area is wholly or mainly in England, or persons representing them, and

(f) such other persons as the Secretary of State considers appropriate.

(6) The Secretary of State must publish the plan before 1 September 2022.

(7) The Secretary of State may at any time revise the plan, having consulted the persons referred to in subsection (5), and must publish any revised version.

(8) The plan, and any revised version of it, must be laid before Parliament once it is published.

141B Progress reports on storm overflow discharge reduction plan

(1) The Secretary of State must publish reports ("progress reports") relating to the plan under section 141A.

(2) A progress report is to contain the Secretary of State's assessment of—

(a) the progress made, during the period to which the report relates, in implementing the proposals in the plan (or any revised version of it), and

(b) the effect of that progress on the matters referred to in section 141A(1)(a) and (b).

(3) The first progress report must relate to the period of three years beginning with the day on which the plan under section 141A is first published.

(4) Subsequent progress reports must relate to successive periods of five years after the period referred to in subsection (3).

(5) A progress report must be published within 12 weeks following the last day of the period to which it relates.

(6) A progress report must be laid before Parliament once it is published.

141C Annual reports on discharges from storm overflows

(1) A sewerage undertaker whose area is wholly or mainly in England must publish annual reports in relation to the undertaker's storm overflows ("storm overflow reports").

(2) A storm overflow report must specify, for each of the sewerage undertaker's storm overflows—

(a) the location of the storm overflow;

(b) the watercourse, body of water or underground strata into which the storm overflow discharges;

(c) the frequency and duration of discharges from the storm overflow in the period to which the report relates;

(d) where the information is available, the volume of each discharge in that period;

(e) information on any investigations that have taken place or improvement works that have been undertaken in relation to the storm overflow during that period.

(3) Storm overflow reports are to relate to successive calendar years, starting with 2021.

(4) A storm overflow report must be published by a sewerage undertaker before 1 April in the year after the calendar year to which it relates.

(5) A storm overflow report must—

(a) be in a form which allows the public readily to understand the information contained in the report, and

(b) be published in a way which makes the report readily accessible to the public.

(6) The duties of a sewerage undertaker under this section are enforceable under section 18 by—

(a) the Secretary of State, or

(b) the Authority, with the consent of or in accordance with a general authorisation given by the Secretary of State.

141D Environment Agency reports

(1) The Environment Agency must publish annual reports in relation to the operation of storm overflows of sewerage undertakers whose area is wholly or mainly in England.

(2) A report under this section must specify—

(a) the location of the storm overflows;

(b) the watercourse, body of water or underground strata into which the storm overflows discharge;

(c) the frequency and duration of discharges from the storm overflows in the period to which the report relates;

(d) where the information is available, the volume of each discharge in that period.

(3) Reports under this section are to relate to successive calendar years, starting with 2021.

(4) A storm overflow report must be published by the Environment Agency—

(a) before 1 April in the year after the calendar year to which it relates, and

(b) in such manner as the Environment Agency thinks fit.

141E Interpretation of Chapter 4

(1) In this Chapter, references to a storm overflow of a sewerage undertaker are to any structure or apparatus—

(a) which is comprised in the sewerage system of the sewerage undertaker, and

(b) which, when the capacity of other parts of the system downstream or of storage tanks at sewage disposal works is exceeded, relieves them by discharging their excess contents into inland waters, underground strata or the sea.

(2) References in this Chapter to discharges from a storm overflow do not include discharges occurring as a result of—

(a) electrical power failure at sewage disposal works,

(b) mechanical breakdown at sewage disposal works,

(c) rising main failure, or

(d) blockage of any part of the sewerage system downstream of the storm overflow.

(3) Section 17BA(7) (meaning of sewerage system of a sewerage undertaker) applies for the purposes of subsection (1)."

In force 9 January 2022

Application E

Background

S 80 provides for significant amendments to the Water Industry Act 1991 relating to storm overflows, which were introduced by the Government during the final stages of the Bill's progress. The issue became highly politicised and attracted much media attention during the passage of the Bill.

Until the mid-twentieth century most sewers in England were combined, carrying both foul and surface water. Storm overflows were constructed as release mechanisms to allow the discharge of the contents of the sewer into rivers and other waters in times of high rainfall in order to prevent back-flooding of properties connected to the system. There are estimated to be around 15,000 storm overflows in England, with the vast majority discharging into rivers. The operation of storm overflows is legally permitted by the Environment Agency under strict conditions, but with the increased urbanisation and changing weather patterns, they now operate more frequently than originally intended. In August 2020 a Storm Overflow Task Force was established, including representatives of the water industry, the Government, the Environment Agency and Ofwat, with the long-term goal of eliminating harm from storm overflows. The Task Force commissioned a major study of the issue from consultants, the first comprehensive report of its kind, which was published by Stantec in November 2021 – *Storm Flow Evidence Project – Final Report*. Although there are many other sources of water pollution, including agricultural run-offs, the report noted that the Environment Agency had estimated that, aside from public health and aesthetic impacts from overflows, the failure of around 402 inland water bodies to achieve Good Ecological Status under the EU Water Framework Directive was due to intermittent discharges from storm overflows.

The new ss 141A–E of the Water Industry Act provide for the following key changes.

Secretary of State Discharge Reduction Plan: s 141A

The Secretary of State must publish before 1 September 2022 a storm overflow reduction plan. The plan is to be prepared for the purposes of (a) reducing storm overflows of sewerage undertakers, including reducing the frequency, duration and volume of discharge, and (b) reducing the adverse impacts of discharges, including reducing adverse effects on the environment and public health. A storm overflow is defined in new s 141E as a structure or apparatus in the sewerage system which relieves the capacity of other parts of the system by discharging excess contents into inland waters, underground strata or the sea. The plan is intended to cover the planned use of storm overflows, and discharges as a result of a number of specific causes, such as electrical failures and mechanical failures, are excluded (s 141E(1)(2)).

The plan may include proposals for reducing discharges, treatment of discharges, monitoring of receiving waters and obtaining information about the operation of storm overflows (s 141A(4)). Although there is a time limit for producing the plan, the legislation does not specify any precise reduction targets or goals. During the debate in the House of Lords, Lord Goldsmith, the Lords Minister for the Environment, noted that the plan rather than primary or secondary legislation '*is the right place to set out guiding principles to reduce harm from storm overflows, including our level of ambition*' (HL Deb 9 November 2021, vol 815, col 1622). However, s 84 below also requires the Secretary of State to publish before 1 September 2022 a report on actions needed to eliminate discharges from storm overflows, with the costs and benefits of such actions.

The Secretary of State must consult various specified bodies when preparing the plan (s 141A(5)), including the Environment Agency, Ofwat (the Authority), the Consumer Council for Water (the Council), Natural England, sewerage undertakers in England or their representatives, and such other persons considered appropriate. Lord Goldsmith announced in the House of Lords that consultation on the draft plan would take place in spring 2022 (HL Deb 9 November 2021, vol 815, col 1622).

The plan may be revised at any time following consultation, and the plan and any revised version must be laid before Parliament.

Progress Reports by Secretary of State: s 141B

S 141B strengthens the political accountability of the Government by requiring the Secretary of State to publish and lay before Parliament regular progress reports concerning the implementation of the Discharge Reduction Plan, and its effect on reducing discharges and the adverse effects of those discharges.

The first Progress Report relates to the three-year period following publication of the plan, and must be published within 12 weeks of the end of that period. Subsequent reports are to be published at five-year intervals.

Annual Reports on Storm Overflows by Undertakers: s 141C

S 141C imposes duties on sewerage undertakers to be transparent on information concerning discharges from their storm overflows. They are obliged to publish an annual report, which must specify for each of their storm overflows its location, the watercourse into which the overflow discharges, the frequency and duration of any discharges and their volume, where available, and information on any investigation or improvements in relation to each storm overflow. S 83 below imposes a general duty on undertakers to secure a progressive reduction in adverse impacts from discharges from storm overflows, and these annual reports should help to provide information on the extent to which progressive reductions in impacts are being achieved. In addition to the duty to publish annual reports, s 81 below requires undertakers to publish information on any particular discharge from an overflow within one hour of it taking place.

The first such report must relate to 2021 and be published before April 2022, and then in successive years. The report must be in a form that is readily understandable and readily accessible to the public. The report will relate to discharges as defined in s 141E, and will not include certain discharges due to causes such as electrical or mechanical breakdown at sewerage disposal works.

The duties are enforceable by Enforcement Orders made under s 18 Water Industry 1991 by the Secretary of State or Ofwat. On s 18 orders, see further the annotations to s 83 below.

Annual Reports by Environment Agency: s 141D

The Environment Agency must also publish annual reports concerning the operation of storm overflows, which, as with the undertakers' reports, must specify the location of each overflow, the watercourse into which the overflow discharges, the frequency and duration of any discharges and their volume, where available.

The first such report must relate to 2021 and be published before April 2022, and then in successive years. Unlike the undertakers' reports, there is no express legal requirement to make the reports intelligible to the public, but they must be published 'in such manner as the Environment Agency thinks fit'.

81 Reporting on discharges from storm overflows

In Chapter 4 of Part 4 of the Water Industry Act 1991 (as inserted by section 80 above), after section 141D insert—

"141DA Reporting on discharges from storm overflows

(1) Where there is a discharge from a storm overflow of a sewerage undertaker whose area is wholly or mainly in England, the undertaker must publish the following information—

(a) that there has been a discharge from the storm overflow;

(b) the location of the storm overflow;

(c) when the discharge began;

(d) when the discharge ended.

(2) The information referred to in subsection (1)(a) to (c) must be published within an hour of the discharge beginning; and that referred to in subsection (1)(d) within an hour of it ending.

(3) The information must—

(a) be in a form which allows the public readily to understand it, and

(b) be published in a way which makes it readily accessible to the public.

(4) The duty of a sewerage undertaker under this section is enforceable under section 18 by—

(a) the Secretary of State, or

(b) the Authority, with the consent of or in accordance with a general authorisation given by the Secretary of State.

(5) The Secretary of State may by regulations make provision for exceptions from the duty in subsection (1) or (2) (for example, by reference to descriptions of storm overflows, frequency of discharge or the level of risk to water quality).

(6) Before making regulations under this section the Secretary of State must consult such persons as the Secretary of State considers appropriate.

(7) The Secretary of State may not make regulations under this section unless a draft of the statutory instrument containing the regulations has been laid before, and approved by resolution of, each House of Parliament."

In force	Day to be appointed by Secretary of State
Application	E

In addition to the duty to produce an annual report on storm overflows, sewerage undertakers will now have to make public immediately information about any discharges that take place. S 81 introduces into the Water Act 1991 a new s 141DA, which provides that where a discharge from a storm overflow takes place an undertaker must within one hour publish information that there has been a discharge, and the location, time and duration of the discharge.

The information must be in a form that is readily intelligible and accessible to the public. Discharges will have the meaning contained in the new s 141E Water Industry Act 1991 (see previous section), which excludes discharges from certain causes. The Secretary of State may also make regulations providing for exceptions to the duty, though there must be prior consultation, and regulations must be approved by affirmative resolution in Parliament.

The duty is enforceable by enforcement orders made by the Secretary of State or Ofwat under s 18 Water Industry Act 1991. For further notes on s 18 orders, see the annotations to s 83 below.

82 Monitoring quality of water potentially affected by discharges

(1) In Chapter 4 of Part 4 of the Water Industry Act 1991, after section 141DA insert—

"141DB Monitoring quality of water potentially affected by discharges from storm overflows and sewage disposal works

(1) A sewerage undertaker whose area is wholly or mainly in England must continuously monitor the quality of water upstream and downstream of an asset within subsection (2) for the purpose of obtaining the information referred to in subsection (3).

(2) The assets referred to in subsection (1) are—

(a) a storm overflow of the sewerage undertaker, and

(b) sewage disposal works comprised in the sewerage system of the sewerage undertaker,

where the storm overflow or works discharge into a watercourse.

(3) The information referred to in subsection (1) is information as to the quality of the water by reference to—

(a) levels of dissolved oxygen,

(b) temperature and pH values,

(c) turbidity,

(d) levels of ammonia, and

(e) anything else specified in regulations made by the Secretary of State.

(4) The duty of a sewerage undertaker under this section is enforceable under section 18 by—

(a) the Secretary of State, or

(b) the Authority, with the consent of or in accordance with a general authorisation given by the Secretary of State.

(5) The Secretary of State may by regulations make—

(a) provision as how the duty under subsection (1) is to be carried out (for example, provision as to the type of monitor to be used and where monitors must be placed);

(b) provision for exceptions from the duty in subsection (1) (for example, by reference to descriptions of asset, frequency of discharge from an asset or the level of risk to water quality);

(c) provision for the publication by sewerage undertakers of information obtained pursuant to subsection (1).

(6) Before making regulations under this section the Secretary of State must consult such persons as the Secretary of State considers appropriate.

(7) The Secretary of State may not make regulations under this section unless a draft of the statutory instrument containing the regulations has been laid before, and approved by resolution of, each House of Parliament."

(2) In section 213 of the Water Industry Act 1991 (power to make regulations) in subsection (1), for "or 105A" substitute "105A, 141DA or 141DB".

In force Day to be appointed by Secretary of State

Application E

S 82 introduces a new s 141DA to the Water Industry Act 1991, which strengthens the ability of sewerage undertakers to monitor the quality of waters that could be affected by storm overflows. Monitoring must be continuous, and take place upstream and downstream of storm overflows or a sewerage works discharging into a watercourse.

The information to be obtain relates to water quality criteria, including levels of dissolved oxygen, temperature and pH values, turbidity, ammonia levels and anything else specified in regulations.

The Secretary of State may make regulations as to how the duty is be carried out, with possible exceptions. There is no explicit duty in the Act to publish the information, but the regulations may make provision for publication. Any such information is also likely to be obtainable under Access to Environmental Information requirements. Regulations are subject to the affirmative procedure in Parliament.

The duties of sewerage undertakers under this section are enforceable by an enforcement made under s 18 Water Industry Act 1991 by the Secretary of State or Ofwat. On s 18 enforcement orders, see further the annotations to s 83 below.

83 Reduction of adverse impacts of storm overflows

In Chapter 4 of Part 4 of the Water Industry Act 1991, after section 141DB insert—

"141DC Reduction of adverse impacts of storm overflows

(1) A sewerage undertaker whose area is wholly or mainly in England must secure a progressive reduction in the adverse impacts of discharges from the undertaker's storm overflows.

(2) The reference in subsection (1) to reducing adverse impacts includes—

(a) reducing adverse impacts on the environment, and

(b) reducing adverse impacts on public health.

(3) The duty of a sewerage undertaker under this section is enforceable under section 18 by—

(a) the Secretary of State, or

(b) the Authority with the consent of or in accordance with a general authorisation given by the Secretary of State."

In force Day appointed by Secretary of State

Application E

S 83 introduces a new s 141DCB Water Industry Act 1991, which imposes a general duty on sewerage undertakers to secure a progressive reduction of the adverse environmental and public health impacts of storm overflows in their area. There is no statutory definition of what 'progressive reduction' actually means in terms of scale and speed, though clearly it implies a direction of travel. It should be noted that the provisions refer to reduction of impacts rather than the actual number of storm overflows. During the Parliament debate, Lord Goldsmith, Lords Minister for the Environment, stated that *'"Progressive" means that water companies must continue to take action even after the next price review period and even after they have achieved a significant reduction and tackled high priority sites, as required in the draft policy statement by the regulator, Ofwat'* (HL Deb 9 November 2021, vol 815, col 1623). In July 2021, the Government published a draft statement of its strategic policies for Ofwat under s 2A Water Industry Act 1991, which stated at para 24, *'We want to see far less reliance on storm overflows which discharge sewage into our water courses. We expect companies to significantly reduce the frequency and volume of sewage discharges from storm overflows, so they operate infrequently. We expect overflows that do the most harm or impact on the most sensitive and highest amenity sites to be prioritised first. Water companies should set out how they will improve the performance of their drainage system, including reducing discharges, through drainage and waste water management plans'* (DEFRA, *The Government's Strategic Priorities for Ofwat: Draft for Consultation*, July 2021). The new drainage and sewerage plans required of undertakers under s 79 above are likely to play a significant role in providing evidence of the reduction progress being considered.

The duty is enforceable by enforcement orders under s 18 Water Industry Act made by the Secretary of State or Ofwat. Under s 22A(2)(a) of the 1991 Act, Ofwat or the Secretary of State can also impose a financial penalty where satisfied there is a breach of a statutory duty enforceable by s 18 orders, with a maximum 10 per cent of the company's annual turnover for each breach (Water Industry (Determination of Turnover for Penalties) Order 2005, SI 2005 No 477). Given the express statutory reference to the duty being enforceable by s 18 enforcement orders, it seems unlikely that a court would entertain a judicial review action against undertakers in respect of breaches – see generally the discussion on alternative remedies in M Fordham, *Judicial Review Handbook*, 7th edn (London, Bloomsbury, 2020) 36. In *Marcic v Thames Water Utilities Ltd* [2003] UKHL 66, the House of Lords held that a civil action in nuisance could not be brought against an undertaker in respect of sewer flooding on similar grounds: *"S 94(3) [Water Industry Act 1991] provides, so far as relevant, that a sewerage undertaker's duty to provide an adequate system of public sewers under section 94(1) is enforceable by the Director under section 18, in accordance with a general authorisation given by the Secretary of State. Hence, as provided in section 18, the remedy in respect of a contravention of the sewerage undertaker's general drainage obligation lies solely in the enforcement procedure set out in section 18. Thus, a person who sustains loss or damage as a result of a sewerage undertaker's contravention of his general duty under section 94 has no direct remedy in respect of the contravention. A person in the position of Mr Marcic can bring proceedings against a sewerage undertaker in respect of its failure to comply with an enforcement order if such an order has been made. In the absence of an enforcement order his only legal remedy is, where appropriate, to pursue judicial review proceedings against the Director or the Secretary of State, who has similar enforcement functions regarding section 94, in respect of any alleged failure by the*

Director or the Secretary of State to make an enforcement order as required by section 18(1)' (Lord Nicholls, para 21).

For the same reason, it seems unlikely that the Office for Environmental Protection could bring an environmental review or judicial review proceedings directly against an undertaker for breach of this duty, even though the provision falls within the definition of environmental law in s 46 of this Act and water undertakers should be considered public bodies falling within the OEP's general jurisdiction. Furthermore, s 23 of this Act requires the OEP's strategy to set out how it intends 'to exercise its enforcement functions in a way that respects the integrity of other statutory regimes' (s 23(6)(c)). On the other hand, the OEP could bring enforcement proceedings against Ofwat or the Secretary of State for failures of duty in respect of the use of s 18 orders to enforce this duty. In this context, it is important to note that, unlike many provisions concerning enforcement, s 18 Water Industry Act 1991 does not give complete discretion as to their use. Once satisfied that there is a breach of statutory duties, Ofwat or the Secretary of State must serve a s 18 order subject to the exceptions in s 19. These provide that an order does not have to be made where Ofwat or the Secretary of State is satisfied that the breach is trivial, where the undertaker has given an undertaking to secure compliance with the duty in question or where duties imposed on Ofwat or the Secretary of State in other parts of the Act preclude the making of an order. The last exception may involve a careful balancing of the general duties under the Act, including the core duties in s 2, which include a duty to exercise powers and duties in a manner best calculated to ensure undertakers are able to finance the proper carrying out of their functions. During the parliamentary debate on the predesssor to these provisions (s 20 Water Act 1989), the Minister stressed that the discretion under this heading was unlikely to be exercised where there was a danger to public health (House of Commons Standing Committee D, 9 February 1989, col 924).

84 Report on elimination of discharges from storm overflows

(1) The Secretary of State must prepare a report on—

  (a) the actions that would be needed to eliminate discharges from the storm overflows of sewerage undertakers whose areas are wholly or mainly in England, and

  (b) the costs and benefits of those actions.

(2) The Secretary of State must publish the report before 1 September 2022.

(3) The report must be laid before Parliament once it is published.

In force	9 January 2022
Application	E

S 84 requires the Secretary of State to publish and lay before Parliament before 1 September 2022 a report on the actions needed to eliminate discharges from storm overflows, and the costs and benefits of so doing. The core new duties concerning storm overflows are mainly focused on reducing environmental and public health impacts, which may or may not require their elimination.

The *Storm Flows Evidence Report* published in November 2021 during the final stages of the passage of the Bill (see annotations to s 80 above) was the first such comprehensive study, and the authors acknowledged there remained many uncertainties, particularly as to the costs of tackling the issue. As a result, their estimation of the costs of the complete separation of waste water and storm water resulting in the elimination of storm overflows had a broad scale of between £350 billion and £600 billion. Figures for more focused amelioration were far less. The scale of the figures and their uncertainty attracted considerable media and political attention during the passage of the Bill, and the duty on the Secretary of State to provide a report on the actions needed for total elimination, and their costs and benefits, appears to be designed to produce rather more clarity as to what complete separation of waste and storm water from sewers would involve.

Regulation of water and sewerage undertakers

85 Authority's power to require information

In the Water Industry Act 1991, after section 27 insert—

"**27ZA Power to require information for purpose of monitoring**

(1) The Authority may, for the purpose of performing its duty under section 27(1) or (2), serve a notice under subsection (2) on—

(a) a water undertaker or sewerage undertaker;

(b) a water supply licensee or sewerage licensee.

(2) A notice under this subsection is a notice which requires the person on whom it is served—

(a) to produce to the Authority, at a time and place specified in the notice (which must be reasonable), any documents specified or described in the notice which are in that person's custody or under that person's control, or

(b) to provide to the Authority, at a time and place and in the form and manner specified in the notice (which must be reasonable), information specified or described in the notice.

(3) The requirements imposed by a notice under subsection (2) are enforceable by the Authority under section 18.

(4) Nothing in this section requires a disclosure of information that would contravene the data protection legislation (but in determining whether a disclosure would do so, take into account the duty imposed by this section).

(5) In subsection (4) "the data protection legislation" has the same meaning as in the Data Protection Act 2018 (see section 3(9) of that Act)."

In force	10 May 2022 Commencement Order No 3, so far as relating to undertakers whose areas are wholly or mainly in England and licensees using the systems of such undertakers; Day to be appointed by Welsh Ministers so far as relating to undertakers whose areas are wholly or mainly in Wales
Application	E W

S 85 introduces a new provision in the Water Industry Act 1991 (s 27ZA) giving Ofwat greater power to require undertakers and licensees to provide it with documentation and information. Ofwat has powers under s 203 Water Industry Act to issue notices requiring information from undertakers, but these powers relate to its enforcement functions concerning potential breaches of licences or failure to meet standards. In its consultation document, *Improving Our*

Management of Water in the Environment – Consultation Proposals (DEFRA, January 2019), the Government noted that while Ofwat could informally request more general information, it lacked powers to require the provision of such information or within specific time limits where the information was needed promptly. The new s 27ZA now gives the power to issue notices requiring documents and information from water and sewerage undertakers, and to specify time limits. S 87 below amends s 216 Water Industry Act (provisions relating to the service of document), meaning that notices can now be served by electronic means rather than solely in writing. The duty to respond to the notice is enforceable by enforcement orders made under s 18 Water Industry Act. Amendments introduced to the Water Industry Act 1991 under the Water Act 2003 allow the Secretary of State or the Welsh Assembly to impose financial penalties for the contravention of any statutory requirement enforceable by s 18 enforcement orders. S 207 Water Industry Act 1991 makes it an offence to knowingly or recklessly provide false information under any provision of the Act. In 2008 Seven Trent were fined £2 million following a prosecution by the Serious Fraud Office for deliberately supplying misleading data on leakage to Ofwat.

86 Water and sewerage undertakers in England: modifying appointments

(1) Part 2 of the Water Industry Act 1991 (appointment and regulation of undertakers) is amended as follows.

(2) After section 12 insert—

"Modification of appointment conditions: England

12A Modification by the Authority

(1) This section and sections 12B to 12I apply in relation to a company appointed under this Chapter whose area is wholly or mainly in England.

(2) The Authority may make modifications of the conditions of the company's appointment under this Chapter.

(3) Before making any modifications under this section, the Authority must give notice—

(a) stating that it proposes to make modifications,

(b) setting out the proposed modifications and their effect,

(c) stating the reasons why it proposes to make the modifications, and

(d) specifying the time within which representations with respect to the proposed modifications may be made.

(4) That time must not be less than 42 days from the date of publication of the notice.

(5) A notice under subsection (3) must be given—

(a) by publishing the notice in a way the Authority considers appropriate for bringing it to the attention of persons likely to be affected by the modifications, and

(b) by sending a copy of it to—

(i) each company holding an appointment under this Chapter the conditions of which the Authority proposes to modify,

(ii) any other company holding an appointment under this Chapter, any water supply licensee and any sewerage licensee, whose interests the Authority considers are likely to be materially affected by the modifications,

(iii) the Secretary of State,

(iv) any person whose functions are or include representing those within sub-paragraph (i) or (ii) in respect of interests of theirs that the Authority considers are likely to be materially affected by the modifications, and

(v) the Consumer Council for Water.

(6) The Authority must consider any representations which are duly made.

(7) If, within the time specified under subsection (3)(d), the Secretary of State directs the Authority not to make a modification, the Authority must comply with the direction.

(8) Subsections (9) to (11) apply where, having complied with subsections (3) to (6), the Authority decides to proceed with making modifications.

(9) The Authority must—

(a) publish the decision and the modifications in a way the Authority considers appropriate for bringing them to the attention of persons likely to be affected by the modifications,

(b) state the effect of the modifications,

(c) state how it has taken account of any representations duly made, and

(d) state the reason for any differences between the modifications and those set out in the notice under subsection (3).

(10) Each modification has effect from the date specified by the Authority in relation to that modification (subject to the giving of a direction under paragraph 2 of Schedule 2ZA).

(11) The date specified may not be less than 56 days from publication of the decision to make the modification (except as provided in section 12B).

12B Modification of conditions of appointment: early effective date

(1) The date specified by virtue of section 12A(10) in relation to a modification under that section may be less than 56 days from the publication of the decision to make the modification if—

(a) the Authority considers it necessary or expedient for the modification to have effect before the 56 days expire, and

(b) the consultation condition is satisfied.

(2) The consultation condition is that the notice under section 12A relating to the modification—

(a) stated the date from which the Authority proposed that the modification should have effect,

(b) stated the Authority's reasons for proposing that the modification should have effect from a date less than 56 days from the decision to modify, and

(c) explained why, in the Authority's view, that would not have a material adverse effect on any person holding an appointment under this Chapter.

12C Modifications of conditions under section 12A: supplementary

(1) This section applies where under section 12A the Authority modifies the conditions of any appointment under this Chapter.

(2) The Authority may make such incidental or consequential modifications of the conditions of any appointments as it considers necessary or expedient.

(3) The modification of a condition of an appointment has effect subject to the giving of a direction under paragraph 2 of Schedule 2ZA in relation to the decision to which the modification relates.

12D Appeal to the CMA

(1) An appeal lies to the CMA against a decision by the Authority to proceed with the modification under section 12A of a condition of an appointment under this Chapter.

(2) An appeal may be brought under this section only by—

(a) a company holding an appointment under this Chapter the conditions of which the Authority has decided to modify,

(b) any other company holding an appointment under this Chapter, any water supply licensee or any sewerage licensee, whose interests are materially affected by the decision,

(c) a person whose functions are or include representing those within paragraph (a) or (b) in respect of interests of theirs which are materially affected by the decision, or

(d) the Consumer Council for Water.

(3) The permission of the CMA is required for the bringing of an appeal under this section.

(4) The CMA may refuse permission only on one of the following grounds—

(a) in relation to an appeal brought by a company, water supply licencee or sewerage licensee within subsection (2)(b), that the interests of the company or licensee are not materially affected by the decision;

(b) in relation to an appeal brought by a person within subsection (2)(c), that the interests of the person represented are not materially affected by the decision;

(c) in relation to any appeal, that the appeal is brought for reasons that are trivial or vexatious, or has no reasonable prospect of success.

12E Procedure on appeal to CMA

(1) Schedule 2ZA makes provision about the procedure for appeals under section 12D.

(2) Except where specified otherwise in that Schedule, the functions of the CMA with respect to an appeal under section 12D are to be carried out by a group constituted for that purpose by the chair of the CMA under Schedule 4 to the Enterprise and Regulatory Reform Act 2013.

12F Determination by CMA of appeal

(1) This section applies to an appeal brought under section 12D.

(2) In determining an appeal, the CMA must have regard, to the same extent as is required of the Authority, to—

(a) the Authority's duties under section 2, and

(b) the Authority's strategic priorities and objectives as set out in a statement under section 2A.

(3) In determining the appeal the CMA—

(a) may have regard to any matter to which the Authority was not able to have regard in relation to the decision which is the subject of the appeal, but

(b) must not, in the exercise of that power, have regard to any matter to which the Authority would not have been entitled to have regard in reaching its decision had it had the opportunity of doing so.

(4) The CMA may allow the appeal only to the extent that it is satisfied that the decision appealed against was wrong on one or more of the following grounds—

(a) that the Authority failed properly to have regard to any matter mentioned in subsection (2),

(b) that the Authority failed to give appropriate weight to any matter mentioned in subsection (2),

(c) that the decision was based, wholly or partly, on an error of fact,

(d) that the modifications fail to achieve, in whole or in part, the effect stated by the Authority by virtue of section 12A(9)(b),

(e) that the Authority did not follow the procedure required by sections 12A to 12C, or

(f) that the decision was otherwise wrong in law.

(5) To the extent that the CMA does not allow the appeal, it must confirm the decision appealed against.

12G CMA's powers on allowing an appeal

(1) Where the CMA allows an appeal under section 12D to any extent, it must do one or both of the following—

(a) quash the decision (to the extent that the appeal is allowed);

(b) remit the matter back to the Authority for reconsideration and determination in accordance with any directions given by the CMA.

(2) A direction under subsection (1) must not require the Authority to do anything that it would not have power to do (apart from the direction).

(3) The Authority must comply with a direction given to it under that subsection.

12H Time limits for CMA to determine an appeal

(1) The CMA must determine an appeal within the period of 4 months beginning with the permission date, unless subsection (2) applies.

(2) This subsection applies where—

(a) the CMA has received representations on the timing of the determination from a party to the appeal, and

(b) it is satisfied that there are special reasons why the determination cannot be made within the period specified in subsection (1).

(3) Where subsection (2) applies, the CMA must determine an appeal within the period specified by it, not being longer than the period of 5 months beginning with the permission date.

(4) Where subsection (2) applies, the CMA must also—

(a) inform the parties to the appeal of the time limit for determining the appeal, and

(b) publish that time limit in a way it considers appropriate to bring it to the attention of any other persons likely to be affected by the determination.

(5) References in this section to the permission date are to the date on which the CMA gave permission to bring the appeal in accordance with section 12D(3).

(6) In this section and in section 12I any reference to a party to an appeal is to be read in accordance with Schedule 2ZA.

12I Determination of appeal by CMA: supplementary

(1) A determination by the CMA on an appeal—

(a) must be contained in an order made by the CMA;

(b) must set out the reasons for the determination;

(c) takes effect at the time specified in the order or determined in accordance with provision made in the order;

(d) must be notified by the CMA to the parties to the appeal;

(e) must be published by the CMA—

(i) as soon as reasonably practicable after the determination is made;

(ii) in a way the CMA considers appropriate to bring it to the attention of any person likely to be affected by it (other than a party to the appeal).

(2) The CMA may exclude from publication any information it is satisfied is—

(a) commercial information, the disclosure of which would, or in the CMA's opinion might, significantly harm the legitimate business interests of an undertaking to which it relates, or

(b) information relating to the private affairs of an individual, the disclosure of which would, or in the CMA's opinion might, significantly harm the individual's interests.

(3) The Authority must take such steps as it considers requisite for it to comply with an order of the CMA under subsection (1)(a).

(4) The steps must be taken—

(a) if a time is specified in (or is to be determined in accordance with) the order, within that time;

(b) in any other case, within a reasonable time.

(5) Section 12C applies where a condition of a licence is modified in accordance with section 12G as it applies where a condition of a licence is modified under section 12A."

(3) For the italic heading before section 13 substitute—

"Modification of appointment conditions: Wales".

(4) In section 13 (modification by agreement), before subsection (1) insert—

"(A1) This section and sections 14 to 16B apply in relation to a company appointed under this Chapter whose area is wholly or mainly in Wales."

(5) Before section 17 insert—

"Modification of appointment conditions: England and Wales".

(6) After Schedule 2 insert the Schedule set out in Schedule 13.

(7) In paragraph 35(3) of Schedule 4 to the Enterprise and Regulatory Reform Act 2013 (CMA Panels), in the definition of "specialist utility functions", after paragraph (c) insert—

"(ca) an appeal under section 12D of that Act;".

In force 24 January 2022 Commencement Order No 2

Application E

Modifications of Water Undertakers' Licence Appointments

Under the Water Industry Act 1991, water undertakers are licensed by Ofwat. Ofwat's general statutory duties are to further the interests of consumers, ensure that the undertakers' functions are carried out and that they are able to finance those functions, and to secure the long-term resilience of supply systems (see s 2 Water Industry Act). When it comes to the modification of licences, Ofwat must either secure the agreement of the licence holder or refer to the matter to the Competition and Marketing Authority (CMA), although to date no references to the CMA have needed to be made. S 86 introduces new ss 12A–12G to the Water Industry Act dealing with modifications and designed to modernise and introduce more flexible procedures, more in line with modification provisions in other privatised sectors. The core reform is that Ofwat does not require consent to modifications, but undertakers will have a right of appeal to the CMA, rather than Ofwat having to make a reference to the CMA where there is no consent.

In 2011 an independent review (the Gray Review) supported the need for Ofwat and undertakers to work together to standardise and simplify licences, and recommended that the government should consider legislating for licence changes if need be: *Review of Ofwat and Consumer Representation in the Water Sector* (DEFRA, 2011). This was followed two years later by DEFRA issuing a consultation paper discussing models for reforming the procedure for modification of licence conditions: *Review of Processes for Modifying Appointment Conditions of Water and Sewerage Undertakers* (DEFRA, November 2013). In its consultation document, *Improving Our Management of Water in the Environment – Consultation Proposals* (DEFRA, January 2019) the Government consulted on proposals to change the existing provisions on modifications *'to create a more responsive modern model enabling Ofwat to better regulate and amend licences, taking into account current and future priorities, including the environment'* (p 35). Whether the new procedures will encourage Ofwat to be more forceful in changing licence conditions to improve performance standards of undertakers remains to be seen.

The key features of the new system are:

- Ofwat must first send a notification of the proposed modifications to the undertaker concerned, any other undertakers whom Ofwat considers might be materially affected by the proposals, undertakers' representative bodies (currently Water Industry UK) and the Secretary of State. It must also publish the notice in a way that will bring it to the attention of persons likely to be affected by the modifications (s 12A(3) and (5)).
- Ofwat must specify a time limit for making representations, normally a minimum of 52 days (s 12A(3)(d) and (4)), and must consider any representations duly made (s 12A(6)). Within the period of representation, the Secretary of State may direct Ofwat not to make the proposed modification (s 12A(7)).
- Ofwat must publish its notification of the modification to bring it to the attention of those who might be affected, stating its effect and how it has taken account of representations, and explaining any changes to the modification from that originally proposed (s12A(9)).
- The modification will come into effect on the date specified in the notice, which will generally be a minimum of 56 days from publication of the notice to modify (s 12A(10). However, this time limit may be shortened where Ofwat considers it necessary or expedient, provided it specified an earlier date in the original proposal, provided reasons for so doing and explained why it considers the earlier date will not adversely affect the undertaker (s 12B). If there is an appeal to Competition and Marketing Authority, the CMA may direct that the modification is to be suspended in whole or in part pending its decision (Sch 2ZA, para 2 Water Industry Act introduced by s 12I(6)).
- Rights of appeal to the CMA are introduced by new ss 12D–12I. Appeals may be made by the undertaker holding the licence to be modified, other undertakers, water and sewerage undertakers whose interests are materially affected, industry representative bodies (currently Water UK) and the Consumer Council for Wales (s 12D(2)).
- The CMA must give permission for appeal, and may refuse only on the grounds specified in s 12D(4). For any appellant, it may refuse permission if it considers the appeal is brought for trivial or vexatious reasons or has no prospect of success. Otherwise the undertaker whose

licence is to be affected always has a right of appeal, but in the case of other undertakers or representative bodies, the CMA may also refuse permission if it considers their interests are not materially affected by the modification decision (s 12D(3) and (4)).

- Detailed procedures for appeals are contained in a new Sch 2ZA Water Industry Act introduced by s 121(6).
- The CMA may only allow an appeal on the grounds specified in s 12F(4): Ofwat failed to have proper regard or give appropriate weight to its overall duties and strategy priorities and objectives under s 2 and s 2A of the Water Industry Act; its decision was based wholly or in part on an error of fact; the modifications did not achieve in whole or in part the effects stated by Ofwat in its decision notification; Ofwat failed to follow the statutory procedural requirements for making a modification; or its decision was otherwise wrong in law.
- On appeal, the CMA may not itself change the proposed modification, but must quash the decision and/or send the matter back to Ofwat for reconsideration and a decision in accordance with any directions made by the CMA (s 12G).
- The CMA must make its appeal decision normally within four months of permission being given, but the time limit may be extended by a further month on representation by a party to the appeal if the CMA is satisfied there are special reasons (s 12H(1)–(3)).

87 Electronic service of documents

In section 216 of the Water Industry Act 1991 (service of documents) after subsection (4) insert—

"(4A) Any document required or authorised by virtue of this Act to be served on any person may be served by electronic means.

(4B) But a document may be served by electronic means on a person who is a consumer only if—

(a) the person has consented in writing to the receipt of documents by electronic means (and has not withdrawn that consent), and

(b) the document is sent to the number or address most recently specified by the person for that purpose.

(4C) For the purposes of subsection (4B) "consumer" means a person who is liable to pay charges in respect of—

(a) the supply of water to any premises, or

(b) the provision of sewerage services to any premises,

but does not include a water undertaker, a water supply licensee, a sewerage undertaker, a sewerage licensee, or the Authority."

In force	10 May 2022 Commencement Order No 3 so far as relating to undertakers whose areas are wholly or mainly in England and licensees using the systems of such undertakers; Day to be appointed by Welsh Ministers so far as relating to undertakers whose areas are wholly or mainly in Wales
Application	E W

S 216 Water Industry Act 1991 provides that documents required or authorised to be served under the legislation must be served by delivery or post in hard copy. S 81 modernises the provisions by permitting the service of documents by electronic means. Consumers, as defined in s 216(4)(c), must first give their consent to electronic service.

Abstraction

88 Water abstraction: no compensation for certain licence modifications

(1) In the Water Resources Act 1991, after section 61 insert—

"61ZA No compensation where modification to protect environment: England

(1) This section applies where—

(a) a relevant licence is revoked or varied on or after 1 January 2028 in pursuance of a direction under section 54 or 56, and

(b) the ground for revoking or varying the licence is that the Secretary of State is satisfied the revocation or variation is necessary—

(i) having regard to a relevant environmental objective, or

(ii) to otherwise protect the water environment from damage.

(2) A "relevant licence" is a licence to abstract water that—

(a) is to abstract water in England only, and

(b) is to remain in force until revoked.

(3) Where this section applies, no compensation is payable under section 61 in respect of the revocation or variation of the licence.

(4) In this section the "water environment" means—

(a) any inland waters (including, in relation to a lake, pond, river or watercourse that is for the time being dry, its bottom, channel or bed),

(b) any water contained in underground strata,

(c) any underground strata themselves,

or any flora or fauna dependent on any of them.

(5) In this section "relevant environmental objective" means an environmental objective within the meaning of whichever of the following is applicable—

(a) the Water Environment (Water Framework Directive) (England and Wales) Regulations 2017 (S.I. 2017/407);

(b) the Water Environment (Water Framework Directive) (Solway Tweed River Basin District) Regulations 2004 (S.I. 2004/99);

(c) the Water Environment (Water Framework Directive) (Northumbria River Basin District) Regulations 2003 (S.I. 2003/3245).

61ZB No compensation where variation to remove excess headroom: England

(1) This section applies if a relevant licence is varied in pursuance of a direction under section 54 on or after 1 January 2028 so as to reduce the quantity of water the holder is authorised to abstract.

(2) A "relevant licence" is a licence to abstract water that—

(a) is to abstract water in England only, and

(b) is to remain in force until revoked.

(3) No compensation is payable under section 61 if—

(a) in each year during the 12 year period ending with the relevant date, the quantity of water abstracted in pursuance of the licence did not exceed 75% of the quantity of water the holder was authorised to abstract in that year, and

(b) the ground for varying the licence is that the Secretary of State is satisfied the variation does not reduce the quantity of water the holder is authorised to abstract to a level below that which the holder reasonably requires.

(4) In subsection (3) the "relevant date" is the date on which the notice of the proposals for varying the licence was served on the holder of the licence."

(2) In section 27 of the Water Act 2003 (withdrawal of compensation for certain revocations and variations), after subsection (3) insert—

"(4) This section does not apply in respect of a licence revoked or varied on or after 1 January 2028 if the licence is a "relevant licence" within the meaning of section 61ZA of the Water Resources Act 1991."

(3) Omit paragraph 30(4) of Schedule 8 to the Water Act 2014.

In force 9 January 2022

Application E

Background

The abstraction of water from surface and groundwaters is regulated by licences issued by the Environment Agency in England and Natural Resources Wales in Wales under Part II Chapter II of the Water Resources Act 1991. In September 2011 Ofwat and the Environment Agency published a report arguing for the need for change in the management of water abstraction in the light of future environmental pressures: *The Case for Change – Reforming Water Abstraction Management in England*. Two months later the government published a White Paper, *Water for Life* (Cm 8230), which included proposals to reform the abstraction system, followed later by a consultation exercise on proposed changes in order 'to make the system more flexible and resilient to future pressures'. Its response to the consultation exercise was published in 2016: *UK Government Response to Consultation Reforming the Water Abstraction Management System* (DEFRA, 15 January 2016). The government's *Water Abstraction Plan* (DEFRA, updated September 2020) contained an overall strategy to modernise abstraction management, including the development of a stronger catchment focus.

Many of the proposed strategic changes will be achieved within the existing legislative framework, but some legislative changes were needed, as outlined in the most recent consultation document, *Improving Our Management of Water in the Environment – Consultation Proposals* (DEFRA, January 2019). Since 2001 abstraction licences have been granted with a time limit, making it easier to vary or revoke them at the end of that time. But out of around 20,000 licences, only around 20 per cent have such limits, and in other cases, variation or revocation will generally require compensation if they cannot be voluntarily agreed. The existing legislation contains limited exceptions where no compensation is required when variation or revocation is on the direction of the Secretary of State, including where no abstraction has taken place in the previous four years or where the licence is held by a water company (see s 61 Water Resources Act 1991). The Water Act 2003 extended the circumstances where no compensation is required by providing that no compensation is payable for licences varied or revoked by direction of the Secretary of State after July 2012 where the Secretary of State considers this is necessary to protect waters, underground strata or any dependent flora and fauna from 'serious damage'.

No Compensation for Revocation or Variation of Licences for Environmental Reasons

S 88, applicable to England only, introduces a new s 61Z, which widens considerably the grounds where no compensation is payable where a variation or revocation is made on the direction of the Secretary of State. It applies to variations or revocations taking place after 1 January 2028. No compensation is payable if the Secretary of State is satisfied that the variation or revocation is necessary either in regard to the environmental objectives in the Water Framework Directive Regulations as listed in sub-s (5) or to protect the water environment from damage. The threshold of 'serious' environmental damage is no longer required. The water environment is defined as inland and groundwater, underground strata, and dependent flora and fauna (s 61Z(4)). It appears that the decision of the Secretary of State can only be challenged by way of judicial review. S 61(5) Water Resources Act 1961 allows for questions of 'disputed compensation' to be referred to the Upper Tribunal for determination, but would not be applicable where no compensation is provided under that section.

No Compensation for Removing Excessive Headroom in Licences

Another key issue concerning the current abstraction regime concerns the underuse of licences where licence holders abstract less water than authorised. According to *Improving Our Management of Water in the Environment – Consultation Proposals*, around 12 per cent of existing licence holders abstract less than 50 per cent of the amount authorised under the licence. If the headroom is later taken up, this could cause environmental damage. Excessive unused headroom also means that other potential abstractors may be unable to secure new licences because the regulators must take into account the existing amount of abstraction that has been already licensed even if not all taken up. S 80 introduces a new s 61ZB, applicable to England only, which provides that no compensation is payable for variations designed to reduce the headroom under existing licences. It applies where the Secretary of State has made a direction on or after 1 January 2028 and is subject to two conditions: (i) the quantity of water abstracted during each of the previous 12 years from when notice to vary was served did not exceed 75 per cent of the licensed quantity authorized; and (ii) the Secretary of State is satisfied that the reduction does not reduce the amount to less that the licence holder reasonably requires.

Future Incorporation into Environmental Permitting Regulations

S 80(3) is a technical but important amendment to Sch 8 of the Water Act 2014. As part of the modernising strategy, the government intends in future to incorporate the abstraction regime into the Environmental Permitting Regulations 2016 to provide greater consistency across environmental regulation. Sch 8 of the 2014 Act provides broad powers to make regulations, including those capable of being made, inter alia, under the abstraction provisions of the Water Resources Act 1991, but para 30(4) refers to the legislation as it had effect at the time of the commencement orders for those powers. The removal of this paragraph by s 80(3) means that these regulations can also relate the new amendments to the Water Resources Act introduced in this Act.

Water quality

89 Water quality: powers of Secretary of State

(1) The Secretary of State may by regulations amend or modify any legislation to which this section applies for the purpose of—

(a) making provision about the substances to be taken into account in assessing the chemical status of surface water or groundwater;

(b) specifying standards in relation to those substances or in relation to the chemical status of surface water or groundwater.

(2) This section applies to—

(a) the Water Environment (Water Framework Directive) (England and Wales) Regulations 2017 (S.I. 2017/407);

(b) the Water Environment (Water Framework Directive) (Northumbria River Basin District) Regulations 2003 (S.I. 2003/3245);

(c) the Water Environment (Water Framework Directive) (Solway Tweed River Basin District) Regulations 2004 (S.I. 2004/99);

(d) the Groundwater Regulations (Northern Ireland) 2009 (S.R. (N.I.) 2009 No. 254);

(e) the Water Framework Directive (Classification, Priority Substances and Shellfish Waters) Regulations (Northern Ireland) 2015 (S.R. (N.I.) 2015 No. 351);

(f) the Water Environment (Water Framework Directive) Regulations (Northern Ireland) 2017 (S.R. (N.I.) 2017 No. 81);

(g) any regulations modifying that legislation made under or by virtue of the European Union (Withdrawal) Act 2018.

(3) Regulations under subsection (1) may also, in connection with provision made under subsection (1)(a) or (b), amend or modify legislation to which this section applies so as to make provision—

(a) setting objectives in relation to the substances about which the provision is made, or in relation to the chemical status of surface water or groundwater (including objectives to maintain specified standards or to achieve specified standards by specified dates);

(b) about how objectives set by the regulations are to be met, including provision requiring, or otherwise relating to, measures to be taken to achieve those objectives;

(c) requiring, or otherwise relating to, the monitoring or assessment of any matter relating to the chemical status of surface water or the chemical status of groundwater;

(d) about the classification of bodies of water according to their chemical status or any matter relating to their chemical status.

(4) Regulations under this section may not contain provision that could be contained in—

(a) regulations made by the Welsh Ministers under section 90, or

(b) regulations made by the Department of Agriculture, Environment and Rural Affairs in Northern Ireland under section 91,

unless those Ministers or that Department consents.

(5) Regulations under this section may not contain provision applying to that part of a Scottish cross-border river basin district which is in Scotland, unless the Scottish Ministers consent.

(6) Before making regulations under this section the Secretary of State must consult—

(a) if the regulations apply to England (or part of England), the Environment Agency;

(b) if the regulations do not require the consent of the Welsh Ministers but apply to any part of a Welsh cross-border river basin district, the Welsh Ministers;

(c) if the regulations do not require the consent of the Scottish Ministers but apply to any part of a Scottish cross-border river basin district, the Scottish Ministers;

(d) any persons or bodies appearing to the Secretary of State to represent the interests of those likely to be affected by the regulations.

(7) A "Scottish cross-border river basin district" is a river basin district which is partly in England and partly in Scotland.

(8) A "Welsh cross-border river basin district" is a river basin district which is partly in England and partly in Wales.

(9) Regulations under this section are subject to the negative procedure.

Definitions

'groundwater'	s 93
'river basin district'	s 93
'Scottish cross-border river basin district'	s 89(7)

'surface water'	s 93
'Water Framework Directive'	s 93
'Welsh cross-border river basin district'	s 89(7)

In force	E W S: 9 January 2022; NI: 28 February 2022. Northern Ireland Commencement Order 2022 (for making regulations concerning legislation made under s 89(2)(d)–(f)
Application	E W S (cross-border river basin districts) NI

S 89 gives broad powers to the Secretary of State to make regulations concerning chemicals and standards for chemicals in a range of regulations implementing various EU Water Directives that were rolled over after Brexit. According to the Delegated Powers Memorandum on the Environment Bill provided by DEFRA, the powers are needed to ensure that the lists and standards do not remain fixed following the UK withdrawal from the EU: '*The power would enable action to be taken legislatively to tackle those new priority substances most accurately representing harm to the water environment. Because a degree of flexibility is required to act on the basis of future scientific developments, it is not possible to prescribe these values now on the face of primary legislation. The department expects that the power would need to be exercised whenever significant developments in scientific knowledge about substances of concern, and standards, occur*' (para 370).

The provision caused some political controversy during the passage of the Bill since regulations could be used not solely to add new chemicals of concern into the existing water regulations, but also to remove existing chemicals, or change objectives or monitoring requirements. There is no legal restraint on non-regression of chemical standards in the Act. During the debate in the Public Bill Committee, the Parliamentary Under Secretary of State noted, '*The hon. Member was concerned about a lowering of standards, which is absolutely not the case … The wider regulations require the [Environment Agency] to have an extensive and robust monitoring regime for chemicals in the water environment and refer to the priority substances as those that must be used to assess chemical status in surface waters. The EA will monitor for new and emerging harmful substances through an early warning system and, in consultation with the EA, the updates to the list will be based on the latest science and monitoring data, which currently suggest a potential increase in the number of substances of concern, rather than a reduction*' (House of Commons Public Bill Committee, 17 November 2020).

The ability of the government to reduce existing water standards concerning chemicals could be restrained by provisions in the UK–EU Trade and Cooperation Agreement (TCA). Art 7.1 gives broad autonomy to the parties to determine their levels of environmental protection, but this is qualified by Art 7.2, which provides that '*A Party shall not weaken or reduce, in a manner affecting trade or investment between the Parties, its environmental levels of protection or its climate level of protection below the levels that are in place at the end of the transition period, including by failing to effectively enforce its environmental law or climate level of protection*'. Proving that a reduction in chemical standards for water could affect trade or investment according to Art 7.2 is likely to be challenging, but could be the subject of dispute under the mechanisms provide in the Agreement. As to the status of Art 7.2 in national law, see the European Union (Future Relations) Act 2020. S 31 of that Act provides broad powers to make regulations considered appropriate to implement the TCA, and could be used to incorporate the level playing field obligations into national law. S 29, which provides that existing domestic law has effect with such modifications as are required for implementing the

TCA in that law, would not be applicable since it applies only to law existing at the time when the Agreement took effect.

Regulations under s 83 may not relate to Wales without the consent of Welsh Ministers (see also the powers relating to Wales in the next section), Northern Ireland without the consent of the Department of Agriculture, Environment and Rural Affairs (s 83(4)), or in the case of Scottish cross-border rivers without the consent of Scottish Ministers (s 83(5)).

Consultation requirements are provided for s 83(6), and include the Environment Agency for waters in England, Welsh and Scottish Ministers for cross-border rivers, and any persons appearing to the Secretary of State to represent the interests of those likely to be affected by the regulations.

90 Water quality: powers of Welsh Ministers

(1) The Welsh Ministers may by regulations amend or modify any legislation to which this section applies for the purpose of—

(a) making provision about the substances to be taken into account in assessing the chemical status of surface water or groundwater;

(b) specifying standards in relation to those substances or in relation to the chemical status of surface water or groundwater.

(2) This section applies to—

(a) the Water Environment (Water Framework Directive) (England and Wales) Regulations 2017 (S.I. 2017/407);

(b) any regulations modifying that legislation made under or by virtue of the European Union (Withdrawal) Act 2018.

(3) Regulations under subsection (1) may also, in connection with provision made under subsection (1)(a) or (b), amend or modify legislation to which this section applies so as to make provision—

(a) setting objectives in relation to the substances about which the provision is made, or in relation to the chemical status of surface water or groundwater (including objectives to maintain specified standards or to achieve specified standards by specified dates);

(b) about how objectives set by the regulations are to be met, including provision requiring, or otherwise relating to, measures to be taken to achieve those objectives;

(c) requiring, or otherwise relating to, the monitoring or assessment of any matter relating to the chemical status of surface water or the chemical status of groundwater;

(d) about the classification of bodies of water according to their chemical status or any matter relating to their chemical status.

(4) Before making regulations under this section the Welsh Ministers must consult—

(a) the Natural Resources Body for Wales;

(b) if the regulations apply to any part of a river basin district which is partly in Wales and partly in England, the Secretary of State;

(c) any persons or bodies appearing to the Welsh Ministers to represent the interests of those likely to be affected by the regulations.

(5) Regulations under this section may contain only provision which, if contained in an Act of Senedd Cymru, would (disregarding paragraphs 8(1)(c) and 11(1)(a) and (c) of Schedule 7B to the Government of Wales Act 2006) be within the legislative competence of the Senedd.

(6) Regulations under this section are subject to the negative procedure.

Definitions

'groundwater'	s 93
'river basin district'	s 93
'surface water'	s 93
'Water Framework Directive'	s 93

In force	9 January 2022
Application	W

S 90 gives similar powers to Welsh Ministers relating to chemicals as those given in England under s 89, but is confined to the regulations implementing the Water Framework Directive. Consultation requirements include the obligation to consult with Natural Resources Wales, the Secretary of State for a cross-border river basin district and anu bodies representing interests likely to be affected.

91 Water quality: powers of Northern Ireland department

(1) The Department of Agriculture, Environment and Rural Affairs in Northern Ireland may by regulations amend or modify any legislation to which this section applies for the purpose of—

(a) making provision about the substances to be taken into account in assessing the chemical status of surface water or groundwater;

(b) specifying standards in relation to those substances or in relation to the chemical status of surface water or groundwater.

(2) This section applies to—

(a) the Groundwater Regulations (Northern Ireland) 2009 (S.R. (N.I.) 2009 No. 254);

(b) the Water Framework Directive (Classification, Priority Substances and Shellfish Waters) Regulations (Northern Ireland) 2015 (S.R. (N.I.) 2015 No. 351);

(c) the Water Environment (Water Framework Directive) Regulations (Northern Ireland) 2017 (S.R. (N.I.) 2017 No. 81);

(d) any regulations modifying that legislation made under or by virtue of the European Union (Withdrawal) Act 2018.

(3) Regulations under subsection (1) may also, in connection with provision made under subsection (1)(a) or (b), amend or modify legislation to which this section applies so as to make provision—

(a) setting objectives in relation to the substances about which the provision is made, or in relation to the chemical status of surface water or groundwater (including objectives to maintain specified standards or to achieve specified standards by specified dates);

(b) about how objectives set by the regulations are to be met, including provision requiring, or otherwise relating to, measures to be taken to achieve those objectives;

(c) requiring, or otherwise relating to, the monitoring or assessment of any matter relating to the chemical status of surface water or the chemical status of groundwater;

(d) about the classification of bodies of water according to their chemical status or any matter relating to their chemical status.

(4) Before making regulations under this section the Department must consult any persons or bodies appearing to the Department to represent the interests of those likely to be affected by the regulations.

(5) Regulations under this section may contain only provision which, if contained in an Act of the Northern Ireland Assembly, would be within the legislative competence of the Assembly and would not require the Secretary of State's consent.

(6) Regulations under this section are subject to the negative procedure.

Definitions

'groundwater'	s 93
'surface water'	s 93
'Water Framework Directive'	s 93

In force	28 February 2022. Northern Ireland Commencement Order 2022
Application	NI

S 91 gives similar powers to those in s 89 relating to chemicals to the Department of Agriculture, Environment and Rural Affairs in Northern Ireland, and applicable to the regulations specified in sub-s (2). Before making regulations, the Department must consult persons or bodies appearing to represent the interests of anyone likely to be affected by the proposals (s 91(4)).

92 Solway Tweed river basin district: power to transfer functions

(1) The Secretary of State may by regulations amend or modify the Solway Tweed Regulations in accordance with this section.

(2) The "Solway Tweed Regulations" means the Water Environment (Water Framework Directive) (Solway Tweed River Basin District) Regulations 2004 (S.I. 2004/99).

(3) The regulations may provide for a function under the Solway Tweed Regulations which is exercisable (to any extent)—

(a) by the Secretary of State and the Scottish Ministers jointly,

(b) by the Secretary of State and the Scottish Ministers concurrently, or

(c) only by the Secretary of State or the Scottish Ministers, to be exercised (to any extent) in another of those ways.

(4) The regulations may provide for a function under the Solway Tweed Regulations which is exercisable (to any extent)—

(a) by the Environment Agency and SEPA jointly,

(b) by the Environment Agency and SEPA concurrently, or

(c) only by the Environment Agency or SEPA,

to be exercised (to any extent) in another of those ways.

(5) The regulations may make provision changing the geographical area in relation to which a function under the Solway Tweed Regulations is exercisable (or is exercisable by a specified person).

(6) The regulations may also provide—

(a) for a function within subsection (3) to be exercisable only with the consent of, or after consultation with, the Secretary of State or the Scottish Ministers;

(b) for a function within subsection (4) to be exercisable only with the consent of, or after consultation with, the Environment Agency, SEPA, the Secretary of State or the Scottish Ministers.

(7) The Secretary of State may make regulations under this section only with the consent of the Scottish Ministers.

(8) Regulations under this section are subject to the negative procedure.

(9) In this section "SEPA" means the Scottish Environment Protection Agency.

Definitions

'river basin district'	s 93

In force	9 January 2022
Application	E S

The Solway Tweed River Basin District is a cross-border river basin incorporating English and Scottish waterbodies flowing into the Solway and Tweed estuaries. The Water Environment (Water Framework Directive) (Solway Tweed River Basin District) Regulations 2004, made under the European Communities Act 1972, contain a general duty on the Secretary of State, the Scottish Ministers, the Environment Agency and the Scottish Environment Protection Agency (SEPA) to coordinate their functions in respect of the Water Framework Directive and the Environmental Quality Standards Directive. A common river basin management plan is developed by the Environment Agency and SEPA jointly. S 92 gives power to the Secretary of State to modify these regulations to provide for future changes in the exercise of functions by the Secretary of State, Scottish Ministers, the Environment Agency and SEPA.

93 Water quality: interpretation

In sections 89 to 92—

"groundwater" has the same meaning as in the Water Framework Directive;

"river basin district" means an area identified as such by or under any legislation to which the section in question applies;

"surface water" has the same meaning as in the Water Framework Directive;

"Water Framework Directive" means Directive 2000/60/EC of the European Parliament and of the Council establishing a framework for Community action in the field of water policy.

In force 9 January 2022

Application E W S NI

Land drainage

94 Valuation of other land in drainage district: England

(1) Section 37 of the Land Drainage Act 1991 (apportionment of internal drainage board's drainage expenses) is amended in accordance with subsections (2) and (3).

(2) In subsection (5), in the words before paragraph (a), after "shall" insert ", subject to subsection (5ZA)".

(3) After subsection (5) insert—

"(5ZA) The Secretary of State may by regulations make provision for the value of other land in an English internal drainage district to be determined in accordance with the regulations.

(5ZB) The provision that may be made under subsection (5ZA) includes, in particular, provision—

(a) about methods to be applied, or factors to be taken into account, in determining the value of land;

(b) for the value of land to be determined on the basis of estimates, assumptions or averages;

(c) for the value of land to be determined by reference to such time or times as may be specified in the regulations;

(d) for the value of land to be determined by reference to the value shown for the time being in a list or register prepared for the purposes of another enactment;

(e) for determining the value of land which is only partly within the internal drainage district in question;

(f) for the making of adjustments to what would otherwise be determined to be the value of land;

(g) for land to be taken to have a nil value.

(5ZC) Regulations under subsection (5ZA) may apply in relation to—

(a) English drainage boards specified in the regulations;

(b) English drainage boards of a description specified in the regulations;

(c) all English drainage boards.

(5ZD) Provision made by virtue of subsection (5ZC) may, in particular, include provision for an English drainage board—

(a) to elect that the regulations are to apply to them, and

(b) to make such an election in accordance with the procedure specified in the regulations.

(5ZE) Regulations under subsection (5ZA) may—

(a) make different provision for different cases, including different provision in relation to different circumstances or different descriptions of English drainage board or of land;

(b) make such incidental, supplementary, consequential, transitional, transitory or saving provision as the Secretary of State considers appropriate.

(5ZF) Provision made by virtue of subsection (5ZE)(b) may include provision which amends or repeals any provision of this Act.

(5ZG) Before making regulations under subsection (5ZA) the Secretary of State must consult such persons (if any) as the Secretary of State considers appropriate having regard to the extent to which the regulations are, in the view of the Secretary of State, likely to affect the valuation of any land.

(5ZH) Regulations may not be made under subsection (5ZA) unless a draft of the instrument containing the regulations has been laid before, and approved by a resolution of, each House of Parliament."

(4) In section 65(2) of that Act (regulations) after "Subject to" insert "section 37(5ZH)".

In force Day to be appointed by Secretary of State

Application E

Background

Ss 96–97 are designed to modernise the system of funding Internal Drainage Boards (IDBs) mainly by introducing amendments to the Land Drainage Act 1991. Although the broad underlying policy is apparent from the amendments, the core provisions give wide-ranging powers to make regulations which will flesh out the details of the changes in practice. According to the Explanatory Notes, *'By enabling the technical implementation of this policy to be set out in secondary legislation, future governments will be better able to make any future necessary updates in a timely manner*' (para 794).

IDBs have a long history, but are now governed by the Land Drainage Act 1991, which consolidated previous legislation and provides for their structures, funding and functions. They are independent public bodies, governed by boards of members elected from agricultural drainage rate payers and members appointed by local authorities contributing to their funding. Although their primary role is to supervise the drainage of land within their district, their functions and powers now go wider and include contributing to flood risk management, working closely with the Environment Agency, together with general environmental and recreational duties, including special duties relating to Sites of Special Interest (see Part IVA of the Land Drainage Act 1991). IDBs have been established in areas with special drainage needs, and in England there are currently 122 IDBs, covering just under 10 per cent of the country's land area.

The provisions in this Act are focused on funding. There are currently three main sources of funding for IDBs: drainage rates, collected directly from owners of agricultural land and buildings; 'special levies' relating to non-agricultural land, collected through rates from district and unitary local authorities; and contributions from the Environment Agency, known as Higher Land Water Contributions, for additional costs incurred from water received from higher ground outside the IDB's district.

Valuation of Non-agricultural Land for Special Levies

S 94 relates to the special levies from local authorities in England. S 37 Land Drainage Act provides for the apportionment of contributions from drainage rates and special levies, and how non-agricultural land is to be valued for the purposes of calculating the levies, essentially by reference to 1990 rating valuation lists. See also the Internal Drainage Boards (Finance) Regulations 1992 SI 1992/3079. In its consultation proposals, *Improving Our Management of Water in the Environment – Consultation Proposals* (DEFRA, January 2019), the Government noted that the 1991 Act allowed no other valuation lists to be used, and that some of the data was missing or incomplete in some areas of England. According the consultation, '*There is a desire in parts of the country to create new Internal Drainage Boards or for existing Internal Drainage Boards to be expanded, and the government welcomes these proposals where they are supported by the local community and partners. However, missing ratings data restricts the government's ability to take these forward*' (p 28).

S 94 introduces new sub-ss (5ZA)–(5ZH) into s 37 Land Drainage Act, giving the Secretary of State broad and flexible powers to make regulations concerning the valuation of non-agricultural land for the purposes of the special rates. Regulations may apply to particular drainage boards or may be of general application, and may provide for methodologies for calculation, such as using up-to-date council tax and business rate data. Regulations may allow for Internal Drainage Boards to choose whether to adopt the new methodologies in accordance with procedures laid down in the regulations. As the Government notes in its response to the consultation document, '*it is not currently minded to mandate that all internal drainage boards should automatically convert to any such new valuation methodology, as this could create cost burden. Instead the government is minded to allow internal drainage boards the choice to adopt this where appropriate. This is because the government does not expect all existing internal drainage boards will want to expand, and therefore mandating that they adopt the new valuation methodology would be an unnecessary process for many internal drainage boards*' (DEFRA, *Improving Our Management of Water in the Environment – Summary of*

Responses and Government Response, July 2021, p 50). The power to make new regulations relate to how non-agricultural land is valued, and do not apply to the apportionment between drainage rates and special rates provided in s 37(1)–(3) Land Drainage Act.

Where regulations are made, they will override the existing provisions in s 37 Land Drainage Act 1991 since the amendment provides that they are to be 'subject to' the regulations (s 88(2)). Regulations may amend or revoke existing legislation, an example of a so-called Henry VIII power (5ZF). Regulations are subject to the affirmative procedure in Parliament.

95 Valuation of other land in drainage district: Wales

(1) Section 83 of the Environment (Wales) Act 2016 (which amends the Land Drainage Act 1991) is amended as follows.

(2) In subsection (2)—

(a) for paragraph (a) substitute—

"(a) in subsection (5), in the words before paragraph (a), after "subject to subsection (5ZA)" insert "and subject to subsection (5A),";

(b) in paragraph (b)—

(i) for the inserted subsection (5A) substitute—

"(5A) The Welsh Ministers may by regulations make provision for the value of other land in a Welsh internal drainage district to be determined in accordance with the regulations.";

(ii) in each of the inserted subsections (5B) and (5C) for "The regulations" substitute "Regulations under subsection (5A)";

(iii) for the inserted subsection (5D) substitute—

"(5D) Before making regulations under subsection (5A) the Welsh Ministers must consult such persons (if any) as they consider appropriate having regard to the extent to which the regulations are, in their view, likely to affect the valuation of any land.

(5E) Regulations may not be made under subsection (5A) unless a draft of the instrument containing them has been laid before, and approved by a resolution of, Senedd Cymru."

(3) For subsection (3) substitute—

"(3) In section 65(2) (regulations) after "section 37(5ZH)" insert "and (5E),"."

In force	Day to be appointed by Welsh Ministers
Application	W

S 37 Land Drainage Act 1991 was amended by the Environment (Wales) Act 2016, giving the power to Welsh Ministers to make regulations concerning the valuation of non-agricultural land similar to the powers now being given in England by s 88 above. S 95 introduces some further amendments to those provisions. The key changes are that there is now an express consultation duty on Welsh Ministers (sub-s (5D)) and that regulations are subject to the affirmative resolution procedure by the Welsh Parliament.

96 Valuation of agricultural land in drainage district: England and Wales

(1) The Land Drainage Act 1991 is amended as follows.

(2) In section 41 (rates charged by reference to annual value of agricultural land and buildings), in subsection (2), at the end insert—

"This is subject to section 41A below."

(3) After section 41 insert—

"41A Alternative method of calculating annual value of agricultural land and buildings

(1) The appropriate national authority may by regulations make provision for the annual value of each chargeable property in an internal drainage district to be determined for the purposes of this Chapter by the drainage board for that district in accordance with the regulations.

Any determination made under the regulations is subject to sections 43 and 44 below.

(2) In this section "the appropriate national authority" means—

(a) in the case of any English internal drainage district, the Secretary of State;

(b) in the case of any Welsh internal drainage district, the Welsh Ministers.

(3) Regulations under subsection (1) may, in particular, make provision—

(a) about the date by which a drainage board are to determine the annual value of each chargeable property in their internal drainage district;

(b) about methods to be applied, or factors to be taken into account, in determining the annual value of a chargeable property;

(c) for the annual value of a chargeable property to be determined on the basis of estimates, assumptions or averages;

(d) for the annual value of a chargeable property to be determined by reference to such time or times as may be specified in the regulations;

(e) for the annual value of a chargeable property to be determined by reference to the value shown for the time being in a list or register prepared for the purposes of another enactment;

(f) for the annual value of a chargeable property to be determined by reference to the amount payable under a hypothetical transaction involving the property;

(g) for determining the annual value of a chargeable property which is only partly within the internal drainage district in question;

(h) for the making of adjustments to what would otherwise be determined to be the annual value of a chargeable property;

(i) for the determination of the annual value of a chargeable property to be made on behalf of a drainage board by a person, or a person of a description, specified in the regulations;

(j) about the appointment by the drainage board of such a person.

(4) Provision made by virtue of subsection (3)(f) may, in particular, include provision as to—

(a) the assumptions to be made about—

(i) the date of the transaction;

(ii) the nature of the transaction;

(iii) the characteristics of the parties to the transaction;

(iv) the characteristics of the property;

(v) the terms of the transaction;

(b) any matters relating to the chargeable property which are to be taken into account or disregarded;

(c) any matters relating to comparable transactions which are to be taken into account or disregarded.

(5) Regulations under subsection (1) may make provision which—

(a) applies to a drainage board which have determined the annual values of the chargeable properties in their internal drainage district for the purposes of this Chapter under the regulations (regardless of whether any of those determinations has been replaced under section 43 below or altered on appeal under section 46 below), and

(b) requires the drainage board to make further determinations of those values for those purposes in accordance with the regulations at such times or at the end of such periods as may be specified in the regulations.

(6) Provision made by virtue of subsection (5) may, in particular—

(a) make provision in relation to such a further determination which is the same as or similar to that made in relation to an initial determination, or

(b) apply provision in the regulations relating to an initial determination to a further determination, with or without modifications.

(7) Regulations made by the Secretary of State under subsection (1) may apply in relation to—

(a) English drainage boards specified in the regulations;

(b) English drainage boards of a description specified in the regulations;

(c) all English drainage boards.

(8) Regulations made by the Welsh Ministers under subsection (1) may apply in relation to—

(a) Welsh drainage boards specified in the regulations;

(b) Welsh drainage boards of a description specified in the regulations;

(c) all Welsh drainage boards.

(9) Provision made by virtue of subsection (7) or (8) may, in particular, include provision for an internal drainage board—

(a) to elect that the regulations are to apply to them, and

(b) to make such an election in accordance with the procedure specified in the regulations.

(10) Regulations under subsection (1) may—

(a) make different provision for different cases, including different provision in relation to different circumstances or different descriptions of drainage board or of land;

(b) make such incidental, supplementary, consequential, transitional, transitory or saving provision as the appropriate national authority considers appropriate.

(11) Provision made by virtue of subsection (10)(b) may include provision which amends or repeals any provision of this Act.

(12) Before making regulations under subsection (1) the appropriate national authority must consult such persons (if any) as the authority considers appropriate having regard to the extent to which the regulations are, in the view of the authority, likely to affect the valuation of any chargeable properties.

(13) Regulations may not be made under subsection (1) by the Secretary of State unless a draft of the instrument containing the regulations has been laid before, and approved by a resolution of, each House of Parliament.

(14) Regulations may not be made under subsection (1) by the Welsh Ministers unless a draft of the instrument containing the regulations has been laid before, and approved by a resolution of, Senedd Cymru."

(4) In section 42 (determination of annual value)—

(a) in subsection (4) after "under this section" insert "or under regulations under section 41A(1) above";

(b) in subsection (5) after "subsections (1) and (2) above" insert "or under regulations under section 41A above".

(5) In section 44 (effect of determinations under section 43) in each of subsections (2) and (3) after "Subject to" insert "regulations under section 41A above and to".

(6) In section 45 (appeals against determinations of annual value)—

(a) in subsection (1) after "determination under" insert "regulations under section 41A above or a determination under";

(b) in subsection (3)(b) after "determination under" insert "regulations under section 41A above or a fresh determination under";

(c) in subsection (7) after "determination under" insert "regulations under section 41A above or a determination under".

(7) In section 46 (hearing and determination of appeals under section 45) in each of subsections (2)(a), (3), (4), (5), (6), (7) and (8) after "determination under" insert "regulations under section 41A above or a determination under".

(8) In section 65(2) (regulations) after "section 37A(6) and (7)," insert "section 41A(13) and (14) and".

In force	Day to be appointed by Secretary of State for internal drainage districts wholly or mainly in England; day appointed by Secretary of State for internal drainage districts wholly or mainly in Wales
Application	E W

S 96 is concerned with drainage rates levied by Internal Drainage Boards from agricultural land. S 41 Land Drainage Act prescribes that rates are to be determined by the annual value of such land and buildings, with the annual value essentially based on the annual rent that the property could reasonably be expected to obtain if it were let. S 96 introduces a new s 41A, which gives broad powers to the Secretary of State (in England) and Welsh Ministers to make regulations providing for different methods for valuing agricultural land and buildings. These are very similar in format to the new provisions for regulations concerning non-agricultural land and buildings introduced in s 94, and are designed to allow the use of different, more modern databases.

As with the regulations concerning non-agricultural property, the regulations may apply to specific Internal Drainage Boards or all of them. Provision may be made for IDBs to choose whether to adopt the new methodologies in accordance with procedures contained in the regulations. Regulations may amend enactments, and are subject to the affirmative procedure in Parliament or the Welsh Parliament. Where regulations are made, they override the existing provisions in s 41, since s 41 is amended to make it subject to the regulations (s 96(2)).

97 Disclosure of Revenue and Customs information

(1) The Land Drainage Act 1991 is amended as follows.

(2) After section 37 insert—

"Disclosure of Revenue and Customs information

37A Disclosure of Revenue and Customs information

(1) An officer of the Valuation Office of Her Majesty's Revenue and Customs may disclose Revenue and Customs information to a qualifying person for a qualifying purpose.

(2) Information disclosed to a qualifying person under this section may be retained and used for any qualifying purpose.

(3) Each of the following is a "qualifying person"—

(a) an internal drainage board;

(b) the Agency;

(c) the Natural Resources Body for Wales;

(d) a person authorised to exercise any function of a body within paragraph (a), (b) or (c) relating to drainage rates or special levies;

(e) a person providing services to a body within paragraph (a), (b) or (c) relating to drainage rates or special levies;

(f) the Secretary of State;

(g) the Welsh Ministers;

(h) any other person specified in regulations made by the appropriate national authority.

(4) Each of the following is a "qualifying purpose"—

(a) enabling the qualifying person to whom the disclosure is made, or any other qualifying person, to carry out any functions conferred by or under Chapter 1 or 2 of this Part or section 75 of the Local Government Finance Act 1988;

(b) enabling the qualifying person to whom the disclosure is made, or any other qualifying person, to determine for the purposes of Part 1 how functions mentioned in paragraph (a) might be exercised by—

(i) an internal drainage board which is proposed to be constituted under that Part, or

(ii) the drainage board for an internal drainage district which is proposed to be constituted under that Part.

(5) Regulations under subsection (3)(h) may only be made with the consent of the Commissioners for Her Majesty's Revenue and Customs.

(6) Regulations may not be made under subsection (3)(h) by the Secretary of State unless a draft of the instrument containing the regulations has been laid before, and approved by a resolution of, each House of Parliament.

(7) Regulations may not be made under subsection (3)(h) by the Welsh Ministers unless a draft of the instrument containing the regulations has been laid before, and approved by a resolution of, Senedd Cymru.

(8) In this section—

"the appropriate national authority" means—

(a) the Secretary of State in relation to English internal drainage districts, and

(b) the Welsh Ministers in relation to Welsh internal drainage districts;

"drainage rates" means drainage rates made by an internal drainage board under Chapter 2 of this Part;

"Revenue and Customs information" means information held as mentioned in section 18(1) of the Commissioners for Revenue and Customs Act 2005;

"special levy" means a special levy issued by an internal drainage board under regulations under section 75 of the Local Government Finance Act 1988.

37B Restrictions on onward disclosure of Revenue and Customs information

(1) Information disclosed under section 37A or this section may not be further disclosed unless that further disclosure is—

(a) to a qualifying person for a qualifying purpose,

(b) in pursuance of a court order,

(c) with the consent of each person to whom the information relates,

(d) required under any other enactment, or

(e) permitted under any other enactment.

(2) Information may not be disclosed—

(a) under subsection (1)(a) to a qualifying person within section 37A(3)(d), (e), (f) or (g),

(b) under subsection (1)(a) to a person who is a qualifying person by virtue of regulations under section 37A(3)(h), where those regulations specify that this subsection is to apply in relation to the person, or

(c) under subsection (1)(e),

except with the consent of the Commissioners for Her Majesty's Revenue and Customs (which may be general or specific).

(3) Information disclosed to a qualifying person under this section may be retained and used for any qualifying purpose.

(4) A person commits an offence if the person contravenes subsection (1) or (2) by disclosing information relating to a person whose identity—

(a) is specified in the disclosure, or

(b) can be deduced from it.

(5) It is a defence for a person charged with an offence under this section to prove that the person reasonably believed—

(a) that the disclosure was lawful, or

(b) that the information had already lawfully been made available to the public.

(6) A person guilty of an offence under this section is liable—

(a) on summary conviction, to imprisonment for a term not exceeding 12 months, to a fine or to both;

(b) on conviction on indictment, to imprisonment for a term not exceeding two years, to a fine or to both.

(7) A prosecution under this section may be instituted only by, or with the consent of, the Director of Public Prosecutions.

(8) In relation to an offence under this section committed before the coming into force of paragraph 24(2) of Schedule 22 to the Sentencing Act 2020 (increase in maximum term that may be imposed on summary conviction of offence triable either way) the reference in subsection (6)(a) to 12 months is to be read as a reference to 6 months.

(9) This section is without prejudice to the pursuit of any remedy or the taking of any action in relation to a contravention of subsection (1) or (2) (whether or not subsection (4) applies to the contravention).

(10) In this section—

"qualifying person" has the same meaning as in section 37A; "qualifying purpose" has the same meaning as in that section.

37C Further provisions about disclosure under section 37A or 37B

(1) A disclosure of information under section 37A or 37B does not breach—

(a) any obligation of confidence owed by the person making the disclosure, or

(b) any other restriction on the disclosure of information (however imposed).

(2) But nothing in section 37A or 37B authorises the making of a disclosure—

(a) if the disclosure would contravene the data protection legislation (but in determining whether a disclosure would do so, take the powers conferred by those sections into account), or

(b) which is prohibited by any of Parts 1 to 7 or Chapter 1 of Part 9 of the Investigatory Powers Act 2016.

(3) Until the repeal of Part 1 of the Regulation of Investigatory Powers Act 2000 by paragraphs 45 and 54 of Schedule 10 to the Investigatory Powers Act 2016 is fully in force, subsection (2)(b) has effect as if it included a reference to that Part.

(4) Revenue and customs information relating to a person which has been disclosed under section 37A or 37B is exempt information by virtue of section 44(1)(a) of the Freedom of Information Act 2000 (prohibition on disclosure) if its further disclosure—

(a) would specify the identity of the person to whom the information relates, or

(b) would enable the identity of such a person to be deduced.

(5) In subsection (4) "revenue and customs information relating to a person" has the same meaning as in section 19(2) of the Commissioners for Revenue and Customs Act 2005.

(6) In this section "data protection legislation" has the same meaning as in the Data Protection Act 2018 (see section 3(9) of that Act)."

(3) In section 65(2) (regulations) after "and (5E)," insert "section 37A(6) and (7),".

(4) In section 70 (confidentiality of information obtained by Environment Agency and Natural Resources Body for Wales)—

(a) the existing provision becomes subsection (1);

(b) after that subsection insert—

"(2) Subsection (1) does not apply to information obtained by virtue of section 37A (disclosure of Revenue and Customs information)."

(5) In section 72(1) (interpretation), at the appropriate places insert—

""enactment" includes an enactment comprised in subordinate legislation within the meaning of the Interpretation Act 1978;";

""English drainage board" means a drainage board for an English internal drainage district;";

""English internal drainage district" means an internal drainage district which is wholly or mainly in England;";

""Welsh drainage board" means a drainage board for a Welsh internal drainage district;";

""Welsh internal drainage district" means an internal drainage district which is wholly or mainly in Wales.".

In force	Two months after Act was passed (9 November 2021)
Application	E W

S 97 introduces new ss 37A–C into the Land Drainage Act 1991, and applies to England and Wales. It allows the Valuation Office, an executive agency of Her Majesty's Revenue, to provide information to specific bodies that is not publicly available but may be needed for carrying out new valuations under regulations made under the amendments introduced by ss 89–90 above. These may include council tax valuation lists and non-domestic rating lists maintained by the Valuation Office.

S 37A specifies that the information may be supplied only to 'qualifying persons' for 'qualifying purposes' as defined in the new section. Qualifying persons include Internal Drainage Boards, the Environment Agency, Natural Resources Wales, persons authorised by those bodies to carry out functions relating to drainage rates or special levies or providing services to those bodies in relation of drainage rates or special levies, the Secretary of State and Welsh Ministers (s 37A(3)). Other persons may be included in regulations made by the Secretary of State or Welsh Ministers but only with the consent of the Commissioners of Her Majesty's Revenue and Customs (s 37A(5)) and are subject to the affirmative procedure (s 37A(6) and (7)). The qualifying purposes are defined in s 37A(4) and relate to the raising of finance by drainage rates and special levies under Part IV of the Land Drainage Act 1991 and s 75 Local Government Finance Act 1988 (special levies).

S 37B makes it an offence to disclose information obtained from the Valuation Office if this could reveal the identity of the person to whom it relates unless disclosure is to another qualifying person, pursuant to a court order, with the consent of the person to whom the information relates, or it is required or permitted under another enactment. For disclosure to certain qualifying persons (the Secretary of State, Welsh Ministers and persons authorised to carry out functions on behalf of or providing services to Internal Drainage Boards, the Environment Agency or Natural Resources Wales), consent of the Commissioners of Customs and Exercise is required (s 37B(2)).

S37C makes further provisions about disclosure of information by the Valuation Office under s 37A or onward disclosure to other qualifying persons under S37B. It provides that disclosure is not to be considered a breach of confidence that might be owed, or a breach of any other restriction on disclosure, but no disclosure is authorised if it would breach data protection legislation or is prohibited under specified provisions of the Investigatory Powers Act 2016 (s 37C(1) and (2)). Revenue and customs information which has been disclosed by the Valuation Office under s37A or disclosed to others under s37B is to be treated as exempt information under the Freedom of Information Act 2000 if its release could reveal the identity of the person to whom the information relates (s 37C(4)).

PART 6

NATURE AND BIODIVERSITY

Background

The global decline in biodiversity is causing increasing concern, with most indicators showing rapid declines. According to the Intergovernmental Science-Policy Platform on Biodiversity and Ecosystems, biodiversity loss and environmental degradation poses risks to food security, increases the risk of transmission of zoonotic diseases and makes coasts areas more vulnerable to floods and storm surges (*Summary for Policymakers of the Global Assessment Report on Biodiversity and Ecosystem Services of the Intergovernmental Science-Policy Platform on Biodiversity and Ecosystem Services*, 2019). At the UN COP 26 meeting in November 2021, the significance of biodiversity loss in the context of climate change was increasingly recognised, and para 38 of the resulting Glasgow Climate Pact '*Emphasizes the importance of protecting, conserving and restoring nature and ecosystems to achieve the Paris Agreement temperature goal, including through forests and other terrestrial and marine ecosystems acting as sinks and reservoirs of greenhouse gases and by protecting biodiversity, while ensuring social and environmental safeguards*'.

A report by the House of Commons Environment Audit Committee, published in July 2021, noted that the UK was one of the most nature-depleted countries in the world, and that the country had yet to developed a sophisticated mechanism for restoring the UK's natural environment equivalent to that provided by the Climate Change Act 2008 (House of Commons Environment Audit Committee, *Biodiversity in the UK: Bloom or Bust*, First Report of Session 2021–22, HC 136). It quoted the 2019 State of Nature Report, produced by a partnership of more than 70 organisations involved in monitoring and researching nature conservation, which estimated that since the 1970s 41 per cent of all species surveyed had declined, and that 15 per cent of species were threatened with extinction: DB Hayhow and others, *State of Nature 2019* (The State of Nature partnership, 2019). In its response to the Committee's report, published in September 2021, the Government acknowledged that '*the UK is currently one of the most nature depleted countries in the world, following centuries of species decline*' (https://publications.parliament.uk/pa/cm5802/cmselect/cmenvaud/727/72702.htm).

The UK ratified the 1992 Convention on Biological Diversity in June 1994. At the tenth meeting of the Conference of the Parties in 2010 a Strategic Plan for Biodiversity 2011–2020 was adopted (Decision X/2, www.cbd.int/doc/meetings/cop/cop-10/official/cop-10-27-add1-en.pdf). This included the Aichi Biodiversity Targets. A 2019 assessment report by the Joint Nature Conservation Committee estimated that the UK had failed to meet 14 of the 19 Aichi targets assessed but was on track to meet five, though these mainly concerned process and procedural issues rather than actual outcome targets (JNCC, *United Kingdom's 6th Report to the Convention on Biological Diversity*, 2019). The lack of progress was not out of step with global efforts, where a 2020 stocktaking assessment by the Convention Secretariat showed that none of the targets had been achieved, with only six being partially achieved (Secretariat of the Convention on Biological Diversity, *Global Biodiversity Outlook 5 – Summary for Policy Makers*, 2020). Securing better progress is likely to be a key concern of the 15th meeting of the parties (COP 15), the main meeting being planned for April–May 2022.

Biodiversity loss is now high on the UK political and policy agenda, and helps to account for the fact that, compared with the other environmental media covered by the Act (waste and resources, air, water), the provisions in Part 6 on biodiversity, coupled with the new duty on the Secretary of State to set a species abundance target for 2030 under s 3 of the Act, are rather more cohesive and innovative.

Biodiversity gain in planning

98 Biodiversity gain as condition of planning permission

Schedule 14 makes provision for biodiversity gain to be a condition of planning permission in England.

In force	Day to be appointed by Secretary of State
Application	E

Background

A number of local planning authorities already provide for requirements for biodiversity net gain in local plans, and the current National Planning Policy Framework states that *'Planning policies and decisions should contribute to and enhance the natural and local environment by … (d) minimising impacts and providing net gains for biodiversity'* (Ministry of Housing, Communities and Local Government, *National Planning Policy Framework*, 2020, para 175). Some developers have voluntarily adopted biodiversity gains in their approach to development. In December 2018 the Government consulted on proposals to introduce a general requirement that new developments should deliver net biodiversity gain across England, building on existing experience and providing greater consistency across the country: *Net Gain: Consultation Proposals* (DEFRA, December 2018). The consultation examined whether a more standardised approach to calculating biodiversity gain would be provided by a government metric. According to the proposals, *'An effective net gain policy could enable us to build the houses, commercial premises and local infrastructure we need and at the same time improve our environment by more than compensating for biodiversity loss where it cannot be avoided or mitigated'* (p 4).

The Government also consulted the Natural Capital Committee, an independent advisory committee established in 2012 and wound up in December 2020. The Committee was particularly concerned at the focus on biodiversity rather than wider environmental assets that treated the environment as an integrated system – see *Advice to Government on Net Environmental Gain* (Natural Capital Committee, May 2019) and *Net Environmental Gain: The Natural Capital Committee's Response to Defra's Commission* (Natural Capital Committee, September 2019). Requirements for wider environmental gains are being considered for the future, but as the consultation proposals stated, *'At this stage, the government is only considering mandatory implementation of net gain for biodiversity, but our longer-term commitment is to embed wider environmental net gain principles in development'* (p 16).

The summary of responses to the Government's consultation and the Government's response was published in July 2019: *Net Gain: Summary of Responses and Government Response* (DEFRA, 2019). The response forms the basis of the legislative changes introduced in the Environment Act.

The new provision concerning biodiversity gain sits alongside existing planning policies and provisions designed to protect habitats, including Sites of Specific Scientific Interest, and are not designed to diminish them – see, in particular, s 15 of the *National Planning Policy*

Framework (Ministry of Housing, Communities and Local Government). S 98 and the new Sch 14 introduced into the Town and Country Planning Act 1990 must be read in conjunction with other core provisions in this Act concerning nature and diversity, notably those on biodiversity duties (ss 102–03), nature recovery strategies (ss 104–85) and conservation covenants (ss 117–39), together with the Secretary of State's duties to set a long-term target for biodiversity in s 1(3) and species abundance target in s 3. In 2021 the British Standards Institute published British Standard 8683:2021: *Process for Designing and Implementing Biodiversity Net Gain*.

S 98 and Sch 14 introduce a new s 90A and Sch 7A into the Town and Country Planning Act 1990. Sch 7A contains the details of the new provisions, and in its response to the consultation the Government stated that it would make provision in the Environment Bill for a transition period of two years before the new requirements came into effect. This has not appeared in the Act; instead, s 98 comes into effect on a date to be determined by the Secretary of State (s 150(3)(r) Environment Act 2021). However, in its consultation document published in January 2022 (see below), the Government stated its intention to introduce mandatory net gain for development for applications for planning permission under the Town and Country Planning Act 1990 made two years after royal assent of the Environment Act (9 November 2021).

Core Requirement, Scope and Submission of Biodiversity Plan

The new Sch 7A provides that every planning permission is deemed to be subject to the condition that it may not be begin until a biodiversity gain plan has been submitted to and approved by the planning authority (para 13). The biodiversity plan must relate to the development and specify:

(a) steps taken or to be taken to minimise the adverse effect of the development on biodiversity, both on-site and off-site;
(b) the *pre-diversity* and *post-diversity values* of the on-site habitat;
(c) any *registered off-site biodiversity gain* allocated to the site;
(d) any *biodiversity credits* purchased for the site; and
(e) any other matters specified in regulations by the Secretary of State (para 14(1) and (2)).

The terms in italics are defined in Part 1 of the new Sch 7A, considered below. Regulations may be made by the Secretary of State defining the form of the biodiversity plan, the procedure for its submission, including timings, and who must submit the plan (para 14(3)). Essentially, the proposed on-site biodiversity gains, registered off-site gains and purchased credits under s 102 of the Act must in combination (or individually) secure the overall gain objective, which will generally be a 10 per cent gain in biodiversity. The legislation itself does not specify a hierarchy or prioritisation of the different options available to achieve the gain. However, in its consultation document, the Government noted that a mitigation hierarchy for habitats is already well established in planning policy, as reflected in the National Planning Policy Framework (see para 175) and local planning policies – avoid damage where possible, minimise damage where possible, restore damage or loss where possible, and as a last resort compensate for the damages or lost habitat. This approach will continue. In relation to the biodiversity gain requirements, the government indicated that the preference was for on-site net gains possible, followed by locally achieved off-site gain and, only where opportunities for on-site and locally sourced compensation were not available, the purchase of biodiversity credits. These preferences would be reflected in government guidance, the design of the metric to calculate values and the price of credits. See also the Natural England's publication on Biodiversity Metric 3.0 (July 2021): http://publications.naturalengland.org.uk/publication/6049804846366720.

The new requirement applies to all planning permissions granted under the Town and Country Planning Act, with the exception of permissions granted by a development order (such as the General Development Order), permission relating to urgent Crown development and permissions for any other types of developments specified in regulations made by the Secretary of State. In its response to the consultation exercise, the Government stated it did not favour broad exemptions from the requirements, other than for permitted development or small householder extensions. Sites with no existing habitats would not be required to comply the obligations, while smaller sites, such as minor residential developments, might be subject to longer transition requirements or a lower net gain requirement (DEFRA, *Summary of Responses and Government Response*, 2019, pp 4–5). Power to make regulations modifying the applications of the requirements to certain types of planning permission (including the grant of outline planning permission) is provides in para 18 of Sch 7A.

Finally, there is power to make regulations modifying or excluding the requirements where the on-site habitat is irreplaceable, as defined in the regulations, because it is considered that general net gain requirements would be inappropriate in such cases. The current *National Planning Policy Framework* (Ministry of Housing, Communities and Local Government, February 2019) defines irreplaceable habitat (Annex 2, Glossary) and provides that '*development resulting in the loss or deterioration of irreplaceable habitats (such as ancient woodland and ancient or veteran trees) should be refused, unless there are wholly exceptional reasons and a suitable compensation strategy exists*' (para 175(c)).

Approval of Biodiversity Plan by Planning Authority

Under para 15 of Sch 7A, the planning authority must approve the plan provided it is satisfied that:

(a) the pre-diversity value is correct;
(b) the post-diversity values are at least those stated in the plan;
(c) any registered off-site biodiversity gain specified in the plan has been duly allocated before development begins;
(d) any biodiversity credits have been actually purchased;
(e) the *biodiversity gain objective* has been met. This is defined in para 2 of the Schedule, and essentially means that overall there has been a 10 per cent increase in habitat value (whether on-site, allocated off-site gain, or purchase of diversity credits); and
(f) any other matters specified in regulations under para 14 have been dealt with.

The Secretary of State is given powers to make regulations about the procedures for approval plans, including timescales, factors that must be taken into account and appeals (para 16).

Biodiversity Value and the Biodiversity Gain Objective

The *biodiversity value* attributable to the development site is defined in para 3 of the new Sch 7A. The biodiversity value of any habitat or its enhanced value is to be calculated in accordance with a biodiversity metric produced by the Secretary of State (paras 3 and 4), and power is given to regularly update the metric. A common metric is designed to provide greater consistency and transparency, and the statutory metric will build upon experience with a biodiversity metric that was first developed by DEFRA and English Nature in 2012 for pilot sites.

The *biodiversity gain objective* is defined in para 2 as a 10 per cent gain in biodiversity from the existing pre-development biodiversity value of the site as compared to the biodiversity value attributable to the development from on-site habitat gain, any registered off-site gains and any biodiversity credits purchased from the site. The 10 per cent figure may be changed by regulations made by the Secretary of State. During the parliamentary discussion on the Bill, there was concern that the power could be used to reduce the 10 per cent figure. The Government's response was that the 10 per cent should not be viewed as a cap and that some local planning authorities were already going further. But if the Government did not have the power to reduce the 10 per cent figure, it might be forced to exempt completely development types that could not reach the 10 per cent requirement rather than subjecting such development types to a lower per cent requirement: '*Broader exemptions would be a greater risk to the achievement of wider policy aims than targeted application of a lower percentage gain*' (Rebecca Pow, Parliamentary Under Secretary of State, DEFRA, Public Bill Committee, 17 November 2020).

Pre-development Biodiversity Value

The *pre-development biodiversity value* is defined in para 5 of the new Sch 7A as the biodiversity value of the site, as calculated by the metric, at the date on which planning permission was granted (para 5(1) and (2)). Various adjustments are made for specific categories as defined in paras 6 and 7, including where development has been carried out without planning permission or permission is granted in respect of land already recorded in the biodiversity gain register (see s 101 Environment Act).

Post-development Biodiversity Value

The *post-development biodiversity value* is defined in para 8 as the projected value of the on-site habitat when development is completed as compared with the pre-development value. If the value is decreased, the biodiversity gain objective must be met by greater off-site gains or the purchase of biodiversity credits to make up the required gain. Where the person submitting the biodiversity plan proposes to carry out on-site works to increase its biodiversity value and the planning authority considers the proposed increase significant, para 9 provides that this can be taken into account in calculating the post-biodiversity value provided the condition in para 9(3) is satisfied. This requires that any proposed increase of biodiversity value by on-site works is maintained for at least 30 years, whether by virtue of a planning condition attached to the planning permission, a planning obligation or a conservation covenant as provided in s 108 of the Act.

Registered Off-Site Biodiversity Gains and Biodiversity Credits

Registered off-site biodiversity gains are defined in para 10 as habitat enhancement (itself defined in para 12(2) as enhancement of the biodiversity of the habitat) where the enhancement is required to be carried out under a conservation covenant or planning obligation and has been recorded in the biodiversity gain site register under s 100 below. *Biodiversity credits* are defined in para 11 as those credits under s 102 of the Act.

Consultation on Biodiversity Net Gain Regulations

In January 2022, the Department of Environment, Food and Rural Affairs published its *Consultation on Biodiversity Net Gain Regulations and Implementation*. This is a lengthy document of 109 pages, providing a more detailed account of how the Government is proposing the new system will work in practice.

99 Biodiversity gain in nationally significant infrastructure projects

Schedule 15 makes provision about biodiversity gain in relation to development consent for nationally significant infrastructure projects.

In force Day to be appointed by Secretary of State

Application E

The provisions concerning biodiversity gain originally did not cover national infrastructure projects under Part 3 of the Planning and Development Act 2008 or marine development projects. In its consultation response in 2019 the Government justified the exclusion because it considered that approaches to biodiversity gain for such developments had fundamentally different characteristics from more ordinary development (*Net Gain: Summary of Responses and Government Response, Department of Environment, Food and Rural Affairs*, 2019, p 5). However, as part of its response to the Treasury-commissioned study, *The Economics of Biodiversity: The Dasgupta Review* (HM Treasury, 2021), government amendments introduced during the passage of the Bill through Parliament now apply similar requirements to national infrastructure projects, and provide for their potential application to marine development projects.

S 99 introduces Sch 15, which makes amendments to the Planning Act 2008 relating to biodiversity gain and national infrastructure projects. The key changes are summarised below. The provisions in Sch 2A are closely aligned with biodiversity gain requirements for ordinary planning applications introduced by s 98 above by incorporating the definitions of the biodiversity register and biodiversity credits contain in ss 100 and 101 below (see para 12 of the new Sch 15).

The January 2022 Government Consultation on Biodiversity Net Gain (see above) addresses core policy issues concerning the application of net gain requirements to nationally significant infrastructure projects, though it states that the detail and specific wording of the requirements will be subject to further consultation.

Compliance with National Policy Statements Containing a Biodiversity Statement

A new sub-s (3A) is inserted into s 104 of the 2008 Act, providing that where a national policy statement contains a biodiversity gain statement, the Secretary of State may not grant an application for an order granting development consent unless satisfied that the biodiversity gain objective is met in relation to the proposed development. The duty is subject to the existing derogations concerning the duty to comply with national policy statements in s 104(4)–(8), including where compliance would lead to a breach of international obligations or a breach of law under other enactments, or where the Secretary of State is satisfied that the adverse impacts of the development would outweigh its benefits.

On the first review of an existing national policy statement after these provisions come into force, the Secretary of State must amend the statement to include a biodiversity gain statement for the type of development covered by the NPS (new Sch 2A para 9(2)). See further below on the biodiversity gain statement. During the period before the review takes place, the Secretary of State may publish and lay before Parliament a separate biodiversity gain statement which is to be regarded as contained in the NPS (para 9(7)), and the Secretary of State may amend the NPS to remove any inconsistencies with the biodiversity gain statement without going through the formal review process.

Once the review has taken place and incorporates the biodiversity gain statement, the separate biodiversity gain statement must be revoked (para 9(8) and (9)).

Decisions Where No National Policy Statement is Designated

S 105 of the Planning Act 2008 Act applies where no national policy statement has been designated for the development in question. It is amended to provide that where a biodiversity gain statement relating to the development type in question has been made under the new Sch 2A (see below), the Secretary of State may not grant the application unless satisfied that the biodiversity gain objective has been met in relation to the proposed development.

Biodiversity Gain Statement for National Infrastructure Development

A new Sch 2A (Biodiversity Gain) in inserted into the Planning Act 108. In summary this provides the following:

- A 'biodiversity gain statement' is defined as a statement of government policy in relation to biodiversity gain to be achieved with any description of development. The statement must set out the biodiversity gain objective, defined as the biodiversity value attributable to the development exceeding the pre-development on-site habitat by the percentage specified in the statement. New para 3(2) provides that the figure must be at least 10 per cent, though this can be changed by regulations. The statement may specify how the biodiversity value or relative biodiversity value of any habitat or habitat enhancement is to be calculated, and how development of any description may meet the objective.
- The statement may specify the pre-development biodiversity value of the on-site habitat, including the date by which it is referenced. The pre-development value must include any biodiversity enhancement recorded on the biodiversity gain site register established under s 100 below on that date.
- The statement may specify the biodiversity value attributable to the development, and for these purposes may specify the post-development value of the on-site habitat, the

biodiversity value of off-site gain allocated to the development and any biodiversity credits purchased for the development under s 101 below. In its consultation document on biodiversity credits for ordinary planning applications (DEFRA, *Net Gain: Consultation Proposals*, December 2018), the Government indicated that the preference was for on-site net gains possible, followed by locally achieved off-site gain and, only where opportunities for on-site and locally sourced compensation were not available, the purchase of biodiversity credits. This hierarchy may be reflected in the biodiversity gain statement for national infrastructure projects.

- Where the statement specifies the post-development site habitat value or the biodiversity value of off-site gain (other than registered off-site gain), it must specify that enhancement works are maintained for a period specified in the statement or that maintenance is secured through other means specified in the statement, such as a conservation covenant (see Part 7 of the Act). This is to help ensure the long-term value of enhancement works.
- The statement must set out how the biodiversity objective applies where the on-site habitat is 'irreplaceable', and may specify arrangements for minimising the adverse effect of the development on the on-site habitat. The term 'irreplaceable habitat' is defined by regulations made by the Secretary of State under para 18(1) of the new Sch 7A Town and Country Planning Act inserted by s 98 of this Act.
- The statement must specify the evidence to be supplied by the applicant for the order to be produced to demonstrate how the biodiversity gain objective is to be met.

100 Biodiversity gain site register

(1) The Secretary of State may by regulations make provision for and in relation to a register of biodiversity gain sites ("the biodiversity gain site register").

(2) A biodiversity gain site is land where—

(a) a person is required under a conservation covenant or planning obligation to carry out works for the purpose of habitat enhancement,

(b) that or another person is required to maintain the enhancement for at least 30 years after the completion of those works, and

(c) for the purposes of Schedule 7A to the Town and Country Planning Act 1990 the enhancement is made available to be allocated (conditionally or unconditionally, and whether for consideration or otherwise) in accordance with the terms of the covenant or obligation to one or more developments for which planning permission is granted.

(3) Regulations under this section must provide for the information in the register to be accessible to members of the public.

(4) Regulations under this section may in particular make provision about—

(a) the person who is to establish and maintain the biodiversity gain site register (who may be the Secretary of State, Natural England or another person);

(b) circumstances in which land is or is not eligible to be registered;

(c) applications to register land in the register;

(d) the information to be recorded in relation to any land that is registered;

(e) amendments to the register;

(f) removal of land from the register;

(g) fees payable in respect of any application under the regulations.

(5) Provision under subsection (4)(c) may in particular include provision about—

(a) who is entitled to apply to register land in the biodiversity gain site register;

(b) the procedure to be followed in making an application;

(c) the information to be provided in respect of an application;

(d) how an application is to be determined;

(e) appeals against the rejection of an application;

(f) financial penalties for the supply of false or misleading information in connection with an application.

(6) Provision under subsection (4)(d) may in particular require the recording of the following in relation to any land registered in the biodiversity gain site register—

(a) the location and area of the land;

(b) the works to be carried out on the land and the habitat enhancement to be achieved by them;

(c) information about the habitat of the land before the commencement of those works;

(d) the person who applied to register the land and (if different) the person by whom the requirement to carry out the works or maintain the habitat enhancement is enforceable;

(e) any development to which any of the habitat enhancement has been allocated;

(f) the biodiversity value (for the purposes of Schedule 7A to the Town and Country Planning Act 1990 or Schedule 2A to the Planning Act 2008) of any such habitat enhancement in relation to any such development.

(7) Regulations under this section may amend subsection (2)(b) so as to substitute for the period for the time being specified there a different period of at least 30 years.

(8) Regulations under this section making provision under subsection (4)(g) or (5)(f) are subject to the affirmative procedure.

(9) Other regulations under this section are subject to the negative procedure.

(10) The Secretary of State must keep under review—

(a) the supply of land for registration in the biodiversity gain site register;

(b) whether the period specified in subsection (2)(b) or in paragraph 9(3) of Schedule 7A to the Town and Country Planning Act 1990 can be increased under subsection (7) or paragraph 9(4) of that Schedule without adversely affecting that supply.

(11) In this section "development", "habitat enhancement", "planning obligation" and "planning permission" have the same meanings as in Schedule 7A to the Town and Country Planning Act 1990.

Definitions

'development'	Sch 7A Town and Country Planning Act 1990
'habitat enhancement'	Sch 7A Town and Country Planning Act 1990
'planning obligation'	Sch 7A Town and Country Planning Act 1990
'planning permission'	Sch 7A Town and Country Planning Act 1990

In force	Day appointed by Secretary of State
Application	E

S 100 gives power to the Secretary State to establish by regulations a biodiversity gain register. The register is an important element of the new regime for achieving biodiversity gain for planning developments introduced in s 98, ensuring that developers can only claim for off-site gains where these have been duly registered and meet conditions in the legislation and regulations. It will help ensure that off-site biodiversity credits are only allocated to one development site.

Para 2 provides three conditions for a site to be registered: (a) someone is required under a planning obligation or a conservation covenant (see ss 117–39 below) to carry out habitat enhancement works; (b) the enhancement is required to be maintained by that person or another for at least 30 years after completion of the works; and (c) the enhancement is made available under the covenant or planning obligation to be allocated to one or more developments subject to the new biodiversity gain regime. Payment may be made by developers for the allocation.

Regulations must provide for the register to be made publicly available (s 100(3)), and there is then wide discretion given to the Secretary of State to determine in the regulations detailed operational issues, such as eligibility for registration, information to be included, who may apply to register land, the development to which the habitat gain has been allocated and its biodiversity value for the purposes of calculating biodiversity gain. Regulations may introduce fees for making an application and financial penalties for supplying false or misleading information, but any such provisions are subject to the affirmative procedure (s 100(8)).

101 Biodiversity credits

(1) The Secretary of State may make arrangements under which a person who is entitled to carry out the development of any land may purchase a credit from the Secretary of State for the purpose of meeting the biodiversity gain objective referred to in Schedule 7A to the Town and Country Planning Act 1990 or Schedule 2A to the Planning Act 2008.

(2) A credit is to be regarded for the purposes of that Schedule as having such biodiversity value as is determined under the arrangements.

(3) The arrangements may in particular include arrangements relating to—

- (a) applications to purchase credits;
- (b) the amount payable in respect of a credit of a given value;
- (c) proof of purchase;
- (d) reimbursement for credits purchased for development which is not carried out.

(4) In determining the amount payable under the arrangements for a credit of a given value the Secretary of State must have regard to the need to determine an amount which does not discourage the registration of land in the biodiversity gain sites register.

(5) The Secretary of State must publish information about the arrangements, including in particular the amount payable for credits.

(6) The Secretary of State may use payments received under arrangements under this section for the following purposes (only)—

(a) carrying out works, or securing the carrying out of works, for the purpose of habitat enhancement (within the meaning of Part 7A of the Town and Country Planning Act 1990) on land in England;

(b) purchasing interests in land in England with a view to carrying out works, or securing the carrying out of works, for that purpose;

(c) operating or administering the arrangements.

(7) The references to works in subsection (6) do not include works which the Secretary of State is required to carry out apart from this section by virtue of any enactment.

(8) The Secretary of State must publish reports relating to the discharge of the Secretary of State's functions under subsections (1) and (6).

(9) A report must relate to a period not exceeding a year which—

(a) in the case of the first report, begins on the date on which Schedule 7A to the Town and Country Planning Act 1990 comes into force in relation to any development (within the meaning of Part 3 of that Act), and

(b) in the case of any subsequent report, begins on the day after the last day of the period to which the previous report related.

(10) A report must set out—

(a) the total payments received under arrangements under this section in the period to which the report relates,

(b) how those payments have been used, and

(c) where those payments have been used for the purpose of carrying out or securing the carrying out of works for the purpose of habitat enhancement, the projected biodiversity value of the habitat enhancement at such time or times after completion of the works as the Secretary of State considers it appropriate to specify.

In force Day appointed by Secretary of State

Application E

S 101 gives power to the Secretary of State to set up a scheme at national level for the purchase of biodiversity credits to fulfil obligations to meet the requirement for biodiversity gain under the new Sch 7A Town and Country Planning Act 1971. Any credits purchased will form part of the diversity plan submitted under Sch 7A, but it is clear from the consultation proposals that the preference is for gains to be achieved on site, followed by local off-site gains, and only if neither of these is possible should the gain be secured by the purchase of credits at national level. The price to be charged for biodiversity credits is therefore likely to incentivise this hierarchy rather than making their purchase too easy an option for developers, but it will be a difficult balancing exercise since s 101(4) provides that, in setting prices, the Secretary of State must have regard to the need to set levels that do not discourage the registration of land in the biodiversity gains register.

Sub-s (6) provides that the income from the purchase of credits may only be used for carrying out works for habitat enhancement as defined in para 12(2) of Sch 7A ('enhancement of the biodiversity of the habitat'), together with the purchase of land for such purposes and the administrative costs in running the scheme. But, as provided by sub-s (7), there must be additionality, in that the income may not be used for works that the Secretary of State is already under a statutory duty to carry out under other legislation. In its response to the consultation proposals, the Government indicated that '*Revenue from the sale of statutory biodiversity units will, where possible, be invested directly into pre-determined local habitat creation projects, and government will design the system to discourage any long-term pooling of revenue. Projects for investment will be selected on the basis of their additionality, their long-term environmental benefits and their contribution to strategic ecological networks*' (DEFRA, *Net Gain: Summary of Responses and Government Response*, 2019, p 12).

Accountability for how the funds are spent is provided for in sub-ss (8)–(10), which require the Secretary of State to publish annual reports (though unusually there is no requirement to lay these before Parliament) on the payments received during that year, how they were used and the projected biodiversity value after completion of any biodiversity enhancement works funded by the payments.

Biodiversity objective and reporting

102 General duty to conserve and enhance biodiversity

(1) Section 40 of the Natural Environment and Rural Communities Act 2006 (duty to conserve biodiversity) is amended in accordance with subsections (2) to (7).

(2) In the heading, after "conserve" insert "and enhance".

(3) For subsections (A1) and (1) substitute—

"(A1) For the purposes of this section "the general biodiversity objective" is the conservation and enhancement of biodiversity in England through the exercise of functions in relation to England.

(1) A public authority which has any functions exercisable in relation to England must from time to time consider what action the authority can properly take, consistently with the proper exercise of its functions, to further the general biodiversity objective.

(1A) After that consideration the authority must (unless it concludes there is no new action it can properly take)—

(a) determine such policies and specific objectives as it considers appropriate for taking action to further the general biodiversity objective, and

(b) take such action as it considers appropriate, in the light of those policies and objectives, to further that objective.

(1B) The requirements of subsection (1A)(a) may be satisfied (to any extent) by revising any existing policies and specific objectives for taking action to further the general biodiversity objective.

(1C) The first consideration required by subsection (1) must be completed by the authority within the period of one year beginning with the day on which section 102 of the Environment Act 2021 comes into force.

(1D) Any subsequent consideration required by subsection (1) must be completed no more than five years after the completion of the authority's previous consideration.

(1E) A determination required by subsection (1A)(a) must be made as soon as practicable after the completion of the consideration to which it relates.

(1F) Nothing in this section prevents the authority from—

(a) determining or revising policies and specific objectives at any time, or

(b) taking action to further the general biodiversity objective at any time."

(4) In subsection (2) for "subsection (1)" substitute "subsections (1) and (1A)".

(5) After subsection (2) insert—

"(2A) In complying with subsections (1) and (1A) the authority must in particular have regard to—

(a) any relevant local nature recovery strategy, and

(b) any relevant species conservation strategy or protected site strategy prepared by Natural England.

(2B) The Secretary of State must issue guidance to local planning authorities as to how they are to comply with their duty under subsection (2A)(a) when complying with subsections (1) and (1A) in their capacity as such authorities.

(2C) Guidance under subsection (2B) must be—

(a) published by the Secretary of State in such manner as the Secretary of State thinks fit,

(b) kept under review, and

(c) revised where the Secretary of State considers it appropriate.

(2D) The first guidance under subsection (2B) must be published by the Secretary of State within the period of two years beginning with the day on which section 102 of the Environment Act 2021 comes into force."

(6) For subsection (3) substitute—

"(3) The action which may be taken by the authority to further the general biodiversity objective includes, in particular, action taken for the purpose of—

(a) conserving, restoring or otherwise enhancing a population of a particular species, and

(b) conserving, restoring or otherwise enhancing a particular type of habitat."

(7) After subsection (5) insert—

"(6) This section has effect in relation to Her Majesty's Revenue and Customs with the following modifications—

(a) the omission from subsection (A1) of the words "in England" and "in relation to England";

(b) the omission from subsection (1) of the words from "which" to "England".

(7) In this section references to England include the territorial sea adjacent to England."

(8) In section 41 of that Act (biodiversity lists and action (England))—

(a) in subsection (1), after "conserving" insert "or enhancing";

(b) in subsection (3) for "and (2)" substitute "and (1A)".

In force Day to be appointed by Secretary of State

Application E

S 40(1) of the Natural Environment and Rural Communities Act 2006 introduced a general duty concerning biodiversity: 'A public authority must, in exercising its functions, have regard so far as is consistent with the proper exercise of those functions, to the purpose of conserving biodiversity'. The duty has been raised in argument in a number of reported cases (see, for example, *Smyth v Secretary of State for Communities and Local Government* [2013] EWHC 3844; *Morge v Hampshire County Council [2009]* EWHC 2940; *R on the application of Buglife v Thurrock Thames Gateway Development Corporation* [2008] EWHC 475), but it has not played a decisive role in court judgments. In 2017 a House of Lords committee reported on the Natural Environment and Rural Communities Act, and in relation to the s 40 biodiversity duty concluded, '*A general theme from the evidence we heard was that the duty to "have regard" to biodiversity had been ineffective, and that the state of biodiversity continues to decline. It was considered to have had little practical impact for a range of reasons, including low awareness, poor understanding, a lack of reporting requirements, a lack of biodiversity knowledge and resources, weak wording and lack of enforceability*' (Select Committee on the Natural Environment and Resources Act 2006, *The Countryside at the Crossroads: Is the Natural Environment and Resources Act Still Fit for Purpose?*, Report of Session 2017–2019, HL Paper 99, para 183).

S 102 is designed to strengthen the impact of this duty by introducing amendments to the generality of the s 40 duty by elaborating on what authorities are expected to do. S 103 below introduces an obligation on local authorities and other public bodies designated by the Secretary of State to report regularly on what has been done in respect of the duty.

The heading of the s 40 duty is now to read as a duty to conserve and enhance biodiversity (s 102(2)). From a legal perspective, this might not have been strictly necessary, since the original version of s 40 defined conservation to include 'restoring or enhancing a population or habitat', but the change underlines the general policy of raising the importance of biodiversity enhancement.

The general duty under s 40(1) is replaced with new wording that '*a public authority which has any functions exercisable in relation to England must from time to time consider what action the authority can properly take, consistently with the proper exercise of its functions, to further the general biodiversity objective*' (s 104(3)). According to the Explanatory Notes, '*This represents a proactive, strategic assessment of the public authorities functions rather than considering each function in isolation as required by the original s 40 duty'* (para 831). The 'general biodiversity objective' is defined in a new s 40(A1) as 'the conservation and enhancement of biodiversity England through the exercise of functions in relation to England'. In parliamentary discussion of the Bill, the government emphasised the broad scope of the duty: *'we want public authorities to consider all functions when determining the best action to take. That could be action on limiting their biodiversity footprint or addressing wider, indirect impacts on biodiversity, such as from transport policy, water use or energy consumption'* (Rebecca Pow, Parliamentary Under Secretary of State, DEFRA, Public Bill Committee, 17 November 2020). The original definition of a public authority in s 40(4) is retained, and includes government departments, local authorities, local planning authorities and statutory undertakers, but it is made explicit that the reference to England includes the territorial sea (s 102(7)).

New sub-ss (IA) and (IF) are inserted into s 40 Natural Environment and Rural Communities Act 2006 and elaborate on how the duty to consider action to further the conservation and enhancement of biodiversity is to be fulfilled. The first consideration must take place within one year of the section coming into force and thereafter at any time, but at least every five years (s 40(1C) and (1D)). The body may conclude that no new action can been taken, but otherwise it must determine as soon as practicable after consideration has taken place any policies and specific objectives considered appropriate to achieve the biodiversity objective, and take the action considered appropriate. This may include the revision of existing policies and objectives (s 40(1A), (1B) and (1E)).

In complying with the requirements of ss 40(1) and (1A), the authority must have regard to any relevant local nature recovery strategy (see s 105 below), and any species conservation strategy or protected site strategy produced by English Nature (s 40(2A)). The new s 40(3) elaborates on the original meaning of conservation in the former s 40 by emphasising species and habitat conservation and enhancement. Within two years of s 102 coming into force, the Secretary of State must issue guidance as to how local authorities must have regard to local nature recovery strategies in order to comply with their general conservation duty. Unusually for this Act, there is no express statutory requirement that authorities must have regard to the guidance.

The duties apply to authorities in England only, with the exception of Her Majesty's Revenue and Customs, which also has jurisdiction in Wales (s 40(6)).

103 Biodiversity reports

(1) After section 40 of the Natural Environment and Rural Communities Act 2006 insert—

"40A Biodiversity reports

(1) This section applies to—

(a) a local authority in England other than a parish council,

(b) a local planning authority in England, and

(c) a designated authority (see subsection (8)(a)).

(2) A public authority to which this section applies ("the authority") must publish biodiversity reports in accordance with this section.

(3) A biodiversity report so published must contain—

(a) a summary of the action which the authority has taken over the period covered by the report for the purpose of complying with its duties under section 40(1) and (1A),

(b) a summary of the authority's plans for complying with those duties over the period of five years following the period covered by the report,

(c) any quantitative data required to be included in the report by regulations under subsection (8)(b), and

(d) any other information that the authority considers it appropriate to include in the report.

(4) If the authority is a local planning authority, its biodiversity report must also contain—

(a) a summary of the action taken by the authority in carrying out its functions under Schedule 7A to the Town and Country Planning Act 1990 (biodiversity gain as condition of planning permission) over the period covered by the report,

(b) information about any biodiversity gains resulting or expected to result from biodiversity gain plans approved by the authority during that period, and

(c) a summary of the authority's plans for carrying out those functions over the five year period following the period covered by the report.

(5) A biodiversity report—

(a) must specify the period covered by the report, and

(b) must be published within the period of 12 weeks following the last day of that period.

(6) The authority's first biodiversity report must cover a period chosen by the authority which—

(a) is no longer than three years, and

(b) begins with the day on which the authority first becomes subject to the duty under subsection (2).

(7) A subsequent biodiversity report made by the authority must cover a period chosen by the authority which—

(a) is no longer than five years, and

(b) begins with the day after the last day of the period covered by its most recent biodiversity report.

(8) The Secretary of State may by regulations—

(a) provide for specified public authorities, or public authorities of a specified description, to be designated authorities for the purposes of this section;

(b) require biodiversity reports to include specified quantitative data relating to biodiversity in any area of land in England in relation to which the authority exercises any functions.

In this subsection "specified" means specified in the regulations.

(9) Public authorities with no functions exercisable in relation to England may not be designated under subsection (8)(a).

(10) The power to make regulations under subsection (8) is exercisable by statutory instrument.

(11) A statutory instrument containing regulations under subsection (8) is subject to annulment in pursuance of a resolution of either House of Parliament.

(12) Terms used in this section and section 40 have the same meaning as in that section."

In force Day to be appointed by Secretary of State

Application E

A weakness of the original s 40 general conservation duty was the absence of any reporting requirements. S 103 is aimed at addressing this omission, and introduces a new s 40A into the Natural Environment and Rural Communities Act 2006 requiring the production of biodiversity reports. The general conservation duty as revised applies to all public authorities, but the reporting requirement is confined to local authorities (excluding Parish Councils), local planning authorities and any other authority designated in regulations made by the Secretary of State (s 40A(1) and (8)).

Dates of Reports

Under s 40A (5) and (6) the first biodiversity report must cover a period determined by the authority of no more than three years starting from the date on which s 40A comes into effect and must be published within 12 weeks of the end of that period. Subsequent reports must cover periods of no more than five years, with no gaps in periods from previous reports, and must again be published with 12 weeks of the end of the period chosen (s 40A(5) and (7)).

Scope of Reports

The biodiversity report must contain a summary of action taken by the authority over the period covered for the purpose of complying with its duties under s 40(1) and (1A), and must also look forward to the authority's plans for the five years following that period (s 40A(3)(a) and (b)). S 40(1A) makes it clear that after consideration of its conservation duty, the authority may conclude that no new action can properly be taken. Sub-s 3(a) refers only to 'action' taken by the authority, and it is therefore ambiguous whether the report should also contain information where the authority has decided that no action can be properly taken. However, sub-s 3(d) provides that the authority must include any other information it considers appropriate to include, and it would probably be advisable that reports include information on where it was decided to take no action, and the reason for the decision.

The Secretary of State may make regulations specifying quantitative data relating to biodiversity to be included in reports (s 40A(8)). Biodiversity reports must contain such quantitative data (s 40A(3)(c)).

The report is linked to the biodiversity gain system introduced by s 98 above by requiring that a local planning authority must also include in the biodiversity report a summary of action it has taken in respect of its functions under the new Sch 7A Town and Country Planning Act 1971, information on biodiversity gains resulting or expected to be secured from biodiversity gain plans approved by the authority during the period covered by the report, and its forward plans for carrying out these functions in the five years following the end of that period (s 40A(4)).

Local nature recovery strategies

104 Local nature recovery strategies for England

(1) There are to be local nature recovery strategies for areas in England.

(2) Together the local nature recovery strategies are to cover the whole of England.

(3) The Secretary of State is to determine the areas within England to which individual local nature recovery strategies are to relate.

(4) The area of a local authority, other than a county council, may not be split between local nature recovery strategies.

(5) Section 40(2A) of the Natural Environment and Rural Communities Act 2006 (duty to conserve biodiversity) makes provision about the duties of public authorities in relation to local nature recovery strategies.

Definitions

'local authority'	s 108

In force	24 January 2022 Commencement Order No 2
Application	E

Background

Ss 104–08 make provision for the development of local nature recovery strategies. In 2010 an independent review chaired by Sir John Lawton concluded that the country's protected sites, such as Natural Nature Reserves and Sites of Special Scientific Interest, failed to provide a sufficiently coherent and resilient network to cope with future challenges, including climate change: '*Despite the important contribution designated sites have made, England's wildlife habitats have become increasing fragmented and isolated, leading to declines in the provision of some ecosystem services, and losses to species populations*' (DEFRA, *Making Space for Nature: A Review of England's Wildlife Sites and Ecological Network*, p vi). Building on these proposals, the Government's Biodiversity Strategy published in 2011 (DEFRA, *Biodiversity 2020: A Strategy for England's Wildlife and Ecosystem Services*) endorsed the need to develop ecological networks. The 25-year plan for the environment published in 2018 (HM Government, *A Green Future: Our 25 Year Plan to Improve the Environment*) included a commitment to develop a National Nature Recovery Network 'to complement and connect our best wildlife sites, and provide opportunities for species conservation and the reintroduction of native species'.

Local Nature Recovery Strategies

S 104 provides for the creation of local nature recovery strategies that will cover the whole of England. The area covered by each such strategy is to be determined by the Secretary of State. According to the Explanatory Notes, it is anticipated that each strategy will be approximately county-scale and align with administrative boundaries, and the power will be used to ensure alignment of boundaries between neighbouring strategies to avoid gaps or overlap (para 852). S 104(4) provides that, with the exception of county councils, local authority areas may not be split between different local nature recovery strategies. According to the Explanatory Notes, this will make it easier for local authorities to produce and implement strategies by making each area for a strategy an aggregate of local authority areas. County councils are exempted from the requirement because of their size and the fact that ecological and other practical considerations may not require local nature recovery strategies to align with county council boundaries (paras 854 and 855).

The new s 40(2A) Natural Environment and Rural Communities Act 2008, referred to in sub-s (5), provides that in complying with the general biodiversity duty, public authorities 'must in particular have regard to (a) any relevant local nature recovery strategy' (see annotations to s 102 above).

105 Preparation of local nature recovery strategies

(1) A local nature recovery strategy for an area ("the strategy area") is to be prepared and published by the responsible authority.

(2) The responsible authority for a local nature recovery strategy is such one of the following authorities as is appointed by the Secretary of State—

- (a) a local authority whose area is, or is within, the strategy area;
- (b) the Mayor of London;
- (c) the mayor for the area of a combined authority established under section 103 of the Local Democracy, Economic Development and Construction Act 2009;
- (d) a National Park authority in England;
- (e) the Broads Authority;
- (f) Natural England.

(3) A local nature recovery strategy is to be reviewed and republished from time to time by the responsible authority.

(4) The Secretary of State may by regulations make provision about the procedure to be followed in the preparation and publication, and review and republication, of local nature recovery strategies.

(5) Regulations under this section may, for example, include provision—

- (a) requiring the provision of information by a local authority whose area is, or is within, the strategy area but which is not the responsible authority;
- (b) for a local nature recovery strategy to be agreed by all of the local authorities whose areas are within the strategy area;
- (c) for the procedure for reaching such agreement and for the resolution of disagreements (including resolution by the Secretary of State or by a public inquiry);

(d) for consultation, including consultation of members of the public;

(e) for the times at or after which a local nature recovery strategy is to be reviewed and republished.

(6) Regulations under this section are subject to the negative procedure.

Definitions

'local authority'	s 108
'responsible authority'	s 105 (2)

In force	24 January 2022 Commencement Order No 2
Application	E

S 105 is concerned with the preparation of local nature recovery strategies. They are to be developed by authorities appointed by the Secretary of State from the list of bodies contained in sub-s (2), and are to be reviewed and republished *'from time to time'* by the authority concerned (s 105(3)). Procedures for preparing the strategies and their later review are to be contained in regulations made by the Secretary of State. Regulations may, inter alia, provide for all local authorities to agree on the strategy within their area, procedures for resolving disagreements and public consultation. Regulations may also provide for the times at which strategies are to be reviewed and republished.

106 Content of local nature recovery strategies

(1) A local nature recovery strategy relating to an area ("the strategy area") is to include—

(a) a statement of biodiversity priorities for the strategy area, and

(b) a local habitat map for the whole strategy area or two or more local habitat maps which together cover the whole strategy area.

(2) The statement of biodiversity priorities referred to in subsection (1)(a) is to include—

(a) a description of the strategy area and its biodiversity,

(b) a description of the opportunities for recovering or enhancing biodiversity, in terms of habitats and species, in the strategy area,

(c) the priorities, in terms of habitats and species, for recovering or enhancing biodiversity (taking into account the contribution that recovering or enhancing biodiversity can also make to other environmental benefits), and

(d) proposals as to potential measures relating to those priorities.

(3) A local habitat map referred to in subsection (1)(b) is a map identifying—

(a) national conservation sites in the strategy area,

(b) any nature reserves in the strategy area provided under section 21 of the National Parks and Access to the Countryside Act 1949, and

(c) other areas in the strategy area which in the opinion of the responsible authority—

(i) are, or could become, of particular importance for biodiversity, or

(ii) are areas where the recovery or enhancement of biodiversity could make a particular contribution to other environmental benefits.

(4) A local habitat map which does not relate to the whole of the strategy area must relate to the area of one or more local authorities within the strategy area.

(5) The Secretary of State may issue guidance as to—

(a) information to be included in a local nature recovery strategy pursuant to the requirements in subsections (1) to (3), and

(b) any other matters to be included in a local nature recovery strategy.

(6) A responsible authority must have regard to the guidance when preparing a local nature recovery strategy.

(7) The Secretary of State must lay before Parliament, and publish, the guidance.

Definitions

'National conservation site'	s 108(3)

In force	24 January 2022 Commencement Order No 2
Application	E

S 106 provides that the local nature recovery strategy for any area must include a statement of '*biodiversity priorities*' for the area and a local habitat map or maps covering the whole area. In order to promote consistency, the Secretary of State may give guidance on the information to be included in the strategy, and under s 107 below must also provide certain information to assist authorities in the production of local nature recovery strategies.

The statement of biodiversity priorities must include a description of the area and its biodiversity, and a description of opportunities for recovering or enhancing biodiversity in terms of habitats and species. It must then identify priorities for biodiversity recovery and enhancement, and potential measures to address those priorities (s 107(2)). There is no formal legal duty on the authorities to take action to secure the opportunities identified in the biodiversity statement, but in complying with the revised general biodiversity duty under s 40(1A) Natural Environment and Rural Communities Act, an authority must have particular regard to a local nature recovery strategy (see annotations to s 102 above). An authority which fails to take action in respect of opportunities identified in the strategy could find itself in breach of this duty.

The local habitat map must identify national conservation sites with the area, as defined in s 109(3) (which includes Sites of Special Scientific Interest, Ramsar sites and National Nature Reserves), local nature reserves and areas that the authority responsible for drawing up the strategy considers are or could become of particular importance to biodiversity and/or areas where biodiversity recovery or enhancement could make a particular contribution to other environmental benefits (s 106(3)). The reference to areas considered of potentially particular biodiversity importance is sometimes known in practice as 'biodiversity opportunity mapping', and the intention is to build upon best practice that already exists (para 871). Technical guidance on opportunity mapping was published by English Nature in 2006 (*Planning for Biodiversity – Opportunity Mapping and Habitats Networks: A Technical Guide*, English Nature Research Report ENRR687).

The reference in sub-s (3c)(ii) to other environmental benefits that may result from biodiversity gain is intended to encourage opportunities that may have multiple environmental benefits. The example given in the Explanatory Notes is the planting of a new woodland to enhance biodiversity but which could also sequester carbon and reduce flooding (para 872). Concern was expressed during parliamentary debate on these provisions as to how these strategies would fit into the government's proposed reforms to the planning system (see Ministry for Housing, Communities and Local Government White Paper, *Planning for the Future*, August 2020). The government responded that the spatial information provided by local nature recovery strategies would support the development of local plans, and that *'the Department of Environment, Food and Rural Affairs will continue to work closely with the Ministry of Housing, Communities and Local Government to set out clearly the role of local nature recovery strategies as part on the ongoing planning reforms'* (Rebecca Pow, Parliamentary Under Secretary of State, DEFRA, Public Bill Committee, 17 November 2020).

107 Information to be provided by the Secretary of State

(1) For the purpose of assisting responsible authorities in their preparation of local nature recovery strategies, the Secretary of State must prepare and publish a national habitat map for England.

(2) The national habitat map must in particular identify—

  (a) national conservation sites, and

  (b) other areas that in the opinion of the Secretary of State are of particular importance for biodiversity.

(3) The Secretary of State may from time to time review and republish the national habitat map.

(4) The Secretary of State must inform a responsible authority of any area in the authority's strategy area which falls within subsection (5).

(5) An area falls within this subsection if in the Secretary of State's opinion—

  (a) the area could be of greater importance for biodiversity, or is an area where the recovery or enhancement of biodiversity could make a contribution to other environmental benefits, and

  (b) the area could contribute to the establishment of a network of areas across England for the recovery and enhancement of biodiversity in England as a whole.

(6) The Secretary of State must provide a responsible authority with any other information—

  (a) that is held by the Secretary of State, and

  (b) that the Secretary of State considers might assist the authority in preparing a local nature recovery strategy.

Definitions

'National Conservation Site'	s 108 (3)
'Responsible Authority'	s 105 (2)

In force	24 January 2022 Commencement Order No 2
Application	E

S 107 requires the Secretary of State to provide certain information to assist in the production of local nature recovery strategies. This includes a national habitat map identifying national conservation sites as defined in s 109(3) and other areas considered of particular importance to biodiversity (sub-s (2)). The Secretary of State must also inform the authority responsible for drawing up the strategy of areas that the Secretary of State considers could be of greater biodiversity importance, or where biodiversity recovery or enhancement could contribute to other environmental benefits and where the area could contribute to a network of biodiversity areas across the England (sub-ss (4) and (5)). The lack of a coherent and resilient national network of biodiversity sites was a core criticism of existing approaches to biodiversity protection (see annotations to s 104 above), and this provision is intended to ensure that authorities do not necessarily view their local nature recovery strategies in isolation from the broader national perspective.

108 Interpretation

(1) This section has effect for the purposes of sections 104 to 107.

(2) "Local authority" means—

- (a) a county or district council in England;
- (b) a London borough council;
- (c) the Common Council of the City of London;
- (d) the Council of the Isles of Scilly.

(3) "National conservation site" means—

- (a) a site of special scientific interest, within the meaning of Part 2 of the Wildlife and Countryside Act 1981;
- (b) a national nature reserve declared in accordance with section 35 of that Act;
- (c) a Ramsar site, within the meaning of section 37A of that Act;
- (d) a marine conservation zone designated under section 116 of the Marine and Coastal Access Act 2009;
- (e) a European site, within the meaning of regulation 8 of the Conservation of Habitats and Species Regulations 2017 (S.I. 2017/1012).

In force	24 January 2022 Commencement Order No 2
Application	E

Conservation

109 Species conservation strategies

(1) Natural England may prepare and publish a strategy for improving the conservation status of any species of fauna or flora.

(2) A strategy under subsection (1) is called a "species conservation strategy".

(3) A species conservation strategy must relate to an area (the "strategy area") consisting of—

(a) England, or

(b) any part of England.

(4) A species conservation strategy for a species may in particular—

(a) identify areas or features in the strategy area which are of importance to the conservation of the species,

(b) identify priorities in relation to the creation or enhancement of habitat for the purpose of improving the conservation status of the species in the strategy area,

(c) set out how Natural England proposes to exercise its functions in relation to the species across the whole of the strategy area or in any part of it for the purpose of improving the conservation status of the species in the strategy area,

(d) include Natural England's opinion on the giving by any other public authority of consents or approvals which might affect the conservation status of the species in the strategy area, and

(e) include Natural England's opinion on measures that it would be appropriate to take to avoid, mitigate or compensate for any adverse impact on the conservation status of the species in the strategy area that may arise from a plan, project or other activity.

(5) Natural England may, from time to time, amend a species conservation strategy.

(6) A local planning authority in England and any prescribed authority must co-operate with Natural England in the preparation and implementation of a species conservation strategy so far as relevant to the authority's functions.

(7) The Secretary of State may give guidance to local planning authorities in England and to prescribed authorities as to how to discharge the duty in subsection (6).

(8) The Secretary of State must lay before Parliament, and publish, the guidance.

(9) A local planning authority in England and any prescribed authority must in the exercise of its functions have regard to a species conservation strategy so far as relevant to its functions.

(10) In this section—

"England" includes the territorial sea adjacent to England, which for this purpose does not include—

(a) any part of the territorial sea adjacent to Wales for the general or residual purposes of the Government of Wales Act 2006 (see section 158 of that Act), or

(b) any part of the territorial sea adjacent to Scotland for the general or residual purposes of the Scotland Act 1998 (see section 126 of that Act);

"local planning authority" means a person who is a local planning authority for the purposes of any provision of Part 3 of the Town and Country Planning Act 1990;

"prescribed authority" means an authority exercising functions of a public nature in England which is specified for the purposes of this section by regulations made by the Secretary of State.

(11) Regulations under subsection (10) are subject to the negative procedure.

Definitions

'England'	s 109(10)
'local planning authority'	s 109(10)
'prescribed authority'	s 109(10)

In force	30 September 2022 Commencement Order No 3
Application	E

The provisions on species conservation strategies and protected site strategies in ss 110 and 111 were introduced by government amendments during passage of the Bill through Parliament.

S 109 provides that Natural England must produce a species conservation strategy relating to England or any part of the country (the '*strategy area*'), and may amend it from time to time. A strategy may include information on areas or features of importance to the conservation of species, priorities for the conservation and enhancement of habitats for improving the conservation of species, and Natural England's own proposals for the exercise of its functions in relation to the species conservation (sub-ss (4)(a)–(c)). The strategy may also include Natural England's opinion on the giving of consents or approvals by public authorities which might affect the conservation status of species (such as planning consents) and its opinion on measures to take to avoid, mitigate or compensate for adverse impacts on species conservation that could arise from any plan, project or activity (sub-ss (4)(d) and (e)). The inclusion of these opinions should provide planning authorities in particular and developers with greater advance insights on Natural England's strategic approach concerning species conservation in order to anticipate and avoid potential conflicts. The amended general conservation duty in the Natural Environment and Rural Communities Act 2006 requires public authorities to have regard to any relevant species conservation strategy produced by Natural England (s 40(2A) introduced by s 102 of this Act – see annotations to s 102 above).

Local planning authorities and any other authority prescribed by the Secretary of State must cooperate with Natural England in the preparation and implementation of a relevant species conservation strategy, and in accordance with any guidance on cooperation given by the Secretary of State. In the exercise of their functions, local planning authorities and any other prescribed authority must have regard to the relevant species conservation strategy (sub-ss (6)–(8)).

110 Protected site strategies

(1) Natural England may prepare and publish a strategy for—

(a) improving the conservation and management of a protected site, and

(b) managing the impact of plans, projects or other activities (wherever undertaken) on the conservation and management of the protected site.

(2) A strategy under subsection (1) is called a "protected site strategy".

(3) A "protected site" means—

(a) a European site,

(b) a site of special scientific interest, or

(c) a marine conservation zone,

to the extent the site or zone is within England.

(4) A protected site strategy for a protected site may in particular—

(a) include an assessment of the impact that any plan, project or other activity may have on the conservation or management of the protected site (whether assessed individually or cumulatively with other activities),

(b) include Natural England's opinion on measures that it would be appropriate to take to avoid, mitigate or compensate for any adverse impact on the conservation or management of the protected site that may arise from a plan, project or other activity,

(c) identify any plan, project or other activity that Natural England considers is necessary for the purposes of the conservation or management of the protected site, and

(d) cover any other matter which Natural England considers is relevant to the conservation or management of the protected site.

(5) In preparing a protected site strategy for a protected site, Natural England must consult—

(a) any local planning authority in England which exercises functions in respect of an area—

(i) within which any part of the protected site is located, or

(ii) within which a plan, project or other activity that Natural England considers may have an adverse impact on the conservation or management of the protected site is being, or is proposed to be, undertaken,

(b) any public authority in England—

(i) That is undertaking or proposing to undertake, a plan, project or other activity that Natural England considers may have an adverse impact on the conservation or management of the protected site,

(ii) the consent or approval of which is required in respect of a plan, project or other activity that Natural England considers may have an adverse impact on the conservation or management of the protected site, or

(iii) that Natural England considers may otherwise be affected by the strategy,

(c) any IFC authority in England which exercises functions in respect of an area—

(i) the conservation or management of which Natural England considers may be affected by the strategy, or

(ii) the sea fisheries resources of which Natural England considers may be affected by the strategy,

(d) the Marine Management Organisation, where—

(i) any part of the protected site is within the MMO's area, or

(ii) Natural England considers any part of the MMO's area may otherwise be affected by the strategy,

(e) the Environment Agency,

(f) the Secretary of State, and

(g) any other person that Natural England considers should be consulted in respect of the strategy, including the general public or any section of it.

(6) In subsections (4) and (5), a reference to an adverse impact on the conservation or management of a protected site includes—

(a) in relation to a European site, anything which adversely affects the integrity of the site,

(b) in relation to a site of special scientific interest, anything which is likely to adversely affect the flora, fauna or geological or physiographical features by reason of which the site is of special interest,

(c) in relation to a marine conservation zone, anything which hinders the conservation objectives stated for the zone pursuant to section 117(2) of the Marine and Coastal Access Act 2009, and

(d) any other thing which causes deterioration of natural habitats and the habitats of species as well as disturbance of the species in the protected site, in so far as such disturbance could be significant in relation to the conservation or management of the protected site.

(7) A person whom Natural England consults under subsection (5)(a) to (e) must co-operate with Natural England in the preparation of a protected site strategy so far as relevant to the person's functions.

(8) The Secretary of State may give guidance as to how to discharge the duty in subsection (7).

(9) The Secretary of State must lay before Parliament, and publish, the guidance.

(10) A person must have regard to a protected site strategy so far as relevant to any duty which the person has under—

(a) the Conservation of Habitats and Species Regulations 2017 (S.I. 2017/1012),

(b) sections 28G to 28I of the Wildlife and Countryside Act 1981, or

(c) sections 125 to 128 of the Marine and Coastal Access Act 2009.

(11) Natural England may, from time to time, amend a protected site strategy.

(12) The duty to consult a person under subsection (5) also applies when Natural England amends a protected site strategy under subsection (11) so far as the amendment is relevant to the person's functions.

(13) In this section—

"England" has the meaning given in section 109;

"European site" has the meaning given in regulation 8 of the Conservation of Habitats and Species Regulations 2017;

"IFC authority" means an inshore fisheries and conservation authority created under section 150 of the Marine and Coastal Access Act 2009;

"local planning authority" has the meaning given in section 109;

"marine conservation zone" means an area designated as a marine conservation zone under section 116(1) of the Marine and Coastal Access Act 2009;

"MMO's area" has the meaning given in section 2(12) of the Marine and Coastal Access Act 2009;

"public authority" has the meaning given in section 40(4) of the Natural Environment and Rural Communities Act 2006;

"sea fisheries resources" has the meaning given in section 153(10) of the Marine and Coastal Access Act 2009;

"site of special scientific interest" means an area notified under section 28(1) of the Wildlife and Countryside Act 1981.

Definitions

'England'	s 109(9)
'European site'	s 110(13), referring to meaning in reg 8 Conservation of Habitats and Species Regulations 2017
'IFC authority'	s 109(9), referring to an inshore fisheries and conservation authority created under s 150 of the Marine and Coastal Access Act 2009
'local planning authority'	s 109(9)
'marine conservation zone'	s 110(13): an area designated as a marine conservation zone under s 116(1) of the Marine and Coastal Access Act 2009

'MMO's area'	s 110(13), referring to meaning in s 2(12) of the Marine and Coastal Access Act 2009
'public authority'	s 110(13), referring to meaning in s 40(4) of the Natural Environment and Rural Communities Act 2006
'sea fisheries resources'	s 110(9), referring to meaning in s 153(10) of the Marine and Coastal Access Act 2009
'site of special scientific interest'	s 110(9): an area notified under s 28(1) of the Wildlife and Countryside Act 1981

In force 24 January 2022 Commencement Order No 2

Application E

S 110 complements the duty to produce a s 110 Species Conservations Strategy by giving power to Natural England to produce strategies in relation to certain protected sites – European sites as defined in reg 8 Conservation of Habitats and Species Regulations 2017 (which include special areas of conservation), Sites of Special Scientific Interest and Marine Conservation Areas to the extent they lie within England. The purpose of the strategy is to improve the conservation and protection of such sites, and manage the impact of plans, projects and activities on their conservation and protection.

S 110(4) provides examples of what may be included in the strategy, and includes an assessment of the impact that plans, projects and other activities may have on the conservation and management of the protected sites; Natural England's opinion on appropriate measures to be taken to avoid or mitigate adverse effects on conservation and management; and the identification of plans, projects and other activities that it considers necessary for the conservation and management of sites. Other matters that Natural England considers relevant for the conservation and management may also be included. Adverse impacts on conservation and management of protected sites are defined in sub-s (6).

In contrast to the provisions on the Species Conservation Strategy under s 109, there are extensive consultation requirements on Natural England in preparing the strategies (sub-s (5)) and when amending them. The difference in approach is probably explained by the fact that protected site strategies will impact more directly on specified localities. The requirements include the duty to consult local planning authorities; public authorities undertaking or proposing plans, projects and activities requiring consent or approval which may have an adverse impact (as defined in sub-s (6)) on the site; public authorities whom Natural England considers might otherwise be affected by the proposed strategy; the Environment Agency; and the Secretary of State. Inshore fisheries and conservation authorities affected by the strategy must also be consulted, as must be the Marine Management Organization where a protected site falls within its jurisdiction or where Natural England considers its area may be affected by the strategy. Other bodies, including the general public, may also be consulted.

The named consultation bodies (other than the Secretary of State) have a mandatory duty to cooperate with Natural England in the preparation of protected site strategies and in accordance with any guidance issued by the Secretary of State (sub-ss (7) and (8)). Sub-s (9) provides that regard must be had to the guidance in respect of specified statutory duties – those under the Conservation of Habitats and Species Regulations 2017, the duties of statutory undertakers in relation to Sites of Special Scientific Interest under s 28G–I Wildlife and Countryside Act 1981 and the duties of public authorities in respect of marine conservation areas under ss 125–28 Marine and Coastal Access Act 2009. The amended general conservation duty in s 40 Natural

Environment and Rural Communities Act 2006 requires public authorities to have regard to any relevant protected site strategy – s 40(2A) of the 2006 Act and see annotations to s 102 of this Act above.

111 Wildlife conservation: licences

(1) In section 10 of the Wildlife and Countryside Act 1981 (exceptions to section 9 of that Act), in subsection (1)—

- (a) in paragraph (a), omit the final "or";
- (b) at the end insert "or

  (c) anything done in relation to an animal of any species pursuant to a licence granted by Natural England under regulation 55 of the Conservation of Habitats and Species Regulations 2017 (S.I. 2017/1012) in respect of an animal or animals of that species".

(2) In section 16 of that Act (power to grant licences), in subsection (3)—

- (a) in paragraph (h), omit the final "or";
- (b) at the end insert "or

  (j) in England, for reasons of overriding public interest".

(3) In that section, after subsection (3A) insert—

"(3B) In England, the appropriate authority shall not grant a licence under subsection (3) unless it is satisfied—

- (a) that there is no other satisfactory solution, and
- (b) that the grant of the licence is not detrimental to the survival of any population of the species of animal or plant to which the licence relates."

(4) In that section, in subsections (5A)(c) and (6)(b), after "two years," insert "or in the case of a licence granted by Natural England five years,".

(5) In that section, in subsection (9)(c), after "to (e)" insert "or (j)".

(6) In the Conservation of Habitats and Species Regulations 2017 (S.I. 2017/1012), in regulation 55(10), for "two years" substitute—

"(a) five years, in the case of a licence granted by Natural England, or

(b) two years, in any other case."

In force	30 September 2022 Commencement Order No 3
Application	E

S 112, amending provisions concerning licensing under the Wildlife and Countryside Act 1981, was also introduced by government amendments to the Bill during its passage through Parliament.

S 9 Wildlife and Countryside Act 1981 provides a number of offences concerning wild animals belonging to protected species, but subject to exceptions contained in s 10 of the Act which relate inter alia to government orders made under a number of Agricultural Acts and the Animal Health Act 1981. By the amendments introduced in sub-s (1), a new general exception is provided in respect of anything done under a licence granted by Natural England under reg 55 Conservation of Habitats and Species Regulations 2017, implementing the EU Habitats Directive, which gives powers to grant licences for a range of specified purposes. In 2015 the Law Commission published a major report on Wildlife Law, accompanied a draft Bill designed to secure greater consistency and coherence across wildlife legislation, including licensing provisions where there was room for confusion and overlap: *Wildlife Law*, Law Com No 362 (Law Commission, 2015). Particular complexities have arisen because the Wildlife and Countryside Act was used largely used to transpose the requirements of the 1979 EU Wild Birds Directive (now Directive 2009/147/EC), while the 2017 Regulations were introduced to transpose the requirements of the Habitats Directive (Directive 92/43/EEC). In 2017 the Government decided to delay progress on the Law Commission's proposed Bill because of the need for re-evaluation in the light of Brexit. The amendment here is a modest contribution towards integration across two regimes with respect to wild animals.

S 16(3) Wildlife and Countryside Act provides for the granting of licences by appropriate authorities as defined in the Act and covering 10 specified purposes, including the prevention of serious damage to livestock and crops. A number of core offences under the Act, including those under s 9, do not apply where the activity was in accordance with such a licence. The amendment introduced by sub-s (2) adds an additional purpose, in England only, of 'reasons of overriding public interest'. The existing purposes that can be covered by licences already include a broad category of 'any other social, economic or environmental purposes', but in relation to this category a licence may not be granted unless the authority is satisfied that the licensed activity will give rise to significant social, economic or environmental benefit and that there is no other satisfactory solution (s 16(3A) Wildlife and Countryside Act 1981). It is not immediately clear how the new category of 'overriding public interest' adds to this. But, as with the previous amendment, this is intended to create better alignment with the provisions on the purposes of licences granted under reg 55 Conservation of Habitats and Species Regulations, though it should be noted that reg 55 refers to 'imperative' reasons of overriding public interest, which appears to be a somewhat stricter hurdle.

Sub-s (3) adds an important proviso to the overall licensing provisions under s 16(3) Wildlife and Countryside Act 1981 by providing that a licence may not be granted unless the authority is satisfied there is no other satisfactory solution, and that the granting of the licence will not be detrimental to survival of the population of the species of animal or plant to which it relates. The no satisfactory solution requirement aligns these provisions with licences granted under s 16(1) of the 1981 Act, where this requirement applies. For a discussion of 'no satisfactory solution' in the context of s 16(1) Wildlife and Countryside Act, see *R (McMorn) v Natural England and another* [2015] EWHC 3297 and *R (Royal Society for the Protection of Birds v Natural England* [2019] EWHC 585 (on appeal). The species conservation strategies to be produced by Natural England under s 102 of this Act should help to underpin compliance with the new condition concerning population survival, and provide better information for potential licence applicants.

The amendments introduced under s 112(4) and (5) extend the maximum period of licences granted by Natural England under s 16(1)–(3) Wildlife and Countryside Act 1981 or under reg 55 Conservation and Habitats Regulations 2017 from two years to five years. In its report of Wildlife Law, the Law Commission recommended against having maximum time limits for licences, and the amendment here is a compromise, extending the potential length but still with a maximum limit. In appropriate cases, a licence longer than two years will improve the confidence of developers and planning authorities that a scheme has some stability, and reduces the need for the unnecessary reissuing of licences every two years.

Habitats Regulations

112 Habitats Regulations: power to amend general duties

(1) The Secretary of State may by regulations amend the Conservation of Habitats and Species Regulations 2017 (S.I. 2017/1012) (the "Habitats Regulations"), as they apply in relation to England, for the purposes in subsection (2).

(2) The purposes are—

(a) to require persons within regulation 9(1) of the Habitats Regulations to exercise functions to which that regulation applies—

(i) to comply with requirements imposed by regulations under this section, or

(ii) to further objectives specified in regulations under this section, instead of exercising them to secure compliance with the requirements of the Directives;

(b) to require persons within regulation 9(3) of the Habitats Regulations, when exercising functions to which that regulation applies, to have regard to matters specified by regulations under this section instead of the requirements of the Directives.

(3) The regulations may impose requirements, or specify objectives or matters, relating to—

(a) targets in respect of biodiversity set by regulations under section 1 or 3;

(b) improvements to the natural environment which relate to biodiversity and are set out in an environmental improvement plan.

(4) The regulations may impose any other requirements, or specify any other objectives or matters, relating to the conservation or enhancement of biodiversity that the Secretary of State considers appropriate.

(5) Regulations under this section may also, in connection with provision made for the purposes in subsection (2), amend other provisions of the Habitats Regulations, as they apply in relation to England, which refer to requirements, objectives or provisions of the Directives.

(6) In making regulations under this section the Secretary of State must have regard to the particular importance of furthering the conservation and enhancement of biodiversity.

(7) The Secretary of State may make regulations under this section only if satisfied that the regulations do not reduce the level of environmental protection provided by the Habitats Regulations.

(8) Before making regulations under this section the Secretary of State must lay before Parliament, and publish, a statement explaining why the Secretary of State is satisfied as mentioned in subsection (7).

(9) Before making regulations under this section the Secretary of State must consult such persons as the Secretary of State considers appropriate.

(10) Regulations under this section may not come into force before 1 February 2023.

(11) In this section—

"the Directives" has the same meaning as in the Habitats Regulations (see regulation 3(1));

"England" includes the territorial sea adjacent to England, which for this purpose does not include—

(a) any part of the territorial sea adjacent to Wales for the general or residual purposes of the Government of Wales Act 2006 (see section 158 of that Act), or

(b) any part of the territorial sea adjacent to Scotland for the general or residual purposes of the Scotland Act 1998 (see section 126 of that Act);

"environmental improvement plan" has the same meaning as in Part 1.

(12) Regulations under this section are subject to the affirmative procedure.

Definitions

'the Directives'	reg 3(1) Habitats Regulations (Habitats Directive 92/43/EEC and Birds Directive 2009/147/EC (s 112(11))
'England'	s 112(11)
'environmental improvement plan'	s 8(1) of this Act (s 112(11))

In force	24 January 2022 Commencement Order No 2, but no regulations to come into force before 1 February 2023 (s 112(10))
Application	E

The provisions concerning the power to amend the 2017 Conservation of Habitats and Species Regulations were introduced by the Government during the passage of the Bill through Parliament. The 2017 Regulations, implementing the EU Habitats Directive, were made under the European Communities Act 1972, and power to amend them more substantially than permissible under s 8 European Union (Withdrawal) Act 2018 would now require specific legislative authority. According to the Supplementary Delegated Powers Memorandum, the purposes of the powers are to realign the provisions to enable the Secretary of State *'to take into account the evolution of domestic biodiversity priorities, while not diminishing the overall level of environmental protection provided'*.

Reg 9(1) of the 2017 Habitats Regulations imposes a general duty that requires the Secretary of State, Natural England, Ministers of the Crown, statutory undertakers, local authorities and other public bodies (as defined in reg 7) to comply with the requirements of the Habitats Directive 92/43/EEC and the Birds Directive 2009/147/EC. In addition, reg 9(3) of the regulations requires competent authorities (Ministers of the Crown, statutory undertakers, local authorities and other public bodies as defined in s 7) to have regard to the requirements of the Directives when exercising any of their functions. See the Introduction for the legal meaning of *'have regard to'*.

S 122 (1) gives the Secretary of State the general power to amend the regulations in relation to s 9, but any amendments may not come into force before 1 February 2023 (sub-s (10)). This is to ensure that amendments take into account the setting of long-term priority targets under s 1 of the Act (one of which must include a biodiversity target), the species abundance target made by regulations under s 3 and the first revision of the environmental improvement plan, which must be completed by 31 January 2023 (s 10(3) of the Act). Under sub-s (2) the regulations may require persons falling within s 9(1) or 9(3) to comply with requirements in the regulations instead of the Directives. Sub-s (3) links the power to amend to allow them to include reference to the long-term priority targets under s 1 and the species abundance target under s 3 of the Act. During the parliamentary debates, the Government noted that the reg 9 duties are not specified anywhere else: '*This has provided scope for differing interpretations and disagreement, as well as potential for legal challenge. Instead of spending time and taxpayers' money on battles in the courtroom, we want to try to focus on ensuring that the protection of our designated sites and species is based on robust science and technical expertise*' (Lord Goldsmith, HL Deb 15 September 2021, vol 814, col 1399).

S 122 provides two legal constraints on the scope of the amending regulations. Under sub-s (6), in making the regulations, the Secretary of State must have regard to the particular importance of furthering the conservation and enhancement of biodiversity. For further comments of the meaning of 'have regard to', see the Introduction. Sub-s (7) is more forceful, providing that regulations may only be made if the Secretary of State is satisfied that the regulations 'do not reduce the level of environmental protection provided by the Habitats Regulations'. Greater political accountability is provided in sub-s (8), which requires the Secretary of State, before making any regulations, to publish and lay before Parliament a statement explaining why the Secretary of State is satisfied the regulations do not reduce the level of protection as required under sub-s (7).

During the lively parliamentary debates in the House of Lords on these provisions, it was pointed out that there may be an uncomfortable mismatch between the provisions in that the biodiversity priority targets, the species abundance target and the environmental improvement plan are likely to focus on overall national improvements, while the Habitats Regulations are primarily aimed at the protection of individual protected sites. The reference in sub-s (7) to the 'level of protection' provided by the Habitats Regulations is still a little ambiguous in that it might be interpreted as referring to the overall protection, though the wording seems to more naturally refer to the level of protection of individual sites falling within the regulations. Lord Goldsmith, the House of Lords Environment Minister, noted that the provision in sub-s (8) '*requires certainty on his part that there have been no reductions in protections from the existing habitats regulations. The Secretary of State will also have to demonstrate this by making a statement to this House and subjecting that statement to scrutiny. If the judgment of the Secretary of State is proven, or even thought, to be wrong, it can subsequently be challenged in court*' (HL Deb 15 September 2021, vol 814, col 1399).

Sub-s (9) imposes a duty on the Secretary of State to consult persons considered appropriate before making the regulations. During the parliamentary debate, the Government committed to consulting with, amongst others, the Office for Environmental Protection, the statutory nature conservation bodies, key environmental NGOs, farmers and land managers, as well as publishing a Green Paper '*which will set out clearly, plainly and transparently our view of the current requirements of Regulation 9 and remove that uncertainty*' (Lord Goldsmith, HL Deb 15 September 2021, vol 814, col 1399) that was introduced by the Government during the passage of the Bill through Parliament. The 2017 Regulations, implementing the EU Habitats Directive, were made under the European Communities Act 1972, and the power to amend them more substantially than permissible under s 8 European Union (Withdrawal) Act 2018 would now require specific legislative authority. According to the Supplementary Delegated Powers Memorandum, the purposes of the powers are to realign the provisions to enable the Secretary of State '*to take into account the evolution of domestic biodiversity priorities, while not diminishing the overall level of environmental protection provided*'.

113 Habitats Regulations: power to amend Part 6

(1) The Secretary of State may by regulations amend Part 6 of the Conservation of Habitats and Species Regulations 2017 (S.I. 2017/1012) (the "Habitats Regulations") (assessment of plans and projects) as they apply in relation to England.

(2) In making regulations under this section the Secretary of State must have regard to the particular importance of furthering the conservation and enhancement of biodiversity.

(3) The Secretary of State may make regulations under this section only if satisfied that the regulations do not reduce the level of environmental protection provided by the Habitats Regulations.

(4) Before making regulations under this section the Secretary of State must lay before Parliament, and publish, a statement explaining why the Secretary of State is satisfied as mentioned in subsection (3).

(5) Before making regulations under this section the Secretary of State must consult such persons as the Secretary of State considers appropriate.

(6) In this section "England" has the same meaning as in section 112.

(7) Regulations under this section are subject to the affirmative procedure.

In force	24 January 2022 Commencement Order No 2
Application	E

S 113 provides similar powers to amend the 2017 Conservation of Habitats and Species Regulations as s 112 above but in relation to Part 6, which deals with the assessment of plans and projects. However, the coming into force of such regulations are not subject to the time limit specified in s 112.

As with s 112, before making regulations, the Secretary of State must have regard to the particular importance of further conservation and the enhancement of biodiversity, and must be satisfied that the regulations do not reduce the level of protection provided by the Habitats Regulations (sub-s (2) and (3). A statement explaining why he is so satisfied must be published and laid before Parliament (sub-s (4)). See further the annotations to s 112 above.

In its Supplementary Delegated Powers Memorandum, the Government affirmed that the network of European sites protected under the regulations remained important for the UK international obligations and in meeting domestic biodiversity objectives: '*Ensuring that plans and projects that could impact upon these sites are properly assessed and adverse impacts upon them avoided, will be important in meeting the Government's ambitions in relation to biodiversity. At the same time however, the Government continues to look to improve the operation of these provisions, where this is possible, eg adding additional clarity as to the requirements into the legislation. The Government would like to explore more strategic approaches to achieving these requirements*' (DEFRA, Supplementary Delegated Powers Memorandum, 2021, p 2). During the parliamentary debate in the House of Lords, the Government confirmed that a Green Paper would be published on options for proposals to amend the assessment process under the Habitats Regulations, and that a working group under the chair of Lord Benyon had to be established to consult experts in the field and provide input to the Green Paper. According to Lord Goldsmith, '*A clearer, quicker and more easily understood process will support environmental protection by focusing on the issues that really matter for protected sites*' (HL Deb 15 September 2021, vol 814, col 1399).

Tree felling and planting

114 Controlling the felling of trees in England

Schedule 16 makes amendments to Part 2 of the Forestry Act 1967 in relation to the enforcement of the power to control the felling of trees in England.

In force	Day to be appointed by Secretary of State
Application	E

S 9 Forestry Act 1967 requires licences for the felling of trees over certain quantities (over five cubic metres per quarter and where more than two cubic metres is sold) and subject to various exceptions specified in the Act. Licences are granted in England by the Forestry Commission, in Wales by Natural Resources Wales. Sch 16, introduced by this section, makes various amendments to the Forestry Act designed to improve the enforcement of controls. The proposed measures were included as part of the Government's 2019 consultation on trees and woodlands – see *Protecting and Enhancing England's Trees and Woodlands: Consultation* (DEFRA, December 2018) and *Summary of Responses and Government Response* (DEFRA, October 2019).

The changes brought about by the amendments that apply to England only are:

- The penalty for the summary offence of felling without a licence is raised to an unlimited fine.
- A notice under s 17A of the Act from the Forestry Commission requiring restocking following felling without a licence becomes a land charge. Subsequent purchasers of the land in question will be bound by the notice unless and until the charge is removed. Similarly, a notice requiring compliance with conditions or directions served under s 24 of the Act becomes a land charge.
- Under a new s 24A Forestry Act, the Commissioners may serve the new owner of land already subject to a notice which has not be been complied with a new notice requiring the steps that must be completed.
- Under a new s 24B, following conviction of failure to comply with a notice under s 24, a magistrates' court may make a restocking order, including requirements to maintain the restocked trees for a period not exceeding 10 years. Enforcement of such orders is under s 63 Magistrates' Courts Act 1980, which provides for a daily fine of £50 for every day in default, a penalty of not more that £5000 or a custodial sentence until the order is complied with or not exceeding two months.
- Where documents such as s 17A enforcement notices are served under the Forestry Act on a company or body, s 30 of the Act is amended to allow service on a director as well as the secretary or clerk, as currently provided.
- S 30 Forestry Act currently gives power to the Forestry Commission to require occupiers of land or anyone receiving rent to provide information on others, including owners, who have an interest in the land in question. This is now amended to give the Commission additional powers to seek information from the owner of the land about other interests in the land, such as tenants and leaseholders.

115 Local highway authorities in England to consult before felling street trees

After section 96 of the Highways Act 1980 insert—

"96A Duty of local highway authorities in England to consult before felling street trees

(1) A local highway authority in England must consult members of the public before felling a tree on an urban road (a "street tree").

(2) A local highway authority must have regard to any guidance given by the Secretary of State to local highway authorities about how to discharge the duty under subsection (1).

(3) The duty under subsection (1) does not apply in a case where—

(a) the street tree has a diameter not exceeding 8 centimetres (measured over the bark, at a point 1.3 metres above ground level),

(b) the authority considers that the street tree is dead,

(c) the authority considers that the street tree is required to be felled—

(i) by virtue of an order under the Plant Health Act 1967, or

(ii) under any enactment on the basis that the tree is dangerous,

(d) the authority considers that the street tree is required to be felled in order to comply with—

(i) a duty to make reasonable adjustments in the Equality Act 2010 because the tree is causing an obstruction (see section 20 of that Act), or

(ii) a duty in section 29 of that Act (prohibitions on discrimination etc in the provision of services) because the tree is causing an obstruction, or

(e) the felling of the street tree is required for the purpose of carrying out development authorised by—

(i) planning permission granted under section 70, 73, 76D, 77 or 79 of the Town and Country Planning Act 1990, or

(ii) outline planning permission granted under section 92 of that Act.

(4) In subsection (1) "urban road" means a highway, other than a trunk road or classified road, which—

(a) is a restricted road for the purposes of section 81 of the Road Traffic Regulation Act 1984 (30 miles per hour speed limit),

(b) is subject to an order made by virtue of section 84(1)(a) of that Act imposing a speed limit not exceeding 40 miles per hour, or

(c) is otherwise a street in an urban area."

In force Day appointed by Secretary of State
Application E

S 115 introduces a new s 96A Highways Act 1980 requiring local highway authorities in England to consult the public before felling trees on an urban road, but subject to various exceptions specified in the new section. The proposed measures were included as part of the Government's 2019 consultation on trees and woodlands – see *Protecting and Enhancing England's Trees and Woodlands: Consultation* (DEFRA, December 2018) and *Summary of Responses and Government Response* (DEFRA, October 2019). The issue largely arose from the political controversy in 2015 surrounding Sheffield City Council's programme of highway maintenance, which included the removal and replacement of several thousand trees. In *R (on the application of David Dillner) v Sheffield City Council and Amey Hallam Highways Ltd* [2016] EWHC 945, Mr Justice Gilbart held that the felling of the trees concerned fell under the authority's duty to maintain highways under the Highways Act 1980, and that there was no legal duty to consult with the public under those provisions. He concluded his judgment by noting, '*It may be that those who will be disappointed by the terms of this Judgment will want to see a different legislative regime in place. That is a matter for Parliament, and not for this Court.*'

The new s 96A requires highway authorities to consult the public before felling a tree on an urban road as defined in sub-s (4). The authority must have regard to any guidance issued by the Secretary of State on consultation (sub-s 9(2)). For the legal meaning of 'have regard to', see the Introduction.

S 96A(3) provides a number of important exceptions to the duty to consult:

- The tree to be felled is below a specified diameter (8 cm at 1.3 m above ground level).
- The authority considers that the tree to be felled is dead.
- The tree is required to be felled under an order under the Plant Health Act 1967. Orders made under the Act may, inter alia, require the destruction of trees or bushes infected with a pest (see s 3 Plant Health Act).
- The tree is required to be felled under other legislation because it is dangerous. In the *Dillner* case, noted above, the court noted that a highway authority's statutory duty to maintain highways under s 4(1) Highways Act 1980 would include the removal of dangerous trees.
- The authority considers the tree is required to be felled in order to comply with duties under ss 20 (adjustments for disabled persons) and 29 (discrimination in the provision of services to the public) Equality Act 2010.
- Felling is required for carrying out development authorised by planning permission under the Town and Country Planning Act 1990.

Use of forest risk commodities in commercial activity

116 Use of forest risk commodities in commercial activity

(1) In Schedule 17—

(a) Part 1 makes provision about the use of forest risk commodities in commercial activity,

(b) Part 2 makes provision about enforcement, and

(c) Part 3 contains general provisions.

(2) Regulations under the following provisions of Schedule 17 are subject to the affirmative procedure—

(a) paragraph 1;

(b) paragraph 2(4)(c);

(c) paragraph 5 (except for paragraph 5(2)(b) and (5));

(d) paragraph 7;

(e) Part 2.

(3) Regulations under the following provisions of Schedule 17 are subject to the negative procedure—

(a) paragraph 3;

(b) paragraph 4;

(c) paragraph 5(2)(b) and (5).

In force	30 September 2022 Commencement Order No 3
Application	E W S NI

Background

S 116 introduces Sch 17, which is designed to ensure that larger businesses do not use commodities in their supply chain that are derived from agricultural land in overseas countries that has been illegally converted from forestry. The Government's 25-year plan for the environment (HM Government, *A Green Future: Our 25 Year Plan to Improve the Environment*, 2018) contained a commitment to support companies to implement zero-deforestation supply chains. Proposals were developed in the report of a Government Task Force published in 2020 (Global Resource Initiative, *Final Recommendation Report*, March 2020), and the government response (Department for Business, *Government Response to the Recommendations of the Global Resource Initiative Response to the Report*, Energy and Industry Strategy, Department of Environment, Food and Rural Affairs and Foreign, Commonwealth and Development Office, November 2020). The proposals concerning forest-risk commodities were the subject of government consultation in 2020 – see *Due Diligence on Forest Risk Commodities: Consultation Document* (DEFRA, August 2020) and *Summary of Responses and the Government's Response* (DEFRA, November 2020).

According to the consultation document, deforestation is the second leading cause of climate change after the burning of fossil fuels, and responsible for around 11 per cent of all greenhouse gas emissions. In the last 60 years more than half of tropical forests have been destroyed, with around 80 per cent driven by conversion to agricultural land. Globally, around half of recent deforestation is the result of illegal clearance, with higher proportions in some areas. Controls of the use of timber from illegal sources were introduced under EU Regulation 995/2010. For implementation in the UK, see Timber and Timber Products (Placing on the Market) Regulations 2013, SI 2013/233, and Forest Law Enforcement, Government and Trade Regulations 2012, SI 2012/178 (FLEGT). Post-Brexit, see Timber and Timber Products and FLEGT (EU Exit) Regulations 2018, SI 2018/1025, and Timber and Timber Products and FLEGT (Amendments) (EU Exit) Regulations 2020, SI 2020/1315. The new proposals will extend controls to other commodities from illegal sources, and according to the Government will be the first legislation in the world with such wide reach.

At the Glasgow Climate Conference in 2021, COP 26, the protection of forestry and land-use in the context of climate change featured strongly, leading to the Glasgow Leader's Declaration on Forest and Land-Use, signed by more than 141 countries, and covering over 90 per cent of the world's forests. The Declaration included a commitment *'to working collectively to halt and reverse forest loss and land degradation by 2030 while delivering sustainable development and promoting an inclusive rural transformation'*. The overall goal of forestry commodities provisions introduced in s 116 were reflected in the Declaration, where parties agreed to shared efforts to *'Facilitate trade and development policies, internationally and domestically, that promote sustainable development, and sustainable commodity production and consumption, that work to countries' mutual benefit, and that do not drive deforestation and land degradation'*.

Sch 17 provides the core framework for the new controls, but much of the detail is to be made by regulations which will be subject to consultation. The core provisions that are applicable to the whole of the UK are:

Scope of Controls on Forest Risk Commodities

The provisions apply to *'forest risk commodities'* as defined in regulations made by the Secretary of State. The regulations may specify only commodities that have been produced from living organisms, including plants and animals, and only where forestry is being or has been converted to agricultural use. They may not cover timber or timber products within the meaning of EU Regulation 995/2010 (para 1).

The requirements apply only to *'regulated persons'*, meaning businesses carrying on commercial activities in the UK that meets certain conditions in respect of turnover as defined in regulations, or subsidiaries of such businesses (para 7). In its consultation, the Government indicated that it would focus on a relatively small number of larger businesses that use forest risk commodities in UK production and trade.

There is a further exemption for regulated persons who have notified enforcement authorities in any year that the amount of the forest risk commodity will not exceed the amount prescribed in regulations (para 5).

Waste to be used for making renewable transport fuel, or renewable transport fuel derived from waste (see Renewable Transport Fuel Obligations Order 2007/3072), is excluded (paras 2(7) and (8)).

Obligation Only to Use Forest Risk Commodities Where Local Laws were Complied with

Regulated persons are prohibited from using forest risk commodities, or products derived from such commodities, in their UK commercial activities unless relevant local laws are complied with. A relevant local law is defined as a law relating to the ownership of the land on which the organism from which the commodity was produced was grown, the use of the land or the land itself, and is specified in regulations made by the Secretary of State (para 2).

Obligation to Establish a Due Diligence System

Regulated persons using a forest risk commodity must establish a *'due diligence system'* for identifying and obtaining information about the commodity in question, assessing the risk that local laws were not complied with and mitigating that risk (para 3(1)). The Secretary of State may make regulations elaborating on these requirements (para 3(2)).

Annual reports on the operation of the due diligence system must be provided to the relevant authorities, with further details to be provided by regulations made by the Secretary of State. The reports must be made available to the public in a way and to the extent provided in regulations (para 4).

Enforcement and Sanctions

The Secretary of State is given wide powers to make regulations concerning the enforcement of the requirements. These can include the nomination of enforcement authorities, powers of entry and inspection, the keeping of records and disclosure of information (paras 9–11).

Core sanctions under the regulations are the imposition of civil penalties under the Regulatory Enforcement and Sanctions Act 2008 (fixed or variable monetary penalties, stop notices and enforcement undertakings) for failure to comply with the obligations, or obstruction of or failure to assist an enforcement officer. But in relation to the prohibition under para 2 of using forest risk commodities or products derived from them where the agricultural land was not in compliance with local laws, the regulations must include provisions that no civil sanction can be imposed where the enforcement authority is satisfied that all reasonable steps have been taken to implement a due diligence system (paras 13(1) and (2)). Due diligence or an equivalent is often provided as a defence to statutory offences, but generally the burden is on the defendant to prove due diligence on the balance of probabilities. Here the question is concerned with a due diligence system and whether all reasonable steps have been taken to establish such a system. The wording implies that the regulations must provide that it is for the enforcement authority to determine whether reasonable steps have been taken to establish a system, and if it is so satisfied, it cannot then impose a civil sanction. In practice, if the regulated person provides convincing evidence that all reasonable steps have been taken to establish a due diligence system, the enforcement authority would need to be able to provide counterarguments on the evidence provided before proceeding to impose a civil sanction.

Regulations may also provide for the imposition of criminal sanctions punishable with a fine for failing to comply with civil sanctions or for obstructing or failing to assist an enforcement officer (para 13(3)). Enforcement authorities must have regard to any guidance issued by the Secretary of State (para 6) and regulations may require them to make reports or provide information to the Secretary of State (para 11). The reports and information will be important to allow the Secretary of State to comply with obligations to provide reports on the implementation of the controls (see next para). See the Introduction on the meaning of *'have regard to'*.

Reviews by Secretary of State

The Secretary of State must carry out a review of the effectiveness of the legislation and any regulations made under it. It is rare for national environmental legislation to provide for such reviews, and this provision probably reflects the innovative scope of the new controls. The review must consider in particular the amount of forest being converted to agricultural use for producing commodities, the impact of the provisions on the conversion for producing forest risk commodities, the impact of the provisions on the use of such commodities or products derived from them in UK commercial activities where local laws were not complied with and changes to local laws in relation to forest risk commodities (para 17(1)).

A report of the review, including any steps the Secretary of State intends to take to improve the effectiveness of the provisions in the light of the review, must be completed every two years and published and laid before Parliament.

Part 7

Conservation covenants

Creation of conservation covenant

117 Conservation covenant agreements

(1) For the purposes of this Part, a "conservation covenant agreement" is an agreement between a landowner and a responsible body where—

(a) the agreement contains provision which—

(i) is of a qualifying kind,

(ii) has a conservation purpose, and

(iii) is intended by the parties to be for the public good,

(b) it appears from the agreement that the parties intend to create a conservation covenant, and

(c) the agreement is executed as a deed by the parties.

(2) The reference in subsection (1)(a) to provision of a qualifying kind is to provision—

(a) requiring the landowner—

(i) to do, or not to do, something on land in England specified in the provision in relation to which the landowner holds a qualifying estate specified in the agreement for the purposes of the provision, or

(ii) to allow the responsible body to do something on such land, or

(b) requiring the responsible body to do something on such land.

(3) For the purposes of subsection (1)(a)(ii), provision has a conservation purpose if its purpose is—

(a) to conserve the natural environment of land or the natural resources of land,

(b) to conserve land as a place of archaeological, architectural, artistic, cultural or historic interest, or

(c) to conserve the setting of land with a natural environment or natural resources or which is a place of archaeological, architectural, artistic, cultural or historic interest.

(4) In this Part—

a reference to conserving something includes a reference to protecting, restoring or enhancing it;

"qualifying estate" means—

(a) an estate in fee simple absolute in possession, or

(b) a term of years absolute granted for a term of more than seven years from the date of the grant and in the case of which some part of the period for which the term of years was granted remains unexpired;

a reference to "the qualifying estate", in relation to an obligation under a conservation covenant, is to the estate in land by virtue of which the condition in subsection (1)(a)(i) was met in relation to—

(a) if the obligation is not an ancillary obligation, the provision giving rise to the obligation, or

(b) if the obligation is an ancillary obligation, the provision giving rise to the obligation to which it was ancillary;

(and for this purpose "ancillary obligation" means an obligation under provision falling within section 118(2)(b));

"natural environment", in relation to land, includes—

(a) its plants, animals and other living organisms;

(b) their habitats;

(c) its geological features.

Definitions

'ancillary obligation'	s 118(2(b))
'conservation covenant agreement'	s117(1)
'conservation purpose'	s 117(3)
'natural environment'	s 117(4)
'qualifying estate'	s 117(4)
'responsible body'	s 119

In force	30 September 2022 Commencement Order No 3
Application	E

Background

This part of the Act introduces into England a new form of voluntary agreement between landowners and bodies such as public authorities and conservation organisations designed to promote the conservation of the land in question, and one that binds the successor in title to the land. Following consultation by the Law Commission (see *Conservation Covenants: A Consultation Paper (2013)*, Law Commission Consultation Paper No 211) the Commission published a report on the subject in 2014 – *Conservation Covenants*, Law Com No 249 (Law Commission, June 2014) – where it summarised a conservation covenant as 'a private and voluntary arrangement in the public interest, which continues to be effective even after the land changes hands'. The Law Commission published a draft Bill with its report, and the provisions in the Act largely follow the Law Commission's draft, often word for word. The Commission's report related to both England and Wales, but the provisions here apply to land in England only (s 117(2)(i)(a)). In 2016 the Government responded to the report, noting that it 'broadly agrees with the Law Commission that a statutory scheme of conservation covenants could contribute to the protection of England's natural and historic assets' (*Law Commission Report on Conservation Covenants*: *Government Response*, DEFRA, January 2016). The Government consulted on the issue in 2019 (*Conservation Covenants*, DEFRA, February 2019; *Consultation Outcome: Summary of Responses and Government Response*, DEFRA, July 2019).

Conservation covenants are found in some other jurisdictions and have been introduced in Scotland – see Abolition of Feudal Tenure etc (Scotland) Act 2000 and the Title Conditions (Scotland) Act 2003. As the Law Commission identified, the limitation in current land law in England and Wales is that it is generally not possible to make an agreement containing positive obligations concerning the land that would bind successive owners of the land in question. A restrictive covenant not to do something might run with the land, but there has to be some neighbouring land that would benefit from it. Covenants running with the land but relating to issues that would be of public benefit rather than neighbouring land are not permissible. There were examples of landowners and conservations using legal workarounds to avoid the problem (such as using transfers and leasebacks), but the Law Commission concluded they were often cumbersome or complex – hence the need for a new form of land obligations in the form of a conservation covenant.

Conservation covenants are likely to prove environmentally valuable in themselves, but they also have a role in ensuring biodiversity gain under Part 6 of the Act. The provisions concerning biodiversity gain under the new Sch 7A of the Town and Country Planning Act as introduced by s 92 above provide that proposed works for on-site gain may be satisfied by a planning permission condition, a planning condition or a conservation covenant having effect for at least 30 years (Sch 7A para 9(3)). Registered off-site biodiversity gains are defined as habitat enhancement, recorded in the biodiversity gain register, where it is required to be carried out under a conservation covenant for 30 years or more or a planning obligation (Sch 7A para 10(1)).

Elements of a Conservation Covenant

S 117(1) describes in general terms a conservation covenant agreement as an agreement between a landowner and a 'responsible body' (bodies as designated by the Secretary of State under s 119 below). The agreement must contain a provision that has a conservation purpose as defined in sub-s (3), is intended to be for the public good and is of a '*qualifying kind*'. This term is defined in sub-s (2) as a provision requiring the landowner to do or not do something on the land in question or one that allows or obliges the responsible body to do something on the land. The landowner must have a 'qualifying estate' in the land, which is defined in sub-s (4) as meaning either a freehold or a leasehold estate of more than seven years, provided the agreement is made within the period of the lease (ie not during any statutory continuation of the lease). The part of the agreement that is a conservation covenant within the meaning of s 118 below is given statutory effect and becomes a land charge.

There is no specified form of a conservation covenant agreement other that it is executed as a deed by the parties (sub-s (1)(c)), but it must appear from the agreement that the parties intend to create a conservation covenant (sub-s (1)(b)). This is intended to ensure that parties do not inadvertently create a conservation covenant under these provisions unless they expressly wish to do so. Presumably the evidence of intention would be met by an express reference in the agreement to a conservation covenant under this part of the Act, and the nature of the provisions in the agreement. Appendix G of the Law Commission's report contains a model template for a conservation covenant agreement.

The agreement must contain provision for a conservation purpose as defined in sub-s (3). This encompasses conserving the natural environment of land or its natural resources, conserving land as a place of archaeological, architectural, artistic, cultural or historic interest, or conserving the setting of land with a natural environment or natural resources or which is a place of archaeological, architectural, artistic, cultural or historic interest. The 'natural environment' is defined in sub-s (4) as including plants, animals and other living organisms, their habitats and geological features. The reference to habitats was added to the definition of the natural environment provided in the Law Commission's draft Bill, underlying the significance of habitat conservation. The reference to the 'setting of the land' in sub-s (3)(c) is intended to provide protection of land around a conservation site that might affect its conservation status. The example given in the Explanatory Notes is where the architectural or artistic value of a country house derives in part from the landscape in which it is set.

The agreement must be intended by the parties to be 'for the public good' to qualify as a conservation covenant (sub-s (1)(iii)). There is no statutory definition of this term, and presumably this will be determined and in most cases be obvious from the nature of the obligations and other provisions of the agreement, such as creating public access to land. The provisions leave it to the parties to decide the extent to which financial payments should form part of the agreement and which party should pay. The Law Commission gave the example of a conservation body that wished to sell land it owned to a private party but wished to ensure that its conservation value was maintained. Conversely, the landowner might be paid by the other party to carry out conservation work: see *Payment for Ecosystem Services: A Best Practice Guide* (DEFRA, May 2013). But there might be situations where the amount of the payments made to the landowner, and the nature of the provisions, appear to be predominantly intended to improve the value of the property concerned, so it is no longer considered to be for the public good.

118 Conservation covenants

(1) A conservation covenant is so much of a conservation covenant agreement as is given statutory effect by this section.

(2) The following provisions of a conservation covenant agreement have statutory effect as a conservation covenant—

(a) provisions in respect of which the conditions in section 117(1)(a) are met, and

(b) provisions ancillary to any provision falling within paragraph (a).

(3) If the agreement includes provision for public access to land to which other provision of the agreement (being provision which meets the conditions in section 117(1)(a)) relates, the provision for public access is to be treated as ancillary to that other provision.

(4) In this Part—

(a) references to an obligation under a conservation covenant are to an obligation of the landowner or the responsible body given statutory effect by this section as part of the conservation covenant, and

(b) references to the land to which an obligation under a conservation covenant relates are, in the case of an obligation given statutory effect by this section by virtue of being ancillary to another provision, to the land to which the obligation under the other provision relates.

In force Day to be appointed by Secretary of State

Application E

S 118 defines what provisions of a conservation covenant agreement are to have statutory effect as a conservation covenant and will, for example, become a land charge under the next section. They include those that fall within s 117(1)(a) – ie those that have a conservation purpose, are intended to be for the public good, and either require the landowner to do or not do something or oblige or enable the other party to do something on the land (see annotations to s 117). They also include provisions that are ancillary to these provisions. The Explanatory Notes describe these as provisions which by themselves may not have a conservation purpose (such as those relating to payments of money), but 'are nevertheless closely linked with provision of the agreement that does meet the relevant conditions'. Sub-s (3) provides that provision for public access to the land in question is to be treated as an ancillary provision. Sub-s (4) provides that both the core conservation provisions and the ancillary provisions are referred to as 'conservation obligations' in this part of the Act.

119 Responsible bodies

(1) The following are responsible bodies for the purposes of this Part—

(a) the Secretary of State;

(b) bodies which are designated under this section (referred to in this Part as "designated bodies").

(2) The Secretary of State may, on the application of a local authority or other body, designate it as a responsible body for the purposes of this Part.

(3) The Secretary of State may only designate a local authority if satisfied that it is suitable to be a responsible body.

(4) The Secretary of State may only designate a body that is not a local authority if satisfied that it—

(a) meets the condition in subsection (5), and

(b) is suitable to be a responsible body.

(5) The condition is that—

(a) in the case of a public body or a charity, at least some of its main purposes or functions relate to conservation, or

(b) in any other case, at least some of the body's main activities relate to conservation.

(6) The Secretary of State may revoke a designation by notice to the body concerned if—
   (a) the body has applied to the Secretary of State for its designation to be revoked,
   (b) the Secretary of State is satisfied that the body is not suitable to remain as a responsible body, or
   (c) in the case of a body other than a local authority, the Secretary of State is satisfied that the body does not meet the condition in subsection (5).

(7) The Secretary of State may determine the criteria to be applied in deciding whether a body is suitable to be or to remain a responsible body (which may include criteria relating to the body's connection with the United Kingdom).

(8) The Secretary of State must publish (and keep up to date)—
   (a) a document setting out the criteria applicable for the purposes mentioned in subsection (7), and
   (b) a list of the bodies who are designated under this section.

(9) In this section—

"charity" means a charity registered under the Charities Act 2011 or an exempt charity (within the meaning of that Act);

"conservation" means conservation of—
   (a) the natural environment or natural resources of land,
   (b) places of archaeological, architectural, artistic, cultural or historic interest, or
   (c) the setting of land with a natural environment or natural resources or which is a place of archaeological, architectural, artistic, cultural or historic interest;

"local authority" means—
   (a) a county or district council in England;
   (b) a London borough council;
   (c) the Common Council of the City of London;
   (d) the Council of the Isles of Scilly.

Definitions

'charity'	s 119(9)
'conservation'	s 110(9)
'local authority'	s 119(9)
'natural environment'	s 117(4)

In force	Day to be appointed by Secretary of State
Application	E

Under s 117 a conservation agreement must be between a landowner and a 'responsible body'. S 119 provides that responsible bodies are either the Secretary of State or bodies designated by the Secretary of State under this section.

A body may be designated a responsible body on application to the Secretary of State. In the case of a local authority, the Secretary of State may only designate if satisfied that the body is 'suitable', in accordance with published criteria on suitability published by the Secretary of State (sub-ss (7) and (8)). Other bodies applying to be a responsible body must also be considered satisfactory in accordance with the criteria, and in the case of a public body or a charity must have at least some of its main purposes or functions relating to conservation as defined in sub-s (9). Non-charitable bodies may also apply, provided their main activities relate to the environment (sub-s (5)). The Law Commission's original proposals and draft Bill would have confined applicants to local authorities, public bodies and charities, but the Commission conceded that the consultees were almost equally split on whether private for-profit companies should be entitled to apply to be a responsible body, and that it was one of most difficult questions it had to consider.

The position of statutory undertakers such as water utilities remains unclear. Because of their distinct powers, statutory undertakers have been held to be 'public authorities' for the purposes of the Environment Information Regulations 2004 (*Fish Legal v Information Commissioner and others* [2015] UKUT 52 (AAC)) following a reference to the Court of Justice of the European Union (Case C-279/12 *Fish Legal v Information Commissioners and others* [2014] QB 521).

It does not necessarily follow that they would be considered a 'public body' within the context of s 119(5), and as the Law Commission noted, the meaning of a public body within legislation can vary according to context. The Commission's draft Bill therefore contained a definition of a public body to provide clarity, but one which would have excluded statutory undertakers. Here no definition of a public body is provided. A non-public body must have at least some of its main activities relating to conservation to be eligible (sub-s 5(b)). Water utilities, for example, have general duties relating to conservation in formulating or considering proposals relating to their functions (s 3 Water Industry Act 1991), but it is questionable whether this is equivalent to meeting the test that some of their main activities relate to conservation as defined in the section.

Sub-s (6) gives power to the Secretary of State to revoke a designation either on application of the body concerned or where it is considered the body is no longer suitable, or, in the case of bodies other than local authorities, does not meet the tests in sub-s (5).

A list of the bodies designated as responsible bodies under this section must be published and maintained by the Secretary of State (sub-s (8)(b)). This is likely to be helpful to landowners to identify potential partners to a conservation covenant agreement.

Effect of conservation covenant

120 Local land charge

(1) A conservation covenant is a local land charge.

(2) For the purposes of the Local Land Charges Act 1975 the originating authority, as respects a conservation covenant, is the person by whom an obligation of the landowner under the covenant is enforceable.

(3) In section 2 of the Local Land Charges Act 1975 (matters which are not local land charges), the references in paragraphs (a) and (b) to a covenant or agreement made between a lessor and a lessee do not include a conservation covenant.

(4) In its application to a conservation covenant, section 10(1) of the Local Land Charges Act 1975 (compensation for non-registration or defective official search certificate) has effect as if—

(a) in the words preceding paragraph (a), the words from the beginning to "but" were omitted,

(b) paragraph (a) (non-registration) were omitted, and

(c) in paragraph (b), for the words from "in existence" to the end there were substituted the words "registered in that register at the time of the search but was not shown by the official search certificate as so registered".

In force	Day to be appointed by Secretary of State
Application	E

S 120 provides that a conservation covenant is a local land charge, meaning that successors in title will generally be bound by the covenant. Provisions on discharge and modification by agreement are provided in ss 127–30 below. In the case of non-agreement, provision for application for modification or discharge to the Upper Tribunal by one of the parties is provided by s 130 and Sch 18.

Under s 5(2) Local Land Charges Act 1975 there is a duty on the responsible body to apply for registration of the covenant as a local land charge. Generally local land charges are enforceable whether or not registered, but under s 122(5)(b) below a conservation covenant will not bind a successor in title until it has been registered. Sub-s (4) therefore modifies the provisions in s 10(1) Local Land Charges Act relating to compensation for non-registration to reflect this position, since the registering body cannot incur liability to subsequent purchasers for the failure to register. Liability for defective searches remains unaffected.

Conservation covenant agreements can be made between a responsible body and a lessee of more than 7 years. S 2 of the Local Land Charges Act provides that covenants or agreements between a lessor and a lessee cannot be a local land charge, and this is therefore amended by s 120(3) to allow conservation covenants to be included where a lessee is a party.

121 Duration of obligation under conservation covenant

(1) An obligation under a conservation covenant has effect for the default period, unless the covenant provides for a shorter period.

(2) The default period for the purposes of subsection (1) is—

(a) if the qualifying estate in relation to the obligation is an estate in fee simple absolute in possession, a period of indefinite duration, and

(b) if the qualifying estate in relation to the obligation is a term of years absolute, a period corresponding in length to the remainder of the period for which the term of years was granted.

Definitions

'conservation covenant'	s 118(1)
'qualifying estate'	s 117(4)

In force	Day to be appointed by Secretary of State
Application	E

Parties to a conservation covenant can agree to its duration, though it must be for more than 30 years for the purposes of the biodiversity gain provisions introduced in the amendments to the Town and Country Planning Act 1971 under s 98 above and Sch 14. S 121 provides that in the absence of agreement as to duration, there is an indefinite default period in the case of a freehold estate, or the remainder of a leasehold term in the case of a leaseholder estate.

122 Benefit and burden of obligation of landowner

(1) An obligation of the landowner under a conservation covenant is owed to the responsible body under the covenant.

(2) Subject to the following provisions, an obligation of the landowner under a conservation covenant binds—

(a) the landowner under the covenant, and

(b) any person who becomes a successor of the landowner under the covenant.

(3) In subsection (2)(b) "successor" (in relation to the landowner under the covenant) means a person who holds, in respect of any of the land to which the obligation relates—

(a) the qualifying estate, or

(b) an estate in land derived (whether immediately or otherwise) from the qualifying estate after the creation of the covenant.

(4) An obligation of the landowner under a conservation covenant ceases to bind the landowner under the covenant, or a person who becomes a successor of that landowner, in respect of—

(a) land which ceases to be land to which the obligation relates,

(b) in the case of the landowner under the covenant, land in relation to which the landowner ceases to be the holder of the qualifying estate, or

(c) in the case of a successor, land in relation to which the successor ceases to be the holder of the qualifying estate or of the estate derived from the qualifying estate, as the case may be.

(5) Subsection (2)(b) does not apply if—

(a) the obligation is positive and the person becomes a successor by virtue of holding a term of years absolute granted for a term of seven years or less from the date of the grant,

(b) the conservation covenant was not registered in the local land charges register at the time when the successor acquired the estate in land concerned, or

(c) the successor's immediate predecessor was not bound by the obligation in respect of the land to which the successor's interest relates.

(6) In the case of a conservation covenant relating to land in an area in relation to which section 3 of the Local Land Charges Act 1975 (as substituted by paragraph 3 of Schedule 5 to the Infrastructure Act 2015) does not yet have effect, the reference in subsection (5)(b) to the local land charges register is to the appropriate local land charges register.

(7) The reference in subsection (5)(b) to the time when the successor acquired the estate in land concerned is, if the successor acquired that interest under a disposition which

took effect at law only when registered in the register of title kept under the Land Registration Act 2002, to be read as a reference to the time when the disposition was made.

(8) In subsection (5)(c) the successor's "immediate predecessor" is, unless subsection (9) applies, the successor's immediate predecessor in title.

(9) If the successor is the first holder of an estate in land which is derived from another estate in land (whether the other estate is the qualifying estate or an estate derived, immediately or otherwise, from it) the successor's immediate predecessor is the holder of that other estate when the derived estate was created.

Definitions

'conservation covenant'	s 118(1)
'responsible body'	s 119
'qualifying estate'	s 117(4)
'successor'	s 122(3))

In force	Day to be appointed by Secretary of State
Application	E

S 122 concerns the obligations of a landowner under a conservation covenant. Sub-s (1) makes it clear that the obligations are owed to the responsible body, who will be able to enforce these obligations under the provisions of s 125 below.

Sub-s (2) provides that generally the obligations bind both the landowner and any successors in title. However, there are three important exceptions under sub-s (5) where successors in title will not be bound:

(i) Positive obligations in the covenant will not bind a subsequent lessee of the land where the term of the lease is seven years or less. The Explanatory Notes give the example of a freeholder who creates and registers a conservation covenant, then grants a tenancy of less than seven years. The lessee is bound by the covenant's negative obligations but not by the positive ones.

(ii) The covenant has not been registered in the local land charges register at the time when the successor acquired the interest in the land. This contrasts with the general position of local land charges, which have effect whether or not registered, though in the case of non-registration compensation may be payable under s 10 Local Land Charges Act 1975. Because of the provision here that an unregistered conservation covenant does not bind successors, s 120(4) above amends the Land Charges Act to provide that the compensation provisions do not apply to conservation covenants. Sub-s (7) provides that the time at which the interest was acquired was the time a deposition (such as a sale, gift or grant of a lease) was made, even if it only has legal effect after registration under s 27 Land Registration Act 2002.

(iii) Successors where the immediate predecessor was not bound by the covenant. Sub-ss (8) and (9) define what is meant by an immediate predecessor. The Explanatory Notes give the example of a landowner who transfers part of his land before registering the conservation covenant. The new owner of the transferred part then transfers it to a third party.

Even if the covenant is subsequently registered, the third party is not bound because the predecessor was not bound at the time of transfer.

Sub-s (4) provides that the landowner's liabilities in respect of obligations under a conservation covenant cease when the land is no longer bound by the obligations or the owner ceases to be the holder of the land in question. Similarly, a successor in title will no longer be bound once the successor ceases to be the holder.

123 Benefit of obligation of responsible body

(1) Subject to the following provisions, an obligation of the responsible body under a conservation covenant is owed—

(a) to the landowner under the covenant, and

(b) to any person who becomes a successor of the landowner under the covenant.

(2) In this section "successor" (in relation to the landowner under the covenant) means a person who holds, in respect of any of the land to which the obligation relates—

(a) the qualifying estate, or

(b) an estate in land derived (whether immediately or otherwise) from the qualifying estate after the creation of the covenant.

(3) An obligation of the responsible body under a conservation covenant ceases to be owed to the landowner under the covenant, or to a person who becomes a successor of that landowner, in respect of—

(a) land which ceases to be land to which the obligation relates,

(b) in the case of the landowner under the covenant, land in relation to which the landowner ceases to be the holder of the qualifying estate, or

(c) in the case of a successor, land in relation to which the successor ceases to be the holder of the qualifying estate or of the estate derived from the qualifying estate, as the case may be.

(4) Subsection (1)(b) does not apply if the obligation is ancillary to an obligation of the landowner under the covenant which does not bind the successor.

Definitions

'conservation covenant'	s 118(1)
'responsible body'	s 119
'qualifying estate'	s 117(4)
'successor'	s 122(3))

In force	Day to be appointed by Secretary of State
Application	E

S 123 provides that obligations of the responsible body are owed under the covenant to the original landowner with whom the responsible body made the covenant, and any successors under the covenant holding a qualifying estate – an estate in fee simple or a lease of more than seven years (s 117(4)).

Similar to the provisions on a landowner's obligations under s 122, the obligations of the responsible body cease to be owed under a conservation covenant when the land is no longer bound by the obligations, or where the owner or successor ceases to be the holder of the land in question (sub-s (3)). Sub-s (4) provides that where an obligation under a covenant does not bind a successor (such as positive obligations where the successor holds a lease of less than seven years), any obligations of the responsible body ancillary to these (the payment of money, for example) are not owed to the successor.

Breach and enforcement

124 Breach of obligation

(1) A person bound by a negative obligation under a conservation covenant breaches the obligation by—

(a) doing something which it prohibits, or

(b) permitting or suffering another person to do such a thing.

(2) A person bound by a positive obligation under a conservation covenant breaches the obligation if it is not performed.

Definitions

'conservation covenant'	s 118(1)

In force	Day to be appointed by Secretary of State
Application	E

S 124 defines breaches of obligations under a conservation covenant which will be relevant to the enforcement provisions in s 125 and 136 below. The Law Commission considered that compliance with covenant obligations was likely to be high in early years, but could then decrease as the land subsequently changes hands. The Commission also advised that in order to reduce the possibilities of subsequent disagreement or litigation, parties to a covenant must ensure that their respective obligations are drafted with clarity. As the Explanatory Notes state, these provisions are likely to be relevant considerations where the landowner grants a lease of the land after the creation of the covenant.

Breach of a negative obligation occurs where the person bound does something which the obligation prohibits or permits, or suffers someone else to do so. According to the Law Commission, the terminology 'permitting or suffering' is derived from case law and is language commonly found in restrictive covenants (see Law Commission, *Easements, Covenants and Profits a Prendre*, Consultation Paper 18, 2008, para 9.39). See in particular *Tophams v Earl of Sefton* [1967] 1 AC 50 on permitting and *Barton v Reed* [1932] I Ch 362 where the court accepted that 'suffer' had a rather wider meaning than 'permit'. For an extensive discussion of the case law on permit and suffer, see GL Newsom and E Paton, *Preston and Newsom: Restrictive Covenants Affecting Freehold Land*, 11th edn (London, Sweet & Maxwell, 2020) chapter 7, s 6. Action by a trespasser, for example, is unlikely to create a breach of a landowner's obligations unless, say, they had taken no action to prohibit repeated trespassers on their land. See also the defence in s 126 (1)(a) below, where the event was outside the defendant's control. A person bound by a positive obligation under the covenant is in breach where it is not performed.

125 Enforcement of obligation

(1) In proceedings for the enforcement of an obligation under a conservation covenant, the available remedies are—
  (a) specific performance,
  (b) injunction,
  (c) damages, and
  (d) order for payment of an amount due under the obligation.

(2) On an application for a remedy under subsection (1)(a) or (b), a court must, in considering what remedy is appropriate, take into account any public interest in the performance of the obligation concerned.

(3) Subject to subsection (4), contract principles apply to damages for breach of an obligation under a conservation covenant.

(4) In the case of breach of an obligation of the landowner under a conservation covenant, a court may award exemplary damages in such circumstances as it thinks fit.

(5) For the purposes of the Limitation Act 1980, an action founded on an obligation under a conservation covenant is to be treated as founded on simple contract.

Definitions

'conservation covenant'	s 118(1)

In force	Day to be appointed by Secretary of State
Application	E

S 125 provides the remedies that are available for the enforcement of obligations, either in the county court or the High Court – specific performance, injunction, damages or an order for payment of any money due under an obligation in the covenant. S 126 below provides a number of defences to such actions. Specific performance and injunctions are discretionary remedies of the court, and sub-s (2) provides that a court, in considering whether such a remedy is appropriate, must take into account any public interest in the performance of the obligation in question. The court has the power to award damages in lieu of an injunction (s 50 Senior Courts Act 1981). See *Coventry and others v Lawrence and another* [2014] AC 822, where the Supreme Court emphasised how the public interest could be a relevant factor in deciding to award damages in lieu of an injunction in a common law nuisance action. This was in the context of an activity causing the nuisance having a public interest, such as providing local employment. Here one of the core definitions of a conservation covenant is that it is intended to be for the public good (s 118(1)(a)(iii) above), and this is likely to strengthen the case for the award of specific performance or an injunction rather than damages in lieu.

Sub-s (3) provides that contract principles will apply to a claim for damages in relation to a covenant obligation, with the limitation period applying for contract under Limitation Act 1980 – six years from the date on which the cause of action arose (s 5 Limitation Act 1980). As the Law Commission noted, direct losses resulting from a breach by the landowner or successors to the responsible body that is party to the covenant may well be insignificant, and in most cases claims for specific performance or an injunction are likely to be sought.

Under sub-s (4), the court also has the power to award exemplary damages if it thinks fit. Exemplary damages provide deterrence and punishment rather than compensation, and the Explanatory Notes provide the example of a landowner who develops land in breach of covenant obligations knowing that the profits will be greater than any ordinary claim for damages. See also the review, by Lord Devlin in *Rookes v Barnard* [1964] AC 1129, of the limited number of situations where, without statutory authority, courts should be able to award exemplary damages, and the considerations that should apply. One category of case was where *'the defendant's conduct has been calculated by him to make a profit for himself which may well exceed the compensation payable to the plaintiff'*.

126 Defences to breach of obligation

(1) In proceedings for breach of an obligation under a conservation covenant it is a defence to show—

(a) that the breach occurred as a result of a matter beyond the defendant's control,

(b) that the breach occurred as a result of doing, or not doing, something in an emergency in circumstances where it was necessary for that to be done, or not done, in order to prevent loss of life or injury to any person, or

(c) that at the time of the breach—

(i) the land to which the obligation relates was, or was within an area, designated for a public purpose, and

(ii) compliance with the obligation would have involved a breach of any statutory control applying as a result of the designation.

(2) If the only reason for the application of subsection (1)(c) was failure to obtain authorisation, the defendant must also show that all reasonable steps to obtain authorisation had been taken.

(3) The defence under subsection (1)(c) does not apply if the designation was in force when the conservation covenant was created.

(4) The defence of statutory authority (which applies in relation to the infringement of rights such as easements by a person acting under statutory authority) applies in relation to breach of an obligation under a conservation covenant.

(5) In this section—

"authorisation" means any approval, confirmation, consent, licence, permission or other authorisation (however described), whether special or general;

"statutory control" means control imposed by provision contained in, or having effect under, an Act.

Definitions

'conservation covenant'	s 118(1)
'authorisation'	s 126(5)
'statutory control'	s 126(5)

In force	Day to be appointed by Secretary of State
Application	E

S 126 provides a number of defences to proceedings for the enforcement of obligations, with the burden of proof on the defendant.

Beyond the Defendant's Control

The defence in sub-s (1)(a) applies where the matters are beyond the defendant's control. The Law Commission provided an example of a covenant containing an obligation not to use insecticides. A neighbouring farmer sprays insecticides on his own land but inadvertently sprays on part of the land subject to the covenant. The landowner could invoke the defence unless it had happened regularly and the landowner had taken no steps to try to prevent it happening. For a useful discussion of the concept of control in connection with causation for water offences, see W Howarth and D McGillivray, *Water Pollution and Water Quality Law* (Crayford, Shaw & Sons, 2001) 9.6.3.

Acting in an Emergency

Sub-s (1)(b) provides a defence of acting in an emergency to prevent loss of life or injury to any person. This could happen, say, where it was necessary to control a flood, or where it was necessary to fell trees to create a firebreak.

Subsequent Statutory Designation

Sub-s (1)(c) provides a defence where the land is subject to a statutory designation (such as a Site of Special Scientific Interest) after the conservation covenant was agreed (sub-s (3)) and compliance with an obligation under the covenant would breach the statutory controls applicable. The example given in the Explanatory Notes is where obligations in the covenant would be likely to damage a Site of Special Scientific Interest and Natural England refused to give consent to the works involved. In effect, the statutory system prevails. The Law Commission was particularly impressed with the views of English Heritage, Natural Resources Wales and Natural England. who did not see that conflicts between the two systems would be significant, and indeed that in practice they should be supportive of each other. If there was incompatibility, it might be appropriate to agree to modify the covenant under s 129 below.

Statutory Authority

Sub-s (4) provides a defence of statutory authority. This would apply, say, where the land had been compulsorily purchased by a public authority, and is in line with the position on easements where the owner of an easement cannot enforce against the authority while it owns the land and is acting in accordance with its statutory authority: see *Kirby v School Board for Harrogate* [1896] 1 Ch 437. However, in the absence of specific statutory provision, the easement is overridden in relation to the acquiring authority rather than wholly extinguished, and can be revived against subsequent owners should the authority sell the land. The same principle would presumably apply to conservation covenants.

Sch 20, introduced by s 139 below, amends s 12 of the Acquisition of Land Act 1981 by providing that a person entitled to the benefit of an obligation under a conservation covenant is given due notice of a compulsory purchase under the Act by local authorities, other authorities and Ministers. This provides the person with an opportunity to make objections.

Provisions in s 203 Housing and Planning 2016 are also amended to provide that the power to override easements on land acquired for planning development by local authorities and other authorities within the meaning of the Act extends to conservation covenants other than those owed to the National Trust. S 204 of that Act is amended so that compensation payable for interference with easements and other rights authorised by s 203 does not extend to breaches of obligations under conservation covenants.

Provisions in the Neighbourhood and Planning Act 2017 relating to the powers of authority to take temporary possession of land are amended to ensure that: a person having the benefit of a conservation covenant is given due notice of a compulsory temporary possession (s 20); the provisions on compensation for loss or injury for temporary possession do not apply to persons entitled to a benefit of a conservation covenant (s 23); the authority acquiring temporary possession is not bound by obligations under a conservation covenant (s 27); and, with the exception of obligations owed to the National Trust under a conservation covenant, the authority may use the land even if it causes a person to be in breach of an obligation owed under a conservation covenant.

Discharge and modification

127 Discharge of obligation of landowner by agreement

(1) The responsible body under a conservation covenant and a person who holds the qualifying estate in respect of any of the land to which an obligation of the landowner under the covenant relates may, by agreement, discharge from the obligation any of the land in respect of which the person holds that estate.

(2) Subsection (3) applies to—

(a) the responsible body under a conservation covenant, and

(b) a person who is a successor of the landowner under the covenant by virtue of holding an estate in land which—

(i) is an estate in respect of any of the land to which an obligation of the landowner under the covenant relates, and

(ii) is derived (whether immediately or otherwise) from the qualifying estate.

(3) Those persons may, by agreement, discharge the estate in land mentioned in subsection (2)(b) from the obligation in respect of any of the land to which the obligation relates.

(4) Any power under this section is exercisable by agreement executed as a deed by the parties which specifies—

(a) the obligation to which the discharge relates,

(b) the land to which the discharge relates, and

(c) the estate in land by virtue of which the power is exercisable.

Definitions

'conservation covenant'	s 118(1)
'qualifying estate'	s 117(4)
'responsible body'	s 119

In force	Day to be appointed by Secretary of State
Application	E

S 127 provides that the parties to a conservation covenant or the successors holding a qualifying estate may agree to discharge all or any of the land from obligations under the covenant. Any such agreement must be executed by deed (sub-s (4)). Any modification or discharge of the covenant must be notified under the Local Land Charges Registration Rules 1977. The Law Commission discussed whether responsible parties should have the power to discharge the covenant unilaterally where, say, it serves no further purpose and where the parties could not agree. The Commission rejected the proposal as undermining the consensual nature of the scheme, though it noted that parties could build in provisions concerning unilateral discharge into the covenant. A responsible body also has the power to appoint another responsible body under s 131 below.

128 Discharge of obligation of responsible body by agreement

(1) A person to whom an obligation of the responsible body under a conservation covenant is owed by virtue of the person holding an estate in land may, by agreement with the responsible body, discharge the obligation, so far as owed in relation to that estate, in respect of any of the land in respect of which the person is entitled to the benefit of the obligation.

(2) The power under this section is exercisable by agreement executed as a deed by the parties which specifies—

(a) the obligation to which the discharge relates,

(b) the land to which the discharge relates, and

(c) the estate in land by virtue of which the power is exercisable.

Definitions

'conservation covenant'	s 118(1)
'responsible body'	s 119

In force	Day to be appointed by Secretary of State
Application	E

S 128 is the counterpart to s 127, and allows an obligation owed by the responsible party under a conservation covenant to be discharged by agreement executed by deed by the responsible body and the person holding the relevant estate. This amounts to a modification of the covenant and must be notified under the Local Land Charges Registration Rules 1977.

129 Modification of obligation by agreement

(1) A person bound by, or entitled to the benefit of, an obligation under a conservation covenant may, by agreement with the responsible body under the covenant, modify the obligation in its application to any of the land in respect of which the person is bound by, or entitled to the benefit of, it.

(2) The power under subsection (1) does not include power to make a change which, had it been included in the original agreement, would have prevented the provision of the agreement that gave rise to the obligation being provision in relation to which the conditions in section 117(1) were met.

(3) The power under this section is exercisable by agreement executed as a deed by the parties which specifies—

(a) the obligation to which the modification relates,

(b) the land to which the modification relates, and

(c) the estate in land by virtue of which the power is exercisable.

(4) If an obligation under a conservation covenant is modified by an agreement under this section, the modification binds—

(a) the parties to the agreement, and

(b) any person who, as respects any of the land to which the modification relates, becomes a successor of a person bound by the modification.

(5) In subsection (4)(b) "successor of a person bound by the modification", means a person who holds, in respect of any of the land to which the modification relates—

(a) the estate held by the person bound by the modification when the modification was agreed, or

(b) an estate in land derived (whether immediately or otherwise) from that estate after the modification is agreed.

Definitions

'conservation covenant'	s 118(1)
'responsible body'	s 119

In force	Day to be appointed by Secretary of State
Application	E

S 129 allows obligations under the conservation covenant to be modified by agreement. But any change must also meet the core conditions of a conservation covenant agreement as defined in s 117(1) – ie the change must still have a conservation purpose, be intended to be for the public good and require the landowner to do or not do something, or require the responsible body to do something, on the land in question. The agreement must be executed as a deed specifying the obligation being modified, the land to which the modification relates and the estate in land by which the modification power is exercised (sub-s (3)). Any modification must be notified under the Local Land Charges Rules 1977.

Sub-s (5) provides that the modification will bind the parties to the agreement, and successors in title to the land after the modification was made. The example given in the Explanatory Notes is of a landowner who had entered a conservation covenant and after registration sells part of the land. The new owner of that land will also be bound by the original covenant. If the first landowner then agrees a modification, this will only bind the owner and his successors in respect of the retained land, but not the new owner of the part of the land that had previously been sold.

130 Discharge or modification of obligation by Upper Tribunal

(1) Schedule 18 makes provision about the discharge or modification of an obligation under a conservation covenant on application to the Upper Tribunal.

(2) Where any proceedings by action or otherwise are taken to enforce an obligation under a conservation covenant, any person against whom the proceedings are taken may in such proceedings apply to the High Court or the county court for an order giving leave to apply to the Upper Tribunal under Schedule 18 and staying the proceedings in the meantime.

(3) No application under section 84(1) of the Law of Property Act 1925 (which enables the Upper Tribunal on application to discharge or modify a restriction arising under covenant or otherwise) may be made in relation to an obligation under a conservation covenant.

In force	Day to be appointed by Secretary of State
Application	E

Where the parties cannot agree a discharge or modification under ss 127–29 above, s 130 and Sch 18 provide for an application to the Upper Tribunal, in practice the Lands Chamber.

Where enforcement proceedings are initiated under s 125, it may sometimes be useful for the defendant to seek to modify or discharge the obligation as a response. Sub-s (2) allows the defendant to apply to the High Court or county court for any order to stay the enforcement proceedings and leave to apply to the Upper Tribunal to modify or discharge the obligation in question.

Sub-s (3) makes it clear that applications may not be made under the Law of Property Act 1925 to discharge or modify restrictive obligations in a conservation covenant. The bespoke provisions in Sch 18 must be used.

Part 1 of Sch 18 relates to the discharge of obligations under a conservation covenant, and provides that application may be made by either the holder of an estate bound by an obligation or entitled to a benefit under the covenant, or the responsible body. Where the holder of the estate makes the application, the Upper Tribunal must add the responsible body as a party to proceedings. Where the responsible body makes the application, the Tribunal must add as a party any person bound by or entitled to benefits of an obligation concerned (paras 1 and 2).

Para 3(1) of Sch 18 provides that the Upper Tribunal may exercise its powers to discharge 'if it considers it reasonable to do so in all the circumstances of the case'. Para 3(2) then provides matters to which the Tribunal must have regard in considering whether to discharge. These include material changes of circumstances since the making of the original conservation agreement and, in particular, changes in the character of the land or neighbourhood, changes affecting its enjoyment, whether the obligation serves the public good and changes affecting the extent to which performance of the obligation is or is likely to be affordable or practicable. But in considering affordability or practicability, the Tribunal must apply an objective test and ignore the personal circumstances of the person bound by the obligation (para 3(4)). The Tribunal must also consider whether the conservation purpose of the original agreement could be equally served by a conservation covenant created on different land in which the applicant for the discharge owns an estate. Under para 5, the Tribunal may make a discharge order conditional on the applicant and the responsible making a new conservation covenant, provided the parties consent.

Para 4 gives the Tribunal the power to require the applicant to pay compensation in respect of a loss of benefit resulting for the discharge order.

Part 2 of Sch 18 concerns the powers of the Upper Tribunal to modify obligations, and is written in the same terms as those relating to the discharge. The general provision that the Tribunal may modify the covenant where it considers it reasonable to do so applies, and the Tribunal must have regard to the same factors as in Part 1. The modification will bind the parties to the order, and any successors following modification.

S 84 Law of Property Act 1925, providing for the power of the Upper Tribunal to discharge or modify restrictive covenants, contains some similar language to Sch 18, such as a change in the character of the property or neighbourhood, and there is a reference to the restriction being contrary to the public interest. For a recent discussion by the Court of Appeal on the operation of s 84 and in particular the meaning of public interest, see *Alexander Devine Children's Cancer Trust v Millgate Developments Ltd* (2018) EWCA Civ 2679. Sales LJ noted at 56 that '*The grant of planning permission in relation to the applicant's proposed use of his land is not at all the same as saying that upholding a restrictive covenant which restricts some reasonable user of land is contrary to the public interest … There is a public interest in having private contractual and property rights respected in dealings between private persons. Further, if private contractual/property rights under a restrictive covenant are to be overridden in the public interest, the Upper Tribunal should be astute to see that the public interest reasons for discharge or modification of the covenant are clearly made out.*' Nevertheless, one should be wary of reading too much from case law on s 84 into the interpretation and operation of Sch 18. The statutory language is different, and conservation covenants are a distinct form of land agreement made for the public interest rather than private benefit.

Replacement etc of responsible body

131 Power of responsible body to appoint replacement

(1) The responsible body under a conservation covenant may appoint another responsible body to be the responsible body under the covenant, unless the covenant otherwise provides.

(2) The power under subsection (1) is exercisable by agreement executed as a deed by the appointor and appointee.

(3) In the case of a conservation covenant registered in the local land charges register, an appointment under subsection (1) only has effect if the appointor supplies to the Chief Land Registrar the information necessary to enable the Registrar to amend the registration.

(4) In the case of a conservation covenant relating to land in an area in relation to which section 3 of the Local Land Charges Act 1975 (as substituted by paragraph 3 of Schedule 5 to the Infrastructure Act 2015) does not yet have effect—

(a) the references in subsection (3) to the local land charges register and the Chief Land Registrar are to the appropriate local land charges register and the authority responsible for that register, but

(b) subsection (3) does not apply to an appointment by that authority.

(5) Appointment under subsection (1) has effect to transfer to the appointee—

(a) the benefit of every obligation of the landowner under the conservation covenant, and

(b) the burden of every obligation of the responsible body under the covenant.

(6) Appointment under subsection (1) does not have effect to transfer any right or liability in respect of an existing breach of obligation.

(7) A body appointed under subsection (1) as the responsible body under a conservation covenant must notify its appointment to every person who is bound by an obligation of the landowner under the covenant.

Definitions

'conservation covenant'	s 118(1)
'responsible body'	s 119

In force	Day to be appointed by Secretary of State
Application	E

S 131 allows the responsible body to appoint another responsible body to fulfil its role, unless provisions in the covenant prohibit this. A covenant could identify and specify any responsible body to whom a transfer is to be made, provided they agree. The Law Commission discussed whether transfer should only take place on extinction of the responsible body (see s 135) or whether the landowner's prior consent should be required in all cases. But the Commission concluded that it was preferable to give flexible powers to the responsible party unless the covenant specified otherwise.

The transfer has to made by agreement executed as a deed between the responsible body making the transfer and the new responsible body (sub-s (2)). The appointment must be notified to every person bound by a landowner's obligations under the covenant (sub-s (7)), though, subject to any provisions in the covenant, they have no right to object or prohibit the transfer. Sub-s (5) provides that the appointed replacement takes on the benefit of any obligation of the landowner and the burden of any obligations. But this does not extend to transferring rights or liabilities in respect of breaches of the obligation existing at the time of the appointment (sub-s (6)). As the Explanatory Notes provide, this means that the new body cannot take or continue enforcement action in relation to a breach that predates the transfer, but in the case of a continuing breach, it could do so in respect of the breaches occurring after transfer.

Conservation covenants only take affect after registration as a land charge (see s 122(5)(b) above). Sub-s (3) is consistent with this provision by providing that a transfer only takes place after the transferring body has provided sufficient information to allow the registration to be amended. The information is to be provided to the Chief Land Registrar or, in the areas where s 3 Local Land Charges Act 1975 has not yet come into effect, the local authority responsible for local land charges register. Since 2018 the Chief Land Registrar has been incrementally assuming responsibility from local authorities for maintaining the charges registers. For a list of authorities where transfer of responsibility has taken place, see www.gov.uk/government/publications/hm-land-registry-local-land-charges-programme/local-land-charges-programme#local-authorities.

132 Body ceasing to be a responsible body

(1) Subsections (2) and (3) apply if a body which is the responsible body under a conservation covenant ceases to be a designated body.

(2) The body ceases to be the responsible body under the conservation covenant.

(3) The following transfer to the Secretary of State—

  (a) the benefit of every obligation of the landowner under the covenant, and

  (b) the burden of every obligation of the responsible body under the covenant.

(4) Subsection (3) does not have effect to transfer any right or liability in respect of an existing breach of obligation.

(5) If subsection (3) has effect in relation to a conservation covenant, the Secretary of State becomes custodian of the covenant until—

  (a) an appointment under section 131(1) by the Secretary of State has effect in relation to the covenant, or

  (b) the Secretary of State makes an election under subsection (6) in relation to the covenant.

(6) If custodian of a conservation covenant, the Secretary of State may elect to be the responsible body under the covenant by giving written notice of election to every person who is bound by an obligation of the landowner under the covenant.

(7) The Secretary of State may, as custodian of a conservation covenant—

(a) enforce any obligation of the landowner under the covenant, and

(b) exercise in relation to the covenant any power conferred by this Part on the responsible body under the covenant.

(8) In relation to any period as custodian of a conservation covenant, the Secretary of State has no liability with respect to performance of any obligation of the responsible body under the covenant.

Definitions

'conservation covenant'	s 118(1)
'responsible body'	s 119

In force	Day to be appointed by Secretary of State
Application	E

S 132 provides for the Secretary of State to be the holder of last resort where the responsible body ceases to be a designated body under s 119 above. This could happen where the body ceases to exist before it has exercised transfer powers under s 131 or where the Secretary of State is satisfied the body is not suitable to remain as a responsible body because, say, its main activities no longer relate to conservation. It could also happen where the body has applied to the Secretary of State for its designation to be revoked, though the Secretary of State retains discretion as to whether or not to revoke (see s 119(6)).

Once it is no longer designated, the body ceases to be the responsible body under the covenant (sub-s (2)), and the landowner's benefits from obligations and the burden of the responsible body's obligations pass to the Secretary of State as custodian of the covenant, with the exception of any rights or liabilities in respect of existing breaches of obligations (sub-ss (3) and (4)).

As custodian of the covenant, the Secretary of State has the power to enforce the landowner's obligations and exercise any power conferred on the previous responsible body, but no enforcement can be taken against the Secretary of State in respect of the obligations of the responsible body (sub-ss (7) and (8)).

On becoming the custodian of the covenant, the Secretary of State has two options. First, the covenant may be transferred by the Secretary of State to another responsible body under s 131 above (sub-s 5(a)), but note that s 131 refers only to the power of responsible bodies to transfer, and as custodian of the covenant the Secretary of State is strictly not yet a responsible body. Alternatively, the Secretary of State may choose to become the responsible body under the covenant by given written notice to every person bound by an obligation of the landowner under the covenant. At the same time, notification must be made under the Local Land Charges Regulations. There appears to be no time limit for the Secretary of State to make his decision whether to transfer or become the responsible body. This could result in the rather unsatisfactory situation of covenants being held by the Secretary of State as custodian for lengthy periods where the Secretary of State has no liability in respect of the obligations of the responsible body under the covenant.

Miscellaneous

133 Effect of acquisition or disposal of affected land by responsible body

If the responsible body under a conservation covenant acquires an estate in land to which an obligation under the covenant relates (whether an obligation of the landowner or of the responsible body under the covenant)—

(a) the acquisition does not have effect to extinguish the obligation,

(b) section 122(2)(b) applies to the body as it would apply to any other person acquiring the estate in land in the same circumstances, and

(c) any obligation of the responsible body under the covenant continues to bind the body in accordance with this Part.

Definitions

'conservation covenant'	s 118(1)
'responsible body'	s 119

In force	Day to be appointed by Secretary of State
Application	E

S 133 deals with the situation where the responsible body acquires an estate in the land to which the covenant relates. The obligations under the covenant are not extinguished and s 122(2)(b) (successors of landowners bound by obligations under the covenant) applies. This is in contrast to the general position concerning restrictive covenants and other easement, where, under the doctrine of unity of seisin, the relevant lands come into one ownership.

134 Effect of deemed surrender and re-grant of qualifying estate

(1) Subsection (2) applies if a term of years absolute which is the qualifying estate in relation to an obligation under a conservation covenant is deemed to be surrendered and re-granted by operation of law.

(2) In the application of sections 122, 123 and 127 to the period after the deemed surrender, references to the qualifying estate are to be read as including a reference to the term of years deemed to be granted.

Definitions

'conservation covenant'	s 118(1)
'qualifying estate'	s 117(4)

In force	Day to be appointed by Secretary of State
Application	E

A conservation covenant can be created by a leaseholder of more than seven years. S 134 is concerned with the situation where a lease is surrendered and regranted by operation of law, as can happen where a lease is varied by the parties to such an extent that the variation is deemed to be a surrender and regrant of the lease whatever the intention of the parties – see *Friends Provident Life Office v British Railways Board* [1996] 1 All ER 336. Sub-s (2) provides that ss 125 (benefits and obligations of landowner), 126 (benefits of obligation of responsible body) and 130 (discharge by agreement) apply to the tenant or successors of the extended lease but, since s 124 (duration of covenant) continues to apply, only for the period of the original lease, or any shorter period agreed by the parties.

135 Declarations about obligations under conservation covenants

(1) The court or Upper Tribunal may on the application of any person interested declare—

(a) whether anything purporting to be a conservation covenant is a conservation covenant,

(b) whether any land is land to which an obligation under a conservation covenant relates,

(c) whether any person is bound by, or entitled to the benefit of, an obligation under a conservation covenant and, if so, in respect of what land,

(d) what, upon the true construction of any instrument by means of which an obligation under a conservation covenant is created or modified, is the nature of the obligation.

(2) No application under section 84(2) of the Law of Property Act 1925 (which enables the court on application to make declarations about restrictions under instruments) may be made in relation to an obligation under a conservation covenant.

(3) In this section "the court" means the High Court or the county court.

Definitions

'conservation covenant'	s 118(1)
'the court'	s 135(3)

In force	Day to be appointed by Secretary of State
Application	E

S 135 provides a procedure analogous to s 84(2) Law of Property Act 1925 and allows an application to be made to the county court, High Court or Upper Tribunal to seek a declaration about the status of a covenant – whether it is a conservation covenant in law, the land to which an obligation relates, who is bound by obligations or entitled to benefits of an obligation, and the nature of the obligations in question. Application must be made by an 'interested' person – a question to be determined by the court or Upper Tribunal – but is clearly not confined to the responsible bodies or landowners. In dealing with such an application, the court or Tribunal only has powers of declaration and cannot modify or discharge the covenant in question, though the Upper Tribunal has powers to modify or discharge in accordance with the provisions of s 130 and Sch 18. In certain circumstances, seeking a declaration concerning the covenant may be a more effective and less costly tactic that initiating enforcement proceedings under s 125 above.

136 Duty of responsible bodies to make annual return

(1) A designated body must make an annual return to the Secretary of State stating whether, during the period to which the return relates, there were any conservation covenants under which an obligation was owed to it as the responsible body.

(2) If there were any such conservation covenants, the annual return must—

(a) state the number of conservation covenants;

(b) state, for each conservation covenant, the area of the land in relation to which the body was owed any obligation as the responsible body.

(3) The annual return must also give any information that is prescribed under subsection (4).

(4) The Secretary of State may by regulations make provision about annual returns to be made by a designated body.

(5) The provision which may be made under subsection (4) includes, in particular, provision—

(a) prescribing information to be included in an annual return (but see subsection (10)), and

(b) provision as to the period to which an annual return is to relate and the date by which an annual return is to be made.

(6) Subject to any provision made as mentioned in subsection (5)(b)—

(a) the period to which an annual return is to relate, and

(b) the date by which an annual return is to be made,

are such period and date as the Secretary of State may direct.

(7) On giving a direction under subsection (6) the Secretary of State must take all reasonable steps to draw the direction to the attention of each responsible body affected by it.

(8) A direction under subsection (6) may be varied or revoked by a further such direction.

(9) Regulations under subsection (4) and directions under subsection (6) may make—

(a) provision of general application, or

(b) provision applicable only to one or more particular responsible bodies or to responsible bodies of a particular description.

(10) Any information prescribed for inclusion in an annual return made by a designated body must be information about or connected with—

(a) the designated body;

(b) its activities over the period to which the return relates;

(c) any conservation covenant under which an obligation was owed to it as the responsible body during that period;

(d) the land in relation to which it was owed such an obligation.

(11) Regulations under this section are subject to the negative procedure.

Definitions

'conservation covenant'	s 118(1)
'designated body'	s 122(1)(b)

In force	Day to be appointed by Secretary of State
Application	E

S 136 requires a responsible body designated under s 119 to make an annual return to the Secretary of State. The return must state whether there were any conservation covenants containing obligations owed to the responsible body. If there were such covenants, the return must state the number of covenants and the area of land concerned for each.

The Secretary of State is given power to make regulations prescribing further information that must be included, together with the period for the annual returns and the date by which they must be made. Subject to any provisions in the regulations concerning dates, the Secretary of State may also issue directions as to the period of the annual return and the date by which it must be made. The regulations may be of general application, be applicable to responsible bodies of a particular description, or only applicable to one or more particular bodies.

There is no statutory requirement here for the Secretary of State to publish the information provided in annual returns. The returns are likely to be used by the Secretary of State in making the annual report on progress in meeting the current environmental improvement plan (see s 9 above) and in meeting any statutory biodiversity targets established under s 1 of this Act.

Supplementary

137 Crown application

Schedule 19 makes provision about the application of this Part to Crown land.

In force	Day to be appointed by Secretary of State
Application	E

Sch 19 provides that the provisions concerning conservation covenants can apply to Crown land, but with various modifications to reflect its distinct and sometimes complex legal nature. Para 2 defines Crown land by reference to various different types of estates, such as those of the Duchy of Cornwall, and specifies who is the appropriate authority for each. Essentially, the appropriate authority can enter into a covenant as landowner and be bound by the covenant.

Para 3 relates to demesne land, where the Crown holds the land but no freehold has been granted. For the purposes of Part 7 of this Act, the Crown is to be treated as holding a freehold estate and can, through the appropriate authority, enter into and be bound by conservation covenants in respect of such land.

Para 4 deals with land subject to escheat, where, in certain circumstances, such as a disclaimer by a liquidator, the Crown may be entitled to take possession of the land. The provisions provide that any conservation covenant is not terminated, but that the appropriate authority for the Crown has no liability in respect of a covenant obligation until the Crown takes possession.

Para 5 deals with land that has become ownerless and becomes vested in the Crown as *bona vacantia*. This can happen, for example, where someone dies intestate and without relatives, or where companies are dissolved. The appropriate authority has no liability under any conservation covenant relating to the land until it takes possession or control, or enters into occupation of the land. In effect, the covenant is suspended until the Crown chooses to make that choice or until the land passes to a new owner.

Parts 2 and 3 (paras 6–21) introduce various modifications to the provisions of the Act concerning conservation covenants where the covenants relate to Crown land held by a person other than an appropriate authority.

138 Index of defined terms in Part 7

The following Table sets out expressions defined or explained in this Part for general purposes.

Expression	*Provision*
conservation covenant	section 118(1)
conservation covenant agreement	section 117(1)
conservation purpose	section 117(3)
conserving (something)	section 117(4)
designated body	section 119(1)(b)
natural environment (in relation to land)	section 117(4)
qualifying estate (generally)	section 117(4)
the qualifying estate (in relation to an obligation under a conservation covenant)	section 117(4)
responsible body	section 119

In force Day to be appointed by Secretary of State

Application E

139 Consequential amendments relating to Part 7

Schedule 20 makes consequential amendments relating to this Part.

In force Day to be appointed by Secretary of State

Application E

Sch 20 contains various amendments to existing legislation relating to powers of local authorities which override easements and applying them to conservation covenants. See further annotations to s 126 above.

S 12 of the Acquisition of Land Act 1981 is amended to require a person entitled to the benefit of an obligation under a conservation covenant to be given due notice of a compulsory purchase under the Act by local authorities, other authorities and Ministers, and allow them to make objections.

Provisions in s 203 Housing and Planning 2016 are also amended to provide that the power to override easements on land acquired for planning development by local authorities and other authorities within the meaning of the Act extends to conservation covenants other than those owed to the National Trust. S 204 of that Act is amended so that compensation payable for interference with easements and other rights authorised by s 203 does not extend to breaches of obligations under conservation covenants.

Provisions in the Neighbourhood and Planning Act 2107 relating to powers of authority to take temporary possession of land are amended to ensure that a person having the benefit of a conservation covenant is given due notice of a compulsory temporary possession. The provisions on compensation for loss or injury for temporary possession do not apply to persons entitled to a benefit of a conservation covenant, the authority acquiring temporary possession is not bound by obligations under a conservation covenant and, with the exception of obligations owed to the National Trust under a conservation covenant, the authority may use the land even if it causes a person to be in breach of an obligation owed under a conservation covenant.

Part 8

Miscellaneous and general provisions

Regulation of chemicals

140 Amendment of REACH legislation

Schedule 21 confers powers to amend the REACH Regulation and the REACH Enforcement Regulations 2008.

In force	Day on which Act was passed (9 November 2021) except for provisions relating to regulations in Northern Ireland under Sch 21 para 2, which come into force on day determined by DAERA
Application	E W S

Sch 21 is concerned with the key EU regulation on chemicals, Regulation (EC) 1907/2006 concerning the Registration, Authorisation, Evaluation and Registration of Chemicals (REACH). REACH had been rolled over into England, Wales and Scotland following Brexit, but with various amendments to make it operational in a domestic context. In particular, the Health and Safety Executive has now assumed the functions and powers of the European Chemicals Agency as the competent authority under the Regulation. See REACH etc (Amendment etc) (EU Exit) Regulations 2019, SI 2019/758, REACH etc (Amendment etc) (EU Exit) (No 2) Regulations 2019, SI 2019/858, REACH etc (Amendment etc) (EU Exit) (No 3) Regulations 2019/1144 and REACH etc (Amendment etc) (EU Exit) Regulations 2020, SI 2020/1577.

UK REACH applies to chemical substances manufactured in the UK as well as imports. See further *End of Brexit Transition: Chemicals Regulation (REACH)*, Briefing Paper CBP 8403 (House of Commons Library, March 2021).

UK REACH was originally intended to apply throughout the UK, but in line with the Ireland/Northern Ireland Protocol in the Brexit Withdrawal Agreement, the EU REACH system will continue to apply in Northern Ireland – see REACH etc (Amendment etc) (EU Exit) Regulations 2020, SI 2020/1577.

The various amendments that have been made to the REACH Regulation to date were made under the European Union (Withdrawal) Act 2018, where the powers to amend were essentially confined to making the EU law operate effectively in a national context, such as removing references to EU entities that no longer have functions. Sch 20, introduced by this section, gives much broader powers to amend the REACH regulation, though they are constrained.

Power to Amend REACH Regulation

Para 1(1) of Sch 20 gives the Secretary of State powers to amend by regulations the REACH Regulation, but with two significant provisos:

(i) Any amendments must be considered by the Secretary of State to be consistent with Art 1 of the REACH Regulation (paras 1(2)). Art 1 provides that the purpose of the Regulation *'is to ensure a high level of protection of human health and the environment, including the promotion of alternative methods for assessment of hazards of substances, as well as free circulation on the internal market while enhancing competitiveness and innovation'*. Before making regulations, the Secretary of State must publish an explanation of why he considers proposed amendments are consistent with Art 1. The explanation must be published no later than the time when statutory consultation begins under para 5 – see below.

(ii) Regulations may not amend certain provisions of the Regulation ('protected provisions') unless they relate to supplementary, incidental, transitional or saving provisions under s 133(1)(a) of the Act (paras (3) and (4)). A list of the protected provisions is provided in para 6 and, according to the Explanatory Notes, relates to fundamental principles of REACH (including, inter alia, 'no data, no market' (Art 5), animal testing as a last resort (Art 25 (1)), communication to the public on risks of substances (Art 123) and various provisions on transparency. The Annexes to the Regulation are also included as protected provisions because they can be amended under provisions with the REACH Regulation itself.

According to an answer given in Parliament in 2020 by the DEFRA Minister of State: *'We will not seek ongoing alignment with the EU Regulatory system but will not diverge simply for the sake of it. There may be good reasons for taking a different approach on a particular substance to reflect UK circumstances, but that does not mean reducing standards or levels of protection'* (Lord Goldsmith, HL Deb 16 March 2020, col 1273). The Policy Statement on the Environment Bill states the amending powers *'will allow the Secretary of State to take further steps where necessary to ensure a smooth transition to a UK chemicals regime following the UK's exit from the EU. It will also make it possible to keep the legislation up to date and respond to emerging needs and ambitions for the effective management of chemicals'* (DEFRA, 30 January 2020, s 7). In the House of Lords' consideration of the Bill in 2021, the Government stated, *'this power will ensure that legislation can keep up to date with and respond to emerging needs or ambitions for the management of chemicals. We will build on our global reputation and continue to provide a strong and influential voice on the world stage as an active party to the four UN conventions on chemicals and waste. We will continue our work to improve regulation, strengthening the evidence base and ambition globally. The intention is to make sure that we have the means to keep REACH fit for purpose'* (Lord Goldsmith, HL Deb 7 June 2021, vol 812, col 1198).

Regulations made under para 1(1) are subject to the affirmative procedure.

Power to Amend REACH Enforcement Regulations

Para 2(1) gives the Secretary of State or devolved authorities in respect of devolved matters under the regulations the power to amend the REACH Enforcement Regulations 2008, SI 2008/2852. These regulations were made under the European Communities Act 1972, and without Sch 21 there would be no power to amend them following Brexit.

The power to amend includes creating or widening the scope of criminal offences and providing for penalties, but subject to maximum amounts specified in para 4.

Consent of the Devolved Administrations

Art 4A of the REACH Regulation was introduced by REACH etc (Amendment etc) (EU Exit) Regulations 2019 (SI 2019/758), and requires the consent of the devolved administrations to provisions in the Regulation that are stated to be subject to the requirement and are within their competence. Chemicals policy including REACH engages a complex mixture of reserved and devolved competences. Product safety, animal testing and health and safety at work are reserved, while environmental protection, waste management and public health are devolved. Para 3 of Sch 21 provides that the power to make regulations is subject to these Art 4A consent requirements. In addition, under para 4, the Secretary of State must consider any request made by a devolved authority to make regulations under the Schedule.

Consultation

Before making regulations under Sch 21, the Secretary of State must consult the Health and Safety Executive, any person nominated by a devolved authority and any other persons the Secretary of State considers appropriate (para 5(1) and (2)). The Secretary of State must publish an explanation of why the amendments are considered to be consistent with the overall aims of the REACH in Art 1 of the REACH Regulation (para 1(5)). Where a devolved authority is proposing regulations in relation to the REACH enforcement regulations, it must consult the Health and Safety Executive and any other persons it considers appropriate.

Concurrent functions in Wales

141 Amendments of Schedule 7B to the Government of Wales Act 2006

(1) Schedule 7B to the Government of Wales Act 2006 (general restrictions on legislative competence of Senedd Cymru) is amended as follows.

(2) In paragraph 9(8)(b) (exceptions to restrictions relating to reserved authorities)—

(a) omit the "or" at the end of paragraph (v);

(b) after paragraph (vi) insert "; or

(vii) the Environment Act 2021."

(3) In paragraph 11(6)(b) (exceptions to restrictions relating to Ministers of the Crown)—

(a) omit the "or" at the end of paragraph (v);

(b) after paragraph (vi) insert "; or

(vii) the Environment Act 2021."

In force	Day on which Act was passed (9 November 2021)
Application	W

General provisions

142 Consequential provision

(1) The Secretary of State may by regulations make provision that is consequential on this Act or regulations under this Act.

(2) The Welsh Ministers may by regulations make provision that is consequential on—

(a) a provision within section 147(4) (provisions to be commenced by Welsh Ministers), or

(b) regulations under this Act made by the Welsh Ministers.

(3) The Scottish Ministers may by regulations make provision that is consequential on—

(a) a provision within section 147(5) (provisions to be commenced by Scottish Ministers), or

(b) regulations under this Act made by the Scottish Ministers.

(4) The Department of Agriculture, Environment and Rural Affairs in Northern Ireland may by regulations make provision that is consequential on—

(a) a provision within section 147(6) (provisions to be commenced by the Department), or

(b) regulations under this Act made by that Department.

(5) The Department for the Economy in Northern Ireland may by regulations make provision that is consequential on regulations under this Act made by that Department.

(6) Regulations under this section may amend or repeal provision made by or under any legislation (whenever passed or made).

(7) Regulations under this section are subject to the affirmative procedure if they amend or repeal any provision of—

(a) an Act of Parliament,

(b) a Measure or Act of Senedd Cymru,

(c) an Act of the Scottish Parliament,

(d) Northern Ireland legislation, or

(e) retained direct principal EU legislation.

(8) Regulations under this section to which subsection (7) does not apply are subject to the negative procedure.

(9) Regulations under this section—

(a) made by the Welsh Ministers, may contain only provision which, if contained in an Act of Senedd Cymru, would be within the legislative competence of the Senedd;

(b) made by the Scottish Ministers, may contain only provision which, if contained in an Act of the Scottish Parliament, would be within the legislative competence of the Parliament;

(c) made by a Northern Ireland department, may contain only provision which, if contained in an Act of the Northern Ireland Assembly, would be within the legislative competence of the Assembly and would not require the Secretary of State's consent.

(10) Regulations under this section made by the Secretary of State may not contain provision that could be contained in regulations under this section—

(a) made by the Welsh Ministers, unless the Welsh Ministers consent;

(b) made by the Scottish Ministers, unless the Scottish Ministers consent;

(c) made by a Northern Ireland department, unless the department consents.

In force Day on which Act was passed (9 November 2021)

Application E S W NI

143 Regulations

(1) A power to make regulations under any provision of this Act includes power to make—

(a) supplementary, incidental, transitional or saving provision;

(b) different provision for different purposes or areas.

(2) Subsection (1) does not apply to regulations under section 147 or 148.

(3) Regulations under this Act made by—

(a) the Secretary of State, or

(b) the Welsh Ministers,

are to be made by statutory instrument.

(4) A power of a Northern Ireland department to make regulations under this Act is exercisable by statutory rule for the purposes of the Statutory Rules (Northern Ireland) Order 1979 (S.I. 1979/1573 (N.I. 12)).

(5) Where regulations under this Act made or to be made by the Secretary of State—

(a) are subject to the negative procedure, the statutory instrument containing them is subject to annulment in pursuance of a resolution of either House of Parliament;

(b) are subject to the affirmative procedure, they may not be made unless a draft of the statutory instrument containing them has been laid before, and approved by a resolution of, each House of Parliament.

(6) Where regulations under this Act made or to be made by the Welsh Ministers—

(a) are subject to the negative procedure, the statutory instrument containing them is subject to annulment in pursuance of a resolution of Senedd Cymru;

(b) are subject to the affirmative procedure, they may not be made unless a draft of the statutory instrument containing them has been laid before, and approved by a resolution of, Senedd Cymru.

(7) Where regulations under this Act made or to be made by a Northern Ireland Department—

(a) are subject to the negative procedure, they are subject to negative resolution within the meaning given by section 41(6) of the Interpretation Act (Northern Ireland) 1954 (c. 33 (N.I.));

(b) are subject to the affirmative procedure, they may not be made unless a draft of the regulations has been laid before and approved by a resolution of the Northern Ireland Assembly.

(8) See sections 28 and 29 of the Interpretation and Legislative Reform (Scotland) Act 2010 (asp 10) for the meaning of "the negative procedure" and "the affirmative procedure" in relation to regulations under this Act made or to be made by the Scottish Ministers.

(9) Any provision that may be made by regulations under this Act subject to the negative procedure may be made by regulations subject to the affirmative procedure.

In force Day on which Act was passed (9 November 2021)

Application E S W NI

144 Crown application

(1) This Act binds the Crown, subject to subsection (2).

(2) An amendment or repeal made by this Act binds the Crown to the same extent as the provision amended or repealed.

In force Day on which Act was passed (9 November 2021)

Application E W S NI

145 Financial provisions

There is to be paid out of money provided by Parliament—

(a) any expenditure incurred under or by virtue of this Act by the Secretary of State, and

(b) any increase attributable to this Act in the sums payable under any other Act out of money so provided.

In force Day on which Act was passed (9 November 2021)

Application E W S NI

146 Extent

(1) In Part 1 of this Act (environmental governance)—

(a) the following provisions extend to England and Wales—

(i) Chapter 1 (improving the natural environment), except for sections 17 to 20;

(ii) section 28 (monitoring and reporting on environmental improvement plans and targets);

(b) sections 17 to 19 (policy statement on environmental principles) extend to England and Wales and Scotland;

(c) the remaining provisions extend to England and Wales, Scotland and Northern Ireland.

(2) Part 2 of this Act (environmental governance: Northern Ireland) extends to Northern Ireland, except that—

(a) in Part 1 of Schedule 3, paragraphs 16 and 17(7) extend to England and Wales, Scotland and Northern Ireland;

(b) an amendment or repeal made by Part 2 of Schedule 3 has the same extent as the provision amended or repealed.

(3) In Part 3 of this Act (waste and resource efficiency)—

(a) the following provisions extend to England and Wales, Scotland and Northern Ireland—

(i) section 50 and Schedule 4 (producer responsibility obligations);

(ii) section 51 and Schedule 5 (producer responsibility for disposal costs);

(iii) section 52 and Schedule 6 (resource efficiency information);

(iv) section 53 and Schedule 7 (resource efficiency requirements);

(v) section 63 (procedure for regulations under the Environmental Protection Act 1990);

(b) the following provisions extend to England and Wales and Northern Ireland—

(i) section 54 and Schedule 8 (deposit schemes);

(ii) sections 55 and Schedule 9 (charges for single use items);

(c) the following provisions extend to England and Wales—
  (i) section 60 (hazardous waste);
  (ii) section 66 and Schedule 10 (enforcement powers);
  (iii) section 68 (littering enforcement);

(d) section 71 (waste regulation: amendment of Northern Ireland Order) extends to Northern Ireland;

(e) an amendment or repeal has the same extent as the provision amended or repealed, except where contained in a provision for which a different extent is provided by this subsection.

(4) In Part 4 of this Act (air quality and environmental recall)—

(a) section 73 and Schedule 12 (smoke control areas) extend to England and Wales;

(b) sections 74 to 77 (recall of motor vehicles) extend to England and Wales, Scotland and Northern Ireland;

(c) an amendment or repeal has the same extent as the provision amended or repealed, except where contained in a provision for which a different extent is provided by this subsection.

(5) In Part 5 of this Act (water)—

(a) section 84 (report on elimination of discharges from storm overflows) extends to England and Wales;

(b) sections 89 and 93 (water quality) extend to England and Wales, Scotland and Northern Ireland;

(c) section 90 (water quality - powers of Welsh Ministers) extends to England and Wales;

(d) section 91 (water quality - powers of Northern Ireland Department) extends to Northern Ireland;

(e) section 92 (Solway Tweed river basin district) extends to England and Wales and Scotland;

(f) an amendment or repeal has the same extent as the provision amended or repealed.

(6) Part 6 of this Act (nature and biodiversity) extends to England and Wales, except that—

(a) the amendments made by Schedule 15 (biodiversity gain in nationally significant infrastructure projects) have the same extent as the provisions amended, and

(b) section 116 and Schedule 17 (use of forest risk commodities in commercial activity) extend to England and Wales, Scotland and Northern Ireland.

(7) Part 7 of this Act (conservation covenants) extends to England and Wales.

(8) This Part (miscellaneous and general provisions) extends to England and Wales, Scotland and Northern Ireland.

In force Day on which Act was passed (9 November 2021)

Application E W S NI

147 Commencement

(1) The following provisions of this Act come into force on the day on which this Act is passed—

(a) section 63 (procedure for regulations under the Environmental Protection Act 1990);

(b) this Part of this Act (miscellaneous and general provisions), except section 140 and Schedule 21 so far as relating to powers of a Northern Ireland department to make regulations under paragraph 2 of that Schedule.

(2) The following provisions of this Act come into force at the end of the period of 2 months beginning with the day on which this Act is passed—

(a) section 51 and Schedule 5 (producer responsibility for disposal costs) so far as relating to England and Wales and Scotland;

(b) section 52 and Schedule 6 (resource efficiency information) so far as relating to England and Wales and Scotland;

(c) section 53 and Schedule 7 (resource efficiency requirements) so far as relating to England and Wales and Scotland;

(d) section 54 and Schedule 8 (deposit schemes) so far as relating to England and Wales;

(e) section 55 and Schedule 9 (charges for single use items) so far as relating to England and Wales;

(f) section 56 (carrier bag charge) so far as relating to England and Wales;

(g) section 58 (electronic waste tracking);

(h) section 66 and Schedule 10 (enforcement powers);

(i) section 70 (regulation of polluting activities);

(j) section 80 (storm overflows) and section 84 (report on elimination of discharges from storm overflows);

(k) section 88 (water abstraction in England);

(l) section 89 (water quality), except so far as relating to legislation within section 89(2)(d) to (f) and any regulations modifying that legislation made under or by virtue of the European Union (Withdrawal) Act 2018;

(m) sections 90, 92 and 93 (water quality);

(n) section 97 (disclosure of HMRC information).

(3) The following provisions of this Act come into force on such day as the Secretary of State may by regulations appoint—

(a) Part 1 (environmental governance);

(b) section 50 and Schedule 4 (producer responsibility obligations), so far as relating to England;

(c) section 57 (separate collection of waste);
(d) section 60 (hazardous waste), so far as relating to England;
(e) section 62 (transfrontier shipments of waste);
(f) section 64 (charging powers), so far as relating to the Environment Agency;
(g) section 68 (littering enforcement), so far as relating to England;
(h) in section 69 (fixed penalty notices), subsections (2) and (4) and subsection (1) so far as relating to those subsections;
(i) section 72 and Schedule 11 (local air quality management framework);
(j) Parts 1 and 3 of Schedule 12 (smoke control areas) and section 73 so far as relating to those Parts;
(k) sections 74 to 77 (recall of motor vehicles);
(l) sections 78 and 79 (water management plans etc), so far as relating to undertakers whose areas are wholly or mainly in England;
(m) sections 81 and 82 (reporting and monitoring duties relating to discharges from storm overflows etc);
(n) section 83 (reduction of adverse impacts of storm overflows);
(o) sections 85 and 87 (amendments to Water Industry Act 1991), so far as relating to undertakers whose areas are wholly or mainly in England and licensees using the systems of such undertakers;
(p) section 86 and Schedule 13 (appointment of water and sewerage undertakers in England);
(q) section 94 (valuation of other land in drainage districts: England);
(r) section 96 (valuation of agricultural land in drainage districts), so far as relating to internal drainage districts which are wholly or mainly in England;
(s) Part 6 (nature and biodiversity);
(t) Part 7 (conservation covenants).

(4) The following provisions of this Act come into force on such day as the Welsh Ministers may by regulations appoint—

(a) section 50 and Schedule 4 (producer responsibility obligations), so far as relating to Wales;
(b) section 60 (hazardous waste), so far as relating to Wales;
(c) section 64 (charging powers), so far as relating to the Natural Resources Body for Wales;
(d) section 68 (littering enforcement), so far as relating to Wales;
(e) in section 69 (fixed penalty notices), subsections (3) and (5) and subsection (1) so far as relating to those subsections;
(f) Part 2 of Schedule 12 (smoke control areas) and section 73 so far as relating to that Part;
(g) sections 78 and 79 (water management plans etc), so far as relating to undertakers whose areas are wholly or mainly in Wales;

(h) sections 85 and 87 (amendments to Water Industry Act 1991), so far as relating to undertakers whose areas are wholly or mainly in Wales and licensees using the systems of such undertakers;

(i) section 95 (valuation of other land in drainage districts: Wales);

(j) section 96 (valuation of agricultural land in drainage districts), so far as relating to internal drainage districts which are wholly or mainly in Wales.

(5) The following provisions of this Act come into force on such day as the Scottish Ministers may by regulations appoint—

(a) section 50 and Schedule 4 (producer responsibility obligations), so far as relating to Scotland;

(b) section 64 (charging powers), so far as relating to the Scottish Environment Protection Agency.

(6) The following provisions of this Act come into force on such day as the Department of Agriculture, Environment and Rural Affairs in Northern Ireland may by order appoint—

(a) Part 2 (environmental governance: Northern Ireland);

(b) section 50 and Schedule 4 (producer responsibility obligations), so far as relating to Northern Ireland;

(c) section 51 and Schedule 5 (producer responsibility for disposal costs) so far as relating to Northern Ireland;

(d) section 52 and Schedule 6 (resource efficiency information) so far as relating to Northern Ireland;

(e) section 53 and Schedule 7 (resource efficiency requirements) so far as relating to Northern Ireland;

(f) section 54 and Schedule 8 (deposit schemes) so far as relating to Northern Ireland;

(g) section 55 and Schedule 9 (charges for single use items), so far as relating to Northern Ireland;

(h) section 56 (carrier bag charge) so far as relating to Northern Ireland;

(i) section 59 (electronic waste tracking: Northern Ireland);

(j) section 61 (hazardous waste: Northern Ireland);

(k) section 65 (waste charging: Northern Ireland);

(l) section 67 (enforcement powers: Northern Ireland);

(m) section 71 (waste regulation: amendment of Northern Ireland Order);

(n) section 89 (water quality: powers of Secretary of State), so far as relating to legislation within section 89(2)(d) to (f) and any regulations modifying that legislation made under or by virtue of the European Union (Withdrawal) Act 2018;

(o) section 91 (water quality: powers of Northern Ireland Department);

(p) section 140 and Schedule 21 (amendment of REACH legislation) so far as relating to powers of a Northern Ireland department to make regulations under paragraph 2 of that Schedule.

(7) An order under subsection (6) may not appoint a day for the coming into force of the following provisions of Schedule 3 (OEP's Northern Ireland functions), unless the Secretary of State consents—

(a) paragraphs 16 and 17(7);

(b) Part 2.

(8) The power to make an order under subsection (6) is exercisable by statutory rule for the purposes of the Statutory Rules (Northern Ireland) Order 1979 (S.I. 1979/1573 (N.I. 12)).

(9) An order under subsection (6) may not be made unless a draft of the order has been laid before and approved by a resolution of the Northern Ireland Assembly.

(10) A power to make regulations or an order under this section includes power to appoint different days for different purposes or areas.

In force	Day on which Act was passed (9 November 2021)
Application	E W S NI

148 Transitional or saving provision

(1) The Secretary of State may by regulations make transitional or saving provision in connection with the coming into force of any provision of this Act.

(2) The Welsh Ministers may by regulations make transitional or saving provision in connection with the coming into force of any provision within section 147(4) (provisions to be commenced by Welsh Ministers).

(3) The Scottish Ministers may by regulations make transitional or saving provision in connection with the coming into force of any provision within section 147(5) (provisions to be commenced by Scottish Ministers).

(4) The Department of Agriculture, Environment and Rural Affairs in Northern Ireland may by regulations make transitional or saving provision in connection with the coming into force of any provision within section 147(6) (provisions to be commenced by Department).

(5) Regulations under this section—

(a) made by the Welsh Ministers, may contain only provision which, if contained in an Act of Senedd Cymru, would be within the legislative competence of the Senedd;

(b) made by the Scottish Ministers, may contain only provision which, if contained in an Act of the Scottish Parliament, would be within the legislative competence of that Parliament;

(c) made by the Department of Agriculture, Environment and Rural Affairs in Northern Ireland, may contain only provision which, if contained in an Act of the Northern Ireland Assembly, would be within the legislative competence of the Assembly and would not require the Secretary of State's consent.

(6) Regulations under this section made by the Secretary of State may not contain provision that could be contained in regulations under this section—

(a) made by the Welsh Ministers, unless the Welsh Ministers consent;

(b) made by the Scottish Ministers, unless the Scottish Ministers consent;

(c) made by the Department of Agriculture, Environment and Rural Affairs in Northern Ireland, unless the Department consents.

(7) Any provision which could be made by regulations under this section made by the Department of Agriculture, Environment and Rural Affairs in Northern Ireland may be made by an order made by the Department under section 147.

(8) A power to make regulations or an order under this section includes power to make different provision for different purposes or areas.

In force	Day on which Act was passed (9 November 2021)
Application	E W S NI

149 Short title

This Act may be cited as the Environment Act 2021.

In force	Day on which Act was passed (9 November 2021)
Application	E W S NI

Schedules

Commentary on provisions in the Schedules will be found in the annotations to the sections of the Act to which they refer.

SCHEDULE 1

The Office for Environmental Protection

Membership

1 (1) The OEP is to consist of—

(a) a Chair (who is to be a non-executive member),

(b) at least two, but not more than five, other non-executive members,

(c) a chief executive (who is to be the accounting officer), and

(d) at least one, but not more than three, other executive members.

(2) The members are to be appointed by the Secretary of State and the OEP in accordance with paragraphs 2 and 3.

(3) In making those appointments, the Secretary of State and the OEP must ensure, so far as practicable, that the number of non-executive members is at all times greater than the number of executive members.

Appointment of non-executive members

2 (1) Non-executive members are to be appointed by the Secretary of State.

(2) The Secretary of State must consult the Chair before appointing any other non-executive member.

(3) The Secretary of State must, in appointing non-executive members, have regard to the desirability of the members (between them) having experience of—

(a) law (including international law) relating to the natural environment,

(b) environmental science,

(c) environmental policy, and

(d) investigatory and enforcement proceedings.

(4) A person may not be appointed as a non-executive member if the person is an employee of the OEP.

Appointment of executive members

3 (1) The chief executive is to be appointed by the non-executive members of the OEP, other than the first chief executive who is to be appointed by the Chair.

(2) The other executive members are to be appointed by the OEP.

(3) The Secretary of State must be consulted before a person is appointed as chief executive.

(4) An executive member must be an employee of the OEP.

Interim chief executive

4 (1) The Secretary of State may appoint a person as an executive member to act as chief executive of the OEP ("an interim chief executive") until the appointment of the first chief executive by the Chair under paragraph 3(1).

(2) Where the OEP has fewer members than are needed to hold a meeting that is quorate (see paragraph 11(2)), an interim chief executive may incur expenditure and do other things in the name and on behalf of the OEP.

(3) In exercising the power in sub-paragraph (2), an interim chief executive must act in accordance with any directions given by the Secretary of State.

(4) Neither paragraph 3(4) (requirement that executive members are employees) nor paragraph 5(2) (requirement that members are not civil servants) apply to an interim chief executive.

Terms of membership

5 (1) A member of the OEP holds and vacates office in accordance with the terms of the member's appointment, subject to the provisions of this Schedule.

(2) A person may not hold office as a member of the OEP if the person is employed in the civil service of the State.

(3) A non-executive member must be appointed for a fixed term of no more than 5 years.

(4) The Secretary of State must, in determining the length of a non-executive member's term, have regard to the desirability of securing that the appointments of non-executive members expire at different times.

(5) The previous appointment of a person as a non-executive member does not affect the person's eligibility for re-appointment.

(6) A non-executive member—

(a) ceases to be a member of the OEP upon becoming its employee,

(b) may resign from office by giving notice to the Secretary of State, and

(c) may be removed from office by notice given by the Secretary of State on the grounds that the member—

(i) has without reasonable excuse failed to discharge the member's functions, or

(ii) is, in the opinion of the Secretary of State, unable or unfit to carry out the member's functions.

Remuneration of non-executive members

6 (1) The OEP must pay its non-executive members such remuneration and allowances as the Secretary of State may determine.

(2) If a person ceases to be a non-executive member, other than by reason of their term of office expiring, and the Secretary of State determines that the person should be compensated, the OEP must pay compensation of such amount as the Secretary of State may determine.

(3) The Secretary of State must consult the Chair before making a determination under this paragraph.

Staffing and remuneration

7 (1) The OEP may—

(a) appoint employees on such terms as it determines, and

(b) make such other arrangements for the staffing of the OEP as it determines.

(2) The terms of the first chief executive's appointment are to be determined by the Chair.

(3) The OEP must pay its employees such remuneration as the OEP may determine.

(4) The OEP must pay, or make provision for paying, to or in respect of a person who is or has been an employee of the OEP, such sums as the OEP may determine with the approval of the Secretary of State in respect of pensions, allowances and gratuities.

(5) In the Superannuation Act 1972 ("the 1972 Act"), in Schedule 1 (kinds of employment to which a scheme under section 1 of the 1972 Act can apply), in the list of "other Bodies", at the appropriate place insert—

"The Office for Environmental Protection."

(6) The OEP must pay to the Minister for the Civil Service, at such times as the Minister may direct, such sums as the Minister may determine in respect of any increase attributable to sub-paragraph (5) in the sums payable out of money provided by Parliament under the Superannuation Act 1972.

Powers

8 (1) The OEP may do anything (other than something mentioned in sub-paragraph (2)) it thinks appropriate for the purposes of, or in connection with, its functions.

(2) The OEP may not—

(a) accept gifts of money, land or other property, or

(b) form, participate in forming, or invest in, a company, partnership, joint venture or other similar form of organisation.

Committees

9 (1) The OEP may establish committees.

(2) A committee may include persons who are not members of the OEP (whether or not they are employees of the OEP).

(3) A member of a committee who is neither a member nor an employee of the OEP is not entitled to vote at meetings of that committee.

(4) The OEP may pay such allowances as it may determine to any person who—

(a) is a member of a committee, but

(b) is neither a member, nor an employee, of the OEP.

Delegation to members, committees and employees

10 (1) The OEP may delegate any of its functions (other than a function mentioned in sub-paragraph (4)) to—

(a) a member of the OEP,

(b) any of the OEP's employees authorised for that purpose, or

(c) a committee of the OEP.

(2) The OEP must prepare a document that sets out its policy on how its functions may be appropriately delegated (a "delegation policy").

(3) A function is delegated under this paragraph to the extent, and on the terms, that the OEP determines in accordance with its delegation policy.

(4) The OEP may not delegate the following functions—

(a) approving the strategy under section 23(3) (or a revision of it);

(b) approving a report under section 28 or 29;

(c) approving written advice to a Minister of the Crown under section 30(1) or (3);

(d) deciding whether to give an information notice;

(e) deciding whether to give a decision notice;

(f) deciding whether to apply for an environmental review (see section 38);

(g) deciding whether to apply for judicial review or a statutory review, or to intervene in proceedings that relate to a judicial review or a statutory review (see section 39);

(h) approving a delegation policy under sub-paragraph (2);

(i) approving a report on the exercise of the OEP's functions under paragraph 13(1) or a statement of accounts under paragraph 14(2).

Procedure

11 (1) The OEP may determine its own procedure, subject to sub-paragraph (2), and the procedure of its committees.

(2) A meeting of the OEP is not quorate unless—

(a) there are at least three members present, and

(b) a majority of the members present are non-executive members.

(3) The validity of any proceedings of the OEP is not affected by any vacancy among its members or by any defect in the appointment of such a member.

Funding

12 (1) The Secretary of State must pay to the OEP such sums as the Secretary of State considers are reasonably sufficient to enable the OEP to carry out its functions.

(2) The Secretary of State may provide further financial assistance to the OEP (including by way of grants, loans, guarantees or indemnities) subject to such conditions as the Secretary of State may determine.

Annual Report

13 (1) As soon as reasonably practicable after the end of each financial year the OEP must prepare a report on the exercise of its functions during that financial year.

(2) The OEP must—

(a) arrange for its report to be laid before Parliament, and

(b) publish it.

Annual accounts

14 (1) The OEP must keep proper accounts and proper records in relation to them.

(2) The OEP must prepare a statement of accounts in respect of each financial year in the form specified by the Secretary of State.

(3) A statement of accounts must include an assessment by the OEP of whether, in the financial year to which the statement relates, the Secretary of State provided it with sufficient sums to carry out its functions.

(4) The OEP must send a copy of each statement of accounts to the Secretary of State and the Comptroller and Auditor General as soon as reasonably practicable after the end of the financial year to which it relates.

(5) The Comptroller and Auditor General must—

(a) examine, certify and report on the statement of accounts, and

(b) send a copy of the certified statement and the report to the Secretary of State and the OEP.

(6) The OEP must arrange for the laying before Parliament of a copy of—

(a) its certified statement of accounts, and

(b) the Comptroller and Auditor General's report on its statement of accounts.

Meaning of "financial year"

15 In this Schedule "financial year" means—

(a) the period beginning with the date on which the OEP is established and ending with 31 March following that date, and

(b) each successive period of 12 months.

Status

16 (1) The OEP is not to be regarded—

(a) as a servant or agent of the Crown, or

(b) as enjoying any status, immunity or privilege of the Crown.

(2) The OEP's property is not to be regarded as property of, or property held on behalf of, the Crown.

(3) Service as a member, or as an employee, of the OEP is not service in the civil service of the State.

Independence of the OEP

17 In exercising functions in respect of the OEP, the Secretary of State must have regard to the need to protect its independence.

Disqualification from membership of legislatures

18 In Part 2 of Schedule 1 to the House of Commons Disqualification Act 1975, at the appropriate place insert—

"The Office for Environmental Protection."

19 In Part 2 of Schedule 1 to the Northern Ireland Assembly Disqualification Act 1975, at the appropriate place insert—

"The Office for Environmental Protection."

Public records

20 In Part 2 of the Table in paragraph 3 of Schedule 1 to the Public Records Act 1958 (definition of public records), at the appropriate place insert—

"The Office for Environmental Protection."

Freedom of Information

21 In Part 6 of Schedule 1 to the Freedom of Information Act 2000 (other public bodies), at the appropriate place insert—

"The Office for Environmental Protection."

Investigation by the Parliamentary Commissioner

22 In Schedule 2 to the Parliamentary Commissioner Act 1967 (departments subject to investigation), at the appropriate place insert—

"The Office for Environmental Protection."

Public sector equality duty

23 In Part 1 of Schedule 19 to the Equality Act 2010 (authorities subject to the public sector equality duty), under the heading "Environment, housing and development", at the appropriate place insert—

"The Office for Environmental Protection."

SCHEDULE 2

SECTION 48

IMPROVING THE NATURAL ENVIRONMENT: NORTHERN IRELAND

PART 1

ENVIRONMENTAL IMPROVEMENT PLANS

Environmental improvement plans

1 (1) The Department must prepare an environmental improvement plan.

(2) An "environmental improvement plan" is a plan for significantly improving the natural environment.

(3) The plan may—

(a) relate to a period specified in the plan, or

(b) be of no specified duration.

(4) An environmental improvement plan must set out—

(a) the steps that the Department intends to take to improve the natural environment, and

(b) any steps that any other Northern Ireland department intends to take to improve the natural environment.

(5) It may also set out steps that any Northern Ireland department intends to take to improve people's enjoyment of the natural environment (and if it does so references in this Schedule to improving the natural environment, in relation to that plan, include improving people's enjoyment of it).

(6) In preparing an environmental improvement plan, the Department must consult such other Northern Ireland departments as it considers appropriate.

(7) The Department must lay before the Northern Ireland Assembly, and publish, an environmental improvement plan before the end of the 12 month period beginning with the day on which this paragraph comes into force.

(8) References in this Schedule to the current environmental improvement plan are to the environmental improvement plan for the time being in effect.

Annual reports on environmental improvement plans

2 (1) The Department must prepare annual reports on the implementation of the current environmental improvement plan.

(2) An annual report must—

(a) describe what has been done, in the period to which the report relates, to implement the environmental improvement plan, and

(b) consider, having regard to any data obtained under paragraph 5, whether the natural environment has, or particular aspects of it have, improved during that period.

(3) Annual reports on an environmental improvement plan must relate to—

(a) the 12 month period beginning with the day on which the plan is published, and

(b) each subsequent 12 month period.

(4) An annual report must be laid before the Northern Ireland Assembly before the end of the 4 month period beginning immediately after the last day of the period to which the report relates.

(5) The Department must publish annual reports laid before the Northern Ireland Assembly under this paragraph.

Reviewing and revising environmental improvement plans

3 (1) The Department must—

(a) review the current environmental improvement plan in accordance with this paragraph, and

(b) if the Department considers it appropriate as a result of the review, revise the plan.

(2) The first review of an environmental improvement plan must be completed before the end of the 5 year period beginning with—

(a) if it is the first environmental improvement plan, the day on which it is published, and

(b) otherwise, the day on which it replaces the previous plan (see paragraph 4(6)).

(3) Subsequent reviews of an environmental improvement plan must be completed before the end of the 5 year period beginning with the day on which the previous review was completed.

(4) In reviewing an environmental improvement plan, the Department must—

(a) consider what has been done to implement the plan in the period since it was published or (if it has been reviewed before) last reviewed,

(b) consider whether, having regard to data obtained under paragraph 5, the natural environment has, or particular aspects of it have, improved during that period, and

(c) consider whether any Northern Ireland department should take further or different steps to improve the natural environment (compared to those set out in the plan).

(5) In reviewing and revising an environmental improvement plan, the Department must consult such other Northern Ireland departments as it considers appropriate.

(6) If as a result of a review the Department considers it appropriate to revise the plan, the Department must lay before the Northern Ireland Assembly—

(a) a revised environmental improvement plan, and

(b) a statement explaining the revisions and the reasons for them.

(7) If as a result of a review the Department does not consider it appropriate to revise the plan, the Department must lay before the Northern Ireland Assembly a statement explaining that and the reasons for it.

(8) The Department must publish the documents laid under sub-paragraph (6) or (7).

(9) A review is completed when the Department has laid and published the documents mentioned in sub-paragraph (6) or (7).

(10) References in this Schedule to an environmental improvement plan include a revised environmental improvement plan.

Renewing environmental improvement plans

4 (1) This paragraph applies where an environmental improvement plan relates to a period specified in the plan.

(2) Before the end of the period to which the environmental improvement plan (the “old plan”) relates, the Department must prepare a new environmental improvement plan (the “new plan”).

(3) If the new plan relates to a period specified in the plan, that period must begin no later than immediately after the end of the period to which the old plan relates.

(4) In preparing the new plan the Department must—

(a) consider what has been done to implement the old plan,

(b) consider whether, having regard to data obtained under paragraph 5, the natural environment has improved since the beginning of the period to which the old plan relates,

(c) consider whether any Northern Ireland department should take further or different steps to improve the natural environment (compared to those set out in the old plan) after the end of that period, and

(d) consult such other Northern Ireland departments as it considers appropriate.

(5) At or before the end of the period to which the old plan relates the Department must lay before the Northern Ireland Assembly, and publish, the new plan.

(6) The new plan replaces the old plan when—

(a) it has been laid and published, and

(b) if it relates to a period specified in the new plan, that period has begun.

Environmental monitoring

5 (1) The Department must make arrangements for obtaining such data about the natural environment as the Department considers appropriate for the purpose of monitoring whether the natural environment is, or particular aspects of it are, improving in accordance with the current environmental improvement plan.

(2) The Department must lay before the Northern Ireland Assembly, and publish, a statement setting out the kinds of data to be obtained under sub-paragraph (1).

(3) The first statement must be laid before the end of the 4 month period beginning with the day on which this paragraph comes into force.

(4) The Department may revise the statement at any time (and sub-paragraph (2) applies to any revised statement).

(5) The Department must publish any data obtained under sub-paragraph (1).

Part 2

Policy statement on environmental principles

Policy statement on environmental principles

6 (1) The Department must prepare a policy statement on environmental principles in accordance with this paragraph and paragraph 7.

(2) A "policy statement on environmental principles" is a statement explaining how the environmental principles should be interpreted and proportionately applied—

(a) by Northern Ireland departments when making policy, and

(b) by Ministers of the Crown when making policy so far as relating to Northern Ireland.

(3) It may also explain how Northern Ireland departments and Ministers of the Crown, when interpreting and applying the environmental principles, should take into account other considerations relevant to their policy.

(4) The Department must be satisfied that the statement will, when it comes into effect, contribute to—

(a) the improvement of environmental protection, and

(b) sustainable development.

(5) In this Schedule "environmental principles" means the following principles—

(a) the principle that environmental protection should be integrated into the making of policies,

(b) the principle of preventative action to avert environmental damage,

(c) the precautionary principle, so far as relating to the environment,

(d) the principle that environmental damage should as a priority be rectified at source, and

(e) the polluter pays principle.

Policy statement on environmental principles: process

7 (1) The Department must prepare a draft of the policy statement on environmental principles.

(2) The Department must consult—

(a) the other Northern Ireland departments,

(b) the Secretary of State, and

(c) such other persons as the Department considers appropriate, in relation to the draft statement.

(3) The Department must lay the draft statement before the Northern Ireland Assembly.

(4) If before the end of the 21 day period the Northern Ireland Assembly passes a resolution in respect of the draft statement, the Department must produce a response and lay it before the Assembly.

(5) The Department must prepare and lay before the Northern Ireland Assembly the final statement, but not before—

(a) if sub-paragraph (4) applies, the day on which the Department lays the response required by that sub-paragraph, or

(b) otherwise, the end of the 21 day period.

(6) The final statement has effect when it is laid before the Northern Ireland Assembly.

(7) The Department must publish the statement when it comes into effect.

(8) The "21 day period" is the period of 21 sitting days beginning with the first sitting day after the day on which the draft statement is laid under sub-paragraph (3).

(9) "Sitting day" means a day on which the Northern Ireland Assembly sits.

(10) The requirements in sub-paragraphs (1) and (2) may be met by the preparation of a draft statement, and consultation, before this paragraph comes into force.

(11) The Department may prepare a revised policy statement on environmental principles at any time (and sub-paragraphs (1) to (9) apply in relation to any revised statement).

Policy statement on environmental principles: effect

8 (1) A Northern Ireland department must, when making policy, have due regard to the policy statement on environmental principles currently in effect.

(2) A Minister of the Crown must, when making policy so far as relating to Northern Ireland, have due regard to the policy statement on environmental principles currently in effect.

(3) Nothing in this paragraph requires a Northern Ireland department or a Minister of the Crown to do anything (or refrain from doing anything) if doing it (or refraining from doing it)—

(a) would have no significant environmental benefit, or

(b) would be in any other way disproportionate to the environmental benefit.

(4) Sub-paragraph (1) does not apply to policies so far as relating to taxation, spending or the allocation of resources within government.

(5) Sub-paragraph (2) does not apply to policies so far as relating to—

(a) the armed forces, defence or national security, or

(b) taxation, spending or the allocation of resources within government.

Part 3

Interpretation

Meaning of "natural environment"

9 In this Schedule the "natural environment" means—

(a) plants, wild animals and other living organisms,

(b) their habitats,

(c) land (except buildings or other structures), air and water,

and the natural systems, cycles and processes through which they interact.

Meaning of "environmental protection"

10 In this Schedule "environmental protection" means any of the following—

(a) protection of the natural environment from the effects of human activity;

(b) protection of people from the effects of human activity on the natural environment;

(c) maintenance, restoration or enhancement of the natural environment;

(d) monitoring, assessing, considering, advising or reporting on anything in paragraphs (a) to (c).

General interpretation

11 (1) In this Schedule—

"current environmental improvement plan" has the meaning given by paragraph 1(8);

the "Department" means the Department of Agriculture, Environment and Rural Affairs in Northern Ireland;

"environmental improvement plan" has the meaning given by paragraph 1 (and see also paragraph 3(10));

"environmental principles" has the meaning given by paragraph 6(5);

"improving the natural environment", in relation to an environmental improvement plan, is to be read in accordance with paragraph 1(5);

"making" policy includes developing, adopting or revising policy;

"Minister of the Crown" has the same meaning as in the Ministers of the Crown Act 1975;

"policy" includes proposals for legislation, but does not include an administrative decision taken in relation to a particular person or case (for example, a decision on an application for planning permission, funding or a licence, or a decision about regulatory enforcement);

"policy statement on environmental principles" has the meaning given by paragraph 6.

(2) Section 41(3) of the Interpretation Act (Northern Ireland) 1954 (c. 33 (N.I.)) applies in relation to the laying of a document before the Northern Ireland Assembly under this Schedule, as it applies in relation to the laying of a statutory document under an Act of the Northern Ireland Assembly.

SCHEDULE 3

Section 49

The Office for Environmental Protection: Northern Ireland

Part 1

The OEP's Northern Ireland functions

Monitoring and reporting on the Department's environmental improvement plans

1 (1) The OEP must monitor progress in improving the natural environment in accordance with the current environmental improvement plan.

(2) The OEP must prepare a progress report for each annual reporting period.

(3) A progress report for an annual reporting period is a report on progress made in that period in improving the natural environment in accordance with the current environmental improvement plan.

(4) An annual reporting period is a period for which the Department must prepare a report under paragraph 2 of Schedule 2 (a "Schedule 2 report").

(5) In reporting on progress made in an annual reporting period, the OEP must consider—

(a) the Schedule 2 report for that period,

(b) the data published by the Department under paragraph 5 of Schedule 2 that relates to that period, and

(c) any other reports, documents or information it considers appropriate.

(6) A progress report for an annual reporting period may include—

(a) consideration of how progress could be improved, and

(b) consideration of the adequacy of the data published by the Department under paragraph 5 of Schedule 2.

(7) The OEP must—

(a) arrange for its reports under this paragraph to be laid before the Northern Ireland Assembly, and

(b) publish them.

(8) A progress report for an annual reporting period must be laid no later than 6 months after the Schedule 2 report for that period is laid before the Northern Ireland Assembly.

(9) The Department must—

(a) respond to a report under this paragraph, and

(b) lay before the Northern Ireland Assembly, and publish, a copy of the response.

(10) Where a report under this paragraph contains a recommendation for how progress could be improved, the response must address that recommendation.

(11) The response—

(a) must be laid no later than 12 months after the report is laid, and

(b) may be included in a Schedule 2 report.

Monitoring and reporting on environmental law

2 (1) The OEP must monitor the implementation of Northern Ireland environmental law.

(2) The OEP may report on any matter concerned with the implementation of Northern Ireland environmental law.

(3) But the OEP must not monitor the implementation of, or report on, a matter within the remit of the Committee on Climate Change.

(4) A matter is within the remit of the Committee on Climate Change if it is a matter on which the Committee is, or may be, required to advise or report under Part 1, sections 34 to 36, or section 48 of the Climate Change Act 2008.

(5) The OEP must—

(a) arrange for its reports under this paragraph to be laid before the Northern Ireland Assembly, and

(b) publish them.

(6) The Department must—

(a) respond to a report under this paragraph, and

(b) lay before the Northern Ireland Assembly, and publish, a copy of the response.

(7) The response to a report under this paragraph must be laid no later than 3 months after the report is laid.

Advising on changes to Northern Ireland environmental law etc

3 (1) The OEP must give advice to any Northern Ireland department about—

(a) any proposed change to Northern Ireland environmental law, or

(b) any other matter relating to the natural environment, on which that department requires it to give advice.

(2) The Northern Ireland department may specify matters which the OEP is to take into account in giving the required advice.

(3) The OEP may give advice to any Northern Ireland department about any changes to Northern Ireland environmental law proposed by that department.

(4) Advice under this paragraph is to be given in writing to the Northern Ireland department concerned.

(5) The OEP must publish—

(a) its advice, and

(b) if the advice is given under sub-paragraph (1), a statement of the matter on which it was required to give advice and any matters specified under sub-paragraph (2).

(6) The Northern Ireland department concerned may, if it thinks fit, lay before the Northern Ireland Assembly—

(a) the advice, and

(b) any response that department may make to the advice.

Failure of relevant public authorities to comply with environmental law

4 (1) Paragraphs 6 to 15 make provision about functions of the OEP in relation to failures by relevant public authorities to comply with relevant environmental law.

(2) For the purposes of those paragraphs, a reference to a relevant public authority failing to comply with relevant environmental law means the following conduct by that authority—

(a) unlawfully failing to take proper account of relevant environmental law when exercising its functions;

(b) unlawfully exercising, or failing to exercise, any function it has under relevant environmental law.

Meaning of relevant environmental law, relevant public authority etc

5 (1) The following definitions apply for the purpose of this Part of this Schedule.

(2) "Relevant environmental law" means—

(a) in relation to a Northern Ireland public authority, UK environmental law or Northern Ireland environmental law;

(b) in relation to any other relevant public authority, Northern Ireland environmental law.

(3) "Relevant public authority" means—

(a) a Northern Ireland public authority, or

(b) a person, other than a Northern Ireland public authority, carrying out any function of a public nature in or as regards Northern Ireland that is not a parliamentary function or a function of any of the following persons—

(i) the OEP;

(ii) a court or tribunal;

(iii) either House of Parliament;

(iv) the Northern Ireland Assembly.

(4) "Northern Ireland public authority" means—

(a) a Northern Ireland department, or

(b) a person carrying out a Northern Ireland devolved function (including an implementation body carrying out such a function) that is not a function in connection with proceedings in the Northern Ireland Assembly or a function of any of the following persons—

(i) the OEP;

(ii) a court or tribunal;

(iii) the Northern Ireland Assembly.

(5) "Northern Ireland devolved function" means a function of a public nature exercisable in or as regards Northern Ireland that could be conferred by provision included in an Act of the Northern Ireland Assembly made without the consent of the Secretary of State (see sections 6 to 8 of the Northern Ireland Act 1998).

Complaints about relevant public authorities

6 (1) A person may make a complaint to the OEP under this paragraph if the person believes that a relevant public authority has failed to comply with relevant environmental law.

(2) The OEP must prepare and publish a document which sets out the procedure by which complaints can be made.

(3) A complaint under this paragraph must be made in accordance with that procedure (as most recently published).

(4) A complaint under this paragraph may not be made by any person whose functions include functions of a public nature.

(5) A complaint about a relevant public authority may not be made under this paragraph if—

(a) the authority operates a procedure for considering complaints ("an internal complaints procedure") under which the complaint could be considered, and

(b) that procedure has not been exhausted.

(6) A complaint under this paragraph may not be made after the later of—

(a) the end of the 1 year period beginning with the day on which the alleged failure that is the subject of the complaint last occurred, and

(b) if the substance of the complaint was subject to an internal complaints procedure, the end of the 3 month period beginning with the day on which that procedure was exhausted.

(7) The OEP may waive the time limit in sub-paragraph (6) if it considers that there are exceptional reasons for doing so.

Investigations: relevant public authorities

7 (1) The OEP may carry out an investigation under this paragraph if it receives a complaint made under paragraph 6 that, in its view, indicates that—

(a) a relevant public authority may have failed to comply with relevant environmental law, and

(b) if it has, the failure would be a serious failure.

(2) The OEP may carry out an investigation under this paragraph without having received such a complaint if it has information that, in its view, indicates that—

(a) a relevant public authority may have failed to comply with relevant environmental law, and

(b) if it has, the failure would be a serious failure.

(3) An investigation under this paragraph is an investigation into whether the relevant public authority has failed to comply with relevant environmental law.

(4) The OEP must notify the relevant public authority of the commencement of the investigation.

(5) The OEP must prepare a report on the investigation and provide it to the relevant public authority.

(6) The OEP is not required to prepare a report until it has concluded that it intends to take no further steps under this Part of this Schedule in relation to the alleged failure to comply with relevant environmental law that is the subject of the investigation.

(7) The OEP is not required to prepare a report if it has made a review application, or an application for judicial review by virtue of paragraph 13(1), in relation to the alleged failure.

(8) The report must set out—

(a) whether the OEP considers that the relevant public authority has failed to comply with relevant environmental law,

(b) the reasons the OEP came to that conclusion, and

(c) any recommendations the OEP may have (whether generally or for the relevant public authority) in light of those conclusions.

(9) The OEP may publish the report or parts of it.

(10) If the public authority is not a Northern Ireland department, the OEP must also—

(a) notify the relevant department of the commencement of the investigation, and

(b) provide the relevant department with the report prepared under sub-paragraph (5).

(11) In this Part "the relevant department", in relation to a failure (or alleged failure) of a relevant public authority to comply with relevant environmental law, means the Northern Ireland department that the OEP considers appropriate having regard to the nature of the authority and the nature of the failure.

Duty to keep complainants informed

8 (1) Where a person makes a complaint to the OEP alleging that a relevant public authority has failed to comply with relevant environmental law, the OEP must keep the complainant informed about its handling of the complaint.

(2) In particular, the OEP must—

(a) notify the complainant if it does not intend to consider the complaint because the complaint was not made in accordance with paragraph 6;

(b) notify the complainant if it has concluded that it will not be commencing an investigation under paragraph 7 in relation to the complaint;

(c) notify the complainant if it commences an investigation under paragraph 7 in relation to the complaint;

(d) if such an investigation is commenced, notify the complainant—

(i) where it provides a report under paragraph 7(5) to the relevant public authority that is the subject of the investigation, that it has provided it;

(ii) where it makes a review application (see paragraph 12), or an application for judicial review by virtue of paragraph 13(1), in relation to the alleged failure to comply with relevant environmental law that is the subject of the investigation, that it has made such an application;

(e) provide the complainant with a copy of any document published under paragraph 7(9) in relation to any investigation in relation to the complaint.

Information notices

9 (1) The OEP may give an information notice to a relevant public authority if—

(a) the OEP has reasonable grounds for suspecting that the authority has failed to comply with relevant environmental law, and

(b) it considers that the failure, if it occurred, would be serious.

(2) An information notice is a notice which—

(a) describes an alleged failure of a relevant public authority to comply with relevant environmental law,

(b) explains why the OEP considers that the alleged failure, if it occurred, would be serious, and

(c) requests that the authority provide such information relating to the allegation as may be specified in the notice.

(3) The recipient of an information notice must—

(a) respond in writing to the notice, and

(b) so far as is reasonably practicable, provide the OEP with the information requested in the notice.

(4) The recipient of an information notice must comply with sub-paragraph (3) by—

(a) the end of the 2 month period beginning with the day on which the notice was given, or

(b) such later date as may be specified in the notice.

(5) The written response to an information notice must set out—

(a) the recipient's response to the allegation described in the notice, and

(b) what steps (if any) the recipient intends to take in relation to the allegation.

(6) The OEP may—

(a) withdraw an information notice;

(b) give more than one information notice in respect of the same alleged failure of a relevant public authority to comply with relevant environmental law.

(7) Where the OEP intends to give an information notice to a relevant public authority in respect of an alleged failure to comply with relevant environmental law which relates to emissions of greenhouse gases (within the meaning of the Climate Change Act 2008), the OEP—

(a) must notify the Committee on Climate Change of its intention before it gives the notice to the authority, and

(b) must provide that Committee with such information relating to the alleged failure as the OEP considers appropriate.

Decision notices

10 (1) The OEP may give a decision notice to a relevant public authority if—

(a) the OEP is satisfied, on the balance of probabilities, that the authority has failed to comply with relevant environmental law, and

(b) it considers that the failure is serious.

(2) A decision notice is a notice that—

(a) describes a failure of a relevant public authority to comply with relevant environmental law,

(b) explains why the OEP considers that the failure is serious, and

(c) sets out the steps the OEP considers the authority should take in relation to the failure (which may include steps designed to remedy, mitigate or prevent reoccurrence of the failure).

(3) The recipient of a decision notice must respond in writing to that notice by—

(a) the end of the 2 month period beginning with the day on which the notice was given, or

(b) such later date as may be specified in the notice.

(4) The written response to a decision notice must set out—

(a) whether the recipient agrees that the failure described in the notice occurred,

(b) whether the recipient intends to take the steps set out in the notice, and

(c) what other steps (if any) the recipient intends to take in relation to the failure described in the notice.

(5) The OEP—

(a) may not give a decision notice to a relevant public authority unless it has given at least one information notice relating to the failure of the authority to comply with relevant environmental law that is described in the decision notice;

(b) may withdraw a decision notice.

Linked notices

11 (1) If the OEP gives an information notice or a decision notice to more than one relevant public authority in respect of the same or similar conduct, it may determine that those notices are linked.

(2) A Northern Ireland department may request that the OEP determine that information notices or decision notices are linked and the OEP must have regard to that request.

(3) The OEP must provide the recipient of an information notice or a decision notice (a "principal notice") with a copy of every information notice or decision notice which is linked to it (and such a notice is referred to in this section as a "linked notice").

(4) The OEP must provide the recipient of a principal notice with a copy of any relevant correspondence, relating to a linked notice, between the OEP and the recipient of that linked notice.

(5) The OEP must provide the recipient of a principal notice with a copy of any relevant correspondence between the OEP and the relevant department that relates to a linked notice.

(6) Sub-paragraph (5) does not apply where either the recipient of the principal notice or the linked notice is a Northern Ireland department.

(7) If the OEP considers that an information notice or a decision notice relates to conduct that is the same as or similar to conduct that is the subject of a UK information notice or UK decision notice, it may determine that those notices are linked.

(8) The OEP must provide the recipient of an information notice or a decision notice with—

(a) a copy of every UK information notice or UK decision notice which is linked to it, and

(b) a copy of any relevant correspondence, relating to such a notice, between the OEP and the recipient of that notice.

(9) The obligation to provide a copy of any notice or correspondence under this paragraph does not apply where the OEP considers that in the circumstances it would not be in the public interest to do so.

(10) For the purposes of this paragraph, correspondence is relevant if—

(a) it is not correspondence in connection with a review application or any other legal proceedings, and

(b) it is not correspondence sent by virtue of paragraph 14(1)(a) or (b).

(11) In this Part of this Schedule—

"UK decision notice" means a notice given under section 36;

"UK information notice' means a notice given under section 35.

Review application

12 (1) The OEP may make a review application in relation to conduct described in a decision notice given to a relevant public authority as a failure of the authority to comply with relevant environmental law, but only if—

(a) it is satisfied, on the balance of probabilities, that the authority has failed to comply with relevant environmental law, and

(b) it considers that the failure is serious.

(2) A review application is an application for judicial review in respect of conduct of a relevant public authority, and any reference in this Part of this Schedule to a review application is to an application made by virtue of sub-paragraph (1).

(3) A review application may not be made before the earlier of—

(a) the end of the period within which the authority must respond to the decision notice that precedes the application (see paragraph 10(3)), and

(b) the date on which the OEP receives the authority's response to that notice.

(4) Subject to that, the OEP may make a review application at any time (and accordingly any time limit, that would otherwise apply to the making of a review application, does not apply).

(5) The High Court may grant a remedy on a review application only if Condition A or Condition B is met.

(6) Condition A is that the court is satisfied that granting the remedy would not—

(a) be likely to cause substantial hardship to, or substantially prejudice the rights of, any person other than the authority, or

(b) be detrimental to good administration.

(7) Condition B is that Condition A is not met but the court is satisfied that—

(a) granting the remedy is necessary in order to prevent or mitigate serious damage to the natural environment or to human health, and

(b) there is an exceptional public interest reason to grant it.

(8) If, on a review application, there is a finding that a relevant public authority has failed to comply with relevant environmental law, and the finding has not been overturned on appeal, the authority must publish a statement that sets out the steps it intends to take in light of the finding.

(9) A statement under sub-paragraph (8) must be published before the end of the 2 month period beginning with the day the proceedings relating to the review application (including any appeal) conclude.

(10) In this Part of this Schedule reference to an application for judicial review includes an application for the permission of the High Court to apply for judicial review.

Judicial review: powers to apply to prevent serious damage and to intervene

13 (1) The OEP may make an application for judicial review in relation to conduct of a relevant public authority (whether or not it has given an information notice or a decision notice to the authority in respect of that conduct) if—

(a) the OEP considers that the conduct constitutes a serious failure to comply with relevant environmental law, and

(b) the urgency condition is met.

(2) The urgency condition is that making an application under sub-paragraph (1) (rather than proceeding under paragraphs 9 to 12) is necessary to prevent, or mitigate, serious damage to the natural environment or to human health.

(3) If, on an application for judicial review made by virtue of sub-paragraph (1), there is a finding that a relevant public authority has failed to comply with relevant environmental law, and the finding has not been overturned on appeal, the authority must publish a statement that sets out the steps it intends to take in light of the finding.

(4) A statement under sub-paragraph (3) must be published before the end of the 2 month period beginning with the day the proceedings relating to the application for judicial review (including any appeal) conclude.

(5) Sub-paragraph (6) applies to proceedings (including any appeal) that—

(a) are in respect of an application for judicial review, and

(b) relate to an alleged failure by a relevant public authority to comply with relevant environmental law (however the allegation is framed in those proceedings).

(6) If the OEP considers that the alleged failure, if it occurred, would be serious, it may apply to intervene in the proceedings (whether it considers that the relevant public authority has, or has not, failed to comply with relevant environmental law).

Duty of the OEP to involve the relevant department

14 (1) Where the recipient of an information notice or a decision notice is not a Northern Ireland department, the OEP must—

(a) provide the relevant department with—

(i) a copy of the notice, and

(ii) a copy of any correspondence between the OEP and the recipient of the notice that relates to the notice (apart from correspondence sent by virtue of paragraph (b)), and

(b) provide the recipient of the notice with a copy of any correspondence between the OEP and the relevant department that relates to the notice (apart from correspondence sent by virtue of paragraph (a)).

(2) The obligation to provide a copy of any notice or correspondence under sub-paragraph (1) does not apply where the OEP considers that in the circumstances it would not be in the public interest to do so.

(3) Where the OEP makes a review application, or an application for judicial review by virtue of paragraph 13(1), in which the relevant department is not a party, it must provide the relevant department with—

(a) a copy of the application, and

(b) a statement of whether the OEP considers the relevant department should participate in the review (for example, by applying to be a party).

Public statements

15 (1) Where the OEP gives an information notice or a decision notice, makes a review application or an application for judicial review by virtue of paragraph 13(1) or applies to intervene in a judicial review, it must publish a statement that—

(a) states that the OEP has taken that step,

(b) describes the failure (or alleged failure) of a relevant public authority to comply with relevant environmental law in relation to which that step was taken, and

(c) sets out such further information as the OEP considers appropriate.

(2) Sub-paragraph (1) does not apply if the OEP considers that in the circumstances it would not be in the public interest to publish a statement.

Disclosures to the OEP

16 (1) No obligation of secrecy imposed by statute or otherwise prevents a person from—

(a) in accordance with section 27(1), providing the OEP with information in connection with an investigation under paragraph 7, an information notice or a decision notice, or

(b) providing information to the OEP in accordance with paragraph 9(3)(b).

(2) But nothing in this Part of this Schedule—

(a) requires a person to provide the OEP with information that the person would be entitled to refuse to provide in civil proceedings on grounds of legal professional privilege (or, in Scotland, confidentiality of communications), or

(b) requires a person to provide the OEP with information that the person would be entitled, or required by any rule of law, to refuse to provide in civil proceedings on grounds of public interest immunity.

(3) No obligation of secrecy imposed by statute or otherwise prevents the Northern Ireland Public Services Ombudsman from providing information to the OEP—

(a) for purposes connected with the exercise of the OEP's functions under paragraph 7;

(b) for purposes connected with the co-ordination of the OEP's functions that relate to investigations under paragraph 7 and the Ombudsman's functions that relate to investigations by the Ombudsman.

(4) Nothing in this Part of this Schedule requires or authorises a disclosure of information that would contravene the data protection legislation (but in determining whether a disclosure would do so, take into account the duties imposed and powers conferred by this Part of this Schedule).

(5) In this paragraph "the data protection legislation" has the same meaning as in the Data Protection Act 2018 (see section 3(9) of that Act).

Confidentiality of proceedings

17 (1) The OEP must not disclose—

(a) information obtained under paragraph 9(3)(b), or

(b) correspondence between the OEP and a relevant public authority that—

(i) relates to a particular information notice or decision notice, or

(ii) is, or contains, such a notice.

(2) Sub-paragraph (1) does not apply to a disclosure—

(a) other than a disclosure of an information notice or a decision notice, made with the consent of the person who provided the information or correspondence;

(b) made for purposes connected with an investigation under paragraph 7 or section 33;

(c) made for purposes connected with the co-ordination of the OEP's functions that relate to investigations under paragraph 7 and the Northern Ireland Public Services Ombudsman's functions that relate to investigations by the Ombudsman;

(d) made for purposes connected with the co-ordination of the OEP's functions that relate to investigations under section 33 and functions of a relevant ombudsman that relate to investigations by that ombudsman;

(e) made for the purposes of any publication of a report (or part of it) on an investigation under paragraph 7 or section 33;

(f) made for purposes connected with the exercise of the OEP's functions under paragraphs 9 to 15 or sections 35 to 41 (enforcement);

(g) made to a devolved environmental governance body for purposes connected with the exercise of a devolved environmental governance function;

(h) made for purposes connected with the protection of the natural environment in a country or territory outside the United Kingdom, to an authority of that country or territory, or an international organisation, that has functions in connection with the protection of the natural environment in that country or territory;

(i) of information, or correspondence, that relates only to a matter in relation to which the OEP has concluded that it intends to take no further steps under this Part of this Schedule or under Chapter 2 of Part 1 of this Act.

(3) A relevant public authority must not disclose correspondence between the OEP and that, or any other, relevant public authority that—

(a) relates to a particular information notice, decision notice, UK information notice or UK decision notice, or

(b) is, or contains, such a notice.

(4) Sub-paragraph (3) does not apply to a disclosure—

(a) made—

(i) in the case of a disclosure of correspondence between another relevant public authority and the OEP other than correspondence that is, or contains, an information notice, a decision notice, a UK information notice or a UK decision notice, with the consent of that authority and the OEP, or

(ii) in any other case, with the specific or general consent of the OEP;

(b) made for purposes connected with co-operating with any investigation under paragraph 7 or section 33;

(c) made for purposes connected with responding to any information notice or decision notice;

(d) made for purposes connected with any proceedings in relation to a review application, an environmental review, a judicial review or a statutory review (within the meaning given by section 39(8)(b)).

(5) The OEP may not give a person consent to disclose an information notice, a decision notice, a UK information notice or a UK decision notice unless that notice relates only to a matter in relation to which the OEP has concluded that it intends to take no further steps under this Part of this Schedule or under Chapter 2 of Part 1 of this Act.

(6) If a relevant public authority requests the consent of the OEP to disclose correspondence that relates only to a matter in relation to which the OEP has concluded that it intends to take no further steps under this Part of this Schedule or under Chapter 2 of Part 1 of this Act, the OEP may not withhold that consent.

(7) If information referred to in sub-paragraph (1) and held by the OEP, or referred to in sub-paragraph (3) and held by a relevant public authority, is environmental information for the purposes of the Environmental Information Regulations 2004 (S.I. 2004/3391) or the Environmental Information (Scotland) Regulations 2004 (S.S.I. 2004/520), it is held by that person, for the purposes of the application of those regulations to that information, in connection with confidential proceedings.

Meaning of UK environmental law and Northern Ireland environmental law

18 (1) In this Part of this Schedule "UK environmental law" means anything that is environmental law for the purposes of Part 1 of this Act (see section 46), but not anything that is environmental law only for the purposes of section 20.

(2) In this Part of this Schedule "Northern Ireland environmental law" means any Northern Ireland legislative provision that—

(a) is mainly concerned with environmental protection, and

(b) is not concerned with an excluded matter.

(3) Excluded matters are—

(a) disclosure of or access to information;

(b) taxation, spending or the allocation of resources within government.

(4) "Northern Ireland legislative provision" means—

(a) legislative provision contained in, or in an instrument made under, Northern Ireland legislation, and

(b) legislative provision not within paragraph (a) which, if contained in an Act of the Northern Ireland Assembly, would be within the legislative competence of the Assembly and would not require the Secretary of State's consent.

(5) The Department may by regulations provide that a Northern Ireland legislative provision specified in the regulations is, or is not, within the definition of "Northern Ireland environmental law" in sub-paragraph (2) (and this Part of this Schedule applies accordingly).

(6) Before making regulations under sub-paragraph (5) the Department must consult—

(a) the OEP, and

(b) any other persons the Department considers appropriate.

(7) Regulations under sub-paragraph (5) are subject to the affirmative procedure.

Interpretation of Part 1 of this Schedule: general

19 (1) In this Part of this Schedule—

"application for judicial review" is to be read in accordance with paragraph 12(10);

"current environmental improvement plan" has the meaning it has in Schedule 2 (see paragraph 1(8) of that Schedule);

"decision notice" means a notice given under paragraph 10;

"the Department" means the Department of Agriculture, Environment and Rural Affairs in Northern Ireland;

"devolved environmental governance body" has the meaning it has in Part 1 of this Act (see section 47);

"devolved environmental governance function" has the meaning it has in Part 1 of this Act (see section 47);

"environmental improvement plan" has the meaning it has in Schedule 2 (see paragraphs 1 and 3(10) of that Schedule);

"environmental protection" has the meaning it has in Schedule 2 (see paragraph 10 of that Schedule);

"environmental review" has the meaning it has in Part 1 of this Act (see section 38);

"implementation body" has the meaning it has in section 55 of the Northern Ireland Act 1998 (see subsection (3) of that section);

"improving the natural environment", in relation to an environmental improvement plan, is to be read in accordance with paragraph 1(5) of Schedule 2;

"information notice" means a notice given under paragraph 9; "natural environment" has the meaning it has in Schedule 2 (see paragraph 9 of that Schedule);

"Northern Ireland devolved function" has the meaning given by paragraph 5(5);

"OEP" has the meaning given by section 22;

"parliamentary function" means a function in connection with proceedings in Parliament or the Northern Ireland Assembly;

"relevant department" has the meaning given by paragraph 7(11); "relevant environmental law" has the meaning given by paragraph 5(2);

"relevant ombudsman" has the meaning it has in Part 1 of this Act (see section 23);

"relevant public authority" has the meaning given by paragraph 5(3); "review application" has the meaning given by paragraph 12(2);

"UK decision notice" has the meaning given by paragraph 11(11);

"UK information notice" has the meaning given by paragraph 11(11).

(2) Section 41(3) of the Interpretation Act (Northern Ireland) 1954 (c. 33 (N.I.)) applies in relation to the laying of a document before the Northern Ireland Assembly under this Part of this Schedule, as it applies in relation to the laying of a statutory document under an Act of the Northern Ireland Assembly.

Part 2

Amendments of the OEP's general functions

20 This Act is amended in accordance with paragraphs 21 to 30.

21 (1) Section 23 (principal objective of the OEP and exercise of its functions) is amended as follows.

(2) In subsection (6)—

(a) after paragraph (a) insert—

"(aa) how the OEP intends to determine whether failures to comply with relevant environmental law are serious for the purposes of paragraphs 7(1)(b) and (2)(b), 9(1)(b), 10(1)(b), 12(1)(b) and 13(1) and (6) of Schedule 3,";

(b) at the end of paragraph (b) insert "or paragraph 13(2) of Schedule 3,";

(c) omit the "and" at the end of paragraph (d);

(d) after paragraph (d) insert—

"(da) how the OEP intends to avoid any overlap between the exercise of its functions under paragraphs 6 to 8 of Schedule 3 (complaints) and the exercise by the Northern Ireland Public Services Ombudsman of its functions, and".

(3) In subsection (7)(c) after "environmental law" insert "or Northern Ireland environmental law".

(4) After subsection (7) insert—

"(7A) In this section "relevant environmental law" and "Northern Ireland environmental law" have the meanings they have in Part 1 of Schedule 3 (see paragraphs 5 and 18(2) of that Schedule)."

(5) In subsection (8) after "sections 32 to 41" insert "and paragraphs 6 to 15 of Schedule 3".

22 In section 24 (the OEP's strategy: process), in subsection (1)(a) after "Parliament" insert "and the Northern Ireland Assembly".

23 (1) Section 25 (guidance on the OEP's enforcement policy and functions) is amended as follows.

(2) At the end of subsection (1) insert ", so far as relating to the OEP's Part 1 enforcement functions."

(3) In subsection (2)—

(a) in paragraph (a) after "policy," insert "so far as relating to its Part 1 enforcement functions,";

(b) in paragraph (b) for "enforcement functions" substitute "Part 1 enforcement functions".

(4) In subsection (3) for "enforcement functions" substitute "Part 1 enforcement functions".

24 After section 25 (guidance on the OEP's enforcement policy and functions) insert—

"25A Guidance on the OEP's Northern Ireland enforcement policy and functions

(1) The Department of Agriculture, Environment and Rural Affairs in Northern Ireland may issue guidance to the OEP on the matters listed in section 23(6) (OEP's enforcement policy), so far as relating to the OEP's Northern Ireland enforcement functions.

(2) The OEP must have regard to the guidance in—

(a) preparing its enforcement policy, so far as relating to its Northern Ireland enforcement functions, and

(b) exercising its Northern Ireland enforcement functions.

(3) The OEP's "Northern Ireland enforcement functions" are its functions under paragraphs 6 to 15 of Schedule 3.

(4) Before issuing the guidance, the Department must—

(a) prepare a draft, and

(b) lay the draft before the Northern Ireland Assembly.

(5) If before the end of the 21 day period the Northern Ireland Assembly passes a resolution in respect of the draft guidance, the Department must produce a response and lay it before the Assembly.

(6) The Department may prepare and lay before the Northern Ireland Assembly the final guidance, but not before—

(a) if subsection (5) applies, the day on which the Department lays the response required by that subsection, or

(b) otherwise, the end of the 21 day period.

(7) The final guidance has effect when it is laid before the Northern Ireland Assembly.

(8) The Department must publish the guidance when it comes into effect.

(9) The "21 day period" is the period of 21 sitting days beginning with the first sitting day after the day on which the draft guidance is laid under subsection (4).

(10) "Sitting day" means a day on which the Northern Ireland Assembly sits.

(11) The Department may revise the guidance at any time (and subsections (4) to (10) apply in relation to any revised guidance)."

25 (1) Section 27 (co-operation duties of public authorities and the OEP) is amended as follows.

(2) In subsection (2)—

(a) in paragraph (d) for ", the Welsh Ministers, a Northern Ireland department or a Minister within the meaning of the Northern Ireland Act 1998" substitute "or the Welsh Ministers";

(b) in paragraph (f) for "devolved functions" substitute "Scottish devolved functions or Welsh devolved functions".

(3) In subsection (3) for "devolved functions", in both places it occurs, substitute "Scottish devolved functions or Welsh devolved functions".

(4) After subsection (3) insert—

"(3A) An implementation body is only required to co-operate with the OEP by virtue of subsection (1) to the extent that co-operation is in relation to functions of that body exercisable in or as regards Northern Ireland.

In this subsection "implementation body" has the meaning it has in section 55 of the Northern Ireland Act 1998 (see subsection (3) of that section)."

26 In section 37 (linked notices), after subsection (6) insert—

"(6A) If the OEP considers that an information notice or a decision notice relates to conduct that is the same as or similar to conduct that is the subject of a Northern Ireland information notice or Northern Ireland decision notice, it may determine that those notices are linked.

(6B) The OEP must provide the recipient of an information notice or a decision notice with—

(a) a copy of every Northern Ireland information notice or Northern Ireland decision notice which is linked to it, and

(b) a copy of any relevant correspondence, relating to such a notice, between the OEP and the recipient of that notice."

27 (1) Section 43 (confidentiality of proceedings) is amended as follows.

(2) In subsection (2)—

(a) in paragraph (b) after "(investigations)" insert "or paragraph 7 of Schedule 3 (functions of the OEP in Northern Ireland)";

(b) after paragraph (c) insert—

"(ca) made for purposes connected with the co-ordination of the OEP's functions that relate to investigations under paragraph 7 of Schedule 3 and the Northern Ireland Public Services Ombudsman's functions that relate to investigations by the Ombudsman;";

(c) in paragraph (d) after "section 33" insert "or paragraph 7 of Schedule 3";

(d) in paragraph (e) after "sections 35 to 41" insert "or paragraphs 9 to 15 of Schedule 3";

(e) in paragraph (h) after "this Chapter" insert "or Part 1 of Schedule 3".

(3) In subsection (3)(a) for "or decision notice" substitute ", decision notice, Northern Ireland information notice or Northern Ireland decision notice".

(4) In subsection (4)—

(a) in paragraph (a)(i) for "or a decision notice" substitute ", a decision notice, a Northern Ireland information notice or a Northern Ireland decision notice";

(b) in paragraph (b) after "section 33" insert "or paragraph 7 of Schedule 3";

(c) in paragraph (d) after "judicial review" insert "(which includes a review application)".

(5) In subsection (5)—

(a) for "or a decision notice" substitute ", a decision notice, a Northern Ireland information notice or a Northern Ireland decision notice";

(b) after "this Chapter" insert "or Part 1 of Schedule 3".

(6) In subsection (6) after "this Chapter" insert "or Part 1 of Schedule 3".

28 (1) Section 47 (interpretation of Part 1 of the Act) is amended as follows.

(2) The existing text becomes subsection (1).

(3) In that subsection—

(a) in the definition of "devolved environmental governance function"—

(i) for "devolved function" substitute "Scottish devolved function or Welsh devolved function";

(ii) after "this Part" insert "or Part 1 of Schedule 3 (functions of the OEP in Northern Ireland)";

(b) at the appropriate places insert—

""Northern Ireland decision notice" means a notice given under paragraph 10 of Schedule 3 (functions of the OEP in Northern Ireland);";

""Northern Ireland information notice" means a notice given under paragraph 9 of Schedule 3;";

""review application" has the meaning it has in Part 1 of Schedule 3 (see paragraph 12 of that Schedule);";

""Scottish devolved function" means a function exercisable in or as regards Scotland, the exercise of which would be within devolved competence (within the meaning of section 54 of the Scotland Act 1998);";

““Welsh devolved function” means a function exercisable in or as regards Wales that could be conferred by provision falling within the legislative competence of Senedd Cymru (see section 108A of the Government of Wales Act 2006).”.

(4) After that subsection insert—

“(2) Section 41(3) of the Interpretation Act (Northern Ireland) 1954 (c. 33 (N.I.)) applies in relation to the laying of a document before the Northern Ireland Assembly under this Part, as it applies in relation to the laying of a statutory document under an Act of the Northern Ireland Assembly.”

29 (1) Schedule 1 is amended as follows.

(2) In paragraph 1—

(a) in sub-paragraph (1), after paragraph (a) insert—

“(aa) a Northern Ireland member (who is to be a non-executive member),”;

(b) in sub-paragraph (2) after “Secretary of State” insert “, the Northern Ireland Department”;

(c) in sub-paragraph (3)—

(i) for “In making those appointments,” substitute “When exercising their functions of appointment”;

(ii) after “non-executive members” insert “(including the Northern Ireland member)”.

(3) In paragraph 2 for sub-paragraphs (1) and (2) substitute—

“(1) The Chair is to be appointed by the Secretary of State acting jointly with the Northern Ireland Department, other than the first Chair who is to be appointed by the Secretary of State.

(2) The Northern Ireland member is to be appointed by the Northern Ireland Department after consulting the Secretary of State and the Chair.

(2A) The other non-executive members are to be appointed by the Secretary of State after consulting the Northern Ireland Department and the Chair.

(2B) The Northern Ireland Department must appoint as the Northern Ireland member a person with experience of—

(a) Northern Ireland environmental law (within the meaning of Part 1 of Schedule 3),

(b) environmental science in Northern Ireland, or

(c) environmental regulation in Northern Ireland.”

(4) In paragraph 3(3) after “Secretary of State” insert “and the Northern Ireland Department”.

(5) In paragraph 5—

(a) in sub-paragraph (4) after "of non-executive members" insert "(including the Northern Ireland member)";

(b) after that sub-paragraph insert—

"(4A) The Northern Ireland Department must, in determining the length of a Northern Ireland member's term, have regard to the desirability of securing that the appointments of non-executive members expire at different times.";

(c) for sub-paragraph (6) substitute—

"(6) A non-executive member ceases to be a member of the OEP upon becoming its employee.

(7) A non-executive member, other than the Northern Ireland member—

(a) may resign from office by giving notice to the Secretary of State, and

(b) may be removed from office by notice given by the Secretary of State, after consulting the Northern Ireland Department, on the grounds that the member—

(i) has without reasonable excuse failed to discharge the member's functions, or

(ii) is, in the opinion of the Secretary of State, unable or unfit to carry out the member's functions.

(8) The Northern Ireland member—

(a) may resign from office by giving notice to the Northern Ireland Department, and

(b) may be removed from office by notice given by the Northern Ireland Department after consulting the Secretary of State, on the grounds that the member—

(i) has without reasonable excuse failed to discharge the member's functions, or

(ii) is, in the opinion of the Northern Ireland Department, unable or unfit to carry out the member's functions."

(6) In paragraph 10(4)—

(a) in paragraph (b) after "section 28 or 29" insert ", or a report under paragraph 1 or 2 of Schedule 3 (functions of the OEP in Northern Ireland)";

(b) in paragraph (c) after "section 30(1) or (3)" insert ", or written advice to a Northern Ireland department under paragraph 3(1) or (3) of Schedule 3";

(c) in paragraph (d) after "information notice" insert "or a Northern Ireland information notice";

(d) in paragraph (e) after "decision notice" insert "or a Northern Ireland decision notice";

(e) after paragraph (g) insert—

"(ga) deciding whether to make a review application (see paragraph 12 of Schedule 3) or an application for judicial review by virtue of paragraph 13(1) of that Schedule or to intervene in proceedings that relate to a judicial review (see paragraph 13 of that Schedule);".

(7) In paragraph 12—

(a) in sub-paragraph (1)—

(i) after "Secretary of State", in the first place it occurs, insert "and the Northern Ireland Department";

(ii) after "must" insert ", between them,";

(iii) for "the Secretary of State considers" substitute "they consider";

(b) in sub-paragraph (2)—

(i) after "Secretary of State", in the first place it occurs, insert ", or the Northern Ireland Department,";

(ii) after "Secretary of State", in the second place it occurs, insert ", or that department,".

(8) In paragraph 13(2)(a) after "Parliament" insert "and the Northern Ireland Assembly".

(9) In paragraph 14—

(a) in sub-paragraph (3) after "Secretary of State" insert "and the Northern Ireland Department";

(b) in sub-paragraph (4) after "Secretary of State" insert ", the Northern Ireland Department";

(c) in sub-paragraph (5)(b) after "Secretary of State" insert ", the Northern Ireland Department";

(d) in sub-paragraph (6) after "Parliament" insert "and the Northern Ireland Assembly".

(10) In paragraph 17 after "Secretary of State" insert "and the Northern Ireland Department".

(11) After paragraph 23 insert—

"Meaning of "the Northern Ireland Department"

24 In this Schedule "the Northern Ireland Department" means the Department of Agriculture, Environment and Rural Affairs in Northern Ireland."

30 (1) Schedule 2 (improving the natural environment: Northern Ireland) is amended as follows.

(2) In paragraph 3(4)(b) after "under paragraph 5" insert "and reports made by the OEP under paragraph 1 of Schedule 3".

(3) In paragraph 4(4)(b) after "under paragraph 5" insert "and reports made by the OEP under paragraph 1 of Schedule 3".

(4) In paragraph 11(1), at the appropriate place insert— ""OEP" has the meaning given by section 22;".

SCHEDULE 4

Section 50

Producer responsibility obligations

Part 1

Requirements

General Power

1 (1) The relevant national authority may by regulations make provision for imposing producer responsibility obligations on specified persons in respect of specified products or materials.

(2) The regulations may be made only for the purpose of—

(a) preventing a product or material becoming waste, or reducing the amount of a product or material that becomes waste;

(b) sustaining a minimum level of, or promoting or securing an increase in, the re-use, redistribution, recovery or recycling of products or materials.

(3) In this Schedule "producer responsibility obligations" means steps required to be taken, in respect of products or materials, for a purpose in sub-paragraph (2).

Examples of provision that may be made

2 (1) The regulations may make provision about—

(a) the persons to whom producer responsibility obligations apply;

(b) the products or materials in relation to which producer responsibility obligations apply;

(c) the obligations imposed by the regulations.

(2) The regulations may make provision about targets to be achieved in relation to the proportion of products or materials (by weight, volume or otherwise) to be re-used, redistributed, recovered or recycled (either generally or in a specified way).

(3) The regulations may make provision about circumstances in which a producer responsibility obligation is to be treated as met (in whole or in part) by payment of a sum of money, including provision about—

(a) the manner in which and persons by whom the amount of such sums is to be determined, and

(b) the persons to whom such sums are to be paid.

Registration of persons subject to producer responsibility obligations

3 (1) The regulations may make provision requiring the registration of persons who are subject to a producer responsibility obligation.

(2) The regulations may make provision about—

(a) applications for registration,

(b) the imposition and variation of requirements in connection with registration,

(c) the period for which registration is to remain in force, and

(d) the cancellation of registration.

(3) The regulations may require registers to be published or made available for inspection.

Compliance schemes

4 (1) The regulations may make provision authorising or requiring persons who are subject to a producer responsibility obligation to become members of a compliance scheme.

(2) The regulations may make provision about—

(a) the approval, or withdrawal of approval, of compliance schemes by the relevant national authority,

(b) the establishment, maintenance or management of a compliance scheme by a person appointed by the relevant national authority.

(3) In this Schedule "compliance scheme" means a scheme under which producer responsibility obligations of members of the scheme are discharged by the scheme operator on their behalf.

Registration of compliance schemes

5 (1) The regulations may make provision about the registration of compliance schemes, including provision about—

(a) requirements and criteria to be met before a compliance scheme may be registered,

(b) applications for registration,

(c) the imposition and variation of conditions in connection with registration,

(d) the period for which registration is to remain in force,

(e) the cancellation of registration.

(2) The regulations may make provision about—

(a) appeals against the refusal of registration, the imposition of conditions in connection with registration, or the cancellation of registration,

(b) the procedure on the appeals.

(3) The regulations may make provision about the position of persons and compliance schemes pending determination or withdrawal of an appeal, including provision about cases in which—

(a) a compliance scheme is, or is not, to be treated as registered, or

(b) a person is, or is not, to be treated as a member of a registered compliance scheme.

(4) The regulations may require registers to be published or made available for inspection.

Power to direct compliance scheme operators

6 (1) If it appears to the relevant national authority that any action proposed to be taken by the operator of a compliance scheme would be incompatible with an international agreement to which the United Kingdom is a party, it may direct the operator not to take the action in question.

(2) If it appears to the relevant national authority that any action which the operator of a compliance scheme has power to take is required for the purpose of implementing an international agreement to which the United Kingdom is a party, it may direct the operator to take the action in question.

(3) A direction under this paragraph—

(a) may include consequential, supplementary, incidental, transitional or saving provision;

(b) on the application of the relevant national authority, is enforceable—

(i) by injunction, or

(ii) in Scotland, by interdict or by an order for specific performance under section 45 of the Court of Session Act 1988.

Certificates of compliance

7 (1) The regulations may make provision about certificates of compliance.

(2) The regulations may make provision—

(a) requiring persons who are not members of compliance schemes to provide certificates of compliance to an enforcement authority;

(b) about the approval of persons by an enforcement authority for the purposes of issuing certificates of compliance.

(3) In this Schedule "certificate of compliance" means a certificate which—

(a) is issued by a person approved by an enforcement authority, and

(b) states that the person issuing the certificate is satisfied that the person to whom it relates is complying with their producer responsibility obligations.

(4) The regulations may include provision requiring an enforcement authority to give guidance to persons issuing certificates of compliance, including guidance as to matters which are, or are not, to be treated as evidence of compliance or non-compliance.

(5) In this paragraph "enforcement authority" means a person on whom functions are conferred by regulations under Part 2 of this Schedule.

Consultation etc requirements

8 (1) Before making regulations under this Part of this Schedule the relevant national authority must consult persons appearing to it to represent the interests of those likely to be affected.

(2) The requirement in sub-paragraph (1) may be met by consultation carried out before this paragraph comes into force.

9 (1) Before making regulations under this Part of this Schedule the relevant national authority must be satisfied that—

(a) making the regulations would be likely to achieve one or more of the purposes in paragraph 1(2);

(b) making the regulations would produce environmental or economic benefits;

(c) those benefits are significant as against the likely costs resulting from the imposition of the producer responsibility obligations;

(d) the burdens imposed on businesses by the regulations are the minimum necessary to secure those benefits;

(e) those burdens are imposed on the persons most able to make a contribution to securing those benefits—

(i) having regard to the desirability of acting fairly between persons who manufacture, process, distribute or supply products or materials, and

(ii) taking account of the need to ensure that the proposed producer responsibility obligation is so framed as to be effective in achieving the purposes for which it is imposed.

(2) Nothing in sub-paragraph (1)(e)(i) prevents regulations imposing a producer responsibility obligation on any class or description of person to the exclusion of any others.

(3) Sub-paragraph (1) does not apply to regulations for the implementation of an international agreement to which the United Kingdom is a party.

10 The relevant national authority must exercise the power to make regulations under this Part in the way it considers best calculated to secure that—

(a) the regulations do not have the effect of restricting, distorting or preventing competition, or

(b) if the regulations are likely to have that effect, the effect is no greater than is necessary for achieving the environmental or economic benefits mentioned in paragraph 9(1).

Interpretation

11 (1) In this Part of this Schedule—

"operator", in relation to a compliance scheme, includes any person responsible for establishing, maintaining or managing the scheme; "product" and "material" include a product or material at a time when it becomes, or has become, waste;

"recovery", in relation to products or materials, includes—

(a) composting them, or any other transformation of them by biological processes, or

(b) obtaining energy from them by any means;

"specified" means specified in, or determined in accordance with, the regulations.

(2) The regulations may specify, in relation to products or materials, activities, or the activities, which are to be treated for the purposes of this Part of this Schedule and the regulations as re-use, redistribution, recovery or recycling.

PART 2

ENFORCEMENT

General power

12 The relevant national authority may by regulations ("Part 2 regulations") make provision about the enforcement of requirements imposed by regulations ("Part 1 regulations") made by the authority under Part 1 of this Schedule.

Powers to confer functions

13 (1) Part 2 regulations may include provision conferring functions on one or more persons specified in the regulations (each of whom is an "enforcement authority" for the purposes of this Part).

(2) Part 2 regulations may include provision—

(a) conferring functions involving the exercise of discretion;

(b) for the functions of an enforcement authority to be exercised on its behalf by persons authorised in accordance with the regulations.

(3) Part 2 regulations may include provision requiring an enforcement authority to issue guidance about the exercise of its functions.

Monitoring compliance

14 Part 2 regulations may include provision conferring on an enforcement authority the function of monitoring compliance with requirements imposed by Part 1 regulations.

Records and information

15 Part 2 regulations may include provision—

(a) requiring persons on whom requirements are imposed by Part 1 regulations to keep records;

(b) requiring persons on whom requirements are imposed by Part 1 regulations to provide records or other information to an enforcement authority;

(c) requiring an enforcement authority to make reports or provide information to the relevant national authority.

Powers of entry etc

16 (1) Part 2 regulations may include provision conferring on an enforcement authority powers of entry, inspection, examination, search and seizure.

(2) Part 2 regulations may include provision—

(a) for powers to be exercisable only under the authority of a warrant issued by a justice of the peace, sheriff, summary sheriff or lay magistrate;

(b) about applications for, and the execution of, warrants.

(3) Part 2 regulations must secure that the authority of a warrant is required for the exercise of any powers conferred by the regulations to—

(a) enter premises by force;

(b) enter a private dwelling without the consent of the occupier;

(c) search and seize material.

Sanctions

17 (1) Part 2 regulations may include provision—

(a) for, about or connected with the imposition of civil sanctions in respect of—

(i) failures to comply with Part 1 regulations or Part 2 regulations, or

(ii) the obstruction of or failure to assist an enforcement authority;

(b) for appeals against such sanctions.

(2) Part 2 regulations may include provision—

(a) creating criminal offences punishable with a fine in respect of—

(i) failures to comply with Part 1 regulations or Part 2 regulations,

(ii) failures to comply with civil sanctions imposed under Part 2 regulations, or

(iii) the obstruction of or failure to assist an enforcement authority;

(b) about such offences.

(3) In this paragraph "civil sanction" means a sanction of a kind for which provision may be made under Part 3 of the Regulatory Enforcement and Sanctions Act 2008 (fixed monetary penalties, discretionary requirements, stop notices and enforcement undertakings).

18 Part 2 regulations may include provision for the imposition of sanctions of that kind whether or not—

(a) the conduct in respect of which the sanction is imposed constitutes an offence,

(b) the Regulatory Enforcement and Sanctions Act 2008, or

(c) the relevant national authority may make provision for the imposition of sanctions under that Part.

Charges and costs

19 Part 2 regulations may include provision—

(a) requiring persons on whom requirements are imposed by Part 1 regulations to pay charges, as a means of recovering costs incurred by an enforcement authority in performing its functions;

(b) authorising a court or tribunal dealing with any matter under Part 1 regulations or Part 2 regulations to award to an enforcement authority costs incurred by it in performing its functions under the regulations in relation to that matter.

Consultation requirement

20 (1) Before making Part 2 regulations the relevant national authority must consult any persons the authority considers appropriate.

(2) The requirement in sub-paragraph (1) may be met by consultation carried out before this paragraph comes into force.

SCHEDULE 5

SECTION 51

PRODUCER RESPONSIBILITY FOR DISPOSAL COSTS

PART 1

REQUIREMENTS

General power

1 (1) The relevant national authority may by regulations make provision requiring the payment of sums by specified persons, in respect of specified products or materials.

(2) The regulations may be made only for the purpose of securing that those involved in manufacturing, processing, distributing or supplying products or materials meet, or contribute to, the disposal costs of the products or materials.

"Disposal costs" and "disposal"

2 (1) In this Schedule the "disposal costs" of products or materials means such costs incurred in connection with the disposal of the products or materials as may be specified in the regulations.

(2) In this Schedule the "disposal" of products or materials includes their re-use, redistribution, recovery or recycling.

(3) Disposal costs may include the costs of—

(a) collecting and transporting products or materials for disposal,

(b) sorting and treating products or materials,

(c) other steps preparatory to disposal of products or materials, and

(d) providing public information about the disposal of products or materials.

(4) They may include costs incurred in relation to products or materials that have been disposed of unlawfully.

(5) The regulations may make provision as to how the disposal costs of products or materials are to be calculated.

Calculation of sums payable

3 (1) The regulations may make provision as to how the sums payable under the regulations are to be calculated.

(2) They may include provision for the sums payable under the regulations to vary according to the design or composition of the products or materials to which the regulations relate, the methods by which they were produced or any other factor.

Administration

4 (1) The regulations may appoint, or make provision for the appointment of, a person (an "administrator") to administer provision made by the regulations.

(2) More than one person may be appointed as an administrator.

(3) The regulations may confer functions on an administrator (including functions involving the exercise of discretion).

(4) References in this Schedule to an administrator include a person appointed by an administrator or exercising functions on an administrator's behalf.

Registration

5 (1) The regulations may require—

(a) persons required to pay sums under the regulations to register with an administrator;

(b) administrators to register with an enforcement authority appointed by regulations under Part 2 of this Schedule.

(2) The regulations may make provision—

(a) about applications for registration;

(b) about the period for which registration has effect;

(c) about the cancellation of registration.

(3) The regulations may require persons required to register to pay, in connection with their registration, fees of an amount determined by or in accordance with the regulations.

(4) The regulations may require registers to be published or made available for inspection.

Payment of sums

6 (1) The regulations may make provision for the sums payable under the regulations to be payable to an administrator.

(2) The regulations may make provision as to how sums paid to the administrator are to be held by the administrator.

Distribution of sums paid

7 The regulations may make provision for sums paid to an administrator—

(a) to be distributed by the administrator, in accordance with the regulations, among persons who have incurred disposal costs in relation to products or materials to which the regulations relate, or

(b) to be paid to another administrator to be so distributed by that administrator.

Repayment of sums paid

8 (1) The regulations may make provision for sums paid to an administrator to be repayable, in whole or in part, to the persons by whom they were payable ("liable persons").

(2) The regulations may make provision as to how sums repayable under the regulations are to be calculated.

(3) They may include provision for the sums repayable under the regulations to vary according to the extent to which, or manner in which, liable persons dispose of products or materials to which the regulations relate, or meet or contribute to their disposal costs.

Charges

9 The regulations may include provision requiring the payment of charges to administrators, as a means of recovering costs incurred by administrators in performing functions under the regulations.

Consultation requirements

10 (1) Before making regulations under this Part of this Schedule the relevant national authority must consult persons appearing to it to represent the interests of those likely to be affected.

(2) The requirement in sub-paragraph (1) may be met by consultation carried out before this paragraph comes into force.

Part 2

Enforcement

General power

11 The relevant national authority may by regulations ("Part 2 regulations") make provision about the enforcement of requirements imposed by regulations ("Part 1 regulations") made by the authority under Part 1 of this Schedule.

Powers to confer functions

12 (1) Part 2 regulations may include provision conferring functions on one or more persons specified in the regulations (each of whom is an "enforcement authority" for the purposes of this Part).

(2) Part 2 regulations may include provision—

(a) conferring functions involving the exercise of discretion;

(b) for the functions of an enforcement authority to be exercised on its behalf by persons authorised in accordance with the regulations.

(3) Part 2 regulations may include provision requiring an enforcement authority to issue guidance about the exercise of its functions.

Monitoring compliance

13 Part 2 regulations may include provision conferring on an enforcement authority the function of monitoring compliance with requirements imposed by Part 1 regulations.

Records and information

14 Part 2 regulations may include provision—

(a) requiring persons on whom requirements are imposed by Part 1 regulations to keep records;

(b) requiring persons on whom requirements are imposed by Part 1 regulations to provide records or other information to an enforcement authority or (where the person is not an administrator) an administrator;

(c) requiring an enforcement authority to make reports or provide information to the relevant national authority.

Powers of entry etc

15 (1) Part 2 regulations may include provision conferring on an enforcement authority powers of entry, inspection, examination, search and seizure.

(2) Part 2 regulations may include provision—

(a) for powers to be exercisable only under the authority of a warrant issued by a justice of the peace, sheriff, summary sheriff or lay magistrate;

(b) about applications for, and the execution of, warrants.

(3) Part 2 regulations must secure that the authority of a warrant is required for the exercise of any powers conferred by the regulations to—

(a) enter premises by force;

(b) enter a private dwelling without the consent of the occupier;

(c) search and seize material.

Sanctions

16 (1) Part 2 regulations may include provision—

(a) for, about or connected with the imposition of civil sanctions in respect of—

(i) failures to comply with Part 1 regulations or Part 2 regulations, or

(ii) the obstruction of or failure to assist an enforcement authority;

(b) for appeals against such sanctions.

(2) Part 2 regulations may include provision—

(a) creating criminal offences punishable with a fine in respect of—

(i) failures to comply with civil sanctions imposed under Part 2 regulations, or

(ii) the obstruction of or failure to assist an enforcement authority;

(b) about such offences.

(3) In this paragraph "civil sanction" means a sanction of a kind for which provision may be made under Part 3 of the Regulatory Enforcement and Sanctions Act 2008 (fixed monetary penalties, discretionary requirements, stop notices and enforcement undertakings).

(4) Part 2 regulations may include provision for the imposition of sanctions of that kind whether or not—

(a) the conduct in respect of which the sanction is imposed constitutes an offence,

(b) the enforcement authority is a regulator for the purposes of Part 3 of the Regulatory Enforcement and Sanctions Act 2008, or

(c) the relevant national authority may make provision for the imposition of sanctions under that Part.

Charges and costs

17 Part 2 regulations may include provision—

(a) requiring persons on whom requirements are imposed by Part 1 regulations to pay charges, as a means of recovering costs incurred by an enforcement authority in performing its functions;

(b) authorising a court or tribunal dealing with any matter under Part 1 regulations or Part 2 regulations to award to an enforcement authority costs incurred by it in performing its functions in relation to that matter.

Consultation requirements

18 (1) Before making regulations under this Part of this Schedule the relevant national authority must consult any persons the authority considers appropriate.

(2) The requirement in sub-paragraph (1) may be met by consultation carried out before this paragraph comes into force.

SCHEDULE 6

Section 52

Resource efficiency information

Part 1

Requirements

General power

1 (1) The relevant national authority may by regulations make provision for the purposes of requiring specified persons, in specified circumstances, to provide specified information about the resource efficiency of specified products.

(2) The regulations may not make such provision in relation to a product which is—

(a) a medicinal product, within the meaning of the Human Medicines Regulations 2012 (S.I. 2012/1916);

(b) a veterinary medicinal product, within the meaning of the Veterinary Medicines Regulations 2013 (S.I. 2013/2033);

(c) food, within the meaning of article 2 of Regulation (EC) No. 178/2002 of the European Parliament and of the Council of 28 January 2002 laying down the general principles and requirements of food law, establishing the European Food Safety Authority and laying down procedures in matters of food safety.

(3) Sub-paragraph (2) does not prevent the regulations making provision in relation to a product which is not within that sub-paragraph, but is packaging for a product which is within that sub-paragraph.

Meaning of "information about resource efficiency"

2 (1) Information about resource efficiency, in relation to a product, means information which—

(a) is within sub-paragraph (2) or (3), and

(b) is relevant to the product's impact on the natural environment.

(2) The information within this sub-paragraph is information about—

(a) the expected life of the product;

(b) aspects of the product's design which affect its expected life;

(c) the availability or cost of component parts, tools, or anything else required to repair or maintain the product;

(d) whether the product can be upgraded, and the availability or cost of upgrades;

(e) any other matter relevant to repairing, maintaining, remanufacturing or otherwise prolonging the expected life of, the product;

(f) the ways in which the product can be disposed of at the end of its life (including whether and to what extent it can be recycled, and whether materials used in it can be extracted and reused or recycled).

(3) The information within this sub-paragraph is information about—

(a) the materials from which the product is manufactured;

(b) the techniques used in its manufacture;

(c) the resources consumed during its production or use;

(d) the pollutants (including greenhouse gases within the meaning of section 92 of the Climate Change Act 2008) released or emitted at any stage of the product's production, use or disposal.

Persons on whom requirements may be imposed

3 The regulations may impose requirements to provide information in relation to a product on a person only if the person is a person connected with the manufacture, import, distribution, sale or supply of the product.

Examples of provision that may be made

4 The regulations may include provision—

(a) about how information about a product is to be provided (for example, by affixing a label to the product);

(b) conferring on specified persons the function of determining whether specified products or materials have specified properties or characteristics (for example, whether they can be recycled) and publishing the results of such determinations;

(c) specifying a scheme for classifying products by reference to matters about which resource efficiency information must be provided;

(d) requiring information provided about a product to be determined according to specified criteria (for example, according to results published by virtue of paragraph (b) or classification schemes under paragraph (c)).

Consultation etc requirements

5 (1) Before making regulations under this Part of this Schedule the relevant national authority must—

(a) consult any persons the authority considers appropriate, and

(b) have regard to the matters in sub-paragraph (2).

(2) The matters are—

(a) the extent to which the proposed regulations are likely to reduce the product's impact on the natural environment at any stage of its production, use or disposal;

(b) the environmental, social, economic or other costs of complying with the regulations;

(c) whether exemptions should be given, or other special provision made, for smaller businesses.

(3) The requirement in sub-paragraph (1)(a) may be met by consultation carried out before this paragraph comes into force.

Interpretation

6 In this Part of this Schedule—

"natural environment" has the same meaning as in Part 1 of this Act (see section 44);

"product" includes a product which is a component part of, or packaging for, another product;

"specified" means specified in, or determined in accordance with, the regulations.

Part 2

Enforcement

General power

7 The relevant national authority may by regulations ("Part 2 regulations") make provision about the enforcement of requirements imposed by regulations ("Part 1 regulations") made by the authority under Part 1 of this Schedule.

Powers to confer functions

8 (1) Part 2 regulations may include provision conferring functions on one or more persons specified in the regulations (each of whom is an "enforcement authority" for the purposes of this Part).

(2) Part 2 regulations may include provision—

(a) conferring functions involving the exercise of discretion;

(b) for the functions of an enforcement authority to be exercised on its behalf by persons authorised in accordance with the regulations.

(3) Part 2 regulations may include provision requiring an enforcement authority to issue guidance about the exercise of its functions.

Monitoring compliance

9 Part 2 regulations may include provision conferring on an enforcement authority the function of monitoring compliance with requirements imposed by Part 1 regulations (which may include the function of testing or assessing products).

Records and information

10 Part 2 regulations may include provision—

(a) requiring persons on whom requirements are imposed by Part 1 regulations to keep records;

(b) requiring persons on whom requirements are imposed by Part 1 regulations to provide records or other information to an enforcement authority;

(c) requiring an enforcement authority to make reports or provide information to the relevant national authority.

Powers of entry etc

11 (1) Part 2 regulations may include provision conferring on an enforcement authority powers of entry, inspection, examination, search and seizure.

(2) Part 2 regulations may include provision—

(a) for powers to be exercisable only under the authority of a warrant issued by a justice of the peace, sheriff, summary sheriff or lay magistrate;

(b) about applications for, and the execution of, warrants.

(3) Part 2 regulations must secure that the authority of a warrant is required for the exercise of any powers conferred by the regulations to—

(a) enter premises by force;

(b) enter a private dwelling without the consent of the occupier;

(c) search and seize material.

Sanctions

12 (1) Part 2 regulations may include provision—

(a) for, about or connected with the imposition of civil sanctions in respect of—

(i) failures to comply with Part 1 regulations or Part 2 regulations, or

(ii) the obstruction of or failure to assist an enforcement authority;

(b) for appeals against such sanctions.

(2) Part 2 regulations may include provision—

(a) creating criminal offences punishable with a fine in respect of—

(i) failures to comply with civil sanctions imposed under Part 2 regulations, or

(ii) the obstruction of or failure to assist an enforcement authority;

(b) about such offences.

(3) In this paragraph "civil sanction" means a sanction of a kind for which provision may be made under Part 3 of the Regulatory Enforcement and Sanctions Act 2008 (fixed monetary penalties, discretionary requirements, stop notices and enforcement undertakings).

(4) Part 2 regulations may include provision for the imposition of sanctions of that kind whether or not—

(a) the conduct in respect of which the sanction is imposed constitutes an offence,

(b) the enforcement authority is a regulator for the purposes of Part 3 of the Regulatory Enforcement and Sanctions Act 2008, or

(c) the relevant national authority may make provision for the imposition of sanctions under that Part.

Costs

13 Part 2 regulations may include provision—

(a) requiring persons on whom requirements are imposed by Part 1 regulations to pay costs incurred by an enforcement authority in performing its functions;

(b) authorising a court or tribunal dealing with any matter under Part 1 regulations or Part 2 regulations to award to an enforcement authority costs incurred by it in performing its functions in relation to that matter.

Consultation requirement

14 (1) Before making Part 2 regulations the relevant national authority must consult any persons the authority considers appropriate.

(2) The requirement in sub-paragraph (1) may be met by consultation carried out before this paragraph comes into force.

SCHEDULE 7

Section 53

Resource efficiency requirements

Part 1

Requirements

General power

1 (1) The relevant national authority may by regulations make provision for the purposes of requiring specified products, in specified circumstances, to meet specified resource efficiency requirements.

(2) The regulations may not make such provision in relation to a product which is—

(a) an energy-related product, within the meaning of the Ecodesign for Energy-Related Products Regulations 2010 (S.I. 2010/2617);

(b) a medicinal product, within the meaning of the Human Medicines Regulations 2012 (S.I. 2012/1916);

(c) a veterinary medicinal product, within the meaning of the Veterinary Medicines Regulations 2013 (S.I. 2013/2033);

(d) food, within the meaning of article 2 of Regulation (EC) No. 178/2002 of the European Parliament and of the Council of 28 January 2002 laying down the general principles and requirements of food law, establishing the European Food Safety Authority and laying down procedures in matters of food safety.

(3) Sub-paragraph (2) does not prevent the regulations making provision in relation to a product which is not within that sub-paragraph, but is packaging for a product which is within that sub-paragraph.

Meaning of "resource efficiency requirements"

2 (1) "Resource efficiency requirements", in relation to a product, means requirements which—

(a) are within sub-paragraph (2) or (3), and

(b) are relevant to the product's impact on the natural environment.

(2) The requirements within this sub-paragraph are requirements relating to—

(a) aspects of the product's design which affect its expected life;

(b) the availability or cost of component parts, tools, or anything else required to repair or maintain the product;

(c) whether the product can be upgraded, and the availability or cost of upgrades;

(d) any other matter relevant to repairing, maintaining, remanufacturing or otherwise prolonging the expected life of, the product;

(e) the ways in which the product can be disposed of at the end of its life (including whether and to what extent it can be recycled, and whether materials used in it can be extracted and reused or recycled).

(3) The requirements within this sub-paragraph are requirements relating to—

(a) the materials from which the product is manufactured;

(b) the techniques used in its manufacture;

(c) the resources consumed during its production or use;

(d) the pollutants (including greenhouse gases within the meaning of section 92 of the Climate Change Act 2008) released or emitted at any stage of the product's production, use or disposal.

(4) Resource efficiency requirements may be specified by reference to standards prepared by a specified person.

Persons on whom requirements may be imposed

3 The regulations may impose resource efficiency requirements on a person only if the person is connected with the manufacture, import, distribution, sale or supply of the product.

Examples of provision that may be made

4 (1) The regulations may include provision—

(a) prohibiting a product being distributed, sold or supplied unless it meets resource efficiency requirements;

(b) requiring persons connected with the manufacture, import, distribution, sale or supply of a product to provide information to other such persons.

(2) The regulations may include provision—

(a) about how and by whom a product's compliance with resource efficiency requirements is to be determined;

(b) for appeals against such determinations;

(c) about how a product's compliance with resource efficiency requirements is to be evidenced (for example, by affixing a label or applying a marking to a product).

Consultation etc requirements

5 (1) Before making regulations under this Part of this Schedule the relevant national authority must—

(a) consult such persons as the authority considers appropriate, and

(b) where sub-paragraph (3) or (4) applies, publish for the purposes of the consultation—

(i) the authority's assessment of the matters it must be satisfied of, and

(ii) a draft of the regulations.

(2) The requirements in sub-paragraph (1) may be met by consultation carried out, and assessments and draft regulations published, before this paragraph comes into force.

(3) Before making regulations under this Part of this Schedule in relation to a new product, the relevant national authority must be satisfied that—

(a) the product has a significant impact on the natural environment at any stage of its production, use or disposal,

(b) the proposed regulations would be likely to reduce the product's impact on the natural environment,

(c) the benefit of that would be significant as against the likely environmental, social, economic or other costs of the proposed regulations, and

(d) a reduction in the product's impact on the natural environment could not be achieved as effectively without making the regulations.

(4) Before making regulations under this Part of this Schedule which—

(a) specify additional resource efficiency requirements in relation to a product, or

(b) specify additional persons who must meet resource efficiency requirements in relation to a product,

the relevant national authority must be satisfied of the matters in sub-paragraph (3)(b) to (d).

(5) A "new product" means a product in relation to which there are no existing regulations made by the relevant national authority under this Part of this Schedule.

(6) Before making regulations under this Part of this Schedule the relevant national authority must consider whether exemptions should be given, or other special provision made, for smaller businesses.

Interpretation

6 In this Part of this Schedule—

"natural environment" has the same meaning as in Part 1 of this Act (see section 44);

"product" includes a product which is a component part of, or packaging for, another product;

"specified" means specified in, or determined in accordance with, the regulations.

Part 2

Enforcement

General power

7 The relevant national authority may by regulations ("Part 2 regulations") make provision about the enforcement of requirements imposed by regulations ("Part 1 regulations") made by the authority under Part 1 of this Schedule.

Powers to confer functions

8 (1) Part 2 regulations may include provision conferring functions on one or more persons specified in the regulations (each of whom is an "enforcement authority" for the purposes of this Part).

(2) Part 2 regulations may include provision—

(a) conferring functions involving the exercise of discretion;

(b) for the functions of an enforcement authority to be exercised on its behalf by persons authorised in accordance with the regulations.

(3) Part 2 regulations may include provision requiring an enforcement authority to issue guidance about the exercise of its functions.

Monitoring compliance

9 Part 2 regulations may include provision conferring on an enforcement authority the function of monitoring compliance with requirements imposed by Part 1 regulations (which may include the function of testing or assessing products).

Records and information

10 Part 2 regulations may include provision—

(a) requiring persons on whom requirements are imposed by Part 1 regulations to keep records;

(b) requiring persons on whom requirements are imposed by Part 1 regulations to provide records or other information to an enforcement authority;

(c) requiring an enforcement authority to make reports or provide information to the relevant national authority.

Powers of entry etc

11 (1) Part 2 regulations may include provision conferring on an enforcement authority powers of entry, inspection, examination, search and seizure.

(2) Part 2 regulations may include provision—

(a) for powers to be exercisable only under the authority of a warrant issued by a justice of the peace, sheriff, summary sheriff or lay magistrate;

(b) about applications for, and the execution of, warrants.

(3) Part 2 regulations must secure that the authority of a warrant is required for the exercise of any powers conferred by the regulations to—

(a) enter premises by force;

(b) enter a private dwelling without the consent of the occupier;

(c) search and seize material.

Sanctions

12 (1) Part 2 regulations may include provision—

(a) for, about or connected with the imposition of civil sanctions in respect of—

(i) failures to comply with Part 1 regulations or Part 2 regulations, or

(ii) the obstruction of or failure to assist an enforcement authority;

(b) for appeals against such sanctions.

(2) Part 2 regulations may include provision—

(a) creating criminal offences punishable with a fine in respect of—

(i) failures to comply with civil sanctions imposed under Part 2 regulations, or

(ii) the obstruction of or failure to assist an enforcement authority;

(b) about such offences.

(3) In this paragraph "civil sanction" means a sanction of a kind for which provision may be made under Part 3 of the Regulatory Enforcement and Sanctions Act 2008 (fixed monetary penalties, discretionary requirements, stop notices and enforcement undertakings).

(4) Part 2 regulations may include provision for the imposition of sanctions of that kind whether or not—

(a) the conduct in respect of which the sanction is imposed constitutes an offence,

(b) the enforcement authority is a regulator for the purposes of Part 3 of the Regulatory Enforcement and Sanctions Act 2008, or

(c) the relevant national authority may make provision for the imposition of sanctions under that Part.

13 Part 2 regulations may include provision—

(a) requiring persons on whom requirements are imposed by Part 1 regulations to pay costs incurred by an enforcement authority in performing its functions;

(b) authorising a court or tribunal dealing with any matter under Part 1 regulations or Part 2 regulations to award to an enforcement authority costs incurred by it in performing its functions under the regulations in relation to that matter.

Consultation requirement

14 (1) Before making Part 2 regulations the relevant national authority must consult any persons the authority considers appropriate.

(2) The requirement in sub-paragraph (1) may be met by consultation carried out before this paragraph comes into force.

SCHEDULE 8

SECTION 54

DEPOSIT SCHEMES

Power to establish deposit schemes

1 (1) The relevant national authority may by regulations establish deposit schemes for any of the following purposes—

(a) sustaining, promoting or securing an increase in the recycling or reuse of materials;

(b) reducing the incidence of littering or fly-tipping.

(2) A deposit scheme is a scheme under which—

(a) a person supplied with a deposit item by a scheme supplier pays the supplier an amount (a "deposit"), and

(b) a person who provides a deposit item to a scheme collector is entitled to be paid an amount (a "refund") in respect of that item by the collector.

(3) A "deposit item" is a specified item that is supplied—

(a) by way of sale, or

(b) in connection with the supply of goods or services.

(4) A deposit scheme may make provision about the circumstances in which a deposit or refund is to be paid in respect of a deposit item.

(5) A person may be specified—

(a) as a scheme supplier if the person is a supplier or producer of deposit items;

(b) as a scheme collector if the person is a supplier or producer of deposit items or is a scheme administrator (see paragraph 4).

(6) A deposit scheme may provide that the amount of the deposit or refund in respect of a deposit item is—

(a) an amount specified,

(b) an amount determined and published by the relevant national authority in accordance with the scheme, or

(c) an amount determined by a scheme administrator in accordance with the scheme.

(7) In this paragraph "specified" means specified or described in a deposit scheme.

Scheme suppliers

2 (1) A deposit scheme may impose requirements on a scheme supplier in connection with the scheme, including requirements—

(a) to take steps to ensure deposits are paid in respect of deposit items in accordance with the scheme (which may include a requirement to include the amount of the deposit in the sale price of the item, or in the price of goods or services the item was supplied in connection with);

(b) as to the marking of deposit items to identify them as such;

(c) as to the retention of deposits;

(d) to pay amounts received as deposits to other scheme suppliers, scheme collectors or to a scheme administrator;

(e) in connection with securing that a specified proportion of deposit items supplied by scheme suppliers, or by individual scheme suppliers, are returned to scheme collectors;

(f) to keep records in connection with the scheme;

(g) to provide those records or other information in connection with the scheme to a scheme administrator.

(2) A deposit scheme may impose different requirements on different scheme suppliers.

(3) In this paragraph "specified" means specified in a deposit scheme.

Scheme collectors

3 (1) A deposit scheme may impose requirements on a scheme collector in connection with the scheme, including requirements—

(a) to pay a person who provides a deposit item a refund in accordance with the scheme;

(b) to pay a person who provides a deposit item under another deposit scheme an amount determined in accordance with the scheme (and the scheme may provide for that amount to be determined by reference to the other deposit scheme);

(c) to pay a person who provides articles or packaging that are the subject of a Scottish deposit and return scheme an amount determined in accordance with the scheme (and the scheme may provide for that amount to be determined by reference to the Scottish deposit and return scheme);

(d) to recycle, re-use, or arrange or facilitate the recycling or re-use of any item provided to them in accordance with the scheme (which may include articles or packaging that are the subject of a Scottish deposit and return scheme);

(e) to otherwise dispose of such items in accordance with the scheme;

(f) where a scheme collector receives any payment in connection with the recycling or disposal of such an item, to retain that amount or to pay it, or a part of it, to a scheme administrator;

(g) as to the retention of any amounts received from scheme suppliers, other scheme collectors or a scheme administrator;

(h) to pay such amounts received to scheme suppliers, other scheme collectors or a scheme administrator;

(i) in connection with securing that a specified proportion of deposit items supplied by scheme suppliers, or by individual scheme suppliers, are returned to scheme collectors;

(j) to keep records in connection with the scheme;

(k) to provide those records or other information in connection with the scheme to a scheme administrator.

(2) A deposit scheme may impose different requirements on different scheme collectors.

(3) In this paragraph "specified" means specified in a deposit scheme.

Deposit scheme administrators

4 (1) A person may be appointed as a scheme administrator of a deposit scheme by, or in accordance with, that scheme.

(2) A deposit scheme may confer functions (including functions involving the exercise of discretion) on a scheme administrator, including—

(a) any requirement that could be imposed on a scheme collector by virtue of paragraph 3(1)(a) to (e);

(b) functions relating to the registration of scheme suppliers and scheme collectors;

(c) a power to charge fees for registration (the amounts of which may be such as to recover the costs referred to in paragraphs (d) and (e));

(d) a power to use such fees to meet the costs of exercising its functions under, or in connection with, the scheme;

(e) requirements to pay such fees to persons exercising functions conferred by virtue of paragraph 5 for the purpose of meeting the costs of the exercise of those functions;

(f) a power to give general or specific directions to scheme suppliers and scheme collectors as to the matters mentioned in paragraphs 2(1) and 3(1);

(g) a power to make payments to scheme collectors to reimburse them in respect of the payment of refunds or payments made by virtue of a requirement under paragraph 3(1)(a), (b) or (c);

(h) a power to make payments to another scheme administrator of the deposit scheme;

(i) a power to make payments to a scheme administrator of another deposit scheme in connection with the operation of the scheme, or the operation of the other scheme;

(j) a power to make payments to a Scottish deposit administrator in connection with the operation of the scheme, or the operation of the Scottish deposit and return scheme in relation to which the Scottish deposit administrator is exercising functions;

(k) requirements to retain amounts received by it under or by virtue of the scheme;

(l) a power to use such amounts, or to pay such amounts to another person, for purposes connected with the scheme, or other deposit schemes;

(m) a power to use such amounts for purposes connected with the protection of the environment;

(n) requirements to pay such amounts to the relevant national authority;

(o) functions relating to securing compliance by scheme suppliers and scheme collectors with their obligations under the scheme;

(p) requirements in connection with securing that a specified proportion of deposit items supplied by scheme suppliers, or by individual scheme suppliers, are returned to scheme collectors;

(q) requirements to keep records in connection with the scheme;

(r) requirements to provide any such records or other information in connection with the scheme to the relevant national authority;

(s) requirements as to the exercise of the administrator's functions.

(3) Where there is more than one scheme administrator, a deposit scheme may confer different functions on different scheme administrators.

(4) A deposit scheme may confer a power on the relevant national authority to give directions to a scheme administrator of the scheme as to the exercise of the administrator's functions under the scheme.

(5) In this paragraph "specified" means specified in a deposit scheme.

Enforcement

5 (1) The relevant national authority may by regulations make provision about the enforcement of requirements under deposit schemes.

(2) The provision that may be made under sub-paragraph (1) includes provision—

(a) conferring functions (including functions involving the exercise of discretion) in connection with the enforcement of requirements under deposit schemes on specified persons (which may include scheme administrators);

(b) for such functions of such a person to be exercised on the person's behalf by persons authorised in accordance with the regulations;

(c) requiring scheme suppliers, scheme collectors or scheme administrators to provide records and other information relating to deposit schemes to specified persons;

(d) for, about or connected with the imposition of civil sanctions in respect of failures to comply with relevant requirements, or the obstruction of or failure to assist a person having functions in connection with the enforcement of relevant requirements;

(e) for appeals against such sanctions;

(f) creating criminal offences punishable with a fine in respect of failures to comply with civil sanctions, or the obstruction of or failure to assist a person having functions in connection with the enforcement of relevant requirements;

(g) about such offences.

(3) For the purposes of this paragraph "civil sanction" means a sanction of a kind for which provision may be made under Part 3 of the Regulatory Enforcement and Sanctions Act 2008 (fixed monetary penalties, discretionary requirements, stop notices and enforcement undertakings).

(4) Regulations under sub-paragraph (1) may include provision for the imposition of sanctions of that kind whether or not—

(a) the conduct in respect of which the sanction is imposed constitutes an offence,

(b) the person imposing them is a regulator for the purposes of Part 3 of the Regulatory Enforcement and Sanctions Act 2008, or

(c) the relevant national authority may make provision for the imposition of sanctions under that Part.

(5) In this paragraph—

"relevant requirement" means any requirement imposed by or under a deposit scheme or regulations under sub-paragraph (1);

"specified" means specified in, or determined in accordance with, regulations under sub-paragraph (1).

Interpretation

6 In this Schedule—

"deposit" has the meaning it has in paragraph 1(2)(a);

"deposit item" has the meaning it has in paragraph 1(3);

"deposit scheme" has the meaning it has in paragraph 1(2);

"refund" has the meaning it has in paragraph 1(2)(b);

"scheme administrator", in relation to a deposit scheme, means a person appointed as a scheme administrator of the scheme;

"scheme supplier" or "scheme collector" means a person specified as such (see paragraph 1(5));

"Scottish deposit administrator" means a person exercising the functions of a scheme administrator in relation to a Scottish deposit and return scheme;

"Scottish deposit and return scheme" means a deposit and return scheme under section 84 of the Climate Change (Scotland) Act 2009 (asp 12).

SCHEDULE 9

SECTION 55

CHARGES FOR SINGLE USE ITEMS

General power

1 (1) The relevant national authority may by regulations make provision about charging by sellers of goods or services for items specified in the regulations.

(2) Regulations made by the Secretary of State or the Welsh Ministers may specify only items which—

(a) are single use items, and

(b) are supplied in connection with goods or services.

(3) Regulations made by the Department of Agriculture, Environment and Rural Affairs in Northern Ireland may specify only items which—

(a) are single use items,

(b) are made wholly or partly of plastic, and

(c) are supplied in connection with goods or services.

(4) A "single use item" is a manufactured item which is likely to be used only once, or used only for a short period of time, before being disposed of.

(5) An item is supplied in connection with goods or services if it is supplied—

(a) at the place the goods or services are sold or provided, for the purpose of enabling the goods to be taken away, used or consumed, or enabling the services to be received, or

(b) for the purpose of enabling goods to be delivered.

(6) In particular, a container or other packaging into which goods are placed at the point of sale is supplied in connection with goods.

Requirement to charge

2 The regulations may make provision requiring sellers of goods or services to charge for items specified in the regulations.

Sellers of goods and services

3 (1) "Seller", in relation to goods or services, has the meaning given by the regulations.

(2) The regulations may define that term by reference (in particular) to—

(a) a person's involvement in selling the goods or services,

(b) a person's interest in goods or services, or

(c) a person's interest in the place at or from which the goods or services are sold or provided,

or any combination of those factors.

(3) The regulations may make provision for the regulations to apply—

(a) to all sellers of goods or services, or

(b) to sellers of goods or services identified by reference to factors specified in the regulations.

(4) The factors which may be specified in the regulations include—

(a) the place or places at or from which a seller supplies goods or services,

(b) the type of goods or services that a seller supplies,

(c) the value of goods or services that a seller supplies, and

(d) a seller's turnover or any part of that turnover.

Amount of charge

4 The regulations may specify the minimum amount that a seller must charge for an item specified in the regulations, or provide for that amount to be determined in accordance with the regulations.

Administration

5 (1) The regulations may appoint a person (an "administrator") to administer provision made by the regulations.

(2) More than one person may be appointed as an administrator.

(3) The regulations may confer functions on an administrator (including functions involving the exercise of discretion).

(4) References in this Schedule to an administrator include a person appointed by an administrator or exercising functions on an administrator's behalf.

Registration

6 (1) The regulations may require sellers to register with an administrator.

(2) The regulations may make provision—

(a) about applications for registration;

(b) about the period for which registration has effect;

(c) about the cancellation of registration.

(3) The regulations may require sellers to pay to the administrator, in connection with their registration, fees of an amount determined by or in accordance with the regulations.

(4) The regulations may provide for the amount of the fees to be such as to recover the costs incurred by the administrator in performing its functions under the regulations.

Record-keeping and publication of records

7 (1) The regulations may require records to be kept relating to charges made for items specified in the regulations.

(2) The regulations may require the records, or such other information as may be specified—

(a) to be published at such times and in such manner as may be specified;

(b) to be supplied on request and in such manner as may be specified to—

(i) the relevant national authority,

(ii) an administrator, or

(iii) members of the public.

(3) The regulations may (in particular) require the publication or supply of records or information relating to any of the following—

(a) the amount received by a seller by way of charges for items specified in the regulations;

(b) the seller's gross or net proceeds of the charge;

(c) the uses to which the net proceeds of the charge have been put.

(4) In this paragraph—

"gross proceeds of the charge" means the amount received by the seller by way of charges for items specified in the regulations;

"net proceeds of the charge" means the seller's gross proceeds of the charge reduced by such amount as may be specified.

Enforcement

8 (1) The regulations may confer functions on an administrator to enforce provision made by the regulations.

(2) The regulations may (in particular) confer powers on an administrator to—

(a) require the production of documents or the provision of information, or

(b) question a seller or officers or employees of a seller.

(3) Regulation under sub-paragraph (2) must contain provision for ensuring that the power in question is exercised by a person only where the person reasonably believes there has been a failure to comply with a requirement of regulations under this Schedule.

9 (1) The regulations may make provision for, about or connected with the imposition of civil sanctions in respect of failures to comply with the regulations, or the obstruction of or failure to assist a person on whom functions are conferred by the regulations.

(2) The regulations may make provision for appeals against such sanctions.

(3) In this paragraph "civil sanction" means a sanction of a kind for which provision may be made under Part 3 of the Regulatory Enforcement and Sanctions Act 2008 (fixed monetary penalties, discretionary requirements, stop notices and enforcement undertakings).

(4) The regulations may include provision for the imposition of sanctions of that kind whether or not—

(a) the conduct in respect of which the sanction is imposed constitutes an offence,

(b) the enforcement authority is a regulator for the purposes of Part 3 of the Regulatory Enforcement and Sanctions Act 2008, or

(c) the relevant national authority may make provision for the imposition of sanctions under that Part.

SCHEDULE 10

Section 66

Enforcement powers

Powers to search and seize vehicles in connection with waste offences

1 In section 5(6) of the Control of Pollution (Amendment) Act 1989 (constable's power to seize vehicles and contents)—

(a) in paragraph (b) after "presence of" insert "or at the request of";

(b) in paragraph (c) for "without such an officer present" substitute "in any other case".

2 In section 34B(6) of the Environmental Protection Act 1990 (constable's power to seize vehicles and contents)—

(a) in paragraph (b) after "presence of" insert "or at the request of";

(b) in paragraph (c) for "without such an officer present" substitute "in any other case".

Powers of direction in relation to waste

3 (1) Section 57 of the Environmental Protection Act 1990 (power to give directions) is amended as follows.

(2) In subsection (2) omit the words from "with a view" to the end.

(3) After subsection (2) insert—

"(2A) The appropriate Minister may, by notice in writing—

(a) direct a registered waste carrier to collect waste which is being kept on specified land and deliver it to a specified person on specified terms;

(b) direct any person who—

(i) is keeping waste on any land, or

(ii) owns or occupies land on which waste is being kept,

to facilitate collection of the waste by a specified registered waste carrier to whom a direction in respect of the waste is given under paragraph (a)."

(4) In subsection (4), for "of treating or disposing of" substitute "in relation to".

(5) After subsection (4) insert—

"(4A) A direction under subsection (2A)(b) may require the person to whom it is given—

(a) to pay to the specified registered waste carrier the reasonable costs of collecting and delivering the waste;

(b) to pay to the specified person to whom the waste is delivered ("P") the reasonable costs incurred by P in relation to the waste (including any costs P is required by a direction under this section to pay to another person)."

(6) In subsection (7) for the words from ", where" to the end substitute "pay any costs mentioned in subsection (4)."

(7) After subsection (7) insert—

"(7A) The appropriate Minister may pay any costs mentioned in subsection (4A)."

(8) In subsection (8), before the definition of "specified" insert— ""appropriate Minister" means—

(a) the Secretary of State, in relation to waste being kept on land in England, and

(b) the Welsh Ministers, in relation to waste being kept on land in Wales;

"registered waste carrier" means a person registered under the Control of Pollution (Amendment) Act 1989 as a carrier of controlled waste;".

Powers of entry in relation to pollution control etc

4 The Environment Act 1995 is amended as follows.

5 (1) Section 108 (powers of enforcing authorities and their authorised officers) is amended as follows.

(2) In subsection (4), after paragraph (k) insert—

"(ka) as regards any premises which an English or Welsh authorised person has power to enter by virtue of paragraph (a), for the purposes of an examination or investigation under paragraph (c)—

(i) to search the premises;

(ii) to seize and remove documents or anything else found on the premises (other than an article or substance within paragraph (g));

(iii) to require any information which is stored in electronic form and is accessible from the premises to be produced in a form in which it can be removed and—

(a) in which it is visible and legible, or

(b) from which it can readily be produced in a visible and legible form;

(iv) to operate any equipment found on the premises for the purposes of producing such information in such a form;".

(3) In subsection (6), omit paragraph (a).

(4) After subsection (7) insert—

"(7A) An English or Welsh authorised person may not exercise the powers in subsection (4)(ka) without—

(a) the consent of a person entitled to grant access to material on or accessible from the premises, or

(b) the authority of a warrant by virtue of Schedule 18 to this Act.

This is subject to subsections (7B) and (7C).

(7B) An English or Welsh authorised person may exercise a power in subsection (4)(ka)(ii) to (ka)(iv) in relation to a thing without consent or the authority of a warrant if the person has reasonable grounds for believing that—

(a) it is evidence of a failure to comply with any provision of the pollution control enactments or flood risk activity enactments, and

(b) exercising the power is necessary to prevent it being concealed, lost, altered or destroyed.

(7C) Subsection (7A) does not require consent or the authority of a warrant for doing something within the powers in subsection (4)(ka) if, and so far as, it may be done without them in exercise of another power conferred by subsection (4).

(7D) Where anything seized or removed from premises under subsection (4)(ka) contains protected material, that material—

(a) may not be used for the purposes of an examination or investigation under subsection (4)(c), and

(b) must be returned to the premises from which it was removed, or to the person who had possession or control of it immediately before it was removed, as soon as reasonably practicable after it is identified as protected material.

(7E) Subsection (7D) does not prevent any part of a thing containing protected material which is not protected material being used for the purposes of an examination or investigation, retained or copied.

(7F) "Protected material" means—

(a) material subject to legal professional privilege,

(b) excluded material within the meaning of section 11 of the Police and Criminal Evidence Act 1984, or

(c) journalistic material, within the meaning of section 13 of that Act, which is not excluded material."

(5) After subsection (12) insert—

"(12A) Subject to subsection (7D), anything seized or removed under subsection (4)(ka) may be retained for so long as is necessary in all the circumstances."

(6) In subsection (15)—

(a) after the definition of "authorised person" insert—

""document" includes anything in which information of any description is recorded (by any means) and any part of such a thing;";

(b) after the definition of "enforcing authority" insert—

""English or Welsh authorised person" means a person authorised under subsection (1) or (2) by the Secretary of State, the Welsh Ministers, the Agency, the Natural Resources Body for Wales, a waste collection authority or a local enforcing authority in England or Wales;";

(c) in the definition of "pollution control functions" in relation to a waste collection authority, in paragraph (a) after "46" insert "to 46D".

6 (1) Schedule 18 (supplemental provision about powers of entry) is amended as follows.

(2) In paragraph 2—

(a) after sub-paragraph (2) insert—

"(2A) A justice of the peace may by warrant authorise an English or Welsh authorised person, designated for the purpose by the person who authorised them, to exercise the powers in section 108(4)(ka) in accordance with the warrant and, if need be, by force.

(2B) The justice may do so only if satisfied that there are reasonable grounds for believing that—

(a) there is material on or accessible from the premises in question which is likely to be of substantial value (by itself or together with other material) to an examination or investigation under section 108(4)(c), and

(b) it is impracticable to communicate with a person entitled to grant access to it, or access to it is unlikely to be granted unless a warrant is produced.";

(b) omit sub-paragraph (3).

(3) In paragraph 3 after "shall" insert ", if so required,".

SCHEDULE 11

Section 72

Local air quality management framework

1 The Environment Act 1995 is amended as follows.

2 (1) Section 80 (national air quality strategy) is amended as follows.

(2) Omit subsection (3).

(3) After subsection (4) insert—

"(4A) The strategy must be reviewed, and if appropriate modified—

(a) within the period of 12 months beginning with the day on which this subsection comes into force, and

(b) within each period of 5 years beginning with the day on which the person carrying out the review completed their most recent review under this subsection."

3 After that section insert—

"80A Duty to report on air quality in England

As soon as reasonably practicable after the end of each financial year, beginning with the financial year in which this section comes into force, the Secretary of State must lay a statement before Parliament that sets out—

(a) the Secretary of State's assessment of the progress made in meeting air quality objectives, and air quality standards, in relation to England, and

(b) the steps the Secretary of State has taken in that year in support of the meeting of those objectives and standards."

4 After section 81 insert—

"81A Functions of relevant public authorities etc

(1) The following persons must have regard to the strategy when exercising any function of a public nature that could affect the quality of air—

(a) relevant public authorities;

(b) local authorities in England;

(c) county councils for areas in England for which there are district councils.

(2) In this Part, "relevant public authority" means a person designated in accordance with subsection (3) as a relevant public authority in relation to an area in England.

(3) The Secretary of State may by regulations designate a person as a relevant public authority in relation to an area in England if the person's functions include functions of a public nature in relation to that area.

(4) Before making regulations under subsection (3) the Secretary of State must consult—

(a) the person that is proposed to be designated, and

(b) such other persons as the Secretary of State considers appropriate.

(5) The requirement in subsection (4) may be met by consultation carried out before this section comes into force.

(6) For the purposes of subsections (2) and (3), reference to England includes the territorial sea adjacent to England, which for this purpose does not include—

(a) any part of the territorial sea which is adjacent to Wales for the purposes of the Government of Wales Act 2006 (see section 158 of that Act), or

(b) any part of the territorial sea which is adjacent to Scotland for the purposes of the Scotland Act 1998 (see section 126 of that Act)."

5 (1) Section 82 (local authority reviews) is amended as follows.

(2) In subsection (3)—

(a) for "If" substitute "This subsection applies to a local authority where";

(b) omit the words from ", the local authority shall" to the end.

(3) After subsection (3) insert—

"(4) Where subsection (3) applies to a local authority, it must identify any parts of its area in which it appears that air quality standards or objectives are not likely to be achieved within the relevant period.

(5) Where subsection (3) applies to a local authority in England, it must also—

(a) identify relevant sources of emissions that it considers are, or will be, responsible (in whole or in part) for any failure to achieve air quality standards or objectives in its area,

(b) in the case of a relevant source within the area of a neighbouring authority, identify that authority, and

(c) in the case of a relevant source within an area in relation to which a relevant public authority or the Agency has functions of a public nature, identify that person in relation to that source.

(6) For the purposes of subsection (5), a source is "relevant" if—

(a) it is within the area of the local authority,

(b) it is within the area of a neighbouring authority in England, or

(c) it is within an area in relation to which a relevant public authority or the Agency has functions of a public nature and the local authority considers that the exercise of those functions is relevant to the source of the emissions."

6 After section 83 insert—

"83A Duties of English local authorities in relation to designated areas

(1) This section applies in relation to a local authority in England.

(2) A local authority must, for the purpose of securing that air quality standards and objectives are achieved in an air quality management area designated by that authority, prepare an action plan in relation to that area.

(3) An action plan is a written plan that sets out how the local authority will exercise its functions in order to secure that air quality standards and objectives are achieved in the area to which the plan relates.

(4) An action plan must also set out how the local authority will exercise its functions to secure that air quality standards and objectives are maintained after they have been achieved in the area to which the plan relates.

(5) An action plan must set out particular measures the local authority will take to secure the achievement, and maintenance, of air quality standards and objectives in the area to which the plan relates, and must in relation to each measure specify a date by which it will be carried out.

(6) A local authority may revise an action plan at any time, and must revise an action plan if it considers that there is a need for further or different measures to be taken to secure that air quality standards and objectives are achieved or maintained in the area to which the plan relates.

(7) Subsections (8) to (10) apply where a district council in an area for which there is a county council is preparing an action plan, or a revision of an action plan.

(8) Where the county council disagrees with the contents of the proposed plan, or the proposed revision of a plan, a referral of the matter may be made to the Secretary of State by—

(a) the county council;

(b) the district council preparing the plan or revision.

(9) The Secretary of State may, on a reference made under subsection (8), confirm (with or without modifications) or reject the proposed action plan, or revision of an action plan.

(10) Where a reference has been made under subsection (8), the district council may not finally determine the proposed action plan or revision of an action plan, except in accordance with the decision of the Secretary of State on the reference or in pursuance of a direction made by the Secretary of State under section 85."

7 (1) Section 84 (duties of local authorities in relation to designated areas) is amended as follows.

(2) In the heading, after "of" insert "Scottish and Welsh".

(3) Before subsection (2) insert—

"(1A) This section applies in relation to a local authority in Scotland or Wales."

(4) Omit subsection (5).

8 After section 85 insert—

"85A Duty of air quality partners to co-operate

(1) For the purposes of this Part, an "air quality partner" of a local authority means a person identified by that authority in accordance with section 82(5)(b) or (c).

(2) An air quality partner of a local authority must provide the authority with such assistance in connection with the carrying out of any of the authority's functions under this Part as the authority requests.

(3) An air quality partner may refuse a request under subsection (2) to the extent it considers the request unreasonable.

85B Role of air quality partners in relation to action plans

(1) Where a local authority in England intends to prepare an action plan it must notify each of its air quality partners that it intends to do so.

(2) Where an air quality partner of a local authority has been given a notification under subsection (1) it must, before the end of the relevant period, provide the authority with proposals for particular measures the partner will take to contribute to the achievement, and maintenance, of air quality standards and objectives in the area to which the plan relates.

(3) An air quality partner that provides proposals under subsection (2) must—

(a) in those proposals, specify a date for each particular measure by which it will be carried out, and

(b) as far as is reasonably practicable, carry out those measures by those dates.

(4) An action plan prepared by a local authority in England must set out any proposals provided to it by its air quality partners under subsection (2) (including the dates specified by those partners by virtue of subsection (3)(a)).

(5) The Secretary of State may direct an air quality partner to make further proposals under subsection (2) by a date specified in the direction where the Secretary of State considers the proposals made by the partner under that subsection are insufficient or otherwise inappropriate.

(6) A direction under subsection (5) may make provision about the extent to which the further proposals are to supplement or replace any other proposals made under subsection (2) by the air quality partner.

(7) An air quality partner must comply with any direction given to it under this section."

9 (1) Section 86 (functions of county councils for areas for which there are district councils) is amended as follows.

(2) Omit subsection (1).

(3) In subsection (2), for the words before paragraph (a) substitute "A county council for an area in England for which there are district councils may make recommendations to any of those district councils with respect to the carrying out of—".

(4) After subsection (2) insert—

"(2A) Where a district council of a district in England for which there is a county council intends to prepare an action plan it must notify the county council that it intends to do so."

(5) For subsections (3) to (5) substitute—

"(3) Where a county council has been given a notification by a district council under subsection (2A) it must, before the end of the relevant period, provide the district council with proposals for particular measures the county council will take to contribute to the achievement, and maintenance, of air quality standards and objectives in the area to which the plan relates.

(4) A county council that provides proposals under subsection (3) must—

(a) in those proposals, specify a date for each particular measure by which it will be carried out, and

(b) as far as is reasonably practicable, carry out those measures by those dates.

(5) An action plan prepared by a district council of a district in England for which there is a county council must set out any proposals provided to it by the county council under subsection (3) (including the dates specified by the county council by virtue of subsection (4)(a))."

(6) In subsection (6), in paragraph (a), after "district council" insert "of a district in England for which there is a county council".

(7) In subsection (7)—

(a) in paragraph (a), omit the words from "above or" to the end;

(b) in paragraph (b)—

(i) omit "or statement";

(ii) omit "or (4) above";

(c) in paragraph (c)—

(i) omit "or statement";

(ii) omit "or (4) above".

10 For section 86A substitute—

"86A Role of the Mayor of London in relation to action plans

(1) Where a local authority in London intends to prepare an action plan it must notify the Mayor of London (referred to in this section as "the Mayor").

(2) Where the Mayor has been given a notification under subsection (1) by a local authority in London the Mayor must, before the end of the relevant period, provide the authority with proposals for particular measures the Mayor will take to contribute to the achievement, and maintenance, of air quality standards and objectives in the area to which the plan relates.

(3) Where the Mayor provides proposals under subsection (2), the Mayor must—

(a) in those proposals, specify a date for each particular measure by which it will be carried out, and

(b) as far as is reasonably practicable, carry out those measures by those dates.

(4) An action plan prepared by a local authority in London must set out any proposals provided to it by the Mayor under subsection (2) (including the dates specified by the Mayor by virtue of subsection (3)(a)).

86B Role of combined authorities in relation to action plans

(1) Where a local authority in the area of a combined authority intends to prepare an action plan it must notify the combined authority.

(2) Where a combined authority has been given a notification under subsection (1) by a local authority, the combined authority must, before the end of the relevant period, provide the local authority with proposals for particular measures the combined authority will take to contribute to the achievement, and maintenance, of air quality standards and objectives in the area to which the plan relates.

(3) Where a combined authority provides proposals under subsection (2), the combined authority must—

(a) in those proposals, specify a date for each particular measure by which it will be carried out, and

(b) as far as is reasonably practicable, carry out those measures by those dates.

(4) An action plan prepared by a local authority in the area of a combined authority must set out any proposals provided to it under subsection (2) (including the dates specified by virtue of subsection (3)(a)).

(5) In this section "combined authority" has the meaning it has in Part 6 of the Local Democracy, Economic Development and Construction Act 2009 (see section 120 of that Act)."

11 (1) Section 87 (regulations) is amended as follows.

(2) In subsection (2)—

(a) in paragraph (c), after "authorities" insert ", relevant county councils, relevant public authorities or the Agency";

(b) in paragraph (j), after "otherwise)" insert ", relevant county councils, relevant public authorities, the Agency";

(c) in paragraph (l), after "authorities" insert ", relevant county councils, relevant public authorities or the Agency";

(d) in paragraph (m)—

(i) after "local authority" insert ", a relevant county council, a relevant public authority or the Agency";

(ii) after "the authority", in both places it occurs, insert ", council or Agency".

(3) After that subsection insert—

"(2A) In subsection (2) "relevant county council" means a county council for an area in England for which there are district councils."

12 In section 88, in subsection (3), after "district councils" insert ", relevant public authorities and the Agency".

13 In section 91 (interpretation), in subsection (1)—

(a) for the definition of "action plan" substitute—

""action plan" is to be construed—

(a) in relation to England, in accordance with section 83A;

(b) otherwise, in accordance with section 84(2);";

(b) at the appropriate places insert—

""air quality partner" has the meaning given by section 85A(1);";

""neighbouring authority", in relation to a local authority ("the principal authority"), means another local authority whose area is contiguous with the area of the principal authority;";

""relevant public authority" has the meaning given by section 81A(2);".

14 In Schedule 11 (air quality: supplemental provisions), in paragraph 1(2), for paragraph (d) substitute—

"(d) every neighbouring authority;".

SCHEDULE 12

Section 73

Smoke control in England and Wales

Part 1

Principal amendments to the Clean Air Act 1993: England

1 The Clean Air Act 1993 is amended as follows.

2 After section 19 insert—

"Regulation of smoke and fuel in smoke control areas in England

19A Penalty for emission of smoke in smoke control area in England

Schedule 1A makes provision for financial penalties in relation to the emission of smoke in smoke control areas in England."

3 After Schedule 1 insert—

"SCHEDULE 1A

PENALTY FOR EMISSION OF SMOKE IN SMOKE CONTROL AREA IN ENGLAND

Key definitions

1 In this Schedule—

"relevant chimney" means—

(a) a chimney of a building to which a smoke control order in England applies, or

(b) a chimney which serves the furnace of any fixed boiler or industrial plant to which a smoke control order in England applies;

"person liable", in relation to a relevant chimney, means—

(a) if the chimney is the chimney of a building, the occupier of the building, or

(b) if the chimney serves the furnace of any fixed boiler or industrial plant, the person having possession of the boiler or plant.

Notice of intent

2 (1) This paragraph applies where a local authority is satisfied, on the balance of probabilities, that on a particular occasion smoke has been emitted from a relevant chimney within a smoke control area declared by that authority.

(2) The local authority may give to the person liable a notice under this paragraph (a "notice of intent").

(3) A notice of intent must—

(a) inform the person that the local authority is satisfied as specified in sub-paragraph (1),

(b) specify the occasion referred to in sub-paragraph (1),

(c) inform the person that the local authority proposes to impose a financial penalty under this Schedule (including the proposed amount of the penalty), and

(d) give details regarding the person's right to object to the imposition of a financial penalty.

Amount of penalty

3 (1) The minimum amount of a financial penalty that may be imposed under this Schedule is £175.

(2) The maximum amount of a financial penalty that may be imposed under this Schedule is £300.

(3) The Secretary of State may by regulations amend sub-paragraph (1) or (2) so as to substitute a different amount for the amount specified there.

(4) Regulations under sub-paragraph (3) may not be made unless a draft of the regulations has been laid before, and approved by resolution of, each House of Parliament.

Right to object to proposed financial penalty

4 (1) A person to whom a notice of intent is given may, within the period of 28 days beginning with the day after that on which the notice was given—

(a) object in writing to the local authority on a ground specified in sub-paragraph (2), and

(b) provide evidence that supports the objection.

(2) The grounds of objection referred to in sub-paragraph (1) are—

(a) that there was no emission of smoke from the chimney on the occasion specified in the notice of intent;

(b) that the chimney was not a chimney to which a smoke control order applied on the occasion specified in the notice of intent;

(c) that the person to whom the notice of intent was given was not a person liable in relation to the chimney on the occasion specified in the notice of intent;

(d) that there are other compelling reasons why the financial penalty should not be imposed.

(3) Where a person objects on the ground specified in sub-paragraph (2)(c), the objection must include the name and address of the person who was the person liable on the occasion specified in the notice of intent (if known).

(4) The Secretary of State may by regulations amend this paragraph so as to amend the grounds of objection listed in sub-paragraph (2).

(5) Before making regulations under sub-paragraph (4) the Secretary of State must consult anyone that the Secretary of State considers may have an interest in the proposed regulations.

(6) Regulations under sub-paragraph (4) may not be made unless a draft of the regulations has been laid before, and approved by resolution of, each House of Parliament.

Decision regarding a final notice

5 (1) Where a local authority in England has given a notice of intent to a person, the authority may impose a financial penalty on the person if the local authority so decides within—

(a) the period of 56 days beginning with the day on which an objection is made under paragraph 4, or

(b) if no such objection is made, the period of 56 days beginning with the day after the day on which the period mentioned in paragraph 4(1) ended.

(2) If the local authority decides not to impose a financial penalty on a person, or does not decide to impose a financial penalty on the person within the period specified in sub-paragraph (1), the authority must give a notice to that person that informs the person that a financial penalty will not be imposed.

Final notice

6 (1) This paragraph applies where a local authority in England decides to impose a financial penalty on a person who was given a notice of intent.

(2) The local authority may impose a financial penalty by a notice given to that person (a "final notice").

(3) A final notice must specify—

(a) the amount of the financial penalty,

(b) the reasons for imposing the penalty,

(c) information about how to pay the penalty,

(d) the period for payment of the penalty, and

(e) information about rights of appeal.

(4) The final notice must require the financial penalty to be paid within the period of 28 days beginning with the day after that on which the notice was given.

Withdrawal or amendment of notices

7 (1) A local authority may at any time—

(a) withdraw a notice of intent or a final notice, or

(b) reduce the amount of the financial penalty specified in a final notice.

(2) The power in sub-paragraph (1) is to be exercised by giving notice to the person to whom the notice of intent or final notice was given.

Appeals

8 (1) A person on whom a financial penalty is imposed by a final notice may, within the period of 28 days beginning with the day after that on which the notice was given, appeal against the notice to the First-tier Tribunal.

(2) The grounds for an appeal under this paragraph are that the decision to impose the financial penalty was—

(a) based on an error of fact,

(b) wrong in law, or

(c) unreasonable.

(3) If a person appeals under this paragraph, the final notice is suspended until the appeal is finally determined or withdrawn.

(4) On an appeal under this paragraph the First-tier Tribunal may—

(a) quash the final notice,

(b) confirm the final notice,

(c) vary the final notice by reducing the amount of the financial penalty, or

(d) remit to the local authority the decision whether to—

(i) withdraw or confirm the final notice, or

(ii) vary the final notice by reducing the amount of the financial penalty.

Recovery of penalties

9 A financial penalty is recoverable as a civil debt due to the local authority that imposed the penalty.

Delegation

10 (1) A local authority may delegate to a person the exercise of any of the authority's functions under this Schedule.

(2) A delegation under this paragraph must be made by giving notice to the person.

Notices

11 (1) A notice under this Schedule must be in writing.

(2) A notice under this Schedule may be given to a person by—

(a) handing it to the person,

(b) leaving it at the person's address,

(c) sending it by post to the person at their address, or

(d) with the person's consent, sending it to them electronically.

Notices: vessels which are moored

12 (1) This paragraph applies in relation to a vessel which is moored in a smoke control area in England and is subject to the operation of this Schedule (see section 44).

(2) If the local authority is unable to give a notice of intent to the occupier of the vessel who is not the registered owner of the vessel, the local authority may give the notice to the registered owner of the vessel instead.

(3) In such a case, the ground for objecting to the proposed financial penalty mentioned in paragraph 4(2)(c) does not apply.

(4) Where a notice of intent is given to a person in respect of a vessel, that person may object under paragraph 4 on the further ground that, on the occasion specified in the notice, the emission of smoke was solely due to the use of the vessel's engine to propel the vessel or to provide electric power to the vessel."

4 After section 19A (as inserted by paragraph 2 above)—

"19B Acquisition and sale of controlled solid fuel in England

(1) A person who acquires in England any controlled solid fuel for use in—

(a) a building to which a smoke control order in England applies,

(b) a fireplace to which such an order applies, or

(c) a fixed boiler or industrial plant to which such an order applies,

is guilty of an offence.

(2) Where a smoke control order in England applies to a moored vessel (see section 44), subsection (1)(a) does not apply in relation to the acquisition of controlled solid fuel for use in the propulsion of the vessel or to provide electric power to the vessel.

(3) Subsection (1)(b) does not apply where the fireplace was an approved fireplace at the time of the acquisition.

(4) A person who—

(a) offers controlled solid fuel for sale by retail in England where the fuel is to be taken away by a purchaser, and

(b) fails to take reasonable steps to notify potential purchasers that it is an offence to acquire that fuel for any of the uses mentioned in subsection (1),

is guilty of an offence.

(5) A person who sells any controlled solid fuel by retail in England for delivery by that person, or on that person's behalf, to—

(a) a building to which a smoke control order in England applies, or

(b) premises in which there is any fixed boiler or industrial plant to which such an order applies,

is guilty of an offence.

(6) In proceedings for an offence under subsection (5) it is a defence for the person accused to prove that the person believed and had reasonable grounds for believing that—

(a) the building referred to in subsection (5)(a) was not one to which the smoke control order in question applied, or

(b) the fuel was acquired for use in—

(i) a fireplace that was, at the time of the delivery, an approved fireplace, or

(ii) a boiler or plant to which the smoke control order did not apply.

(7) A person guilty of an offence under subsection (1) is liable on summary conviction to a fine not exceeding level 3 on the standard scale.

(8) A person guilty of an offence under subsection (4) or (5) is liable on summary conviction to a fine.

19C Exemptions relating to particular areas in England

(1) The Secretary of State may, if it appears to the Secretary of State to be necessary or expedient to do so, by order suspend or relax the operation of—

(a) Schedule 1A (penalty for emission of smoke), or

(b) section 19B(1), (4) or (5) (offences relating to acquisition and sale of fuel),

in relation to the whole or part of a smoke control area in England.

(2) Before making an order under subsection (1) the Secretary of State must consult the local authority that declared the smoke control area in question unless satisfied that, on account of urgency, such consultation is impracticable.

(3) As soon as practicable after the making of such an order the local authority must take such steps as appear to them suitable for bringing the effect of the order to the notice of persons affected.

19D Interpretation: "approved fireplace" and "controlled solid fuel"

(1) In section 19B, "approved fireplace" means a fireplace of a type specified in a list published by the Secretary of State.

(2) The Secretary of State may only specify a type of fireplace in the list if satisfied that such a fireplace can, if used in compliance with any conditions specified in the list, be used for burning controlled solid fuel without producing any smoke or a substantial quantity of smoke.

(3) In section 19B and this section, "controlled solid fuel" means any solid fuel other than an approved fuel.

(4) In subsection (3), "approved fuel" means a solid fuel specified in a list which has been published by the Secretary of State for the purposes of this section."

5 After section 26 insert—

"26A Duty of local authority to reimburse for adaptations of vessels in England

(1) This section applies where—

(a) a local authority in England makes a smoke control order,

(b) as a result of the order a vessel will, when the order comes into operation, be within a smoke control area and subject to the operation of Schedule 1A,

(c) the owner or occupier of the vessel has a right to moor the vessel at a single mooring place within that area for the period which—

(i) begins on the day on which the smoke control order is made, and

(ii) ends six months after it comes into operation, and

(d) the owner or occupier does not have access to a mains electricity or gas supply at the mooring place.

(2) If—

(a) before the coming into operation of the order, the owner or occupier incurs expenditure on adaptations to or in connection with the vessel to avoid the imposition of a penalty under Schedule 1A,

(b) the expenditure is incurred with the approval of the local authority given for the purpose of this section, and

(c) the adaptations are completed to the satisfaction of the local authority,

the authority must pay to the owner or occupier of the vessel 70% of the expenditure.

(3) That amount must be paid in equal instalments every month for a period of six months.

(4) But the duty to pay instalments under this section ceases if, at any time after the coming into operation of the smoke control order—

(a) the owner or occupier of the vessel ceases to have the right to moor the vessel at the single mooring place mentioned in subsection (1)(c), or

(b) the vessel is absent from the smoke control area for a period of, or periods together totalling, three months."

6 After section 28 insert—

"28A Guidance for local authorities in England

A local authority in England must have regard to any guidance published by the Secretary of State about the exercise of the authority's functions under this Part."

7 In section 44 (vessels), after subsection (2) insert—

"(2A) A smoke control order made under section 18 by a local authority in England may provide for vessels which are moored in the smoke control area to be subject to the operation of Schedule 1A.

(2B) For the purposes of a smoke control order which so provides—

(a) any reference in Part 3 and in section 54 to a building is to be read with any necessary modifications as a reference to such a vessel, but

(b) references in sections 24 and 25 to dwellings do not include such vessels.

(2C) In subsection (2A) the reference to vessels which are moored includes a vessel which is unmoored but which is stationary at a mooring place in circumstances where it might reasonably be moored."

8 In section 56 (rights of entry and inspection etc), for subsection (2) substitute—

"(2) Subsection (1) does not apply in relation to a private dwelling except in relation to—

(a) a private dwelling in relation to which adaptations are required under section 24(1), or

(b) a private dwelling that is a vessel in relation to which there is a duty to make payments under section 26A(3)."

Part 2

Principal amendments to the Clean Air Act 1993: Wales

9 The Clean Air Act 1993 is amended as follows.

10 (1) Section 20 (prohibition on emission of smoke in smoke control area) is amended as follows.

(2) After subsection (5C) insert—

"(5D) In the application of this Part to Wales, "authorised fuel" means a fuel included in a list of authorised fuels kept by the Welsh Ministers for the purposes of this Part.

(5E) The Welsh Ministers must—

(a) publish the list of authorised fuels, and

(b) publish a revised copy of the list as soon as is reasonably practicable after any change is made to it.

(5F) The list must be published in such manner as the Welsh Ministers consider appropriate."

(3) Omit subsection (6).

11 (1) Section 21 (power to exempt certain fireplaces) is amended as follows.

(2) After subsection (4) insert—

"(4A) For the purposes of the application of this Part to Wales, the Welsh Ministers may exempt any class of fireplace from the provisions of section 20 (prohibition of smoke emissions in smoke control area) if they are satisfied that such fireplaces can be used for burning fuel other than authorised fuels without producing any smoke or a substantial quantity of smoke.

(4B) An exemption under subsection (4A) may be made subject to such conditions as the Welsh Ministers consider appropriate.

(4C) The Welsh Ministers must—

(a) publish a list of those classes of fireplace that are exempt under subsection (4A) including details of any conditions to which an exemption is subject;

(b) publish a revised copy of the list as soon as is reasonably practicable after any change is made to the classes of fireplace that are so exempt or to the conditions to which an exemption is subject.

(4D) The list must be published in such manner as the Welsh Ministers consider appropriate."

(3) Omit subsection (5).

PART 3

MINOR AND CONSEQUENTIAL AMENDMENTS

Minor and consequential amendments to the Clean Air Act 1993

12 The Clean Air Act 1993 is amended as follows.

13 (1) Section 18 (declaration of smoke control area by local authority) is amended as follows.

(2) In subsection (2)—

(a) in paragraph (b)—

(i) after "smoke" insert "in Wales";

(ii) before "to" insert "or Schedule 1A (penalty for emission of smoke in England)";

(b) in paragraph (c), after "section" insert "or Schedule".

(3) After subsection (2) insert—

"(2A) For the purposes of this Part a smoke control order in England "applies" to a building, fireplace, fixed boiler or industrial plant if the operation of Schedule 1A is not excluded in relation to it by virtue of subsection (2)(b) or (c)."

14 (1) Section 20 (prohibition on emission of smoke in smoke control area) is amended as follows.

(2) In the heading, at the end insert "in Wales".

(3) In subsections (1) and (2), after "area" insert "in Wales".

(4) Omit subsections (5ZA) to (5ZC).

(5) If at the time of the coming into force of this paragraph Part 2 of this Schedule is not in force, in subsection (6)—

(a) omit "Except as provided by subsection (5ZA),";

(b) for "Secretary of State" substitute "Welsh Ministers".

15 (1) Section 21 (power to exempt certain fireplaces) is amended as follows.

(2) In the heading, at the end insert "in Wales".

(3) Omit subsections (A1) to (A4).

(4) If at the time of the coming into force of this paragraph Part 2 of this Schedule is not in force, in subsection (5)—

(a) omit "Except where subsection (A1) applies,";

(b) for "Secretary of State" substitute "Welsh Ministers";

(c) for "he is" substitute "they are".

16 (1) Section 22 (exemptions relating to particular areas) is amended as follows.

(2) In the heading, at the end insert "in Wales".

(3) In subsection (1)—

(a) for "Secretary of State" substitute "Welsh Ministers";

(b) for "him" substitute "them";

(c) after "area", in both places, insert "in Wales".

(4) In subsection (2)—

(a) for "Secretary of State" substitute "Welsh Ministers";

(b) for "he is" substitute "they are".

17 (1) Section 23 (acquisition and sale of unauthorised fuel in a smoke control area) is amended as follows.

(2) In the heading, at the end insert "in Wales".

(3) In subsection (1)—

(a) in paragraph (a), after "area" in both places insert "in Wales";

(b) in paragraph (b), after "area" insert "in Wales";

(c) in paragraph (c)—

(i) after "fuel" insert "in Wales";

(ii) in sub-paragraph (i), after "area" insert "in Wales".

(4) In subsection (3), after "area" insert "in Wales".

(5) In subsection (4)—

(a) for "Secretary of State" substitute "Welsh Ministers";

(b) after first "area" insert "in Wales".

(6) In subsection (5)—

(a) after first "fuel" insert "in Wales";

(b) after "premises" insert "in Wales".

18 In section 24 (power to require adaptations of fireplaces), in subsection (1)—

(a) after second "area" insert "in Wales";

(b) at the end insert "or the imposition of a financial penalty under Schedule 1A (penalty for emission of smoke in England)".

19 In section 26 (power to make grants for fireplaces in churches etc)—

(a) in subsection (1)—

(i) after second "area" insert "in Wales";

(ii) before ", the local authority" insert "or the imposition of a financial penalty under Schedule 1A (penalty for emission of smoke in England)";

(b) after subsection (2) insert—

"(3) Where a smoke control order in England applies to a vessel which is moored (see section 44), subsection (2)(c) applies to the vessel as it applies in relation to premises."

20 In section 27 (references to adaptations)—

(a) in the heading, at the end insert "or Schedule 1A";

(b) in subsection (1)—

(i) after "area" insert "in Wales";

(ii) before "shall be read" insert "or the imposition of a financial penalty under Schedule 1A (penalty for emission of smoke in England)";

(iii) at the end insert "or incurring liability under Schedule 1A";

(c) in subsection (3), after "Act" insert "or liability under Schedule 1A to this Act";

(d) in subsection (4), at the end insert ", and to any vessel to which section 26 or 26A (adaptations of vessels in England) applies".

21 In section 28 (expenditure on execution of works), in subsection (3), at the end insert ", and to any vessel to which section 26 or section 26A (adaptations of vessels in England) applies".

22 In section 29 (interpretation)—

(a) in the definition of "old private dwelling", omit the final "and";

(b) in the definition of "smoke control order", at the end insert "and";

(c) after that definition insert—

""smoke control order in England" means a smoke control order made by a local authority in England."

23 In section 63 (orders and regulations)—

(a) in subsection (2), after "47(2)" insert "or paragraph 3(4) or 4(6) of Schedule 1A";

(b) in subsection (3), after "section" insert "19C,".

24 (1) Schedule 1 (coming into operation of smoke control orders) is amended as follows.

(2) In paragraph 5—

(a) after "area" insert "in Wales";

(b) before "may" insert "or Schedule 1A (penalty for emission of smoke in England)".

(3) After paragraph 6 insert—

"6A When a local authority in England has made an order, the authority must—

(a) inform the Secretary of State that it has done so, and

(b) provide the date on which the order is to come, or came, into operation."

Minor amendments to other legislation

25 In section 79 of the Environmental Protection Act 1990 (statutory nuisances), in subsection (3)(i), insert "in Wales".

PART 4

SMOKE CONTROL AREAS IN ENGLAND: TRANSITIONAL PROVISION

26 Where a local authority in England has made a smoke control order under section 18 of the Clean Air Act 1993, any limitations or exemptions from the operation of section 20 of that Act (prohibition of emissions of smoke) made by that order under section 18(2)(b) or (c) of that Act that apply immediately before the commencement of Parts 1 and 3 of this Schedule continue to apply as if they were limitations or exemptions from the operation of Schedule 1A to that Act (penalty for emission of smoke), as inserted by paragraph 3 of this Schedule.

SCHEDULE 13

SECTION 86

MODIFYING WATER AND SEWERAGE UNDERTAKERS' APPOINTMENTS: PROCEDURE FOR APPEALS

"SCHEDULE 2ZA

SECTION 12E

PROCEDURE FOR APPEALS UNDER SECTION 12D

Application for permission to bring appeal

1 (1) An application for permission to bring an appeal may be made only by sending a notice to the CMA requesting the permission.

(2) Only a person entitled under section 12D to bring the appeal if permission is granted may apply for permission.

(3) Where the Authority publishes a decision to modify the conditions of any appointment under section 12A(9), any application for permission to

appeal is not to be made after the end of 20 working days beginning with the first working day after the day on which the decision is published.

(4) An application for permission to appeal must be accompanied by all such information as may be required by appeal rules.

(5) Appeal rules may require information contained in an application for permission to appeal to be verified by a statement of truth.

(6) A person who applies for permission to bring an appeal in accordance with this paragraph is referred to in this Schedule as the appellant.

(7) The appellant must send the Authority—

(a) a copy of the application for permission to appeal at the same time as it is sent to the CMA, and

(b) such other information as may be required by appeal rules.

(8) The CMA's decision whether to grant permission to appeal is to be taken by an authorised member of the CMA.

(9) Before the authorised member decides whether to grant permission under this paragraph, the Authority must be given an opportunity of making representations or observations, in accordance with paragraph 3(2).

(10) The CMA's decision on an application for permission to appeal must be made—

(a) where the Authority makes representations or observations in accordance with paragraph 3(2), before the end of 10 working days beginning with the first working day after the day on which those representations or observations are received;

(b) in any other case, before the end of 14 working days beginning with the first working day after the day on which the application for permission was received.

(11) The grant of permission may be made subject to conditions, which may include—

(a) conditions which limit the matters that are to be considered on the appeal in question,

(b) conditions for the purpose of expediting the determination of the appeal, and

(c) conditions requiring that appeal to be considered together with other appeals (including appeals relating to different matters or decisions and appeals brought by different persons).

(12) Where a decision is made to grant or to refuse an application for permission, an authorised member of the CMA must notify the decision, giving reasons—

(a) to the appellant, and

(b) to the Authority.

(13) A decision of the CMA under this paragraph must be published, in a way an authorised member of the CMA considers appropriate, as soon as reasonably practicable after it is made.

(14) Section 12I(2) applies to the publication of a decision under sub-paragraph (13) as it does to the publication under section 12I of a determination by the CMA on an appeal.

Suspension of decision

2 (1) The CMA may direct that, pending the determination of an appeal against a decision of the Authority—

(a) the decision is not to have effect, or

(b) the decision is not to have effect to such extent as may be specified in the direction.

(2) In the case of an appeal against a decision of the Authority which already has effect by virtue of section 12B, the CMA may direct that the modification that is the subject of the decision—

(a) ceases to have effect entirely or to such extent as may be specified in the direction, and

(b) does not have effect, or does not have effect to the specified extent, pending the determination of the appeal.

(3) The power to give a direction under this paragraph is exercisable only where—

(a) an application for its exercise has been made by the appellant at the same time the appellant made an application in accordance with paragraph 1(3) for permission to bring an appeal against a decision of the Authority,

(b) the Authority has been given an opportunity of making representations or observations, in accordance with paragraph 3(2),

(c) the appellant (or, where the appellant is within section 12D(2)(c) or (d), those represented by the appellant, or consumers, respectively) would incur significant costs if the decision were to have effect before the determination of the appeal, and

(d) the balance of convenience does not otherwise require effect to be given to the decision pending that determination.

(4) The CMA's decision on an application for a direction under this paragraph must be made—

(a) where the Authority makes representations or observations in accordance with paragraph 3(2), before the end of 10 working days beginning with the first working day after the day on which those representations or observations are received;

(b) in any other case, before the end of 14 working days beginning with the first working day following the day on which the application under sub-paragraph (3)(a) is received.

(5) The appellant must send the Authority a copy of the application for a direction under this paragraph at the same time as it is sent to the CMA.

(6) A direction under this paragraph must be—

(a) given by an authorised member of the CMA, and

(b) published, in a way an authorised member of the CMA considers appropriate, as soon as reasonably practicable after it is given.

(7) Section 12I(2) applies to the publication of a direction under sub-paragraph (6) as it does to the publication under section 12I of a determination by the CMA on an appeal.

Time limit for representations and observations by the Authority

3 (1) Sub-paragraph (2) applies where the Authority wishes to make representations or observations to the CMA in relation to—

(a) an application for permission to bring an appeal under paragraph 1;

(b) an application for a direction under paragraph 2.

(2) The Authority must make the representations or observations in writing before the end of 10 working days beginning with the first working day after the day on which it received a copy of the application under paragraph 1(7) or 2(5) as the case may be.

(3) Sub-paragraph (4) applies where an application for permission to bring an appeal has been granted and the Authority wishes to make representations or observations to the CMA in relation to—

(a) the Authority's reasons for the decision in relation to which the appeal is being brought, and

(b) any grounds on which that appeal is being brought against that decision.

(4) The Authority must make the representations or observations in writing before the end of 15 working days beginning with the first working day after the day on which permission to bring the appeal was granted.

(5) The Authority must send a copy of the representations and observations it makes under this paragraph to the appellant.

Consideration and determination of appeal by group

4 (1) A group constituted by the chair of the CMA under Schedule 4 to the Enterprise and Regulatory Reform Act 2013 for the purpose of carrying out functions of the CMA with respect to an appeal under section 12D must consist of three members of the CMA panel.

(2) A decision of the group is effective if, and only if—

(a) all the members of the group are present when it is made, and

(b) at least two members of the group are in favour of the decision.

Matters to be considered on appeal

5 (1) The CMA, if it thinks it necessary to do so for the purpose of securing the determination of an appeal within the period provided for by section 12H, may disregard—

(a) any or all matters raised by an appellant that were not raised by that appellant at the time of the relevant application, and

(b) any or all matters raised by the Authority that were not contained in representations or observations made for the purposes of the appeal in accordance with paragraph 3.

(2) In this paragraph "relevant application" means an application under paragraph 1 or 2.

Production of documents etc

6 (1) For the purposes of this Schedule, the CMA may, by notice, require—

(a) a person to produce to the CMA the documents specified or otherwise identified in the notice;

(b) any person who carries on a business to supply to the CMA such estimates, forecasts, returns or other information as may be specified or described in the notice in relation to that business.

(2) The power to require the production of a document, or the supply of any estimate, forecast, return or other information, is a power to require its production or, as the case may be, supply—

(a) at the time and place specified in the notice, and

(b) in a legible form.

(3) No person is to be compelled under this paragraph to produce a document or supply an estimate, forecast, return or other information that the person could not be compelled to produce in civil proceedings in the High Court.

(4) An authorised member of the CMA may, for the purpose of the exercise of the functions of the CMA, make arrangements for copies to be taken of a document produced or an estimate, forecast, return or other information supplied under this paragraph.

(5) A notice for the purposes of this paragraph—

(a) may be issued on the CMA's behalf by an authorised member of the CMA;

(b) must include information about the possible consequences of not complying with the notice (as set out in paragraph 10).

Oral hearings

7 (1) For the purposes of this Schedule an oral hearing may be held, and evidence may be taken on oath—

(a) by a person considering an application for permission to bring an appeal under paragraph 1,

(b) by a person considering an application for a direction under paragraph 2, or

(c) by a group with the function of determining an appeal,

and, for that purpose, such a person or group may administer oaths.

(2) The CMA may, by notice, require a person—

(a) to attend at a time and place specified in the notice, and

(b) at that time and place, to give evidence to a person or group mentioned in sub-paragraph (1).

(3) At any oral hearing, the person or group conducting the hearing may require—

(a) the appellant, or the Authority, if present at the hearing to give evidence or to make representations or observations, or

(b) a person attending the hearing as a representative of the appellant or of the Authority to make representations or observations.

(4) A person who gives oral evidence at the hearing may be cross-examined by or on behalf of any party to the appeal.

(5) If the appellant, the Authority, or the appellant's or Authority's representative is not present at a hearing—

(a) there is no requirement to give notice to that person under sub-paragraph (2), and

(b) the person or group conducting the hearing may determine the application or appeal without hearing that person's evidence, representations or observations.

(6) No person is to be compelled under this paragraph to give evidence which that person could not be compelled to give in civil proceedings in the High Court.

(7) Where a person is required under this paragraph to attend at a place more than 10 miles from that person's place of residence, an authorised member of the CMA must arrange for that person to be paid the necessary expenses of attendance.

(8) A notice for the purposes of this paragraph may be issued on the CMA's behalf by an authorised member of the CMA.

Written statements

8 (1) The CMA may, by notice, require a person to produce a written statement with respect to a matter specified in the notice to—

(a) a person who is considering, or is to consider, an application for a direction under paragraph 2, or

(b) a group with the function of determining an appeal.

(2) The power to require the production of a written statement includes power—

(a) to specify the time and place at which it is to be produced, and

(b) to require it to be verified by a statement of truth,

and a statement required to be so verified must be disregarded unless it is so verified.

(3) No person is to be compelled under this paragraph to produce a written statement with respect to any matter about which that person could not be compelled to give evidence in civil proceedings in the High Court.

(4) A notice for the purposes of this paragraph may be issued on the CMA's behalf by an authorised member of the CMA.

Expert advice

9 Where permission to bring an appeal is granted under paragraph 1, the CMA may commission expert advice with respect to any matter raised by a party to that appeal.

Defaults in relation to evidence

10 (1) This paragraph applies if a person ("the defaulter")—

(a) fails to comply with a notice issued or other requirement imposed under paragraph 6, 7 or 8,

(b) in complying with a notice under paragraph 8, makes a statement that is false in any material particular, or

(c) in providing information verified in accordance with a statement of truth required by appeal rules, provides information that is false in a material particular.

(2) An authorised member of the CMA may certify the failure, or the fact that such a false statement has been made or such false information has been given, to the High Court.

(3) The High Court may inquire into a matter certified to it under this paragraph and if, after having heard—

(a) any witness against or on behalf of the defaulter, and

(b) any statement in the defaulter's defence,

it is satisfied that the defaulter, without reasonable excuse, failed to comply with the notice or other requirement, or made the false statement, or gave the false information, that court may punish that defaulter as if the person had been guilty of contempt of court.

(4) Where the High Court has power under this paragraph to punish a body corporate for contempt of court, it may so punish any director or other officer of that body (either instead of or as well as punishing the body).

(5) A person who wilfully alters, suppresses or destroys a document that the person has been required to produce under paragraph 6 is guilty of an offence and shall be liable—

(a) on summary conviction to a fine;

(b) on conviction on indictment, to imprisonment for a term not exceeding two years or to a fine, or to both.

Appeal rules

11 (1) The CMA Board may make rules of procedure regulating the conduct and disposal of appeals under section 12D.

(2) Those rules may include provision supplementing the provisions of this Schedule in relation to any application, notice, hearing, power or requirement for which this Schedule provides; and that provision may, in particular, impose time limits or other restrictions on—

(a) the taking of evidence at an oral hearing, or

(b) the making of representations or observations at such a hearing.

(3) The CMA Board must publish rules made under this paragraph in a way it considers appropriate for bringing them to the attention of those likely to be affected by them.

(4) Before making rules under this paragraph, the CMA Board must consult such persons as it considers appropriate.

(5) Rules under this paragraph may make different provision for different cases.

Costs

12 (1) A group that determines an appeal must make an order requiring the payment to the CMA of the costs incurred by the CMA in connection with the appeal.

(2) An order under sub-paragraph (1) must require those costs to be paid—

(a) where the appeal is allowed in full, by the Authority,

(b) where the appeal is dismissed in full, by the appellant, or

(c) where the appeal is partially allowed, by one or more parties in such proportions as the CMA considers appropriate in all the circumstances.

(3) The group that determines an appeal may also make such order as it thinks fit for requiring a party to the appeal to make payments to another party in respect of costs reasonably incurred by that other party in connection with the appeal.

(4) A person who is required by an order under this paragraph to pay a sum to another person must comply with the order before the end of the period of 28 days beginning with the day after the making of the order.

(5) Sums required to be paid by an order under this paragraph but not paid within the period mentioned in sub-paragraph (4) shall bear interest at such rate as may be determined in accordance with provision contained in the order.

(6) Any costs payable by virtue of an order under this paragraph and any interest that has not been paid may be recovered as a civil debt by the person in whose favour that order is made.

Interpretation of Schedule

13 (1) In this Schedule—

"appeal" means an appeal under section 12D;

"appeal rules" means rules of procedure under paragraph 11;

"authorised member of the CMA"—

(a) in relation to a power exercisable in connection with an appeal in respect of which a group has been constituted by the chair of the CMA under Schedule 4 to the Enterprise and Regulatory Reform Act 2013, means a member of that group who has been authorised by the chair of the CMA to exercise that power;

(b) in relation to a power exercisable in connection with an application for permission to bring an appeal, or otherwise in connection with an appeal in respect of which a group has not been so constituted by the chair of the CMA, means—

(i) any member of the CMA Board who is also a member of the CMA panel, or

(ii) any member of the CMA panel authorised by the Secretary of State (whether generally or specifically) to exercise the power in question;

"CMA Board" and "CMA panel" have the same meaning as in Schedule 4 to the Enterprise and Regulatory Reform Act 2013;

"statement of truth", in relation to the production of a statement or provision of information by a person, means a statement that the person believes the facts stated in the statement or information to be true;

"working day" means any day other than—

(a) Saturday or Sunday;

(b) Christmas Day or Good Friday;

(c) a day which is a bank holiday in England and Wales under the Banking and Financial Dealings Act 1971.

(2) References in this Schedule to a party to an appeal are references to—

(a) the appellant, or

(b) the Authority."

SCHEDULE 14

SECTION 98

BIODIVERSITY GAIN AS CONDITION OF PLANNING PERMISSION

PART 1

BIODIVERSITY GAIN CONDITION

1 In the Town and Country Planning Act 1990, after section 90 insert—

"Biodiversity gain

90A Biodiversity gain in England

Schedule 7A (biodiversity gain in England) has effect."

2 In that Act, after Schedule 7 insert—

"SCHEDULE 7A

SECTION 90A

BIODIVERSITY GAIN IN ENGLAND

PART 1

OVERVIEW AND INTERPRETATION

Overview

1 (1) This Schedule makes provision for grants of planning permission in England to be subject to a condition to secure that the biodiversity gain objective is met.

(2) Paragraphs 2 to 12 have effect for the purposes of this Schedule.

Biodiversity gain objective

2 (1) The biodiversity gain objective is met in relation to development for which planning permission is granted if the biodiversity value attributable to the development exceeds the pre-development biodiversity value of the onsite habitat by at least the relevant percentage.

(2) The biodiversity value attributable to the development is the total of—

(a) the post-development biodiversity value of the onsite habitat,

(b) the biodiversity value, in relation to the development, of any registered offsite biodiversity gain allocated to the development, and

(c) the biodiversity value of any biodiversity credits purchased for the development.

(3) The relevant percentage is 10%.

(4) The Secretary of State may by regulations amend this paragraph so as to change the relevant percentage.

Biodiversity value and the biodiversity metric

3 References to the biodiversity value of any habitat or habitat enhancement are to its value as calculated in accordance with the biodiversity metric.

4 (1) The biodiversity metric is a document for measuring, for the purposes of this Schedule, the biodiversity value or relative biodiversity value of habitat or habitat enhancement.

(2) The biodiversity metric is to be produced and published by the Secretary of State.

(3) The Secretary of State may from time to time revise and republish the biodiversity metric.

(4) Before publishing or republishing the biodiversity metric the Secretary of State must consult such persons as the Secretary of State considers appropriate.

(5) The Secretary of State may by regulations make transitional provision in relation to the revision and republication of the biodiversity metric.

(6) The Secretary of State must lay the biodiversity metric, and any revised biodiversity metric, before Parliament.

Pre-development biodiversity value

5 (1) In relation to any development for which planning permission is granted, the pre-development biodiversity value of the onsite habitat is the biodiversity value of the onsite habitat on the relevant date.

(2) The relevant date is—

(a) in a case in which planning permission is granted on application, the date of the application, and

(b) in any other case, the date on which the planning permission is granted.

(3) But the person submitting the biodiversity gain plan for approval and the planning authority may agree that the relevant date is to be a date earlier than that specified in sub-paragraph (2)(a) or (b) (but not a date which is before the day on which this Schedule comes into force in relation to the development).

(4) This paragraph is subject to paragraphs 6 and 7.

6 If—

(a) a person carries on activities on land on or after 30 January 2020 otherwise than in accordance with—

(i) planning permission, or

(ii) any other permission of a kind specified by the Secretary of State by regulations, and

(b) as a result of the activities the biodiversity value of the onsite habitat referred to in paragraph 5(1) is lower on the relevant date than it would otherwise have been,

the pre-development biodiversity value of the onsite habitat is to be taken to be its biodiversity value immediately before the carrying on of the activities.

7 Where planning permission is granted in respect of land which is registered in the biodiversity gain site register under section 100 of the Environment Act 2021, the pre-development biodiversity value of the land is the total of—

(a) the biodiversity value of the onsite habitat on the relevant date, and

(b) to the extent that it is not included within that value, the biodiversity value of the habitat enhancement which is, on that date, recorded in the register as habitat enhancement to be achieved on the land.

8 (1) In relation to any development for which planning permission is granted, the post-development biodiversity value of the onsite habitat is the projected value of the onsite habitat as at the time the development is completed.

(2) That value is to be calculated by taking the pre-development biodiversity value and—

(a) if at the time the development is completed the development will, taken as a whole, have increased the biodiversity value of the onsite habitat, adding the amount of that increase, or

(b) if at the time the development is completed the development will, taken as a whole, have decreased the biodiversity value of the onsite habitat, subtracting the amount of that decrease.

This is subject to paragraph 9.

9 (1) This paragraph applies in relation to any development for which planning permission is granted where—

(a) the person submitting the biodiversity gain plan for approval proposes to carry out works in the course of the development that increase the biodiversity value of the onsite habitat, and

(b) the planning authority considers that the increase is significant in relation to the pre-development biodiversity value.

(2) The increase in biodiversity value referred to in sub-paragraph (1) is to be taken into account in calculating the post-development biodiversity value of the onsite habitat only if the planning authority is satisfied that the condition in sub-paragraph (3) is met.

(3) The condition is that any habitat enhancement resulting from the works referred to in sub-paragraph (1)(a) will, by virtue of—

(a) a condition subject to which the planning permission is granted,

(b) a planning obligation, or

(c) a conservation covenant,

be maintained for at least 30 years after the development is completed.

(4) The Secretary of State may by regulations amend sub-paragraph (3) so as to substitute for the period for the time being specified there a different period of at least 30 years.

Registered offsite biodiversity gains

10 (1) "Registered offsite biodiversity gain" means any habitat enhancement, where—

(a) the enhancement is required to be carried out under a conservation covenant or planning obligation, and

(b) the enhancement is recorded in the biodiversity gain site register (as to which, see section 100 of the Environment Act 2021).

(2) References to the allocation of registered offsite biodiversity gain are to its allocation in accordance with the terms of the conservation covenant or planning obligation referred to in sub-paragraph (1)(a).

(3) The biodiversity value of registered offsite biodiversity gain is measured, under the biodiversity metric, in relation to development to which it is allocated.

Biodiversity credits

11 "Biodiversity credits" means credits under section 101 of the Environment Act 2021.

General

12 (1) In relation to development for which planning permission is granted—

"onsite habitat" means habitat on the land to which the planning permission relates;

"planning authority" means the local planning authority, except that—

(a) in a case where the planning permission is granted by Mayoral development order under section 61DB, "planning authority" means such of the Mayor of London or the local planning authority as may be specified in the order;

(b) in a case where the planning permission is granted by the Secretary of State under section 62A, 76A or 77, "planning authority" means such of the Secretary of State or the local planning authority as the Secretary of State may determine;

(c) in a case where the planning permission is granted on an appeal under section 78, "planning authority" means such of the person determining the appeal or the local planning authority as that person may direct.

(2) "Habitat enhancement" means enhancement of the biodiversity of habitat.

(3) References to the grant of planning permission include the deemed grant of planning permission.

PART 2

CONDITION OF PLANNING PERMISSION RELATING TO BIODIVERSITY GAIN

General condition of planning permission

13 (1) Every planning permission granted for the development of land in England shall be deemed to have been granted subject to the condition in sub-paragraph (2).

(2) The condition is that the development may not be begun unless—

(a) a biodiversity gain plan has been submitted to the planning authority (see paragraph 14), and

(b) the planning authority has approved the plan (see paragraph 15).

Biodiversity gain plan

14 (1) For the purposes of paragraph 13(2)(a), a biodiversity gain plan is a plan which—

(a) relates to development for which planning permission is granted, and

(b) specifies the matters referred to in sub-paragraph (2).

(2) The matters are—

(a) information about the steps taken or to be taken to minimise the adverse effect of the development on the biodiversity of the onsite habitat and any other habitat,

(b) the pre-development biodiversity value of the onsite habitat,

(c) the post-development biodiversity value of the onsite habitat,

(d) any registered offsite biodiversity gain allocated to the development and the biodiversity value of that gain in relation to the development,

(e) any biodiversity credits purchased for the development, and

(f) such other matters as the Secretary of State may by regulations specify.

(3) The Secretary of State may by regulations make provision about—

(a) any other matters to be included in a biodiversity gain plan;

(b) the form of a biodiversity gain plan;

(c) the procedure to be followed in relation to the submission of a biodiversity gain plan (including the time by which a plan must be submitted);

(d) persons who may or must submit a biodiversity gain plan.

Approval of biodiversity gain plan

15 (1) For the purposes of paragraph 13(2)(b) a planning authority to which a biodiversity gain plan is submitted must approve the plan if, and only if, it is satisfied as to the matters specified in sub-paragraph (2).

(2) The matters are—

(a) that the pre-development biodiversity value of the onsite habitat is as specified in the plan,

(b) that the post-development biodiversity value of the onsite habitat is at least the value specified in the plan,

(c) that, in a case where any registered offsite biodiversity gain is specified in the plan as allocated to the development—

(i) the registered offsite biodiversity gain is so allocated (and, if the allocation is conditional, that any conditions attaching to the allocation have been met or will be met by the time the development begins), and

(ii) the registered offsite biodiversity gain has the biodiversity value specified in the plan in relation to the development,

(d) that any biodiversity credits specified in the plan as purchased for the development have been so purchased,

(e) that the biodiversity gain objective is met, and

(f) any other matters specified in the plan under paragraph 14(2)(f).

Regulations about determinations

16 The Secretary of State may make regulations as to—

(a) the procedure which a planning authority is to follow in determining whether to approve a biodiversity gain plan (including the time by which a determination must be made);

(b) factors which may or must be taken into account in making such a determination;

(c) appeals relating to such a determination.

Exceptions

17 Paragraph 13 does not apply in relation to—

(a) development for which planning permission is granted—

(i) by a development order, or

(ii) under section 293A (urgent Crown development), or

(b) development of such other description as the Secretary of State may by regulations specify.

Modifications for irreplaceable habitat

18 (1) The Secretary of State may by regulations make provision modifying or excluding the application of this Part of this Schedule in relation to any development for which planning permission is granted where the onsite habitat is "irreplaceable habitat" as defined in the regulations.

(2) Regulations under this paragraph must make provision requiring, in relation to any such development, the making of arrangements for the purpose of minimising the adverse effect of the development on the biodiversity of the onsite habitat.

(3) Regulations under this paragraph may confer powers and duties, including powers and duties in relation to the giving of guidance, on Natural England.

Modifications for particular kinds of planning permission

19 (1) The Secretary of State may by regulations make provision modifying the application of this Part of this Schedule in relation to—

(a) the grant of outline planning permission, where the reservation of matters for subsequent approval has the effect of requiring or permitting development to proceed in phases, or

(b) the grant of any kind of planning permission, where the grant is subject to conditions (whether requiring the subsequent approval of any matters or otherwise) having that effect.

(2) Regulations under this paragraph may include provision for a grant of planning permission referred to in sub-paragraph (1)(a) or (b) to be subject to conditions relating to meeting the biodiversity gain objective referred to in paragraph 2.

20 (1) The Secretary of State may by regulations make provision modifying or excluding the application of this Part of this Schedule in relation to development for which—

(a) planning permission is granted under section 73A (planning permission for development already carried out), or

(b) planning permission is granted by an order under section 102 (orders requiring discontinuance of use etc).

(2) Regulations under this paragraph may in particular include provision—

(a) for paragraph 13 not to apply in relation to the grant of planning permission referred to in sub-paragraph (1)(a) or (b);

(b) for the grant of any such planning permission to be subject to other conditions relating to meeting the biodiversity gain objective.

(3) The conditions referred to in sub-paragraph (2)(b) may include conditions requiring—

(a) habitat enhancement on the land to which the planning permission relates;

(b) the allocation of registered offsite biodiversity gain to any development for which the planning permission is granted;

(c) the purchase of biodiversity credits for any such development.

Further application of this Part

21 The Secretary of State may by regulations make provision to apply this Part of this Schedule in relation to development for which planning permission is granted under section 141 or 177(1), with such modifications or exclusions as may be specified in the regulations."

Part 2

Consequential amendments

3 (1) The Town and Country Planning Act 1990 is amended as follows.

(2) In section 56 (time when development begins), in subsection (3), at the end insert "and paragraph 13 of Schedule 7A".

(3) In section 69 (register of applications etc)—

(a) in subsection (1), at the end insert—

"(e) applications for approval of biodiversity gain plans under Part 2 of Schedule 7A.";

(b) in subsection (2)(a), for "and (aza)" substitute ", (aza) and (e)".

(4) In section 70 (determination of applications: general considerations), in subsection (1)(a), after "section 62D(5)" insert ", paragraph 13 of Schedule 7A".

(5) In section 73 (determination of applications to develop land after non-compliance), after subsection (2A) insert—

"(2B) Nothing in this section authorises the disapplication of the condition under paragraph 13 of Schedule 7A (biodiversity gain condition).

(2C) Subsection (2D) applies where—

(a) for the purposes of paragraph 13 of Schedule 7A a biodiversity gain plan was approved in relation to the previous planning permission ("the earlier biodiversity gain plan"),

(b) planning permission is granted under this section, and

(c) the conditions subject to which the planning permission is granted under this section do not affect the post-development biodiversity value of the onsite habitat as specified in the earlier biodiversity gain plan.

(2D) Where this subsection applies, the earlier biodiversity gain plan is regarded as approved for the purposes of paragraph 13 of Schedule 7A in relation to the planning permission granted under this section."

(6) In section 74A (deemed discharge of planning permission conditions), after subsection (2) insert—

"(2A) But this section does not apply to the condition under paragraph 13 of Schedule 7A (biodiversity gain condition)."

(7) In section 76C (provisions applying to applications made under section 62A), in subsection (2), after "Schedule 1" insert ", or by regulations under paragraph 14(3) or 16 of Schedule 7A,".

(8) In section 84 (simplified planning zone schemes: conditions and limitations on planning permission), at the end insert—

"(5) A simplified planning zone scheme may not disapply the condition under paragraph 13 of Schedule 7A (biodiversity gain condition)."

(9) In section 88 (enterprise zones), after subsection (3) insert—

"(3A) Subsection (3) is subject to paragraph 13 of Schedule 7A (biodiversity gain condition)."

(10) In section 96A (power to make non-material changes to planning permission), after subsection (3) insert—

"(3A) The conditions referred to in subsection (3)(b) do not include the condition under paragraph 13 of Schedule 7A (biodiversity gain condition)."

(11) In section 97 (revocation or modification of planning permission), at the end insert—

"(7) Subsection (1) does not permit the revocation or modification of the condition under paragraph 13 of Schedule 7A (the biodiversity gain condition), subject as follows.

(8) The Secretary of State may by regulations make provision—

(a) for the condition under paragraph 13 of Schedule 7A to apply in relation to the modification of planning permission under this section, subject to such modifications as may be specified in the regulations;

(b) for planning permission modified under this section to be subject to other conditions relating to meeting the biodiversity gain objective referred to in paragraph 2 of Schedule 7A (including conditions of a kind referred to in paragraph 20(3) of that Schedule)."

(12) In section 100ZA (restriction on power to impose planning conditions in England), in subsection (13)(c), after "limitation" insert "but do not include the condition under paragraph 13 of Schedule 7A (biodiversity gain condition)".

(13) In section 106 (planning obligations), in subsection (1), in the words before paragraph (a), after "106C" insert ", Schedule 7A".

(14) In section 106A (modification and discharge of planning obligations), after subsection (6) insert—

"(6A) Except in such cases as may be prescribed, the authority may not under subsection (6) discharge or modify the planning obligation if the authority considers that doing so would—

(a) prevent the biodiversity gain objective referred to in paragraph 2 of Schedule 7A from being met in relation to any development, or

(b) give rise to a significant risk of that objective not being met in relation to any development."

(15) In section 333 (regulations and orders), after subsection (3A) insert— "(3AA) No regulations may be made under paragraph 2(4) of Schedule 7A (biodiversity gain condition) unless a draft of the instrument containing the regulations has been laid before, and approved by a resolution of, each House of Parliament."

SCHEDULE 15

Section 99

Biodiversity gain in nationally significant infrastructure projects

Part 1

Principal amendments to the Planning Act 2008

1 The Planning Act 2008 is amended as follows.

2 In section 103 (Secretary of State is to decide applications), after subsection (1) insert—

"(1A) Schedule 2A makes provision about biodiversity gain in relation to decisions of the Secretary of State under sections 104 and 105; and for related matters."

3 (1) Section 104 (decisions in cases where national policy statement has effect) is amended as follows.

(2) For subsection (3) substitute—

"(3) The Secretary of State must decide the application in accordance with any relevant national policy statement.

(3A) In particular, if a relevant national policy statement contains a biodiversity gain statement under Schedule 2A in relation to development of the description to which the application relates, the Secretary of State may not grant the application unless satisfied that the biodiversity gain objective contained in the statement is met in relation to the development to which the application relates.

(3B) Subsections (3) and (3A) do not apply to the extent that one or more of subsections (4) to (8) applies."

(3) In each of subsections (4), (5) and (6), for "any relevant national policy statement" substitute "subsection (3) or (3A)".

(4) In subsection (8), for "a national policy statement" substitute "subsection (3) or (3A)".

4 (1) Section 105 (decisions in cases where no national policy statement has effect), after subsection (2) insert—

"(3) Where there is a biodiversity gain statement under Schedule 2A in relation to development of the description to which the application relates, the Secretary of State may not grant the application unless satisfied that the biodiversity gain objective contained in the statement is met in relation to the development to which the application relates.

(4) Subsection (3) does not apply to the extent that the Secretary of State is satisfied that deciding the application in accordance with that subsection would have an effect referred to in section 104(4), (5), (6) or (7)."

5 After Schedule 2 insert—

"SCHEDULE 2A **Section 103**

Biodiversity gain

Introductory

1 (1) This Schedule applies to development which—

(a) is of a description of development to which a development consent order application may relate, and

(b) is not excluded development,

to the extent that the development is carried out in England.

(2) In this Schedule—

"development consent order application" means an application made under section 37 which falls to be determined under section 104 or 105;

"excluded development" means development of a description specified in regulations made by the Secretary of State.

Biodiversity gain statement

2 (1) A biodiversity gain statement is a statement of government policy in relation to the biodiversity gain to be achieved in connection with any description of development to which this Schedule applies.

(2) In particular the statement must—

(a) set out a biodiversity gain objective for any description of development to which this Schedule applies, and

(b) set out that, where development consent order applications are made for any development of that description during a period specified in the statement, the development must meet that objective.

(3) The statement may specify how development of any description may or must meet the biodiversity gain objective.

(4) In this Schedule, references to the period for which a biodiversity gain statement has effect are to the period referred to in sub-paragraph (2)(b).

3 (1) A biodiversity gain objective is an objective that the biodiversity value attributable to development to which a biodiversity gain statement relates exceeds the pre-development biodiversity value of the onsite habitat by a percentage specified in the statement.

(2) The percentage specified under sub-paragraph (1) must be at least 10%.

(3) The Secretary of State may by regulations amend sub-paragraph (2) so as to change the percentage for the time being specified in it.

4 (1) A biodiversity gain statement may specify for the purposes of a biodiversity gain objective how the biodiversity value or relative biodiversity value of any habitat or habitat enhancement is to be calculated.

(2) That may include calculation by, or by reference to—

(a) a biodiversity metric set out in a document produced by the Secretary of State for the purposes of the statement,

(b) the biodiversity metric referred to in paragraph 4 of Schedule 7A to the Town and Country Planning Act 1990, or

(c) such other biodiversity metric as the Secretary of State considers appropriate.

(3) The Secretary of State must—

(a) lay any document within sub-paragraph (2)(a) before Parliament, and

(b) publish it in such manner as the Secretary of State considers appropriate.

5 (1) A biodiversity gain statement may specify for the purposes of a biodiversity gain objective—

(a) what the pre-development biodiversity value of onsite habitat consists of, and

(b) the date by reference to which it is calculated.

(2) A biodiversity gain statement may in particular under sub-paragraph (1)(b) specify a different date in relation to development on land where activities on the land before the making of a development consent order application have, or have had, the result that the biodiversity value of the onsite habitat is lower than it would otherwise have been.

(3) A biodiversity gain statement must include provision to secure that, where a development consent order application relates to land which is registered in the biodiversity gain site register, the pre-development biodiversity value of the onsite habitat includes the biodiversity value of the habitat enhancement which is, on the date specified under sub-paragraph (1)(b), recorded in the register as habitat enhancement to be achieved on the land.

6 (1) A biodiversity gain statement may specify for the purposes of a biodiversity gain objective what the biodiversity value attributable to any development consists of.

(2) In particular, a biodiversity gain statement may specify any of the following as included in the biodiversity value attributable to any development—

(a) the post-development biodiversity value of the onsite habitat,

(b) the biodiversity value of any offsite biodiversity gain allocated to the development (which may be registered offsite biodiversity gain), and

(c) the biodiversity value of any biodiversity credits purchased for the development.

(3) If pursuant to sub-paragraph (2)(a) a biodiversity gain statement specifies the post-development biodiversity value of the onsite habitat, the statement must specify what that value consists of.

(4) If pursuant to sub-paragraph (2)(b) a biodiversity gain statement specifies the biodiversity value of any offsite biodiversity gain allocated to the development, other than registered offsite biodiversity gain, the statement must specify—

(a) what offsite biodiversity gain consists of, and

(b) how the allocation of offsite biodiversity gain is to be recorded.

(5) Provision under sub-paragraph (3) or (4) must include provision to secure that, where works are carried out for the purposes of any development that increase the biodiversity value of onsite or offsite habitat by an amount that is significant in relation to its previous biodiversity value, the increase is to be taken into account only if—

(a) any habitat enhancement resulting from the works is maintained for a period specified in the statement, and

(b) the maintenance of that habitat enhancement is secured in a way specified in the statement (for example, through conservation covenants or requirements imposed by a development consent order).

7 (1) A biodiversity gain statement must set out whether, and if so how, the biodiversity gain objective applies in relation to development where the onsite habitat is irreplaceable habitat.

(2) A biodiversity gain statement may specify requirements, in relation to any such development, relating to the making of arrangements for the purpose of minimising the adverse effect of the development on the onsite habitat.

8 A biodiversity gain statement must specify the evidence that persons making a development consent order application in relation to which the statement has effect must produce in order to demonstrate how the biodiversity gain objective is met.

Development covered by an existing national policy statement

9 (1) This paragraph applies where, at the time this Schedule comes into force, an existing national policy statement sets out policy in respect of a description of development to which this Schedule applies.

(2) On the first review of the existing national policy statement under section 6 after the coming into force of this Schedule, the Secretary of State must amend the statement under section 6(5)(a) so as to include a biodiversity gain statement for development of that description.

(3) The Secretary of State may issue a separate biodiversity gain statement (a "separate biodiversity gain statement") having effect for any period before that for which the statement included in the existing national policy statement under sub-paragraph (2) has effect.

(4) Before issuing a separate biodiversity gain statement the Secretary of State must consult such persons as the Secretary of State considers appropriate.

(5) The Secretary of State must keep a separate biodiversity gain statement under review and may amend it at any time.

(6) The Secretary of State must—

(a) lay a separate biodiversity gain statement before Parliament, and

(b) publish it in such manner as the Secretary of State considers appropriate.

(7) A separate biodiversity gain statement is for the purposes of section 104(2) to (9) to be regarded as contained in the existing national policy statement.

(8) If it appears to the Secretary of State that the existing national policy statement is inconsistent with a separate biodiversity gain statement, the Secretary of State may amend the existing national policy statement in such manner as seems appropriate to the Secretary of State to remove the inconsistency.

(9) Where the existing national policy statement is amended pursuant to sub-paragraph (2) to include a biodiversity gain statement in relation to any description of development, a separate biodiversity gain statement relating to development of that description must be revoked as from the beginning of the period for which the new statement has effect.

(10) If the existing national policy statement's designation as a national policy statement is withdrawn in relation to any description of development, any separate biodiversity gain statement relating to development of that description has effect as if it were a biodiversity gain statement issued under paragraph 10(2).

(11) References in sub-paragraphs (4) to (10) to separate biodiversity gain statements include amended versions of such statements.

(12) For the purposes of this Schedule, "existing national policy statement" means a national policy statement which is designated under section 5 before the coming into force of this Schedule.

(13) For the purposes of sub-paragraph (2), an existing national policy statement is only reviewed under section 6 after the coming into force of this Schedule if the review begins after that time.

Development not covered by a national policy statement

10 (1) This paragraph applies where, at the time this Schedule comes into force or any subsequent time, no national policy statement sets out policy in respect of a description of development to which this Schedule applies.

(2) The Secretary of State may issue a biodiversity gain statement in relation to that description of development.

(3) Before issuing a biodiversity gain statement under sub-paragraph (2) the Secretary of State must consult such persons as the Secretary of State considers appropriate.

(4) The Secretary of State must keep a statement issued under sub-paragraph (2) under review and may amend or revoke it at any time.

(5) The Secretary of State must—

(a) lay a statement issued under sub-paragraph (2) before Parliament, and

(b) publish it in such manner as the Secretary of State considers appropriate.

(6) References in sub-paragraphs (3) to (5) to statements issued under sub-paragraph (2) include amended versions of such statements.

(7) If after a statement is issued under sub-paragraph (2) a national policy statement relating to the description of development is designated under section 5, the Secretary of State must—

(a) include a biodiversity gain statement in relation to that description of development in the national policy statement, and

(b) revoke the statement issued under sub-paragraph (2).

Development at sea

11 (1) The Secretary of State may by regulations provide for this Schedule to apply, with or without modifications, to any development to which this paragraph applies.

(2) This paragraph applies to development which—

(a) is of a description to which a development consent order application may relate, and

(b) is not excluded development,

to the extent that the development is carried out in the English marine region.

(3) In sub-paragraph (2), the "English marine region" means—

(a) the English offshore region, and

(b) the English inshore region, excluding waters in England.

(4) Regulations under this paragraph may make provision modifying the application of this Schedule in relation to development which is carried out at an inter-tidal location.

(5) In sub-paragraph (4), "inter-tidal location" means a location that—

(a) is in England, and

(b) is also at any time in the English inshore region.

Interpretation

12 For the purposes of this Schedule—

"biodiversity credits" means credits under section 101 of the Environment Act 2021;

"biodiversity gain site register" means the register under section 100 of the Environment Act 2021;

a "biodiversity metric" is a means of measuring the biodiversity value or relative biodiversity value of habitat or habitat enhancement;

"development consent order application" has the meaning given by paragraph 1(2);

"English inshore region" and "English offshore region" have the meanings given by section 322 of the Marine and Coastal Access Act 2009;

"excluded development" has the meaning given by paragraph 1(2);

"existing national policy statement" has the meaning given by paragraph 9(12);

"irreplaceable habitat" has the meaning given in regulations under paragraph 18 of Schedule 7A to the Town and Country Planning Act 1990;

"onsite habitat", in relation to any development, means habitat on the land to which the development consent order application relates, and "offsite habitat" means habitat on other land;

"registered offsite biodiversity gain" has the meaning given by paragraph 10 of Schedule 7A to the Town and Country Planning Act 1990."

Part 2

Supplementary Amendments To The Planning Act 2008

6 The Planning Act 2008 is amended as follows.

7 In section 37 (applications for orders for development consent), after subsection (3) insert—

"(3A) The documents and information prescribed under subsection (3)(d) may include documents and information demonstrating how any biodiversity gain objective in a biodiversity gain statement under Schedule 2A having effect in relation to the development is to be met."

8 In section 120 (what may be included in development consent order), in subsection (2), at the end insert—

"(c) requirements designed to secure that—

(i) the biodiversity gain objective under Schedule 2A relevant to the development is met;

(ii) any proposals included in the application for the order for the purposes of meeting the biodiversity gain objective are implemented."

9 (1) Section 232 (orders and regulations) is amended as follows.

(2) In subsection (5), at the end insert—

"(f) regulations under paragraph 3(3) or 11 of Schedule 2A."

(3) In subsection (7), after "or 105(2)(b)" insert "or paragraph 3(3) or 11 of Schedule 2A".

SCHEDULE 16

Section 114

Controlling the felling of trees in England

Introductory

1 Part 2 of the Forestry Act 1967 (power to control felling of trees) is amended as follows.

Penalty for felling without licence: increase of fine

2 In section 17(1) (penalty for felling without a licence)—

(a) after "and" insert—

"(a) in relation to an offence committed in Wales,";

(b) at the end insert ", or

(b) in relation to an offence committed in England, liable on summary conviction to a fine."

Restocking notices to be local land charges

3 In section 17A (power to require restocking after unauthorised felling), after subsection (1A) insert—

"(1B) A restocking notice served by the Commissioners is a local land charge; and for the purposes of the Local Land Charges Act 1975 the Commissioners are the originating authority as respects the charge."

Enforcement notices to be local land charges

4 In section 24 (notice to require compliance with conditions or directions), at the end insert—

"(6) A notice under this section given by the Commissioners is a local land charge; and for the purposes of the Local Land Charges Act 1975 the Commissioners are the originating authority as respects the charge."

Further enforcement notices for new estate or interest holders

5 (1) In section 17C (enforcement of restocking notice), after "directions)," insert "24A (further notice under section 24 for next estate or interest holders),".

(2) After section 24 insert—

"24A Further notice under section 24 for next estate or interest holders

(1) Subsection (2) applies where—

(a) a notice has been given to a person under section 24 to require compliance with the conditions of a felling licence in relation to land in England,

(b) steps required by the notice have not been taken, and

(c) before the time specified in the notice has expired, the person ceases to have the estate or interest in the land by reference to which the notice was served.

(2) The Commissioners may give to the next estate or interest holder a further notice under section 24 requiring the steps that were not completed under the notice described in subsection (1) to be completed.

(3) In subsection (2) the "next estate or interest holder" means the person who has an estate or interest in the land as is referred to in section 10(1) immediately after the person referred to in subsection (1) ceased to have the estate or interest referred to in subsection (1)(c).

(4) The reference in subsection (1) to a notice under section 24 includes a notice given under subsection (2)."

Power of court to order restocking after conviction for failure to comply with enforcement notice

6 After section 24A (inserted by paragraph 5) insert—

"24B Restocking orders after conviction under section 24 in England

(1) This section applies where a person has been convicted of an offence under section 24(4) in England in relation to a failure to take steps required by a notice given under section 24 to remedy a default in the case of non-compliance with—

(a) the conditions of a felling licence that relate to the restocking or stocking of land with trees, or

(b) the requirements of a restocking notice.

(2) The court may make a restocking order.

(3) A restocking order is an order that requires the person to take such steps as may be specified therein to be taken within such time as may be so specified—

(a) to restock or stock with trees the land in respect of which the notice under section 24 was given, or such other land as the court considers appropriate, and

(b) to maintain those trees in accordance with the rules and practice of good forestry for a period not exceeding ten years specified in the order.

(4) In deciding whether to make a restocking order the court must have regard to—

(a) the interests of good forestry and agriculture and of the amenities of the district to which the restocking order would relate, and

(b) the desirability of promoting the establishment and maintenance of adequate reserves of growing trees in England.

(5) Section 63(3) of the Magistrates' Courts Act 1980 (power of magistrates' court to deal with person for breach of order etc) applies in relation to a restocking order."

Service of notices on directors of companies that have estates or interests in land

7 (1) Section 30 (service of documents) is amended as follows.

(2) In subsection (2), at the end insert "or, in the case of service by the Commissioners, upon a director of the company or body".

(3) In subsection (3), after "clerk" insert "or director".

Requiring information from the owner of land

8 In section 30(5) (power to require information regarding interests in land), after the second "land" insert ", and the owner of any land in England".

SCHEDULE 17

SECTION 116

USE OF FOREST RISK COMMODITIES IN COMMERCIAL ACTIVITY

PART 1

REQUIREMENTS

Meaning of "forest risk commodity"

1 (1) In this Schedule "forest risk commodity" means a commodity specified in regulations made by the Secretary of State.

(2) The regulations may specify only a commodity that has been produced from a plant, animal or other living organism.

(3) The regulations may specify a commodity only if the Secretary of State considers that forest is being or may be converted to agricultural use for the purposes of producing the commodity.

(4) "Forest" means an area of land of more than 0.5 hectares with a tree canopy cover of at least 10% (excluding trees planted for the purpose of producing timber or other commodities).

(5) In sub-paragraph (4) the reference to land includes land that is wholly or partly submerged in water (whether temporarily or permanently).

(6) The regulations may not specify timber or timber products, within the meaning of Regulation (EU) No. 995/2010 of the European Parliament and of the Council of 20 October 2010 laying down the obligations of operators who place timber and timber products on the market.

(7) Before making regulations under this paragraph the Secretary of State must consult such persons as the Secretary of State considers appropriate.

(8) The requirement to consult in sub-paragraph (7) may be met by consultation carried out before this paragraph comes into force.

Prohibition on using illegally produced commodities

2 (1) A regulated person in relation to a forest risk commodity must not use that commodity in their UK commercial activities unless relevant local laws were complied with in relation to that commodity.

(2) A regulated person in relation to a forest risk commodity must not use a product derived from that commodity in their UK commercial activities unless relevant local laws were complied with in relation to that commodity.

(3) In this Schedule "local law", in relation to a forest risk commodity, means any law having effect in the country or territory where the source organism was grown, raised or cultivated.

(4) In this Schedule "relevant local law", in relation to a forest risk commodity, means local law—

(a) which relates to the ownership of the land on which the source organism was grown, raised or cultivated,

(b) which relates to the use of that land, or

(c) which otherwise relates to that land and is specified in regulations made by the Secretary of State.

(5) The regulations may specify a local law only if it relates to the prevention of forest being converted to agricultural use.

(6) The "source organism" means the plant, animal or other living organism from which the forest risk commodity was produced.

(7) Sub-paragraph (1) does not apply to the use of a forest risk commodity where—

(a) the commodity is waste (within the meaning of article 2(1) of the Renewable Transport Fuel Obligations Order 2007 (S.I. 2007/3072)), and

(b) the use of the commodity is for the purpose of making renewable transport fuel—

(i) that qualifies for the issue of an RTF certificate under article 17 of that Order, and

(ii) in respect of which an additional RTF certificate may be issued under article 17A(4) of that Order.

(8) Sub-paragraph (2) does not apply to the use of a product derived from a forest risk commodity where—

(a) the commodity is waste (within the meaning of article 2(1) of the Renewable Transport Fuel Obligations Order 2007 (S.I. 2007/3072)), and

(b) the product is renewable transport fuel—

(i) that qualifies for the issue of an RTF certificate under article 17 of that Order, and

(ii) in respect of which an additional RTF certificate may be or has been issued under article 17A(4) of that Order.

Due diligence system

3 (1) A regulated person in relation to a forest risk commodity who uses that commodity or a product derived from that commodity in their UK commercial activities must establish and implement a due diligence system in relation to that commodity.

(2) In this Schedule a "due diligence system", in relation to a forest risk commodity, means a system for—

(a) identifying, and obtaining information about, that commodity,

(b) assessing the risk that relevant local laws were not complied with in relation to that commodity, and

(c) mitigating that risk.

(3) The Secretary of State may by regulations make further provision about the matters in sub-paragraph (2)(a) to (c), including in particular—

(a) the information that should be obtained;

(b) the criteria to be used in assessing risk;

(c) the ways in which risk may be mitigated.

Annual report on due diligence system

4 (1) A regulated person in relation to a forest risk commodity who uses that commodity or a product derived from that commodity in their UK commercial activities must, for each reporting period, provide the relevant authority with a report on the actions taken by the person to establish and implement a due diligence system in relation to that commodity as required by paragraph 3.

(2) The report must be provided no later than 6 months after the end of the reporting period to which it relates.

(3) The Secretary of State may by regulations make provision—

(a) about the content and form of reports under this paragraph;

(b) about the manner in which reports under this paragraph are to be provided.

(4) The relevant authority must make reports under this paragraph available to the public in the way, and to the extent, specified in regulations made by the Secretary of State.

(5) In this paragraph "relevant authority" means—

(a) the Secretary of State, or

(b) if regulations made by the Secretary of State specify another person as the relevant authority for the purposes of this paragraph, that other person.

(6) In this Schedule "reporting period" means—

(a) the period beginning with the day on which this paragraph comes fully into force and ending with the following 31 March, and

(b) each successive period of 12 months.

Exemption

5 (1) A regulated person in relation to a forest risk commodity is exempt from the Part 1 requirements in respect of their use of that commodity, or a product derived from that commodity, in their UK commercial activities during a reporting period if they satisfy the following two conditions.

(2) Condition 1 is that before the start of the period, the person gives a notice to the relevant enforcement authority containing—

(a) a declaration that the person is satisfied on reasonable grounds that the amount of the commodity used in their UK commercial activities during the period will not exceed the prescribed threshold, and

(b) the prescribed information.

(3) Condition 2 is that the amount of the commodity used in the person's UK commercial activities during the period does not exceed the prescribed threshold.

(4) Sub-paragraphs (5) and (6) apply where—

(a) a regulated person gives a notice under sub-paragraph (2), but

(b) the amount of the commodity used in the person's UK commercial activities during the period exceeds the prescribed threshold.

(5) If, before the relevant date, the regulated person gives a notice to the relevant enforcement authority containing the prescribed information, the person is exempt from the Part 1 requirements in respect of their use of the commodity, or the product derived from the commodity, in their UK commercial activities during the part of the reporting period—

(a) beginning with the start of the period, and

(b) ending with the date the notice is given.

(6) If the regulated person does not give a notice under sub-paragraph (5), the person is not exempt from the Part 1 requirements in respect of their use of the commodity, or the product derived from the commodity, in their UK commercial activities during any part of the reporting period.

(7) In this paragraph—

"prescribed" means prescribed in regulations made by the Secretary of State;

"relevant date" means the date during the reporting period that the amount of the commodity used in the person's UK commercial activities exceeds the prescribed threshold;

"relevant enforcement authority" means the enforcement authority on which the function of receiving notices under this paragraph has been conferred by Part 2 regulations.

(8) Regulations under this paragraph may in particular—

(a) prescribe thresholds by reference to weight or volume;

(b) make provision about how the amount of a forest risk commodity used in a regulated person's UK commercial activities (including in relation to a forest risk commodity from which a product is derived) is to be determined,

and regulations under paragraph (b) may include provision for determining the amount by reference to matters determined or published by the Secretary of State or other persons.

(9) Before making regulations under this paragraph (except under sub-paragraph (2)(b) or (5)) the Secretary of State must consult such persons as the Secretary of State considers appropriate.

(10) The requirement to consult in sub-paragraph (9) may be met by consultation carried out before this paragraph comes into force.

Guidance

6 (1) The Secretary of State may issue guidance to an enforcement authority about the Part 1 requirements.

(2) An enforcement authority must have regard to guidance issued under sub-paragraph (1) when exercising its functions under Part 2 of this Schedule.

Meaning of "regulated person"

7 (1) In this Schedule "regulated person", in relation to a forest risk commodity, means a person (other than an individual) who carries on commercial activities in the United Kingdom, and—

(a) meets such conditions in relation to turnover as may be specified in regulations made by the Secretary of State for the purposes of defining who is a regulated person in relation to that forest risk commodity, or

(b) is an undertaking which is a subsidiary of another undertaking which meets those conditions.

(2) Regulations under sub-paragraph (1) may make provision about how turnover is to be determined.

(3) Before making regulations under sub-paragraph (1) the Secretary of State must consult such persons as the Secretary of State considers appropriate.

(4) The requirement to consult in sub-paragraph (3) may be met by consultation carried out before this paragraph comes into force.

(5) The Secretary of State may by regulations make provision for the Part 1 requirements not to apply, or to apply with modifications, in relation to a person who becomes a regulated person for such transitional period, after they become a regulated person, as may be specified in the regulations.

(6) The Secretary of State may by regulations make provision for a group of undertakings to be treated as a regulated person, in such circumstances, for such purposes and to such extent as may be provided (and may modify the application of the Schedule accordingly).

(7) In this paragraph—

"group" has the meaning given by section 474 of the Companies Act 2006;

"undertaking" has the meaning given by section 1161 of that Act,

and whether an undertaking is a subsidiary of another undertaking is to be determined in accordance with section 1162 of that Act.

PART 2

ENFORCEMENT

General power

8 The Secretary of State may by regulations ("Part 2 regulations") make provision about the enforcement of requirements imposed by or under Part 1 of this Schedule ("Part 1 requirements").

Powers to confer functions

9 (1) Part 2 regulations may include provision conferring functions on one or more persons specified in the regulations (each of whom is an "enforcement authority" for the purposes of this Schedule).

(2) Part 2 regulations may include provision—

(a) conferring functions involving the exercise of discretion;

(b) for the functions of an enforcement authority to be exercised on its behalf by persons authorised in accordance with the regulations.

(3) Part 2 regulations may include provision requiring an enforcement authority—

(a) to issue guidance about the exercise of its functions;

(b) to consult with specified persons before issuing such guidance.

Monitoring compliance

10 Part 2 regulations may include provision conferring on an enforcement authority the function of monitoring compliance with Part 1 requirements.

Records and information

11 Part 2 regulations may include provision—

(a) requiring persons on whom Part 1 requirements are imposed to keep records;

(b) requiring persons on whom Part 1 requirements are imposed to provide records or other information to an enforcement authority;

(c) requiring an enforcement authority to make reports or provide information to the Secretary of State.

Powers of entry etc

12 (1) Part 2 regulations may include provision conferring on an enforcement authority powers of entry, inspection, examination, search and seizure.

(2) Part 2 regulations may include provision—

(a) for powers to be exercisable only under the authority of a warrant issued by a justice of the peace, sheriff, summary sheriff or lay magistrate;

(b) about applications for, and the execution of, warrants.

(3) Part 2 regulations must secure that the authority of a warrant is required for the exercise of any powers conferred by the regulations to—

(a) enter premises by force;

(b) enter a private dwelling without the consent of the occupier;

(c) search and seize material.

Sanctions

13 (1) Part 2 regulations may include provision—

(a) for, about or connected with the imposition of civil sanctions in respect of—

(i) failures to comply with Part 1 requirements or Part 2 regulations, or

(ii) the obstruction of or failure to assist an enforcement authority;

(b) for appeals against such sanctions.

(2) Part 2 regulations must include provision to ensure that in a case where—

(a) a regulated person fails to comply with a requirement in paragraph 2(1) or (2) in relation to their use of a forest risk commodity or a product derived from a forest risk commodity, but

(b) an enforcement authority is satisfied that the regulated person took all reasonable steps to implement a due diligence system in relation to the commodity used by the person in that particular case,

a civil sanction may not be imposed on the regulated person in respect of the failure to comply.

(3) Part 2 regulations may include provision—

(a) creating criminal offences punishable with a fine in respect of—

(i) failures to comply with civil sanctions imposed under Part 2 regulations, or

(ii) the obstruction of or failure to assist an enforcement authority;

(b) about such offences.

(4) In this paragraph "civil sanction" means a sanction of a kind for which provision may be made under Part 3 of the Regulatory Enforcement and Sanctions Act 2008 (fixed monetary penalties, discretionary requirements, stop notices and enforcement undertakings).

14 Part 2 regulations may include provision for the imposition of sanctions of that kind whether or not—

(a) the conduct in respect of which the sanction is imposed constitutes an offence, or

(b) the enforcement authority is a regulator for the purposes of Part 3 of the Regulatory Enforcement and Sanctions Act 2008.

Charges

15 Part 2 regulations may include provision—

(a) requiring persons on whom Part 1 requirements are imposed to pay to an enforcement authority charges, as a means of recovering costs incurred by that enforcement authority in performing its functions;

(b) authorising a court or tribunal dealing with any matter relating to Part 1 requirements or Part 2 regulations to award to an enforcement authority costs incurred by it in performing its functions in relation to that matter.

Consultation requirement

16 (1) Before making Part 2 regulations the Secretary of State must consult any persons the Secretary of State considers appropriate.

(2) The requirement to consult in sub-paragraph (1) may be met by consultation carried out before this paragraph comes into force.

PART 3

GENERAL PROVISIONS

Review

17 (1) The Secretary of State must review the effectiveness of the Part 1 requirements and any Part 2 regulations ("relevant provisions") in accordance with this paragraph.

(2) A review must consider in particular—

(a) the amount of forest being converted to agricultural use for the purposes of producing commodities;

(b) the impact of the relevant provisions on the amount of forest being converted to agricultural use for the purposes of producing forest risk commodities;

(c) the impact of the relevant provisions on the use of forest risk commodities, or products derived from forest risk commodities, in UK commercial activities where relevant local laws were not complied with in relation to those commodities;

(d) any changes to relevant local laws in relation to forest risk commodities.

(3) Having carried out a review the Secretary of State must lay before Parliament, and publish, a report stating—

(a) the conclusions of the review, and

(b) the steps, if any, the Secretary of State intends to take to improve the effectiveness of the relevant provisions (including whether the Secretary of State intends to make any regulations under this Schedule).

(4) The first review must be completed during the period—

(a) beginning with the second anniversary of the first date on which paragraphs 2 to 4 are fully in force, and

(b) ending with the third anniversary of the first date on which paragraphs 2 to 4 are fully in force.

(5) Subsequent reviews must be completed before the end of the 2 year period beginning with the day on which the previous review was completed.

(6) A review is completed when the Secretary of State has laid and published the report.

Interpretation

18 (1) In this Schedule—

"agricultural use" includes use for horticulture and aquaculture; "commercial activity" includes—

(a) producing, manufacturing and processing;

(b) distributing, selling, or supplying;

(c) purchasing for a purpose within paragraph (a) or (b) (but not purchasing as a consumer);

"due diligence system", in relation to a forest risk commodity, has the meaning given by paragraph 3;

"enforcement authority" has the meaning given by paragraph 9; "forest" has the meaning given by paragraph 1;

"forest risk commodity" has the meaning given by paragraph 1;

"local law", in relation to a forest risk commodity, has the meaning given by paragraph 2;

"Part 1 requirements" has the meaning given by paragraph 8; "Part 2 regulations" has the meaning given by paragraph 8;

"regulated person", in relation to a forest risk commodity, has the meaning given by paragraph 7;

"relevant local law", in relation to a forest risk commodity, has the meaning given by paragraph 2;

"reporting period" has the meaning given by paragraph 4;

"UK commercial activity" means commercial activity carried on in the United Kingdom.

(2) References in this Schedule to a product derived from a forest risk commodity are to a product derived from a forest risk commodity in whole or in part (and include any product of an animal fed on a forest risk commodity or a product derived from a forest risk commodity).

SCHEDULE 18

Section 130

Discharge or modification of obligations under conservation covenants

Part 1

Discharge by Upper Tribunal

Power to discharge on application by landowner or responsible body

1 (1) The Upper Tribunal may, on the application of a person bound by, or entitled to the benefit of, an obligation under a conservation covenant by virtue of being the holder of an estate in land, by order discharge the obligation in respect of any of the land to which it relates.

(2) The Upper Tribunal must add as party to the proceedings on an application under sub-paragraph (1) the responsible body under the covenant.

2 (1) The Upper Tribunal may, on the application of the responsible body under a conservation covenant, by order discharge an obligation under the covenant in respect of any of the land to which it relates.

(2) The Upper Tribunal must add as party to the proceedings on an application under sub-paragraph (1) any person who, by virtue of being the holder of an estate in land, is bound by, or entitled to the benefit of, the obligation to which the application relates.

Deciding whether to discharge

3 (1) The Upper Tribunal may exercise its power under paragraph 1(1) or 2(1) if it considers it reasonable to do so in all the circumstances of the case.

(2) In considering whether to exercise its power under paragraph 1(1) or 2(1), the matters to which the Upper Tribunal is to have regard include—

(a) whether there has been any material change of circumstance since the making of the original agreement, in particular—

(i) change in the character of the land to which the obligation relates or of the neighbourhood of that land;

(ii) change affecting the enjoyment of the land to which the obligation relates;

(iii) change affecting the extent to which performance of the obligation is, or is likely in future to be, affordable;

(iv) change affecting the extent to which performance of the obligation is, or is likely in future to be, practicable;

(b) whether the obligation serves any conservation purpose it had—

(i) when the original agreement was entered into, or

(ii) if the obligation has since been modified (whether by agreement or by the Upper Tribunal), when the obligation was modified,

as the case may be; and

(c) whether the obligation serves the public good.

(3) In considering whether to exercise its power under paragraph 1(1), the matters to which the Upper Tribunal is to have regard also include—

(a) whether any conservation purpose which the obligation in question had when the original agreement was entered into could be served equally well by an obligation relating to different land in respect of which the applicant holds a qualifying estate; and

(b) whether, if an order under paragraph 1(1) were made, such an alternative obligation could be created by means of a conservation covenant.

(4) In considering, for the purposes of this paragraph, affordability or practicability in relation to performance of an obligation, change in the personal circumstances of a person bound by the obligation is to be disregarded.

(5) In this paragraph references to the original agreement, in relation to an obligation under a conservation covenant, are to the agreement containing the provision which gave rise to the obligation.

Supplementary powers

4 (1) The Upper Tribunal may include in an order under paragraph 1(1) or 2(1) provision requiring the applicant to pay compensation in respect of loss of benefit resulting from the order.

(2) Compensation under sub-paragraph (1) shall be payable to such person at such time and be of such amount as the order may provide.

5 (1) The Upper Tribunal may, if it considers it reasonable to do so in connection with the discharge under paragraph 1(1) of an obligation under a conservation covenant, include in the order discharging the obligation provision making the discharge conditional on the entry by the applicant and the responsible body under the covenant into a conservation covenant agreement containing such provision as the order may specify.

(2) The power under sub-paragraph (1) is exercisable only with the consent of the applicant and the responsible body.

Part 2

Modification by Upper Tribunal

Power to modify on application by landowner or responsible body

6 (1) The Upper Tribunal may, on the application of a person bound by, or entitled to the benefit of, an obligation under a conservation covenant by virtue of being the holder of an estate in land, by order modify the obligation in respect of any of the land to which it relates.

(2) The Upper Tribunal must add as party to the proceedings on an application under sub-paragraph (1) the responsible body under the covenant.

7 (1) The Upper Tribunal may, on the application of the responsible body under a conservation covenant, by order modify an obligation under the covenant in respect of any of the land to which it relates.

(2) The Upper Tribunal must add as party to the proceedings on an application under sub-paragraph (1) any person who, by virtue of being the holder of an estate in land, is bound by, or entitled to the benefit of, the obligation to which the application relates.

8 The power under paragraph 6(1) or 7(1) does not include power to make a change to an obligation which, had it been included in the original agreement, would have prevented the provision of the agreement which gave rise to the obligation being provision in relation to which the conditions in section 117(1)(a) were met.

Deciding whether to modify

9 (1) The Upper Tribunal may exercise its power under paragraph 6(1) or 7(1) if it considers it reasonable to do so in all the circumstances of the case.

(2) In considering whether to exercise its power under paragraph 6(1) or 7(1), the matters to which the Upper Tribunal is to have regard include—

(a) whether there has been any material change of circumstance since the making of the original agreement, in particular—

(i) change in the character of the land to which the obligation relates or of the neighbourhood of that land;

(ii) change affecting the enjoyment of the land to which the obligation relates;

(iii) change affecting the extent to which performance of the obligation is, or is likely in future to be, affordable;

(iv) change affecting the extent to which performance of the obligation is, or is likely in future to be, practicable;

(b) whether the obligation serves any conservation purpose it had—

(i) when the original agreement was entered into, or

(ii) if the obligation has since been modified (whether by agreement or by the Upper Tribunal), when the obligation was modified,

as the case may be; and

(c) whether the obligation serves the public good.

(3) In considering, for the purposes of this paragraph, affordability or practicability in relation to performance of an obligation, change in the personal circumstances of a person bound by the obligation is to be disregarded.

Supplementary powers

10 (1) The Upper Tribunal may include in an order under paragraph 6(1) or 7(1) provision requiring the applicant to pay compensation in respect of loss of benefit resulting from the order.

(2) Compensation under sub-paragraph (1) shall be payable to such person at such time and be of such amount as the order may provide.

11 (1) The Upper Tribunal may, if it considers it reasonable to do so in connection with the modification under paragraph 6(1) of an obligation under a conservation covenant, include in the order modifying the obligation provision making the modification conditional on the entry by the applicant and the responsible body under the covenant into a conservation covenant agreement containing such provision as the order may specify.

(2) The power under sub-paragraph (1) is exercisable only with the consent of the applicant and the responsible body.

Effect of modification

12 (1) The modification of an obligation by an order under this Part binds—

(a) the parties to the proceedings in which the order is made, and

(b) any person who, as respects any of the land to which the modification relates, becomes a successor of a person bound by the modification.

(2) For the purposes of sub-paragraph (1) "successor of a person bound by the modification" means a person who holds, in respect of any of the land to which the modification relates—

(a) the estate held by the person so bound when the order modifying the obligation was made, or

(b) an estate in land derived (whether immediately or otherwise) from that estate after the order modifying the obligation was made.

Interpretation

13 In this Part, references to the original agreement, in relation to an obligation under a conservation covenant, are to the agreement containing the provision which gave rise to the obligation.

SCHEDULE 19

Section 137

Application of Part 7 to Crown land

Part 1

General

Application of Part 7

1 Part 7 applies in relation to Crown land as it applies in relation to any other land, subject to the provisions of this Schedule.

Interpretation

2 (1) In this Schedule—

(a) "Crown land" means land in relation which there is an estate in land of a kind listed in column 1 of the following Table, and

(b) "the appropriate authority", in relation to any Crown land, means the authority specified in column 2 for the estate in land in question.

Estate in land	*Appropriate authority*
Estate belonging to Her Majesty in right of the Crown (other than estate vesting as bona vacantia)	The Crown Estate Commissioners or other government department having management of the land
Estate vesting in Her Majesty in right of the Crown as bona vacantia	The Treasury Solicitor
Estate belonging to Her Majesty in right of Her private estates	A person appointed by Her Majesty under the Royal Sign Manual, or, if no such appointment is made, the Secretary of State
Estate belonging to Her Majesty in right of the Duchy of Lancaster	The Chancellor of the Duchy of Lancaster
Estate belonging to the Duchy of Cornwall	Such person as the Duke of Cornwall, or the possessor for the time being of the Duchy of Cornwall, appoints
Estate belonging to a government department or held in trust for Her Majesty for the purposes of a government department	That department

(2) References in this Schedule to Part 7 are to Part 7 of this Act (apart from this Schedule and Schedule 20).

(3) If any question arises as to what authority is the appropriate authority in relation to any Crown land, that question is to be referred to the Treasury, whose decision is final.

(4) In this paragraph the reference to Her Majesty's private estates is to be read in accordance with section 1 of the Crown Private Estates Act 1862.

Demesne land

3 (1) Where land belongs to Her Majesty in right of the Crown but is not held for an estate in fee simple absolute in possession—

(a) Her Majesty in right of the Crown is to be regarded for the purposes of Part 7 and this Schedule as holding an estate in fee simple absolute in possession in the land, and

(b) any estate granted or created out of the land is to be regarded for those purposes as derived from that estate in fee simple.

(2) The land referred to in sub-paragraph (1) does not include land which becomes subject to escheat on the determination of an estate in fee simple absolute in possession in the land if—

(a) it is land to which an obligation under a conservation covenant related when the estate determined, or

(b) it is not land to which such an obligation related at that time and Her Majesty in right of the Crown has not taken possession or control of the land, or entered into occupation of it.

Land subject to escheat

4 (1) This paragraph applies where land becomes subject to escheat on the determination of an estate in fee simple absolute in possession in land to which an obligation under a conservation covenant relates.

(2) The conservation covenant is not terminated on the determination of that estate, even though the appropriate authority has no liability in respect of the obligation unless and until the Crown—

(a) takes possession or control of the land, or enters into occupation of it, or

(b) becomes the holder of—

(i) an estate granted by the Crown out of the land, or

(ii) an estate in land derived (whether immediately or otherwise) from an estate falling within sub-paragraph (i).

(3) If the Crown takes possession or control of the land, or enters into occupation of it—

(a) the Crown is to be regarded for the purposes of Part 7 and this Schedule as holding an estate in fee simple in possession in the land, and

(b) that estate is to be regarded for those purposes as immediately derived from the determined estate.

(4) If the Crown grants an estate out of the land after having previously taken possession or control of the land, or entered into occupation of it, the estate

is to be regarded for the purposes of Part 7 and this Schedule as immediately derived from the estate mentioned in sub-paragraph (3)(a).

(5) But if the Crown grants an estate out of the land without having previously taken possession or control of the land, or entered into occupation of it—

(a) the acts of the Crown in granting that estate are not to be regarded for the purposes of Part 7 and this Schedule as taking possession or control of the land, or entering into occupation of it, and

(b) the new estate is to be regarded for those purposes as immediately derived from the determined estate.

(6) In this paragraph and paragraph 5 "the Crown" means Her Majesty in right of the Crown or of the Duchy of Lancaster, or the Duchy of Cornwall, as the case may be.

Bona vacantia

5 (1) This paragraph applies where an estate in land to which an obligation of the landowner under a conservation covenant relates vests in the Crown as bona vacantia.

(2) The appropriate authority has no liability in respect of the obligation in relation to any period before the Crown takes possession or control of the land or enters into occupation of it.

Part 2

Conservation covenants relating to Crown land held by a person other than the appropriate authority

Agreements for the purposes of section 117

6 (1) If Crown land which is a qualifying estate is held by a person other than the appropriate authority, the appropriate authority may, as respects that qualifying estate, enter into a conservation covenant agreement, in place of the holder of the estate.

(2) An authority that enters into such an agreement by virtue of sub-paragraph (1) is to be treated for the purposes of section 117 as the holder of the qualifying estate (instead of the person in whose place the authority is acting).

Modification of Part 7 in relation to obligations under certain Crown conservation covenants

7 (1) Paragraphs 8 to 12 modify Part 7 in its application to obligations under a conservation covenant created by an agreement entered into by virtue of paragraph 6(1).

(2) In those paragraphs, in relation to an obligation under the conservation covenant—

"the appropriate authority" means the appropriate authority with respect to the estate in land of the original landowner which is the qualifying estate in relation to the obligation, and

"the original landowner" means the person who held the qualifying estate when the agreement was entered into.

8 References in Part 7 to an obligation of the landowner under a conservation covenant are to be read as references to an obligation of the appropriate authority under the conservation covenant.

9 (1) Section 122 has effect with the following modifications in its application to an obligation mentioned in paragraph 8.

(2) In subsection (2)—

(a) in paragraph (a), the reference to the landowner under the covenant is to be read as a reference to the appropriate authority, and

(b) in paragraph (b), the reference to the landowner under the covenant is to be read as a reference to the original landowner.

(3) In subsection (3) the reference to the landowner under the covenant is to be read as a reference to the original landowner.

(4) In subsection (4)—

(a) in the opening words and in paragraph (b), the reference to the landowner under the covenant is to be read as a reference to the appropriate authority,

(b) in the opening words, the reference to a successor of that landowner is to be read as a reference to a successor of the original landowner, and

(c) in paragraph (b), the reference to land in relation to which the landowner ceases to be the holder of the qualifying estate is to be read as a reference to land in relation to which the original landowner ceases to be the holder of the qualifying estate.

(5) Subsection (5)(c) has effect, if the successor's immediate predecessor was the original landowner, as if the reference to the successor's immediate predecessor were a reference to the appropriate authority.

10 (1) Section 123 has effect with the following modifications in its application to an obligation of the responsible body under the conservation covenant.

(2) In subsection (1)—

(a) in paragraph (a), the reference to the landowner under the covenant is to be read as a reference to the appropriate authority, and

(b) in paragraph (b), the reference to the landowner under the covenant is to be read as a reference to the original landowner.

(3) In subsection (2) the reference to the landowner under the covenant is to be read as a reference to the original landowner.

(4) In subsection (3)—

(a) in the opening words and in paragraph (b), the reference to the landowner under the covenant is to be read as a reference to the appropriate authority,

(b) in the opening words, the reference to a successor of that landowner is to be read as a reference to a successor of the original landowner, and

(c) in paragraph (b), the reference to land in relation to which the landowner ceases to be the holder of the qualifying estate is to be read as a reference to land in relation to which the original landowner ceases to be the holder of the qualifying estate.

11 In section 129(4)(b) and (5) the references to a successor of a person bound by the modification (where the person bound is the appropriate authority) are to be read as references to a successor of the original landowner.

12 In Schedule 18—

(a) the references in paragraphs 1(1) and 6(1) to a person bound by, or entitled to the benefit of, an obligation under a conservation covenant by virtue of holding an estate in land are to be read as references to the appropriate authority;

(b) the references in paragraphs 2(2) and 7(2) to any person who by virtue of holding an estate in land is bound by or entitled to the benefit of an obligation are to be read as references to the appropriate authority;

(c) the references in paragraph 12(1)(b) and (2) to a successor of a person bound by the modification (where the person bound is the appropriate authority) are to be read as references to a successor of the original landowner.

Part 3

Other modifications of Part 7

Cases where estate in land to which conservation covenant relates has been acquired by the Crown and is held by person other than the appropriate authority

13 (1) Paragraphs 14 to 17 apply where the estate in land by virtue of which a person is a successor of the landowner under a conservation covenant is held by or on behalf of the Crown by a person other than the appropriate authority.

(2) In sub-paragraph (1) "successor" (in relation to the landowner under the covenant) means a person who holds, in respect of any of the land to which any obligation under the covenant relates—

(a) the qualifying estate, or

(b) an estate in land derived (whether immediately or otherwise) from the qualifying estate after the creation of the covenant.

14 In section 122—

(a) subsections (2)(b), (3) and (4) have effect as if the estate in land were held by the appropriate authority, and

(b) subsection (5)(c) has effect, in relation to a disposal of the estate in land, as if the successor's immediate predecessor were the appropriate authority.

15 In section 123—

(a) subsections (1)(b), (2) and (4) have effect as if the estate in land were held by the appropriate authority, and

(b) subsection (4) has effect as if the reference to the successor were a reference to the appropriate authority.

16 (1) In section 129(4)(b) and (5) references to a successor of a person bound by the modification (where the person bound is the appropriate authority) are to be read as references to a successor of the person in whose place the appropriate authority acts.

(2) In section 129(4)(b) and (5) references to a successor of a person bound by the modification (where the person bound is not the appropriate authority) are to be read as if the estate in any of the land to which the modification relates which is held by the person in whose place the appropriate authority acts were held by the appropriate authority.

17 In Schedule 18—

(a) the reference in paragraph 6(1) to a person bound by an obligation under a conservation covenant by virtue of holding an estate in land is to be read as a reference to the appropriate authority;

(b) the reference in paragraph 7(2) to any person who is bound by or entitled to the benefit of an obligation by virtue of holding an estate in land is to be read as a reference to the appropriate authority;

(c) the references in paragraph 12(1)(b) and (2) to a successor of a person bound by the modification (where the person bound is the appropriate authority) are to be read as references to a successor of the person in whose place the appropriate authority is acting.

Agreements under section 127(1) and (3)

18 (1) This paragraph applies where, in respect of any of the land to which an obligation of the landowner under a conservation covenant relates, the qualifying estate is held by or on behalf of the Crown by a person other than the appropriate authority.

(2) The appropriate authority may enter into an agreement under section 127(1) or (3) in place of the holder of that estate.

(3) An agreement entered into by virtue of sub-paragraph (2) is to be treated for the purposes of section 127(4)(c) as entered into by virtue of the estate in land held by the person in whose place the appropriate authority enters into the agreement.

Agreements under section 128(1)

19 (1) This paragraph applies if the responsible body under a conservation covenant enters into an agreement under section 128(1) in relation to an obligation which it owes to the other party to the agreement by virtue of paragraph 10(2)(a) or 15(a).

(2) If the other party is entitled to the benefit of the obligation by virtue of paragraph 10(2)(a), the reference in section 128(2)(c) to the estate in land by virtue of which the power is exercisable is to be read as a reference to the estate in land held by the person in whose place the other party acted in entering into the agreement which gave rise to the obligation.

(3) If the other party is entitled to the benefit of the obligation by virtue of paragraph 15(a), the reference in section 128(2)(c) to the estate in land by virtue of which the power is exercisable is to be read as a reference to the estate in land which the other party is treated by paragraph 15(a) as holding.

Agreements under section 129(1)

20 (1) Sub-paragraph (2) applies where a person who—

(a) is bound by an obligation of the landowner under the covenant by virtue of paragraph 9(2)(a), or

(b) is entitled to the benefit of the obligation of the responsible body under a conservation covenant by virtue of paragraph 10(2)(a),

exercises the power under section 129(1) to modify the obligation.

(2) The reference in section 129(3)(c) to the estate in land by virtue of which the power is exercisable is to be read as a reference to the estate in land held by the person in whose place the person exercising that power acted in entering into the agreement which gave rise to the obligation.

21 (1) Sub-paragraph (2) applies where a person who—

(a) is bound by an obligation of the landowner under a conservation covenant by virtue of paragraph 14(a), or

(b) is entitled to the benefit of an obligation of the responsible body under a conservation covenant by virtue of paragraph 15(a),

exercises the power in section 129(1) to modify the obligation.

(2) The reference in section 129(3)(c) to the estate in land by virtue of which the power is exercisable is to be read as a reference to the estate in land which the person is treated by paragraph 14(a) or 15(a) as holding.

SCHEDULE 20

Section 139

Consequential amendments relating to Part 7

Acquisition of Land Act 1981 (c. 67)

1 The Acquisition of Land Act 1981 is amended as follows.

2 (1) Section 12 (notice of compulsory purchase by local and other authorities) is amended as follows.

(2) In the title, for "and occupiers" insert ", occupiers and others".

(3) In subsection (2)—

(a) omit the "or" at the end of paragraph (a), and

(b) at the end of paragraph (b) insert ", or

(c) the person is entitled to the benefit of an obligation under a conservation covenant (within the meaning of Part 7 of the Environment Act 2021) relating to the land."

3 (1) Paragraph 3 of Schedule 1 (notice of compulsory purchase by Ministers) is amended as follows.

(2) In the title, for "and occupiers" insert ", occupiers and others".

(3) In sub-paragraph (2)—

(a) omit the "or" at the end of paragraph (a), and

(b) at the end of paragraph (b) insert ", or

(c) the person is entitled to the benefit of an obligation under a conservation covenant (within the meaning of Part 7 of the Environment Act 2021) relating to the land."

Housing and Planning Act 2016 (c. 22)

4 The Housing and Planning Act 2016 is amended as follows.

5 (1) Section 203 (power to override easements and other rights) is amended as follows.

(2) In subsections (1)(b) and (4)(b)—

(a) the words after "breaching" become sub-paragraph (i), and

(b) after that sub-paragraph insert ", or

(ii) an obligation under a conservation covenant."

(3) In subsection (10)—

(a) omit the "or" at the end of paragraph (a), and

(b) at the end of paragraph (b)(ii) insert ", or

(c) a breach of an obligation under a conservation covenant owed to the National Trust."

6 (1) Section 204 (compensation for overridden easements etc) is amended as follows.

(2) In subsection (1), after "section 203" insert "(1)(a) or (b)(i) or (4)(a) or (b)(i)".

(3) After subsection (1) insert—

"(1A) But a person is not liable to pay compensation under this section for breaching an obligation under a conservation covenant."

7 In section 205(1) (interpretation), at the appropriate place insert—

""obligation under a conservation covenant" has the same meaning as in Part 7 of the Environment Act 2021;".

Neighbourhood Planning Act 2017 (c. 20)

8 The Neighbourhood Planning Act 2017 is amended as follows.

9 In section 20 (notice requirements relating to taking temporary possession), at the end insert—

"(10) For the purposes of subsection (1), a person entitled to the benefit of an obligation under a conservation covenant is to be treated as having an interest in the land to which the obligation relates."

10 In section 23 (compensation), after subsection (5) insert—

"(5A) For the purposes of subsections (2) and (3), the person is not entitled to compensation under this section by virtue of being the person entitled to the benefit of an obligation under a conservation covenant."

11 (1) Section 27 (powers of acquiring authority in temporary possession of land) is amended as follows.

(2) In subsection (3)—

(a) omit the "or" at the end of paragraph (a), and

(b) at the end of paragraph (b), insert ", or

(c) causing a person to be in breach of an obligation under a conservation covenant relating to the land."

(3) After subsection (4) insert—

"(4A) The acquiring authority is not bound by an obligation under a conservation covenant relating to the land by virtue of acquiring a right to use the land under this section."

(4) In subsection (6)—

(a) omit the "or" at the end of paragraph (a), and

(b) at the end of paragraph (b), insert ", or

(c) a use of land that causes a person (or, if the person were to permit or suffer the use, would cause the person) to be in breach of an obligation under a conservation covenant relating to the land owed to the National Trust."

12 In section 30 (interpretation), at the appropriate place, insert—

""obligation under a conservation covenant" has the same meaning as in Part 7 of the Environment Act 2021;".

SCHEDULE 21

Section 140

Amendment of REACH legislation

Amendment of the REACH Regulation

1 (1) The Secretary of State may by regulations amend the REACH Regulation.

(2) The Secretary of State may make regulations under this paragraph only if the Secretary of State considers that the provision made by the regulations is consistent with Article 1 of the REACH Regulation (aim and scope of the REACH Regulation).

(3) The Secretary of State may not make regulations under this paragraph which amend any protected provision of the REACH Regulation.

(4) But sub-paragraph (3) does not prevent any protected provision of the REACH Regulation from being amended by provision made under this paragraph by virtue of section 143(1)(a).

(5) Before making regulations under this paragraph, the Secretary of State must publish an explanation of why the Secretary of State considers that the provision to be made by the regulations is consistent with Article 1 of the REACH Regulation.

(6) The explanation relating to regulations under this paragraph is to be published—

(a) no later than the time when the Secretary of State begins the consultation on that exercise of the power that is required by paragraph 5, and

(b) in the manner which the Secretary of State considers appropriate.

(7) Regulations under this paragraph are subject to the affirmative procedure.

Amendment of the REACH Enforcement Regulations 2008

2 (1) The Secretary of State or a relevant devolved authority may by regulations amend the REACH Enforcement Regulations 2008 (S.I. 2008/2852).

(2) The Secretary of State or a relevant devolved authority may make regulations under this paragraph only if the Secretary of State or the authority considers that the provision made by the regulations is necessary or appropriate for, or in connection with, enforcement of the REACH Regulation.

(3) The provision that may be made by regulations under this paragraph includes—

(a) provision creating, or widening the scope of, a criminal offence;

(b) provision specifying the punishment for a criminal offence.

(4) But regulations under this paragraph may not provide for a criminal offence—

(a) under the law of England and Wales to be—

(i) punishable on conviction on indictment with imprisonment for more than two years, or

(ii) punishable on summary conviction with imprisonment for more than the prescribed term for England and Wales or with a fine that is calculated on a daily basis of more than £100 a day;

(b) under the law of Scotland to be—

(i) punishable on conviction on indictment with imprisonment for more than two years, or

(ii) punishable on summary conviction with imprisonment for more than the prescribed term for Scotland or with a fine of more than the applicable maximum for Scotland (if not calculated on a daily basis) or a fine of more than £100 a day;

(c) under the law of Northern Ireland to be—

(i) punishable on conviction on indictment with imprisonment for more than two years, or

(ii) punishable on summary conviction with imprisonment for more than three months or with a fine of more than level 5 on the standard scale (if not calculated on a daily basis) or a fine of more than £100 a day.

(5) In sub-paragraph (4)—

"applicable maximum for Scotland" means—

(a) level 5 on the standard scale, where the offence is a summary offence;

(b) the statutory maximum, where the offence is triable either way;

"prescribed term for England and Wales" means—

(a) 51 weeks, where the offence is a summary offence;

(b) 12 months, where the offence is triable either way; "prescribed term for Scotland" means—

(a) 3 months, where the offence is a summary offence;

(b) 12 months, where the offence is triable either way.

(6) But, in the definition of "prescribed term for England and Wales" in sub-paragraph (5)—

(a) the reference to 51 weeks is to be read, until the commencement of section 281(5) of the Criminal Justice Act 2003, as a reference to 3 months;

(b) the reference to 12 months is to be read, until the commencement of section 282(3) of the Criminal Justice Act 2003, as a reference to 3 months.

(7) Regulations under this paragraph—

(a) made by the Welsh Ministers, may contain only provision which, if contained in an Act of Senedd Cymru, would be within the legislative competence of the Senedd;

(b) made by the Scottish Ministers, may contain only provision which, if contained in an Act of the Scottish Parliament, would be within the legislative competence of the Parliament;

(c) made by the Department of Agriculture, Environment and Rural Affairs or the Department for the Economy in Northern Ireland may contain only provision which, if contained in an Act of the Northern Ireland Assembly, would be within the legislative competence of the Assembly and would not require the Secretary of State's consent.

(8) Regulations under this paragraph are subject to the affirmative procedure.

Consent of the devolved administrations

3 (1) The power of the Secretary of State to make regulations under this Schedule is subject to the consent requirement in Article 4A of the REACH Regulation.

(2) Accordingly, in Article 4A(1) of the REACH Regulation, the reference to the REACH Regulation is to be read as including a reference to this Schedule.

Requests by devolved administrations for exercise of powers under this Schedule

4 The Secretary of State must consider any request made by a relevant devolved authority for the Secretary of State to make regulations under this Schedule.

Consultation

5 (1) Before making regulations under this Schedule the Secretary of State must consult—

(a) the Agency,

(b) any person nominated by a relevant devolved authority as a consultee for the consultation in question, and

(c) such other persons the Secretary of State considers appropriate.

(2) The nomination of a person as a consultee by a relevant devolved authority is to be made by that authority to the Secretary of State.

(3) Before making regulations under paragraph 2 a relevant devolved authority must consult—

(a) the Agency, and

(b) such other persons that authority considers appropriate.

The protected provisions

6 In paragraph 1 "protected provision of the REACH Regulation" means any of the provisions of the REACH Regulation set out in the following Table—

Fundamental principles
Article 1 (aim and scope of the REACH Regulation) Article 5 (the principle of "no data, no market") Article 25(1) (animal testing as a last resort)
Article 35 (access to information for workers)
Article 45 (evaluation of substances on the rolling action plan) Article 48 (follow-up to substance evaluation)
Article 55 (the aim of Title VII, which is about authorisation of substances) Article 67(1) (effect of restrictions contained in Annex XVII)
Article 92 or 93 (appeals)
Article 111, first subparagraph (formats and software for submission of information to the Agency)
Article 123 (communication to the public of information on risks of substances)
Role of the devolved administrations
Article 4A (the consent requirement)
Article 129(1) (the safeguard clause: basic principles)
Transparency
Article 54 (publication of information on evaluation) Article 64(6) (publication of Agency authorisation opinions) Article 72(2) (publication of Agency restriction opinions)
Article 77(A4) (Agency to act in a way that ensures a high degree of transparency) and (2)(e) (database(s) of registered substances)
Article 109 (general rules on transparency for the Agency)
Collaboration between the Agency and other bodies
Article 95 (conflicts of opinion with other bodies) Article 108 (contacts with stakeholder organisations)
Article 110 (relations with relevant public bodies)
Annexes
The Annexes

Other interpretation

7 In this Schedule—

"Agency" has the same meaning as in the REACH Regulation (see Article 2A of the Regulation);

"REACH Regulation" means Regulation (EC) No 1907/2006 of the European Parliament and of the Council concerning the Registration, Evaluation, Authorisation and Restriction of Chemicals (REACH), establishing a European Chemicals Agency;

"relevant devolved authority" means—

(a) the Scottish Ministers,

(b) the Welsh Ministers, or

(c) the Department of Agriculture, Environment and Rural Affairs or the Department for the Economy in Northern Ireland.

INDEX